fessor of Hebrew and Semitic Languages and Literatures at the University. One year prior to his death in 1965, he was named University Professor of Oriental Studies, the highest honor that the University of Pennsylvania awards to distinguished faculty members.

Among his many works are: *Mesopotamian Origins; The United States and the Near East; Introduction to Hurrian;* and *Akkadian Myths and Epics*. Co-editor of the Jewish Publication Society translation of the Torah, Speiser also wrote the now famous introduction, translation, and commentary to the *Book of Genesis* in the Anchor Bible Series.

Oriental and Biblical Studies

Collected Writings of E. A. Speiser

E. A. Speiser (1902-1965)
Abraham M. Ellis Professor of Hebrew and Semitic Languages and Literatures; University Professor of Oriental Studies, University of Pennsylvania.

Oriental and Biblical Studies

Collected Writings of
E. A. SPEISER

Edited and with an Introduction
by J. J. FINKELSTEIN and
MOSHE GREENBERG

Philadelphia
University of Pennsylvania Press

Library of Congress Catalogue Card Number: 65-21779

7506

Printed in the United States of America

Introduction

SCHOLARS DIRECTLY CONCERNED WITH BIBLICAL AND ANCIENT Near Eastern studies have long been aware of the original and significant contributions of E. A. Speiser to one or another of the various disciplines that this field comprehends. What has perhaps not been so readily apparent is the underlying unity in approach and conception that informed his work over a period of forty years. Building upon a meticulously prepared philological foundation, he consistently aimed at relating particulars to larger entities: linguistic detail to comprehensive structures valid for the Semitic languages as a whole, literary and historical detail to the larger patterns of Near Eastern cultures. He was ever insistent upon the continuity in outlook and values within the main sectors of Near Eastern civilization from earliest times to the present. The field of vision in which he regarded any given phenomenon embraced at once its antecedent and subsequent manifestations through history. And there was throughout a concern for lucidity and economy of expression that make the reading of his work a delight to the esthetic sense as well as to the intellect. This selection and arrangement of his studies is designed to capture something of this unity and present it to a wider audience.

Some of the most important aspects of Professor Speiser's work are missing from this collection, e.g., his studies in the Hurrian language and in Mesopotamian archaeology—in both of which he was a pioneer. In these areas his thought and achievements ultimately found their unified expression in books or monographs of lasting significance—*Mesopotamian Origins, Excavations at Tepe Gawra I, Introduction to Hurrian*—thus largely obviating the need to search through many scattered publications for his contribution to these fields. But so much else appeared only in specialized journals, jubilee volumes, and the like, that many who would be well served by these studies cannot find access to them. Accordingly, our aim has been to bring together within the covers of a single volume some of Professor Speiser's more notable writings. Our criterion, such as it was, was simply which of our mentor's scholarly articles we should most want to commend to our students and colleagues if we had to limit their reading to the scope of one book.

This selection of material is the responsibility of the undersigned. The original publications have been reprinted unaltered. While this has entailed a lack of uniformity in such matters as the style of citations and references, we have sought to minimize any resultant difficulties by supplying a cross-referenced list of abbreviations. Here and there, however, Professor Speiser added a note—enclosed in brackets—taking account of developments in the intervening years. Though we are aware that valuable insights have been incorporated in Professor Speiser's book reviews or review articles, the necessarily topical and derivative nature of reviews indicated, in our judgment, that they not be included in this volume.

Dr. Aaron Shaffer, to whose initiative and assistance this volume owes much, has also done the important service of compiling, at no small pains, what we believe to be a complete bibliography of Professor Speiser's publications.

For the gracious help extended us in preparing this volume for the press we wish to thank Miss Mary Cole, formerly secretary of the Department of Oriental Studies at the University of Pennsylvania, and her successor, Mrs. Brenda Sjostrom.

In closing, we express our deep appreciation to the following for courteous permission granted us to reprint the material here included (item numbers refer to the Bibliography listing):

American Council of Learned Societies for item no. 72, reprinted from *Studies in the History of Culture.*

American Oriental Society for items no. 48, 73, 75, 98, 109, 112, 113, 139, reprinted from the *Journal of the American Oriental Society.*

American Schools of Oriental Research for items no. 68, 74, 117, 124, 130, and 141, reprinted from the *Bulletin of the American Schools of Oriental Research,* and items no. 78, 97, 108, reprinted from the *Journal of Cuneiform Studies.*

The *Canadian Bar Review* for item no. 103.

Carl Winter Universitätsverlag for item no. 135, reprinted from *Festschrift Johannes Friedrich.*

Catholic Biblical Quarterly for item no. 143.

Hebrew Union College-Jewish Institute of Religion for item, no. 96, reprinted from *Hebrew Union College Annual,* and item no. 119, reprinted from *Hebrew Union College Booklet* (1956).

The International Commission for the Scientific and

Cultural Development of a History of Mankind (UNESCO) for item no. 105, reprinted from the *Journal of World History.*

Israel Exploration Society for item no. 131, reprinted from *Eretz-Israel,* and for items no. 104 and 127, reprinted from *Israel Exploration Journal.*

The Harvard University Press for item no. 144, reprinted from *The Lown Institute Studies and Texts,* Vol. I.

Journal of Biblical Literature for items no. 116, 121, 137.

Linguistic Society of America for items no. 47, and 69, reprinted from *Language.*

The Magnes Press, The Hebrew University, for item no. 138, reprinted from *Yehezkel Kaufmann Jubilee Volume.*

Pontifical Biblical Institute for items no. 121 and 128, reprinted from *Orientalia.*

University of Chicago Press for item no. 6, reprinted from the *American Journal of Semitic Languages and Literatures.*

Yale University Press for item no. 111, reprinted from *The Idea of History in the Ancient Near East.*

J. J. Finkelstein
Moshe Greenberg

Contents

Ancient Near Eastern History and Culture

Linguistic Studies

Perpectives

List of Abbreviations

AAA	Annals of Archaeology and Anthropology
AASOR	Annual of the American Schools of Oriental Research
ABL	R. F. Harper, Assyrian and Babylonian Letters
ACh	Ch. Virolleaud, L'Astrologie Chaldéenne
AfO (AFO)	Archiv für Orientforschung
AHw	W. von Soden, Akkadisches Handwörterbuch
AJA	American Journal of Archaeology
AJSL	American Journal of Semitic Languages and Literatures
ANET	J. B. Pritchard, Ancient Near Eastern Texts
Annual = AASOR	
AOB	Altorientalische Bibliothek
AOS	American Oriental Series
AOT	H. Gressmann, Altorientalische Tetxe zum AT
Arch. Or. = ArOr	

ARM	Archives Royales de Mari
ArOr	Archiv Orientální
AS	Assyriological Studies
AT	D. Wiseman, Alalakh Tablets
ATD	Das Alte Testament Deutsch
BA	Beiträge zur Assyriologie
BASOR	Bulletin of the American Schools of Oriental Research
BAW	B. Meissner, Beiträge zum assyrischen Wörterbuch
Berlin SB	Sitzungberichte der berliner Akademie der Wissenschaften
Bezold Glossar	C. Bezold, Babylonisch-assyrisches Glossar
Bulletin = BASOR	
CAD	The Assyrian Dictionary of the Oriental Institute of the University of Chicago
CCT	Cuneiform Texts from Cappadocian Tablets in the British Museum
CH	Code of Hammurabi
CT	Cuneiform Texts from Babylonian Tablets in the British Museum
GAG	Wolfr. von Soden, Grundriss der akkadischen Grammatik
Gilg. (Ep.)	Gilgameš-Epic
HSS	Harvard Semitic Series
HUCA	Hebrew Union College Annual
JAOS	Journal of the American Oriental Society
JBL	Journal of Biblical Literature
JCS	Journal of Cuneiform Studies

JEN	Joint Expedition with the Iraq Museum at Nuzi
JNES	Journal of Near Eastern Studies
JQR	Jewish Quarterly Review
JRAS	Journal of the Royal Asiatic Society
JSOR	Journal of the Society of Oriental Research
KAH	Keilschrifttexte aus Assur historischen Inhalts
KAR	Keilschrifttexte aus Assur religiösen Inhalts
KAV	Keilschrifttexte aus Assur verschiedenen Inhalts
KB	Keilinschriftliche Bibliothek
KBo	Keilschrifttexte aus Boghazköi
King, STC	L. W. King, The Seven Tablets of Creation
Knudtzon, Amarna	J. A. Knudtzon, Die El-Amarna-Tafeln
Koschaker Volume	Symbolae . . . Paulo Koschaker Dedicatae, Studia et Documenta ad Iura Orientis Antiqui Pertinentia, II
KUB	Keilschrifturkunden aus Boghazköi
Lang.	Language
MAD	Materials for the Assyrian Dictionary
MAOG	Mitteilungen des altorientalischen Gesellschaft
MSL	B. Landsberger, Materialien zum sumerischen Lexikon

MVA(e) G	Mitteilungen der vorderasiatisch (-ägyptisch)en Gesellschaft
OECT	Oxford Editions of Cuneiform Texts
OIP	Oriental Institute Publications
OLZ	Orientalistische Literaturzeitung
PRU	Palais royal d'Ugarit
PSBA	Proceedings of the Society of Biblical Archaeology
RA	Revue d'Assyriologie
RB	Revue biblique
RIU	C. J. Gadd–L. Legrain, Royal Inscriptions of Ur
RLA	Reallexikon der Assyriologie
SAI	B. Meissner, Seltene assyrische Ideogramme
SAW Wien	Sitzungberichte der kaiserlichen Akademie der Wissenschaften, Wien
ST	O. R. Gurney and J. J. Finkelstein, The Sultantepe Tablets I
TCL	Textes cunéiformes. Musée du Louvre
TSBA	Transactions of the Society for Biblical Archaeology
VAB	Vorderasiatische Bibliothek
VS	Vorderasiatische Schriftdenkmäler der königlichen Museen zu Berlin
W.F.A.	William Foxwell Albright
WVDOG	Wissenschaftliche Veröffentlichungen der deutschen Orient-Gesellschaft

WZKM	Wiener Zeitschrift für die Kunde des Morgenlandes
YBT	Yale Oriental Series. Babylonian Texts
YOS = YBT	
YOR	Yale Oriental Series, Researches
YOT = YBT	
ZA	Zeitschrift für Assyriologie
ZAW	Zeitschrift für die alttestamentliche Wissenschaft
ZDMG	Zeitschrift der deutschen morgenländischen Gesellschaft
ZDPV	Zeitschrift des deutschen Palästina-Vereins

BIBLICAL STUDIES

'ED in The Story of Creation

THE TRADITIONAL EXPLANATIONS OF THE TERM *'ēd* IN GEN. 2:6 range from "spring, source" to "cloud" and "mist."[1] Each is no more than a guess based on the context, which happens to leave a large area open to speculation. The only other occurrence of the term, Job 36:27, is equally inconclusive and may itself owe something to the account in Genesis. In these circumstances, no progress towards the solution of the problem is possible without the aid of comparative etymology.

The best prospect of assistance in the matter rests with Akkadian, in view of the locale of the paradise story. The material, however, which is available there has proved to be almost too much of a blessing. Whereas formerly there was no etymology at all, Akkadian now furnishes two possible prototypes of Herb. *'ēd:* (1) *edû;* (2) *id.* Both are loanwords from the Sumerian, yet they are unrelated generically. Each has to be judged on its own merits.

The term *edû* has been known for many decades in the sense of "flood, waves, swell," and it was compared with Heb. *'ēd* well over sixty years ago.[2] The only reason, ap-

[1] For details cf. the standard commentaries.

[2] This comparison is weighed already in A. Dillmann's *Die Genesis* (1892), p. 52, on the authority of an advanced fascicle of F. Delitzsch, *Assyrisches Handwörterbuch;* cf. the complete edition (abbr. HWb), 1896, p. 22 b.

parently, why this equation has enjoyed only limited acceptance is that the passage in Genesis suggests subterranean waters, a meaning that is not automatically implicit in the hitherto known values of Akk. *edû*. Accordingly, P. Dhorme advanced in 1907 a rival etymology based on Akk. *id* (fr. Sumerian ÍD "river").[3] H. Zimmern was undecided between *edû* and *id*.[4] E. Sachsse, in a special article on *'ēd,* abbduced *id* once again, but limited the sense to "canal, watercourse."[4a] It was not until 1939 that W. F. Albright furnished the argument which raised the equation Heb. *'ēd* = Akk. *id* from a casual and precarious suggestion to a highly attractive probability.[5]

Yet all the doubts about this latter identification were not dispelled even then. It could not be denied, for instance, that *id,* when so pronounced, had a specific cultic bearing, notably so in the Assyrian Laws.[6] Generally, moreover, the Sumerian logogram in question was read in Akkadian as *nāru* "river" and could not, as such, have led to Heb. *'ēd*.[7] Such objections need not be decisive in themselves. The whole question, however, remains open; indeed, Albright himself did not regard it as definitely solved.

It so happens that all the facts in favor of equating Heb. *'ēd* with Akk. *edû* have never been jointly brought to bear on that equation. Each has been available separately for a long time. Cumulatively they would seem to

[3] *Revue Biblique,* 1907, 274.
[4] *Akkadische Fremdwörter,* p. 44.
[4a] ZAW 39 (1921) 176 ff.
[5] JBL 58 (1939) pp. 102–3, n. 25.
[6] See *ibid.* for this and other references.
[7] This does not apply necessarily to the passages which Albright cites from L. W. King, *Seven Tablets of Creation* I 128 f. and from the Mari letters (*Syria* XIX 126). Nevertheless, we can be sure of Akkadian *id* as distinct from *nāru* only when the term is spelled out syllabically; and such explicit instances are relatively rare.

add up to a case against which it would be difficult to take valid exception.

(1) In the Vocabulary VAT 10270 iv 44 ff.[8] the following entries are listed in sequence:

(Sum.)	A.GI$_6$.A =	(Akk.)	*e-gu-[u]*
	A.DÉ.A =		*e-du-u*
	A.SI.GA =		*e-si-gu*
	A.ZI.GA =		*me-lu*
	A.MAḪ =		*bu-tuq-tum*

All these are synonyms for certain bodies of water (= A). The first three are direct loanwords from the Sumerian, with the initial *a*-vowel changing to *e*- under the influence of *e/i* in the following syllable (A. DÉ.A > **ede'a'u* > *edû*). The character of the group as a whole is indicated by the last two entries: *butuqtum* "break-through" (of the subterranean water); *mēlu* "flood, (ground) flow."

(2) One of the common usages of *mēlu* is repeatedly attested in the following refrain from the Atraḫasis Epic:

"Above, let Adad make scarce his rain;
Below, let the flow (*mēlu*) be dammed up,
That it rise not from the source."[9]

Thus *mēlu* is used expressly to signify the flow that rises from underground springs. Synonymous with it is the term for water that has broken through to the surface (*butuqtum*), and also *edû*.

(3) In another vocabulary *edû* is defined as *šaqû ša*

[8] Cf. B. Meissner, *Assyriological Studies,* I, p. 10, No. 4.
[9] Cf. ANET 106 iii 44–5. For the use of *našû* as an intransitive ("to rise), particularly with *mēlu* "flow," see Delitzsch. HWb 485 b.

eqli "watering of the field." [10] The terms listed under (2) above make it clear that the process involved is not the result of manual irrigation but the consequence of natural phenomena. It will be recalled that Gen. 2:6 says of *'ēd* that it "would rise (*ya'lê*) from the earth and water (*w^ehišqâ*) the whole face of the ground." We find thus both with Heb. *'ēd* and with Akk. *edû* the same verb (*šqy*) employed to describe the function of the respective nouns.

(4) All in all, Gen 2:6 contains three terms which are represented by cognates in pertinent Akkadian contexts:

(Heb.) *'ēd*	corresponds to	(Akk.) *edû*
ya'lê		*mēlu*
hišqâ		*šaqû*

Plainly, the Biblical verse might have been lifted verbatim from an Akkadian lexical work.[11]

(5) Finally, one could scarcely counter the force of the above argument by pointing out that *edû* should have resulted in some such form as Heb. **'ēdê*. For one, *'ēd* is a rare term, found but twice in the whole OT; and the posited Akkadian original is itself a loanword, lacking the full potential of native terms. For another, even an established **'ēdê* could have developed an alloform *'ēd*. One need only be reminded of Heb. *'ēš* "fire" which has a well attested alloform *'iššê;* note furthermore the Akk. cognate *išātum* (sg.; the corresponding plural is *išātātum*).

[10] This equation has long been known; cf. Deimel, ŠL 579, 324 b; it was cited, e.g., by Sachsse, ZA 39, p. 181.

[11] Which is not to suggest that this actually occurred.

The Rivers of Paradise

ALTHOUGH THE PARADISE OF THE BIBLE WAS MANIFESTLY A place of mystery, its physical setting cannot be dismissed offhand as sheer imagination. To the writer of the account in Gen. 2:8 ff., in any case, and to his ultimate source or sources, the Garden of Eden was obviously a geographic reality. The fantasy in this instance is the unintentional contribution of interpreters, both ancient and modern.[1] In their efforts to locate the site, countless prospectors have roamed over many regions of the earth. The garden and the rivers that circumscribe it have been sought in such places as Armenia and Transcaucasia, Ethiopia, India, and Mongolia. And as A. H. Sayce noted some sixty years ago, even Australia and the North Pole have had their credulous advocates.[2] In short, the storied delights of Eden have been made to cover a multitude of aberrations.

Various recent findings justify a fresh survey of the problem. The relation of the biblical Urgeschichte to its

[1] Cf. especially Friedr. Delitzsch, *Wo lag das Paradies?* (1881); A. H. Sayce, *Dictionary of the Bible I* (1898), pp. 643 ff.; S. R. Driver, *The Book of Genesis,* 8th ed. (1911), pp. 57–60; W. F. Albright, "The Mouth of the Rivers," AJSL 35 (1919), pp. 161–195, and "The Location of the Garden of Eden," AJSL 39 (1922), pp. 15–31. See also M. D. Cassuto, *Genesis: From Adam to Noah* (1953), pp. 75–79 (in Hebrew).

[2] *Loc. cit.*

Mesopotamian analogues has been clarified on many counts. Our knowledge of the geographic history of Lower Mesopotamia has been substantially advanced in the past few years. And above all, our understanding of the cultural attainments of the ancient Near East in general has been greatly improved. All this has a bearing, in one way or another, on the site of the biblical Paradise.

It is well to bear in mind in this connection that "the important question about any statement contained in a source is not whether it is true or false, but what it means."[3] To put it differently, the problem is basically one of methodology: does the issue lend itself to a conclusion consistent with all the known facts in the case? I believe that it does. The pertinent details, however, are at once too numerous and too diffuse to be duly developed at this time. The alternative is to concentrate on the salient points and list them schematically as so many links in a progressive chain of reasoning.[4]

1. The biblical data on the subject either are a valid point of departure, or they are not. The narrative states explicitly that the garden was planted in the east (vs. 8), and that the four rivers involved had a common meeting place in a single body of water (10). Those who regard the two unidentified streams, the Pishon and the Gihon, as fictional need waste no time speculating about the site of Eden as a whole. But when the existence of the pair is conceded, it is fallacious to look for the Pishon in India, far from the meeting place of the Euphrates and the Tigris, and to locate the Gihon in Ethiopia, which was surely not east of either Mesopotamia or Palestine. One simply cannot have it both ways.

[3] R. G. Collingwood, *The Idea of History* (1946), p. 260.

[4] Such an approach has long been characteristic of Professor Johannes Friedrich, to whose honor this paper is a small token contribution.

2. It does no good to argue, as has often been done, that the ancients had weird notions of geography. When the account before us received its present form, hardly later than the 10th century B.C., Israel had just witnessed, under David, its maximum geographic expansion. By that time, Western Asia, the Nile Valley, and the Aegean had long had many mutual ties. Centuries before, the commercial center of Ugarit benefited from contacts with all these regions. A millennium earlier, there were trade relations between Mesopotamia and the Indus valley; the same is true of Egypt and Mesopotamia at the very dawn of history. Even primitive prehistoric centers like Jarmo managed to obtain obsidian from distant places. There is a vast difference between drawing a reasonably accurate map of a country and dumping the Nile in the Persian Gulf. The chances are that no ancient caravan ever strayed that far from its intended objective.

3. The source of most of our geographic troubles with the biblical Paradise is the mention of a land called *Cush* in Gen. 2:13. Normally, the Bible understands by that term the region of the Upper Nile, cuneiform *Kus/šu, Kas/ši,* Eg. *K'š.* But there was also another, and wholly unrelated, Cush; the Nimrod fragment (Gen. 10:8–12) connects this homonym unmistakably with Mesopotamia, by assigning it to the father of the hero who is said to have founded a number of Babylonian and Assyrian capitals.[5] This particular Cush, then, is the eponym of the Kassites, Akk. *Kaššû;* its Nuzi form *Kuššu-*[6] and its Greek derivative *Kossaîoi,* actually contain the same vowel as the biblical name. Now the Kassite rule over

[5] Cf. my paper on "In Search of Nimrod," *Eretz-Israel* 5 (1958), pp. 32*–36* [below, pp. 41–52].

[6] With the Hurrian adjectical suffix *-ḫi;* for the occurrences see E. R. Lacheman, BASOR 78 (1940), pp. 21 f.

Babylonia had ended by the 12th century. It was bound to be remembered locally for some time afterwards. But how many authors in first-millennium Palestine would be familiar with this footnote to distant history? The narrator of the Urgeschichte—or at least his sources—knew about it, to judge from the Nimrod account and our present passage; for only a Kassite context can accord with the phrase "in the east" of Gen. 2:8. The Samaritan version, too, would seem to reflect the same tradition, for it renders Gihon, the name of the river of Cush, by *'Asqop,* evidently the Choaspes, modern Kerkha. With everyone else, however, it was the Ethiopian Cush, naturally enough, that immediately came to mind. Hence LXX translates the present instance as Ethiopia; and Josephus, Jubilees, the new Genesis Apocryphon,[7] and various other ancient sources go on to identify the Gihon with the Nile.[8] Nor could modern scholarship be blamed at first for its ready acceptance of older opinion, especially before the discovery of the form *Kuššu-,* which was used by next-door neighbors at a time when the Kassites were still very much in power. Today, however, no such excuse can be advanced any longer for detouring both Nimrod and the Gihon all the way to Ethiopia.[9]

4. The river names Pishon and Gihon could only add to the confusion. They were bound to be etymologized as something like "the Gamboler" and "the Gusher" respectively; the latter, moreover, is actually found as the

[7] N. Avigad and Yigael Yadin, *A Genesis Apocryphon* (1956), p. 32.

[8] The old rabbinical authorities were fully aware that this interpretation ran counter to the explicit *miqqedem* "in the east" of Gen. 2:8. This is why they took the word to mean "in the past"; cf. L. Ginzberg, *Legends of the Jews* 5 (1925), pp. 13 f.

[9] It should be emphasized, however, that ever since the appearance of Delitzsch's monograph (see fn. 1) a small group of scholars has held to the equation of the present Cush with the Kassites.

name of a spring near Jerusalem (e.g., I Kings 1:33). Besides, each of these streams is described in the present passage as *sōbēb* its given land, the Heb. participle being interpreted to mean "encompassing, encircling." Now a stream with a playful name and the ability to encircle a whole country does not inspire confidence in its genuinness. It belongs in Cloud-Cuckoo-Land. Small wonder, therefore, that rabbinic tradition had the four rivers represent honey, milk, balsam, and wine.[10] Yet this is not much more fanciful than the other attempts, old and recent, to identify the Pishon with the Ganges or the Indus.[11] Furthermore, the names of the first two rivers of Eden may merely be secondary and Hebraized forms, just as the other two found their way into Greek in the guise of the Tigris[12] and the Euphrates. As for the accompanying *sbb,* the primary meaning of the verb is not so much "to circle," as "to turn." One of its established uses, therefore, is "to pursue an irregular path," hence "to wander." This is still clear from the passage in II Kings 3:9 *wayyāsobbū derek šibᶜat yāmīm,* which tells us that the three kings in question "wandered for seven days," and not that they went around in circles for a whole week. The same sense, incidentally, suggestive of a winding course, is conveyed by Aram. *sᵉḥar,* the equivalent of Heb. *sbb.* The Genesis Apocryphon shows this use repeatedly, once even with the very Gihon of our present text.[13] And "to turn, twist, meander" is precisely what any normal river will do.

5. With Cush and its river thus restored to their re-

[10] Cf. Ginzberg, *op. cit.* I (1909), p. 132. Islamic tradition followed suit.

[11] Cf. Sayce (fn. 1).

[12] Derived from an indigenous term which appears as *Idigna* in Sum., *Idiglat* in Akk., *Ḥiddeqel* in Heb., *Deqlat* in Aram., and *Dijlat* in Arab.

[13] Col. xxi 15.

quired eastern location, the theoretical limits of Eden begin to assume manageable proportions. By the same token there emerges this significant fact: the stated order of the last three out of a total of four Paradise rivers—i.e., the Gihon, the Tigris, and the Euphrates—is east to west. This is exactly the opposite of what one would expect from an Israelite vantage point; for from that direction the first one would be the Euphrates, which for that very reason is not infrequently described simply as "the river" (Gen. 31:21; Exod. 23:21; Num. 22.5, etc.), or "the great river" (Gen. 15:18; Deut. 1. 7; Josh. 1:4). And with three positions thus assured, there is the inherent probability that the remaining stream—the Pishon—would have to be sought still farther east, and presumably not too far from the Gihon. Accordingly, the same uniform sequence should apply also to the central river of Eden itself, which ought thus to be the most easterly of all. The original narrator, therefore, of the account before us has to be visualized as looking from the Persian Gulf inland.

It would seem to follow, then, that the "four heads" of which the text speaks (vs. 10) are meant to be viewed upstream rather than down, something that very few authorities appear to have realized.[14] Yet both Akkadian and Hebrew usage support such a view. Thus Akk. *ina rēs Uqnê* stands for "on the upper Kerkha."[15] And A. Ehrlich has pointed out that the Hebrew term for the lower course, of a stream is *qāṣê* (cf. Josh. 15:5, 18:19); hence *rōš* must refer to the opposite end, the upper course or headstream.[16] Now S. N. Kramer has shown independently that to the poets and priests of Sumer it was

[14] So Sayce *loc. cit.;* also J. W. Dawson, *Modern Science in Bible Lands* (cited in Driver's *Genesis,* p. 58, fn. 1).
[15] Cf. H. Tadmor, JNES 17 (1958), p. 138.9'.
[16] *Randglossen 1* (1908), p. 9.

the Persian Gulf that gave the Tigris and the Euphrates their annual overflow, rather than the invisible thaws in far off Armenia.[17] Strong tidal action in the region of the delta, which has left a salt wedge all the way to modern Qurna,[18] may well have helped to foster this ancient illusion.

6. The biblical text itself contains two semantic trail-markers that point unambiguously to the land and lore of Sumer. One is the geographic term Eden, which hardly can be separated from Sum. edin "plain." The other is the *'ēd* of Gen. 2:6, the term for the groundwater that first irrigated the land. Whether one derives the word, with W. F. Albright, from i d "river," or from a. d e. a (Akk. *edû*) "ground flow," as I have recently advocated,[19] its origin would be Sumerian in any case. Near the head of the Persian Gulf lay the celebrated Dilmun which, as Kramer has shown, was "the land of the living," a place that knew neither sickness nor death, a garden of the gods —or in a word, Paradise. The same general region also bore the name of *pī nārāte* "the mouth of the rivers" (sometimes reduced to "the mouth of the two rivers").[20] Through it access could be gained to the abode of Ut(a)-napishtim, whom the gods had placed there after the Flood, to share in the boon of immortality.[21] The area was thus plainly a favored spot of ancient legend and literature.

Another clue that deserves special mention in the

[17] In his paper on "Dilmun, the Land of the Living," *BASOR* 96 (1944), p. 28, fn. 42.

[18] Cf. P. Buringh, "Living Conditions in the Lower Mesopotamian Plain in Ancient Times," *Sumer* 13 (1957), p. 35.

[19] "*'Ed* in the Story of Creation," BASOR 140 (1955), pp. 9–11 [above pp. 19–22].

[20] Cf. BASOR 96, pp. 27 f.

[21] Gilg. Ep. XI 196.

present context is furnished by sacred architecture. Perhaps the most venerated type of Sumerian sanctuary was the reed shrine, the basic "Gotteshaus" of W. Andrae's pioneering study on the subject.[22] Now the characteristic type of construction that the modern inhabitants of the same region—the so-called Marsh Dwellers or Ma'dān—employ to this day is similiarly based on a reed technique. The latest photographs of contemporary buildings[23] cannot but call to mind immediately the selfsame motifs on archaic Sumerian seals and reliefs. It is worth noting in passing that the Marsh Dwellers are a society apart, so much so that their neighbors often question whether the Ma'dān should at all be regarded as Arabs. We thus have here an immemorial tradition that had a profound spiritual effect on the oldest inhabitants, and has remained very much alive down to the present.

7. There is no need, then, to stray far from the Persian Gulf in search of the Garden of Eden. The biblical text was not anticipating an aquatic Nephelococcygia. What the narrative calls for is an extensive body of sweet water, with ample areas of vegetation dotted through it, and with four sizable rivers fanning out from there upstream. All these conditions, moreover, should be applicable to the past, the 10th century B.C. at the latest. To be sure, hydrographic features in the soft alluvium of Lower Mesopotamia have been far from stable through the ages. Nevertheless, recent technical studies[24] have made it probable that, contrary to all previous calculations, the area from modern Amara eastward must always have contained reedy marsh and shallow lagoon, in the past even

[22] *Das Gotteshaus und die Urformen des Bauens im alten Orient* (1930).
[23] Cf. Gavin Maxwell, *People of the Reeds* (1957).
[24] See especially G. M. Lees and N. L. Falcon, *Geographical Journal* (1952), pp. 24 ff.

more so than today. Much of it appears to have been a sweet-water spur of the Persian Gulf,[25] a shallow lake into which numerous rivers descended, among them the as yet unmerged waters of the Tigris and the Euphrates. Significantly enough, aerial photographs still show traces of ancient cultivation under the present northwest reaches of the Persian Gulf.[26]

8. What is the bearing of these data on the identification of the Pishon and the Gihon? The one definite result is that, at the time when the narrative before us originated, neither of these rivers could have had its estuary very far from the mouths of the Tigris and the Euphrates. This in itself is an appreciable gain, in view of the geographic anarchy that is implicit in so many of the attempted solutions of the question. If one wishes, however, to be even more specific, the choice is as yet by no means self-evident, even though the range has been vastly reduced. The most likely solution should be among one of the following:

a. Gihon-Diyala and Pishon-Kerkha. This presupposes, in line with recent hydrographic studies, that the mouth of the Diyala was at the time considerably farther east than it now is. There is no question that the Diyala winds through much of what was once Kassite terriotry, or one of the two widely separated regions which the Bible designates as Cush. In that case, the Pishon would have to be equated with the Kerkha, a river that comes down from the heart of the Iranian plateau. It so happens that Assyrian records mention Median gold;[27] on the other

[25] Cf. fn. 18. This may explain why Akkadian sources sometimes refer to that region as *Nār marratum* "Bitter River."

[26] Buringh, *loc. cit.*, p. 36.

[27] R. Campbell Thompson, *A Dictionary of Assyrian Chemistry and Geology* (1936), p. 58.

hand, the Havilah of our passage was a non-distinctive geographic designation, being applied in the Table of Nations to more than one place (cf. Gen. 10:7, 29), so that an Iranian namesake is not out of the question. More suggestive, perhaps, is the mention of the *šōham*-stone as one of the products of the Pishon territory. If the Pishon was indeed the Kerkha, then its cuneiform name was *Uqnû* (the lapis lazuli river). Now the biblical term for lapis has yet to be pointed out. It can hardly have been *sappīr,* since sapphire is a different type of blue stone. On the other hand, it is worth noting that *šōham* was the only type of stone used in the decoration of the ephod (e.g., Exod. 25.7). Since lapis would be the corresponding decorative material in Mesopotamia, and since neither the meaning nor the etymology of *šōham* [28] has been determined, there is a good chance that the term referred to lapis.[29] There is the further circumstance that *šōham* is almost invariably accompanied by the word for "stone," which is very rarely the case with other mineral-names in Hebrew; the same is true, of course, of lapis lazuli itself, and probably also of the Sumerian equivalent z a. g ì n.[30] Now just as the Pishon is said to come from a country known for its *šōham*-stone, the Kerkha originates in a land from which lapis was imported in antiquity. What is more, the Assyrian name for the Kerkha was *Uqnû* "the Blue River," or the same term that was also used for lapis. None of this adds up to conclusive proof. But there is at least a fair possibility that the biblical reference to the Pishon in connection with the *šōham*-stone showed an

[28] The often adduced Akk. *sāmtu* "red stone" does not have the same sibilant.

[29] It is interesting to note that Job 28:16 mentions *šōham* together with sapphire, which may suggest similarity while precluding actual identity.

[30] Thompson, *op. cit.,* p. 129.

awareness of the native name *Uqnû*. If these combinations stand up, we shall then have not only a positive equation of the Pishon with the Kerkha but also of the *šōham*-stone with lapis lazuli.

b. Gihon-Kerkha and Pishon-Karun. In favor of this assumption is the known propinquity of the Kerkha and Karun estuaries and the further fact that all four Paradise rivers would then have converged within the compass of the shallow lake area. Another favoring argument would be the Samaritan version's apparent identification of the Gihon with the Choaspes/Kerkha. On the other hand, however, the Kerkha would seem to be placed too far from Kassite territory, unless the biblical statement is taken to allude to the Iranian homeland of the Kassites. When it comes to the Pishon, there is little to choose between the Karun and the Kerkha for purposes of geographic comparison.

c. Gihon-Kerkha and Pishon-Wadi er-Rumma. The latter, or one of the other now dry wadis that slope down from the south, would have to be identified with the Pishon if it is deemed necessary to locate the pertinent land of Havilah in Arabia. Gold is known to have been imported from Arabia as far back as the time of the Royal Tombs of Ur. Furthermore, geographers now estimate that the old shore of the Persian Gulf lay farther to the south,[31] indicating deeper penetration into that quarter in ancient times. It remains to be shown, however, that any of the present wadis was sufficiently active during the period in question to constitute a sizable and perennial river. And if *šōham* was actually lapis, Arabia's stake in the matter would have to be given up.

To sum up, the above discussion has not produced any-

[31] Buringh, *loc. cit.*, p. 37.

thing like a Treasure Island[32] map of Eden, for all the reported gold of Havilah. What I have tried to show is that the biblical text, the traditions of ancient Mesopotamia, the geographic history of the land at the head of the Persian Gulf, and the surviving building practices in that marshy country point jointly to an older garden land, richly watered, and favored by religion and literature alike—the kind of Paradise, in short, that local tradition still locates at the confluence of the Euphrates and the Tigris. Accordingly, the physical background of the biblical Garden of Eden outlines a real, though remote and atypical, sector of the ancient Near East.

[32] For mythical accounts of fabulous treasures cf. the Copper Scroll from Qumran see the discussion by J. T. Milik, *Bibl. Arch.* *19* (1956), pp. 60–62, with parallels from Josephus and some Islamic sources; see also S. Mowinckel, JBL 76 (1957), pp. 261–65.

YDWN, Gen 6:3

THE FORM WHICH APPEARS AS *yādōn* IN GEN. 6:3, IN THE midst of the ever troublesome passage about the primeval giants, has long been the subject of exegetical attention. Yet the strict sense of the verb remains unexplained. There is no basic agreements as to its meaning either in the versions or among the commentators. None of the emendations proposed by the moderns has carried any noticeable appeal.[1] Most translations, to be sure, starting with the LXX, give the connotation 'remain, abide,' but this is no more than a guess based on the context. The etymologies that have been attempted fall back on one form or another of the "hollow" stem *d-n* or of the middle-geminate root *dnn*.[2] The results, however, have so far proved to be unsuited to the context or not fully in accord with actual usage at the source.[3] A third group, limited to a small body of rabbinical commentators, favored a link with *ndn,* which is twice attested in the OT as a noun in the sense of 'sheath.' [4] But this particular approach ran into linguistic obstacles and met with rejec-

[1] For details cf. the standard commentaries.

[2] See also the modern comparative dictionaries, including that of F. Zorell, *s. v.*

[3] L. Koehler, *Lexicon,* p. 206, simply lists the form as unexplained, omitting all the literature on the subject.

[4] See below, n. 18.

tion on the part of such authorities as al-Fāsi and Ibn Ezra.

Since none of the suggested solutions based on comparative or textual techniques has had any success, we are obliged to go back to the traditional form and grant it the full benefit of the doubt. The consonantal text is indirectly borne out as far back as the translation of Symmachus whose *krineî* reflects an underlying Heb. *dyn*. But the Masoretic reading is specific also in regard to the vocalization, in that it insists on *yādōn* rather than **yādūn,* which would be the expected form from a posited **dwn*.[5] It should be stressed that the received reading can be reconciled only with **dnn*. Hence in transliterating we have to normalize the form as *yādon,* with short stem vowel. The plene writing with II gem. forms is not the rule, to be sure, yet it occurs often enough to cause no difficulty. It is frequent with Nifals,[6] but there are instances of it with Qals as well, including intransitives; cf. *yāʿōz* (fr. ʿzz 'to be strong') Dan 11:12.

In line with this reasoning the natural tendency would be to connect *yādon* with the very common Akk. *danānu* 'to become strong' and its adjective *dannu* 'mighty.' Yet such a sense could hardly be fitted into the present context. Accordingly, U. Cassuto sought to posit another Akk. **danānu,* as reflected in the attested *madnanu, dinnū, dinnūtu,* 'bedstead'; he assumed the underlying sense to be something like 'to be fixed, to remain in a specified place.'[7] The results cannot be said to inspire the slightest degree of confidence.

There is, however, still another Akk. base *dnn* which

[5] E. Kraeling, in his paper on "The Significance and Origin of Gen. 6:1–4" (*JNES,* VI [1947], 193 ff.), posits an underlying *dwn* in the sense of 'contend, strive,' without adequate linguistic justification. The required vocalization in that case would have had to be **yādūn.*

[6] Cf. e.g., G. Bergsträsser, *Hebräische Grammatik,* II, 27 i.

[7] See his *From Adam to Noah*[2] (1953, in Hebrew), p. 203.

yields the nominal forms *dinānu* and *andunānu.* These interchangeable terms afford an intimate glimpse into Mesopotamian thinking. The sense is that of 'personal substitute, surrogate, scape-goat.'[8] An Old Babylonian petitioner writes: *a(d)dinānikunu ba'irāku* 'as your *dinānu* I suffer hunger.'[9] The normal greeting formula in letters of the Kassite period is *ana dinān bēliya lullik* 'may I serve as my master's *dinānu.*' The same phrase recurs in an Amarna text[10] and in the tablets from Tell Billa (Šibaniba).[11] Among its occurrences in the royal correspondence of Assyria, the most instructive, no doubt, is in ABL 437.10 ff.: here a courtier and his wife, who have been chosen as substitutes (*ana dināni*) and for the redemption (*ana pidīšunu*) of the king and his brother "go to their fate" and are buried with all the ceremony which this melancholy occasion requires.[12]

The term *dinānu* is thus essentially a synonym of *pūhu* 'substitute' in the technical expiatory sense.[13] Indeed it shares with the latter the Sumerian equivalent *sag.íl,* which is reflected in turn in the famous chronicle about the substitute king Enlilbani.[14] The whole concept, in short, is well established throughout the history of ancient Mesopotamia.

Thus far, however, the term in question has been at-

[8] Cf. B. Landsberger, *MAOG,* IV (1928), 300, n. 2; A. L. Oppenheim, *JAOS,* LXIII (1943), 33.

[9] A. Ungnad, *Vorderasiatische Bibliothek,* VI (1914), 180.18 f.

[10] *EA* 12.25.

[11] J. J. Finkelstein, *JCS,* VII (1953), 135 and E. A. Speiser, *Symbolae Koschaker* (1939), p. 149.

[12] Cf. R. Labat, *Le caractère religieux de la royauté assyro-babylonienne* (1939), pp. 359 f.; H. Frankfort, *Kingship and the Gods* (1948), p. 264.

[13] Note the same sense in the Hurrian loanword *puḫugar-* as reflected in the secondary borrowing in Hittite from the Hurrian; cf. Speiser, *Introduction to Hurrian* (1941), p. 136, n. 207.

[14] L. W. King, *Chronicles Concerning Early Babylonian Kings* I (1907), 12.9 (to be read *ana ṣalam pūḫišu*), and cf. Labat ,op. cit., p. 103, Frankfort, *op. cit.,* p. 263.

tested only as a noun, whereas its assumed biblical correspondent appears as a verb. In this dilemma the recently published tablets from Alalakh may prove to be of assistance. A close morphologic parallel of *dinānu* is *durāru* 'freeing' in that both nouns—and only these two—have alloforms with *an–* (*andunānu, andurāru*). Now the latter (which appears in Hebrew as *d'rōr* 'manumission') has been shown to occur in Alalakh as a denominative: *ina andarārim ul inandar* 'she shall not be granted remittance of her financial obligations.'[15] We have here consequently a close parallel to the assumed denominative use of (*an*)-*dinānu* in a similar intransitive application.

The meaning of the biblical term would be, accordingly, something like 'expiate, answer for,' in other words, 'shield, protect.' The whole sentence would read: "My spirit shall not answer for[16] man forever, in that he too is but flesh. His days shall be therefore a hundred and twenty years." I submit that this rendering, supported by abundant evidence in Akkadian and cleared for Hebrew usage against the several obstacles in its way, is far more telling and appropriate in this context than any that has hitherto been ventured, without comparable justification. It is not merely a question of being immanent in man, with all the theological complications that this would entail. It is rather a matter of shouldering the consequences of man's behavior. The passage as a whole, it should be remembered, is a preamble to the story of the Flood and an explanation of the impending universal disaster.[17] New Hurro-Hittite material, taken in conjunction with long-known Phoenician and Greek sources,

[15] Cf. Speiser, "The Alalakh Tablets," *JAOS*, LXXIV (1954), 22.

[16] The force of the preposition *b-* in this instance is not that of 'in' but of 'on behalf of, for the sake of'; cf. Exod 10:12, Amos 2:8, and the like.

[17] See E. Kraeling, cited in n. 5.

adds up to a picture of cosmic concepts which the biblical writer could not but view as morally depraved.[18] A deadline on shielding the guilty much longer is precisely what the text calls for. It would seem that this is also exactly what the text says.

In this connection it is interesting to note that some of the old rabbinical sources and certain of the later writers versed in that material already operated with the same idea of 'shield, protect' in dealing with the form *yādon*.[19] They based this on the occurrences of a nominal form containing the consonants *ndn,* which is found in the Aramaic portion of Daniel (7:15, significantly in association with *rūḥī,* just as in the passage before us) and in I Chron. 21:27. The indicated sense in both instances is that of 'sheath,' which serves to protect the sword and could be used metaphorically, it was felt, as a symbol of protection for mankind. Other medieval grammarians and lexicographers found the combination far-fetched and the suggestion was eventually given up. Now, however, there exists the outside chance that the idea may have been a sound one after all. A direct connection between *yādon* and *ndn* would indeed be difficult to establish. We know, however, that *dinānu* had an alloform *andunānu,* which could serve, at least theoretically, as a suitable source of Heb.*nādān,* BAram. *n'dān* 'sheath.' Nor are the semantic conditions unfavorable to such an assumption. It must be admitted, however, that tre necessary chain of evidence lacks more than one link. This

[18] Cf. my comments in *Journal of World History,* I (1953), 325 [below, pp. 266–269].

[19] Sanhedrin 108a; Bereshit Rabbah 26.11; Sa'dia, *ad loc.* (=*yngmd*); Ibn Quraysh, *Risāla,* ed. M. Katz, p. 73 (I owe this last reference to my colleague Dr. Moshe Greenberg); 'Ali Ben Suleimān (ed. S. Skoss), p. 127. For the rejection of this view see David ben Abraham al-Fāsi, as quoted by S. Skoss, *op. cit.,* p. 128; Ibn Ezra, *ad loc.*

particular case might well rest on no more than a highly intriguing coincidence.

Another possible relative of *dinānu* which might suggest itself in passing is Nuzi *ditennu/tidennu* and its abstract in *–ūtu,* signifying an antichretic pledge to cover a loan, whereby either a person or specified real estate serves to secure the loan while the gain accruing from the use of the pledge covers the interest involved.[20] Semantically, the combination with *dinānu* is faultless, but the morphologic conditions are by no means impeccable. For this reason I am even more disinclined to press this point than I would be to insist on a relationship between *dinānu* and *ndn* 'sheath.' The sole purpose of this brief paper has been to point out the possibility, which I confess to have found highly attractive, of an ultimate connection between Heb, *yādon* and Akk. *dinānu.*

[20] Cf. Speiser, *JAOS,* LII (1932), 350 ff. and contrast P. Koschaker, *Abh. der phil.-hist. Klasse der sächsischen Akad. d. Wiss.,* XLII (1931), 84. Previously (*ibid.,* XXXIX [1928], 131) Koschaker and B. Landsberger had assumed a derivation from *nadānu* or *tadānu* 'to give.' [A denominative formation from *dinānu* has since been attested; cf. A. L. Oppenheim, AFO 18, 278, and W. v. Soden, *Akkadisches Handwörterbuch,* 160.]

In Search of Nimrod

THE FIGURE OF NIMROD HAS CLAIMED ATTENTION ALMOST from the moment that a reference to this hero's exploits strayed into Genesis 10. "The mighty hunter before the Lord" has himself been the object of ceaseless chase. Greek, rabbinical and Islamic sources echo the pursuit of this elusive target.[1] Modern scholarship has taken up the task with redoubled vigor. Yet the prey remains at large.

The ancient attempts to run down Nimrod may not quite range from A to Z, but they do happen to include Amraphel as well as Zoroaster. It is the moderns, however, who really have roamed far and wide in their efforts to explain the hero and his name. Among the diverse suggestions that have been offered, we find gods (Marduk,[2] Ninurta [3]), demigods (Gilgamesh,[4] Lugalbanda [5]), as well as sundry mortals (Amenophis III/*Nimmuria*,[6]

[1] For the rabbinical and Greek references cf. the extensive material cited in Louis Ginzberg's *Legends of the Jews* V, p. 199 ff.

[2] First proposed by Josef Grivel, *TSBA* 3 (1874), p. 136 ff.; cf. also J. Wellhausen, *Die Composition des Hexateuchs*, p. 309 f., and T. G. Pinches, Scribner's *Dictionary of the Bible* III, p. 552 f.

[3] P. Jensen and A. Ungnad, cf. *OLZ* 20, p. 359, n. 2.

[4] Based on the older reading of the name as Izdubar; cf. George Smith, *TSBA* 1, p. 205, and Paul Haupt, *Das Nimrodepos*.

[5] Presupposing an assumed *Nu/En-marad-da;* cf. A. Deimel, *Orientalia* 26 (1927), p. 76 ff., and E. G. Kraeling, *AJSL* 38 (1922), p. 214 ff.

[6] For this suggestion by Kurt Sethe cf. G. von Rad, *Das erste Buch Moses*, p. 122.

Ben-Hadad/*Bir-adda.*[7] Syria, Egypt, and even Libya,[8] aside from Mesopotamia, are among the lands that have been asked to give asylum to Nimrod's prototype. It can be seen at a glance that the participants in these academic sweepstakes comprise some of the most distinguished authorities on the ancient Near East to appear in the past seventy years, not to mention contemporary orientalists.

The first step in a constructive review of the problem should be to reduce the area of search by discarding leads that have proved or can be proved to be false. Gilgamesh and Lugalbanda, e.g., were adduced on faulty onomastic grounds. And the African entries–even though they may carry the endorsement of such illustrious men as Eduard Meyer and Kurt Sethe—lean heavily on the erroneous notion that biblical Cush, here listed as Nimrod's father, always refers to Ethiopia. It is now well known that this name is ambiguous, in that it may point either to the Upper Nile valley or to Mesopotamia. In the latter usage the name corresponds to Akk. *Kaššû (Nuzi Kušš-* [9]), Greek *Kossaîoi* (Kassites/Cossaeans).[10]

All assumptions, moreover, of an extra-Mesopotamian origin of Nimrod have another serious fault in common. They are predicated on the outright rejection of the entire traditional account, including the specific details which it contains. Yet to dismiss, say, the geographic

[7] T. K. Cheyne, *Encyclopaedia Biblica,* col. 3417-19.

[8] Eduard Meyer, *Israeliten und ihre Nachbarstämme,* 1906, p. 448.

[9] It is wholly immaterial in this connection whether the Nuzi form is based on an eponymous deity or not; cf. K. Balkan, *Die Sprache der Kassiten,* 1954 (*AOS* 37), p. 109. That this form is wholly independent of the name of the Hurrian moon-god *Kušuḫ* follows conclusively from the nature of the underlying sibilants (cf. my *Introduction to Hurrian,* p. 34 and contrast Balkan, p. 31 f.). The ethnicon is written with —*šš*—/*s,* whereas the deity is characterized by *š*–/*z* (single writing). The important thing is that the Nuzi form reflects an *u*-vowel, as does bibl. *kuš.*

[10] For an inescapable reference to the land of the Kassites, see Gen. 2:13 [also see above, p. 25].

content of the Nimrod passage as so much aetiology or popular fancy is to persist in the kind of scepticism that modern discoveries have confounded time and again. In the instance before us there is sufficient internal evidence to stamp the physical background of the story as authentic. For in so far as they can be identified at all, the cities assigned to Nimrod bear out the author's knowledge of his setting: each was a prominent Mesopotamian centre, and each served as a major capital at one time or another. This is true of Ashshur,[11] Calah, and Nineveh in Assyria, and is equally true of Babylon, Erech, and Akkad[12] "in the land of Shinar" (Sumer). Now a source familiar with these facts, a source aware of the transient glories of Calah or Uruk or Akkad, would scarcely have credited the building and control of these places to an Amenophis who reigned long before Calah was founded and never even got close to Babylonia or Assyria. Here, in short, is no spurious display of ill-assorted information. What we have instead is a literary piece sketched against a solid backdrop of history and geography. The home of this tale is Mesopotamia. The same must hold true also of its hero and his name.

The Nimrod account, then—Gen. 10:8–12—should not be condemned without a fair trial. An unprejudiced

[11] Although the syntax is ambiguous at this point, the text surely cannot have intended to exclude Ashshur as a city. If Gen. 10:11 is interpreted by many to mean "From that land he [Nimrod] went forth to Ashshur and built Nineveh" etc., nothing further needs to be done. Since stylistic requirements, however, favour the rendering "went forth Ashshur", the alternative would be to assume an ellipsis and understand the clause to mean "he went forth and built Ashshur".

[12] Albright's proposal, improving on a suggestion by A. Poebel, to read *kullānā* for *kalnē* and render "all of them" (*JNES* 3 [1944], p. 254 f.) is so plausible that it has been widely acclaimed by most subsequent commentators; contrast, however, A. S. Yahuda, *JBL* 65 p. 325 f. There is scarcely room for a freak like *Calneh in such company as Babylon, Uruk, and Akkad.

approach to it promises worthwhile dividends. For instance, we know that the hero of our all too brief tale was active throughout the length and breadth of the land. Yet his activities were strictly mundane, no matter how heroic their scope. Nimrod's domain embraced both Assyria and Babylonia. His prowess as a hunter was to become proverbial. These are, to be sure, extraordinary achievements, but they are not of themselves supernatural. In other words, although of heroic stature, Nimrod was not a divine being. Accordingly, it should have been apparent from the start, even without benefit of linguistics, that Nimrod was not to be confused with Marduk. By the same token, however, there is likewise no warrant for equating the hero with Ninurta, for all that the latter was the god of the chase as well as of war, and bore a name that agrees with Nimrod. For if the biblical account has any value at all, Nimrod was clearly a mortal.

Similarly, a re-evaluation of the biblical tale is capable of yielding valid chronological limits which could then be tested independently. The lower terminus is necessarily the date of the actual passage itself. Now it so happens that this particular portion of the Table of Nations is assigned by the critics, with virtual unanimity, to the "J" source. On this basis, therefore, the Nimrod passage cannot be later than the turn of the tenth century B.C.E. The upper terminus, on the other hand, is provided by the mention of Calah, this being the latest known city listed in this connection. According to a statement in the annals of Ashurnasirpal II (iii, 132), Calah was founded by a Shalmaneser. Theoretically this could refer to one of two of Ashurnasirpal's ancestors by that name: either Shalmaneser II (c. 1028–1017[13]), or Shalmaneser I (c. 1272–1243). The younger of these, however, was a shadowy figure whose brief reign was not distinguished for any notable enterprise, whereas his older namesake had proved to be an outstanding ruler in every way. It is not surprising, therefore, that the founding of Calah is generally ascribed to Shalmaneser I. On this basis the date of Nimrod has to be placed in the first half of the thirteenth century at the earliest.

Accordingly, if there is a kernel of truth behind the legend of Nimrod, his historical prototype should fulfill the following conditions. His date must fall somewhere between the thirteenth and the eleventh centuries. He must have been a famous king whose domain included Babylonia but centered about Assyria; for the fact should not be overlooked that to an eighth-century Judean the land of Nimrod was synonymous with Assyria (Micha 5:5). The name of this Mesopotamian, moreover, should have some tangible relation to that of Nimrod. Above all, the man himself must have had in him the stuff of which legends are made.

Given this set of prerequisites, we do not have far to look for the solution of the problem. There is but one Assyrian king who meets every one of these requirements. Indeed, all of them seem to be made to order for him, and him alone. He is known to history as Tukulti-Ninurta I.

The high point of Tukulti-Ninurta's long and eventful reign (ca. 1246–1206) was unquestionably his conquest of

[13] The dates of Middle Assyrian rulers are still subject to minor adjustments. For the sake of convenience I have adopted the absolute dates given by E. Weidner in *AfO* 15, p. 101.

Babylon. The Kassite ruler of this great traditional centre was carried off to Ashshur, as was also the statue of the national god Marduk. The victor could now add to his other titles that of "King of Sumer and Akkad." It was the first time in history that an Assyrian held sway over all of Babylonia. Such an achievement was not to be repeated until five centuries later, under Tiglath-Pileser III. Small wonder, therefore, that these two awesome milestones came to loom large in the minds of Mesopotamians and were highlighted as late as Hellenistic times.[14] But the desecration by Tukulti-Ninurta of the venerated temple of Marduk was bound to shock religious sensibilities throughout the conqueror's realm. This may well have been the reason for the brooding restlessness that marked the latter half of Tukulti-Ninurta's career. The king sought relief in feverish building activity, mostly in his capital city of Ashshur, but also elsewhere, and specifically in Nineveh. Eventually he built himself a new capital a short distance from tradition-ridden Ashshur. And it was within the shining walls of Kār-Tukulti-Ninurta, soon to become a ghost city, that the builder met his death, hemmed in by rebel forces under the command of his own son.[15]

Here, then, was a forceful and independent ruler, resolute and ruthless, enormously successful, yet obviously a prey to dark impulses—in many ways a prototype of Israel's Saul. That he could inspire fierce loyalty as well as implacable hatred is proved by an epic, obviously the work of a contemporary poet, describing in an exalted style and with rich imagery the events that led up to the

[14] See below, n. 31.

[15] Cf. E. F. Weidner, *AfO* 13, p. 109 f.; W. von Soden, *Herrscher im alten Orient,* 1954, p. 68 ff.

fratricidal war wtih Babylon. This epic has no close parallel in all the literature of Mesopotamia.[16] Its nearest analogues have to be sought among the poetic works of the Bible. If Tukulti-Ninurta's life was sufficient inspiration for such a composition, his tragic death could only enhance his standing with posterity and help to superimpose legend upon history.

It should now be immediately apparent how well the slim data about Nimrod fit into the much richer background of Tukulti-Ninurta. In both instances we are confronted with famous rulers whose authority extended over the whole of Mesopotamia. The biblical fragment, incidentally, gains in import as soon as v. 10 is given the only possible logical rendering of "The mainstays (*rēšīt*[17]) of his kingdom were Babylon and Erech and Akkad, all these being (*wᵉkullānā*[18]) in the land of Shinar." Any heir to these three ancient dynastic centres would indeed be "King of Sumer and Akkad." Let us recall further that Ashshur and Nineveh are cities in which building works of Tukulti-Ninurta have been directly attested, while Calah was founded by that same king's father and was, moreover, a city holy to Ninurta, the king's protective deity.[19] Lastly, the Cushitic connections of Nimrod which the biblical account reflects gain a measure of support from the fact that Tukulti-Ninurta reigned within the Kassite period and crowned his political career with a victory over a Kassite ruler.

[16] E. Ebling, *MAOG* 12/2; cf. v. Soden, *op. cit.,* p. 69 ff [Add now W. G. Lambert, *AfO* 18 (1957), p. 38 ff.].

[17] See already v. Rad, *loc. cit.,* p. 122. That the Heb. term can mean "choicest" as well as "first" is, of course, independently attested. But the "beginning of his kingdom" results in an incoherent context whereas the "main/best parts of his kingdom" (cf., e.g., Deut. 33:21; Jer. 49:35) is immediately intelligible.

[18] See above, note 12.

[19] Cf. H. Lewy *JNES* 11 (1952), p. 267.

The one important feature of the Nimrod story for which there is no counterpart in the known records of Tukulti-Ninurta is the celebrated hunting motif. But the extant material cannot be expected to be exhaustive.[20] Besides, the Assyrian's very name carries of itself a plausible reason for the hunting element in the story. The god Ninurta, of course, was himself a famous hunter and patron of hunters; it is to him that Tiglath-Pileser I gives credit for his own prodigious hunting feats (Prism iii, 57). And it is on this very count, as much as on linguistic grounds, that scholars have equated Nimrod with Ninurta, even though this comparison can scarcely be regarded as feasible any longer.

In passing, it may be of interest to point out that the Nimrod fragment in Genesis has been described independently as a survival of what had once been a full-bodied epic tale.[21] Now literary treatments of historical personalities will often overdraw the exotic at the expense of the familiar, or substitute the fictional for the factual. The various legends about Sargon and Naramsin are ample indication of such tendencies.[22] In any case, there are more ways than one to account for the hunting motif in Nimrod.

There remains, finally, the problem of the name *Nimrod* as against *Tukulti-^{d}Ninurta.* Herein lies probably the crux of the whole question, i.e., the reason why this particular comparison has not been pressed to date. The answer may not be apparent at first glance. Nevertheless,

[20] Cf., however, note 34.

[21] See U. Cassuto, *From Noah to Abraham,* 2nd ed. 1953 (in Hebrew), p. 136 ff.

[22] Cf. H. G. Güterbock, Die historische Tradition, *ZA* 42, p. 24 ff.; E. A. Speiser, in *The Idea of History in The Ancient Near East,* 1955 (*AOS* 38), p. 54 ff. [below, pp. 270 ff.].

it is neither complex nor far-fetched. What is more, it leads to a substantial amount of further evidence which bids fair, in turn, to clinch the identification that has here been advocated.

When one deals with proper names, one sometimes tends to forget that long forms tend to be replaced by shorter ones, especially when they are used familiarly or have been transplanted from their native soil. To stay within the biblical and Akkadian fields,[23] I need call attention only to *Baladan* (*bl'dn*),[24] the name of Merodach-Baladan's father (2 Kings 20:12; Isa. 39:1), and *Belteshazzar* (*blṭš'ṣr*), the Babylonian name of Daniel (Dan. 1:7, etc.). There can be little doubt that these are abbreviated forms, the initial element—in these instances Nabû, Marduk, Nergal, Bēl, or the like—having been sloughed off (cf. esp. Dan. 4:5). The process may have taken place on foreign soil, but it could likewise have happened at home; cf. *Aḫa-iddin*: *ᵈNergal-aḫa-iddin* or *Šuma-iddin*: *ᵈMarkud-šuma-iddin*, *Bēl-aḫḫē*: *ᵈNinurta-bēl-aḫḫīšu*, and many others.[25] In these particular examples the dropped initial element happens to be the divine component. But in such examples as: *Ámur-rabūt-Adad*: *Rabūt-Sin* or *Ṭāb-šār-ᵈŠamaš*: *Šār-Aššur* the theophorous part has been left intact. In *Itti-Ea-balātum*: *Itti-Ea*, the final part has been given up.[26] If there is any single principle behind these abbreviations, it would

[23] I may be permitted, however, one outside example because it is both instructive and unfamiliar. In the Italo-American dialect heard on the Atlantic Seaboard, the name *Atlantic City* often becomes *Niksi'ri*, which is easily explained as soon as it is realized that the starting point is not the full name but the abbreviated form "(*Atlan*)*nik-City*'".

[24] As a matter of fact, all that the native sources tell us about Marduk-apla-iddina (II) is that he was *mār Yakina*, i.e., either son or descendant of one *Yakinu;* cf. R. P. Doughterty, *YOR* XIX, p. 44 ff.

[25] Cf. J. J. Stamm, *Die Akkadische Namengebung*, 1939, p. 111 ff.

[26] *Ibid.*, p. 116.

seem to be that the shortened form should be self-sufficient: *Baladan* (*aplam-iddina*) still makes sense as "he has granted a son"; but **Ámur-rabūt* "I beheld the majesty of" could not survive independently, which is why the shortened form had to dispense with the verb and not the divine element, thus becoming *Rabūt-Sin* "the majesty of Sin."

The full name *Tukulti-^{d}Ninurta* is obviously a mouthful. If it was to be simplified, the element to be dropped was *tukulti,* since "the trust of" is a homeless form by itself. The result would thus have to be *Ninurta* alone. Such residual forms of personal names are not common, to be sure, in Mesopotamian records, yet they do occur; cf., e.g., *Marduku* and *Aššur* as names of persons.[27] In foreign use, however, any original hesitancy to misapply divine names in this fashion would readily disappear. In other words, *Tukulti-^{d}Ninurta* would give way to Ninurta > Nimrod.[28]

The suggestion just advanced is not completely speculative. For as a matter of fact, Tukulti-Ninurta I found his way into one known literary tradition in a similarly abbreviated form. I refer to the *Ninus* of the Greek sources. That this is a literary figure is immediately apparent from the many fabulous achievements for which he has been given credit. His composite character, moreover, has recently been brought out by H. Lewy,[29] who

[27] *Ibid.,* p. 117, n. 3.

[28] The Heb. form *Tiglath-pileser for* Tukulti-apal-ešarra III does not refute the above contention since it is found in historical accounts (2 Kings 15:29; 16:7,9) whereas *Nimrod* came in through literary channels. Yet even the great bearer of that royal name found it expedient—although for political reasons, to be sure—to assume the much simpler name of *Pūlu* in his capacity as king of Babylon. Did the sound of the middle element *—apal—* contribute in any way to the choice of the otherwise unrelated *Pūlu?*

[29] *JNES* 11 (1952), 264-70.

has also shown that there is no sound basis for regarding Ninus simply as the eponymous hero of Nineveh.[30] But to restrict Ninus to some of the features of Šhamshi-Adad V and Sennacherib alone—as Dr. Lewy has done—is to stress only a part of the story, and a secondary part at that. Berossos, whose competence as a historian has been vindicated time and again, implies that Ninus was the first Assyrian to rule Babylonia, and that his reign was separated from that of Phul (*Pūlu*/Tiglath-Pileser III) by the reigns of 45 Babylonian kings.[31] In other words, the original Ninus could be none other than Tukulti-Ninurta I.[32] Diodorus Siculus hints at much the same thing by stressing that Ninus' first campaign was directed against Babylonia;[33] for this was likewise Tukulti-Ninurta's most fateful achievement, clearly recorded in the historical works of Assyria and Babylonia and commemorated, besides, in a unique Assyrian epic. It should be noted in this connection that Ninus was also renowned for his encounters with the lion and leopard.[34] Accordingly, the Greek form of the name cannot simply be traced back to Nineveh, a city whose connection with Tukulti-Ninurta was no more than incidental. The source of *Ninus* has to be the name of his Assyrian prototype, or some element therof, hence its divine component *Ninurta.* The association with Nineveh would be a secondary embellishment. All in all, the Greek sources would seem to have arrived at their Ninus by the same

[30] *Ibid.*, p. 270.

[31] See P. Schnabel, *Berossos,* p. 267 (39a)—the identity of Ninus being vouched for in this instance by the mention of Semiramis—and cf. *ibid.*, p. 151 f. See also F. Cornelius, *AfO* 17, p. 295.

[32] Cornelius, *loc. cit.;* cf. v. Soden, *Herrscher,* p. 69.

[33] Cf. H. Lewy, *JNES* 11 (1952), 298.

[34] See the comment and references in Layard, *Nineveh and its Remains* II, p. 431 f.

process that gave the Bible its Nimrod, both being based on a hypochoristic form of Tukulti-Ninurta.

We have, then, before us two distinct legendary figures, each descended from the same historical personality. The evidence would appear to be compelling enough as it is. But there is still a further link, one which assumes added interest and importance in the light of the foregoing discussion. Ninus and Nimrod are no strangers to each other. Various ancient sources connect the two directly.[35] The most noteworthy of these is Berossos, who is quoted as stating explicity that "the Assyrians identify this Ninus with Nimrod." [36] If there was a loophole in the chain of evidence adduced thus far,[37] this last link should close it very effectively.

[35] Cf. Ginzberg, *Legends of the Jews* V, p. 201 f. Note, moreover, the material in Layard, *op. cit.*, p. 222 f.

[36] Apollonius, *Fragmenta,* p. 59; Layard, *loc. cit.*

[37] No special significance attaches, of course, to the fact that the site of ancient Calah bears the modern name of *Nimrud,* since other Mesopotamian sites are similarly linked with the same vivid hero. Nevertheless, all such occurrences add up to an impressive reminder that the appeal of Nimrod carried over undiminished into Islamic times, especially in the land which tradition has steadfastly maintained as his home.

Word Plays on the Creation Epic's Version of the Founding of Babylon

ALL MODERN DISCUSSIONS ABOUT THE BIBLICAL NARRATIVE about the Tower of Babel agree that the traditional version had a concrete starting point in Mesopotamia. Most writers, moreover, trace the specific focus to Etemenanki, the temple tower or *ziqqurrat*[1] adjacent to Esagila, Marduk's sacred precinct in Babylon.[2] To judge from extant descriptions, the argument runs, the Marduk ziqqurrat was sufficiently impressive in appearance and over-all height—ca. 91 m.—to have inspired the biblical account whereby the ancient Babylonians had set out to scale heaven but ended up in a polyglot diffusion on earth. Indeed, the very name *Etemenanki* "foundation structure of heaven and earth" has been cited as the ultimate source of the phrase "with its head in heaven" in Gen. 11.4.[3]

That the tale as a whole rests on some Mesopotamian

[1] I retain the form with *z-* as the more familiar one, even though *siqquarratum* appears to be linguistically preferable; note also *ziq-qur-rat* in E-e VI 62, a passage which will figure prominently in this paper.

[2] For the extensive literature on the subject cf. E. Unger, RLA I 331 f.; A. Parrot, *Ziggurats et Tour de Babel* and *La Tour de Babel:* W. Baumgartner, ArOr 18 75 n. 36; A. Oppenheim, *Encyclopedia Biblica* II 28, and U. Cassuto, *ibid.* 30 f. and *From Noah to Abraham* (2nd ed.) 154 ff. (the last three publications in Hebrew).

[3] Cassuto, *From Noah to Abraham* 165.

foundation can hardly be subject to doubt. The assumption, however, that the actual source was monumental fails to stand the test of closer probing. Babylon's celebrated stage tower was but one of many such temple towers throughout Mesopotamia. It need not even have been the tallest among them. The remains of the ziqqurrat at Borsippa still rise to a height of 47 m.,[4] those at Dūr-Kurigalzu are 57 m. high, thus comparing favorably with the 91 m. given as the original elevation of Etemenanki.[5] Furthermore, the earliest known references to Etemenanki do not antedate the seventh century B.C.[6] The biblical account, on the other hand, is commonly attributed to "J," which would make it no less than two centuries earlier. In other words, the temple tower as rebuilt by Nabopalassar and described by Herodotus could not in the strict sense be the subject of the tale in Genesis. Lastly, the element *-anki* occurs also with other ziqqurrats, notably that of Borsippa.[7] Babylon had no monopoly on this score.

In these circumstances it must come as a surprise that the assumption of a direct visual influence behind the biblical account has never been seriously questioned. Only a few incidental demurrers have been raised altogether. O. E. Ravn, e.g., wondered whether the metaphorical use of *rēšam ullūm* "to raise the head," in the passage in *Enūma eliš* which records the founding of Babylon, might not have inspired the "head in heaven" phrase in the Hebrew and with it the rest of the story.[8]

[4] This is one reason why some looked there for the Tower of Babel, as far back as Talmudic times (*ibid.* 157), but also in relatively recent days (Parrot, *Archéologie mésopotamienne* I 27).
[5] For a recent review cf. Th. A. Busink. *Jaarbericht Ex Oriente Lux* 10 528.
[6] Nabopalassar and Nebuchadnezzar; cf. F. H. Weissbach, DOG 59 42, 46.
[7] *E-ur$_4$-me-imin-an-ki* "house of the seven preceptors of heaven and earth."
[8] ZDMG 91 352 ff.

E. Kraeling saw in the same Hebrew phrase "a secularized echo of *E–sag–ila* 'the house of the lifting up of the head.'" [9] Yet in neither instance was the initial suggestion followed up. Ravn's assumption fails to take account of the fact that *rēšam ullūm* is applied to various structures, whereas the biblical version deals exclusively with Babel. In Kraeling's surmise we have, to be sure, the required link with Babylon through Esagila. Yet "head in heaven" is by no means the same thing as "the lifting up of the head."

The present paper will seek to show that the ultimate inspiration behind the biblical narrative was indeed literary rather than architectural. The chain of evidence appears to be solid and conclusive. It should be made clear, however, from the start that the statement just made applies only to the building of the tower and the purpose ascribed to that project. The recorded consequence is a different matter entirely. All suggestions offered on this latter count, including the one hazarded at the end of this paper, must be designated in all candor as purely speculative.

The key passage is inevitably the pertinent verse in E–e, which reads: *ša Esagila miḫrit apsî ullū rēšī*[*šu*] [10] "they raised the head of Esagila *miḫrit apsî*." It is immediately apparent that *ullū rēšīšu* is here a word play on *Esagila* "structure which raises the head," in a manner that is amply attested elsewhere in the Creation Epic.[11] The Akkadian phrase itself is old and its primary use is

[9] JBL 66 282.

[10] VI 62. The traces in KAR 164 point to *ši* as against the usually supplemented *ša*. For the second vowel (pl. or dual) cf., e.g., JAOS 71 7.32.

[11] Note, e.g., the succession of glosses with the "fifty names of Marduk" (cf. Böhl, AfO 11 191 ff.); the double pun on the name Marduk in I 101 f.; and the glossing of *uškên-* with *iššiq qaqqara* in III 69.

with persons in the sense of "to exalt." [12] With buildings it could nowhere be as effective as when applied to Esagila, precisely because it evokes the value of the Sumerian name. In other words, this expression had a special meaning in connection with Babylon. This being so—what with the extraordinary position of the Creation Epic and the cultural standing of Babylon—*rēšam ullūm* was bound to and did become a stock expression not only with the ziqqurrat of Babylon but with other monumental structures in Babylonia and Assyria.

A point which should be noted in passing is that nothing is said in this account about Etemenanki. This omission is by no means fortuitous, since the very next verse makes it clear that the building involved is the temple tower itself.[13] Evidently, therefore, the name Esagila denoted originally the ziqqurrat of Babylon, or alternatively the entire temple complex including the tower. Etemenanki must be a later designation.

In any event, when Nabopalassar and Nebuchadnezzar refer to the rebuilding of Etemenanki, they both add the phrase *šamāmi ana šitnuni(m)* "to rival the heavens." [14] Since the inscriptions of these rulers are given to archaizing, the question arises whether this expression, too, does not echo some phrase in the canonical Creation Epic. If so, what was that prototype?

In the above version of E-e VI 62 the phrase *miḫrit apsî* was left untranslated. The standard translations take *apsû* in its usual sense of "the Deep." [15] Yet this cannot

[12] E. g., Gilg., Pennsylvania T. vi 36: *ullū eli mūti rēska.*

[13] See below, p. 320.

[14] WVDOG 59 42. I 36 f.; 46. 3.23 ff.

[15] Cf. Heidel, *The Babylonian Genesis* (2nd ed.) 48 and n. 126: "The meaning of this line appears to be that the foundation of Esagila reached down as far as the waters of the *Apsu.*" I was equally at sea in translating "equaling Apsu," ANET 69.

be right, for the text goes on to say (line 63) *ibnūma ziqqurrat ša apsî elīte* "when they had built the temple tower of *apsû*. . . ." [16] The tower, then, was evidently part of the *apsû*, not its counterpart. And since the structure is celebrated for its height, the *apsû* in question has to be sought above the surface of the ground, not below it. It has to be celestial rather than subterranean. Actually, this conclusion is not as startling as it might appear to be at first glance.[17] Lexical texts have preserved the outright equation of *apsû* with *šamū* "sky, heaven," proving that this term could point upwards as well as downwards.[18] In the cited passage the only suitable connotation of *miḫrit apsî* is "towards heaven." And it is this meaning, of necessity, that is reflected in the Neo-Babylonian records which deal with the ziqqurrat of Babylon.

The conclusion just reached is strikingly corroborated by an independent Assyrian source. The text in question is an account by Esarhaddon of his restoration of Esharra, the main temple in the city of Ashur.[19] The relevant lines correspond so closely with the above passage fiom E-e as

[16] The last term is troublesome grammatically. It is generally regarded as modifying *ziqqurrat,* in which case, however, the gen. form is disturbing even in a careless text. To construe it, on the other hand, with *apsî,* which would suit both the word order and the case ending, would entail the wrong gender. I would propose tentatively that we interpret *elīte* either as an abstract in the sense of "the upper (sphere)," or that we regard the fem. as due to the analogy of *Tiāmat elītu, šaplītu,* cf. King, *Seven Tablets of Creation* I 197 10 f. "The lofty stagetower of the *Apsû*" (Heidel, *loc. cit.*) or the like is surely a contradiction in terms if *apsû* signifies "the Deep." But "the temple tower of the upper *apsû*" makes excellent sense in the present context.

[17] It is foreshadowed in E-e IV 142–45 (*apsû*: *šamāmu*).

[18] Cf. Jensen, RLA I 123 and note Jacobsen, JNES 5 139 f., n. 21. The prevailing impression that *apsû* was restricted to the subterranean waters is thus clearly erroneous. The term signified also the source of waters that come down from the sky and hence the farthest reaches above and below the earth. Eventually it must have come to designate the limits of the horizon as well, and thus limit in general, to judge from Heb. *'apsē 'āreṣ,* Ugar, *aps.*

[19] F. R. Steele, "The University Museum Esarhaddon Prism," JAOS 71 1 ff.

to rule out any possibility of coincidence. The following comparison speaks for itself.[20]

E 60 *šattu ištât libittašu iltabnū* [21]	For one year they
P 1 f. *šattu ištēt* [22] *ilbinū libittu*	made the/its brickwork.
E 61 *šanītu šattu ina kašādi*	When the second year
P. 27 f. *šanītu šatti ina kašādi*	arrived,
E 62 *ša Esagila miḫrit apsî ullū rēšīšu*	they/I raised the head
P 31 ff. *ša Ešarra . . . ana šamē ulli rēšēšu*	of Esagila/Esharra. . . .

Since everything else is identical,[23] Esarhaddon's *ana šamē* "toward heaven" must reflect *miḫrit apsî* in much the same sense.[24]

These two texts jointly leave little doubt in turn that the biblical narrative about the Tower of Babel was likewise influenced by the canonical Akkadian formulation of the founding of Babylon. What is more, and this point is worth stressing, the reference to bricks in Gen. 11.3 now receives for the first time its logical explanation. This particular detail is surely not material to the biblical version. In fact, it bothered the Hebrew writer sufficiently to cause him to include a clause for the benefit of his readers to explain that the use of bricks was a peculiarity of Mesopotamia. He would hardly introduce such a distracting element of his own accord. Obviously, therefore,

[20] In the lines below I have used E for E-e VI and P for the Pennsylvania Prism.

[21] For this reading see v. Soden, ZA 47 4.

[22] Written AD.ME.NUN AS.ÁM, cf. Steele, JAOS 71 6 n. 23.

[23] Except only for the incidental difference *ullū* : *ulli.*

[24] For the prepositional use of *meḫret, meḫrat* cf. v. Soden, GAG 115 o. Note also *miḫrat mē* "upon the waters" in Nebuchadnezzar's building account, KBo III/2 vi 1.

the detail was put in because it figured prominently in the original account, the year-long preparation of the individual bricks being a vital part, together with the laying of the foundation brick, of the ritual connected with monumental architecture in Mesopotamia.[25]

Thus far, then, each item in the biblical narrative proves to have its appropriate Mesopotamian antecedent: the solemn preparation of the bricks (*nilbᵉna lᵉbēnīm*), the building of the stage tower (*īr umigdāl*),[26] and the reference to the "head in the heavens" (*wᵉrōšō baššāmayim*. So much detailed correspondence, and particularly the out-of-the-way reference to the bricks, adds up to convincing proof that the underlying source was textual as opposed to monumental. To that extent at least biblical tradition cannot be charged with fanciful invention.

The construction of the tower, however, is only one half of the story. The other half recounts the eventual failure of the ambitious project. How is this to be explained? The unfolding involves a definite criticism; but is that a Palestinian or a Mesopotamian verdict? The finale is based on word symbolism; is this word play inner Akkadian, inner Hebrew, or inter-dialectal? These are but some of the questions entailed. Each of these questions could be answered in more ways than one, with little chance of confirming or refuting the given solution. In these circumstances there could be scarcely any profit in exploring the various possibilities. It may be in order,

[25] The point was misunderstood and misinterpreted by Cassuto, *From Noah to Abraham* 164. For the abiding significance of the brick ritual see Frankfort, *Kingship and the Gods* 272 ff.

[26] This pair of forms is another instance of hendiadys, a common Semitic usage which has been all but neglected by our grammarians. For its occurrence in Hebrew see provisionally E. Z. Melamed, *Tarbiz* 61 (1945) 173 ff. (in Hebrew). I hope to deal with this subject in the near future, with special attention to Akkadian. The sense in this instance is "city crowned by a tower."

on the other hand, to outline a suggested mode of inquiry if it is stressed at the same time that all such approaches must be regarded for the present as stabs in the dark.

It is a probable, though by no means compelling, assumption that biblical tradition took over from Mesopotamia not only the beginning of the Tower of Babel account but its conclusion as well. In that case, the Hebrew word play involving Babel and *bll* "to mix" would link up in some way with Akkadian usage. Interestingly enough, this very verb is found in building records, including the Esarhaddon Prism adduced above (col. v. 20), in the sense of "sprinkle" (a compound of fragrant oils and essences prior to laying the foundation). Once it had been transplanted to Hebrew soil with the rest of the building account about Babylon, *balālu* could have served to undermine all of the Tower of Babel. Yet I am not disposed to look for a solution from that quarter.

I would see a slightly better chance of success in another line of approach. The name *Bāb-ilim,* which Gelb has recently, shown to be itself a possible result of popular etymology,[27] was bound to be associated on many occasions with the common verb *babālum* (ptcple *bābilum*) "to carry."[28] In fact, we have direct evidence of such punning in a bilingual poem in praise of the city, where *Bābilu* is spoken of as *bibil libbišu* "his wish fulfillment."[29] A rival of Babylon, say in some Kassite center or in the entourage of Tukulti-Ninurta I, could have seized on the same wordplay for less friendly purposes. He could have gone on from *babālum* to its cognate

[27] "The Name of Babylon," *Journal of the Institute of Asiatic Studies* I (1955) 1–4. The underlying meaning of *babil* would thus be uncertain.

[28] This was proposed as far back as 1916 by Böhl, ZA 36 110 ff., although much of the appended argument must today be viewed as inapplicable.

[29] KAR 8 ii 7; cf. Böhl, *Jaarbericht Ex Oriente Lux* 10 492 n. 9.

šutābulum, which includes among its connotations that of "to drive out." Then, mindful of the idiom *šutābulum šaptā* "to move the lips," he might even have hit on the paranomasia of "to scatter speech." If this should appear too bold or too base, I need only to call attention to the double pun on the name of Marduk in the ultra-respectable *Enūma eliš* (I 101 f.), which is even more atrocious linguistically and esthetically than the biblical word play on Babel and certainly goes beyond anything that a modern scholar would conjure up. On West Semitic soil, some such pair as *šutābulum* and *šutābulum šaptā,* linked to *Bābilim* through *babālum,* may at length have resulted in "to diffuse" and "to confuse the speech" (*śāpā*). Finally, the derived stem *šutābulum* would be less likely to inhibit a play on *bll* than the base stem *babālum.*

All this is admittedly far-fetched in the extreme, yet stranger combinations have actually been attested. The biblical writer had ample precedent for the sort of approach that has just been outlined. This is not to imply that we can now retrace his every step, or to deny that various other paths could have led to the same ultimate result. All that can now be posited with reasonable confidence is that for the first half of his story—the part about the building of the temple—the narrator followed a Mesopotamian source. This much at least would seem to be clearly established.

The Wife-Sister Motif in the Patriarchal Narratives

I

THE SUBJECT THAT I PROPOSE TO TAKE UP HERE ANEW[1] IS THE central theme of three narratives in the Book of Genesis: namely, (a) 12:10–20, (b) 20:1–18, (c) 26:6[2]–11. Each tells essentially the same story as the others. A patriarch visits a foreign land in the company of his wife. Fearing that the woman's great beauty might prove to be a source of mortal danger to himself as the husband, he resorts to the subterfuge of passing himself off as the woman's brother.

This recurring wife-sister motif in Genesis has had a long history of abundant yet inconclusive speculation and discussion. The results have ranged from embarrassment and apologetics to expressions of gallantry, moralizing comment, and even gloating. Efforts to find mitigating

[1] I made brief reference to this topic in a paper on "The Biblical Idea of History in its Common Near Eastern Setting," *Israel Exploration Journal* 5:201 ff. (1955); see esp. p. 213 [below, p. 204f.].

[2] The episode is usually listed as starting with verse 7. It is better, however, to go back to verse 6 and translate it as a temporal clause: "When Isaac stayed at Gerar," etc.

circumstances in the Patriarchs' conduct are as old as the narratives themselves. Thus Genesis 20:12 has Abraham remark, "What is more, she [Sarah] is in truth my sister, my father's daughter, though not my mother's." Rabbinical sources go to great lengths in stressing Sarah's exceptional beauty, and the same holds true of the recently discovered Genesis Apocryphon.[3] But censorious notes have found their way into more than one presumably objective comment on the subject. The vast majority, however, of serious students has remained baffled. Small wonder, therefore, that scarcely a year goes by without at least one new stab at solving the problem. Yet each fresh try only points up the failure of previous solutions.

In these circumstances it would be sheer folly to rush in where so many angels have feared to tread or have gone nowhere when they did. No, what follows is not yet another attempted explanation of the Patriarchs' behavior, based on the data received, but rather an appeal from tradition's own version of the incidents in question. In other words, given the traditional accounts, it is hopeless to bring in a sensible verdict. The burden of the present argument is that the basic testimony contained judgments contrary to the facts and that the entire case should therefore be reopened.

It goes without saying that no such argument can be allowed, after so many intervening centuries, without new and compelling evidence. Such evidence, however, does in fact exist. It comes from pertinent extra-Biblical sources that have come to light so recently that the results have yet to be brought to bear on the case before us. It

[3] N. Avigad and Y. Yadin, *A Genesis Apocryphon* (Jerusalem, 1956), col. 20, 2–8.

will be our task as a court of appeal to weigh the new data critically, but without prejudice, and then to decide whether the original disposition of the case can be upheld or whether it should be revised in the light of the new information.

Before the question is re-examined, it will be necessary to review the old transcript as embodied in the Book of Genesis. Very briefly, the received report consists of three separte entries, as cited above. In (a) Abraham introduces Sarah to Pharaoh as his sister, hoping to save himself by this ruse. In (b) we have a repetition of the same incident, with the identical motivation, except only that the host is this time another ruler: namely Abimelech of Gerar. Finally, Abimelech reappears in (c), but his visitors are now Isaac and Rebekah. The excuse offered in each instance is that the wife's startling beauty might have provoked attempts on the husband's life, whereas a brother would not have been deemed to stand in the way.

Now these three incidents, which are so very alike in content in spite of differences in cast and locale, are not only repetitive in their present form; they are also mutually incompatible when analyzed side by side. Abraham's narrow escape in Egypt did not deter him from repeating the deception in Gerar. And Abimelech, for his part, was not sobered in the least by his all but fatal involvement with Sarah, for all his protestations of innocence in that affair. He would have had to be either a fool or a knave to accept Isaac's subsequent pretence at face value, yet the record depicts him as both wise and honest. In short, the accounts cannot be homogeneous. Once all three passages are attributed to a single author, we are forced to conclude that the writing is sloppy, or else that the characters do not permit our confidence.

The stories before us, however, are hardly of a piece, even on the surface. In Genesis 12:17 it is YHWH who afflicts Pharaoh and his household with severe plagues; the use of this divine name signifies in Genesis, according to the documentary hypothesis, an author whom the critics have designated as the Yahwist, or J. In Genesis 20, on the other hand, the deity is consistently indicated as Elohim (verses 3, 6, 13, 18). Moreover, God's warning to Abimelech is communicated there in a dream, and both Abraham and his host take great pains to justify their conduct. Now all these features—Elohim, dreams, emphasis on morality–recur elsewhere in passages which the critics have traced to the Elohistic source, or E. As against this, the third episode (Genesis 26:6–11) displays the same economy of thought and phrase as the first, so that it, in turn, points back to J.

As soon as our three instances of the wife-sister motif have been assigned to two individual authors, all our difficulties with the content disappear automatically. J knew of two separate occasions when a Patriarch felt it necessary to present his wife as a sister: one involved Abraham and Sarah in Egypt and the other concerned Isaac and Rebekah at Gerar. Neither the cast of characters nor the scene of action is repeated in these accounts. In E, on the other hand, the two episodes were telescoped, with the result that Abraham and Sarah were shifted from Egypt to Gerar, while Isaac and Rebekah did not figure at all; thus the E source, too, remains consistent within itself. Between the two versions, however, two original reports branched out into three.

It may be remarked in passing that the internal evidence of this trio of narratives alone, quite apart from the testimony of many other passages, would be enough to establish E as an independent document.[4] Alternative hypotheses about the composition of the Pentateuch, not to mention the traditional doctrine of its Mosaic authorship, do grave injustice to the caliber of writing involved. Nevertheless, our present argument does not hinge in any way on the acceptance of the documentary theory. If the reality of separate versions by J and E is conceded, then the circumstance that the wife-sister motif was known to both must point to a common older source. And if the argument from literary analysis is disallowed, the antiquity of tradition looms that much more prominently, since the writing would then be credited to Moses. On either view, therefore, the meaning of the incidents at issue has to be sought in the Patriarchal Age, in which these episodes have been placed. And it is precisely from that remote age that relevant extra-Biblical data have recently come to light..

I had occasion to allude to the end result of this study in several earlier connections.[5] Each time, however, the theme could only be stated, but not duly developed. Yet the subject is much too significant to be dismissed with casual allusions; it calls for adequate documentation. The pertinent evidence, to be sure, is diffuse and intricate enough to deserve a separate monograph. But even a minimal sampling should prove to be instructive. This will now be presented in all conciseness.

[4] For a comprehensive recent summary of the documentary position see C. R. North, "Pentateuchal Criticism," in *The Old Testament and Modern Study,* ed. H. H. Rowley (Oxford, 1951), pp. 48–83. For E as an independent source, attention may be called to my forthcoming volume on Genesis, Introduction (Anchor Books) [published in 1964].

[5] See above, Note 1. The other occasions were oral presentations.

II

The data in question stem from a single society, that of the Hurrians. In the eighteenth century B.C.E. the Hurrians are known to have been thickly settled in Central Mesopotamia, in the general area of Ḫarran (Biblical Ḥārān), as we know from the Mari and the Chagar Bazar texts, and in northern Syria, as shown by the tablets from Alalaḫ. By the middle of the second millennium, Hurrian settlements and influence had spread to Arrapḫa and Nuzi in the east, and all along the Mediterranean coast in the west, to judge from various sources from Nuzi, Amarna, the upper layers of Alalaḫ, and from Ḫattusas (Boghazköi)[6] On the combined evidence of this extensive documentary network it can be stated with confidence that many distinctive features of Hurrian society, especially in the field of family law, remained the same throughout, regardless of chronology, geographic location, or political influence. What was true of Nuzi, Alalaḫ, or eastern Anatolia in the fifteenth century was thus equally true of eighteenth-century Ḫarran, the approximate central area of over-all Hurrian occupation. But Ḫarran was also the home of the Patriarchs, a district where Hurrians and Western Semites lived in close cultural symbiosis, but where Hurrians constituted the dominant social element. It is for these reasons that the Nuzi texts in particular, which happen to be plentiful and rich in content, have a bearing on Ḫarran in the Patriarchal Age, and can hence

[6] The distribution of the Hurrians is summarized, among other publications, in my "The Hurrian Participation in the Civilizations of Mesopotamia, Syria, and Palestine," *Journal of World History* 1:311 ff. (Paris 1953) [below, pp. 244–269].

contribute to the understanding of the patriarchal narratives.

Now, Hurrian family practices contain certain features which have no counterparts in any other contemporary Near Eastern society. This is true especially of the pervasive role of the brother, as a result of an underlying fratriarchal system which the encroachments of patriarchy managed to restrict but could not entirely obliterate. The pioneering work on the subject was done by the distinguished jurist and outstanding authority on cuneiform law, Paul Koschaker.[7] Koschaker's results are basic to all subsequent study on the subject, but they can now be considerably strengthened and expanded, thanks to further work and additional material. Above all, the possibility of Biblical connections has been virtually ignored,[8] and nothing has been done as yet in regard to the wife-sister motif in Genesis.

Before the latter topic can be adduced for comparison, the pertinent evidence of the cuneiform sources may be summarized as follows.

1. The wife as sister. The Nuzi text *HSS*[9] V 80 is a contract whereby Akkulenni son of Akiya gives his sister Beltakkadummi[10] in marriage (*ana aššūti,* literally "into wifehood") to Ḫurazzi son of Ennaya.[11] But in the parallel document *HSS* V 69 the same brother gives the same

[7] In a study entitled "Fratriarchat, Hausgemeinschaft und Mutterrecht in Keilschrifttexten," *Zeitschrift für Assyriologie* 41:1–89 (1933).

[8] For an approach to the Biblical evidence, see C. H. Gordon, "Fratriarchy in the Old Testament," *Journal of Biblical Literature* 54:223–231 (1935). See also E. A. Speiser, "Of Shoes and Shekels," *BASOR* 77:15–20 (1940) [below, pp. 00-00].

[9] *Harvard Semitic Series,* vol. V, text 80. Volume V (*Excavations at Nuzi,* vol. I, *Texts . . .*) was published in 1929 by E. Chiera. In the following year I presented all the family documents in that volume, in transliteration, translation, and with brief comments, in *AASOR* 10:1–73 (1930).

[10] Contracted from *Bēlit-Akkadi-ummi.*

[11] Koschaker, "Fratriarchat . . .," pp. 14 f.

girl to the same husband "as sister" (*ana aḫāti*). It follows that a wife could have simultaneously the status of sister. There can be no question in this instance of close blood ties between husband and wife, since each has a different father, nor is there any indication or likelihood that Beltakkadummi was Ḫurazzi's half-sister. The fact that a separate sistership document was deemed necessary, in addition to the usual marriage contract, points up the importance of the husband's concurrent status as brother. Interestingly enough, a third document, *HSS* V 25, carries the girl's own statement that the marriage was arranged with her personal consent (line 14), thus implying a degree of independence on the part of the woman.

2. *Sistership transferred.* In the sistership document cited above (*HSS* V 69), the girl is made a man's legal sister after her natural brother has ceded his own fraternal rights. The juridical basis of the transaction is thus a form of adoption. The adoptive brother may then marry the girl himself, as is the case in *HSS* V 80, or he may give her in marriage to another in return for the customary bride price.[12] The latter alternative is indicated in *JEN*[13] 78, where Zigiba son of Eḫel-Teshub gives his sister Ḫinzuri "for sistership" (*ana aḫātūti*) to Ḫudarrapḫi, who reserves the right to marry her to whomever he chooses (line 7). This is not the first time that Ḫinzuri has been the object of such a transfer. According to *JEN* 636,[14] the same woman was first given in sistership by her brother Zigiba to Inni, who then gave her back in return for the symbolic payment[15] of one

[12] Amounting to forty shekels of silver.

[13] *Joint Expedition with the Iraq Museum at Nuzi, vols.* I–V (Paris and Philadelphia), E. Chiera; vol. VI (New Haven), E. R. Lacheman. Vol. I is cited throughout.

[14] For this text see H. Lewy, *Orientalia* 10:209 ff. (1941).

[15] Cf. my "Of Shoes and Shekels," pp. 15 ff. [below, pp. 151 ff].

cloth. The status of sister was thus negotiable, yet the woman involved was not altogether a passive party. For just as was the case with Beltakkadummi (in *HSS* V 25), Ḫinzuri, too, explicitly signifies her personal consent (*irramāniya,* "of my own free will," line 23).

3. Sistership by the woman's choice. There are indications, moreover, that the legal status of sister was beneficial to the woman, no matter whether the given brother was natural or adoptive. We learn this from instances in which the woman goes beyond formal acquiescence, as above, and becomes a principal in the transaction. Thus in *AASOR*[16] XVI 54, Kuniyashe daughter of Ḫut-Teshub states that she was previously given in marriage by Akammushni (evidently her adoptive brother) to an unnamed husband, for the full bridal payment of forty shekels of silver. Since both her guardian and her husband are now dead, Kuniyashe appoints her natural brother Akiya son of Ḫut-Teshub as her legal brother, who is given the right to marry her to another. In two other instances (*G*[17] 31; *HSS* V 26), a woman offers herself physically[18] to a prospective legal brother. In the latter document, the "sister" says this of her brother-husband: "He shall watch over me and protect me in every way, act as my brother, and be a help to me."[19] In all three cases, the woman has become a free agent by virtue of the fact that her original guardian had already given up his rights to her through a previous transaction, and the second party then divorced her or died.[20] Now

[16] See Note 9.

[17] C. J. Gadd, "Tablets from Kirkuk," *Revue d'Assyriologie* 33:49 ff., and texts 1–82.

[18] Cf. Koschaker, "Fratriarchat . . .," p. 28, n. 3.

[19] *AASOR* 10:29 (1930); Koschaker, "Fratriarchat . . .," p. 34.

[20] The Code of Hammurapi (e.g., CH 172) says of similar instances that "a man of her own choice may marry her."

she seeks a new legal relationship as sister because, as *HSS* V 26 has so strongly intimated, such a status affords her all the aid and comfort that local society obviously associated with a brother. But the new status has to be ratified, with actual brothers no less than with adoptive ones.

4. Special safeguards for the sister. As a matter of fact, so intent was Hurrian society on protecting the favored position of a duly accredited sister that it borrowed certain safeguards from the sphere of ritual practices. This socioreligious aspect is made apparent by the solemn form of the payment involved. In ordinary marriage transactions the bride price amounted to forty shekels, payable in various commodities computed at the current rate for silver. In sistership contracts, however, the price remains the same, but thirty shekels of it must be computed as a rule in terms of animals, at the fixed rate of one ox, one ass, and ten sheep. Now this rigid mode of payment is always reserved for cases of unusual gravity,[21] and it is imposed either as a special punishment for serious offences in the past or as a deterrent against possible future violations. The animals play here a monitory part, based on the fate of sacrificial beasts. The payment, in other words, is related to the sanctions of a covenant, and the use of animals recalls the description of God's covenant with Abraham in Genesis 15:9 ff.

It is highly significant, therefore, that this ominous type of payment is typical of the sistership transactions. A striking illustration is provided by *HSS* V 79, which is on the surface a case of adoption into "daughtership" as

[21] For the character and significance of this special type of payment, see E. A. Speiser, "Nuzi Marginalia 4: Ceremonial Payment," *Orientalia* 25:15–20 (1956).

a prelude to marriage (to one of the adoptor's sons). The payment is set at the normal bride price of forty shekels of silver. The money goes, however, to the girl's brother, and the essential "sistership" aspect of the contract is further emphasized by the girl's direct statement.[22] The payment is broken down as follows: "thirty-six minas of tin in lieu of [*kīma*] [23] one ox; twenty-four minas of tin in lieu of one ass; ten sheep;[24] ten shekels of . . .[25] silver." In other words, out of the total of forty shekels, thirty shekels represent the fixed "covenant" payment in the standard proportions of one ox: one ass: ten sheep. And although the animals are converted into metal currency, the record goes out of its way to show that each animal is accounted for, instead of stating simply that the required payment has been made in full. The monitory features are thus retained as a reminder that the implicit sanctions have not been bypassed.

In two similar instances (*HSS* V 80; *JEN* 78) the payment for a sister adds up only to twenty shekels, since the remaining half is retained for the girl as her "dowry." Hence the symbolic equation can no longer apply in full but is prorated. Thus *HSS* V 80 specifies "one ox, ten shekels of silver" (that is, twenty shekels in all), and *JEN* 78 itemizes "one ox . . .[26] sheep, one imer of barley, two minas of copper, nine minas of wool, making up

[22] Lines 27 f.

[23] The Biblical term in similar instances is *ᶜerkĕkā*, on which see my "Leviticus and the Critics," *Yehezkel Kaufmann Jubilee* Volume, ed. M. Haran (Jerusalem, 1960), pp. 30–33 [below, pp. 124–128].

[24] Sheep as currency (cf. Lat. *pecūnia*) were computed at one shekel a head.

[25] The silver is qualified by the term *ḫašaḫušenni*, for which see *AASOR* 25:11, n. 1. The entire payment takes up lines 9–13.

[26] The text is damaged at this point, but the figure could conceivably have been 5, which together with the ten shekels for one ox would add up to fifteen shekels, or half of the normal "covenant" payment.

[*kīma*] twenty shekels of silver." Even here, therefore, the sanction component is not eliminated but merely modified: the reduced total must still include a token entry of animals. Nothing could show more convincingly that Hurrian society went to great lengths to uphold the status of sister through the medium of brother, or the husband as brother.

5. *Practice rejected by outsiders.* That other societies found this Hurrian practice strange and unacceptable is strikingly demonstrated by a treaty between the powerful Hittite king Suppiluliumas and a certain Hukkanas, the vassal ruler of a Hurrian principality in Armenia.[27] As a political measure not uncommon in that period, the Hittite monarch gave his sister in marriage to his Hurrian vassal. By Hurrian custom, this would have made the girl her husband's sister as well. As brother, however, he would have fratriarchal authority over the woman's female siblings, since they, too, would be technically his legal sisters.[28] But such an arrangement was naturally distasteful to the Hittite overlord. He would have none of it, so he made sure to spell out in a formal treaty that the odd Hurrian practice would not be invoked in this particular case. It follows, incidentally, that fratriarchy among the Hurrians was a normal feature of the upper classes, not merely among ordinary citizens, but even in the ruling families.

6. *Evidence of personal names.* There is, finally, one other source of information that remains to be tapped in this connection: namely, the evidence of personal names. Hurrian masculine names reflect a particular liking for

[27] Koschaker, "Fratriarchat . . .," pp. 1–13.
[28] *Ibid.*, p. 33.

compounds with *šenni* "the brother"[29] (from *šena* "brother").[30] As has already been noted by Koschaker,[31] this points suggestively to underlying fratriarchal conditions. And even though fratriarchy had been considerably weakened in the meantime under the influence of a patriarchal orientation,[32] onomastic customs remained conservative enough to echo earlier habits. We have, however, one particular type of name, in common use, which tells us more than all the compounds with *šena*. This type features the element *aḫu* "brother" together with a feminine personal pronoun: *Aḫūša,* "her brother"; *Aḫūšina,* "their [feminine] brother"; *Aḫummiša,* "her mother's brother."[33] All these forms are Akkadian, but we know from the family relations of their bearers that the persons in question were Hurrians. Moreover, while a name like Aḫūšina is known from Akkadian sources, and tells us merely that the new-born boy has older sisters (analogously, Aḫūša has one such sister), Aḫummiša is not used in Akkadian circles. There the corresponding name is *Aḫummišu* ("his mother's brother"): that is, the boy was named after his maternal uncle. Yet the seemingly paradoxical form with feminine suffix cannot be charged to peculiarities of Hurrian grammar,[34] or to scribal errors,[35] for it occurs too often (over twenty times) to be explained

[29] Cf. I. J. Gelb, P. M. Purves, and A. A. MacRae, *Nuzi Personal Names, Oriental Institute Publications* no. LVII (Chicago, 1943), pp. 130–131.

[30] The suffix *-ne/i* (for which see E. A. Speiser, *Introduction to Hurrian* [New Haven, 1941]) serves here as a definite article.

[31] Koschaker, "Fratriarchat . . .," p. 33.

[32] *Ibid.*

[33] See Gelb, Purves, and MacRae, *Nuzi Personal Names,* p. 291.

[34] Which does not recognize grammatical gender, so that Hurrians writing Akkadian usually employ one form for masculine and feminine alike; but the common form is then masculine, not feminine.

[35] This is immediately ruled out by the fact that this particular suffix is written either as ŠA or as ŠÁ (Gelb, Purves, and MacRae, *Nazi Personal Names,* p. 10).

away.[36] In short, both the writing and the construction are correct. Accordingly, "Aḫummiša" must be understood to signify that the bearer of the name shall give his older sister the same kind of support that their mother received from her own brother.

This last example may well help to explain how the exceptional rights of the brother in Hurrian society originated in the first place. The fratriarchal system goes back ultimately to matriarchy. The mother was the dominant figure in the family, and her position was not to be usurped by an exogamous husband. But even a matriarchally governed family often has need of masculine strength and guidance; for these the mother will look to her own brother.[37] Fratriarchy is thus an extension of the part played by the maternal uncle. The name Aḫummiša, with its emphasis on the sister's maternal uncle, would be accordingly a residual witness of an antecedent matriarchal system.

To sum up, the Hurrian family system contained various fratriarchal features, one of which was the wife-sister concept. Under it, a woman given in marriage by her brother, either natural or adoptive, became legally her husband's sister. Such a wife-sister had the advantage of exceptional socioreligious solicitude and protection which was not enjoyed by ordinary wives. The practice was characteristic of, though not restricted to, the top levels of Hurrian society. It was evidently a mark of superior status.

It is worth stressing again that the wife-sister customs were peculiar to the Hurrians. There is no trace of them among the Akkadians, and they were expressly stigmatized

[36] Gelb, Purves, and MacRae, *Nuzi Personal Names,* pp. 10, 291.
[37] Koschaker, "Fratriarchat . . .," p. 80.

by the Hittites, who otherwise had so much culturally in common with the Hurrians. The institution of the levirate affords no parallel at all, since it operates with altogether different presuppositions[38] and is solely concerned with maintaining the line of a deceased brother. Nor can it be compared with the brother-sister marriages of the ruling houses of Egypt, Persia, and certain Hellenistic states,[39] for the Hurrian practice applied to women who were sisters by law and not by blood. The Hurrian family system in general[40] and the wife-sister feature in particular stand thus isolated within the larger social complex of the ancient Near East.

III

The foregoing review of certain marriage customs of the Hurrians can now be applied to a re-examination of the wife-sister incidents in the patriarchal account. No apology is needed for thus bringing the pertinent material from the two respective sources, the cuneiform and the Biblical, into close comparison. Abraham migrated to Canaan from the Central Mesopotamian district of Harran, and it was to that same area that Isaac and Jacob eventually owed their wives. Now, Ḫarran was not only the home base of the patriarchal clan but at the same time also the central link in the far-flung chain of Hur-

[38] *Ibid.*, pp. 85 ff.

[39] *Ibid.*, p. 82.

[40] In this connection, attention may be called once again to the use of the housegods (Akk. *ilāni,* Heb. *tĕrāpīm* or sometimes *ʾelōhīm*) as a symbol of property transfer to a son-in-law, which readily explains Rachel's act as recorded in Genesis 31:19, 30; see A. E. Draffkorn, "Ilāni/Elohim," *JBL* 76:216–224 (1957). This is perhaps the outstanding example of an exclusively Hurrian custom which the patriarchal account records, but which became incomprehensible later on in Canaanite surroundings; it offers an excellent parallel to the wife-sister theme.

rian settlements. In the Bible, the wife-sister theme is confined to two successive generations; elsewhere in the ancient Near East the only society that featured an analogous concept was the Hurrian. Since time, place, and opportunity point thus uniformly to one and the same quarter, it would be surprising indeed if such isolated acts of the patriarchs did not reflect a normal Hurrian practice. It remains then only to inquire how the assumption of such an interrelationship works out in detail.

In the case of Abraham, a few laconic notices about his family are found in Genesis 11:26–32. Even the critics agree that this passage includes relatively old data, since they ascribe verses 28–30 to J, the oldest documentary source in the Pentateuch. The credibility of the section is further enhanced by repeated occurrences of the name Nahor, a name shared by Abraham's grandfather and one of Abraham's brothers. The same form (written *Na-ḫu-ur*^{KI}) is now independently attested to in the approximately contemporary Mari records as the name of a city in the vicinity of Ḫarran.[41] The use of the same name for both places and persons is familiar from many sources.[42]

We are told, furthermore, that Abraham's brother Nahor married his own neice Milcah, daughter of a younger brother named Haran.[43] This agrees closely with a practice which Hurrian law recognizes by a *ṭuppi mārtūti u kallūti* ("tablet of daughtership and daughter-in-law-ship"), whereby a man adopts a girl as his daughter

[41] Cf. the list of occurrences in *Archives royales de Mari* XV (Paris, 1954), 130. The town lay in the valley of the Baliḫ, a tributary of the Euphrates.

[42] The practice is amply attested in the Nuzi records, where virtually any personal name could be made into a place name by the addition of the Hurrian genitive suffix *-we*.

[43] Not to be confused, of course, with the city-name *Hārān,* which has a different initial consonant in Hebrew.

for the declared purpose of either marrying her himself or giving her in marriage to his son.[44] In the present instance, adoption could well have been prompted by the untimely death of Milcah's father (verse 28). Since the latter was Nahor's brother, the marriage would come simultaneously, in accordance with Hurrian law, under the classification of "brothership."

In the face of such detail regarding Nahor's wife, it would seem strange that Abraham's own wife Sarah is introduced without any notice about her parents. This omission is partially rectified in 20:12 (where the author is E!), where we are informed that Sarah was Terah's daughter, though not by Abraham's mother—in other words, she is Abraham's half-sister. Yet this particular entry only serves to bring into that much sharper relief the earlier failure to give Sarah as much genealogical attention as was paid not only Milcah but even the wholly inconsequential Iscah. The likeliest solution under the circumstances would seem to be that Sarah was Terah's daughter by adoption, which is why the relationship was not duly recorded in Genesis 11. At all events, Sarah had adequate credentials to qualify, in one way or another, as Abraham's sister in the broader sense of the term. This would make her eligible, under the law of the land from which Abraham migrated to Canaan, for the *aḫātūtu* or "sistership" status with all its attendant safeguards and privileges.

Thus far it has been fairly clear, if roundabout, sailing. It will be readily agreed that Abraham had ample opportunity to be exposed to the distinctively Hurrian legal concept of wife-sister and to act upon it even after his

[44] The status, however, of a girl acquired under such an arrangement was inferior to that of a principal in an *aḫātūtu* transaction.

arrival in Canaan. But would Isaac, born as he was in non-Hurrian surroundings, be expected to continue a Hurrian practice? Perhaps not, by himself. It was different, however, with Rebekah, a native of Hurrian-dominated Ḫarran. What is more, the details of Rebekah's assignment to Isaac, as recorded in Genesis 24:53–61, are significant enough to yield a recognizable *ṭuppi aḫātūti*, or "sistership document" in typical Nuzi style.

A composite document of that kind would embody the following specifications: (a) the principals in the case, (b) the nature of the transaction, (c) details of payment, (d) the girl's declaration of concurrence, (e) a penalty clause. It so happens that all but the last of these points are touched upon, however, nontechnically, in the corresponding account in Genesis. It goes without saying that a penalty clause would be entirely out of keeping with the literary character of the narrative.

Let us go over the respective points, one by one. (a) For principals we have here, on the one hand, Abraham's servant as spokesman for the prospective bridegroom, and, on the other hand, Laban as the responsible party representing the bride. It is noteworthy that Laban is cited repeatedly (verses 53, 55) as "her brother," in which capacity he is listed both times ahead of the mother. All of this serves to bring out Laban's authority as the brother. The father was apparently dead,[45] and the mother's position was only incidental and without legal standing. (b) The transaction falls thus specifically under the heading of "sistership," since it is the girl's brother

[45] Rebekah's father Bethuel could not otherwise have been ignored in this account. Significantly enough, the Nuzi documents never employ the *aḫātūtu* formula when the bride's father is still alive; cf. Koschaker, "Fratriarchat . . .," p. 31.

who acts on the request. (c) The emissary gives costly presents to Rebekah, but does not neglect the "gifts" for her "brother and mother" (verse 53), covering the bride payment. (d) Perhaps most significant of all, in view of the pertinent Nuzi evidence, is the statement that Rebekah should be consulted (verse 57). Her reply is in the affirmative: *'ēlēk* ("I will go") (verse 58). The Nuzi texts record similarly *ramāniya u aḫūya* ("myself and my brother [agree to this marriage]"),[46] or *irramāniya* ("of my own free will [I am being given into sistership]").[47] To emphasize still further the fratriarchal aspect of the case, the Biblical narrative goes on to speak of "their sister" (*'ăḥōtām*) (verse 59), followed by a festive parting couplet beginning with "Our sister (*'ăḥōtēnū*) (verse 60); the plural pronouns apply to the entire household. In short, we have here a reasonable facsimile of a standard Hurrian *aḫātūtu* documents.

There are thus ample grounds for placing the marriages of Abraham and Sarah and of Isaac and Rebekah in the legal wife-sister class. We come back now to the Biblical narratives which feature the theme that a wife was introduced as sister, with admittedly ulterior motives. Something is obviously wrong there. According to Genesis 20:12, the sisterly relationship was genuine enough; moreover, it was legally correct throughout, in the light of independent evidence. At most, therefore, the statement in each case involves not an outright invention but a half-truth. To that extent, at least, the narratives themselves prove to be misleading. And since the matter at issue is one of adequate data rather than questionable morality, the error may not be irretrievable..

[46] *HSS* V, 25, lines 14 f.

[47] *JEN* I, 78, lines 23 f. In the Biblical instance Laban acts as a real *Aḫummiša:* that is, "her mother's brother."

It should be borne in mind that the accounts before us were committed to writing several centuries after the events and hundreds of miles away from the center where the wife-sister institution was immediately understood and appreciated. The underlying concept could not have long retained its original significance on foreign soil. When the memory of an incident is preserved, but its import has been lost, a new interpretation is likely to be substituted, an interpretation in keeping with local conditions and in conformance with common human instincts. In the present instance, tradition had to deal with certain incidents the meaning of which had been lost in the course of centuries. In due time a new explantion was bound to emerge. Small wonder that the intrusive motive was just so much anachronism.

We cannot be sure, of course, what really happened on those visits to Egypt, and Gerar, assuming that they actually did take place. Such background evidence, however, as we now have may justify the following reconstruction. Both Abraham and Isaac were married to women who enjoyed a privileged status by the standard of their own society. It was the kind of distinction that may well have been deemed worthy of special mention in the presence of royal hosts, since it raised the standing of the visitors. Status has always been an important consideration in international relations, as far back as available records can take us. But popular lore has seldom been internationally oriented.

One important observation remains to be made in conclusion. No matter how tradition interpreted the wife-sister theme, it clearly regarded it as significant, since it saw fit to dwell on it in three separate narratives. Why was tradition so interested in the matter? The answer is no longer far to seek, and it is fortunately free from undue speculation. In the light of the pertinent extra-Biblical evidence which this discussion has adduced, it is clear that the wife-sister status was simultaneously a mark of a cherished social status, as has repeatedly been stressed. Such an affirmation of the wife's favored position was, hence, an implicit guarantee of the purity of her children. Now the ultimate purpose of the Biblical genealogies was to establish the superior strain of the line through which the Biblical way of life was transmitted from generation to generation. In other words, the integrity of the mission had to be safeguarded in transmission, the purity of the content protected by the quality of the container. This is why the antecedents of the wife in the early stages —the mother of the next generation—were of extraordinary significance. Hence all such details, among them the wife-sister theme, were invariably emphasized, even when the appropriate background had in the meantime faded from memory. They were obligatory entries in a proto-canonical body of material.

The demonstrated prestige status of the wife-sister in Hurrian society, which was normative for the Patriarchs in many ways, provides a self-evident reason for the importance of the theme to early Biblical tradition. By the same token, we have here perhaps added circumstantial encouragement that this entire discussion has not been seriously out of focus.

"Coming" and "Going" at the "City" Gate

IN GEN 23, WHICH RECOUNTS THE PURCHASE OF THE CAVE of Machpelah, there occurs twice (vv. 10, 18) the phrase "all those who went in at the gate of his city." Gen 34, on the other hand, contains the contrasting expression "all those who went out by the gate of his city," which is likewise repeated, but this time in the same verse (24). Both statements appear to be direct enough on the surface and have hence attracted little critical attention. A moment's reflection, however, is bound to give one pause. The use of a city gate is hardly a distinctive activity; it is something that is normally open to all the inhabitants. Moreover, "all and sundry," or the like, would not be appropriate in either of the above narratives, for each singles out a specific segment of the population. Lastly, why does one passage refer only to "coming in" and the other to "going out"? The two terms are surely not interchangeable. There is also the further fact that neither phrase is used elsewhere in the OT, at least not in this precise form. Yet the repeated use of each in its particular context is evidence of both accuracy and importance. In short, we are confronted with two idiomatic phrases whose full force remains to be determined.

As a matter of fact, the scholar who was the first to question the face value of these two clauses was also the one who indicated their idiomatic signification. Arnold B. Ehrlich brought out the essential facts as far back as 1908,[1] but his argument appears to have been overlooked. It may well be that his hectoring style and his tendency to disregard other views obscured Ehrlich's actual contribution. Yet in this instance, as in countless others, Ehrlich's learning, penetration, and unerring sense of usage led him to conclusions which later findings could but confirm. If the following remarks about the phrases in question carry the argument a little further and deeper, it is mainly because of added evidence that was not available to Ehrlich at the time.

The two idioms before us feature between them three key terms: two verbs and a noun. It is significant—indeed basic to the problem—that each of these terms may have various secondary meanings aside from its primary one. This is especially true of the verbs, *bā'* "he came in" and *yāṣā'* "he went out," as a mere glance at any standard dictionary will readily attest.[2] Both verbs, moreover, are used together in the expression *lāṣēt wᵉlābō'* "to engage in customary activities." This particular usage, however, has no bearing at all on the phrases under discussion. For the clause in Gen 23 employs *bā'* alone, whereas in Gen 34 only *yāṣā'* is used. Nor would there be the slightest warrant for the assumption that either verb by itself can ever yield the idiom in which they appear jointly. It should be stressed, furthermore, that any such allusion to routine activities would be out of place in both the

[1] *Randglossen zur hebräischen Bibel,* I, pp. 100, 174 f.

[2] Not all of these derived uses have been cleared up by any means; note especially II Kings 6, 7 (perh. referring to going on and off duty on the Sabbath).

Machpelah and the Dinah accounts. In each of these narratives it is a particular and unusual detail that the respective idioms are intended to highlight.

The two expressions, however, have this one thing in common: both lean on the same noun, namely, *šaʿar*. In the great majority of its many occurrences this term stands for "gate." Another familiar connotation is "place of justice, court." Still another meaning is "assembly, community"; note especially Ruth 3:11 "for the whole body of my people knows." In this latter sense *šaʿar* comes close to the Akkadian term *bābtu,* which is familiar from the Code of Hammurabi in the sense of "district, quarter," [3] and is known to be an extension of *bābu* "entrance, gate." It is in this specialized sense, as will be shown presently, that *šaʿar* is employed in the two phrases before us and is the real basis of their idiomatic significance.

Gen 34:24 reads literally, "And all those who went out by his city gate heeded Hamor and his son Shechem; and all the males were circumcised, all those who went out by the gate of his city." The "going out by the city gate" is linked here explicitly to the male inhabitants, and in particular to those who had undergone circumcision. This detail was regarded as sufficiently important to the point of the narrative to be underscored through repetition. The sequel shows clearly what it was that the author thus wished to stress. As a result of their physical ordeal, the patients became incapacitated so that Simeon and Levi had little trouble in wiping out the whole city. This is the main point of the story, and the author makes it by stating twice that the victims were "all those who went out by the gate of his city." It follows that this phrase

[3] This is, however, but one of several distinctive uses of *bābtu;;* cf. B. Landsberger, *Materialien zum sumerischen Lexikon,* I, 1937, pp. 142 f.

must signify "those capable of bearing arms." How, then, is this meaning conveyed by the idiom that was used for the purpose?

It is independently established that *yāṣā'* by itself can be used in the sense of "to go forth to battle"; cf. e.g., Amos 5:3, I Chron 20:1. If *ša'ar* were then added, the whole could mean only "to represent one's community in battle," especially where the qualifying term "of his city" is appended. The primary sense "city gate" would be altogether pointless in such an instance, since warriors would obviously go out by the gate if there was one. The participial form—which is what we have—must stand thus for "those capable of bearing arms." The repetition makes this sense unmistakable. Any other interpretations, as Ehrlich has emphasized, would be unjust to the quality of the narrative before us.

A measure of support for this technical usage can now be adduced from Akkadian literature. The Akkadian verb for "to go out" (*waṣû*), like that for "to come in," can be employed, among many other uses, for communication between a city and the outside world, including even traffic with the enemy.[4] But this of itself does not describe true military operations. There is, however, one pertinent passage which does just that. It reads: "I constructed siege works against him and" *aṣê abul ālišu uterra ikkibuš* "the going out through his city gate I made utterly repugnant for him." In other words, as a result of the siege towers brought up by the attackers, any sallies from within the besieged city became much too

[4] Cf. the picturesque account of the siege of Urshu, *Keilschrifttexte aus Boghazköi,* I, 1916, No. 11:22 ff. (esp. 24, with which cf. Joshua 6:1); the text has been treated by H. G. Güterbock, *Zeitschrift für Assyriologie,* NF, 1938, pp. 126 f. For a discussion of siege tactics in the ancient Near East see Yigael Yadin, *Bulletin,* 137 (1955), pp. 23–32.

costly and hence taboo (*ikkibu*). This time the technical term employed is not just (*w*)*āṣû* "to go out" but the combination of that verb with 'his city gate," or precisely the same phrase as in Gen 34.[5]

The idiom just cited is to the best of my recollection a unique occurrence in cuneiform records. It may not be pure coincidence, therefore, that it should have been used against the background of the same land in which the Dinah episode took place; specifically, in Sennacherib's account of the siege of Jerusalem.[6] In other words, this particular turn of phrase might well have echoed local Hebrew usage. And lest this appear far-fetched, it should be recalled that the Assyrian command could handle Hebrew much too well for the morale of the defenders. When the Rabshakeh was begged to use Aramaic instead of the "language of Judah," he promptly made his persuasive Hebrew carry to all who had assembled on the wall of the city.[7]

There remains Gen 23 with its repeated reference to "all those who went in at the gate of his (i.e., Ephron's) city." The events here described are of an entirely different order, to be sure, from those related in Gen 34. Yet their import is just as far-reaching, and the description fully as skillful and dramatic. For what is ultimately involved is the change in Abraham's status from that of a landless alien to one of a legally approved landowner. The title to a property which has such obvious national implications must have a juridically foolproof basis. The transaction has to be unshakable. In other words, it must be witnessed by the highest city authorities, that is, the

[5] The only difference is in the use of the infinitive in Akkadian as against the participle in the Hebrew occurrence.

[6] Taylor Prism, III 30.

[7] II Kings 18:26, 28 and Isa 36:11, 13.

city fathers or elders.[8] The phrase selected to convey this meaning is "all those who entered at the gate of his city." Now that "the gate of one's city" has emerged as an old idiom for "community," the whole clause yields the comprehensive sense of "all who have a choice in the affairs of the community." [9]

The two cognate phrases with which we have been concerned prove thus to be idiomatic expressions for the two groups which jointly represented the source of governmental authority in most of the ancient Near East. The underlying concept is traceable to the Sumerians. Before he can embark upon his critical contest with the rival ruler of Kish, Gilgamesh must obtain the consent of two separate bodies, the assembly of the "city fathers" (*abba uru*) and the assembly of the "able-bodied men" (*guruš*).[10] It is not surprising, therefore, that early Hebrew society, which in many ways had so much in common with Mesopotamian society, should have employed special phrases for both these institutions. To be sure, the Machpelah account is commonly ascribed to "P." It is conceded, however, that in this instance the account betrays a descriptive flare and a subtle humor for which "P" is not otherwise noted. The hand may thus be indeed that of a later source, for which the story loomed large on various grounds. Yet the voice is evidently that of ancient and genuine tradition.[11]

[8] It may be worth stressing in this connection that the Akk. term for "witness" *šību* has the primary meaning of "greybeard, elder."

[9] The special force of the verb in this phrase is perhaps "attain," as in "advanced in days, years."

[10] See Th. Jacobsen, *Journal of Near Eastern Studies,* II (1943), p. 166, n. 44.

[11] Cf. my paper "A Vivid Sidelight on the Machpelah Episode," *Israel Life and Letters,* 1953 (May-June), p. 56–59. [Attention should be directed to the critical remarks of Geoffrey Evans in BASOR 150 (1958), pp. 28–33.]

"I Know Not the Day of My Death"

Genesis 27 can scarcely be said to have suffered from critical neglect. The confusion that attended Isaac's blessing was bound to yield a profusion of comments of exegetical, theological, and moralizing nature. In this cumulative mass, however, of secondary interpretation certain primary features of the account seem to have been overlooked. The blame for this oversight rests by no means with modern scholarship alone. The received account itself—an ancient and exceptionally skilful blend of still older sources—exhibits marked ethnologic and aetiologic characteristics. Small wonder therefore that sight has been lost of significant juridical and sociological aspects of the story which are, after all, basic to the whole episode.

That literary graces may have an allusive rather than a literal bearing is immediately apparent from the phrase in vs. 2 which reads, "I know not the day of my death." As it stands, this clause is a truism in that it might well be applied to anyone at any time. The intended meaning, of course, is "I may die at any moment," which goes logically with the preceding statement, "See now, I have grown (so) old [1] (that) . . ." That much is clear enough.

[1] There is surely no warrant in good Hebrew usage for translating *zāqantī* "I am old," as is commonly done. The stative sense would be conveyed by the adjective combined with the personal pronoun. In the third

The only question is whether the whole sentence is just a casual expression of personal sentiment, or whether it is instead an accepted formula in a specific context. There are good grounds, I believe, in favor of the second alternative.

The Nuzi [2] text *HSS*, IX, 34 includes this clause: *u inanna anāku altīb* (line 9) "now that I have grown old." [3] The biblical clause just cited parallels this Akkadian passage very closely. Yet the Targum *ad loc.* is closer still: *hā ḵe'an sābet,* where the verb is etymologically and semantically the same as Akk. *altīb* (< **aštib,* from *šīb,* WSem *śyb*) .

Taken by itself, such a sentiment could be, and no doubt was, expressed independently on innumerable occasions. Hẹre, however, there is more to it than mere sententiousness. The Mesopotamian who made the statement, a certain Hanaya, was a functionary [4] under an official whose direct superior was a Nuzian named Shilwateshub, the local representative of the feudal overlord of the kingdom of Mitanni.[5] Because of his advanced age,

---

person, where the adjective and the verb coincide, the language might be ambiguous. In the present instance, however, "I have become old" is favored by the form and required by the context.

[2] The reasons for my using "Nuzi" as opposed to "Nuzu" have been given in detail in JAOS, LXXV, 52–55.

[3] Nuzi *u* seldom has the ordinary copula. For the most part it is resumptive, "then" or the like, shading off at times into a conjunction. The abbreviation *HSS* stands for *Harvard Semitic Series.*

[4] The text refers to him as *(w)ardu,* here not "slave" but "servant" in a technical and official rather than a domestic sense.

[5] The text refers to Mitanni as Hanigalbat, which is the normal Nuzi designation, here abbreviated to ^{KUR}*Ha-lì* (line 3), for *Ha-lì-gal-bat;* cf. E. R. Lacheman, *BASOR,* No. 78, p. 20. Incidentally, Shilwateshub is described as *mār šarri,* which has invariably been rendered literally, i.e., "son of the king, prince." But this translation is certainly wrong. P. Koschaker made the important point in *ZA,* XLVIII, 168, that *šarratu ša Nuzi* cannot be "queen of Nuzi," for the simple reason that Nuzi was not an independent royal center; he suggested that the term stood for the local head priestess. The same argument holds good for *mār šarri,* a title held by a

Hanaya had made orally a final disposition (the technical term here used is *ṭēma šakānu*) of the extensive property in his charge,[6] by entrusting it to five named executors[7] from the nearby administrative center of Paharrashwe.[8] The document before us was made out by Shilwateshub to confirm the appointees and to stipulate that if any portion of the property involved was lost, the town of Paharrashwe would be held responsible.[9]

It should be remembered that in documents of this kind there is little room for casual observations. The various clauses employed are for the most part formulaic and have a well-established legal bearing. In other words, the pronouncement "I have now grown old" was at Nuzi a recognized formula accompanying a solemn final declaration; and such declarations had special standing precisely because they expressed a man's last wish. The phraseology, in short, had definite socio-juridical implications.

That a death-bed statement could be legally binding is shown conclusively by a Nuzi lawsuit, *AASOR,* XVI, 56. In it the plaintiff, one Tarmiya, says explicitly: "My father Huya was ill and he lay on (his) bed. And my

---

number of Nuzi individuals. It means in all likelihood something like "official representative of the king (or Mitanni)" and its principal significance is administrative.

[6] The title of the document, which is given on the envelope (the use of which hints indirectly at the importance of the text), is "tablet of land holdings."

[7] They are appointed *ana šamallūti,* lit. "for apprenticeship," again a technical term signifying that the appointees are expected to render specific services.

[8] This city figures prominently in the important Letter of Saushshattar, King of Mitanni, published in *HSS,* IX, 1, with translation and discussion by Speiser in *JAOS,* XLIX, 269–75.

[9] Lines 30–34: *šumma mimmušu ša Ḫanaya ša iḫalliqu ibašši āl Paḫarrašwe umalla,* "If there occurs any loss in the property of Hanaya, the city of Paharrashwe shall repay it."

father took my hand and spoke to me thus: 'My other, older sons have taken wives, but you have not taken a wife. Therefore I am giving you Sulūli-Ishtar as your wife.' "[10] The judges, on obtaining eye-witness testimony that Tarmiya had told the truth, decided the case in his favor; the purchase price of the girl had to be shared by all the brothers, instead of being paid by the husband alone.[11] This time there is no mention of the father's formulaic reference to his old age, but the death-bed scene is vividly described and the main point at issue is cited verbatim. What is clear, moreover, once again is that a final oral disposition by the head of a household had solid legal standing.

Taken together, the two Nuzi texts just given are strong presumptive evidence that Isaac's blessing was fundamentally a solemn disposal of his property made in the approved fashion of his time and social group. The identifying formula which was customary in such cases, found in Gen. 27:2 and in *HSS,* IX, 34.9, was "I have now grown old." The close correspondence between the two passages in question is surely not a matter of pure chance, just as the other parallels involving the patriarchal narratives and the Nuzi texts cannot be ascribed to

[10] Lines 8–16: ***abuya Huya maruṣ-mi u ina erši nāl u qāti abuya ṣabtu u kinanna ana yāši iqtabi allūtu mārūya rābūti aššata it(t)aḫzū-mi u atta aššata lā taḫḫuz-mi u Ṣulūlištar kīma aššatika akkāša addanakku.*** The phrase "my father took my hand" deserves special attention. It could be conceivably a gesture of affection, cf. Gilgamesh, *ANET,* p. 90, col. iii, l. 12. But in view of what has just been said about the formality of such proceedings, we have here with greater probability a required or customary symbolic touch. In that case, Gen 27 21 might well hark back to the same kind of motive which became meaningless to a later age and had to be reinterpreted.

[11] Code of Hammurabi 166 provides expressly for just such a contingency. In Nuzi law, however, the result was not automatic; the father retained apparently full discretionary rights.

mere coincidence.[12] For the Nuzi region was inhabited by an offshoot of the Hurrian society whose main political center half-way through the second millennium B.C. lay in the Ḫabur valley, which was also the home of the Patriarchs. Since the Hurrians were the dominant ethnic element of that region, many of their customs and institutions, including some which are not duplicated elsewhere, were bound to have been adopted by the local Semitic elements and to be reflected eventually in the patriarchal narratives.[13]

Away from their native environment, however, such borrowed customs may become cut off in due time from their original import. Tradition may preserve or recall the usage, but not always the purpose. Secondary interpretations spring up, reflecting the changed environment. But if the tradition continues faithful, and if its witnesses are blessed with a genius of a J or an E, posterity remains in a position to recover, or at least glimpse, the underlying processes. This cannot be accomplishmed, to be sure, without the aid of archeological discoveries. In so far as the Patriarchal Age is concerned, the Nuzi results in particular have helped to right the balance, so much so that scholars today are favored in a number of instances with a truer perspective than was available to J or E. Indeed, the whole issue of paternal bounty, which is the main topic of Gen. 27, has to be reviewed in this light.

A highly instructive document in this connection is

[12] See provisionally Speiser, *AASOR,* XIII, 44, and *Cahiers d'Histoire Mondiale,* I, 323 f. C. H. Gordon, *RB* (1935), pp. 34–41, and *Biblical Archaeologist,* III, 1–12. There remain, however, links which have not been pointed out so far, and some that have been cited prove to be superficial on further probing. The whole matter deserves a methodical inquiry.

[13] Cf. Speiser, *Cahiers d'Histoire Mondiale,* I, 311 ff.

HSS, V, 48. It pertains to a legal dispute concerning the rightful heir to the estate of one Shurihil. The key witness is a certain Paitilla who had been delegated by a court of eight [14] judges to head a committee of six officials which was to visit Shurihil, then apparently on his deathbed, and have him declare formally who his heir was to be. Paitilla's statement to Shurihil is reported in full, as follows:

(12) *umma lū dayyānū-ma inanna balṭāta-mi u ina arkika išassū* (15) *šumma atta* [15] *tamāt kī-mi* [16] *mārka kullimanni-mi u nīnu nīdē-mi*	Thus indeed (say) the judges: "You are now alive and claims are being raised against you. Since you may die, then point out your son to us so that we may know."

Shurihil accedes to this request and names his nephew Shennima as his son and heir. In a colophon (41–45) Shurihil's widow adds her testimony to the same effect.

The text just cited is but an unusually vivid confirmation of the repeatedly established fact that at Nuzi, and by extension also in Hurrian society in general, sonship could legally be determined by fiat, i.e., adoption, as much as by birth. The practice was widespread in all of Mesopotamia and it was exceedingly common at Nuzi.[17] Its possible bearing, however, on Gen. 27 does not become

[14] This is an exceptionally large panel; it reflects perhaps the high standing of the party concerned.

[15] Reading *at!-ta,* with P. Koschaker, *OLZ* (1932), p. 402. My earlier reading of this passage in *AASOR,* X, 66 is herewith revised.

[16] Koschaker, *loc. cit.,* reads *ta-ma-at-ti*$_4$*-mi,* which would be grammatically untenable. The fourth sign, moreover, is clearly *ki;* the resulting *kīmi* is established in the sense of "so, then."

[17] See the monograph by E. M. Cassin, *L'adoption à Nuzi* (1938).

apparent until attention has been directed to one specific detail which is spelled out for us in several documents, notably so in *HSS*, V, 7. Here we find Akabshenni, another nephew of the above Shurihil, adopting his own brother Shelluni with this emphatic stipulation:

(10) *šumma māriya!*[18] *ša ulladu ibašši rabi u šitta zittēn ileqqi lū 10 ašassu ša Akab-šenni mārē ša!*[19] *ullada rabū* (15) *Šelluni terdennu*

If a son of my own is born to me, he shall be the oldest, receiving two inheritance shares. Indeed, should the wife of Akab-shenni bear ten sons, they shall (all) be major (heirs), Shelluni (becoming) a secondary heir.

In other words, Shelluni can be the principal heir only if Akabshenni's wife remains childless. Should she bear sons, however, each would outrank Shelluni. Thus the primacy of the birthright is here a matter of the father's discretion and not of chronological priority. To be sure, in the present instance the distinction involves actual offspring as against an adopted relative. Elsewhere, however, a similar distinction is made between sons of the same father but of different mothers, an understandable procedure in a polygamous society. In any case, in matters of birthright the father's decree could reverse the natural order. In Hurrian society, in short, the term "older" was a relative concept from a sociojuridical viewpoint.

Against this kind of background, which patriarchal circles are known to have shared, the transfer of birth-

[18] The correct form would have been *māri*.
[19] The text omits the plural marker.

right from Esau to Jacob can no longer be regarded as a singular event. Tradition succeeded in this instance in preserving the recollection of a practice that was at home in central Mesopotamia; the circumstantial details could scarcely have been invented. There is no indication, on the other hand, that identical usages were practiced on Palestinian soil. Thus the underlying significance of the tradition on which Gen 27 is based would be lost with the passage of centuries. New formulations would be introduced, conforming to the altered environment and resulting in the chapter as we now have it, itself an account of great antiquity.[20]

Yet how did tradition arrive at the formulation contained in Gen 27? To such a question there can be no conclusive answer at this time. The best that can be hazarded is a working hypothesis. There was a time apparently in the dim past when Edom, in common perhaps with related elements east of the Jordan, enjoyed a position superior to that of the early Israelite settlers in Palestine. Gradually, however, the balance shifted in favor of the western settlers.[21] Could not such a shift be explained as the sequel to a patriarchal act, an authentic memory of which was still alive? All this, of course, is sheer speculation. What is far more concrete is the societal framework in which the received account has been placed. Yet the recovery of that framework alone would seem to be a substantial gain.

[20] The documentary composition, however, remains in doubt and some modern critics see the text as an original unit; for a recent statement on this point cf. G. von Rad, *Das erste Buch Mose,* p. 240.

[21] A similar shift appears to have taken place within the Israelite tribal confederacy in so far as the vicissitudes of Reuben are concerned; cf. M. Noth, *Geschichte Israels,* pp. 54 f.

The Verb *SHR* in Genesis and Early Hebrew Movements

In Number 163 of the Bulletin W. F. Albright has presented a new interpretation of "Abram the Hebrew." [1] It has come as a surprise to no one that the essay is comprehensive, packed with information, closely reasoned—and provocative. Its central thesis as well as its maze of detail will be weighed and discussed for a long time to come. If I now single out for comment one such detail, it is precisely because the particular point does not seriously affect Albright's main conclusions. It is, however, a critical detail on other grounds. That the dissident statement which follows has been afforded hospitality in a medium so intimately identified with Albright himself is but another instance of the Editor's unfailing objectivity.

In Section III of his study Albright states: '[C. H. Gordon] is probably right to insist on the interpretation of the finite forms of the stem *shr* in Gen. 34:10, 34:21 and 42:34 as meaning "trade," just as the participial forms mean "trader (s) " in Gen. 23:16 and 37:28. It may be observed that the Revised Standard Version agrees with Gordon, while the new Jewish Publication Society

[1] BULLETIN 163 (October, 1961), pp. 36–54.

translation adheres to the more general meaning.[2] It so happens that I was the one who introduced the JPS rendering to which Albright alludes, so that it is now my responsibility to get my colleagues on the JPS translation committee off the hook. The subject has already been dealt with briefly in an address which the JPS subsequently published for private circulation.[3] But a fuller and more readily accessible statement is now clearly in order.

The question before us, then, is whether the verb *sḥr* in the passages cited above refers to trade or something else. The answer must be sought in the pertinent data of linguistics and context. Let us review both types and see whether they add up to a uniform and self-consistent solution.

1. The Hebrew verb *sḥr* is represented in the Old Testament by verbal as well as nominal forms. The finite forms of the verb are found only five times altogether: aside from the three Genesis occurrences (Gen. 34:10, 21; 42:34) once in Jer. 14:18 and once in Ps. 38:11 (in the reduplicated form *s^eḥarḥar*). More common is the verbal noun *sōḥēr* (act. participle).[4] In addition, we find scattered instances of the nominal forms *saḥar, s^eḥōrāh,* and *misḥār*.[5] The meaning "trader" for *sōḥēr* has never been in doubt, and related values are likewise assured for the three independent noun formations. The only matter at issue is thus the meaning of the finite verb.

[2] *Ibid.*, p. 44. For Gordon's statement see *Journal of Near Eastern Studies*, XVII (1958), p. 29.

[3] "New Light on the Eternal Book" (1957).

[4] Thirteen occurrences.

[5] The isolated *sōḥērāh* (Ps. 91:4), an article of armament, and *sōḥeret* (Esther 1:6), a precious stone, are not directly pertinent, although the former at least may be plausibly linked to the verb *sḥr* but not to the specialized nominal forms.

2. The original connotation of the stem is vouched for by comparative etymology. The Akkadian cognate *saḫā-rum* is abundantly certified in the sense of "to turn, circle traverse"; the same is true also of its Aramaic counterpart *sᵉḥar*. This underlying significance accounts readily for the specialized application to trade as reflected in the nominal uses of *sḥr* in Hebrew: the active participle describes someone who travels about, more particularly the peddler and the merchant; and the outright nouns signify other aspects of trade. What we need to decide is whether this derived connotation was already operative in the extant verbal forms. To be sure, we know that back formation yielded a secondary verb *sḥr* "to trade" in post-biblical Hebrew and Jewish Aramaic. But can we posit, let alone demonstrate, the same usage in the early narratives of Genesis?

3. It should be noted in passing that the concepts "to circle" and "to trade" are by no means mutually interchangeable. Akkadian never used its exceedingly common *saḫārum* as a semantic basis for its ubiquitous "merchant." To designate this characteristic occupation, Akkadian employed the more direct services of Semitic **mkr* "to trade," arriving thereby at the noun *tamkārum*, which Sumerian appropriated very early as d a m . g a r, and Aramaic much later as *taggārā*. Heb. *sōḥēr*, on the other hand, is an indirect and circuitous development, lacking even the outward credentials of a professional term, which would have called for **saḥḥār*. In other words, the semantic route "to circle, traverse > trader" is itself a detour, yet negotiable. But there is scarcely any communication from the opposite direction. The normal verbal associate of "merchant" is "to trade," not "to circle." It is essentially a case of one-way traffic all around.

4. Our next step, therefore, will be to ascertain whether the Heb. verb *sḥr* still carries the original meaning of the stem in any of its extant occurrences in the Old Testament. We ignore for the moment the three instances in Genesis, since they are the cases at issue. Furthermore, the passage in Jer. 14:18 is much too obscure for dependable analysis. The text is uncertain, so that many authorities have felt obliged to resort either to emendation or to outright guesses. As the text stands, "for both the prophet and the priest 'trade to' land" (*sāḥ^a^rū 'el 'ereṣ* is obviously impossible; "but turn to land" (to use one of the attested meanings of the Semitic stem) [6] is not at all incongruous; nevertheless, such speculation could not be admitted as evidence. There remains thus only one further instance, *libbī s^e^ḥarḥar* in Ps. 38:11 [10]. Here we find general agreement on at least one point: no one has yet proposed to translate the phrase by "my heart has gone commercial." KJ has "panteth," old JPS "fluttereth," RSV "throbs," SB "le coeur me bat," and so forth. Actually, the ascertained etymology surely speaks for itself: "my heart goes round and round, pitapat." It follows that Heb. *sḥr* could "circle" no less actively than its cognates in Akkadian and Aramaic.

5. We come back now to the three problematic passages in Genesis. The ultimate criterion of meaning is, of course, not etymology but usage, and usage has to be determined from the context. But before we analyze the respective passages, we have a valuable clue in the syntax, which one has no business to ignore. Gen. 34:10 reads

[6] Interestingly enough, the old JPS translation has here "are gone about to a land," even though it retains "trade" and "traffic" in the Genesis passages.

(u)s^{e}*ḥārūhā* "(and) *sḥr* it," with the pronoun pointing back to "land"; Gen. 34:21 has *w*^{e}*yisḥ*^{a}*rū 'ōtāh* "let them *sḥr* it," with "land" once again as the antecedent; finally, Gen. 42:34 states explicitly *w*$^{e'}$*et hā'āreṣ tisḥārū* "and you shall *sḥr* the land." In each instance, then, the verb is construed with a direct object. If we interpret *sḥr* as "to trade," we ought to be consistent and take the direct object with it; but in that case we obtain not "to trade *in* the land," but "to trade *the* land." Understandably enough, no translator has been rash enough so far to saddle these narratives with real estate transactions. Yet to stop half way is to do violence to elementary requirements of Hebrew construction.

6. One could legitimately counter this last argument with the following question: if we restore to the above occurrences of *sḥr* the inherited connotation of "to circle" or the like, and more specifically "to wander about" (as will be presently suggested), would Hebrew still tolerate the direct object in such cases? For an answer we need not go farther than the instructive parallel of Jewish Aramaic, in spite of the fact that the secondary influence of the established Heb. *sōḥēr* is not negligible in that dialect. I quote the following passage from the recently discovered "Genesis Apocryphon": [7]

> So I, Abram, set out to traverse and inspect the land (*lmsḥr wlmḥzh 'r'h*). I starter on the journey (*lmsḥr*) from the River Gihon and came to the shore of the sea, arriving at the Mount of the Ox. I journeyed on (*wsḥrt*) from that Great Salt Sea and continued along the Mount of the Ox towards the east, through the breadth of the land, until I reached the River Euph-

[7] N. Avigad and Y. Yadin, *A Genesis Apocryphon: a Scroll from the Wilderness of Judaea* (Jerusalem, 1956).

> rates. I journeyed (*wsḥrt*) along the Euphrates to the east until I reached the Red Sea.[8] I kept on along the Red Sea until I reached the tongue of the Sea of Reeds, which issues from the Red Sea. I then journeyed (*wsḥrt*) southwards until I reached the River Gihon.[9]

In this single connected passage we find no less than five occurrences of Aram. *sḥr,* each time with the indisputable sense of "to journey, wander." Significantly enough, the first instance is construed with the direct object, and—more important still—that object happens to be "the land," exactly as in the three Hebrew passages in Genesis.

7. The goal of our own wanderings has at last been reached. We are ready to leave the issue to the decisive criterion of content. Let us start with Gen. 42:34. The situation there is clear at first glance. To teach his brothers a lesson long overdue, and to force them to return with Benjamin, Joseph invents the charge that they came to spy on Egypt. He detains Simeon under house arrest and permits the others to go home with emergency food supplies, but warns them not to come back unless they bring Benjamin with them. On that condition only can they effect the release of Simeon and *sḥr* in the land.

How does this verb fit into the context? The ancient versions and the vast majority of commentators,[10] operate

[8] *I.e.,* the Indian Ocean, *op. cit.,* p. 31; the same terminology is used by Herodotus.

[9] The geography becomes confused towards the end, cf. *ibid.,* p. 32. On the Gihon see now E. A. Speiser, "The Rivers of Paradise," in the *Festschrift Johannes Friedrich* (Heidelberg, 1959), pp. 473–485 [above, pp. 23–34].

[10] It is worth noting, however, that Rashi understood this occurrence in the sense of "to move about." Among the moderns, A. Dillmann, *e.g.,* (*Die Genesis,* 6th ed., *Leipzig,* 1892), p. 422, has *durchziehen,* but adds "des Handels wegen," although he explains the two occurrences in Gen. 34 as meaning "to move about freely," without reference to commercial purposes. G. von Rad, *Das erste Buch Mose* (Göttingen, 1953), p. 333, translates *umherziehen* here and *sich umtun* in ch. 34. SB (*La Sainte Bible,* Jerusalem,

with "to trade (in the land)." Yet quite aside from the syntactical incongruence mentioned above, nothing could be more inappropriate in the circumstances. The brothers came to Egypt on a life-saving errand. They were anxious to go back as quickly as possible. To have them settle as land traders at a time of unprecedented famine would have been the farthest thing from anybody's mind. The only sense that the context permits, and the immediate situation calls for, is release from detention and unrestricted travel in the land. The attested basic sense of the verb supplies this very meaning: you can traverse the land, move about freely in it.

The other two instances—actually two variations on the same theme—yield similar results. The narrative in question (Gen. 34) concerns Jacob's daughter Dinah. After his act of violence, young Shechem discovers that he is deeply in love with Dinah and asks for her hand in marriage. If her family would only agree, the remorseful youth pleads, the sojourning Israelites would be free to settle in the land and intermarry with the Shechemites (vv. 10, 21); the land would then be theirs to *sḥr*. The translators, once again all the way back to the Targumim and the LXX, render "to trade in." But the opposite of sojourner, or resident alien who is in the country on sufferance, is one who has the freedom of the land; and this is precisely the connotation of the stem in Semitic.

8. To summarize, the combined evidence of etymology, syntax, and context requires us to interpret the three verbal forms of *sḥr* in Genesis as analogues of Akk. *saḫā-rum,* common Aram. *s*ᵉ*ḥar,* and biblical *s*ᵉ*ḥarḥar* itself.

1956) renders *trafiquer* here, yet *circuler* in the two other instances. This spot check shows that acceptance of the traditional interpretation has been far from unanimous.

Nor is this all. The incidental background of the patriarchal narratives also points to the same conclusion: Joseph "tended the flocks along with his brothers" (Gen. 37:2). While at Shechem, the locale of Gen. 34, Joseph is reported as saying, "I am looking for my brothers. Could you tell me where they are pasturing?" (Gen. 37:16). He describes his family to Pharaoh in these words, "The men are shepherds, having long been keepers of livestock, and they have brought with them their flocks and herds and everything they own" (Gen. 46:32, and cf. 46:34). Similarly, Joseph's brothers declare to Pharaoh, "We your servants are shepherds, just as our fathers were" (Gen. 47:3). In none of these passages do we find the slightest hint about trading. To be sure, this is merely the self-image of the patriarchs, or rather their image as seen by the narrators. But the same applies to the particular narratives in which the verb *sḥr* occurs. Whatever the sociological status of the people may have been in reality—and this a point that has been left open so as not to beg the question—in their own literary retrospect it was the Ishmaelites and the Midianites, and the Canaanites and the Phoenicians who were traders, not the Israelites. As was remarked above, early Hebrew did not even boast a special term for "merchant," and hence had to harness for the purpose the participle *sōḥēr* by raiding a stem with a much more general semantic range. Every bit of evidence points thus uniformly to the same result, which is that the verb *sḥr* in Genesis had nothing whatever to do with trading.

9. In conclusion, one may ask why the verbal uses of the stem, so wide-spread in Akkadian and Aramaic, came to be dispensed with in Hebrew, so much so that only five instances survived in the entire Old Testament, their

meaning eventually lost to tradition and translators alike. The answer should not be far to seek. A settled society could not long maintain itself in the ancient Near East without growing attention to trade, and the necessary terminology to go with it. This is why the descriptive form *sōḥēr* in Hebrew became in due time an indispensable technical term. As this derivative connotation became increasingly prominent, the original meaning of the verb was driven out of use until it became obsolete and eventually forgotten altogether. This could not have happened, however, without a suitable replacement, which was supplied by the stem *sbb*. This stem has not only the sense of "to circle" but also, especially in the base or Qal form, the further connotation of "to wind through" (Gen. 2:11, 13), "to wander" (2 Kings 3: 9), and the like, much the same as *sḥr*. Hence the Targumim normally render Heb. *sbb* by Aram. *sḥr*. All of this helps to explain why later interpretation was to wander so far afield in evaluating the surviving instances of the verb *sḥr* in Biblical Hebrew.

[For a dissenting view see W. F. Albright, BASOR, No. 164 (1961), p. 28.]

An Angelic "Curse": Exodus 14:20

LANGUAGE ADJUSTS INEVITABLY TO THE NEEDS OF THE TIMES. As against the recent bulge in the lexicon of science and technology, there has been steady attrition in the terminology of such areas as cult and magic, areas which loomed much larger in the past than they do today. For instance, we are poorly equipped to reflect the elaborate vocabulary of the ancient Near East on the subject of sin. Similarly, standard translations of the Bible employ the term "curse," noun or verb, to render at one time or another the biblical Hebrew stems *'ārar, qillēl, 'ālā(h)*,[1] *qābab/nāqab, zā'am*, as well as the nouns *šᵉbū'ā(h)* and *ḥerem*. Yet it goes without saying that these terms started out with fundamentally different connotations.[2] Our tendency to lump them together can only blur the context; sometimes it casts gratuitous suspicion on the text. The answer is not to permit our impoverished lexical equipment to affect the recovery of the content.

A case in point is the Heb. verb *'ārar*[3] with its per-

[1] Primarily "adjuration, imprecation," the semantic equivalent of Akk. *māmītu*, Aram. *mōmātā;* note especially the Akk. hendiadys *adê u māmīt* "pact adjuration(s)," var, *riksu u māmītu*, Heb. *'ālōt habbᵉrīt* (Deut. 29:20).

[2] The subject as a whole requires detailed study; one such pertinent investigation has been announced and another is known to be in progress.

[3] Cf. J. Hempel, *ZDMG*, 79 (1925), 20 ff., and M. Noth, *Gesammelte Studien zum Alten Testament*, pp. 155 ff.

tinent noun *m*^{e}*'ērā(h)*; the corresponding Akkadian cognates are *arārum* and *arratum/erretum* respectively. In all instances the all but invariable translation is "curse." This is barely adequate at best. Occasionally, moreover, it is not only misleading but demonstrably wrong. The concept "curse" may be a convenient substitute for the execrations listed in Deut. 27:16 ff. and 28:16 ff., or the sanctions cited in the Epilogue to the Code of Hammurabi and in various Akkadian vassal treaties—the relevant term in each case being based on the root 'RR. But the basic sense of the term is clearly more specific than "curse." The Akk. phrase *arrat lā napšuri . . . līrurūšu*[4] shows that *arratum* was something that could be "loosened, unbound" (verb *pašārum*), hence a form of restraint or bond. Accordingly, the stem 'RR connotes "to bind, hem in with obstacles, render powerless to resist." When such an effect was achieved by magical means, the counteraction (*pašārum*) required corresponding supernatural intervention; hence the *lipšur* formulae in the series *Šurpu* and related texts, which have recently received expert treatment at the hand of Erica Reiner.[5] But if the Akkadian phrase just cited, namely, "may they [the gods] apply to him [the victim] an *arratum* that cannot be loosened" was not idle malevolence, it would follow that some of these spells were past reversing.

The same basic meaning of supernatural spell underlies Heb. *'ārar* in severel unambiguous passages. The celebrated diviner Balaam is engaged for the express purpose of immobilizing Israel, his mandate being "come, cast a spell (imperative of *'ārar*) for me against that

[4] Cf. D. D. Luckenbill, OIP II 148.28.
[5] *AfO*, Beiheft 11, and *JNES*, 15 (1956), 129 ff.

people" (Num. 22:6).[6] With the preposition *mi*(*n*) the verb denotes "to anathematize, ban." Thus in Gen. 3:14, when the serpent is being sentenced for his role in the fall of Adam and Eve, the traditional translation "cursed (*'ārūr*) are you above all cattle and all the beasts of the field" is totally out of place, since the other animals have done nothing to draw a curse upon themselves. What the syntax and context require is "you are banned from all the other animals." Similarly, in Gen. 4:11, Cain's sentence can scarcely read, with RSV (and others), "you are cursed from the ground," whatever this may mean; both the plain text and sense agree on "you are banned from the soil." Nor can "curse" be made to fit the passage that deals with the woman accused of adultery (Num. 5:18 ff.). The form there is *m^{e}'ār^{e}rīm* (factitive participle of *'ārar*). It is applied to a specific potion,[7] which could not in any circumstances voice a violent denunciation (the customary meaning of "curse"). The potion is utilized as an agent "that implements the spell/ordeal," which is exactly how it is described.[8]

The foregoing comment leads up to a critical passage in Exod. 14:20, which was given up as hopeless by the Septuagint, and has not been put back together again ever since. The Israelites had just fled from Egypt, but

[6] How eagerly such diviners (techn. term *mašmašu* or *āḫiz šēri*) were sought after, once they had established their reputation, may be judged from the Mari letter ARM I 18.

[7] Just what that potion was, and how it was called, is beside the point. The syntax of the received *mēy-mārīm* does not accord with the traditional rendering "waters of bitterness."

[8] Another critical passage is Exod. 22:27, where *'ārar* is applied to "an elected chieftain among your people" and is used in parallelism with *qillēl*. It is clear, at all events, that the mechanical translations "curse," and "revile" are altogether out of place in that passage. Cf. provisionally G. Boyer, ARM VIII 174 n. 1. For a possible clue cf. Lev. 19:14, where *qillēl* is paralleled by "you shall not place obstacles before [the handicapped]," which would be an excellent paraphrase of *'ārar* in the sense in which the verb is here being considered.

the pursuing Egyptians are about to overtake them. At this juncture, the angel and the luminous cloud that have led the Israelites hitherto move from front to back [9] and interpose themselves between the fugitives and the pursuers. The text continues, "Thus there was the cloud with the darkness, *wayyā'er 'et-hallaylā(h)* . . ." All is clear enough until we come to the verbal form *wayyā'er*. This is invariably interpreted as a causative form of the verb *'ōr* "to be right as day." But what sense could be made in the present context of the phrase "and it turned the night into daylight"? None whatever. No brightness has ever been less enlightening.

The fact is that the context calls for precisely the opposite turn of events. And indeed, the parallel reference in Josh. 24.7 says explicitly "and he [God] put darkness between you and the Egyptians." [10] Later lexicographers and commentators did their best to torture darkness out of light, but it could not be done.[11] AV translates: "and it was a cloud and darkness *to them*, but it gave light by night *to these*." [12] But the pronouns [13] are not in the text, and the syntax of *'et-hallaylā(h)* will not yield "by night" except through sinful distortion. In this dilemma most

[9] If in a requested omen a star moves from front to back, the prognosis is regarded as unfavorable; cf. E. Reiner, *JNES,* 19 (1960), 31, 106. Unless the correspondence with the biblical passage before us is purely coincidental, the portent in the latter instance would affect the Egyptians alone.

[10] Darkness was commonly regarded as ominous, hence it could be used figuratively for "curse." Note the contrast between *māmītu* and *nūru* in the refrain found in Šurpu V-VI 72, 82, 102, 112, 122 (see below, note 18). Cf. also "dense is the darkness, light there is none," Gilg. IX iii 11 ff., and the Sargon omen "who encountered darkness, but light emerged for him," A. Goetze, *JCS,* I (1947), 255 f.

[11] The usual starting point for this particular exegesis (*'ōr* > "darkness.. is Mishna Pes. 1. 1, with occasional reference to Psalm 139:11. The correct explanation, however, in both instances is quite different.

[12] This interpretation is as old as Targum Onkelos and Symmachus; cf. also Syr.

[13] Which AV marks by means of italics. Later translations add to the confusion by omitting the italics, thereby suggesting to the reader that the original actually has these readings.

moderns help themselves to the Septuagint version which ventures "and the night passed." Yet no amount of sound textual surgery will produce the required *wy'br* (*way-ya'bor*) out of the indicated *wy'r 't*, or vice versa. The Greek translators did not have a different text before them; they were simply guessing as best they could. Small wonder, therefore, that M. Noth, in his recent translation of *Exodus*, leaves this particular passage blank.[14]

Nevertheless, it is possible to do full justice to this context while leaving the text intact. The form *wayyā'er* need not be derived from *'ōr*. It can be traced back as it stands to *'ārar* (Hiphil jussive). And if it should be argued that the causative of *'ārar* is not otherwise attested,[15] one can easily point the text to yield *wayyā́'ŏr* (Qal), which can readily be justified. It should be remembered that the received vocalization reflects later tradition, which in this instance operated with *'ōr*.

How does this alternative derivation work out? Our verse would then read as follows: "And it [the pillar of cloud] came between the Egyptian camp and the Israelite camp. Thus there was the cloud with the darkness, and it cast a spell (*wy'r*) upon the night, so that one side could not make contact with the other all through that night." The last clause now falls naturally into place, in that it spells out the consequences of the intercession by the angel with his magical cloud. The celestial barrier made the resulting darkness so thick that the two camps were effectively sealed off from each other. To the Egyptians

[14] Göttingen Series 5, p. 81. Aside from the negative textual evidence, which lends no support to the Septuagint rendering, the concluding clause of the verse is also unfavorable to it: failure to make contact does not go naturally with "the night passed."

[15] The form *yū'ar* (Num. 22.7) is generally interpreted as Hophal, in which case the Hiphil would be indirectly attested; but this particular occurrence could well reflect the passive form of Qal. Incidentally, the terms in which Balaam is described in the passage here cited are a virtual paraphrase of Akk. *takil* "reliable" as applied to the diviner featured in ARM I 18.

it was black magic. But for the Israelites it was a benign and protective intervention.

Three brief points remain to be made in further support of the interpretation that has just been outlined.

First, the Bible itself furnishes a close parallel to such a magical treatment of the night. For alongside the reclaimed use of *'ārar* with *laylā(h)* as object, we find the unambiguous phrase *'ōrᵉrēy-yōm* (Job 3:8), which may now be meaningfully rendered "those who cast a spell upon the day." The two occurrences are mutually complementary.

Second, an old Akkadian omen contributes a significant analogue to the elemental content of Exod. 14:20. It reads as follows: *šumma padānu II-ma ina bīrišunu dīḫu nurrub nadi*^{di} *amūt*^{ut} *Šarru-kên ša ummānšu rādu īsiruma bēlīšunu ana aḫāmeš ušpîlu*[16] "if the 'path' is twofold and in between there is a break which shows moisture, it is an omen of Sargon whose (split) troops were so hemmed by a cloudburst that they interchanged one another's arms." This laconic notice refers manifestly to a rift that developed between two hostile factions within Sargon's army.[17] Then the elements intervened, with the result that nobody could tell which arms belonged to whom. Thus bloodshed was averted by a meteorological miracle.

Third, and last, if the context is so self-evident, how did its meaning come to be so badly distorted? The answer, I believe, is not far to seek. In course of time, and in view of Israel's progressive aversion to magic practices,[18] *'ārar* lost its earlier occult connotation and became a mere synonym for "curse" in the conventional

[16] E. Weidner, *MAOG*, IV, 230.
[17] Cf. H. G. Güterbock, *ZA*, 42 (1934), 61.
[18] See Deut. 18:10 ff.

sense of the term. As such, its pertinence to Exodus 14:20 was far from obvious. In these circumstances, it was natural to interpret the verb as a form of *'ōr* and let the meaning take care of itself. The Greek translators, to be sure, couldn't do much with such a reading and resorted to a council of desperation. Orthodox tradition had recourse to all sorts of ingenuity, but to little avail. The passage had come up with its own kind of roadblock.

By restoring the verb in question to its ancient meaning, we may now invoke one of the familiar refrains of the Akkadian incantator and say with him, in regard to Exod. 14:20, *māmīt littaṣi anāku nūram lūmur*[19] "Let the curse depart that I may see the light."

[*Addendum.* See now *The Problem of "Curse" in the Hebrew Bible,* JBL Monograph Series XIII (1963), by Herbert C. Brichto. Special interest in this connection attaches to a recently discovered tomb cave in the vicinity of Lachish, with inscriptions including several occurrences and combination of *'rr* and drawings of circles; see Y. Naveh, *Yediot* XXVII, 4 (1963), pp. 242 ff. and pl. 12. The author conjectures a magical objective, perhaps a curse directed against a specific enemy. The above conclusions may help to carry the interpretation a step farther: the purpose of the inscription, and of the accompanying drawings, would seem to be a summary restraint (*'rr*) against any hostile beings that might threaten the peace of the interred. The underlying meaning would thus be precisely that which has been independently established in this paper.]

[19] Šurpu V-VI 72, 72, etc.

Background and Function of the Biblical Nasi'

THE HEBREW TERM *nāśī'* DESIGNATES ONE OF THE KEY FIGures in early biblical society. Yet to this day there is little agreement about the nature and background of this title. The noun has been variously translated through the centuries. Perhaps the commonest, and certainly the most familiar, Western rendering is "prince," or its given equivalent. It so happens, however, that this is also the least appropriate of the attempted translations. We shall see presently that LXX did much better with its *archōn*, as did the Targumim with their *rab*, inasmuch as "leader, chieftain" reflects adequately enough the function, if not the etymology, of *nāśī'*.

The title *nāśī'* occurs over a hundred times in the Hebrew Bible. The distribution is noteworthy in itself. Virtually all the occurrences are crowded into two widely separated periods: an early stage which starts with the patriarchs and ends with Joshua, and a late stage which begins with Ezekiel. In other words, the term is practically dormant during the period of the monarchies; although correlated to some extent with *mäläk* "king," *nāśī'* undergoes an eclipse as soon as kingship has been instituted. It is no mere coincidence, therefore, that the premonarchic Covenant Code cites the *nāśī'* (Ex 22,27) but fails to mention the *mäläk*; by the same token the *nāśī'* reappears on the eve of the Exile, and is to enjoy a new lease on life in postbiblical times.

Ezekiel makes a distinction between *mäläk* and *nāśī'* which is partly qualitative and partly ideological. His *mäläk* is primarily the head of a major political power, such as Egypt or Babylonia. Lesser foreign rulers, on the other hand, are given the title of *nāsī,* as is also the ideal future ruler of Judah. Thus in Ezekiel's view, great temporal power does not appear conducive to spiritual excellence, hence the prophet's personal preference for a modest principality as opposed to an ambitious empire.[1]

It is this special role of the *nāśī'* in the world view of Ezekiel that led to the eventual renditions of the term in the sense of "prince," assisted in large measure by the traditional Latin *princeps*. But it should be borne in mind that Ezekiel's own usage was archaizing and derivative; accordingly, the key to the meaning of the title in question must be sought in sources which Ezekiel himself employed, that is, in material dealing with the premonarchic age. Fortunately, evidence bearing on that early stage is ample and varied enough to justify reasonably safe conclusions.

The subject as a whole has been treated in recent years by two distinguished biblical authorities. Their results may be summed up as follows.

Martin Noth[2] regards the *nāśī'* as the byproduct of a posited amphictyony. Each of the participating tribes would send to the central council a delegate who bore the title *nāśī'*. The name *nāśī'*, Noth believes, may have

[1] Cf. M. North, *Das System der zwölf Stämme Israels* (1930) 151 ff.
[2] Ibid., Exkurs III, "Gebrauch und Bedeutung des Wortes [*nāśī'*]," 151–62.

been based on some such phrase as *nāśā' qōl* "to raise one's voice, speak up," or on *n^eśū' pānīm* "an honored person," lit., "one with lifted up countenance." That Noth still maintains the amphictyonic origin of the term, and favors the first of the above derivations, is evident from his latest study of the Book of Exodus;[3] although he leaves *nāśī'* untranslated in one particularly troublesome passage (Ex 22,27), he retains the translation *Sprecher* "spokesman" in the other pertinent passages (Ex 16,22; 34,31; 35,27), thereby implying that the various occurrences of this title elsewhere in the Hexateuch are to be similarly derived and interpreted.

J. van der Ploeg, in his comprehensive restatement of the evidence,[4] finds himself obliged to reject Noth's basic premise. The *nāśī'*, van der Ploeg argues, is a secular rather than a religious title, having no direct or indirect connection with an amphictyony. If the term is found at times against the background of twelve tribal units, it is solely because that many groups happened to be involved in the given instances. In other instances the number of the same functionaries may be as low as one, or as high as 250.[5] The title itself, van der Ploeg suggests, need mean no more than that the *nāśī'* was a leader who had raised himself (passive formation from the stem *nāśā'* "to raise") above his fellows.[6]

Van der Ploeg's criticism of Noth's position is wholly cogent; but his own interpretation, though objective and lucid, fails to take full advantage of the data that the sources provide. It goes without saying that a satisfactory explanation must account for every distinctive usage of

[3] *ATD* 5, *Das zweite Buch Mose.*
[4] "Les chefs du peuple d'Israël et leur titres," *RB* 57 (1950) 40 ff.
[5] Cf. the references cited below.
[6] *Loc. cit.*, 50.

the term, preferably by relating all of them to a common denominator. Etymology can be useful, of course, provided that it is in keeping with the established connotations. In the case before us it can be shown, I believe, that both usage and etymology yield a harmonious and self-consistent picture. The end result, moreover, has an important bearing on the basic structure of early Israelite society.

The normative evidence, as was intimated above, is contained in records dealing with the premonarchic age. To begin with, those records describe the *nāśī'* unambiguously as a tribal leader. Thus Nm 7,2 speaks of the *neśī'īm* of Israel as "heads of their respective patriarchal groups (*bātē-'abōtām*), that is (*hem*), *neśī'īm* of the tribes (*maṭṭōt*), in charge of the enrollment." [7] Analogously, "[Phineas] had with him ten *neśī'īm* one *nāśī'* from each *bēt-'āb*—each tribe of Israel—all of them heads of their respective *bātē-ābōt*," Jos 22:14. Evidently, therefore, the phrase *bēt-'āb* could characterize the tribe as a group which traced its descent to a common ancestor; and at the head of such a group stood the *nāśī'*. But the explicit and repeated stress on the *bēt-'āb* makes it likely at the same time that the *nāśī'* owed his position ultimately to his patriarchal standing.[8] In other words, in order to qualify as tribal leader, the *nāśī'* had to be a duly recognized head of a *bēt-'āb*.

This last conclusion is not purely conjectural. We know that tribal subdivisions or clans were also designated as *bātē-'ābōt*, each of which in turn could have its own *nāśī*. Thus the three Levite clans had individual

[7] For this technical sense of *peqūdim see* E. A. Speiser, "Census and Ritual Expiation in Mari and Israel," *BASOR* 149 (1958) 17 ff.; lit., "those recorded, enrolled" [see below, pp. 171 ff.].

[8] Cf., e.g., Nm 36,1.

ne'śī'īm, with a chief *nāśī'* over them (Nm 3,32). This particular practice may well have served as the model for Ezekiel's "*nāśī'*-in-chief" (Ez 38,2 f.; 39,1). It follows that any patriarchal grouping, large or small, was headed by its own *nāśī'*.

But how did a *nāśī'* attain his position? The smallest units, or families, were led by elders or patriarchs whose rise was more or less automatic. When it came, however, to larger groupings, such as clans made up of families, or tribes composed of clans (cf. 1 Sm 9,21), seniority could not have been the sole qualification for top rank. Various other criteria and conditions must have played a part. At all events, we need not speculate on this point. The extant sources give us a clear answer.

Nm 1,16, following a list of the individual tribal leaders who were to assist Moses with the census, sums up the entire slate in these terms: "These are the nominees of the assembly (*q^{e}rū/ī'ē hā'ēdā*), the *n^{e}śī'īm* of their ancestral tribes." Analogously, Nm 16, 2 speaks of "250 *n^{e}śī'īm* of the assembly, nominees of the council (*q^{e}rī'ē mō'ēd*), distinguished men." It follows that the *nāśī'* was called, that is to say elected, by the assembly or council of the particular body in question. More often, the two coordinate phrases, "nominees of the assembly/council: *n^{e}śī'īm* of the assembly" are telescoped into the single expression *n^{e}śī'ē hā'ēdā* (Nm 4,34; 31,13; 32,2; Jos 9,15.18; 22,30). Any doubt about the specific force of this possessive compound is immediately dispelled by Ex 34,31, which states unambiguously *w^{e}kol hann^{e}śī'īm bā'ēdā* "and all the *n^{e}śī'īm* in the assembly," where the preposition "in" explicates the precise connection. In short, a *nāśī'* was someone elected to that position by the appropriate council.

The results that have just been obtained have a bearing also on the derivation of the term under discussion. The juxtaposition of "nominees of the assembly: *nᵉśīʾīm* of the assembly/council" proves that *nāśīʾ* is closely correlated with "nominee." The correlation, moreover, is not only semantic but morphological. For in Nm 1,16 the consonantal text (Ktīb) reads *qᵉrīʾē* as opposed to *qᵉrūʾē* of the vocalized text (Qrē); [9] thus *nāśīʾ* is formally matched by **qārīʾ*. Now the Heb. stem-form *qāṭīl* describes *nomina professionis,* or the like, usually passival in aspect.[10] Here **qārīʾ* is self-explanatory: it designates an official who has been "called up, nominated"—from the common verb *qārāʾ*. Analogously, *nāśīʾ* goes back to *nāśāʾ* "to raise," as has been generally recognized. But the noun has nothing to do with raising the voice, let alone with having one's countenance lifted, as proposed by Noth; nor does *nāśīʾ* describe a leader who raised himself above his peers, as suggested by van der Ploeg. Rather, *nāśīʾ* carries with it the complement *bāʿēdā* (or *hāʿēdā* in construct phrases), as expressly supplied in Ex 34,31 (for the analogous *hāʿēdā* see above). Even where *nāśīʾ* is used elliptically, the complement is still implicit as a rule. The title, in short, stands for a duly elected chieftain.

In this connection, it may not be amiss to cite an illuminating account from the literature of a country in

[9] The converse is true of Nm 26,9.

[10] Actually, this Heb. form represents two distinct Semitic formations: an active participle **qātil* (cf. J. Barth, *Die Nominalbildung in den semitischen Sprachen,* 1889, 182 ff.), and a passive participle **qatīl* (ibid., 185 f.). Owing to their phonologic coalescence in Hebrew, they are sometimes difficult to trace back. For unambiguous instances of the passival class cf., e.g., *śākīr* "hireling," *ʾāsīr* "prisoner," *māšīᵃḥ* "anointed." An indisputable active descendant is *qāṣīr* "harvester" (Is 17,5). Inevitably, however, a number of such nouns must be classified as capable of either derivation. These include *nāgīd* and *nādīb,* both of them approximate analogues of *nāśīʾ* and especially *nābīʾ* "prophet," all three of which Barth (op. cit., 184) regards as active. Parenthetically, the description of the *nābīʾ* in Dt 18,18 strongly favors Barth's attribution.

which the consent of the assembly was a traditional feature of government. The Babylonian Epic of Creation goes into considerable detail to describe Tiamat's appointment of Kingu as chief of her insurgent host. We are told, among other things, that Tiamat *ušašqī ᵈKinga ina bērišunu šāšu ušrabbiš* "elevated Kingu and made him chief over all of them" (Enūma eliš I 147). She then *ušēšibaššu ina karri* "caused him to take his (proper) seat in the Council" (158), whereupon *ᵈKingu šušqū* "Kingu was duly elevated" (158). Now the council or assembly of the Babylonians is much the same as the *'ēdā* of the Israelites, and *šušqū* is semantically identical with Heb. *nāśī'*.

This is not to suggest that the Israelites took over the institution of the *nāśī'* from Mesopotamia, at least not directly. It is not without some relevance, however, that the Babylonian Talmud (Pes. 66a) describes the elevation of Hillel in the following terms: *miyyad hōšībūhū bᵉrōš uminnūhū nāśī' ʿᵃlēhem* "they promptly seated him at the head and appointed him their *nāśī'*." [11] Thus both Kingu and Hillel are represented clearly as presiding officers. Obviously, the writers of the Talmudic account had not just come from a session with Enūma eliš, for all that their story appears in the Babylonian Talmud. But it is a fact that the elective process had a long tradition behind it in certain areas of the ancient Near East. And "president," by the way, might be as good a translation of Heb. *nāśī'* as any that has yet been attempted.

It remains only to comment briefly on the less typical occurrences of *nāśī'* in the Bible. These should cause little, if any, difficulty in the light of the above evidence. In regard to the much discussed instance in Ex 22,27, it is clear at any rate that the *nāśī* represents there the chief

[11] This illuminating passage was recalled to my attention by Dr. H. Brichto.

political authority, comparable to the later *mäläk* "king." Since it is generally conceded that the passage is both old and authentic,[12] its evidence merits special attention. It would seem to follow, therefore, that just as clans and tribes had each their respective *nāśī'*, the same title was applied also to the head of a combination or confederation of a number of tribes. In all likelihood, that office too was an elective one, with the further inherent probability that election by the assembly was deemed to enjoy the approval of the Deity.

We have a roughly comparable situation in Gn 34,2, where the Shechemite Hamor is described as "the *nāśī'* of the country." We cannot tell from this isolated account whether the author chose this particular title in purposeful contrast to "king," or whether he merely used a designation for highest local authority with which he happened to be most familiar. In any case, it is interesting to note that Hamor's dealings with his fellow townsmen, for whose approval he appeals so eloquently, are not the actions of an autocrat. Another case in point is that of the four Midianite rulers whom Nm 31,8 identifies as kings, whereas Jos 13,8 describes them as *nᵉśī'īm;* they were obviously no more than local chieftains, no matter how they gained that status.

There is further the celebrated account of the Machpelah episode, in which "the children of Heth" address Abraham as a *nᵉśī' 'ᵉlōhīm* (Gn 23,6). In this instance even the LXX version departs from its customary *archōn* for *nāśī'* and substitutes *basileús.* The traditional English translation of the phrase is "mighty prince." The trouble

[12] Noth himself refrains from pressing this particular occurrence into the amphictyonic mold and leaves it untranslated (*ATD* 5,138). Even more patently secular are the occurrences of this term in Gn 23,6 and 34,2 (for which see below), both manifestly authentic and now commonly conceded to be old. In short, it is precisely the oldest instances that pose an insuperable obstacle to Noth's interpretation of *nāśī'*.

with this familiar rendering is that "prince" as an occupational term accords ill with a patriarchal figure, and that *'ᵉlōhīm* never means "mighty" as such.[13] But there is no need here to force an unattested meaning upon either component of this phrase. In the ancient Near East in particular, any leader would be expected to affirm that his position was achieved "under God." When an assembly chose a *nāśī'*, it could do no less than aspire to divine approval. And when the same title was employed in a gesture of elaborate politeness, as it certainly was in the present instance, assertion of celestial collaboration would be virtually routine. Accordingly, *nᵉśī' 'ᵉlōhīm* in this context calls for the unforced and separately attested rendering "elevated by God," "elect of God."

After the introduction of kingship, the position of the *nāśī'* became of necessity limited and localized. He is rarely mentioned in records that relate to the monarchic age. 3 Kgs 8,1 applies the title to heads of families, and 1 Chr 5,2 to heads of tribes. In 3 Kgs 11,34 God is said to have made Solomon a *nāśī'* for life. This usage recalls immediately the context of Gn 23,6, which has just been discussed. And the same is true essentially of Ezekiel's idealistic employment of the term. As opposed to the fleeting grandeur of the hereditary *mäläk*, the more modest status of the elected *nāśī'*—elected not only by his assembly but by God—promised to be far more enduring in the long run.

On the basis of the foregoing analysis, the translation of the term would have to vary with the circumstances and the context. With clans and tribes the title is best reproduced as "chieftain." With larger units, notably political states, "leader" or "president" should satisfy the

[13] Used as an adjective, the term may describe something "numinous," which is by no means the same thing as "mighty."

requirements. In no case is "prince" justified; as a translation of *nāśīʾ*, this term is misleading in its primary sense and meaningless in its customary derivative usage.

In conclusion, a brief comment is in order about the relationship between the *nāśīʾ* and the *šōpēṭ*. It is worth noting that those sources which use *nāśīʾ* as an analogue of *mäläk* do not similarly employ the title *šōpēṭ*; and conversely, where *šōpēṭ* is employed as a political title, *nāśīʾ* is absent in that connection. Thus Deuteronomy and Judges feature the *šōpēṭ* but ignore the *nāśīʾ*, whereas the Tetrateuch, Joshua, and Ezekiel follow the opposite course. Only the Chronicler manages to accommodate both titles, which is not surprising in the work of so late a period. In other words, on the basis of these terminological criteria, one may distinguish two distinct traditions: the "Priestly" or *nāśīʾ* school, which includes Ezekiel appropriately enough, and the "Deuteronomic" or *šōpēṭ* school, to which Judges belongs with equal propriety.

Now although both terms are used to designate the premonarchic leaders of Israel, the two are by no means precise synonyms. The *nāśīʾ* was part of the normal administrative process. The *šōpēṭ*, on the other hand, as a political authority, was resorted to only in times of great emergency. The former was a regular feature of early Israelite society; the latter was exceptional and sporadic. In reconstructing the past, the Deuteronomic tradition concentrated—anachronistically, one may add—on the *šōpēṭ*. The Priestly school, on the other hand, Ezekiel included, showed a surer grasp of historical detail by emphasizing the role of the *nāśīʾ* in the past and projecting it into the future. Small wonder that the *nāśīʾ* succeeded in reasserting himself in postbiblical times.

Leviticus and the Critics

EVER SINCE THE CLASSIC FORMULATION OF THE DOCUmentary Hypothesis by Julius Wellhausen it has been all but axiomatic for the critics to regard the Priestly Code as essentially post-exilic. The strongest dissenting opinion by a ranking modern scholar has been that of Ezekiel Kaufmann, whose monumental *History of Israelite Religion* embodies the conclusion that the P source is in its entirety a pre-exilic composition.[1]

The substance of the present paper was worked out without any reference to the controversy about the date of P. As one of a Committee that has been preparing a revised translation of the Bible for the Jewish Publication Society of America, I had occasion in recent months to re-examine a number of passages in Leviticus in the light of related cuneiform material. Each of these passages had long posed a problem to interpreters, ancient as well as modern; and each can now be elucidated with the aid of extra-biblical sources. The question, then, is primarily one of detailed exegesis rather than comprehensive theories. Nevertheless, Leviticus figures so prominently

[1] For a convenient summary and discussion of Kaufmann's position in this matter cf. M. Greenberg, "A new Approach to the History of the Israelite Priesthood," *JAOS* 70 (1950), pp. 41–47 [see now Y. Kaufmann, *The Religion of Israel* (Chicago, 1963), pp. 175–200].

in Kaufmann's work that it would be altogether appropriate in any case to offer a selection of sundry cuneiform analects to Leviticus as a small contribution to a volume in honor of a scholar to whom all of us owe so much.

But this paper cannot content itself with exegesis alone. For when the separate results are combined and compared, they prove to be part of an integral and self-consistent pattern. All bear on the problem of dating, and the over-all conclusion lends color to Kaufmann's central position. In other words, the exegesis, though an end in itself, points automatically to further results. The evidence is all the more suggestive precisely because it is independent and unforseen.

In the interests, however, of clarity as well as methodology, the exegesis and the argument will be presented in separate sections. Accordingly, the first and major part of this discussion (I) will deal with selected passages and terms in Leviticus. The remainder of the paper (II) will review the results in so far as they have a bearing on the date and character of the book as a whole.

I

1. *'erkeḵā* in Lev. 5:15,18,25. The term *'erkeḵā* is troublesome grammatically, but the main problem is one of usage in several of the instances in which the word is found. The grammatical difficulty is less serious than would appear on the surface. The pronominal suffix cannot be taken literally, as is still often done (e.g., JPS "thy valuation"; RSV "your valuation"); for the form is found in construct state (Lev. 27:2,12), and also with the definite article (*hā'erkeḵā* Lev. 27:23). This is why A.

Ehrlich proposed to view the noun as a *Piʿlāl* form and vocalize it as *ʿerkāḵ,* const. st. *ʿerkaḵ* [2]; but this would imply an error in vocalization repeated over twenty times. S. Feigin saw in the final *-ḵā* not a pronominal suffix but a general afformative,[3] without showing, however, where this afformative came from or what its function was.

The only explanation that fits all the facts is to interpret the final *-ḵā* as a pronominal suffix that became fossilized and thus absorbed in the nominal stem. Biblical Hebrew itself offers a good analogue in *bōʾᵃḵā* (Gen. 10:19,30, etc.), "your coming" > "as you come" > "as far as." Similarly, Akk. *mimma šumšu,* "whatever be its name" > "what's-its-name," and is eventually fused into a new noun which can in turn take a (second !) pronominal suffix: *mimmušunšu-ya,*[4] "my what's-its-name," i.e., "anything of mine." In other words, such annexed and fossilized pronouns are by no means a puzzle. In the present instance, *ʿerkᵉḵā* started out as "your valuation" and through common usage became simply "valuation" (by an outside party), with the pronoun inactivated and absorbed. The formation is thus perfectly in order. It calls for no emendation, forced interpretations, or—worst of all—inconsistent and meaningless translations.

Turning now from form to meaning, *ʿerkᵉḵā* occurs in Lev. 27 as many as 21 times. Each case involves commutation of a vow. Human beings are to be redeemed on the basis of a tariff fixed according to age and sex. Similar tariffs are optional with animals, houses, and land. The specified monetary equivalent is called *ʿerkᵉḵā.* The mean-

[2] *Randglossen zur hebraischen Bibel* (1909) II, p. 18.
[3] *AJSL* 41 (1925), pp. 277 f.
[4] H(arvard) S(emitic) S(eries) V (1929), 72. 29.

ing is clear throughout, even though a smooth yet accurate translation may not always be easy to achieve.

An analogous treatment is prescribed in the case of a child that has been "offered" to God (Num. 18:15). Commutations is mandatory (*pādō tifdê*), at the fixed sum (*b^{e}ʿerk^{e}ḵā*) of five shekels (vs.16).

In Lev. 5:15 ff., however, conditions are quite different. What is involved this time is an offense of one kind or another, which calls for a guilt offering or penalty payment (*ʾăšām*). Aside from making good the respective stake and adding a fifth to the amount in question, the offender must bring "a ram without blemish" as *ʾăšām*. This ram is further qualified as *b^{e}ʿerk^{e}ḵā kesef š^{e}qālīm* in vs. 15, and as *b^{e}ʿerk^{e}ḵā* alone in 18 and 25, the remainder of the phrase being apparently understood and hence omitted. But what would "at a valuation of silver shekels" mean, It is precisely in such instances that an explicit figure is essential; cf. Num. 18:16. The Rabbis' dictum that the number "two" must be understood here as the minimum plural figure is unsupported by usage.[5] Nor is it economically plausible, since the value of a ram would scarcely exceed a single shekel as a rule. Ehrlich, who is seldom at a loss, and ordinarily gives the right explanation, can do no better this time than delete the whole phrase. Yet there is no need at all to violate either the text or the context. The phrase is perfectly all right as it stands. It reflects an authentic practice that goes back at least to the middle of the second millennium B.C.E.

In a recent study of certain problems in the Nuzi texts, I discussed, among other things, a distinctive and un-

[5] Ehrlich, *loc. cit.*

usual type of payment.[6] Every instance in which this payment is required is invariably a solemn one. In one case a man was guilty of assault and battery after trespassing on his brother's pasture. When he refused to exonerate himself by taking the oath, he was sentenced to make good the damage and pay the special fine. Another defendant has to pay the same kind of fine double, after losing the ordeal by oath. The payment is not always punitive; it can also be preventive or protective, as in "sistership" transactions in which the bride price is payed to the woman's brother. Under Hurrian law the brother enjoyed special rights and privileges, and the atypical payment served to underscore that status.

What immediately betrays the above type of payment as extraordinary is the fact that it is always listed in terms of animals rather than metal currency. What is more, it is not just any kind of animal that may make the required amount. The standard sum is thirty shekels; and this has to be remitted, when the special payment is in order, in terms of one bull, one ass, and ten sheep, always in the same 1-1-10 ratio. Evidently, these animals have the same symbolic and monitory significance as in covenants; cf. Gen. 15:9 ff. They serve to bring home the solemn aspect of the occasion.

There were times, however, when it was impracticable to pay such a fine or contractual obligation in the specified fashion. In such cases commutation to metal currency was permissible, but only by recording explicitly the proper amount for each of the required animals, e.g., "36 minas of tin in lieu of one bull, 24 minas of tin in

[6] "Nuzi Marginalia 4: Ceremonial Payment," *Orientalia,* N. S. 25 (*1956*). pp. 9–15.

lieu of one ass," etc.[7] In other words, even though metal is substituted for the animals, the record must indicate the substitution. As far as the law was concerned, the remittance was still in terms of animals, with the payer assuming all the risks that such a payment implied.

When I worked out and published these results, I had no idea that they might one day prove to have an intimate bearing on Lev. 5:15 ff. Yet the connection is unmistakable, and all the stronger for not having been seen at the time. The offenses recorded in the biblical passage in question are grave enough to call for an *'āšām* over and above the actual damages involved. The guilt payment is here "a ram without blemish," that is, a ritual animal; the animals and their numbers in the Nuzi instances may differ, but the purpose is the same. Moreover, the biblical fine may be commuted to currency, precisely as in Nuzi, it being clearly understood, however, that a substitution is made and what the substitution is for. And the term that makes this clear is *bᵉ'erkᵉḵā*. Accordingly, *bᵉ'erkᵉḵā kesef šᵉqālîm* stands for "convertible into payment in silver." The precise sum to be paid is not given, because that sum would vary with time and place. It could not be fixed in routine fashion as was the case with vows. The emphasis was on the ram rather than the silver and was not to be minimized by a fixed tariff. For the offender must bear his built (*wᵉnāśā 'ᵃwōnō*).

2. *biqqōreṯ,* Lev. 19:20. The circumstances leading up to the provision that is indicated here—but nowhere else in the Bible—as *biqqōreṯ tihyê* are clear enough: A man has had sexual relations with a slave girl who is designated (*neḥrefeṯ* "assigned in advance") as wife of another, but has not as yet been redeemed or given her freedom

[7] *Ibid.,* p. 11.

outright. Because the girl's status is thus still that of a slave, the offense cannot be treated as adultery and there is no death penalty. Instead, there is to be *biqqōreṯ*. But what does this term mean?

Tradition (cf. Rashi), followed by most modern translators, answers "investigation" (e.g., Chicago Translation). "inquiry" (e.g., RSV); the assumed derivation is from the Pi'el in the sense of "to visit," cf. **baqqārā,* "care, solicitude." Ezek. 34:12. However, what is there to investigate? The offense is clear, and the verdict is surely implicit in the decision that there shall be no death penalty. Moreover, the form *biqqōreṯ* is very different morphologically from *baqqārat-*. On these and similar grounds the biblical dictionaries prefer "punishment"; cf. Gesenius-Buhl, Zorell, Koehler-Baumgartner, and note already KJ "scourge." Yet would such punishment be left unspecified?

Ramban alone was bold enough to venture a dissenting opinion. He regards the present occurrence as a hapax in the Bible but homogenous with the common Mishnaic *hbqr,* Talmudic *hfqr*. In conformance with such post-biblical usage, the present instance means, according to Ramban, that the woman is to be declared free of marital commitments, so that the usual penalty for adultery would not apply. The sole penalty in the case would thus be the ram of guilt offering (vs. 21). This solitary explanation has the notable merit of operating with established legal terminology. It presupposes, however, that the offending male is the owner of the slave girl; for otherwise he would lose the customary bride price with no redress whatever. To be sure, the text is not specific on this point. Yet it implies a third party; one's own slave girl would be expresed as *šifḥāṯō,* not *šifḥā.*

All one has to do is go a step farther than Ramban, to the terms and underlying usage from which *hbqr* and *hfqr* are ultimately derived. In old Babylonian legal documents the verb *baqārum* designates recovery by the proper owner of any property that happens to be in the possession of another; it is a technical term for "to vindicate" in the legal sense. The vindicator is called *baqirum* or *bāqirānum*, and the obligation to make good the valid claim or furnish compensation for losses incurred in this connection is *baqrum*. The latter term, which is found both in the Code of Hammurabi (par. 279) and in documents pertaining to the legal practice, is actually translated "Schadensersatzpflicht" by Mr. San Nicolò,[8] the first scholar to subject the terminology and usage to the thorough discussion. The above practice and characteristic phraseology are not restricted to Babylonia; they turn up, among other places, in Assyria (where the spelling is often with initial *p*-) and are particularly common in Nuzi. There the abstract noun is *pirqu*, metathesized from **piqru*, alongside the agent noun *pāqirānu*.

The post-biblical usage of *hbqr* and *hfqr* still harks back to the established earlier meanings of the Akkadian terms. By then, however, the Hiph'il had acquired a broader range: not only to restore property to its rightful claimant but also to declare anything free, forfeit, or ownerless; hence the occasional anarchic and uncomplimentary connotation of the terms involved.

The bearing of the above discussion on Lev. 19:20–21 should now be perfectly clear. A slave girl has been spoken for, but she has not yet been delivered to her designated husband. The price agreed upon remains to

[8] *Die Schlussklauseln der altbabylonischen Kauf- und Tauschverträge* (1922), pp. 154 ff.

be paid, in part or in full. In the meantime another man has slept with her. Since the marriage has not been formalized, this is not a case of adultery. Nevertheless, the girl is no longer a virgin and cannot therefore command the ordinary bride price. A double offense has thus been committed: an impairment of economic values and a sin against morality. Each must be redressed. The moral wrong is to be expiated by means of "the ram of guilt offering." At the same time, the economic damage must also be repaired, whatever the cost may turn out to be. The obligation to make good this economic damage is called *biqqōreṯ*, a cognate of Babylonian *baqrum* and Nuzi *pirqu*. Incidentally, the latter form helps to explain the Hebrew formation. It is now plain that *biqqōreṯ* has nothing to do with the Pi'el stem, but actually represents **biqurtu*, which is based on the simple stem, exactly as *baqrum* and *pirqu* are. The sole purpose, therefore, of the traditional form is to protect the first vowel from reduction or loss. Thus both usage and formation testify to the antiquity of the noun before us, an authentic technical term, for all that it is used but once in the Bible.

3. Lev. 25:35–54. This long passage of 20 verses forms a connected section which deals with various stages and consequences of indebtedness. It is virtually a separate chapter in itself, which long gave trouble to interpreters because they lacked suitable material with which to compare it. Today such material is available in a variety of cuneiform sources; but the evidence has not yet been utilized for the clarification of Lev. 25:35 ff. The following discussion hopes to make a start towards rectifying this costly neglect.

It should be immediately apparent that the section before us is subdivided into three parts, which deal with as many stages in the status of an Israelite debtor: (a) the creditor is a fellow-Israelite who is enjoined from exacting interest from his brother (35–38); (b) the debtor has been driven to self-enslavement (*nimkar*), yet the master shall not treat him as slave (39–46); (c) the debtor has fallen into the hands of a resident alien and must be redeemed. These cases are now abundantly illustrated from extra-biblical sources and prove to conform perfectly to old and well-established legal practices. I shall cite here examples from two pertinent centers, namely Alalaḫ in Old Babylonian, and Nuzi in Middle Babylonian times (18–17 and 15–14th centuries respectively). The former is significant in that it represents old Northwest Semitic territory; the other is important because it reflects the laws of the Hurrians with whom the patriarchs had so much cultural matter in common.

Alalaḫ debtors who could not meet their payments entered the household of the creditor as pledges. The term for such a pledge is *manzazānu*,[9] literally something like "stand-in."[10] The status in question was called *manzazānūtu*, and it required that the debtor remain in the house of the creditor (*ina/ana bīt C wašābum*). The whole is summed up in the following clause: *D*(ebtors) *kīma kaspim annīm ana bīt C*(reditor) *wašbū*,[11] "on account of that sum D shall remain in the household of C." The situation was legally one of antichresis; that is to say, no new interest charges were involved. The debtor, often with his wife and children, secured the loan personally,

[9] Cf. already P. Koschaker, *Abh. Sächs. Akad. Wiss.*, Vol. 42 (1931), pp. 106 f.

[10] Cf. D. J. Wiseman, *The Alalakh Tablets* (1933), abbr. AT, 18 ff.; see E. A. Speiser, *JAOS* 74 (1954), p. 22.

[11] Cf. e.g., AT 32. Often such personal security consists not only of the debtor but also of his wife and children; e.g. AT 20, 38. The same is true of Lev. 25:41.

while his labor covered the interest. When the original loan was repayed in full, the debtor was free to go where he pleased *(ušallamšu ašar libbišu illakma)*.[12]

Occasionally, debtors so bound were redeemed by third parties. In one such instance[13] "A. king of Alalaḫ redeemed (*ipṭur*) Sh. together with his wife and his sons from his creditor (*bēl ḫubullišu*)." In any case, we learn from texts of a later period (15th cent.) that under this particular arrangement the original loan was not subject to further interest (*kaspu ṣipta lā išu*),[14] and the detained debtor received no wages for his obligatory labor. It was strictly an antichretic arrangement both ways.

The Nuzi documents take us a step further. There a loan with antichresis is called *ditennūtu* and a detained debtor becomes a *ditennu.*[15] If the amount involved is not paid up within the specified period, the detention and the services of the detained are continued on a basis that amounts to indefinite self-enslavement. At most a small second loan may be granted without additional collateral.[16] It is doubtful whether the combined burden of two loans was often overcome and slavery averted.

In the light of this material, which thus provides a detailed and authentic commentary that reaches far back into the second millennium, the provisions in Lev. 25:35 ff. can be interpreted with a considerable degree of confidence. In each of the three cases involved the debtor

[12] E.g., AT 21.10–15.
[13] AT 29.
[14] AT 50.
[15] E. A. Speiser, "New Kirkuk Documents Relating to Security Transactions," *JAOS* 52, (1932), pp. 350–367; 53 (1933), pp. 22–46. The security consists ordinarily of land, whose usufruct then covers the interest involved. But instances of personal security are not lacking. Thus No. 10 (*JAOS* 53, pp. 35 f.) names the debtor's son as *ditennu;* and in No. 11 (*ibid.,* pp. 36 f.) it is the debtor himself who enters the creditor's house for *ditennūtu.*
[16] E.g., No. 15 (*JAOS* 53, pp. 40 f.).

is not able to repay the loan or meet the charges incurred. This is self-evident in instances b-c (39 ff.), since the text speaks explicitly of self-enslavement (*nimkar*). But the situation differs only in degree, and not in kind, in instance (a) (35–38): the debtor falls under the authority of the creditor, although this dependence shall terminate as soon as the debt has been paid, precisely as in the *manzazānūtu* provisions at Alalaḫ. Two sets of details confirm this comparison. Linguistically, the repeated *'immāḵ* corresponds to the Alalaḫ clause *ina/ana bīt C wašābum,* "to stay in the creditor's household/remain under his authority";[17] and *wᵉheḥᵉzaqtā* can only mean "and you seize him/lay hold on him," not the traditional "you shall uphold him" (which would require an added *yāḏō*): furthermore, the sequel shows plainly that matters could go from bad to worse. Substantively, the injunction against exacting interest goes hand in hand, as we have seen, with the ancient antichretic arrangement whereby interest was covered by the detained debtor's labor. Accordingly, all of verse 35 constitutes the protasis which must be translated as follows: "If your brother's fortunes decline so that he is reduced (*māṭā yāḏō*) to being under your authority/staying in your household (*'immāḵ*), and you hold him as though a resident alien (*gēr wᵉṯōšāv*), and he lives in your household (*wᵉḥay 'immāḵ*), (36) "he shall remain with you as your brother." The second instance provides (39 f.) that even though the debtor has been driven to self-enslavement, he must not be treated as an ordinary slave but only as though he were a resident laborer (*kᵉśāḵīr kᵉṯōšāv*). At the time of the jubilee he is to be freed from the creditor's authority (*mē'immāḵ*) and leave with his sons (41); note that the detention of other

[17] Note also the last Nuzi instance cited in the preceding note.

members of the debtor's family is explicitly documented at Alalaḫ.[18] Finally, an Israelite debtor who falls under the authority (*'immō*) of a resident alien (47 ff.) must be redeemed. Again, cases of debtors' redemption are known from Alalaḫ, although the exact circumstances are not specified there.

Manifestly, the Levitical provisions before us reflect a solicitude that is not apparent in the matter-of-fact cuneiform parallels adduced above. Nevertheless, the sociolegal framework is exactly the same in both sets of circumstances. The cuneiform analogues demonstrate, among other things, that the long passage in Leviticus had its roots in life rather than in cultic speculation. These roots, moreover, reach far back into the past.

4. Lev. 27:12. This verse has long been a source of trouble to interpreters. It concerns the commutation of vows referring to unclean cattle. After specifying that the priest shall assess the animal (*wehe'erīḵ hakkōhēn 'ōṯāh*), the verse continues: *bēn ṭōv uvēn rā' be'erkeḵā hakkōhēn kēn hū'*. The accents place a major break after *r'*. This analysis is as old as LXX. Later translations follow suit; cf. e.g., KJ, JPS, Leeser ("And the priest shall value it,) whether it be good or bad"; (La) S(aint) B(ible) of the Dominican School in Jerusalem gives "le jugeant bon au mauvais"; and the Chicago Translation (AT), following Ehrlich, offers "midway between high and low," which surely forces the sense and construction of *bēn . . . uvēn*.[19] Yet the other renderings are not much better, in that they construe the masculines *ṭōv, rā'* with the fem. *'ōṯāh* (i.e., *behēmā*). Worst of all, what would be the meaning? If it is a matter of accepting the offering,

[18] Cf. note 11, above.

[19] When the text wishes to express "between fine (good) and poor (bad)" it says *bēn ṭōv lāra'* Lev. 27:33.

whether it is good or bad, the priest's appraisal is pointless; and to strike a balance between high and low would scarcely be within the province of the priest or in the interests of the sanctuary.

The cuneiform documents from Nuzi point clearly to the correct interpretation, which has the added advantage of validating the grammar of the verse as it stands, and clarifying its syntax in the process. Interestingly enough, all the material involved is economic, and much of it concerns actual exchange transaction (*šupeultu*), precisely as in the case before us.

All the texts in question happen to deal with exchanges of fields; yet there can be little doubt that the same formula was applied also to other types of exchange. In its full version this formula reads as follows: *šumma eqlu mād lā inakkis šumma ṣeḫer/mīṣ lā uradda,*[20] "if the land proves to be too large, it shall not be curtailed; if too small, it shall not be increased." The clause means that the stated measurements of the land are to be accepted as final, and no future rectifications would be allowed. Elsewhere the formula is reduced to *miṣā mādā,*[21] "small or large" (pl.), or *lū mād lū ṣeḫer,*[22] "whether it be large or small." The latter version, it should be noted, is virtually the same as our *bēn ṭōv uvēn rāʿ*.

Now our case of commutation is basically the same as an exchange transaction; cf. vs. 10 which explicitly forbids exchange of clean animals. In all such instances it was deemed essential to guard against future contests and appeals. Official valuations had to be regarded as final and incontestable. In the case before us, the assessment

[20] E.g., HSS IX, 104.22 f.; 105.24 f.
[21] *J(oint) E(xpedition . . . at) N(uzi)*, 256.11.
[22] *Ibid.*, 239.14–15.

was made by the priest; once made, it could not be appealed. The final clause says it in so many words. The sentence as a whole must therefore be rendered as follows: "The priest shall assess it (viz., the animal); high or low, whatever the priest's assessment, it shall so be." In other words, the disjunctive accent belongs after *'ōṯāh*, not after *rā'*. And the two adjectives do not qualify *'ōṯāh* or *bᵉēhēmā*, in violation of the proper gender, or *hakkōhēn*, as Ehrlich proposed,[23] which would be a strain both on the sense and the syntax. They go instead with *kᵉ'erkᵉḵā*, which is precisely what the context demands.

Thanks to Nuzi analogues, a troublesome passage has thus been elucidated in all its aspects. Instead of being a cultic curiosity and a grammatical anomaly, Lev. 27:12 turns out to be an authentic reflex of old and well-established economic procedures applied to religious practices. The correct meaning must have been lost early enough to cause LXX to start a chain reaction of mistranslations. But an argument from silence does not become dependable merely because the silence could not be avoided.

II

As was pointed out at the beginning of this paper, the instances just discussed were not chosen to prove or to disprove any given theories. They were singled out solely because each needed elucidation for its own sake. It is only in retrospect that all four cases prove to have a significant and uniform bearing on the date and nature of the legislation involved.

The examples before us, it will have been noted, are

[23] *Randglossen*, II, p. 106.

not limited to any particular section of Leviticus. Two instances, to be sure (Nos. 2, 3), stem from the so-called Law of Holiness (H), which critical analysis ascribes to an older stage than the Priestly Code proper. The other two cases, however, are independent of H: No. 1 belongs to ch. 5, which deals with sacrifices; and No. 4 is part of ch. 27, which summarizes provisions relating to vows. In other words, the evidence is widely distributed.

The four passages in question have now been illuminated with the aid of extra-biblical sources. It is not too much to say, I believe, that each is now perfectly clear thanks to this outside evidence. It is all the more interesting, therefore, to note that every item of the supporting cuneiform material dates either from the Old Babylonian or from the Middle Babylonian period, i.e. from the 15th century B.C.E. at the latest. In short, to understand the practices concerned we have to go back invariably to pre-Mosaic times. This does not mean, of course, that the practices themselves were discontinued so early. But there can no longer be any doubt about either their authenticity or their antiquity.

This conclusion can now be backed up by internal evidence which could not be utilized or appreciated heretofore. I refer to the fact that tradition itself was unable to do justice to these passages, precisely because their meaning had become obscure in course of the intervening centuries. Let us look briefly at the pertinent proof.

In Lev. 5:15 (No. 1), failure to grasp the sense of *bᵉʻerkᵉḵā* led to distortion of the accompanying *kesef šᵉqālīm*. The consequence was the traditional dictum that in such cases the number "two" was implied, although this interpretation violates linguistic usage and economic logic. Tradition failed to come up with the correct answer because that answer had long been lost, there being nothing in the post-exilic experience to keep alive the meaning of the underlying practice.

Another case in point is the use of *biqqōreṯ* in Lev. 19:20 (No. 2). The term, though no longer in its primary meaning, is echoed in rabbinic literature.[24] According to Mishna Ketubbot 11.5 the sale of orphans' property became final and incontestable if the courts executed in this connection an *'Iggereṯ Biqqōreṯ*. This is later explained as "public announcement" (*'aḵrāzā*),[25] to the accompaniment of some fanciful etymologies;[26] tradition had clearly misplaced some vital links and was baffled as a result. But even the deduced sense of "announcement, proclamation" is incidental and secondary. The primary meaning of the term, as indicated above, was "justified claim, vindication."[27] In the Mishnaic instance the objective of the *biqqōreṯ* document is to invite all those who may have a proper claim against the estate to come forward within a specified time. The main thing is the claim itself and not the invitation to submit it to the court. It thus follows that the passage in Leviticus, where the actual claim is featured, and no public announcement whatever could possibly be in order, had not become part of rabbinic tradition. The essential background must have become obliterated long before then, perhaps

[24] I am deeply indebted to Prof. S. Lieberman and Prof. M. Greenberg for calling to my attention a number of post-biblical references, some of which are incorporated below.

[25] Pal. Talm. Ketubbot 34c. The fact that the point needs explaining, Prof. Lieberman suggests, is itself an indication that the sense of *biqqōreṯ* was no longer clear.

[26] Rashi *ad loc.;* cf. C. Albeck's Commentary on the Mishna, S. Nashim (1954), p. 128. Prof. Lieberman voiced some doubts on the subject in his *Tōsefeṯ Rīšōnīm,* II, p. 278.

[27] Thus the root is not to be confused with the familiar *biqqer,* an instance of which is found in Lev. 27:33.

even far back in pre-exilic times. Moreover, the civil aspect of the damages involved point up the non-priestly origin of this particular item of legislation.

The antiquity of the provisions in Lev. 25:35 ff. (No. 3) finds support not only in the cuneiform evidence discussed above but also, indirectly, in tradition's loss of contact with two specific details: (a) *w^{e}heḥ^{e}zaqtā bō* was misunderstood as "you shall uphold, support him," which is in marked contrast with the actual connotation of the phrase, namely "you shall seize him" (for debt); and (b) *nešeḵ* and *t/marbīṯ* came to be regarded as synonymous. On this latter point in particular the following comment may be of interest.

Cuneiform analogues indicate that *nešeḵ* and *t/marbīṯ* were not interchangeable terms from the start. In Mesopotamia interest was normally discounted in advance. The technical term for such advance deduction was *ḫubullû* (not "loan without interest" as the term is sometimes erroneously rendered, but loan with interest already deducted). This is the *nešeḵ* of Biblical Hebrew; [28] significantly enough, Onkelos translates it *ḥibbulyā* in our very passage (vs. 36). When the set time has elapsed, loans that have not been paid off begin to accumulate fresh interest. This is called *ṣiptu,* lit. "increase," which is semantically the same as Heb. *t/marbīṯ*. Assyrian contracts state this explicitly: *edannu etiqma še'u/kaspu ana ṣipti illak,* "when the time has elapsed, the grain/money starts bearing (new) interest." [29]

[28] For the latest discussion see E. Neufeld, "The Prohibitions Against Loans at Interest in Ancient Hebrew Law," HUCA XXVI (1955), pp. 355–412, esp. 355–57. M. Greenberg calls my attention to the fact that this interpretation of *nešek* is already given by Eliezer of Beaugency; cf. his comment on Ezek. 18:8, in S. Posnański's *Kommentar zu Ezechiel von Eliezer aus Beaugency* (1909).

[29] Cf. J. J. Finkelstein, "Cuneiform Texts From Tell Billa," *Jour. Cun. Stud.* VIII (1933), No. 1.16–17.

The arrangement to which Lev. 25:35 ff. alludes is one of antichretic pledge; that is to say, the debtor's person (and this may include various members of his family)[30] secures the loan, while his labor covers the interest. Accordingly, no other interest may be charged, whether discounted in advance or compounded eventually. These conditions must still have been perfectly clear when the provisions of this passage were originally put down in writing. But they were no longer obvious to post-exilic generations. Hence not only the misunderstanding of the key verb, but also the mixing up of the two nouns for the respective forms of interest. The original law itself cannot have opposed interest as such, since it permits the debtor to hand himself over to the creditor, even though he be a non-Israelite. It bars interest in the cases before us because that is the nature of antichresis. Later extrapolations of this law do not alter the basic facts. But tradition no longer had a recollection of these facts.

Finally, it is apparent that tradition was not aware of the precise bearing of the phrase *bēn ṭōv uvēn rāʿ* in Lev. 27:12 (No. 4). We have seen that such elliptical clauses were customary in exchange transaction (as is still hinted at in our own passage), the full wording being: If X proves too large or high, it shall not be diminished; if too small or low, it shall not be increased. But transactions of this sort are part and parcel of normal economy. They cannot be readily reconstructed from secondary cultic usage alone. The same is true, of course, of the other instances that have been discussed in this paper. Each has its proper *Sitz im Leben*. None can be fully understood in terms of ecclesiastical usage exclusively. And this is another way of saying that all the pas-

[30] Lev. 25:41.

sages in question bear the unmistakable imprint of pre-exilic times.

I would not wish this last statement to be misconstrued as implying that all of Leviticus is homogeneous and archaic. The conclusion just drawn applies here only to the passages that have been analyzed above. The fact remains, however, that these passages are scattered through out the book and are not limited to the admittedly early section known as H. To this extent, therefore, the present discussion tends to bear out Kaufmann's position that the late date which critics assign to most of Leviticus cannot be upheld on closer probing. It goes without saying that pre-exilic is by no means synonymous with Mosaic. Some of the instances here discussed are manifestly pre-Mosaic in origin. Others could well be considerably later.

The Shibboleth Incident (Judges 12:6)

ALTHOUGH THE BIBLICAL TERM ŠIBBOLET HAS LONG BEEN naturalized outside Hebrew in the sense of "criterion, catchword," the exact basis of this usage is far from clear. After more than two thousand years of interpretation the matter is still open. The postulates and queries set down by the medieval Hebrew commentators are reflected to this day in the most recent discussions on the subject.

The substance of the incident is plain enough. Some time in or close to the eleventh century B.C. a group of Ephraimites sought to escape a band of vengeful Gileadites by attempting to get across the Jordan back into Palestine. Halted at the fords the fugitives pretended to be natives of Gilead. They were betrayed, however, by their inability to pronounce a chosen test word in the proper Gileadite manner, with consequences that can hardly be called academic. The telltale element was the initial sound of the word *šibbólet,* which at that time probably had the form **šubbult^{u}*. The best that the Ephraimites could do was **subbult^{u}*, which was not good enough.

The test was thus a phonetic one, involving a dialectal difference. The dialect boundary was represented by the Jordan. That much is beyond dispute. It has also been assumed universally that the dialectal peculiarity in question set off the Ephraimites from other speakers of Hebrew, in Palestine and Transjordan alike, thus constituting an Ephraimite isogloss.[a] Ready to hand as such an assumption may be, it will scarcely bear closer investigation. What is more, it appears that this erroneous premise has been chiefly responsible for our failure to reconstruct the primary details of the shibboleth incident, even though the catchword itself has long since become proverbial. We have yet to learn how suspects were caught by the catchword. A review of the problem, therefore, may not be without interest.

The meaning of the test word is of minor importance. Elsewhere in the Old Testament it has the sense of "ear of corn"[1] or, less commonly, "flood, torrent."[2] In our passage it is taken in the former sense by such versions as the Greek Codex Vaticanus and Aquila,[3] as well as some modern scholars.[4] On the other hand, reference to flowing water is assumed by the medieval Hebrew commentators and a majority of the moderns, evidently because such an allusion would be more appropriate to the occasion.

The prevailing explanation of the phonetics involved operates with the contrast between *š* and *s*. The *š*-phoneme is said to have been pronounced by the Ephraimites as *s*, so that *šubbult^u* became *subbult^u*. But it is difficult to reconcile this view with the available facts. We have no knowledge of any West Semitic language that fails to include both *š* and *s* as independent phonemes. The two

[a] [I.e., a linguistic phenomenon characteristic of a given area.—W. F. A.]
[1] Gen. 41:5 ff.; Ruth 2:2; Zach. 4:12.
[2] Psalms 69:3, 16; Isa. 27:12.
[3] The usual Septuagint interpretation, however, is "password."
[4] Cf. Liebmann, ZAW 25 (1905) 161.

may be opposed interdialectally, but neither is absent from any single relevant speech group. Now the account of the incident under discussion is explicit on this important point: The Ephraimites were not asked, "How do you call such-and-such a thing?" Instead they were challenged specifically, "say *šubbult*ᵘ." Even if inherited *š* had changed to *s* in their own dialect—and for this there is not the slightest independent indication—they surely would have used the required sound to save their necks. For it was not a sound unknown to them.[5]

Less commonly advanced is an attempted solution based on the premise that the Ephraimites employed the spirant *ṯ* in place of the Gileadite *š*. On this assumption *subbult*ᵘ would be the necessarily inadequate writing for a spoken **ṯubbult*ᵘ. This approach to the problem was foreshadowed by David Qimḥî (13th cent. A.D.).[6] It was developed by J. Marquart[7] and has been endorsed cautiously by Z. S. Harris.[8] Marquart's reasoning was as follows: The Aramaic correspondents of *šibbólet* are *šᵉḇaltâ* and *tuḇla*. This pair presupposes an original initial *ṯ* which may yet turn up in Arabic. Accordingly, Proto-Semitic possessed a root *šbl* from which is derived the word meaning "ear of corn"; furthermore, another root **ṯbl* which yielded the Hebrew homonym of that form meaning "flood, torrent." By the time of Jephthah the Ephraimites had not yet lost the *ṯ*-phoneme; that is why they said **ṯubbult*ᵘ.

There are three serious objections to this view. The

[5] To assume some peculiar differences in the pronunciation of the *š*-phoneme itself, as is done, e.g., by Budde, *Richter* 89, is to resort to speculation unrelieved by any semblance of fact.

[6] *Miqrāʾôth Gedôlôth,* ad loc.

[7] ZAW 8 (1888) 151 ff.

[8] *Development of the Canaanite Dialects* (1939) 64.

first is etymological. The Aramaic variant with *t*- signifies "ear of corn" and not "flood." [9] The latter value can scarcely be separated from Arab. *sbl* "rain, flow,"so that a sibilant is assured in the cognate forms of Canaanite and Aramaic. The second objection is chronological. Goetze has pointed out that there is no valid reason for dating the merging of *ṯ* with *š* in Palestine later than in Phoenicia, where the process is attested at least as far back as the eleventh century.[10] This argues for an Ephraimite *š* from *ṯ* in Jephthah's time. Thirdly, there is the question of plausibility which applies here no less than it does to the alleged mispronunciation of *š* as *s*. For even if we grant that the Ephraimites had retained the *ṯ*-phoneme, there are no grounds for denying them the possession of the normal Canaanite sibilants. In other words, they were in a position to duplicate cheerfully the *šubbult*^{u} of the Gileadite sentries.

Plainly, then, the current explanations of the shibboleth incident leave it with all the characteristics of a "tall story." And yet, the account as we have it bears the marks of authenticity. Something must be wrong, therefore, with the explanations of the episode rather than the recorded statement about it.

In these circumstances it will not be amiss to approach the matter from a new angle. We know that the Ephraimites found unpronounceable the initial sound of the catchword as it was rendered by the Gileadites. Supposing now that in the Gilead dialect the phoneme under dispute was *ṯ*, which was lacking in the Canaanite speech of Palestine, what would the result be? Much the same, no

[9] Cf. Gesenius-Buhl, ad loc.

[10] *Language* 17 (1941) 168. [On the date of the oldest true Phoenician inscriptions see now *Studies in the History of Culture* (Leland Volume), 1942, pp. 34 ff.—W. F. A.]

doubt, as the efforts of those to whom the English voiceless phoneme expressed by *th* (in *thing*) is foreign.[11] Even more to the point is the experience of non-Arab Moslems who try to reproduce the Arabic *ṯ*. The best that the average Turk, Kurd, or Persian can achieve by way of pronouncing Arabic *ṯâliṯ-* is a mere [sa: lis]. The Ephraimites of the eleventh century B.C. who did not have the phoneme in their own speech must have been equally helpless. Their rendering of **ṯubbult*^{u} could result in little else than an inadequate *subbult*^{u}. And that is precisely what the biblical text reflects.

All of this is as yet less than a working hypothesis. To make it work we have to account for the presence of *ṯ* in the Gileadite form of *šubbult*^{u}. We have seen that etymological data point to an initial sibilant. It is a fact, however, that the Aramaic for "ear of corn' may have either initial *š* (*s*^{e}*ḇaltâ, šuḇaltâ*) or *t* (*tuḇlâ*). This points to a Proto-Semitic doublet with *ṯ* (*ṯubbult*^{u}) alongside the normal form with a sibilant. How such a doublet arose is beside the point.[11a] It may have been due to some analogic interference. At all events, its existence is definitely assured for Aramaic. Since it was present in one Northwest Semitic dialect it may well have been current in another, say, Gileadite.

At this point the objection might be raised that the

[11] In this connection it is interesting to note the statement of John Earle: "The *th*, with its twofold value, is the *shibboleth* of foreigners" (quoted in Webster's *New International Dictionary* [2nd ed., s.v. shibboleth]).

[11a] [In view of the vast number of known loanwords in Semitic, it seems to me that the original stem began with *ṯ* and that Aramaic *tublâ*, etc., is thus genuinely Aramaic, whereas *šib(b)altâ* and *šubbaltâ* have been borrowed from Canaanite or Accadian. Arabic *súnbulah* is in any event a loan from Aramaic, and so is presumably Arab. *sábalah* (from *š*^{e}*baltâ*). Original *ṯ* is strongly suggested by the Canaanite cognate word for "tendril, vine," preserved in New Egyptian as *sabir*, since original *ṯ* appears regularly in Egyptian transcription of this age as *s*.—*W. F. A.*]

argument thus far differs but little from Marquart's, and that we are still tracing the "ear of corn" whereas our concern is really with "flood." Quite so. But Marquart went astray in trying to separate the two spheres of meaning on an etymological basis. In reality, however, there is no reason for deriving the established homonyms for "ear of corn" and "flood" from two distinct roots. Arabic *sbl* may underlie both "hang down" (whence we get *sunbulat-, sabalat-* "ear of corn") and "rain, flow." The two ranges are thus easily linked semantically, which accords fully with their apparent etymological identity.

There is, therefore, no logical obstacle to the assumption of a Gileadite **ṯubbult*^{u} "flood" at the time of Jephthah. Neither is such an assumption inconsistent with the requirements of dialect chronology and geography. We have learned that the merging of *ṯ* with *š* in Phoenician is established as early as the 11th century and that the corresponding process in Palestine need not have been later. But there is nothing to show that the same change had diffused beyond the Jordan and into Gilead until a materially later date. Transjordan has frequently been characterized by cultural and political developments at variance with those in Palestine. The frontier status of Gilead at the time of our episode is best exemplified by the career of Jephthah himself. Still more suggestive from our standpoint is the fact that Gilead bordered on territory which has not given up the *ṯ*-phoneme to this day, as Arabic clearly demonstrates. In the light of the foregoing remarks the absence of that phoneme from the dialect of Gilead in Jephthah's time would indeed be surprising.

One detail remains to be cleared up before our hypothesis may be allowed to proceed on its course. The posited *ṯ*-phoneme is expressed in the text by *š*. A glance at the relevant evidence will show, however, that this is the only way in which that phoneme could have been expressed altogether. In the first place, inherited *ṯ* became *š* in Canaanite and is thus represented regularly in Hebrew. Secondly, Accadian phonology furnishes a complete parallel in this instance. Lastly, where a distinction between original *ṯ* and *š* is maintained orthographically, it is the spirant that is written invariably as *š*, whereas the sibilant may appear either as *š* or *s*.[12] This is true of Old Accadian, the Nuzi dialect, and Amarna. In short, *ṯ* had to be written *š*. It could not be set down as *s* unless such a writing was meant to express an unsuccessful imitation of the required sound, which is exactly what happened.

To sum up, the *shibboleth* incident reveals a peculiarity of the Gileadite dialect at the time of Jephthah as contrasted with the Hebrew of Palestine. That peculiarity consisted in the retention of the phoneme *ṯ* which the Hebrews of Palestine had lost and were unable to reproduce. The resulting misfortune might have affected speakers from Judea or Galilee just as painfully as it did strike the Ephraimites. The dialectal feature in question stemmed from the other side of the Jordan. The current interpretations of the incident suffer primarily from their location on the wrong side of the river.

In conclusion, may I be permitted a fictitious illustration, necessarily provincial, which is designed to show how easy it is to slip into errors of this kind. Let us assume that a particularly bitter sports contest had taken place at Ebbets Field, Brooklyn. A riot among the spectators ensued and the followers of the invading team

[12] Cf. Speiser, JAOS 59 (1939) 187 ff.; Goetze, *Language* 14 (1938) 136 f.

from Manhattan had to take to their heels. But they were overtaken just as they were attempting to cross the Brooklyn Bridge. Their one chance of escape was to pretend that they were Brooklynites. But the local partisans were not to be fooled by such a ruse. "How do you say W-O-R-D? The answer was [wərd]. It was a fatal mistake. The next day readers in England were treated to a description of the incident. They promptly concluded that it was a peculiarity of the Manhattan dialect to say [wərd], whereas Brooklyn and all the rest of the country said [wəyd].

Such a result might well be viewed as self-evident. But that does not make it right.

[*Addendum*. Some of the above conclusions were discussed and disputed by R. Marcus in *BASOR* 87 (1942), p. 39, with the result that W. F. Albright switched his support to Marcus (*ibid.*). Although a great deal of water has flowed down more than one *šubbultu* since then, the issue remains unchanged. Nor can it be resolved until and unless new evidence can put an end to further speculation, without endangering, one would hope, the modern connotation of "shibboleth."]

Of Shoes and Shekels

(I SAMUEL 12:3; 13:21)

I

SHOES WERE USED IN THE ANCIENT ORIENT NOT ONLY AS AN article of dress but also for symbolical purposes. One of these was plainly of a legal nature. This is evident from the well-known statement in Ruth 7:4 that ". . . to confirm anything, a man would take off his shoes and give it to his neighbor; and this was the attestation in Israel." According to Deut: 25:9 the removal of the shoe serves to disgrace publicly the man who has refused to discharge his obligation under the levirate law. These two occurrences have in common the same outward symbol. They differ, however, in substance according to the attitude of the parties involved. In the passage in Ruth there is complete agreement among the participants; in Deuteronomy the action is strictly one-sided. We shall see presently that the mention of "a pair of shoes" in Amos 2:6 and 8:6 harks back to an analogous usage.

At the beginning of the statement in Ruth just cited we are told that the act of taking off the shoe was a custom once prevalent in Israel. As a matter of fact, there is one other passage, in addition to the above occurrences, which alludes to this custom: I Samuel 12:3. That this passage is not linked generally with Ruth 4:7 is due to our present Masoretic text. The ceremony of the shoe is introduced as obsolete at the time of Ruth; it may have become restricted in course of time to a special connection with the levirate marriage. All traces of a wider legal application in early times tended to disappear, until the ceremony was lost entirely to later tradition. But the Septuagint still preserves the original reading of the passage, and a related statement in Ben Sira bears out the Greek version.

The passage in question gives us Samuel's farewell address to the people. According to the present Hebrew text, this address ends as follows: ". . . or from whose hands have I taken ransom that I might hide my eyes with it? And I will restore it to you." In spite of the abruptness of the concluding sentence, the great majority of the modern commentators lean towards the Masoretic text. To be sure, the Targum had to amplify the phrase "that I might hide my eyes with it" by adding significantly "in a lawsuit." But the phrase happens to make sense, which cannot be said offhand about the reading of the Septuagint (followed by Old Latin) and its independent confirmation in Ben Sira. The Masoretic text offers

kofer, w^{e}a'līm 'eynay bô.

The Septuagint presupposes instead [1]

kofer w^{e}na'al(ayim); '^{a}nû vî.

The paraphrase in Ben Sira furnishes for the disputed words the letters [2]

wn'lm . . . 'nh bw,

[1] ἐξίλασμα καὶ ὑπόδημα; ἀποκρίθητε κάτ' ἐμοῦ.

[2] This passage (46:19) is available both in Greek and in Hebrew in identical versions.

thus agreeing with the Septuagint in all respects, since the substitution of the third person for the first does not affect the context. Reduced to a purely consonantal basic text, the two rival readings involve only the difference between ' and *n*. But the Greek version presents a radical difference in context: ". . . (for from whose hand have I taken) ransom and a shoe? Testify against me and I will return it to you." While "testify against me" is an excellent antecedent to "I will return it to you," one that is lacking in the traditional text,[3] what would "a shoe" (or Ben Sira's "pair of shoes") mean in apposition to "ransom"? This difficulty explains the rather unusual preference of the critics of the Masoretic Hebrew reading as against the Septuagint,[4] reinforced so unexpectedly by Ben Sira. The tested principle of textual criticism that the more difficult reading deserves preference was not applied in this instance. It could not be without some outside support. Such support is now found in the Nuzi texts.

Among the Nuzi documents published so far there are two which mention shoes not as items in the local economy[5] but as legal symbols. In H(arvard) S(emitic) S(eries) V, 76[6] we are told of a dowry (*mulugu*) which consists of real estate. We know that such property was inalienable under the law of the land, the only sanctioned method of transfer being formal adoption in cases where the law of inheritance did not operate automatically. In this instance the assignee is the owner's daughter who would not ordinarily share in the inheritance; moreover, a dowry represents an outright gift effective while the

[3] Cf. S. R. Driver, *Notes on the Hebrew Text of the Books of Samuel* (2nd ed.), p. 89.

[4] Kittel-Kahle, *Biblia Hebraica, ad loc.* weighs the Greek reading as "perhaps right."

[5] Cf. D. Cross, *Movable Property in the Nuzi Documents,* p. 52.

[6] Translated by Speiser, in *Annual* X, p. 66.

donor was alive. In short, the transaction does not fall under the head of normal legal practice. Now the daughter reciprocates with a present consisting of "one pair of shoes, one garment, one sheep, one sow with her ten pigs" (lines 6–8). The barter value of animals is self-evident, but the gift of a garment and, particularly, of shoes is difficult to explain in this connection on a purely economic basis. Even more suggestive is HSS V, 17 [7] where a man receives from another the latter's daughter as an outright gift (*makannu*), this gift having some relation to a pending lawsuit. In return for this *makannu* the father gets only "a cloak and a pair of shoes" (lines 9–10). There can be no question in this case of an ordinary exchange, and P. Koschaker is clearly right when he holds that shoes and garments must be regarded in such instances as token payments to validate special transactions by lending them the appearance of normal business practice.[8]

Reviewing the two documents together, we find that in both cases there are elements which do not fall within the regular legal framework. What saves them from being irregular under the law is the ceremonial transfer of shoes to the party that might otherwise have been guilty of an illegal practice. This transfer may accompany a gift (called *qištu,* HSS V, 76), or it may be made in consideration of a "gift" (*makannu,* HSS V, 17; this term is a close analogue to Akk *ṭâtu* which means both "gift" and "bribe"); [9] and it may be connected specifically with lawsuits on which the verdict is pending.

[7] *Ibid.,* pp. 63–4. The translation of both these texts will now bear improvement.

[8] Cf. *ZA* XLI, p. 27, note. Koschaker translates *iltenūtu šēnu* as "one shoe," but this usage is idiomatic for "a pair of shoes"; see Cross, *op. cit.* and Goetze, *ZA* XL, p. 79 f.

[9] Cf. *Annual* XVI, p. 86.

These two Nuzi documents involving shoes provide now a common basis for Ruth 4:7 as well as I Sam. 12:3. In the former instance Boaz cannot claim a legal right to Ruth until he had "purchased" that right (verse 8) from the next-of-kin. The "price" is a shoe, which serves "to confirm all things" and as "attestation." Here the Biblical verse gives us a definition of the ceremony of the shoe which applies admirably to the above cuneiform passages: it is to validate arrangements by circumventing legal obstacles. But the same definition imparts now unusual force to Samuel's final remarks. In his capacity as judge he had never accepted bribes or gratuities from any litigant; what is more, he had had nothing to do with cases where the law could be circumvented through some technicality.

In the light of these remarks the allusions in Amos to "the selling of the needy for a pair of shoes" can easily be appreciated. We have here a proverbial saying which refers to the oppression of the poor by means which may be legal but do not conform to the spirit of the law. The ordinary interpretation of this saying that the poor could be enslaved for so trifling a thing as a pair of shoes is unconvincing, by comparison, and economically improbable.

It is hardly necessary that this particular type of the ceremonial use of the shoe does not exhaust the symbolical application of the object even in the legal-economic sphere. Dr. E. R. Lacheman has attempted recently to connect the above passage in Ruth with the Nuzi custom of "lifting up the foot" as a symbol of property release.[10] This was undoubtedly true in certain dealings of a

[10] See *JBL* LVI, 53 ff.

normal business nature. In the above instances, however, this explanation is colorless and irrelevant.

II

Until quite recently, the text of I Sam. 13:21 was regarded by all critics as hopelessly corrupt. The passage to which this verse belongs speaks of the lack of smiths among the Israelites and the consequent dependence of the people upon Philistine artisans who took full advantage of their profitable monopoly. The verse itself describes apparently in detail the exorbitant charges of the Philistine smiths; [11] but the situation was obscured by the occurrence of several words of unknown meaning. The chief difficulty lay in the word which is represented in the Hebrew text by the letters *pym*. The logical derivation of this word would seem to be from *pê* "mouth, edge." It was clear, however, that the plural of *pê* is attested nowhere else in the masculine form; moreover, "edges" did not yield a suitable meaning in this particular context. That the crux was a very old one indeed is shown by the versions, all of which grope hopelessly and along diverse lines towards the elusive solution.

The correct solution was reserved for modern archaeology. Once again etymologized—incorrectly, of course—as *šinā* "two" + **pû* "a third," i.e., the text is upheld against ancient and modern editors alike. For we have

[11] Incidentally, the statement in I Sam. 13:19 that "there was no smith found throughout all the land of Israel" has to be interpreted with the aid of archaeology. If we take this statement literally, we borrow trouble unnecessarily. There can be no doubt that Palestine did not lack copper-smiths at the time of Samuel. What the text wants to convey is that iron-smiths could not be found among the Israelites, but had to be sought in Philistine settlements. This corresponds closely enough to the known cultural conditions.

now specimens of actual weights inscribed with the letters *pym*,[12] precisely as in the Samuel verse under discussion. The actual weight of these specimens shows that the term denoted "two-thirds (of a shekel)." The verse tells us, therefore, that some of the simple repairs of implements and weapons cost as much as two-thirds of a shekel, while others required one-third,[13] very considerable amounts in either case.

But this welcome demonstration of the significance of the term *pym* does not accounnt for its etymology. The derivation from *pê*, always questionable on morphological grounds, is even less probable now for semantic reasons: *pê* is not used to denote fractions. There is, however, another way to settle this problem. It must be sought in the cultural background, specifically in the field of metrology.

It is a well-known fact that the names for cultural importations frequently accompany the articles imported. This is true especially of such concrete items as weights and measures. The spread of the Sumerian term *mana*, which designates 1/60th of a talent, throughout the Near East and thence to the Graeco-Roman world (Akk. *manû*, Heb. *mānê*, Latin *mina*, etc.) is a case in point. Such borrowings are natural for fractional values based on the sexagesimal system, since this system is characteristic of the Sumerian culture.[14] Now "two-thirds" is a fraction

[12] Cf. G. A. Barton, *Archaeology and the Bible* (6th ed.), p. 207; A. Barrois, *Revue Biblique*, 1932, pp. 67 f., 76.

[13] This plausible interpretation was suggested by Pilcher in the *Quarterly Statement of the Palestine Exploration Fund*, 1914, p. 99.

[14] The term *pî-s^{e}nayim*, which might be adduced in this connection, is not a real objection to this statement. For Deut. 21:17 shows that this phrase was applied to the inheritance share of the first-born, which was twice as large as that of the other heirs. The division was thus two-thirds as against one-third; hence *pî-s^{e}nayim* comes to be used derivatively for "two-thirds" in general (cf. Zech. 13:8; II Kings 2:9). The origin of this expression may be sought in phrases like *k^{e}fî naḥ^{a}lathô* "according to his inheritance" Num-

of the sexagesimal system,[15] being properly another formulation of "four-sixths." If these premises are right, our *pym* should have a good Sumerian etymology.

As a matter of fact, such an etymology can be proposed. It is indirect, but the intermediate steps are all clear, so that the ultimate derivation is plausible enough. We know that Sumerian had special terms for all fractions from 1/6 to 5/6, and we know also that these terms were applied to the respective subdivisions of the shekel (Sumerian *gín*) without the mention of the weight-unit in question. In other words, a term like *kingusila* meant not only "5/6," but also specifically "5/6 shekel." The corresponding term for "4/6" was *šanabi*. This was taken over into Akkadian as *šinipû*, where it was used for "two-thirds." So far the entire process has been relatively simple. It so happens, however, that the Akkadian word for "two" is *šinā*. Inevitably, the loanword *šinipû*, was "two-thirds." The *Glossar* of Bezold still gives this etymology, but the more recent work of Deimel traces *šinipû* back to its proper Sumerian prototype *šanabi*.

The fate of this term on Canaanite soil[17] could have been predicted by any student of the language. While Akkadian uses the dual exclusively for things which occur in pairs, Canaanite will express by the dual any two iden-

bers 35:8; it corresponds in substance to Akk. *kimā šinišū* "according to his double (portion)" which is used specifically of the part of the eldest son. There is no connection, therefore, between *pî-* "according to" and the singular of *pym*.

[15] For the latest discussion of this subject see F. Thureau-Dangin, "Sketch of the History of the Sexagesimal System," *Osiris*, Vol. VII (1939), pp. 95–141.

[16] Cf. A. Poebel, *Sumerische Grammatik*, p. 122.

[17] For its actual occurrence in West Semitic as *snb* see M. Lidzbarski, *Handbuch der nordsemitischen Epigraphik*, 329. But the identification with *pî-sᵉnayim* (cf. H. Zimmern, *Ber. d. Sächs. Ges. d. Wiss.* 53, p. 51) is erroneous; see above, note 14.

tical objects. Since *šinipû* "two-thirds of a shekel" was analyzed as *šinā* + **pû*, with the latter abstraction being understood as the word for "a third," the Canaanite form for the whole was naturally the dual of **pû*, i.e., *payim*. That this dual need not be connected with the Semitic word for "mouth" has already been indicated. If the view expressed above is right, this form had nothing to do with any Semitic word or, for that matter, with any known Sumerian independent vocable. It would be a secretion pure and simple, much like the *-en* in English *oxen* or the *-er* in German *Bücher*.*

[*Addendum*. The number of *pym* weights has increased considerably. Cf. J. B. Pritchard, *Hebrew Inscriptions and Stamps from Gibeon* (University Museum Monographs, 1959), p. 30, and the literature there cited.]

* Linguistically there can be no objection to Professor Speiser's derivation of *pym* from a misunderstood *šinipû* (also *šinipât*). However, the matter is more complex, since similar expressions for "two-thirds" appears in Egyptian (*rʾwi*, "two mouths," i.e. "two parts") since the Fifth Dynasty, in Biblical Hebrew, and elsewhere; see the discussion by K. Sethe, *Von Zahlen und Zahlworten bei den alten Agyptern* (Strassburg, 1916), pp. 91 ff.—W.F.A.

"People" and "Nation" of Israel

WORDS CAN SERVE NOT ONLY TO REVEAL FACTS BUT ALSO TO conceal them. Such catchwords as "people" and "nation" are often used with greater freedom, not to say abandon, than the situation warrants. This is frequently the case when these terms are applied to ancient Israel, particularly when they are made the basis for sweeping political, sociological, and theological conclusions. Actually, there is need for a good deal of tidying up at both ends, the modern and the biblical.

In current usage, the terms "people" and "nation" are not sharply differentiated. Only in technical discussions does one find a serviceable, if not quite precise, distinction of meaning. *People* tends to emphasize common cultural and social characteristics, while *nation* is mainly a political designation associated as a rule with state and government. In neither instance is there any explicit stress on racial origins.[1]

The Bible, for its part, uses a similar pair of terms, *'ām* and *gōy*. These nouns are always translated mechanically as "people" and "nation" respectively. This gives us rough approximations, but does not really tell us very

[1] For a convenient analysis of current usage see Webster's *Dictionary of Synonyms* (1942), under "race," p. 672.

much. For translation involves here not just words but the very fabric of a highly significant society. Hence the modern interpreter need be clear about what is meant today by "people" and "nation," what the Bible means by *'ām* and *gōy*, and how these two sets of terms relate to each other. The key question, however, is the overall problem of *'ām* and *gōy*, a problem that is as yet far from settled.[2]

This paper seeks to focus on the Bible's view of Israel as reflected by the use of *'ām* and *gōy*. The discussion is divided into three parts: (1) The uses of *'ām* and *gōy* in the Bible; (2) extrabibilcal data; and (3) ancient Israel in the light of the combined evidence. The whole theme can be treated here only in brief outline. This should be enough, however, to indicate the principal results.

I. THE USES OF *'AM* AND *GOY* IN THE BIBLE

The latest lexicon of the Bible, that of Koehler and Baumgartner, still carries the statement that *gōy* is not clearly differentiated ("nicht deutlich verschieden") from *'ām* insofar as biblical usage is concerned.[3] Yet this judgment is sharply at variance with the vast bulk of the evidence in the case. Our lexicographers and all others who share this view could not have probed very deep. A check of the pertinent occurrences—there are more than 1800

[2] A useful philological discussion on the subject is furnished by Leonhard Rost, "Die Bezeichnungen für Land und Volk im Alten Testament," *Festschrift Otto Procksch,* pp. 125–44. To the limited extent to which our independent lines of inquiry coincide (a portion of Section I, below), they are in substantial agreement and mutually complementary. [The etymologically preferable form for "people" is *ᶜam* (with short vowel), originally * *ᶜamm*—.]

[3] See p. 174. Contrast Rost, *loc. cit.,* p. 142.

instances of *'ām* and over 550 of *gōy*—should demonstrate conclusively that the weight of the evidence points in the opposite direction.

There is, to be sure, a small number of passages in which *'ām* and *gōy* are interchangeable. But the cases in question are relatively late and due in the main to stylistic variation or poetic parallelism; e.g., *gōy ḥoṭē'*: *'am kebed 'āwōn* (Isa 1:4); *kᵉlimmaṯ haggōyīm wᵉḥerpaṯ 'ammīm* (Ezek 36:15). Contrast, however, the older use of *šᵉnē gōyīm*: *šᵉnē lᵉ'ummīm* (Gen 25:23), where the literary term *l'om* [4] rather than the familair *'ām,* is employed as the poetic counterpart of *gōy.*

At any rate, against the slender minority of passages that do correlate *'ām* with *gōy,* the overwhelming majority indicate a clear and manifold distinction between the two nouns. The evidence may be summarized as follows:

a. Unlike *'ām, gōy* is never possessively construed with YHWH; there is no such construction as *gōy*-YHWH. Even with alien deities the pertinent term is *ām*; cf. *'am kᵉmōš* (Num 21:29). This particular point has been frequently noticed but has not been followed through.[5]

b. Similarly, when Israel is spoken of as God's people, the forms employed are *'ammī, 'ammᵉḵā,* or *'ammō,* but never *gōy* with possessive suffix. In fact, *'ām* is found hundreds of times with pronominal endings, as against only seven with *gōy,* each in connection with land.[6] Evidently, therefore, *'ām* is something subjective and per-

[4] Neither this rare term nor the still rarer *'umma(h)* has a bearing on the present discussion.

[5] Strictly speaking, therefore, all references to Yahweh as a "national" God at any given time are terminologically inaccurate. Yahweh is not specifically traced to a single locality as, say, Enlil is traced to Nippur, or Marduk to Babylon, or Ashur to his homonymous city. Theophanies on sacred mountains are not to be equated with political ties.

[6] Gen 10:5, 20, 31, 32; Ezek 33:13, 14, 15. For the affinity of *gōy* to land and the like see below under (e).

sonal, *gōy* objective and impersonal. Note *ur'ē kī 'ammᵉḵā haggōy hazzê* (Exod 33:13). The same utterance with the two nouns interchanged would be unthinkable in a biblical context, though not in translation. One begins to see now that the renderings "people" and "nation" are not one-to-one correlatives of *'ām* and *gōy*.

c. To go a step further, *'ām* appears often as an element in personal names, but *gōy* never; cf. Ammishaddai, Amminadab, Ammiel, and the like. The function this time is that of a kinship term, on a par with Abi-, Ahi-, and others.

d. The kinship connotation of *'ām* is still alive in such idioms as *wayyē'āsēf 'el-'ammāw* "he was gathered to his kin" (Gen 25:8, 17, etc.), and *niḵrat mē'ammāw* (e.g., Exod 30:33, 38), and the like, "he was sundered from his kin." In such instances the noun is normally in the plural, but not always. Cf., e.g., *wᵉhāyīnū lᵉ'am 'eḥāḏ* (Gen 34:16) "we shall thus become one family"; note also Ruth 1:16. It follows that *'ām* was essentially a term denoting close family connections, and hence secondarily the extended family, that is, people in the sense of a larger, but fundamentally consanguineous, body.

e. In contrast, there is not the least hint of personal ties under the concept of *gōy*. The noun labels large conglomerates held together, so to speak, from without rather than from within. It is surely no accident that the so-called Table of Nations (Gen 10) speaks of *gōyīm* exclusively, all such entries being classified according to geographic (*bᵉarṣōṯām*) and linguistic (*lilᵉšōnōṯām*) principles. The subgroups there are designated as *mišpāḥōṯ*, thus showing that *mišpāḥā(h)* was basically an administrative rubric.

f. A word, like a person, is sometimes typified by the company it keeps. It is significant, therefore, that the usual coördinate of *gōy* is *mamlāḵā(h)* "kingdom." Cf. *gōy*: *mamlāḵā* (e.g., I Kings 18:10; Jer 18:7, 9; II Chron 32:15), or *mamlāḵā*: *gōy* (I Kings 18:10); note especially *mamleḵeṯ kōhᵃnīm wᵉgōy qāḏōš* (Exod 19:6), and cf. also the four kingdoms out of one *gōy* (Dan 8:22). Correspondingly, the Israelites demand a king so that they may become like all the *gōyīm* (I Sam 8:20).

g. Furthermore, it is highly instructive to identify the indivisible units of the *gōy* and the *ʿām* respectively. In the former case it is *ʾāḏām*, the earthling, mortal, one of a crowd, or in short, a statistic; cf. *wᵉʿal gōy wᵉʿal ʾāḏām yaḥaḏ* (Job 34:29), and note Ezek 36:13). Small wonder that *ʾāḏām* is itself originally a collective noun, a mass term, which is why it cannot form a plural. On the other hand, the ultimate component of the *ʿām* is *ʾīš*, that is, the individual; cf. e.g., II Sam 15:30; 16:18. Analogously, one says *ʾaḥaḏ-hāʿām* (Gen 26:10). All of which casts added doubt on the authenticity of the phrase *haggōy gam ṣaddīq tahᵃroḡ* (Gen 20:4); it can be nothing else than an unfortunate textual corruption.

h. It thus becomes clear that where the Bible juxtaposes *ʿām* and *gōy*, it does so deliberately and for purposes of subtle distinction. Aside from *urʾē kī ʿammᵉḵā haggōy hazzê* (Exod 33:13), which has already been cited, note *raq ʿam-ḥāḵām wᵉnāḇōn haggōy haggāḏōl hazzê* (Deut 4:6). The phrase amounts to the same thing as: After all, this large mass of humanity is made up of wise and discerning individuals!

i. In the light of the above facts, the typical verbs that may accompany the two nouns under discussion should prove to be of more than casual interest. A *gōy* can be made (*'sh*), established (*ntn*), founded (*śīm*), or the like. Egypt "came into being" as a *gōy* (Exod 9:24). Such states are not "born" all at once (Isa 66:8). They can, however, go out of existence (Jer 31:35). As opposed to all this, an *'ām* just is; it is a physical fact. As for its behavior, an *'ām* can eat and drink, be faint and suffer thirst, quarrel and complain and weep, tremble or flee or hide in caves, come into the world and eventually be buried. It is a group of persons. The *gōy*, on the other hand, even when not tied to the land or linked to a state, is a regimented body, e.g., when it crosses a stream [7] or makes war. The one, in sum, is discrete, the other collective.

To recapitulate, the modern concept of "people" is at best only a rough approximation to the biblical concept of *'ām*. The main difference lies in the suggestion of blood ties and the emphasis on the individual, both of which features are peculiar to the Hebrew term. On the other hand, *gōy* comes rather close to the modern definition of "nation." In any case, the gap between Hebrew *'ām* and *gōy* is greater than that between our "people" and "nation."

II. EXTRABIBLICAL DATA

Once the various uses of *'ām* and *gōy* have been established within Hebrew, it is safe to venture outside and consult the evidence of cognate languages. What we find there is routine in some respects, but quite unexpected, and highly significant, in others.

'ām is a common West-Semitic term. It still carries in

[7] Josh 4:1.

Arabic its original connotation of "paternal uncle." By extension, the noun came to designate the nuclear family as a whole (cf. Heb. *'ammīm*), and thence the family deity in personal names, notably in Amorite (cf Hammurapi), Aramaic, and early Hebrew. The ethnic sense of the term is clearly secondary and based on kinship. In such occurrences the word stands primarily for a consanguineous group, or the extended family in the widest sense of the term. Its individual correlate is *'īš* which, significantly enough, has approximately the same dialectal distribution as *'ām*.

In marked contrast, Hebrew *gōy* has practically no cognates. Its only established relative is found in the Mari dialect of Akkadian, where it turns up as one of a number of borrowings from West-Semitic. The meaning of Mari *gāw/yum* is "group, work gang," [8] in striking agreement with the posited original connotation of Hebrew *gōy*.

What is especially noteworthy, however, is the hitherto unappreciated fact that Akkadian shows no trace of the West-Semitic pair *'ām* and *'īš*. The concept "men" collectively is expressed there by *nīšū* or *nīšūtu*, cognates of Hebrew *'ᵃnāšīm* and *'ᵉnōš*, but not of *'īš*. The group term is *ṣābum*, which is etymologically the same as Hebrew *ṣāḇā*, but semantically approximates Hebrew *'āḏām*. For "nation" Akkadian resorts to *mātum*, a word with the primary meaning of "country," and a secondary ethnogeographic value that appears also in Hebrew *gōy*. The Akkadian singular for "man" is *awēlum*, ultimately an adjective describing the upper class of the population, the citizenry alongside *muškênum* "tenant" and *wardum* "slave."

In other words, in Mesopotamian society man was

[8] Cf. *Chicago Assyrian Dictionary*, Vol. 5 (G), *s. v.*

fitted into a pattern that differed sharply from the biblical, and with it from other West-Semitic groups. The main emphasis in Mesopotamia rested on the political unit and its administrative subdivisions. The overriding factor had come to be the state, regardless of ethnic composition, indeed a structure composed of diverse ethnic elements. The family played a part, inevitably, but its autonomy was severely restricted by political and economic considerations. Though blood was thicker than water, bread and taxes rated still higher. That is why adoption, which tends to loosen blood ties, became such a prominent factor in Mesopotamian society; contrariwise, the institution of the levirate, which stands guard over blood relationship, never took hold in Mesopotamia proper. And the ultimate component of the Mesopotamian community was the citizen rather than the individual as such, *awēlum,* as opposed to *'īš*. In short, the Akkadian terminology on the subject, in sharp contrast with the Hebrew, reflects, a highly sophisticated urban society, one that set little store by consanguineous groupings.

By the same token, the Hebrew pair *'ām* and *'īš* should presuppose a nonurban background, in common with other West-Semitic elements. Now in nomadic society the isolated individual has little chance of survival. Such an environment imposes unremitting group effort and a constant struggle against rival groups. In these circumstances, careful attention to blood ties promises maximum security. The family is paramount; but it will prosper or fail depending on the initiative and enterprise of its individual members.

These theoretical premises are supported by several concrete facts. There is not a single attested case of adoption in the whole of the Hebrew Bible, in marked contrast to Mesopotamia. On the other hand, the levirate, much though its hold may have been loosened through progressive urbanization, is never completely eliminated. Nor is the nomadic background, though obviously a thing of the past, altogether forgotten. It is recalled nostalgically by the prophets time and again. The period of wanderings in the desert was a golden age, an ideal that may yet be realized again in the future (Hos 2:16 f.; 12:10).[9] Urban life, on the other hand, contributes to corruption (Amos 6:8). Significantly enough, such remembrance of the past is often expressed in terms of family relations. Israel was then the bride, and God her bridegroom (Hos 13:15; Jer 2:2); or Israel was the son, and God the father (Hos 11:1). With so venerable a background, it is not at all strange that the accent on the family should have carried over into the postbiblical stage, and have remained prominent in Jewish life down to the present.

In sum, *'īš* as individual in an originally nomadic-pastoral family, and *awēlum* as citizen in an urban community,[10] epitomize two divergent modes of existence. The two terms are not interchangeable, nor are they found together in the same language. Each helps to circumscribe the group to which it appertains, the *'ām* in the one instance, and the *mātum* in the other. The dichotomy is complete and deep-rooted. As such it pro-

[9] For the so-called nomadic "ideal" of Israel see most recently R. de Vaux, *Les Institutions de l'Ancien Testament,* I, pp. 30 ff. Whether such an ideal was ever actually recognized, or whether it was as strong as is often alleged, is not altogether certain, in view of some noteworthy arguments that have recently been raised against that view. The issue, however, is of no particular relevance to the present discussion.

[10] See W. von Soden, *Assyrisches Handwörterbuch,* p. 90.

vides a major criterion for the sociological analysis of the ancient Near East.

III. ANCIENT ISRAEL IN THE LIGHT OF THE ABOVE EVIDENCE

We are now ready to apply the terms *'ām* and *gōy*, as elucidated in the foregoing discussion, to the case of ancient Israel. The question, then, is not whether Israel was a people or a nation, since these concepts are neither indigenous nor sufficiently defined; rather, the question is whether Israel was an *'ām* or a *gōy*. The answer is plainly that Israel was both. And the direct evidence on which this answer is based yields further significant disclosures.

According to the biblical record, the history of ancient Israel begins with Abraham's migration from Mesopotamia. A mass of circumstantial evidence, both internal and external, tends to validate the substance of the passage in Gen 12 beyond the fondest expectations of the most confirmed traditionalists. Right now, however, we are concerned with the wording of the call that led to the migration. It contains the promise *wᵉ'e'eśᵉḵā lᵉgōy gāḏōl* (Gen 12:2) "I will make you into a great nation." The term in question is *gōy*, not *'ām*; and rightly so. For Abraham was an *'ām* to begin with, in the primary sense of the word, so long as he had a nephew named Lot.

There is nothing casual or accidental about this phraseology. It is consistent, invariable, and exclusive. It is applied again to Abraham in Gen 18:18, to Jacob in Gen 46:3 and Deut 26:5, and to Moses in Exod 32:10, Num 14:12, and Deut 9:13.[11] The reason, then, behind

[11] Similarly to Ishmael, Gen 17:20; 21:13, 18.

the patriarch's departure from Mesopotamia and the Israelites' liberation from Egypt was that Israel might be a nation. The *'ām* had been in Egypt for centuries anyway, where its numbers are stated to have become very large (Exod 1:9).

Yet we are told also on many occasions—and have the independent evidence of grammar and phraseology to the same effect—that, in terms of God's own connection with the people, Israel was his *'ām*. It was chosen and treated as such. But to carry out God's purpose, as that purpose is expressed by the Bible as a whole, the *'ām* was not enough; what was needed was the added status and stability of nationhood in a land specifically designated for that purpose.

With this last affirmation, one that is dictated by direct and explicit evidence, as we have seen, we touch on one of the very roots of the biblical process. The essence of that process was the undeviating quest for a worthy way of life, "the way of Yahweh," in the words of Gen 18:19. To be successful, that quest could not be confined to the care of an obsolescent nomadic society. It required the medium of an up-to-date civilization, a medium that could not function short of the institution of nationhood. But such an institution alone is but an empty form unless animated by the human element. As a historic process, therefore, a process that made world history, Israel can be understood only as both an *'ām* and a *gōy*. One without the other would be at best only a footnote to history.

Census and Ritual Expiation in Mari and Israel

REFERENCES TO THE CENSUS PLAY A SIGNIFICANT PART IN the Old Testament and take up considerable space. The law on the subject is contained in Exod 30:11–16. The book of Numbers, which owes its very name to the census, deals with it in chapters 1–4 and 26. And in II Samuel 24 the sequel of the same institution is a pestilence of unusual severity. Yet there is much about the census in the Bible that has long been a puzzle.

We do know that the underlying purpose was military. Those involved were males from twenty years old and upwards. (Exod 30:14, etc.) who were capable of bearing arms (e.g., Numbers 1:3, 26:2). The results could be used as a basis for new land grants, in which case the actual distribution was determined by lot (Number 26:55). Nevertheless, some of the technical terms employed in this connection have caused trouble and led to makeshift translations. Above all, however, it has never been made clear why such an essential administrative measure should require offerings of expiation or atonement (*kofer*, Exod 30:12) in order to ward off plagues; nor is it immediately apparent how one such plague in the reign of David could be traced back to the census (II Samuel 24).

The issue as a whole involves various problems in the fields of linguistics, government, and religion. It goes without saying that complex issues of this kind had best be left alone unless and until there is new evidence to justify a review of the case. In the present instance, the required new evidence has fortunately come to light recently with the publication of the Mari letters. The relevant material from Mari bids fair to solve the outstanding difficulties connected with the biblical census; and it stands to gain much, in turn, from a comparison with the biblical evidence. The respective sources, in short, can be mutually illuminating, more so in fact than is apparent at first glance. A closer look at their combined testimony is therefore in order.

Parallel texts have to be handled with due caution, particularly when the distances between them amount to several centuries and hundreds of miles. In the case before us, however, the correspondence is at once too detailed and manifold to be distrusted. For one, the terms in question—and there are several of them in each instance—reflect the same technical idioms, and sometimes also the same etymologies. For another, the institutions involved are identical in character and objectives. And for still another, we find in both instances the same ritualistic component.

Furthermore, Mari and the Bible share certain other ties that have nothing to do with the census, while no comparable links exist between the Mari records and other cuneiform sources. The independent status of prophecy in Mari is one such case in point.[1] Another is

[1] For a recent statement on the subject and the pertinent older literature, cf. A. Malamat, " 'Prophecy' in the Mari Documents," *Annual of the Israel Exploration Society* IV (1955), pp. 1–12 (in Hebrew).

the form of the covenant.[2] The pertinent Mari phrase *ḫayarum* DUMU (prob. *bin*) *atānim*[3] is reproduced verbatim in the biblical *'īrô bnī 'atōnô* "his ass's colt" (Gen 49:11; cf. Zech 9:9). Then there is the prominent employment in Mari of the term *šipṭu* in the sense of a disciplinary warning or measure, on a par with Heb. *šᵉfāṭīm*; with this goes the action noun *šāpiṭum*, in significant harmony with the biblical *šōfēṭ*, which is universally mistranslated as "judge." In the light of so much detailed agreement, the mention of nomadic Benjaminites in the Mari documents, or of military leaders who bore the title of *dawidûm*, gains added suggestive appeal. All in all, therefore, a close connection between the biblical census and that of Mari, in their administrative application as well as religious overtones, should occasion little if any surprise.

A comprehensive statement on the subject of the census in Mari was published in 1950 by J. R. Kupper.[4] In his penetrating analysis Kupper surveyed the relevant cuneiform material and called attention to the biblical analogues. The one thing that gave him pause was the use of the word *tēbibtum* (and related forms) as the technical term for the institution as such. In a subsequent statement, which appeared in 1957,[5] Kupper modified his position, on etymological grounds; he restored *tēbib-*

[2] See G. E. Mendenhall, "Puppy and Lettuce in Northwest-Semitic Covenant Making," BULLETIN 133 (1954), pp. 26–30; M. Noth, "Das alttestamentliche Bundschliessen im Lichte eines Mari-Textes," *Mélanges Isidore Lévy* (1955), pp. 433–444 [*Ges. Studien zum Alten Testament*, pp. 142–154].

[3] Cf. G. Dossin, *Syria*, 1938, p. 108.

[4] See his "Le recensement dans les textes de Mari," *Studia mariana* (ed. A. Parrot), 1950, pp. 99–110.

[5] See his book on *Les nomades en Mésopotamie au temps des rois de Mari*, pp. 23–29.

tum to its primary sense of "purification," thus reducing the census to a secondary and incidental procedure.

It goes without saying that where etymology and usage would seem to diverge, the interpretation should be guided by usage and not the other way about. Nevertheless, M. Kupper's change of position is easy enough to understand in view of the prominent place which the texts accord not only to the abstract designation *tēbibtum* but also to the corresponding action nouns *ebbum* and *mubbibum* and the verb *ubbubum*, all of which have a common denominator in the adjective *ebbum* "pure." Accordingly, in any attempted re-evaluation of M. Kupper's present stand, the burden of proof rests with the critic. He must show that *tēbibtum* was indeed a process that was primarily administrative rather than cultic; and, to make his case, he should also be able to indicate the steps whereby a cultic term came to describe such an administrative act. I believe that both these requirements can be fulfilled. To do this, however, it is necessary to place the biblical and Mari evidence in closer juxtaposition than has yet been done. This will involve a brief survey of certain intricate idioms on both sides, as well as reference to significant religious beliefs and practices. I trust that results will repay the effort.

To concentrate, then, for the moment on the question of usage alone, the texts under review make it abundantly clear that *tēbibtum* and the several forms related to it refer specifically to the institution and process of census taking. Thus the characteristic phrase *aššum ṣābim ubbubim* "in regard to the *u.* of the troops" alternates with *aššum ṣābim paqādim* (cf. ARM[6] III 21. 5:19. 5); hence

[6] *Archives royales de Mari* (transliterations and translations); for the texts, see TCL (*Textes cunéiformes, Louvre*) XXII ff.

ubbubum is in this context a synonym of *paqādum* (for which see below), except that the latter verb lacks any cultic implication. The process itself may be carried out under the supervision of the ruler's sons or some of the higher officials, who in turn appoint (*aškun* ARM III 21. 10) or deputized (*alput* 19. 14) the appropriate functionaries (who are called *ebbū* in both instances). It is evident, therefore, that an *ebbum* (or *mubbibum*) was not a priest or even a permanent official, but someone appointed *ad hoc*. This fact should suffice in itself to bring out the essentially secular character of the *tēbibtum*. And this is borne out by the further fact that among the groups involved in the process were the Benjaminites.[7] It is scarcely conceivable that the efficient and tolerant regime of Shamshi-Addu [8] would seek to impose on the fractious Benjaminite elements any religious constraints whatsoever.

There is, moreover, ample evidence to the effect that the main purpose of the *tēbibtum* was to furnish dependable records of the available military manpower. Virtually every reference to the *tēbibtum* involves writing and tablets.[9] The lists are to be prepared methodically, place by place (*ālišam*, e.g., ARM III 19. 13; 21. 13), and name by name (*šumišam*, e.g. ARM II 42. 9, 23). They are sometimes detailed enough to cite separately (*ana ramānimma*) the soldiers and their reserves, the men who have been requisitioned for campaigns and

[7] See G. Dossin, *Mélanges Dussaud* (1939), pp. 981–996; Kupper, *Nomades*, pp. 47–81.

[8] Most of the texts in question are dated to the period when his son Yasmah-Addu was vice-regent of Mari. The relevant material from Chagar Bazar (see below) stems from the local archives of Yasmah-Addu.

[9] This fact is duly emphasized by M. Kupper himself, whose discussion (cf. n. 4, above) affords a fuller survey of the material than is possible in the present paper.

those too old for such tasks (cf. ARM III 19.23 ff.ff).[10] The normal subject matter is the military personnel; lands and towns are mentioned only by metonymy. Occasionally, the *tēbibtum* has as its objective the allotment of land to the conscripted personnel,[11] which must be carried out with utmost care (ARM I 7. 39 f.).[12] In short, the Mari *tēbibtum* covers the same ground as the biblical census, even down to such details as readiness for combat (cf. *yōṣē' ṣāvā'* Numbers 1:3, etc.) and new land grants (Numbers 26).

Were if not, therefore, for etymological considerations, no one would hesitate today to view the *tēbibtum* texts as straight census records. Why, then, does the terminology have a cultic bearing? M. Kupper would seek the answer in a "ceremony of purification" aimed at the absolution of sins and hence capable of affording spiritual relief to the absolved.[13] It is extremely doubtful, however, as was suggested earlier, that piety was so potent a factor in the case. At a minimum, such a purging ceremony should have been a regularly scheduled and countrywide festival in the charge of duly qualified priests; yet none of this is known to apply to the *tēbibtum*. The passage on which M. Kupper bases this particular suggestion does state that, after the *tēbibtum* had been per-

[10] This significant passage may be retranslated in full as follows: "The men (*ṣābum*), whose replacements went off to Babylon while they remained behind, have been recorded (reading *šaṭrū*, with v. Soden, *Orientalia* 21, 1952, p. 84) separately; the men not called up (*ṣabṭū*) for a (military) campaign— whether officials (*sāliḫu* is approximately the same as *gugallu*) or free citizens—have been recorded separately; and the old men unable to go [on campaigns] have been recorded separately."

[11] According to Numbers 26:55 such lands were apportioned by lot. And the Nuzi text JEN 333. 13–14 makes the significant distinction between a *bel zitti* and a *bel pūri*, that is, between those who acquired their lands by inheritance and those who obtained them by lot from the crown.

[12] The order reads *ina tēbibtimma ḫ[uṭṭ]iṭ sunniqma* "make that *tēbibtum* precise and accurate."

[13] Cf. *Nomades*, p. 24.

formed, *libbi mātim uttiḫ* (ARM IV 57. 12) "the heart of the land was at peace." But even if one were to take this phrase at face value, it does not follow that it denotes here an edifying religious response. For the same phraseology reappears in a familiar later passage about the death of a substitute king, which ends on this note: "The Akkadians were in fear (*iptalḫū*). We have reassured them; they are at peace" (*libbi nušaškinšunu ittūḫū*).[14] Evidently, therefore, the *tēbibtum* could give rise to fears, which it was important to forestall. Such a need might well account for the cultic bearing of the pertinent terminology. But why would a routine census engender fear and require the help of ritual as a prophylactic measure? It is on this point that the relevant biblical parallels can shed fresh light.

The technical Hebrew terminology on the subject comprises the phrase *nāśā' rōš* and the verb *pqd*. The two appear to be used interchangeably (cf., e.g., Numbers 1:2 and 3:14). The men thus enrolled are called *peqūdīm* (passim). How did these terms come to be employed for this particular purpose?

The literal meaning of *nāśā' rōš* "he lifted the head" lends itself to a variety of uses. The act may be a symbol of pride (Psalms 24:7) or a sign of pardon (Gen 40:13; II Kings 25:27); but it also can signify an execution (Gen. 40:19). In addition, however, we find the same phrase in the idiomatic sense of "to take stock, notice." A striking case in point is Gen. 40:20, where it is stated that Pharaoh "took notice" of his two incarcerated courtiers; the author had already made subtle use of the identical phrase to refer to a pardon in one instance (v. 13), and a death sentence (cf. our "beheading") in

[14] Harper, ABL 437, rev. 7–8.

another (v. 19). Apparently, "to lift the head" had developed the specialized meaning of "to pick out the essentials," or the like. It is in this derived sense that *nāśā' rōš* figures so prominently in connection with the census (Exod. 30:12; Numbers 1-4; 26, passim). And we learn from Numbers 31:26 that the term could be applied to animals as well as human beings. It is worth stressing that what is involved in all such cases is more than a mere tally, which would scarcely make any sense in Gen. 40:20. The point throughout is not "to take count" but "to take into account."

Since *nāśā' rōš* interchanges in the census passages with *pqd,* it should not be surprising to discover that the idiomatic sense of the former matches the basic meaning of the latter. To be sure, there is probably no other Hebrew verb that has caused translators as much trouble as *pqd.* Its semantic range would seem to accommodate "to remember, investigate, muster, miss, punish, number," and the like. Actually, however, this seemingly lawless profusion reduces itself readily to the single common denominator of "to attend to with care." The important thing in each instance is to start out with this underlying common value and not pay undue heed to a specialized and remote application of the verb. Failure to observe this principle, for instance, has saddled *pqd* with the meaning "to number," which this verb never actually possesses as such.[15] Counting can be the incidental result

[15] An amusing sequel to one such old misinterpretation is found in I Samuel 11. The clear original intent of the passage was to demonstrate Saul's courage against forbidding odds. His rescue of the besieged garrison of Jabesh Gilead was a perfect case in point. When people responded to his call, "he mustered them (*wayyifqᵉdēm*) at Bezeq" (v. 8). But later readers took the verb to mean "he numbered them." In that case, what was the total? According to the present Hebrew text, the Israelites alone (not counting the Judeans!) added up to 300,000; and the Septuagint doubles this number. Yet, quite apart from their inherent improbability, such figures are directly contrary to the purpose of the account, which was to point up Saul's heroism.

of attending to given tasks, whether the performer is a shepherd or a census taker. But *pqd* itself does not specify such possible byproducts. Where a tally is desired, the text will say *mnē(h)* (II Samuel 24:1) or add *mispar-* (v. 3).

Now, associated with the biblical census is the ritual act of furnishing a *kofer* (*-nefeš*). This amounted to the payment of half a shekel, so as to ward off a plague in the wake of the census (Exod. 30:12). The phrase designates a personal (*nefeš*) payment for purposes of propitiation or expiation (*kofer*). But the connection between such an offering and the census is not immediately apparent. We are told, however, in II Samuel 24 that a devastating pestilence afflicted the land following a census which had been ordered by David. Since nothing is said there about a *kofer*, one is justified in assuming that the omission of that precautionary measure was somehow linked with the subsequent plague.

We are now ready to compare the combined biblical evidence on the census with the pertinent material from Mari—as well as added pertinent texts from Chagar Bazar.[16] Both the Hebrew and the Akkadian texts feature distinctive technical terms. The one group yields *nāśā' rōš*, *pqd*, and *kofer;* the other displays *tēbibtum/ubbubum* and *paqādum*. The verbs *pqd* and *paqādum* are, of course, identical etymologically; and we shall see presently that their special technical meaning is also the same. And just as *pqd* interchanges with *nāśā' rōš* in

[16] For these cf. C. J. Gadd, *Iraq* 7 (1940), pp. 22 ff The Chagar Bazar material (see above, note 8) reflects the same age and society as the Mari texts. The Mari letters, however, deal with the *tēbibtum* as something that has either been ordered or carried out. On the other hand, the administrative documents from Chagar Bazar have more to say, naturally, about the economic details involved. Exact counterparts of the latter type should turn up among the as yet unpublished texts from Mari.

Hebrew, Akk. *paqādum* alternates with *ubbubum,* which thus yields the technical equation Heb. *naśā' rōš:* Akk. *ubbubum.* Semantically, however, *ubbubum* must be placed alongside Heb. *kipper* (Exod. 30:15); and *tēbibtum* is the same as *kofer.* In other words, Akk. *ubbubum/tēbibtum* has the special census meaning of Heb. *nāśā' rōš,* together with the cultic bearing of Heb. *kipper/kofer.* This juxtaposition is immensely helpful in more ways than one. It shows at a glance how closely related the respective institutions really were; and it points the way to a solution of the cultic tie in both instances, as we shall see directly. The sole difference between the biblical and the cuneiform material is the employment of *nāśā' rōš* in the Hebrew passages under review. Yet even on this score, Akkadian supplies a complete semantic analogue, although this does not figure in the census texts. Interestingly enough, however, the meaning of the pertinent Akk. idiom, *rēša(m) našû(m)* can now be defined more precisely than was possible hitherto, thanks to the established value of Heb. *nāśā' rōš.*

In analyzing the occurrences of *rēša našû* in the Harper letters, A. L. Oppenheim assigned to this phrase three distinct derivative values: (a) "to cite, summon"; (b) "to examine, control"; (c) "to start," [17] But in the light of the Hebrew evidence that was summed up above, these three separate connotations can be more sharply evaluated and brought under a single heading. The decisive criterion, of course, is actual usage and not interdialectal correspondence. Nevertheless, when all the instances cited by Oppenheim have been rechecked, it becomes clear that the common concept of "to take into account, to take notice of"—as established for the Hebrew passages—

[17] See JAOS 61 (1941), pp. 254–55.

will not only suit each Akkadian occurrence in question, but do it better. And the same meaning stands up also in other passages; cf., e.g., the Middle Assyrian version of the Etana Epic: *Šamaš ina šaggišī rēsu lissi* "may Shamash call him to account in common with murderers." [18] This is obviously the nuance of Heb. *pqd* in *pōqēd 'āwōn* "visiting iniquity."

In respect to the census passages, the technical parallels obtained thus far may be tabulated schematically as follows (with divergent semantic analogues shown in brackets):

OT	Mari (and Chagar Bazar)
nāśā' rōš	*ubbubum* [*rēša(m) našû(m)*]
pqd	*paqādum*
kofer [*cf. kippūrīm* Exod. 30:16]	*tēbibtum*

The direct link is furnished by *pqd/paqādum*. In view of all the other manifold ties, this specific and complete correspondence cannot possibly be ascribed to pure chance. It argues the most intimate kind of agreement between the underlying institutions under review. The respective terms, however, are sufficiently specialized otherwise to raise this further question: are Heb. *pqd: nāśā rōš* and Akk. *paqādum: ubbubum* mere stylistic variants in these contexts, as they would seem to be on the surface? It can now be shown that this is not the case, and that *pqd/paqādum* adds a highly significant detail to the census process. The essential clue is provided by the cuneiform sources.

[18] Cf. E. Ebeling, AfO 14 (1941–44), pl. 9.5 and p. 299, n. 5.

It was previously mentioned in passing that the Mari census involved detailed written records. "Let the troops . . . be recorded on a tablet by name" (*ṣābum . . . šumišam lû šaṭer*) is a characteristic request (ARM I 42. 22-24; cf. 8-9). Indeed, *ṣābam šaṭārum* "to record the troops" may alternate with *ṣābam paqādum* (ARM III 21:10-11:19. 7). The *tēbibtum* calls for experienced scribes; cf. eg., ARM I 7. 37-8: *u mārū*^{pl} *edubbi*[19] *ummēnu ina qātim šutamṣū* "there are enough skilled scribes on hand"; the Chagar Bazar texts say the same thing repeatedly.[20] It follows, therefore, that in these census documents from Amorite centers *paqādum* has the technical sense of "to make note in writing, to conscript." [21] Nor can there be much doubt that in the parallel biblical passages *pqd* must be given the same specialized meaning. For definite confirmation we need look no further than the census passage in Numbers 4:32. The text reads there *b*^{e}*šēmōt tifq*^{e}*dū,* which cannot mean anything but "you shall record by name," cf. Mari *šumišam lū šaṭer*. Therefore all the occurrences of *pqd* in the OT census passages can now be rendered simply, and significantly, "to record, enroll." Hence *p*^{e}*qūdīm* becomes "the enrolled ones"; and the hitherto troublesome *'ōvēr 'al happ*^{e}*qūdīm* (Exod. 30:13, 14) emerges as "one who is entered among the enrolled."

[19] Not *gá-dub-bi* as given in the transliteration in ARM I, both on account of the Chagar Bazar parallels (see next note) and on internal grounds. The initial syllable could be read either *gá* or *é*, the actual difference between the two signs being very slight. But the preceding "sons of" goes with *edubba* "school" and not GA. DUB.BA/ *šadubba,* which signified a high administrative official, cf. B. Landsberger, JCS 9 (155), p. 125, n. 22. And this point is clinched here by the appended *ummēnū* "men of skill."

[20] DUMU.MES *é-dub-bi,* Iraq 7, Nos. 971, 978, 990, 996; DUMU.MES *um-me-ni,* Nos. 920, 988, 989, 995.

[21] A semantic parallel is provided by Akk. *ḫasāsum* "to think," *taḫsistum* "memorandum."

With this demonstration of the special technical force of *pqd/paqādum* we have all that is needed to clear up the one major difficulty of the census texts, one which the respective biblical and cuneiform documents have in common, namely, their cultic connection. For under "the dramatic concept of nature" [22] which is known to us from Mesopotamia and is echoed in the Old Testament, the writing down of names could on certain occasions be a very ominous process. "In the House of Dust . . . [lives] Ereshkigal, Queen of the Nether World. [And Bēlit-]ṣēri, recorder of the Nether World, kneels before her. [She holds a tablet] and reads out to her" (Gilg. VII iv 49-52). Further, "The Anunnaki, the great gods, foregather. Mammetum, maker of fate, with them the fates decrees: Death and life they determine. (But) of death, its days are not revealed" (Gilg. X vi 36-39). Thus, on periodic occasions, the higher powers made lists which determined who among the mortals was to live and who was to die.

Now, the same basic concept confronts us throughout the history of Jewish religious thought. Moses says to God: "Efface me, I pray Thee, from Thy book which Thou hast written," and God replies, "Him only who has sinned against Me will I efface from My book" (Exod. 32:32-33). According to the Mishna *Rosh ha-shana,* the mortals are judged by God on New Year's Day, passing before him in review like *troops* [23] (I 3). The appertaining liturgies carry this thought further. "On New Year's Day they are recorded, and sealed on the Day of Atonement: how many are to pass away and how many to be

[22] Cf. H. and H. A. Frankfort, in *The Intellectual Adventure of Ancient Man* (1946), p. 24.

[23] Reading *bnwmrwn* (*b^{e}nūmrōn*), with Dalman, for the enigmatic traditional *bnēy mārōn* "lambs," cf. P. Fiebig's edition, p. 76.

brought into being, who is to live and who is to die." [24] More relevant still is a passage from another old Jewish poem which refers to the same occasion: "On it are the creatures recorded (*yippāqēdū*), to assign them to life or to death." [25] We have here the technical verb *pqd* itself, in its special idiomatic sense, which tradition had somehow managed to hand down although the correct meaning of the corresponding biblical occurrences had long been lost.

To be sure, these are views relating especially to the New Year. But there are no compelling grounds for assuming that such ideas were always restricted to that one juncture. The two Gilgamesh passages, for instance, which were cited above, lack any reference to the cultic calendar. There must thus have been a time when the ancient Near Easterner shrank from the thought of having his name recorded in lists that might be put to unpredictable uses. Military conscription was an ominous process because it might place the life of the enrolled in jeopardy. The connection with the cosmic "books" of life and death must have been much too close for one's peace of mind. It would be natural in these circumstances to propitiate the unknown powers, or seek expiation as a general precaution. In due time, such a process would be normalized as a *tēbibtum* in Mesopotamia, and as a form of *kippūrīm* among the Israelites.

It should be borne in mind in this connection that the census reflected at Mari and Chagar Bazar on the one hand, and in the Old Testament on the other, is not just a routine mustering process. In both instances it is linked to new land grants and relatively recent political

[24] In the prayer *Unᵉtanne toqef,* see *ibid.*, p. 67.
[25] *Ibid.*, p. 55.

structures. This may well be the reason why we hear nothing about such an institution elsewhere in Mesopotamia, or find no narrative account of it in the Bible after the time of David. Moreover, the "Amorite" states of Mesopotamia had many traditions and practices of their own. At any rate, the fear of enrollment was still so great there in Old Babylonian times that the census took its name from the incidental process of ritual "purification." And such fears would be kept alive by plagues, which must have decimated crowded camps more than once. With the passing centuries, however, society becomes resigned to the inevitable. Unwelcome as the census was in biblical times, it no longer called for a euphemistic designation. To be "called to account" was still something ominous, but not necessarily in a religious sense. The sole survival of older and more awesome concepts was the *kofer,* but by then this had taken the form of a routine monetary payment in the amount of a half of a shekel. Such incidents as the one recorded in II Samuel 24 were manifestly exceptional.

The Mari material has opened up many new vistas. Not a few of the disclosures have an important bearing on the Bible; and the Bible, in turn, may be in a position to reciprocate. When such a comparative treatment is justified, one has the opportunity of dealing, beyond mere words or texts, with the very roots of an integral civilization.

[*Addendum.* Since this was written, statements on the subject have appeared in CAD, 4 and von Soden's AHw, under *ebēbu(m)*, without the opportunity in either instance to take note of the above results. Neither dictionary makes sufficient allowance for the essential difference between the ordinary Old Babylonian uses of *tēbibtum* and the specialized Mari usage, which is echoed in turn in the Biblical sources. Yet a fresh re-examination of the pertinent evidence has only served to underscore the special circumstances as reflected at Mari and Chagar Bazar.

On the other hand, the hitherto customary interpretation of "*dawidûm*" (p. 18) is no longer tenable. As shown by Landsberger and Tadmor (JNES 17, 130), the term is to be read *dawdūm* and interpreted as "defeat"; cf. CAD 3, 14 ff., and AHw 148.]

The Biblical Idea of History in its Common Near Eastern Setting*

AMONG THE MANY CELEBRATED DOCUMENTS FROM MARI, there is a letter containing this invaluable observation: 'No king is powerful on his own. Ten or fifteen kings follow Hammurabi of Babylon. A like number may follow Rim-Sin of Larsa, Ibalpiel of Eshnunna, or Amutpiel of Qaṭanum. There are perhaps twenty who follow Yarim-lim of Yamḫad.' [1] This incidental comment, addressed by Itur-Asdu, governor of Nahor, to King Zimrilim of Mari, is a sage bit of historical wisdom. It shows a keen awareness of the composite sources of authority and is fully alive to the checks and balances of international relations. We have here, furthermore, an unexpected attempt to reach out beyond the specific detail to broader general principles. To our surprise we find that people of that period were not always just so many unreflecting pawns caught in the web of history. Some of them, at any rate, could stand back and appraise impersonally the

* This paper was read at the Second World Congress of Jewish Studies, held in Jerusalem in 1957.

[1] See G. Dossin: Les archives épistolaires du palais de Mari, *Syria,* 19, 1938, p. 117.

historical process. But it is the date of the message that makes it so remarkable. The link with the city of Nahor in the region of Harran and the direct reference to Hammurabi of Babylon point unmistakably to the Patriarchal Age. In short, the generation of Abraham, even the very district where his family was settled, could not have been strangers to the concept of history.

The Bible is first and foremost a unique distillation of history. Now no process of this kind and magnitude can unfold in a vacuum. The people of the Bible, who were to make history in more ways than one, were neither politically nor culturally isolated from other societies. Like the kings mentioned by the governor of Nahor, they did not stand alone. They were an integral part of a larger pattern. Hence the ultimate achievement that is the Bible cannot be properly understood, still less appreciated, except in terms of the setting in which this work originated, and of the initial values which it went on to transfigure and transcend.

As a work that bears on history, the Bible embodies a variety of incidental detail. Its central issues, however, are the larger questions of life and destiny. In other words, the Bible is not so much a chronicle of events worth recording, or thought to be worth recording, as an interpretation of significant happenings. Thus it is essentially a philosophy of history. Now any historiosophy, by definition, presupposes an advanced intellectual and spiritual background. It requires the backdrop of a major civilization. The ancient Near East was the home of two independent historic civilizations, one of which flourished in Mesopotamia and the other in Egypt. Accordingly, the biblical idea of history has to be viewed in the context of the native historiosophies of Egypt and

Mesopotamia. But before this can be done, it will be necessary to restate for purposes of ready reference the salient characteristics of these two dominant civilizations of the region.

All advanced societies must come to grips with two issues above all. One is the relation of the individual to society. The other is the relation of both individual and society to nature and the universe. The former is reflected in law and government. The latter finds expression in religion. The essence of a given civilization will be determined in the main by its distinctive answer to these two basic questions. The most pressing political and economic problems of the day are secondary and ephemeral in comparison.[2]

The two issues just mentioned are, in turn, interdependent. Yet they are seldom in true equilibrium. It is this that makes for the immemorial rivalry between church and state. As we go back in time, moreover, our scientific horizons shrink progressively. There may still be a measure of truth in the saying that just as mythology is the science of the past, science is the mythology of the future. The fact remains, nevertheless, that mythology

[2] Cf. my remarks in *Mid-East: World Center* (Science of Culture Series, ed. Ruth Nanda Anshen, 7). New York, 1956, p. 35. The following remarks on Mesopotamia contain a summary of various themes which I have had occasion to develop in the following publications: (a) Some Sources of Intellectual and Social Progress in the Ancient Near East, *Studies in the History of Culture* (W. G. Leland Volume), Menasha, Wisconsin, 1942, pp. 51–62; [cf. below, pp. 517 ff.] (b) The Ancient Near East and Modern Philosophies of History, *Proceedings of the American Philosophical Society,* 95, 1951, pp. 583–588; (c) Early Law and Civilization, *The Canadian Bar Review,* 31, 1953, pp. 863–877; [cf. below, pp. 534 ff.] (d) Authority and Law in Mesopotamia, *Journ. American Oriental Society,* Suppl. No. 17, 1954, pp. 8–15; [cf. below, pp. 313–323] and especially (e) Ancient Mesopotamia, in R. C. Dentan, ed.: *The Idea of History in The Ancient Near East* (American Oriental Series, 38), New Haven, 1955, pp. 35–76 [cf. below, pp. 270 ff.], and the literature cited in all these publications. The present summary was thought desirable for purposes of minimal background.

—or what we would today call mythology—had a vastly greater effect on ancient society than theology has on modern life. Hence religion in general was the overriding factor in the older civilizations and a powerful influence on law and government. And because the religious solution of Mesopotamia differed radically from that of Egypt, the two respective societies were sharply at variance with each other, far more than is commonly realized.

The outstanding single feature of the cosmos of the ancient Mesopotamians was the tenet that no single god is the ultimate source of power and authority; none is truly omnipotent. All the leading figures of the Mesopotamian pantheon had themselves been created. Final authority resided in the community of the gods as a body. Only the assembly of the gods had the power to choose the head of the pantheon, as in the case of Marduk, or to bestow immortality on a human being, as was the case with Utnapishtim. This restriction served as an important buffer against absolutism, but it also made for uncertainty and insecurity, in heaven no less than on earth. The destiny of the universe had to be decided afresh each year. Nothing was settled for all time, nothing could be taken for granted.

Another fundamental tenet of the world-view of the Mesopotamians was that human society was an exact replica of the society of the gods, with the temple tower, or *ziggurrat,* constituting a tangible link between heaven and earth. No mortal ruler, therefore, could lay claim to absolute authority, inasmuch as that privilege was withheld even from the highest god. The authority of the ruler was thus doubly restricted. On the one hand, his mandate stemmed from the gods, to whom he was accountable for his every action. And on the other hand, the king was subject to the will of the assembly of his elders, just as the head of the pantheon was bound by the wishes of his celestial assembly.

These twin checks on the power of the mortal ruler —one cosmic and the other societal—had a direct effect on the Mesopotamian concept of state. In these circumstances, the state could evolve into nothing but a kind of democracy.[3] For government by assembly and the circumscribed authority of the king could scarcely add up to anything else. The main beneficiary was the individual, whose rights were protected by the law—more specifically the cosmic, unalterable, and impersonal law called *kittum*,[4] an approximate synonym of Hebrew *'ᵉmeth*. The ruler was ever the humble servant of the *kittum*, never its master. The presence of writing was a further safeguard against abuses or distortions on the part of the king. Written compilations of laws are now known to go back to the third millennium. The deeply entrenched legal tradition of the land is reflected, moreover, in the hundreds of thousands of documents about the practice of law which have been dug up in Mesopotamia proper. The law becomes a powerful magnet that draws other areas into the orbit of the expanding Mesopotamian civilization—Elam and Anatolia, the Hurrians and the Hittites, Alalakh and Ugarit. In all these instances the Akkadian language remains the internationally accepted legal medium and goes on to serve as a vehicle for cultural fertilization in other fields. This dynamic legal tradition was to be reflected in part long after the parent civilization had been supplanted, notably in the very

[3] Cf. Th. Jacobsen: Primitive Democracy in Ancient Mesopotamia, *JNES*, 2, 1943, pp. 159–172.

[4] Speiser, *op. cit.* (supra, n. 2d), pp. 12–13 [below, pp. 319–321].

name of the Babylonian Talmud and in the several legal schools of Islam which flourished on Mesopotamian soil.

In the light of all this, there is no need to refute the all too common assumption that Mesopotamia subscribed to the concept of a divine king. This view is based on superficial evidence lifted out of its proper context. Deification of rulers in Mesopotamia was never a consistent, widespread, or thoroughgoing practice; it was rather a sporadic and surface manifestation devoid of any lasting influence. Hammurabi was never guilty of this practice, nor was any of the long line of Assyrian kings, even at a time when their authority extended over Egypt. The very idea of a divine ruler was incompatible with the fundamental tenets and spirits of Mesopotamian civilization.[5]

All in all, Mesopotamia's solution of the ubiquitous societal problem proved to be enormously successful and productive. The same cannot be said of her concurrent religious solution. Since nothing in the cosmos was permanent and secure, there could be no values that were truly enduring. The celestial regime was unpredictable and capricious. The gods had to be forever propitiated if a favourable decision was to be obtained from them at all. This called for constant watchfulness and increasingly elaborate ritual. The cosmos, in short, lacked a true basis for an ethical approach to life. Form rather than content promised the best protection against the whims of heaven. In terms of a philosophy of history, the past was desperately important to be sure, but only as a check against

[5] For the subject in general, cf. R. Labat: *Le caractère religieux de la royauté assyro-babylonienne.* Paris, 1939; H. Frankfort: *Kingship and the Gods.* Chicago, 1948; C. J. Gadd: *Ideas of Divine Rule in the Ancient East.* London, 1948; Speiser, *op. cit.* (supra, n. 2e), pp. 63–64 [below, pp. 300–301].

the recurrence of previous disasters. It was not a positive factor in the understanding of the present or a more confident facing of the future. In the end, this emphasis on outward forms became a barrier to inward progress. The collapse of Nineveh and of Babylon was due not so much to the superiority of outside powers as to the crushing weight of the internal structure.[6] By that time, however, the civilization of Mesopotamia had long outgrown its earlier ethnic, linguistic, and political boundaries.

The Egyptian way was in its essential religious aspects the direct opposite of the Mesopotamian. The cosmos of the Egyptians was the outcome of a single creative process. The demiurge continued his absolute rule on earth through a king in whom the creator was perpetually incarnate. The king was thus himself a god whose world was as stable as the rhythm of the Nile. Because the land was ruled by a divine mediator, the alignment of society with nature was perfect and complete. In this static cosmos, unveiled once and for all in serene splendour, there could be no question about the wishes of heaven. Neither was there any room for the kind of impersonal law that the Mesopotamian had in his *kittum*. The pharaoh could never be the servant of any law; he could be only its source and master. In the words of John A. Wilson,

> He, as a god, *was* the state . . . To be sure, it was necessary for a new state to have rules and regulations for administrative procedures and precedent, but our negative evidence suggests that there was no codification of law, impersonally conceived and referable by magistrates without consideration of the crown. Rather, the customary law of the land was conceived to be the word of the pharaoh . . . The authority of codified law would have competed with the personal authority of the pharaoh.[7]

[6] *Ibid*, pp. 72–73 [below, pp. 311–312].
[7] *The Burden of Egypt*. Chicago, 1951, pp. 49–50.

How does this particular blend of religion and government influence the Egyptian idea of history? On this point one cannot do better than quote a statement from the pen of H. Frankfort:

> . . . the Egyptians had very little sense of history or of past and future. For they conceived their world as essentially static and unchanging. It had gone forth complete from the hands of the Creator. Historical incidents were, consequently, no more than superficial disturbances of the established order, or recurring events of never-changing significance. The past and the future—far from being a matter of concern—were wholly implicit in the present . . . the divinity of animals and kings, the pyramids, mummifications—as well as several other and seemingly unrelated features of Egyptian civilization—its moral maxims, the forms peculiar to poetry and prose—can all be understood as a result of a basic conviction that only the changeless is truly significant.[8]

The deep, indeed the unbridgeable, chasm between the civilizations of Egypt and Mesopotamia—the one with its static and the other with its dynamic worldview—should now be fully apparent. The two existed side by side over a longer period than the whole of the present era. In fact, their interrelations go back to prehistoric times. Material interchanges between them were unavoidable, and important intellectual achievements could not escape diffusion. Nevertheless, the widely-held view of the essential similarity of these two great centres of civilization proves to be a modern myth. Socially and spiritually they differed fundamentally. And their disparity was decisive, since it outweighed their similarities.

It would thus seem that our current practice of classifying civilizations according to their material forms fails to stand the test of subsurface probing. For that matter,

[8] *The Birth of Civilization in the Near East.* London, 1951, pp. 20–21.

even our methods of evaluating material remains may need refining where such products are but the symptoms of underlying spiritual conditions. The mere listing of outward differences may not be sufficient to reflect adequately the inner contrasts. Thus the architectural singularity of the Mesopotamian *ziggurrat* as compared with the Egyptian pyramid does not begin to suggest the depth of the conceptual break between the two. The *ziggurrat* embodied the aspiration of the Mesopotamians to forge a living bond between heaven and earth, between the abode of immortals and the world of mortals. The pyramid, on the other hand, was a monumental tribute —impressive but jejune—to a dead king. The one tells of hope; the other of resignation. Small wonder, then, that the Mesopotamian way was to survive, in countless transpositions, long after the physical collapse of the parent states. The Egyptian way lacked any comparable means of survival. Consequently, Mesopotamia has left firmer links with the modern West, in spite of the intervening distance of space and time, than she ever shared with contemporary Egypt, her partner in the limelight of history over a period of several millennia. And the dominant factor in these relations was the underlying concept of society and the place of the individual in it. Egypt and Mesopotamia were as mutually incompatible as totalitarianism and democracy—and for precisely the same reasons.

The biblical idea of history must be similarly viewed against a background of ideas of the universe and society —of God, man, and the state. These ideas, in turn, have to be judged in terms of their general Near Eastern setting, since the world of the Bible was an integral part of the ancient Near East. The question, then, narrows down at the outset to this: How does the biblical ideal compare with the mutually contrasted ways of Egypt and Mesopotamia? For the setting is automatically circumscribed by the two dominant civilizations of the region. And when it comes to substance, the Bible is both a primary and a unique source on the subject of the idea of history, for the book as a unit is essentially a work of history. All the other aspects of the Scriptures are subordinated to this central theme.

The truth of this last statement must surely be self-evident. The Pentateuch deals with primeval history, the times of the patriarchs, and the gradual incubation of national consciousness among a people unused to independence. There follow accounts of the conquest, the settlement, and the monarchies. Several of the later books concentrate on post-Exilic history. But the prophetic books, too, are by no means oblivious of the historical process: they are invaluable commentaries on current political and military events. Thus the only portions of the Bible that do not address themselves to history in one way or another are the Psalms, the three wisdom books —Proverbs, Job, Ecclesiastes—and the Song of Solomon. Yet the very fact that these books were included in the canon, and the further fact that certain non-historical matter was introduced into the other books, should help to remind us that the Bible as a whole, although conceived as history, was meant to be history of a very special kind.

For the Scriptures were never intended to be a mere chronicle of events, a story of certain states, or even the biography of a nation. The reader who is interested in such things is told time and again where he can find them: in the *Book of the Wars of the Lord,*[9] the *Book of Jasher,*[10] the *Chronicles of the Kings of Israel,*[11] the *Chronicles of the Kings of Judah.*[12] The aim of the biblical authors was of a wholly different order. Their purpose was not so much to tell the story of a nation or of nations, as to give the history of a society embarked on a particular quest, the quest for an enduring way of life, a way of life that had universal validity.

This inspired objective is implicit both in the tone and in the content of the biblical narratives; and it was honoured and implemented by the successive compilers—perceptive, faithful, and anonymous—to whom we owe the composition of most of the individual works, and by the later sages to whom we are indebted for the final canon. The story of such a society cannot be told in terms of action and events alone. It has to be woven into an intricate fabric and enriched with a variety of pertinent detail: the laws which provide the framework that holds the community together; the religious beliefs and practices; the hymns and the secular poems, the songs gay and sad, the homely maxims, the affirmations and the doubts. This is how the non-historical sections and books came to be included. But at no time did the compilers lose sight of the basic truth that what was thus being put together was the composite record of a profound experience of mankind, perhaps the most profound of all if we are to judge from the influence of the Bible on subsequent generations. The Bible, in short, is basically a work of history, and more especially a work of histo-

[9] Num. xxi, 14.
[10] Joshua x, 13.
[11] 1 Kings xiv, 19.
[12] 2 Kings xxiii, 28.

riosophy. And while the history with which it deals is necessarily limited in time and space and action, its ultimate significance is ageless and universal.

Now at what point in the course of the growth of the Scriptures did the conviction gain hold that this was a subject matter of extraordinary importance, inspired and sacred? The final canon afirms this conviction for the Bible as a whole. The emergence of the Pentateuchal canon carries back the same belief, as applied to a portion of the Bible, several centuries earlier. The reception accorded the book of *torah* that was recovered under Josiah is proof that the concept of canonicity was already known in pre-Exilic days. And the references to the *Book of the Wars of the Lord* and the *Book of Jasher* suggest by their implied distinction between special and routine writings that works of the non-secular kind were earlier still and were immediately recognized as being out of the ordinary.

What is, then, the earliest feasible date for the emergence of a canon—no doubt in oral form at first—which was eventually to develop into the Scriptures? As yet we have no sure means of arriving at a definite and absolute answer to that question. But this much can be asserted even now: the date must be earlier than is commonly supposed. It has to be put ahead of the earliest narrative portions of the Pentateuch, quite probably before the time of Moses, indeed close to the age of the patriarchs. I realize that such an assertion is certain to provoke objections from many quarters. It is my duty, therefore, to develop the theme, and to justify and defend my position. Before this is done, however, we must turn once again to the subject of the biblical idea of history as seen in its general Near Eastern setting.

It is abundantly clear today that, of the two major

centres of civilization in the area, it was distant Mesopotamia and not neighbouring Egypt that left the deeper cultural impress upon Israel. This was to be expected. For in the first place, the patriarchs had their roots in the land across the Euphrates and they continued to maintain ties with their original home. And in the second place, the Egyptian way was static and isolationist, whereas the Mesopotamian way was dynamic and expansive—naturally suited to reach out to other lands, Israel included.

These theoretical premises are borne out by concrete evidence. The biblical concept of state can be described as 'democratic' with at least as much justice as the Mesopotamian form of government. It is the 'people' (i.e. *demos*) of Israel who have a decisive say as to how and by whom they are to be ruled; it is they who set up their kings time and again. The leaders of Israel are invariably presented as mortal and fallible. Even a Moses could be guilty of faults all too human, faults that were to keep him from setting foot in the Promised Land. All this is a very far cry from the Egyptian image of a divine king. To be sure, an analogous belief in divine rulers is still occasionally ascribed to the Bible.[13] However, in our present state of considerably increased knowledge of these matters, such allegations amount to little more than an academic anachronism, utterly irreconcilable with attested biblical theory and practice.

The independent evidence of the law, moreover, serves to emphasize the fact that in the wide area of cultural correspondence between Mesopotamia and Israel, we are

[13] See M. Noth: Gott, König, Volk im Alten Testament, *Zeitschrift für Theologie und Kirche*, 47, 1950, pp. 157–191 (=*Gesammelte Studien zum Alten Testament*. München, 1957, pp. 188–229).

likely to be confronted with cases of actual kinship as opposed to mere coincidence. In both societies the law was impersonal and supreme; the king was its servant and not its source and master. Furthermore, the respective legal disciplines are closely linked in spirit and in content, notwithstanding numerous differences in detail. And because many of the features that are common to both lands can now be traced back to the very beginnings of Mesopotamian civilization, Israel has to be regarded in this respect as the cultural descendant of Mesopotamia. Israel and Mesopotamia were jointly separated from Egypt by a conceptual curtain that could and did prove to be more difficult to penetrate than the most formidable physical barriers.

Such then is the general cultural background against which the biblical narrative depicts the dawn of Israel's history by recounting the story of the patriarchs. It is a story told in terms of its leading characters. As such it is an undisputed literary masterpiece. But is it history? Certainly not in the conventional sense of the term. Yet it cannot be set down as fancy. The author [14] retells events in his own inimitable way: he does not invent them. What is thus committed to writing is tradition, in the reverent care of a literary genius. Where that tradition can be independently checked, it proves to be authentic. This much has been evident for some time in respect of a number of incidental details. It now turns out that the main framework of the patriarchal account has also been accurately presented.

[14] I use here such terms as 'author' or 'narrator' in the singular throughout, without implying thereby that there was but one narrative source in the Pentateuch. For purposes of the present discussion it is entirely immaterial to what document a given passage may be assigned. The basic attitude to the subject matter is the same in each instance. The nicer distinctions in regard to numerous details do not affect the major theme under discussion.

The very opening of that account records God's command to Abraham to leave his birthplace in Mesopotamia and journey to another land on a spiritual mission which will be gradually disclosed. There have been those who would dismiss this episode as a pious invention by the author, or as a decorative literary form. We now know, however, that wilful devices were not within the writer's scope—a point that will be presently developed more fully. To the narrator, at least, this particular command was a genuine experience on the part of Abraham. As such, it was to be honoured by a long line of later writers, all of whom saw in God's covenant with Abraham the very cornerstone of the spiritual history of Israel. Small wonder, therefore, that this covenant is made into one of the two dominant notes which the Bible uses as a recurrent refrain.

Now the country that Abraham was thus bidden to leave had achieved, as we indicated earlier, enormous social gains along side an ever-growing spiritual deficit. The societal system of Mesopotamia was to spread in course of time to other lands, Israel included. But the concurrent spiritual solution lacked the same broad appeal. Israel, for one, would have none of it. Can it, then, be pure coincidence that Abraham's departure from his homeland is attributed by tradition to a need for a healthier religious climate? The stated reasons for this departure correspond so closely with the facts of the local religious life as to make fortuitous agreement in this instance highly improbable. Were Abraham, or tradition, or the literary executor of the patriarchal traditions to have improvised an excuse for the fateful journey to the Promised Land, none of them could have dreamed up a motive more closely in consonance with the actual state of affairs.

Arrival in Canaan brings the patriarchs within the orbit of Egypt and into contact with the Egyptian world-view. But if the Mesopotamian way, in spite of its congenial societal features, was to Israel's forefathers sufficient grounds for departure, the Egyptian way could be little short of abomination. Exposure to Egypt was bound to lead to oppression, spiritually as much as socially. The exodus from Egypt was accordingly much more than just a physical undertaking. It was more truly and profoundly an act of liberation from intolerable spiritual bondage. Indeed, the Hebrew verb employed in this connection (*yṣ'*) means both 'to leave' and 'to go free.' The term 'exodus' stresses unduly the less significant aspect of that event. The real emphasis belongs instead to 'liberation,' and more particularly to spiritual liberation; for we are told again and again that it was God who freed the Israelites from the bondage of Egypt for the express purpose of making them His own people.[15] This then is the aspect with which the Bible is principally concerned. Hence the remembrance of the Egyptian experience becomes the other dominant note in all biblical history, a note that is echoed through all the portions of the Scriptures and made into a recurrent refrain together with the covenant between God and Abraham. Only an indelible spiritual experience could sink so deep into the national consciousness.

Thus covenant and liberation, the two focal points of the biblical idea of history, link up unerringly with the two respective centres of civilization which for more than half of all recorded history set the tone for the Near East as a whole. The covenant adverts to Mesopotamia, the liberation to Egypt. Each reflects unalterable opposition

[15] Exod. vi, 7; Jer. xi, 4; xxx, 22; etc.

to the spiritual values at which one or the other of the dominant civilizations had arrived. All the other aspects of biblical historiosophy—its evolution and its pioneering insights, its literary expression and the characteristics of the various writers who left us these accounts—are secondary questions by comparison. The migration from Mesopotamia and the rejection of Egypt are basic to all that is to follow; they add up jointly to mankind's first declaration of spiritual independence, the resolute proclamation of a new and different faith.

We come, lastly, to what is perhaps the keynote of this essay: to what period should we trace back the idea that Abraham's migration did not entail a change in the physical environment alone but that it meant also, and far more so, a decisive turn in the spiritual orientation of mankind? It was suggested earlier in this discussion that the emergence of this idea may have to be dated to the age of the patriarchs themselves—that is to a time close to the covenant with Abraham as recorded in the biblical narrative. One could reason, of course, that since the tradition about the covenant agrees so intimately with the pertinent internal conditions in Mesopotamia, its accepted dating should likewise be given credence. But this would be begging the question. Independent support is desirable. Can such support be adduced?

We need not look far for an answer. Vast stretches of the second millenium in the ancient Near East, hitherto hidden from view, have been brilliantly illumined in recent years by the finds from Mari, Nuzi, Alalakh, Boghazköi, Ugarit, and elsewhere; these have shed much incidental light on the dawn of biblical history. The separate episodes in the patriarchal account have thus acquired a new status in terms of antiquity and authenticity of background. The work and purpose of the biblical narrator consequently stand out in bolder relief.

Among the patriarchal narratives which have won, or deserve to win, a new respect as a result of the recent discoveries, there are several of exceptional significance in that they had come to be used for centuries as criteria of Israel's moral and ethical principles. These include the repeated motif of passing off one's wife as a sister (Gen. xii, 10–xiii, 1; xx, 1–8; xxvi, 1–11); the transfer of the blessing from Esau to Jacob (Gen. xxvii); and the removal by Rachel of her father's household gods (Gen. xxxi, 19, 30, 32). Each of these passages lends itself to a moralizing interpretation; each has been handled apologetically by followers and friends, and with indignation or malicious delight by assorted illwishers. Yet all such moral judgments, if indeed they were in order in the past, now prove to be entirely out of place. For the incidents in question turn out to reflect with startling accuracy the customs and usages appropriate to the patriarchal period; they were peculiar to the societies with which the patriarchs maintained relations, and they are—above all—wholly devoid of any ethical implications whatsoever.

The present context will permit only brief comments on the episodes just mentioned as they can now be restored to their proper social setting. The sister-wife motif emerges as a prominent feature of the laws of the Hurrians,[16] a people with whom western Semites are known to have lived in close symbiosis. Similar practices have also been traced to the Hittites.[17] A wife who had at the same time the status, though not necessarily the blood

[16] Cf. P. Koschaker: Fratriarchat, *Zeitschrift für Assyriologie,* 41, 1933, p. 14. [See above, pp. 62–82].

[17] *Ibid.,* pp. 1–13.

ties, of a sister happened to command greater protection and prestige than an ordinary wife. In the matter of birthright, the direct legal consequence was the title to a double and preferential share in the paternal estate. Yet the birthright—again in Hurrian society—did not always go with the eldest son. In given circumstances the incumbent could be designated by the father from among the younger sons. The primacy of such a position was thus a matter of the father's discretion rather than of chronological priority.[18] And finally, the Nuzi texts revealed some thirty years ago that transfer of the father's household gods was a prerequisite in certain cases where property was to pass to a daughter's husband.[19]

In the light of these discoveries, all three biblical stories assume a new and unsuspected significance. The wife-sister act was based on recognized northern practices. The bypassing of an older son in favour of a younger was in harmony with the Hurrian habit which left such matters to the discretion of the father. And Rachel's removal of the household gods has ample basis in Nuzi law: it was to all intents and purposes the act of a resolute young woman who literally took the law into her own hands as a precautionary measure against a greedy father.

Why is it, then, that the examples just cited, each capable of a simple and straightforward explanation, puzzled and misled so many generations of Bible translators and exegetes? With the help of hindsight, the answer becomes clear enough. The full meaning of these

[18] E. A. Speiser: 'I Know not the Day of my Death,' *JBL*, 74, 1955, pp. 252–256 [cf. above, p. 89 ff.]; cf. also: The Hurrian Participation in the Civilizations of Mesopotamia, Syria and Palestine, *Journ. of World Hist.*, 1, 1953, pp. 323–324. [See below, pp. 264–265.]

[19] S. Smith, apud C. J. Gadd: Tablets from Kirkuk, *Revue d'Assyriologie*, 23, 1926, p. 127.

episodes was hidden from Bible interpreters because it had already been lost to the narrator himself; otherwise he would surely have taken the trouble to enlighten his readers just as he did so often elsewhere. Instead, the traditional narrative reflects puzzlement, as in the case of Rachel, or introduces speculation, as in the other instances. That this should be so is not at all surprising. The full significance of each episode depends on specific practices of a particular society remote in time and space from the immediate background of the narrator. Much of the motivation had been lost in transit. Only the bare details had come down intact.

In these circumstances, why were the narratives in question included at all? The manifest fact that the narrator no longer knew the explanation, yet set down the details—details which prove to be authentic reflections of a forgotten civilization—can mean but one thing: his aim was not to question or to reason why, but only to record faithfully what tradition had handed down to him. His task was to retell, not to originate. He might lavish his genius on the form, but not on the substance. To put it differently, the lives of the patriarchs had already become part of an oral canon some time between the period that was being depicted and the date of their earliest written presentation.

Now canon implies sanctity, and sanctity presupposes that extraordinary importance is thus being attached to the object or objects so venerated. The patriarchal narratives must have acquired such a status well before the date of the literary work in which they were incorporated; otherwise the writer would have felt free to recast them in terms of his own time and environment. In other words, the author approached this particular material as part of the living *torah*. In that context *torah* was not 'law'—which never was the primary sense of this term anyway—nor yet teaching and instruction in general. In its canonical sense *torah* stands for the body of teachings which collectively comprise a design for a divinely ordained way of life. Law enters into it only indirectly, in so far as the inner content requires a shell of formal regulations.

It is altogether appropriate, therefore, that the narrative portions which eventually came to be included in the Pentateuch should early have been viewed as integral components to the *torah*, and that they should have been so treated by their writer. By approaching the patriarchal episodes as inviolable, by faithfully reproducing details whose meaning had grown obscure, the narrator bears testimony to the prior canonical, or quasi-canonical, standing of such material. Patriarchal traditions had to be viewed with awe because they reflected and illuminated the divine plan for an enduring way of life, an ideal not envisioned by other societies. The seeds of this concept had been planted far away and long ago. Their subsequent growth is but another way of describing the entire course of biblical history.

That the basic concept had a capacity for growth is abundantly demonstrated as we move from milestone to milestone, from the patriarchs to the prophets, from the prophets to the scribes. The record in which the whole experience has been distilled is the product of a thousand years and of many, many hands. Its insights are composite and cumulative. It reflects many variables. But through it all there runs a single central theme, the theme of a quest for a life worth living and, if need be, worth dying for. And basic to this theme is a single constant which embodies Israel's own solution of the problem of the relation of society to the cosmos. This solution proceeds from the affirmation that a sole and omnipotent master is responsible for all creation. But his ways are just and purposeful. Man's destiny is not foredoomed or preordained, for it is affected largely by man's own conduct and by his readiness to embrace the eternally valid teachings of God's *torah*. By thus being granted a share in influencing its own destiny, by being liberated from the whims of capricious and unpredictable cosmic powers, and by being freed from the authority of mortal rulers with divine pretensions, mankind was launched on a new course of responsibility, dignity and hope.

Once glimpsed and embraced, this ideal could prove to be enormously productive and capable of infinite enrichment. It was so in the historic career of Israel. In its simplest form it was certainly not beyond the reach of the sophisticated society of which the patriarchs were a part. Yet the available records would seem to suggest that Abraham alone had the vision and the determination to make this ideal his goal. Such at least is the meaning of God's covenant with Abraham in the light of the cultural history of his age.[20] As an earlier generation used to say of Moses—if Abraham did not exist in reality he would have to be reconstructed in theory. This might appear to

[20] The machinery of covenant is already in full swing in Mari, especially among the west-Semitic tribes; and west-Semitic terms are used to describe it. On the other hand, the Hebrew word for 'covenant' (*b^erît*) may ultimately be Akkadian; cf. M. Noth, Das alttestamentliche Bundschliessen im Lichte eines Mari-Textes, *Annuaire de l'Institut de Philologie et d'Histoire Orientales et Slaves,* 13 (Mélanges Isidore Lévy), 1955, pp. 433–444 (=*Ges. Studien,* supra, n. 13, pp. 142–154).

oversimplify the whole issue. Yet the most intricate problems can often be reduced to deceptively simple fundamentals.

Thus the covenant with Abraham is the biblical answer to the religious solution evolved by the civilization of Mesopotamia, a civilization with which the biblical way was otherwise in essential harmony. But as a new design for living, a new faith of limitless scope, the ideal that the patriarchs had embraced was destined to be put to its severest test in the other major centre of Near Eastern and ancient-world civilization. The Bible proclaims and the results confirm the fact that the patriarch's original ideal proved sturdy enough to withstand the temptation of the fleshpots of Egypt and the Pharaoh's political and military might. The Egyptian way was rejected as a horror and an abomination. Abraham and Moses became the spiritual fathers of the biblical experience, and the covenant and the liberation emerged as its enduring historic cornerstones.

The pursuit of such an ideal, however, demands unflagging devotion and dedication. Such a spirit of sacrifice and self-denial cannot long be sustained unless it has become deeply ingrained in the sponsoring society. We thus come back to our earlier assertion that the canonical tradition among the people of the Book must be older than the age of the Pentateuchal writers, older indeed than the time of Moses himself. The foregoing discussion has advanced the argument that certain significant elements in that tradition have to be traced back to the period of the patriarchs. If this were not so, the patriarchal narratives could not have been recorded with such startling accuracy, although the writers lacked full knowledge of their social implications. If this were not so, the tradition of God's covenant with Abraham would not have been one of the two principal refrains in all the Scriptures. And if this were not so, the historic experience of Israel could not have become a decisive experience of mankind. Indeed, if it were otherwise, there could never have been the unique phenomenon of Israel.

ANCIENT NEAR EASTERN HISTORY AND CULTURE

The Sumerian Problem Reviewed

THE SUMERIANS PLAYED A DECISIVE PART IN THE FORMATION and development of the historic civilization of Mesopotamia. Their tangible influence on the region's law and society, religion and literature, and its arts and sciences persisted well into the Hellenistic age, although the last Sumerian state had become but a dim memory as early as the days of Hammurabi. Moreover, the introduction of writing by the Sumerians ushered in the recorded history of mankind as a whole. Lastly, the vitality of the composite Sumero-Akkadian civilization is attested not only by its spread in antiquity beyond the confines of Mesopotamia, but also by its tenaciousness in the later Near East and its sundry survivals in the West, down to our own times. The Sumerians, in short, may be said to have made history in more ways than one.[1]

The problem of Sumerian origins is thus of more than strictly local and temporary interest. It is rather a question concerning a pioneering element in the evolution of civilization in general. But because history proper was made possible by the Sumerians, and because Sume-

[1] Cf. *Studies in the History of Culture* (in honor of Waldo G. Leland). 1942, pp 55 ff.; Attention may be called also to the general summary in my *The United States and the Near East* (1947, 1950), 28 ff.

rian beginnings go back of necessity to prehistoric times, the problem of these beginnings in prehistory cannot be solved by the direct evidence of historic data alone. We have to fall back for much of our material on the circumstantial testimony of inarticulate sources. The pertinent material is diversified, unwieldy, and often inconclusive. Some of the basic details are still missing and quite possibly may never be recovered. Any proposed reconstruction of the underlying pattern will be subject, therefore, to the customary test of a working hypothesis: how comprehensive and efficient is the suggested solution?

The whole problem of Sumerian origins is of relatively recent date. In the days when the First Dynasty of Ur was still thought to be legendary—a scarce thirty years ago—Sumerians and Semites were generally regarded as the only significant factors in the early history and prehistory of Lower Mesopotamia. Furthermore, since Sumerian records antedated Akkadian sources, this precedence was usually viewed as an index of absolute origins. With the rapid progress, however, of achaeological investigations in the nineteen-twenties there came a corresponding broadening of horizons and deepening of insight. Early literary documents could be coordinated for the first time with carefully analyzed stratigraphic evidence, thus leading to a proper appreciation of the great depth and complexity of the antecedent preliterate occupations. And as additional cultures came to light, each with its own peculiar geographic and chronological features, the larger issue of origins and interrelations could no longer be restricted to Sumerians and Semites.[2]

[2] For an important sidelight on this question see Th. Jacobsen, "The Assumed Conflict Between Sumerians and Semites in Early Mesopotamian History," *JAOS* 59 (1939), 485 ff.

Accordingly, Sumerian beginnings emerged as a complex and many-sided problem.

Within the past twenty years the proposed interpretations of this problem have followed one of two main lines of approach: (a) The Sumerians were not the first in the land, having arrived in Lower Mesopotamia after the foundation of its earliest culture, but before the start of the first historic age. (b) The Sumerians were themselves the founders of the earliest prehistoric culture of Lower Mesopotamia—historic Sumer—and were hence the authors of the so-called el-Obeid stage. The first of these theories has been traced back at times to my *Mesopotamian Origins* (1930).[3] While this ascription is not strictly correct,[4] it is true that when my formulation was attempted it was possible to make far more extensive use of the combined archaeologic-epigraphic evidence than had been the case previously, so that a fuller and broader analysis could hardly be avoided. On the other hand, the alternative view of absolute Sumerian priority has been sponsored consistently by Professor Henri Frankfort, who first expressed it with all his usual persuasiveness and penetration in a monograph entitled *Archaeology and the Sumerian Problem* (1932).[5]

Since the appearance of these two studies various writers have indicated preference for the one position or the other. The current division would seem to be in doubt. Seton Lloyd, for instance, writing in 1947, de-

[3] Abbreviated henceforth as *MO.*

[4] Painted pottery in the south had caused R. C. Thompson to assume a pre-Sumerian ethnic element as early as 1920; cf. *Archaeologia* LXX, 109 ff.; and the non-Sumerian character of the oldest place names was mentioned in passing by B. Meissner, *AfO* V (1929), 8.

[5] *Studies in Ancient Oriental Civilizations,* No. 4 (Chicago Oriental Institute); abbreviated *ASP.*

clared: "In the years which followed, Speiser's conclusion, though not his reasoning, came to be increasingly favoured." [6] But Father R. T. O'Callaghan, writing a few months later (1948), stated: "This stand [referring to the same conclusion] is rejected by most scholars." [7] At least one of these statistical estimates obviously must be wrong. Nor is the truth of the matter of any particular significance. The only pertinent question is whether the total available evidence justifies as yet a definite preference either way. Neither Frankfort's formulation nor mine could be reprinted today without very extensive modifications in detail. Much new material has come to light in the meantime, and older sources have been re-examined in several notable instances. The whole Sumerian problem merits, therefore, a comprehensive review in the form of a brief situation report.

II

The main areas of potential information on the question before us may be analyzed as follows:

1. Linguistically, the structure of Sumerian stands out today with unusual clarity and transparent inner logic, for all that countless minor details remain to be worked out.[8] The literary treasures of the Sumerians are steadily adding to our knowledge and appreciation of mankind's early historic progress. Nevertheless, all efforts to link Sumerian to some larger linguistic stock have failed thus far, although such efforts have ranged all the way from

[6] *Sumer* III, 92.
[7] *Aram Naharaim* (Analecta Orientalia 26), 12, note 1.
[8] The highly advanced status of Sumerian grammatical studies today may be judged from A. Falkenstein's *Grammatik der Sprache Gudeas von Lagaš*, I (Analecta Orientalia 28), 1949.

Central Africa to East Asia and Oceania.[9] This line of inquiry, therefore, promises no direct answer to the question regarding the original home of the Sumerians. The negative results obtained to date can have only an indirect and circumstantial bearing.

2. Anthropometrically, the evidence is ambiguous and confused. The number of crania examined is as yet very small, relatively speaking, especially when the prodigious time span involved is taken into consideration. The consensus would seem to be, with all the necessary reservations, that the basic population of the whole region consisted of Mediterranean longheads, who were joined in course of time and relatively late by several groups of Alpine roundheads.[10] Both these physical types, of course, could have been represented by more than one linguistic stock. In this connection it should be stressed that there is a marked discrepancy between the evidence of the cemeteries uncovered in Sumer and the appearance of the historic Sumerians as depicted on the monuments. For it has been repeatedly observed that the monumental representations of the Sumerians point for the most part to pronounced roundheads.[11]

[9] Cf. V. Christian's *Die sprachliche Stellung des Sumerischen, Babyloniaca* XII, fascs. 3–4 (1943). The author concludes that Sumerian resulted from a mixture of a relatively pure type of Caucasic with an earlier blend of Hamitic and Asiatic-Sudanese (p. 125)—a theory which speaks for itself. Note also Karl Bouda, *Die Beziehungen des Sumerischen zum Baskischen, Westkaukasischen und Tibetischen, MAOG* XII/3 (1938).

[10] Cf. W. M. Krogman's study in H. H. von der Osten's *The Alishar Hüyük* III (1937), pp. 213 ff., especially 269 ff. To the full bibliography which this monograph contains may now be added R. J. Braidwood's "Asiatic Prehistory and the Origin of Man," *JNES* VI (1947), 30 ff., for purposes of broader orientation. Charlotte M. Otten, in her preliminary study of the skeletal material from the Obeid cemetery at Eridu (*Sumer* IV, 1948, 125 ff.), concludes (p. 125): "This is unquestionably a Caucasoid population."

[11] A. Moortgat, *Die Entstehung der sumerischen Hochkultur* (Der Alte Orient 43, 1945), 60.

3. Archaeologically, the evidence has been growing steadily in volume and in complexity. Prior to the first historic age in Mesopotamia we can now distinguish a long succession of distinctive strata which—for Mesopotamia as a whole—add up to some thirty separate occupational levels. These levels fall into several individual cultural units. In the south, which includes Sumer proper, we find, starting with the latest of these protohistoric cultures and, moving back into the past, the following groups: [12] (a) The so-called "Protoliterate," [13] corresponding roughly to what used to be called "Jemdet Nasr." (b) "Uruk" or "Warka." (c) "Obeid" or "Ubaid." Until the recent discoveries at Eridu it was thought that the oldest Obeid levels marked the beginning of stratigraphically attested occupations in Sumer. The discovery, however, of (c') the "Eridu" ware poses a new problem which will be touched upon later.

The above groups have their counterparts in the north which can be correlated chronologically with their respective southern analogues and show in addition a number of important material links. Because of its greater geologic antiquity, however, the north has proved to contain major cultural centers antedating the oldest known from the south. Thus it has yielded multiple levels of (d) the "Halaf" culture which underly the oldest northern analogues of Obeid. Moreover, we have now a series of (e) "Hassunah" deposits anterior to Halaf. Finally, there are abundant witnesses of yet another culture which has come to be known under the name of (e') "Samarra."

[12] For purposes of ready reference, the terminology here followed is that used in Ann Louise Perkins' comprehensive study, *The Comparative Archaeology of Early Mesopotamia* (*Studies in Ancient Oriental Civilization*, No. 25), 1949.

[13] An unsatisfactory designation, to my thinking, in that it really begs the question.

Where its straification and classification have been established beyond all doubt, Samarra has been found to co-exist with the later phases of Hassunah; for instance, at the site of Hassunah itself.[14] For the purpose of the present review it will suffice to note the presence of Samarra and its approximate chronologic place without giving it an independent listing.

How many separate ethnic-cultural groups does this archaeological evidence oblige us to assume? There are enough ties between the Protoliterate stage (a) and the earliest historic Sumerians to warrant our positing of an underlying ethnic link. This would still leave us, however, with five major cultural groups (b-e) before the Protoliterate period, if Mesopotamia as a whole is to be considered, as it properly must be. There is, to be sure, the possibility that more than one ethnic element participated in the evolution of a single distinctive prehistoric culture. Conversely, the same ethnic group may have had a part in the development of more than one culture. Furthermore, the absolute cultural individuality of Eridu and Samarra (c', e') may be open to doubt for one reason or another; this is why neither has been given an independent listing, so as not to prejudge the issue. Nevertheless, it would be extremely hazardous to argue, in the face of the mass of cumulative evidence available to us, that Uruk, Obeid, Halaf, and Hassunah, or any smaller combination of these units, went back ultimately to a single ethnic strain. All our evidence would seem to point to the conclusion that the prehistoric composition of Mesopotamia was as complex ethnically as it was culturally.

[14] Cf. R. J. Braidwood, *JNES* IV (1945), 261. For the characteristics of the cultural stages just listed see the studies of Perkins and Moortgat mentioned above, and add André Parrot, *Archéologie mésopotamienne* (1946).

4. Geographically, the historic Sumerians are first seen concentrated at the head of the Persian Gulf, whence they advance gradually up the Tigris-Euphrates valley. Their script and their cylinder seals are the tracers that enable us to follow the spread of Sumerian civilization, or of sundry elements thereof, to the shores of the Mediterranean and beyond. Yet the Sumerians themselves were never entrenched past the confines of Lower Mesopotamia. This rigid geographic limitation contributes an argument whose significance has all too often been entirely overlooked.

5. Lastly, due weight must be given to the combined linguistic-geographic testimony of the place names. It is certainly very suggestive that nearly all, if not all, of the known oldest cities of Sumer have proved to bear non-Sumerian names. In fact, it was this particular onomastic feature that led me, twenty years ago, to probe more extensively into the whole question of Sumerian origins.[15] Since the very prominence and antiquity of the cities involved pointed to the logical conclusion that non-Sumerian meant in this case pre-Sumerian, the further assumption was in order that we were faced here with a pre-Sumerian linguistic substratum. With this premise as a starting point, the other lines of investigation appeared to yield readily a consistent pattern. The isolated character of Sumerian could be explained by the intrusion of its speakers into an area in which totally different stocks had long been at home. Roundheads arriving from a considerable distance, and hence presumably in relatively small numbers, would not alter drastically the prevailing ratio of longheads. Since the Obeid culture and its analogues occupied vast areas of the ancient Near

[15] *MO*, 26 ff. Cf. also the supplementary remarks in *AJA* 37 (1933), 459 ff., and *JAOS* 59 (1939), Supplement, 17 ff.

East and appeared to be autochthonous in that general neighborhood, the sharp geographic restriction of the Sumerian centers called for a correlation with a culture that was far less extensive than the Obeid. The Uruk culture, or a sub-phase of it, answered these requirements. All in all, the combined evidence of all the major sources of potential information—as they were known and understood at the time—seemed to favor the conclusion that the Sumerians were not the first settlers in Lower Mesopotamia. Their arrival, accordingly, would have to be placed after the Obeid occupation, and hence in the Uruk period.[16]

When Frankfort, nevertheless, came out two years later in favor of Sumerian priority, he did not attempt to refute the opposing argument point by point. The onomastic results could not be ignored, but Frankfort countered with the suggestion that non-Sumerian was not necessarily synonymous in this case with pre-Sumerian. The cities in question might have borne Sumerian names originally, only to have their names changed at some period when the basic population was temporarily overshadowed by heterogeneous ethnic elements.[17] This would imply, however, something like the following sequence of events: The Sumerians establish the Obeid civilization and found the cities which are destined to maintain their importance far into the historic period. A foreign group supplants the Sumerians and renames their major centers. The Sumerians eventually throw off the foreign yoke and recapture their cities—but they retain

[16] The Protoliterate period is too late since it has yielded many typically Sumerian features.

[17] Lest these critical remarks be misunderstood, it may be in order to emphasize that the advantage of hindsight is likely to place earlier opinions in an unfavorable light which they by no means merit. The steadily increasing debt under which Frankfort has placed all students of the ancient Near East is too obvious to require stressing.

the alien place-names, even though it is precisely these very centers that come to symbolize Sumerian culture and political authority. The explanation, in short, is highly improbable.

The heart of Frankfort's thesis, however, is its archaeological argument. It is this part of his presentation that has rightly attracted most serious attention. Frankfort regarded as decisive the existing evidence for cultural continuity from the Obeid period on, as exemplified by recurring points of similarity which link the earliest age with its several successors; most especially in the physical type of the inhabitants, their dress, and their hair styles. These features outweigh, in Frankfort's view, the parallel evidence for discontinuity, best observed in the drastic break in pottery styles which signalizes the end of the Obeid and the beginning of the Uruk stages. In other words, the archaeological side of the Sumerian problem would narrow down to an emphasis on the legato theme in cultural progress by the one side, and on the staccato theme by the other.

Frankfort's thoughtful thesis left admittedly a number of questions unanswered. Among these may be mentioned the following: (a) How definite was the similarity of the material features compared? (b) Was the weight of that argument sufficient to offset the undisputed evidence for a sharp break in continuity which attended the termination of the Obeid period? (c) Most important of all, could a working hypothesis be set up without due regard to the other elements in the dispute, namely: the linguistic isolation of Sumerian; the anthropometric disparity between the typical Sumerians of the monuments and the people in the cemeteries of Sumer; the vast expanse of the Obeid culture as contrasted with the sharply limited spread of the known Sumerians; and the un-Sumerian names of the oldest cities in Sumer? All these were weighty obstacles to a ready acceptance of Frankfort's theory of Sumerian priority. Nevertheless, the opposing view likewise contained enough uncertainties to cause the whole dispute to remain hung up for some time.

III

The first scholar to revive the issue was Benno Landsberger. In a series of three articles, which appeared between 1943 and 1945,[18] Landsberger concentrated on the problem of a pre-Sumerian linguistic substratum to which I had already devoted considerable attention a dozen years earlier. He was able, however, to evoke from his sources an incomparably greater amount of suggestive material than had been the case hitherto. Not only could pre-Sumerian names be isolated, to Landsberger's discernment, from comparable Sumerian elements, but even spoken Sumerian could be shown likewise to follow a similar division. The substratum was thus credited with the basic vocabulary for farming, gardening, brewing, pottery, leather work, and building. To the Sumerians, on the other hand, have been assigned, by the same methodical procedure, the terms involving shipping, cattle feeding, jewelry, sculpture, glyptics, land measurement, writing, education, and law. Sumerian economy and society could thus be demarcated with a considerable show of reason from their earlier counterparts.[19] Sumerian

[18] *Ankara Fakültesi Dergisi:* (a) I (1943), 97–102; (b) II (1944), 431–38; (c) III (1945), 150–59.

[19] Ibid. (b). Landsberger distinguishes in fact two distinct substrata. The full import of these studies, however, cannot be properly evaluated so long as the detailed presentation remains unpublished.

thinking is seen to reflect a neatly ordered synthesis between things celestial and things terrestrial, tangibly symbolized by the ziggurat and the temple at its summit, a visible link between heaven and earth, between nature and society.[20] Landsberger's conclusion is that the Sumerians first appeared at the end of the Obeid period, having arrived by sea from a considerable distance—a conclusion that is thus in detailed and gratifying accord with my earlier assumptions, which were based in large part on entirely different arguments.

Anton Moortgat's monograph, *Die Entstehung der sumerischen Hochkultur* (1945),[21] analyzes the over-all archaeological yield from the several prehistoric periods of Western Asia. He, too, feels obliged to sort out the manifestly Sumerian from the indigenous. As undisputed Sumerian contributions Moortgat names the cycle of the mother goddess and the fertility god, and the ziggurrat surmounted by a temple. In this last-name ascription in particular Moortgat is in full agreement with Landsberger, although each worked with sources not utilized by the other. While admitting the complexity of the problem as a whole, Moortgat is inclined to date the arrival of the Sumerians in the Uruk period, without in any way pressing this conclusion.[22]

S. N. Kramer's approach to the problem of Sumerian origins is strictly unique.[23] He proceeds from a consideration of the Sumerian Heroic Age in the light of other such ages in world literature. The heroic age, he argues, presupposes a superior underlying civilization which had

[20] Ibid. (c).

[21] Cf. above, note 11.

[22] Op. cit., 94. See also the review by A. Falkenstein in *Bibliotheca Orientalis* V (1948), 93 f.

[23] Cf. his "New Light on the Early History of the Ancient Near East," *AJA* 52 (1948), 156 ff.

attracted in course of time a people of primitive culture but endowed with youthful vigor and mobility. The invaders in the present instance were the Sumerians, who gradually gained the upper hand. Their arrival is dated to the period of transition between Obeid and Uruk. The nature of Kramer's argument is such that it can neither be proved nor disproved as a whole, although many of its details are admittedly vulnerable and capable of a clearer correlation with the known archaeological data. It may not be wholly gratuitous, however, to add in this connection that this theory is the product of an intimate student of Sumerian thought and that it has, at a minimum, the merit of a fresh and independent viewpoint.

The highly specialized subject of ancient Mesopotamian numeration may be in a position to shed some incidental light on the problem under discussion. In a recent article on the sexagesimal system Dr. Hildegard Lewy arrived at the conclusion that "the entire development leading from the decimal to the sexagesimal system was an accomplished fact when the Sumerian numerals were named." [24] This would seem to constitute yet another link in the lengthening chain of cumulative evidence which points to substantial cultural progress prior to the arrival of the Sumerians, thus rendering that much less probable the thesis of absolute Sumerian priority.

As against this manyside agreement about the relative lateness of Sumerians in Lower Mesopotamia, there is one contrary recent opinion based on evidence not hitherto adduced. This evidence stems from the latest Iraqi excavations at Eridu. Seton Lloyd's first account on the subject, published in 1947, stressed the discovery of a group of temples from Levels VIII-VI, dated to the Obeid

[24] *JAOS* 69 (1949), 11.

period.[25] Their ground plan agrees with one from Gawra XIII,[26] likewise of Obeid date, and foreshadows the plans of the admittedly Sumerian temples from the Protoliterate period at Warka. This architectural continuity, Lloyd asserted, offsets the existing instances of discontinuity and becomes decisive in confirming Frankfort's thesis that the Sumerians were the founders of the Obeid culture and the first settlers in the land.[27]

However, this sole new prop of the principle of continuity collapsed with the very next campaign at Eridu. For below the Obeid desposits there turned up several layers of an earlier culture, the so-called Eridu phase, which is characterized in particular by a novel ware. It was Lloyd himself who said about the painted ornament on this Eridu ware that it presents "elements reminiscent both of Tell Halaf and of Samarra, although technically the ware does not in the least resemble either." [28] It would be premature to inquire at this early date into the precise relations of the Eridu culture, the oldest yet unearthed in Lower Mesopotamia. One is bound, however, to agree with the discoverers in maintaining the distinctiveness of Eridu as compared with Obeid. It would follow, then, that if the Sumerians were the founders of the Obeid culture, which succeeded Eridu, they can no longer be viewed as the earliest settlers in that area. That more than

[25] *Sumer* III (1947), 91 ff.

[26] Until the second volume of *The Excavations at Tepe Gawra* (by Mr. A. J. Tobler), which went to the printers three years ago, is published, the reader must be referred to my field account in *BASOR* 66 (1937), 2 ff., with the plan on p. 5.

[27] Cf. note 25 above. Lloyd's assertion (ibid. p. 91) that my "contrary theory" was "largely based on philological evidence" would seem to leave the curious impression that theories based on such evidence lack sufficient validity. Besides, a considerable amount of archaeological evidence was utilized by me in that connection.

[28] *Sumer* IV (1948), 125.

one cultural phase preceded the northern counterpart of Obeid, and that there could therefore be no question of Sumerian priority in the north—even if the Sumerian authorship of the Obeid phase be granted for the sake of the argument—has been abundantly clear for a number of years.

IV

The chronologic angle of the Sumerian problem has thus been greatly simplified. Since no one would place the Sumerians in the land prior to Obeid proper, and since that cultural phase is not the first in the south—let alone in the north—the question that remains is whether Sumerian connections can plausibly be demonstrated for Obeid times, instead of being relegated to a later period. Let us first take up Lloyd's argument from architecture: namely, because the Protoliterate temples from Warka are Sumerian, and because they correspond to the Obeid temples from Eridu in ground plan, the Obeid builders were Sumerians. Of fundamental importance in this instance is the fact that the Sumerian ziggurrat, which is present at Warka, is lacking both at Eridu [29] and at Gawra XIII. Moreover, we now have from the Obeid period not one temple plan, but three. There is the one to which Lloyd refers; it represents the round-the-corner, or lateral, type. Then there is the longitudinal type, the so-called *Langraum,* which we find in Gawra XI–XVIII,[30] and which is destined to reassert itself in Gawra XI–VIII, and to become eventually characteristic of Assyria.[31] Lastly, there is the circular, or *tholos,* type, known from Gawra

[29] The ziggurrat on that site belongs to a much later historic period.
[30] *The Smithsonian Report,* 1939, p. 443 and Pl. 7.2.
[31] See V. Müller, *JAOS* 60 (1940), 159.
[32] *The Smithsonian Report,* 1939, p. 443 and Pl. 8.1.

XVII and XX,[32] and from Halaf levels at nearby Arpachiyach. Surely, all three of these types were not Sumerian creations. In these circumstances it would seem to be logical to assume that the Sumerians adopted the design already established in the south, adding the temple tower as their own peculiar contribution. Lloyd's argument, at any rate, is no more cogent than would be some hypothetical assumption that because the mosque of Saint Sophia is Muslim, and because it was built under Justinian, therefore its builders must have been Muslims.

The argument from pottery has always militated against the thesis of Sumerian authorship of the Obeid culture. The painted pottery of the Obeid age is by far its most distinctive product. The succeeding Uruk wares are normally undecorated and otherwise different. Furthermore, if the Sumerians initiated the Obeid culture, they must have occupied at one time all of Mesopotamia, not to mention Iran and much of Baluchistan—in short, the known major centers of Obeid and its analogues. Yet at the beginning of the historic age the Sumerians are isolated in a small area at the head of the Persian Gulf. The regions formerly occupied by the Obeid folk are later inhabited by the demonstrably un-Sumerian Elamites, Lullu, Gutians, and others whose names have not been recorded. Elsewhere we find Semitic settlements and the early Hurrian sites. Amidst all this array of ethnic elements which are to remain familiar throughout the history of Mesopotamia—some of these down to our own times—the Sumerians are indeed a small, isolated, and disparate element. Clearly, it is not to their numbers that they owe their outstanding position in history.

No less indicative than the evidence of pottery is the testimony of the seals. Of the two general types, the stamp seal and the cylinder seal, the first one goes back to the

Halaf period at least,[33] and becomes ubiquitous in Obeid times. In the Protoliterate period the cylinder seal is introduced, to become the herald of the advancing Sumerian civilization. Where that civilization has made a mark, the stamp seal disappears; elsewhere, however, the stamps are retained. But when the syncretized Mesopotamian civilization is at long last brought to a close—late in the first millennium B.C.—the stamp returns from its prolonged retreat. Like the underlying physical type itself, the stamp seal had apparently been too firmly rooted to be driven out for ever by intrusive elements.

As regards the physical type, little store can be set by attempted reproductions prior to the historic age. With all due allowance, however, for the inadequacies of primitive techniques, it is scarcely possible to equate the prevailing squat type of the known Sumerians with the narrow-waisted reproductions of earlier times; yet these reproductions are comparable among themselves, whether we find them in Obeid terracottas, engraved on Gawra stamps, or painted on the pottery from Susa. To go beyond such general characteristics and seek to detect from fragmentary reproductions in clay such minute details as beards and hair styles is unprofitable, to say the least. Parenthetically, we now know from the sculptured remains of the Protoliterate period that bearded and beardless types were common in Mesopotamia on the eve of the historic age,[34] and may be presumed to have played their respective parts long before that. Cultural com-

[33] That is to say, the earliest clearly stratified stamp seals belong to the Halaf age (at Gawra). It is not certain, however, whether the actual introduction of these seals is not to be pushed back sufficiently to allow for the necessary period of evolution.

[34] Cf., e.g., the figures on the alabaster vase from Warka, depicted and discussed by E. Heinrich, *Kleinfunde* (1936), pp. 15–17 and Pls. 2–3; Mrs. E. D. Van Buren, *AfO* XIII, 32 ff.; A. Moortgat, op. cit. 88 ff.; F. Basmachi, *Sumer* III (1947), 118 ff.

plexity may be supposed to reflect a variety of underlying ethnic types; it will produce, at any rate (a diversity of concurrent fashions.

Correlations between cranial types and linguistic stocks can never merit much attention, except perhaps as footnotes to conclusions arrived at independently. At all events, the suggestion may be hazarded that the basic Mediterranean type of the region [35] belonged linguistically to Caucasoid and Semitic stocks. Alpine elements appear to have been intrusive. The Sumerians might well have been included among them. On the assumption that they were intruders among long-established and physically related local groups, the Sumerians would not affect appreciably the existing racial balance. Arrival from a considerable distance, especially if they had come by sea, would suggest relatively small numbers. Although they eventually became dominant—within the narrow confines of their settlement—in the political and social sense, they need not have pervaded all the strata of the population. Beyond the limits of southermost Mesopotamia the Sumerian physical type could scarcely have attained prominence in any case. If the skeletal material from a given Sumerian center of a historic period should show a predominance of longheads, while the sculptured figures from the same site show a majority of shortheads, this would be in entire accord with the assumption of a basic native population ruled by physically dissimilar invaders. Analogously, we should expect a future archaeologist excavating a Syrian site of the mid-twentieth century of our era to find ample evidence of Arab culture and Arabic records. But the skeletal remains would hardly conform to the classic Arab type.

[35] See above, note 10.

To sum up, our present material bearing on the problem of Sumerian origins would appear to add up to this: The Sumerians arrived at the head of the Persian Gulf not earlier than the close of the Obeid period, coincident perhaps with the rise of the Uruk stage, or possibly even as its founders. They had come from the east, probably by sea, although their original home seems to have been in a highland zone. That home has to be sought beyond the Iranian province, for that is already pre-empted by others. It would be futile to speculate now—and the prospects do not seem bright for a more profitable attempt of this kind in the foreseeable future—whether that home was in Transcaucasia, Transcaspia, or somewhere in Farther Asia. The Sumerians came to dominate, but did not drive out, the earlier settlers. They took over many of the cultural gains of the past, while adding and developing significant features of their own. In some way which is beyond our means to determine, but not beyond our ability to appreciate, the resulting blend was to become an important factor in the history of all mankind.

If this sketch is approximately right, the Sumerian problem has been clarified in so far as the relative chronology of that people's appearance is concerned. But the question of the ultimate home of the Sumerians is no nearer a solution than it has ever been.

[On the question as a whole, see now especially the symposium organized by the *IXe Recontre assyriologique Internationale* (Geneva, June 20–23, 1960) and published in *Genava,* VIII (1960), pp. 241–314, under the title "Aspects du contact suméro-akkadien."]

Some Factors in the Collapse of Akkad

THE DYNASTY OF AKKAD, WHICH WAS FOUNDED BY SARGON about 2300 B.C., marked in many ways an epoch in the history of Western Asia.[1] Its political and military achievements were felt from Anatolia to Susa. Its economic enterprise may be inferred from demonstrable relations with the Indus Valley.[2] Even more impressive is the growing body of evidence which testifies to consequent social and cultural changes. All in all, so great was the impact of the rulers of Akkad on the contemporary scene that the two most illustrious of these, Sargon and his grandson Naram-Sin, lived on as favorite literary figures, in neighboring lands as well as in their homeland. Evidence of their deeds and fame has survived not only in Akkadian and Sumerian but also in Elamite, Hurrian, and Hittite.

The blend of story and history which characterizes the extant sources dealing with the Sargonids poses a serious problem for the modern historian. In view of the mythopoeic treatment to which the principals came to be

[1] This is a rough figure, approximately half way between the current high and low dates. For a discussion of Mesopotamian chronology cf. E. Weidner, *AfO,* 15, 85 ff., 98.

[2] For the large number of Indian seals from Ur alone see C. J. Gadd, *Proceedings of the British Academy,* XVIII (1932), 191–210. For the Indian gaming piece from Tepe Gawra note Speiser, *Excavations at Tepe Gawra,* I (1935), 82 and 164. Cf. also, H. Frankfort, "The Indus Civilization and the Near East," in the *Annual Bibliography of Indian Archaeology* for 1932, 1 ff.

subjected, can the fictional accretions be separated from the factual core? Are we able with the means now at our disposal to assess the real strength and extent of the Empire of Akkad? How much credence may one give to the laconic original accounts, and how skeptical should one remain with respect to the data preserved in the secondary literary sources? The historian's dilemma is further complicated by the fact that the traditional material, as opposed to the original accounts, is not consistent in itself. H. G. Gütterbock's searching analysis has made it abundantly clear that the literary tradition about the Sargonids, whether in Sumerian, Akkadian, or Hittite, is dominated by two mutually contradictory motifs.[3] The respective protagonists appear here not only as great heroes, but also—and this is true of Naram-Sin in particular—as ill-fated rulers. How is this discrepancy to be explained?

Güterbock approaches the problem by working back from the known fact of the conquest of Akkad by the people of Gutium. Because Naram-Sin was far better known to later generations than were the succeeding members of that dynasty,[4] tradition transferred to him the onus of the disaster that put an end to the dynasty and ushered in a century or so of rule by the hitherto obscure invaders.[5] Yet this explanation is favored neither by the circumstantial evidence of history[6] nor by the historic allusions in the literary sources. The matter calls for a re-examination, especially since certain new data have

[3] See his "Die historische Tradition und ihre literarische Gestaltung bei Babyloniern und Hethitern," *ZA,* 42 (1934), 1–91, and ibid., 44 (1938), 45–149.

[4] *ZA,* 42, 75 f.

[5] The Sumerian King List puts the duration of the Gutian Dynasty at 91 years and 40 days. Weidner, loc. cit., 98 estimates it at just over a hundred years.

[6] Cf. Th. Jacobsen, *The Sumerian King List* (1939), 117, n. 285, and pp. 204 ff., where a strong case is made out in favor of the view that the last kings of Akkad and the first kings of the Gutium Dynasty were con-

recently come to light. The results can be sketched here only in barest outline.[7]

A few words, first, about the credibility of the original—one might say official—Sargonid accounts. The most convincing kind of support for the claims advanced in these laconic sources comes from the hostile territories involved. Susa has yielded monuments and inscriptions of Sargon and his successors.[8] Manishtushu built a temple and left an inscription in Ashur,[9] and an inscription of his son Naram-Sin has been recovered at Nineveh.[10] Farther west there is the long-known stele of Naram-Sin from Diarbekir.[11] In the light of such independent testimony there can be no reason for doubting Naram-Sin's assertion that he had marched to Talḫadum, in Anatolia.[12]

In these circumstances, moreover, we can no longer maintain a cautiously negative attitude towards the epic of *šar tamḫāri,* or 'King of Battle,' which is witnessed in

---

temporaries. Even the King List testifies to a period of chaos immediately following Naram-Sin's son Sharkalisharri; and the omens, which can constitute a good secondary source of historical evidence (cf. A. Goetze, *JCS,* 1 [1947], 265), know the time of "Who was king, who was not king?" as a historical milestone; cf. E. Weidner, *MAOG,* 4 (1929), 234.

[7] It is these secondary historical sources, which Güterbock himself has done so much to elucidate, that make the reign of Naram-Sin end in disaster; cf. especially *ZA,* 42, 52 ff., and Jacobsen, *King List,* 205. The only question that these sources leave ambiguous is the identity of the opponent responsible for Naram-Sin's downfall. The Weidner Chronicle (*ZA,* 42, 47 ff.) ascribes this deed to the Gutians, thus agreeing in part at least with the King List. But the text CT 13, 44, to which further references are made below, seeks the cause ultimately in the action of the Umman-Manda, with the Gutians included among the victims. Güterbock (*ZA,* 42, 76) inclines to favor in this respect the Weidner Chronicle and its analogues. My preference for the Naram-Sin text represented by CT 13, 44 will be explained below.

[8] Cf. the convenient summary in G. C. Cameron, *History of Early Iran* (1936), 28 ff.

[9] Cf. R. Campbell Thompson in *AAA,* XIX (1932), 105 f., and I. J. Gelb, *Hurrians and Subarians* (1944), 36, n. 100.

[10] For references see Gelb, ibid.

[11] Ibid.

[12] Cf. J. Lewy, *Halil Edhem Volume* (1947), 11 ff. The text (RIU 274) is a Larsa copy of an Akkad original.

fragments from Amarna, Ashur, and Boghazköy.[13] For all its fictional overlay, this record of Sargon's invasion of Anatolia would seem to rest on a substantial foundation of fact. Unexpected support for this view comes from a Louvre text, recently published by Jean Nougayrol, which furnishes an independent poetic version of what was apparently the same campaign.[14] The tablet dates back to Old Babylonian times, but the poem itself may well be earlier. In short, the authenticity of the central theme has been considerably enhanced.[15] As a result, various other literary compositions revolving about the great figures of the Akkad Dynasty have gained much in value as potential sources of historical intelligence.

What is especially in need of a fresh approach is the question of the Akkad collapse. Because the empire which Sargon had built and Naram-Sin had expanded has proved more solid and impressive than was generally supposed, the forces that brought about its downfall must likewise have been greater than was previously assumed. Now there is nothing to indicate that Gutium possessed the requisite power; certainly not if that power was actually applied in the course of Naram-Sin's reign—as is becoming increasingly likely[16]—rather than under the chaotic conditions which marked the waning years of the dynasty. The stay of the Gutians in Southern Mesopotamia left no

[13] Cf. Weidner, *Boghazköi-Studien,* 6 (1922), and Güterbock, *ZA,* 42, 86 ff.

[14] *RA,* 45 (1951), 161 ff. Theme, language, and poor state of the tablet combine to make the text extraordinarily difficult to follow at several points, but its general tenor and many of its details are clear nevertheless. In subject matter we have here a source, or one of the sources, for *šar tamḫāri,* and in form a model for the poem of Tukulti-Ninurta I (cf. E. Ebeling, *MAOG,* XII/2).

[15] The legendary touches that characterize *šar tamḫāri* are not a feature of the present composition, which cuts down to about one half the time span between the Amarna age and the events described. The first literary utilization of the theme must obviously be put still closer to the source.

[16] See above, note 6.

discernible cultural trace. There is no measurable influx of Gutian proper names. Following their expulsion the Gutians appear to revert to the relatively minor tribal role which seems to have been theirs before they had moved into the limelight. That they did play a part in displacing the Sargonids cannot, of course, be doubted. What is, however, open to dispute is the importance of their role and the juncture at which they performed it. The whole problem can be reduced, I believe, to manageable proportion after the relevant data of history, archaeology, and tradition have been re-assembled and fitted into a single pattern.

On the basis of the combined evidence it is now clear that there were present at the time, in close proximity to Akkad, several important ethnic groups, each individually more noteworthy than Gutium and each capable of offering a greater challenge to Sargonid aspirations. The case of Elam, the perennial challenger to the east, requires no fresh emphasis. Northwest of Elam was the home of the Lullu, whose contacts with Sumer go back to early historic times.[17] That Naram-Sin held the Lullu in high regard is shown convincingly by the fact that he commemorated their defeat on two great reliefs, one of which is his celebrated Stele of Victory. But the Lullu could counter with steles of their own.[18] One of these, that of Anubanini,[19] testifies both to Akkadian cultural influence and to considerable native power.

[17] Cf. already my remarks in *Mesopotamian Origins* (1930), 88 ff. and the more recent discussion in *JAOS*, 68 (1948), 8.

[18] Cf. *JNES*, 1 (1942), 80 ff.

[19] The name may safely be normalized with single *-n-* in view of the fact that double writing in this text is non-distinctive, as is shown by the form *An-nu-um* for Anu (line 13). The linguistic background of the proper name remains, of course, obscure. As for the name on the Sheikhan stele, usually read *Tar . . . dunni*, the only thing that seems clear about it is that it ended in *-ni*.

Hurrian tradition lists among early world rulers the Lullu king Immashk who is placed before the Sargonids.[20] In Mesopotamian tradition a certain Anubanini is presented as a scourge of the land.[21] The text in question, which is attested in Old Babylonian as well as in Assyrian, is closely related to another literary composition, CT 13, 44, which mentions Naram-Sin by name, in an ominous context.[22] On chronological and substantive grounds, therefore, it is scarcely possible to separate the Anubanini of Babylonian tradition from the very real Lullu king of the same name. It follows that the Lullu must have caused much grief to the Sargonids.

Hurrian opposition to Naram-Sin is reflected in his official accounts which list among his opponents at least two rulers with Hurrian names.[23] Contemporary local documents place Hurrian kings in Namar [24] and probably in Karḫar,[25] both in a northerly direction from Akkad. Hurrian tradition about world kings knows of a Hurrian ruler in Turkish, prior to the Akkad period.[26] More significant, however, than any of these details is the tablet of another Hurrian king by the name of Tišadal, which

[20] KUB XXVII 38, iv 13.

[21] So-called "Legend of the King of Kutha" i 18, discussed by Güterbock, *ZA,* 42, 65 ff. To my thinking, Güterbock would seem to interpret too literally the mythological allusions at the beginning of the text and the following description of the attacking forces. I would see here a mythological setting for an originally historical core comparable roughly to the Utuḫegal text, *RA,* 9, 111 ff.

[22] See Güterbock, loc. cit.

[23] Namely, *Puttim-adal* of Shimurrum and *Hupšumkibi* of Marḫaši, cf. Gelb, *HaS,* 55.

[24] *RA,* 9 (1912), 1–4. The name *Ari-sen* (for discussion and literature cf. Gelb, op. cit., 56) is typically Hurrian.

[25] Gelb (op. cit., 57) has made the plausible suggestion that the name hitherto read ᵈ*Ki-sa-a-ri* should be read *An-ki-sa-a-tal* (i.e., *Ankis-adal*), with a transparently Hurrian final element. For the reading *Kárḫar* see ibid., note 72.

[26] I.e., *Kiklib-adal,* KUB XXVII 38, iv 14. Members of the Akkad Dynasty occur in the same text, lines 22 ff.

has recently been published by Nougayrol.[27] The script dates the document to the Akkad period, yet the language is not Old Akkadian; it is instead the oldest Hurrian text so far recovered.[28] The ruler's city is Urkish, which we know of elsewhere as the seat of the god Kumarbi, head of the Hurrian pantheon.[29] Hurrian pressure against the south was thus sufficiently advanced in the Sargonid age to result in intimate cultural interrelations.[30]

Farther west our information is as yet too spotty for a coherent picture. In any case, it is evident that those regions held a strong attraction for Sargon. His empire endured for over a century, well into Naram-Sin's reign. The kings of Akkad were successful, among other reasons, because they were able to pick off their opponents one by one. Eventually, however, the opposition came to appreciate the need for unity, since historical tradition about Naram-Sin stresses the motif of a coalition involving seventeen hostile kings. According to one context the

[27] *RA*, 42 (1948), 1–20.

[28] With the appearance of this important document the prolonged dispute as to the antiquity of the Hurrians within the orbit of the "cuneiform civilization" is settled definitely in favor of their early arrival. The occurrence of Hurrian names to the north of Akkad can no longer be ascribed to the accidental prominence of sundry individuals. It is instead added proof of ethnic migration on a considerable scale. This fact lends unexpected support, at least in part, to the theory which I advanced in *Mesopotamian Origins* (120 ff.) to the effect that the Hurrians as a people became a factor in Mesopotamia as early as the 3rd millennium B.C. That view had to be modified upon the discovery of the Gasur texts in a stratum underlying the Hurrian settlements at Nuzi, inasmuch as little if any Hurrian evidence could be found in those Old Akkadian documents; cf. my discussion in *AASOR,* XIII (1933), 13–54. (For the Gasur texts see Th. J. Meek, *HSS,* X [1935], and for a discussion of the evolving problem cf. Gelb, *HaS,* 6 ff.) It now becomes apparent that Hurrians had come down in numbers at least as early as Akkad times, but that they settled in various pockets, so to speak, rather than in contiguous stretches of land. Their infiltration increased during Ur III and reached its peak in the middle of the 2nd millennium.

[29] Cf. Güterbock's publication of "The Song of Ullikummi," *JCS,* 5 (1951), 147.5.

[30] These interrelations, which included language, literature, and law, as well as religion and art, cannot be pursued in the present context.

allies were repulsed,[31] but in another, and presumably later, instance they dealt the Akkadians a crushing defeat.[32] By combining these hints with sundry data from other sources we obtain a self-consistent pattern. It would appear that Akkad never did recover fully from the blow which it suffered under Naram-Sin. The empire shrank to provincial proportions and presently proved to be too weak to fend off even the Gutians. The precise time when the Gutians took over remains uncertain.[33] What is important in this re-evaluation of the combined evidence is the strong probability that Gutians had little, if anything, to do with the decisive turn in the fortunes of Akkad. That state may have maintained itself as a local power for some years following the death of Naram-Sin.[34] But the period that made history and was kept alive by legend had already ended. The agents responsible for the end were many, some known and others as yet obscure, but all influenced in some degree by prolonged contact with Akkadian culture.

[31] KBo III, 13 (line 16′), and Güterbock, *ZA*, 44, 67 ff.

[32] CT 13, 44 i 15; cf. *ZA*, 42, 69 ff.; note also the related Hittite material, KBo III, 16–20, edited and discussed by Güterbock, *ZA*, 44, 49 ff.

[33] It is significant that CT 13, 44 ii 10 lists the Gutians among those who were affected by the disaster. It would follow that, once reduced to a local state, Akkad was not markedly superior to its immediate neighbors. Before long the relatively fresh forces of Gutium were able to seize the opportunity to assert themselves for a period of decades. On this reduced basis the temporary success of the northerners would not be out of keeping with the general picture. Incidentally, my assessment of Gutium in *Mesop. Orig.*, 96 ff. has to be substantially modified.

[34] See above, n. 6. The evidence of the Sumerian King List does not necessarily contradict this interpretation in view of the established tendency of such official tabulations to give successive listing to contemporary events in diverse centers; cf. Jacobsen, *King List,* 205 f. At all events, even in the official accounts it is Sharkalisharri alone that separates the end of Naram-Sin from the period of chaos. Significant in this connection is the evidence of the Old Babylonian omen texts according to which no less than three out of the five prominent rulers of the Dynasty of Akkad met their death in palace uprisings. We know now that assassination disposed of Rimush, Manishtushu, and Sharkalisharri (cf. Goetze, *JCS,* 1, 356 ff), leaving only Sargon and apparently also Naram-Sin to their natural fate.

Having utilized thus far the data of tradition as an aid to the recovery of history, we are obliged to pursue the first a step farther. The text that deals explicitly with the Akkadian disaster under Naram-Sin, CT 13, 44, appears to ascribe the initial move—the context is unfortunately fragmentary at that point—to the Umman-Manda.[35] The action originates in Anatolia or beyond. It gathers momentum as it sweeps on with elemental force along the northern perimeter of Akkad towards Elam and onward, until at last it is lost to view, its fury apparently as yet unspent. Who the Umman-Manda may have been is still as much of a puzzle as ever. They turn up stubbornly, however, in texts whose relative antiquity is gradually becoming established, and their inclusion in the Old Babylonian omen material is a noteworthy confirmation of their historical reality.[36] The Umman-Manda are mentioned, moreover, in the Hittite Code,[37] so that the

[35] ii 8; cf. KBo III, 18 + 19, line 20 and the references in n. 32, above.

[36] Cf. Goetze, YBT X, 44.33. The apodosis *ši-ip um-ma-an ma-ad-da* '(it is) a foot of the Umman-Manda' is in parallelism with such portentous signs as *šēp nukurtim* 'foot of hostility,' ibid. 40 and *šēp limuttim* 'foot of evil,' ibid. 58, as well as *šēp elamtim* 'foot of Elam,' 50.3. This indirect association of Umman-Manda and Elam recalls in turn the long-known astrological passage, Virolleaud, *ACh, Sin* IV 21–22, which brings up Elam as a sequel to the irruption of the Ummanmanda; cf. W. F. Albright, *JSOR,* 10 (1926), 242, and L. Oppenheim, *Orientalia,* 5 (1936), 221. The Old Babylonian material furnishes, of course, positive evidence of the long-held view that the events utilized in the omen literature of whatever age rest on old tradition. It follows that the references to the Umman-Manda in later texts of this category can no longer be dismissed as meaningless. One of these instances reports them, interestingly enough, as riding against the land (cf. Oppenheim, loc. cit., 222), a possible indication of the means responsible for their phenomenal success. [Cf. also *ra-ki-ib i-me-ri,* YBT X, 44. 65 in the light of the discussion by S. Feigin in "Studies in Memory of Moses Schorr" (1944), 227–40 and A. Salonen, *ArO,* XVII 3/4 (1949), 320–21.] For the occurrence in the Spartoli Tablets see Albright, loc. cit., 241 ff. and *BASOR,* 88 (1942), 34 ff.

If the association with Elam has any significance at all (in which case Gen. 14 would gain in relevance, cf. Albright. locc. cit.). it may well indicate that Akkad's neighbor to the east and north took advantage of the blow administered to Akkad by the Umman Manda.

[37] Par. 54.

designation seems to have been concrete enough at the time.[38] Does the occurrence of the term in the literary tradition concerning Naram-Sin point, therefore, to a historical event whose significance can only be sensed for the moment?[39] If the details of CT 13, 44 could be taken at face value,[40] we might have here a hint of great ethnic dislocations, precipitated perhaps by profound disturbances in the farther background, such as may well have ultimately brought the Luwians and Hittites into Anatolia. The possibility is attractive and by no means implausible. For the present, however, it remains wholly in the realm of speculation.[41]

What is not open to doubt, on the other hand, is the

[38] That the term came to have an appellative connotation (not unlike SA.GAZ, which is indeed found in the Hittite Naram-Sin fragment, KBo III, 20. 10′) was demonstrated by Landsberger-Bauer, *ZA,* 37, 82. The original meaning, however, is another matter.

[39] Cf. Oppenheim, *Orientalia,* 5, 221 and n. 36, above.

[40] Not the least perplexing of these details is the indicated first objective of the assault by the Umman-Manda, namely, *šu-bat* *^{d}En-*[*lil*] (should ^{ki} be added?), CT 13, 44 ii 8. Is this the Šubat-Enlil of the Mari texts, which is usually equated with Ashur? [Primarily because these texts list no other site as the capital of Shamshi-Adad. This argument from silence is enhanced by Shamshi-Adad's own statement, *AOB,* I, 20. 6–13, that his principal religious edifice in the city of Ashur was named Šubat-Enlil. As a usurper and foreigner, moreover, Shamshi-Adad had good reason to play down the traditional name of the capital in favor of a term with strong southern connections, as his use of the Babylonian inscriptional style independently demonstrates; cf. Landsberger-Balkan, *Belleten,* XIV/53 (1950), 220. The suggested identification of Subat-Enlil with Chagar Bazar (cf. ibid., 252) is rendered unlikely, among other reasons, by the relative insignificance of the latter site as disclosed by the excavations.] If the identity of the Subat-Enlil of the Naram-Sin text in question with Shamshi-Adad's capital should be borne out, we would have an excellent criterion for dating that text. But the problematical character of the equation cannot be over-stated at this juncture.

[41] Another highly speculative point may be mentioned in this connection for what it may be worth. The link between the Umman-Manda and Anatolia brings up anew the question of Tid'al, king of the Goyim, Gen. 14. 1 [for a discussion of that chapter see Albright, *JSOR,* 10, 231 ff and J. H. Kroeze, *Genesis Veertien* (1937)]. The identification of Tid'al with Tudḫaliya has long been current. The name is pre-Hittite, cf. CCT I, 34 *a* 17. A recent onomastic study assigns the name to the proto-Hattic group, cf.

fact of an Akkadian Empire whose extent does not appear to have been overstated unduly in the official sources. The actual duration of this first real empire known to history probably fell short of the 117 years said to have elapsed from the accession of Sargon to the death of Naram-Sin. But the cultural results proved far more enduring. They constitute, incidentally, the most dependable kind of witness for the actual political superstructure. Elam became Akkadianized in official speech and institutions.[42] The Lullu honor Akkadian deities on their reliefs and phrase their inscriptions in Akkadian. The Hurrians take over Akkadian writing and with it important elements of religion, literature, and other aspects of culture, many of which find their way in due time to Hittite centers in a sort of cultural chain reaction.[43] The civilization that had gradually been built up in Southern Mesopotamia [44] over a period of many centuries is transformed from a provincial into a cosmopolitan factor, transcending geographic, ethnic, and political boundaries. That the traffic was not

---

AfO, 15, 6 and 15. This would place the *goyim* likewise in Anatolia and enhance their equation with Umman-Manda. But the basis is as yet too flimsy for serious deductions.

[42] See Cameron, *History of Early Iran,* 33 f.

[43] Cf. Güterbock, *Kumarbi* (1946), 105 ff.; Speiser, *JAOS,* 62 (1942), 98 ff. In Hurrian texts Naram-Sin is mentioned in KUB XXVII, 38 iii 18, and Sargon ibid. iv 23 and KUB XXXI, 3 rev. 6, 10.

[44] Among the important developments which characterize the Sargonid age locally, special attention is due to the concept of *šukênu,* whose origin is traced to Akkad times by Landsberger, *MAOG,* IV (1929), 306 and whose linguistic and cultural implication I have touched upon in a paper scheduled for publication in *JCS* in the near future. Political expansion brought with it marked changes in society, in internal as well as external relations, which paved the way for the rise of the "dependent" class of *muškênu.* Perhaps the clearest support for this particular meaning is to be found in the omen literature; a phrase like *bēl mātim . . . muš-ki-nu-tam illak* (Oppenheim has called attention to it in *Orientalia,* 5, 207, n. 9; illustrations could now be adduced also from Old Babylonian material) does not mean, of course, 'the king will become a pauper,' but rather 'the ruler will become a dependent.'

exclusively one-way goes without saying. But the original impetus appears to have come from Akkad. All in all, the enterprise of Akkad led to the first broad meeting of East and West and became a highly significant milestone in the early history of Western Asia.

[*Addenda.* For the sources from the Dynasty of Akkad see now H. Hirsch, "Die Inschriften der Könige von Agade," AfO, XX (1963), pp. 1–82. Added Old Babylonian references to the Ummān-Manda are given by J. Nougayrol in RA, XLIV (1950), pp. 12–14. And my remarks on the location of Šubat-Enlil (above, note 40) are refuted by the Old Babylonian itinerary published by A. Goetze, JCS, VII (1953), pp. 51 ff., cf. especially p. 58, which favors B. Landsberger's identification of the site with Chagar Bazar.]

The Hurrian Participation in the Civilization of Mesopotamia, Syria and Palestine

THE ETHNO-LINGUISTIC GROUP NOW COMMONLY RECOGNIZED as Hurrian [1] has been known as such to modern scholarship for only slightly over a quarter of a century.[2] Nevertheless, within this short space of time the Hurrians have re-emerged as one of the vital factors in the composite civilization of the ancient Near-East.[3] Their prominence, in one way or another, is attested by a variety of written records which date from shortly after the middle of the third millennium to the early centuries of the first millennium B.C.[4] The area in which the Hurrians were

[1] For a review of the intricate problem of terminology see SPEISER, *JAOS* 68 (1948), 1 ff., and especially note 10.

For the abbreviations employed in this article cf. the appended "Abbreviations and Selective Bibliography."

[2] The principal publications which deal with this question include: CHIERA and SPEISER, "A New Factor in the History of the Ancient East," *AASOR* 6 (1926), 75–91; SPEISER, "Ethnic Movements," *AASOR* 13 (1933), 16 ff.; A. GÖTZE, *Hethiter, Churriter und Assyrer* (1936); A. UNGNAD, *Subartu* (1936); SPEISER, *Introduction to Hurrian* (1941); I. J. GELB, *Hurrians and Subarians* (1944); R. T. O'CALLAGHAN, *Aram Naharaim* (1948).

[3] As foreseen in the first publication cited in note 2.

[4] For the early occurrence of the Hurrians the most important witness is the foundation document of a king of Urkish, written in Hurrian; see J.

active stretched from the Mediterranean to Sumer and from East Anatolia to the borders of Egyt. The documents which witness that activity—at times, to be sure, through mere hints in the form of the distinctive Hurrian personal names—include inscriptions in Sumerian, Akkadian, Hittite, Ugaritic, Egyptian, and Biblical Hebrew, in addition of course to original Hurrian sources.[5]

Such exceptionally wide distribution implies multiple cultural contacts. The results would vary with the number and importance of the intrusive Hurrians in each of the centers involved; and their significance might be expected to diminish in proportion to the distance from the Hurrian homeland. Although this last detail is yet to be settled conclusively, all indications point towards the general region of Armenia as the main area of Hurrian concentration.[6] Accordingly, the nearest major cultural neighbor would have to be sought in the lands of the Hittites. It is not surprising, therefore, that the relations between the Hurrians and the Hittites prove to be unusually intimate, a fact which is abundantly reflected in virtually every phase of the Hittite civilization. Indeed, we are justified in speaking of a Hurro-Hittite symbiosis which for closeness and effect is second only to that blend of Sumerian and Akkadian elements which constitutes the composite culture of Mesopotamia. This particular

---

NOUGAYROL, *RA* 44 (1948), 3 ff., and cf. below; a convenient survey of Hurrian occurrences will be found in UNGNAD, *Subartu,* 135 ff. and in GELB, *HS, passim.* For the latest traces, cf. *ibid.,* 82 ff. The warning is, however, in order that some of the assumed Hurrian occurrences in the first millennium may really be Urartian, since that language was closely related to Hurrian.

[5] For lists of Hurrian personal names from the Ur III and Old Babylonian periods see GELB, *op. cit.,* 100 ff. For the places involved cf. GOETZE, *JNES* 12 (1953), 117–23.

[6] Cf. GOETZE, *Hethiter,* 106.

subject, however, requires separate treatment on the part of Hittite specialists.[7]

Next in importance as meeting grounds in which Hurrian participation can be tested are Mesopotamia on the one hand and Syria-Palestine on the other. Districts to the east and north of the Hurrian center might conceivably have felt the impact of the Hurrians to a greater degree; so far, however, those areas remain inarticulate for our purposes within the period under discussion. In contrast, Mesopotamia is under the full light of history throughout that long stretch of time, and Syria-Palestine is similarly illuminated through most of it. Our knowledge, moreover, of these two major cultural regions is now far enough advanced to enable us to distinguish the indigenous from the intrusive and to discover among the imported elements those features that may be safely, or at least plausibly, credited to the Hurrians. To inquire into this specific phase of Hurrian participation in outside civilizations is the task of the present paper.

It is reasonable to assume in advance that the Hurro-Mesopotamian pattern differed appreciably from the Hurro-Syrian. This assumption is borne out by the actual results, as will be pointed out presently. In Mesopotamia, the seat of a civilization already long-established by the middle of the third millennium, the Hurrians received much more than they appear to have contributed. In the West, on the other hand, the Hurrians had in all probability the advantage of an earlier start in the experience of civilization, and their contribution is consequently more tangible and substantial. The respective details will be presented under separate headings.

[7] *Ibid., passim.*

I. MESOPOTAMIA

The principal actors on the Mesopotamian stage were the Sumerians and Akkadians [8] in the third millennium and the Babylonians, Kassites and Assyrians in the centuries that followed. The Hurrians are included among the supporting cast, so to speak. In other words, the evidence bearing on their participation in Central and Lower Mesopotamia is indirect and circumstantial rather than primary. Such evidence is usually slow to be properly assessed, which is one of the reasons for the realtively late re-discovery of the Hurrians. Another important reason is the paucity of records in Hurrian and the difficulties encountered in their interpretation.[9] We lack thus adequate data from that quarter. In these circumstances it is not possible to reconstruct a comprehensive picture of events and conditions. The sporadic hints that the available material affords are suitable only for a rough outline which is fragmentary at many points. That outline is built up from many sources: political history, religion and law, literature and art, economics and linguistics. It cannot be traced here in detail but has to be suggested in general terms with the aid of spot samples.

Historically, the most significant single source is a recently published calcite tablet which has come down to us from Tišadal,[10] king of Urkiš.[11] It is significant on

[8] It is still uncertain what name, if any, was used for the early Semites in Mesopotamia prior to the rise of Akkad.

[9] On this question cf. my *Introduction to Hurrian,* 1–9.

[10] NOUGAYROL, *RA* 44, 3 ff. I read the ambiguous final RI in this name as *-dal* on inner-Hurrian grounds and in conformity with numerous variant spellings of the form.

[11] On URKIŠ, *see* G. DOSSIN, *Syria* 19, 115.

three main counts: (1) the text dates back to the beginning of the Agade age; (2) it is composed entirely in Hurrian, thus antedating by several centuries the Hurrian texts from Mari, the next-oldest body of documents in that language; [12] (3) the stated royal center is Urkiš, which we know independently as the seat of Kumarbi, the head of the Hurrian pantheon.[13] There can be, therefore, no longer any doubt whatever as to the relative antiquity of cultural contacts between Hurrians and Mesopotamia. These contacts were productive even before the first great expansion of the political influence of Mesopotamia under Sargon and Naramsin.[14] For the Urkiš tablet proves that the script of Sumer had already been adapted by that time to the uses of Hurrian, a move that was to play an important role later on in drawing the Hittites into the orbit of the civilization of Mesopotamia.[15] Furthermore, the indicated prominence of Urkiš as a politico-religious center of the Hurrians draws us a step closer to the solution of the problem of the Hurrian homeland. The site has to be sought in Upper Mesopotamia,[16] apparently in the general area of Mardin-Diarbekir. The geographic center of the people cannot have lain far beyond. It is to that region, then, that we must trace the gradual influx of Hurrian elements in the east and south, a process which we can plot reliably with the aid of Hurrian personal names.[17] These names are excellent

[12] Cf. Fr. THUREAU-DANGIN, Tablettes hurrites provenant de Mâri," *RA* 36 (1939), 1–28.

[13] H. G. GÜTERBOCK, "The Song of Ullikummi," *JCS* 5 (1951), 146.15.

[14] Cf. SPEISER, "Some Factors in the Collapse of Akkad," *JAOS* 72 (1952); [see above. pp. 000.]

[15] *Id., IH* 13; cf. E. STURTEVANT, *Hittite Grammar* (1951), 3.

[16] Cf. note 11, and see GOETZE, *JNES* 12, 119.

[17] The standard study on the subject is that of I. J. GELB, P. M. PURVES, and A. A. MacRAE, *Nuzi Personal Names* (1943).

trail-markers in that they stand out boldly in whatever context they may occur: e.g., in the tablet of Arišen,[18] king of Urkiš and Nawar, a slightly later Akkadian analogue in the Tišadal document; [19] in texts from the Third Dynasty of Ur; [20] in the archives from Mari, and—most abundantly of all—in the tablets from Arrapḫa and Nuzi.

The Hurrian push into Central and Lower Mesopotamia was thus prolonged and persistent. Yet it was not attended by appreciable political gains. Only at the peak of Mitanni power, in the third quarter of the second millennium, do we find substantial sections to the north of Akkad—notably Arrapḫa—under indisputably Hurrian rule.[21] In other words, the whole process is one of ethnocultural interpenetration which did not lead, however, for some centuries at least, to major political changes. The Hurrians cannot be said to have made a lasting impression either on Sumer or on Akkad proper. But they were themselves profoundly influenced in various cultural aspects.

Hurrian religion is a good case in point. The chief gods bear Hurrian names and display many characteristics that appear to be native. There are, however, certain features which Tešub shares, probably through derivation, with Mesopotamian Addu, or Kumarbi with Enlil. [2]
Moreover, the appearance of Alalu and Anu in Hurrian contexts is direct evidence of borrowing from the south.[23]

There is similar eclecticism in regard to law. Although

[18] Written *A-ri-si-en* in accordance with the orthography of that period.

[19] THUREAU-DANGIN, "Tablette de Samarra," *RA* 9 (1912), 1–4.

[20] GELB, *HS*, 58 ff.

[21] SPEISER, "A Letter of Saushshatar and the Date of the Kirkuk Tablets," *JAOS* 49 (1929), 269–275.

[22] H. G. GÜTERBOCK, *Kumarbi* (1946), 105 ff.

[23] For the influence of Mesopotamia see SPEISER, "An Intrusive Hurro-Hittite Myth," *JAOS* 62 (1942), 98–102, and GÜTERBOCK, *loc. cit.*

there is no Hurrian law code that could be used as a basis for comparison, we have an abundance of legal and administrative documents which afford a good illustration of the underlying juridical principles. Most of the pertinent material so far has come from Arrapḫa and Nuzi. It points to this general conclusion: there are significant features, particularly in the realm of family law and societal structure, which cannot be duplicated in Mesopotamia and are therefore in all likelihood original with the Hurrians. Side by side with these features, however, there are others that reflect just as clearly the influence of southern customs and practices as illustrated in the Code of Hammurabi.[24] Native and assimilated elements have thus been blended into a viable pattern.

The field of Hurrian literature promises to be a particularly fruitful and fascinating topic for future study. It is a question of prospects rather than accomplishments primarily because the extant material is as yet scanty and what there is of it in Hurrian itself is circumscribed by our inchoate knowledge of the language. Nevertheless, even the little that we now have and know justifies considerable optimism in regard to much better things to come. Our understanding of Hurrian is progressing and the pertinent material is on the increase. Moreover, Hurrian literary matter has been turning up in a steadily growing volume of Hittite recensions which have enjoyed the signally competent attention of scholars like Güterbock and Friedrich.[25] The result is an emerging picture

[24] From among the many publications that bear on this subject I would single out here only P. KOSCHAKER, *Neue Keilschriftliche Rechtsurkunden aus der El-Amarna Zeit* (1928) and "Fratriarchat, Hausgemeinschaft und Mutterrecht in Keilschriftrechten," *ZA* 41 (1933), 1–89.

[25] See GÜTERBOCK, *Kumarbi,* and "The Song of Ullikummi," *JCS* 5, 135–61, and 6, 8–42; J. FRIEDRICH, "Churritische Märchen und Sagen in hethitischer Sprache," *ZA* 49, 213–55.

of unusually lively literary activity on the part of the Hurrians and of the great popularity of the product. Further examination discloses once again a blend of native and borrowed elements. Manifold adaptability was evidently one of the outstanding characteristics of the Hurrians.

In the Song of Ullikummi, to be sure, there is no substantial evidence of indebtedness to Babylonian sources. The Kumarbi Epic, however, reveals a composite pantheon, the foreign component being demonstrably Mesopotamian.[26] Both these compositions are as yet extant only in Hittite versions, but their Hurrian origin is patent and universally acknowledged. On the other hand, we possess a legendary history of early world rulers written in Hurrian.[27] This contains some intrusive material from the south, although the composition as a whole is obviously independent. Its form, however, recalls Mesopotamian analogues, and the principals involved include members of the Dynasty of Agade alongside kings who had not been known previously. In contrast to this bit of historiography, the Hurrian version of the Gilgamesh Epic, of which we have only a small fragment, implies outright borrowing.[28] Whether the Hittite formulation of the same great theme had been taken from the Hurrian, as was the case with such epics as Ullikummi and Kumarbi, cannot as yet be determined on the basis of the available remnants.

Turning now to the field of art, we soon discover that little conclusive information can be looked for from that quarter. It is true that the distinctive sculptures of North-

[26] Cf. n. 23.
[27] KUB 27.38 iv 8–30.
[28] KUB 8.61; UNGNAD, *ZA* 35 (1924), 133 ff.

ern Syria and Upper Mesopotamia, as well as the cylinder seals of the Kirkuk (the modern representative of Arrapḫa) type, have been ascribed to the Hurrians with a good show of reason.[29] There is in these groups of objects a combination of features that sets them off from the corresponding products of adjoining culture areas. Insofar, however, as Mesopotamia is concerned, the stone monuments in question had less effect than the cylinder seals. The latter flourished, as is natural, in the congenial atmosphere of the Arrapḫa area. The influence of that style, nevertheless, went farther for it shows through the Middle Assyrian seals.[30] Yet Hurrian glyptic art was ultimately indebted to Mesopotamia for many motives, not to speak of the very form of the cylinder seal. Here, too, then, eclecticism would seem to be the keynote.

In the economic field, Hurrians appear in substantial numbers, to judge from the proper names, in the business documents of Ur III and the succeeding periods. Their proportion, however, is insufficient to imply an appreciable Hurrian impact on the commerce of Sumer and Akkad. The situation may have been different on the northern peripheries, back in Agade times, but a distinctly Hurrian settlement of that early age has yet to be excavated. By the middle of the second millennium, of course, Hurrians dominated the economic life of sundry districts such as Arrapḫa. Yet even then neither Babylonia nor Assyria appears to have been seriously affected.

We come, lastly, to the evidence of linguistics. Here Sumerian furnishes a vivid example of what intimate linguistic interaction can be like. Akkadian took over

[29] GOETZE, *Hethiter,* 79 ff. Cf. A. MOORTGAT, *Die bildende Kunst des alten Orients und die Bergvölker* (1932); H. FRANKFORT, *Cylinder Seals* (1939), 273 ff.; E. PORADA, *Seal Impressions of Nuzi* (1947).

[30] FRANKFORT, *op. cit.,* 203, 275.

from Sumerian countless lexical items involving every major phase of cultural communication. To that same source, moreover, Akkadian owed many changes in its phonology and syntax; even its morphology may not have been immune from Sumerian influence.[31] For its part, Sumerian received a modest compensation in the form of certain loanwords from Akkadian.

Nothing comparable can be adduced in terms of Hurro-Mesopotamian contacts in the linguistic sphere. There is just barely enough to indicate that such contacts were not altogether jejune. If we except the script, which the Hurrians borrowed from the south well back in the third millennium, there remains only a handful of loanwords that merit our attention. While we are on this subject, it must be borne in mind that we have as yet very little material in Hurrian from which Akkadian borrowings might be isolated. But the vast mass of Akkadian records reveals precious little that can be ascribed to Hurrian with some measure of probability.

Akkadian loanwords in Hurrian seem to have been assimilated with the same ease with which the Hurrians were able to accommodate other acquired cultural elements. The Akkadian term for "ivory," *šenni-pīri* is readily domesticated in Hurrian into the adjective *šinni-beruḫḫe;* similarly, Akkadian *ḫurāṣu* "gold" acquires Hurrian credentials by assuming the form *ḫiyaruḫḫe.*[32] In analogous fashion, the Akkadian term for "military compound," *ḫalṣu,* takes on the Hurrian occupational suffix to become *ḫalsuḫli* "(military) governor." As an instance of uncompounded borrowing may be suggested Hurrian

[31] A suggestive instance of this has been proposed by GOETZE, *JAOS* 56 (1936), 333.

[32] SPEISER, *IH,* 46.

šarri, from Akkadian *šarru* "king." The same assimilatory quality has already been noted in other phases of Hurrian culture. It confronts us again in the field of personal names, as when a man with a Hurrian name proves to be the father of a person with an Akkadian designation, and *vice versa.*[33] Social factors undoubtedly contributed to such hybrid groupings, but the very fact these interchanges were acceptable is not without significance in the present context. Individual names as well may be compounded of Hurrian and Akkadian elements, e.g., *Tešub-nirāri* and *Nirār-Tešub*; the former has a pure Akkadian analogue in the familiar *Adad-nirāri.*[34]

In the opposite direction there seems to have been less traffic. Akkadian lexical lists recognize various foreign synonyms, some of which are ascribed in a slightly roundabout fashion to Hurrian.[35] There were few such terms, however, in everyday use. The clearest examples come, naturally enough, from Assyria. Among these is the agrarian term *šiluḫi,* which occurs in the Assyrian Laws,[36] and the dialectal term for an official known as *ḫasiḫlu,* which has turned up in the texts from Tell Billa, ancient Šibaniba; [37] an instance of bread cast upon the waters, so to speak, in that *ḫasiḫlu* can hardly be divorced from Nuzi *ḫalsuḫlu,* itself a hybrid Akkado-Hurrian formation, as was pointed out above.

There is, furthermore, the possibility that some loan-

[33] Various instances of such alternation are given by MACRAE, in GELB-PURVES-MACRAE, *NPN,* 282 ff.

[34] Indeed, where the divine element is written with a logogram, it it sometimes difficult to decide how the full name is to be read; for an example of this kind from Alalaḫ see *JAOS* 71 (1951), 152.

[35] Cf. UNGNAD, *Subartu,* 64 ff.; GELB, *HS,* 16; SPEISER, *JAOS* 68, 3, n. 16.

[36] KAV 2 ii 8.

[37] Soon to be published by J. J. FINKELSTEIN in a forthcoming issue of *JCS.* [JCS VII (1953), pp. 111–176].

words from Hurrian entered a relatively old stratum of Akkadian and have escaped detection as borrowed terms precisely because they had a long time to become acclimated. One such word appears to be *aštaperu* which the corresponding Sumerian logogram identifies plainly as "female and male slaves." The word is structurally non-Semitic. We know that Hurrian *ašti/a* meant "woman," and Hurrian onomastic usage is familiar with the element *piru*. The order "female-male" in the Sumerian logogram is an added argument in favor of a Hurrian background for *aštapēru*. Another possibility is Akkadian *papāḫu* "shrine, cella." Since Hurrian *pabaḫḫi* means "mountainous, eastern," and since the Akkadian term is glossed as "mountain of the lands," [38] a Hurrian derivation in this case is highly probable, particularly in view of the fact the word lacks any kind of etymology either in Akkadian or in Sumerian whereas its structure would be transparent in Hurrian. But if the two terms just discussed were acquired from Hurrian, the date of these borrowings would have to be moved back to the third millennium, say, the time of Tišadal or Arišen. The Agade period could well have been congenial to commerce of this type.

All in all, Hurrian participation in the civilization of Mesopotamia proves to have been one-sided to a marked degree: the relationship was enormously profitable for the Hurrians while leaving hardly an imprint on Mesopotamia. In the process the Hurrians acquired writing as an essential instrument of civilization, and with it a number of normative features in such vital fields as law and administration, religion and literature. They were, in short, apt and eager pupils who took full advantage of

[38] KAV 43 rev. 3.

the experience and competence of their masters. There is no indication that Mesopotamia received any substantial cultural values in return, although she was necessarily aware of the Hurrians as a political factor, in the Agade period and more particularly at the time of Mitannian ascendancy.

Yet it does not follow by any means that Hurrian civilization was wholly derivative. Many of its forms were acquired, but much of the content appears to be native. Confronted with the mature attainments of Mesopotamia, the Hurrians failed to display much individuality. To the West however, conditions were different. The Hurrian center was closer and the local civilizations seem to have been less well integrated. The Hurrians had thus a better opportunity to assert their cultural independence. They did this in two ways: by contributing some of their inherited cultural features, and by transmitting others which they had acquired from Mesopotamia. They left their mark as originators and also as middlemen. The extent to which this contribution can now be reconstructed will be outlined briefly in the paragraphs that follow.

II. SYRIA AND PALESTINE

A few words, first, about the evidence for the presence of Hurrians on the eastern coast of the Mediterranean. The clearest testimony is linguistic. Since Mari is known to have maintained close political relations with the region of Aleppo, it is not surprising that the texts from that site, which date from approximately the time of Hammurabi, should contain a sprinkling of Hurrian personal names from that general region; [39] particularly since the Hurrians were sufficiently prominent at Mari to have caused the inclusion in the local archives of a number of texts in their own language.[40] Later on, about the middle of the second millennium and for some two centuries there after, Hurrian material grows more abundant. Leaving Palestine aside for the moment, we find this material in a series of Syrian sites,[41] most notably at Tunip, Qatna, and Alalaḫ, in each of which Hurrian was apparently the principal spoken language.[42] And although Ugarit was Semitic in the main, its Hurrian contingent was far from negligible. To it we owe a number of Hurrian texts in the alphabetic script and, in addition, a Sumero-Hurrian vocabulary [43] and an Akkado-Hurrian bilingual—brief but of extraordinary importance potentially [44]—both in syllabic writing.

The resulting ethnic picture is complex, if not hopelessly confused. We know that other elements also played a part in it.[45] Yet the bulk of the population must have consisted of Western Semites and Hurrians. Some centers were evidently predominantly Semitic. In others, the Hurrians appear to have maintained an effective majority, especially in the north. Elsewhere, e.g., in Ugarit, the

[39] Cf. C. F. JEAN, in *Studia Mariana* (1950), 69. The list could be considerably expanded. For a general statement cf. also W. F. ALBRIGHT, *Archaeology and the Religion of Israel* (1942), 55 ff.

[40] Cf. above, note 12.

[41] Cf. UNGNAD, *Subartu*, 158 ff.

[42] The Amarna letters from the first two of these sites contain Hurrian glosses; on the language of Qatna see Friedrich, *WZKM* 47 (1940), 202 ff. Alalaḫ resembles Nuzi in many ways, and the language on the statue of its king Idrimi is a barbarous form of Akkadian which points to another substratum; cf. S. SMITH, *The Statue of Idrimi* (1949).

[43] SPEISER, *IH*, 6–7.

[44] As yet unpublished at the time of this writing.

[45] Notably, a small but influential group of Indo-Aryans; cf. O'CALLAGHAN, *Aram Naharaim*, 56 ff.

population was mixed. Conditions of this sort are by no means unusual in the Near East and they can be duplicated in our own day, for instance in the Mosul district.[46] Inevitably, they lead to cultural interaction. Where the present is affected, the results can be conveniently studied in the field, for all that adequate advantage has yet to be taken of these opportunities. But where the second millennium B.C. is concerned, accidents of discovery constitute the dominant factor. The pertinent discoveries are of very recent date for the most part; many are as yet unprocessed, some still in progress, others in the offing. The whole question, in short, is just now in a state of flux.

It is clear, at any rate, even now that Hurrian religious practices, say, at Ugarit must have had their effect on the local Semitic inhabitants. The Hurrian god Tešub was intimately identified with Aleppo, a fact that is repeatedly brought home by the phrase *Tešub Ḫalbaḫi* "the Aleppian Tešub." Instances of this kind were scarcely isolated. When the Mitannian king Tushratta wrote to his Egyptian contemporaries, he resorted either to Hurrian or—far more often—to Akkadian, which was the diplomatic language of the day. But Mitanni Akkadian is something like a palimpsest in which the underlying Hurrian is still plainly discernible in vocabulary, morphology, and syntax. And the barbarous Akkadian of Idrimi of Alalaḫ is due, in all probability, to the same Hurrian substratum.[47]

Apart from language as such, Hurrian influence in these parts is attested in art, in social practices, and in certain phases of intellectual life. The first is most clearly

[46] Where Muslims, several Christian sects, and pagan Yazidis may live close together in the same village.

[47] Cf. above, note 42.

in evidence in Syria. The two other fields are best exemplified in Palestine.

The "Kirkuk" type of cylinder seals, reflecting a blend of Hurrian and Mesopotamian elements, has already been touched upon in the preceding section. It is an expression of a larger glyptic school which is sometimes classified as Syro-Mitannian. Genetically related to this category is a massive body of stone monuments widely distributed over North Syria and Upper Mesopotamia. It is a distinctive group featuring a series of peculiar motifs, among them a number of mythical hybrid beings consisting of men and animals in various combinations. These sculptures constitute the artistic stamp of North Syria in the second millennium B.C. Their influence, however, persists into later times and extends to other regions, including the Aegean.[48]

For a full appreciation of the underlying concepts we must await the incidental commentary that is implicit in the mythological literature of the Hurrians which is gradually coming to light. These literary sidelights should suffice to remove the last lingering doubts as to whether the art under discussion is really to be credited to the Hurrians. Traditionally it had been ascribed to the Hittites, and it is one of the achievements of modern scholarship to have corrected this particular error. At that, the misattribution of Hurrian elements to the Hittites is but a recent reflex of a process that goes back to ancient times. Assyrian annals of the first millennium include under the term "Hatti-land" much territory that was demonstrably non-Hittite. The Old Testament attaches the label "Heth" to places and individuals that never were Hittite, and in some instances were clearly Hurrian. The

[48] Cf. GOETZE, *Hethiter,* 82 and the other references in note 29.

Hurrians, it would seem, did not excel in making a direct and indelible impression on others. Their impact appears to have been rather subtle and indirect. Just as they were able to assimilate the products of other cultures, their own products could insinuate themselves into the context of neighboring civilizations. In this particular connection the best examples come to us from Palestine.

It is now a well-established fact that the picture of the Hurrians as such which the Old Testament has preserved is hazy, confused, and distorted by popular etymology. The biblical *Ḥōri*—an accurate derivative of *Ḫurri* as confirmed by the Septuagint *Χορραῖος*—came to be interpreted as "cave dweller" and was hence consigned to that section of the land in which caves were abundant. Internal evidence, however, leaves no room for any doubt whatever that the people in question had been far more widespread and influential in Palestine down to the end of the second millennium than was later realized. For one reason or another, the received text came to read "Hiwwite" or "Hittite" where "Horite" had once stood.[49] It is a measure of the historical genuis of Eduard Meyer that he was able to pierce through these disguises long before the rediscovery of the Hurrians in the cuneiform sources.[50] Eventually, Meyer's brilliant deductions were corroborated by the appearance of Hurrian personal names in cuneiform texts from Central Palestine.[51] The reason for the Egyptian designation of Palestine as *Ḫuru*[52] likewise ceased to be a puzzle, for that name

[49] See SPEISER, *"Ethnic Movements,"* 26 ff.

[50] Cf. his *Die Israeliten und deren Nachbarstamme* (1906), 328 ff.

[51] Primarily from Tell Ta'annek, cf. A. GUSTAVS, *ZDPV* 50 (1927), 1 ff.; 51, 169 ff.

[52] This reading, replacing the previously customary *Ḫaru,* was established by W. F. ALBRIGHT, *The Vocalization of the Egyptian Syllabic Orthography* (1934), 54.

proves to synchronize with the time of maximum Hurrian prominence in the country. The general perspective was further improved by the appearance in the documents from Ugarit of the ethnic name *Ḫry* alongside texts that could be identified independently as Hurrian. The Jebusites of Jerusalem and Uriya "the Hittite" could also be restored at last to their rightful Hurrian status. The requisite evidence, in short, is ample and manifold.

What matters, however, in the present context is not so much the extent of Hurrian penetration far away from their homeland as the reverberations of those wanderings in terms of cultural synthesis. We have seen that in Mesopotamia the Hurrians were barely more than diligent apprentices. In Syria they were in a position to act with greater confidence; for one, they were closer to home, and for another, the local civilization was far less of a piece. Yet an appraisal of the results is complicated just now by the steady flow of new information which remains to be sifted and organized. The situation in Palestine lends itself to a more profitable assessment. Because the Hurrians are here hundreds of miles from their original centers, they stand out in that much bolder relief. The relevant Old Testament material has been subject to intensive scrutiny for many centuries so that the results of modern discovery can readily be integrated. Lastly, and most important of all, the impact of the Old Testament on world culture is self-evident. To the extent, therefore, that the Hurrians contributed to the make-up of the biblical civilization, they were a factor also in the subsequent cultural history of the world.

By and large, it is possible today to distinguish with relative clarity between the Palestinian cultural features that are of West Semitic origin and those that are heterogeneous. Among the latter, Mesopotamian elements played a major part for the very good reason that Hebrew origins are linked traditionally with Mesopotamia and are traceable to the same quarter on innumerable archaeological counts. Yet there is much in the early Hebrew heritage that is neither West Semitic nor outright Mesopotamian. This significant residue is no longer a complete blank. A substantial portion of it can now be certified as Hurrian in that it is illuminated by independent Hurrian sources.

Hurrian features could have been fed into the mainstream of Palestinian culture in one of several ways. The ancestral home of the Patriarchs was located in the Habur Valley, which was also the center of Mitanni, the principal political creation of the Hurrians in the second millenium. Furthermore, Palestine had lively contacts with Syria where Hurrians exercised considerable influence, as we have seen. Finally, it has just been stressed that Hurrians were by no means strangers to Palestine itself. When Ezekiel was reminding Jerusalem that her father was an Amorite and her mother a Hittite (i.e., a Hurrian),[53] he was thus expressing a valid cultural fact and not a mere literary hyperbole.

Where, then, is that "maternal" influence apparent? Even at the present fragmentary state of our knowledge a full discussion of the subject would be far beyond the scope of this article, let alone the little space that has been left in it for this particular section. There is room only for a selective general sketch. The samples to be presented come under the headings of (a) language, (b) communal history, (c) society, and (d) prehistory.

[53] Ezekiel 16.3.

In language, Hebrew shares with certain other West Semitic dialects the strictly un-Semitic peculiarity of spirantizing post-vocalic stops. Long ago I suggested on purely theoretical grounds that this phonologic process could best be explained as due to Hurrian influence.[54] The deduction can now be supported by inner-Hurrian developments.[55] The results constitute unexpected proof of singularly close inter-ethnic relations.

In regard to the communal juxtaposition, there is first the dramatic instance of tension between the Shechemites and the sons of Jacob, as described in Genesis 34. Now the father of Shechem is Hamor "the Hiwwite," and the Hamorites are described as uncircumcised (verse 14), which is tantamount to non-Semitic. Elsewhere, in the Septuagint, as well as in the Hebrew Old Testament itself (Genesis 36, 2 and 20), Hiwwites are equated with Horites.[56] In view of these disclosures, and in the light of the modern evidence concerning the Hurrians, we are in a better position to appreciate the Shechemite agitation against Abimelech of which a vivid account is given in Judges 9. That agitation is justified expressly by the communal differences between the descendants of Hamor and the relatives of Abimelech's father (verse 28). The bitterness of the ensuing struggle can scarcely be explained along political or clannish lines alone. The whole issue gains in sharpness and importance if it is viewed —which has not been done hitherto—as a symptom of the deeper cleavage between two heterogeneous cultures, the Hurrian and the Israelite. Interestingly enough, Shechem and Jerusalem have been frequently in opposite

[54] See *JBL* 48 (1939), vi f.
[55] Cf. *BASOR* 74 (1939), 5, n. 10; *IH*, 61 ff.
[56] SPEISER, *"Ethnic Movement,"* 29 ff.

camps ever since, in ancient and in modern history alike. The reasons for this atavistic antagonism need not, of course, have been the same in each instance. There is, however, a good chance, that the Hurrian component of the culture of North Palestine may have had something to do with the chronic differences between Israel and Judah and the familiar battle cry "Every man to his tents, O Israel!" (e.g., II Samuel 20, 1). The original cause of the incompatibility was naturally bound to become obliterated in course of time.

In societal matters, there are numerous instances of Hurrian influence on the culture of the early Hebrews. The most significant of these will be cited in passing.[57] The source material on the subject is contained in the cuneiform tablets from Arrapḫa and Nuzi. The district in question is remote from Palestine, to be sure. We know, however, that it was in constant touch with the political center of Mitanni, which was also the extra-Palestinian home of the Patriarchs. Furthermore, the recently unearthed tablets from Alalaḫ, in Syria, reveal that Hurrian customs and practices were fairly uniform throughout. In other words, we have the necessary means to bridge the geographic distances.

What is involved in the illustrations that follow is a series of biblical concepts and practices which cannot otherwise be explained either from the local background or from any but Hurrian sources. Perhaps the most impressive single instance involves the appropriation by Rachel of the *teraphim,* or house gods, of her father Laban (Genesis 31). Countless efforts had been made to account for this puzzling act. None had come close to the

[57] I have dealt with some of these points also in the article "Hurrians" which is scheduled to appear in the Hebrew *Biblical Encyclopedia.*

mark because the necessary details about Hurrian family laws had been wanting. But the Arrapḫa and Nuzi documents now make it clear that under certain specific conditions family property could pass to a daughter's husband provided that the son-in-law had been handed the testator's house gods as an outward token of the unorthodox transfer of property.[58]

The case of the daughters of Zelophehad (Numbers 27) can be similarly interpreted, since Nuzi usage provides for conditional inheritance by daughters where male heirs are absent. The strained relations between Sarah and Hagar (Genesis 16) are indirectly illuminated by an explicit Nuzi provision that a childless wife is to furnish her husband with a concubine without surrendering thereby her status as sole legal spouse.[59] The custom of levirate marriage likewise receives welcome socio-juridical support when viewed against the strongly fratriarchal background of Hurrian society.[60] The indicated precedence of a sister as compared with a wife (e.g., Genesis 20) becomes clearer by the same token. Lastly, the fact that biblical law regards land holdings as inalienable, which is not the case in other cultures with a Semitic background and is not otherwise paralleled in Mesopotamia, can best be attributed to Hurrian influence; for it is this particular feature that constitutes the keystone of Nuzi legal practice in regard to real estate.

Finally, the Hurrians can be shown to have had a hand in the formulation of those traditions that deal with world history prior to Abraham, the so-called

[58] See S. SMITH, apud GADD, *RA* 23 (1926), 127. For this and other Nuzi parallels to the Old Testament see also C. H. GORDON, "Parallèles nouziene aux lois et coutumes de l'Ancien Testament," *RB*, 1935, 1 f.

[59] Cf. SPEISER, *AASOR* 10 (1930), 31 ff.

[60] KOSCHAKER, "Fratriachat," 86.

Urgeschichte (Genesis 1-11). Much of the pertinent material points directly to Mesopotamia. This applies to the Garden of Eden, the Tower of Babel, and the exploits of Nimrod. Other significant accounts find striking analogues in Mesopotamian literature: notably, the Creation and the Deluge. Yet an absolute correlation between the two groups of sources cannot be established. The Mesopotamian kings before the Flood do not correspond to the antediluvian Patriarchs. The biblical hero of the Deluge bears no resemblance in name to his Mesopotamian counterpart; and the peak on which the Ark landed is Mount Niṣir in the Gilgamesh Epic, whereas the Old Testament locates it in the Ararat range. Many other differences could readily be cited. Some things had obviously been changed, and others added, in the process of transmission. But to whom are these deviations to be ascribed? Since the biblical version of prehistory has had an enormous influence on world literature and thought, all major participants in its formulation and revision are bound to elicit enduring interest.

It may be in order to stress, for the sake of cogency, that the observed departures from the Mesopotamian originals cannot simply be charged to the Hebrews themselves; certainly not all of them. To be sure, the Hebrews did not leave these accounts intact. They contributed their own paronomastic explanations, moral judgments, and other comments. Nevertheless, the fact of an intermediate link remains. That link needs not have been the same with each individual tradition that was eventually incorporated in the biblical account of prehistory. The names of the antediluvian Patriarchs, for instance, are a far cry from their Sumerian analogues, yet some of them are obviously Semitic. The whole problem cannot be taken up at this time. We are concerned here only with the question of Hurrian participation. The best case for that is tied up with the account of the Flood.

That the Hurrians had the opportunity to handle Mesopotamian traditions is now abundantly clear from the fact of their intimate contacts with Sumer and Akkad well back in the third millennium. Their own literature, moreover, demonstrates that the Hurrians had a keen interest in these matters. Lastly, cultural traffic between the Hebrews and the Hurrians is amply and independently established. In regard to the Flood story, the fact has already been cited that the Hurrians had made a translation of the Gilgamesh Epic, which contains the longest extant account of that story.[61] It is for all these reasons that the change from Mount Niṣir to Ararat in the biblical version should have a special significance. For the original home of the Hurrians cannot have been far from the Lake Van district. And that district is dominated by Ararat.

There is one further important element in this connection. The biblical account of the Deluge is introduced by the dramatic and transparently pagan episode of the Fallen Giants (Genesis 6, 1–4). Now the antecedents of that episode have long been traced, with good reason, to the Uranid phase of Greek mythology: the deadly rivalries between the leading gods and their resort to Titans and Typhon were seen reflected in the laconic biblical statement, which thus served as a basis for the cataclysmic punishment of the Flood.[62] The Greek motifs, in turn, were echoed in Hellenistic fragments of Phoenician mythology.

[61] See above, note 28.

[62] See E. G. KRAELING, "The Significance and Origin of Gen. 6:1–4," *JNES* 6 (1947), 193–208.

The Phoenician tales, however, were commonly viewed as borrowings from the Greeks, until the finds at Ugarit came up to enhance the essential authenticity and originality of these tales.

The gradual recovery of Hurrian literature places now the whole problem in a new light. The Kumarbi Epic supplies parallels to the Uranid succession that are much too close and detailed to be dismissed as coincidence.[63] And the Song of Ullikummi is the obvious source of the Typhon motif at least in these two essentials: the monster Typhon opposes Zeus at precisely the same stage at which the Ullikummi, the stone monster of the Hurrian epic, arises as the adversary of Tešub; and the great battle takes place on Mons Cassius in the Greek version, and on Mount Ḫazzi in Hurrian tradition, the two names being demonstrably identical.[64] It is highly significant in this connection that the motif of hybrid monsters is one of the characteristics of Hurrian sculpture.

Accordingly, the pertinent elements of Greek mythology go back ultimately to the Hurrians. The long suspected link between the Fallen Giants of the Old Testament and Greek mythology must be explained, therefore, in reality as yet another instance of Hurrian influence on the Hebrews. But our reconstruction cannot stop with the Hurrians. The Kumarbi myth points ultimately to Mesopotamian influence in many of its details. Since the Flood story is basically Mesopotamian, these two conclusions suggest themselves as a plausible working hypothesis. First, that the Hurrians took over the basic account but embellished it with certain native touches. And, second, that the Hebrews utilized the Hurrian re-

[63] Cf. the references given in notes 22 and 23, above.
[64] GÜTERBOCK, *JCS*, 5, 145.

daction of the Deluge account, while drawing upon the rich mythological materials of the Hurrians for a frame story, i.e., the episode of the Fallen Giants, to serve as an introduction to the Flood story.

In conclusion, it is appropriate to point out that the indicated vicissitudes of the biblical version of the Deluge would seem to be symptomatic of the nature of the Hurrian participation in the civilization of the Hebrews. There was much that the Hurrians were able to contribute to the civilization of Palestine. A part of that contribution stemmed in the last instance from Mesopotamia. But the original share of the Hurrians in the final product was by no means negligible. And a substantial offshoot of that composite creation found its way ultimately into the mainstream of Western civilization.

The Idea of History in Ancient Mesopotamia

I. NATURE OF THE PROBLEM

IN THE INTELLECTUAL WORLD OF THE SUMERIANS NO CONcepts would seem to be more distinctive and fundamental than the associated ideas of n a m and m e. The first has the approximate force of our "essence" and "destiny" combined. The other has no suitable analogue in the world of ideas with which we are familiar, for m e appears to be the activating feature appropriate to each n a m and required for its proper functioning.[1] Every essential element of nature and society has its individual m e.[2] Cosmic rule and kingship on earth, qualities and emotions noble as well as base, arts and crafts—these and many others become dormant when their special m e is absent.[3]

No rendering of such an intimte cultural term can be

[1] Cf. B. Landsberger, *Archiv für Keilschriftforschung,* 2 (1924–25), 64–8; *Islamica,* 2 (1926), 369; *Fakültesi Dergisi,* 3, 154.

[2] See Kramer, *Sumerian Mythology,* pp. 64–7.

[3] When the Zû bird stole the Tablets of Destinies from Enlil every m e became inoperative; cf. *ANET,* pp. 111 ff. Does this myth imply that the Tablets of Destinies controlled each and every m e or that they constituted the individual m e of the universe on which all others depended?

more than a rough approximation. We may choose "norm" or "decree," "dynamic force" or the like.[4] We may go on to point out that the m e was endowed with esoteric and enduring properties. Yet, for all our efforts, we find ourselves unable to evoke the meaning inherent in the native term. It is in the nature of distinctive civilizations that their distinguishing features cannot be lifted intact out of their context. Neither can their original designations be translated into words stemming from a foreign source and based on alien experiences.

Ideas of history peculiar to a given society are likely to constitute some of that society's most meaningful features. Because they reflect, however, basic societal values, they are difficult for outsiders to apprehend. To appreciate the Mesopotamian idea of history in all its ramifications we should need to know in effect what the Sumerians, who played a major role in the evolution of the civilization of Mesopotamia, conceived as the n a m and the m e of history in general and their own history in particular. This we cannot determine. The two characteristic concepts, which are elusive for us in the first place,[5] are never applied by the sources to an institution or an abstraction which we could confidently equate with "history." All of this is a fair measure of the complexity of the problem that now confronts us.

[4] For a recent discussion see T. Jacobsen, *JNES,* 5 (1946), 139, n. 20, where "*modus operandi*" is proposed as a reasonable approximation.

[5] It is significant in this connection that Frankfort, *The Birth of Civilization in the Near East,,* p. 16, in analyzing the nature of civilization, concludes that its two primary aspects are "form and "dynamics." Now "form," or "the elusive identity " of a given civilization or of any of its distinctive components, is for all practical purposes very close to the Sumerian n a m; and "dynamics" would be as good a rendering of m e as has yet been suggested. Frankfort does not adduce our terms for a possible comparison, but he might easily have done so. It would thus seem that the Sumerians had already anticipated this particular—and altogether convincing—result.

Does this absence of a native term corresponding to our "history" imply that Mesopotamia, in its long career as an integral civilization, failed to evolve a particular idea of history? Hardly. The historic Mesopotamian was keenly aware of his past; he was forever busy recording its details; and he was intent on drawing from the past certain practical lessons. All this can readily be demonstrated. What is less obvious is the over-all system resulting from the sum of such interests and activities. The sense of history varies from place to place and from period to period. In the ancient Near East that sense was highly developed in Palestine [6] but very little, apparently, in Egypt. To the Mesopotamian, history was something involved in the larger issues of life and destiny as manifested in the past, tied up with the present, and projected into the future. But it was also something to be lived, not dissected. Accordingly, the Mesopotamian's awareness of the process was reflected in numerous ways, but it did not lead to a direct statement of principles.

Our conception then, of the idea of history in ancient Mesopotamia has to be pieced together from the incidental reflections of that idea in sundry phases of the underlying civilization. We can thus expect here only a reflection of a reflection or, to paraphrase a distinguished student of historiosophy, a reflection of the

[6] Cf. Meyer, *Geschichte des Altertums* II/2 (1931), 285: "So hat die Blütezeit des judaeischen Königtums eine wirkliche Geschichtsschreibung geschaffen." Contrast, however, Collingwood, *The Idea of History,* p. 12: "two forms of quasi-history, theocratic history and myth, dominated the whole of the Near East until the rise of Greece." This is not the place to demonstrate in detail that Meyer's statement rests on a sounder foundation than Collingwood's. But in justice to Collingwood's provocative study it should be added that its author had not had the opportunity to acquaint himself with much essential information on the progress of historiography among "our forerunners in civilization."

second degree[7]—our analysis of the analysis of the ancients indirectly conveyed. To attempt this we have to approach the subject with the fragmentary data of our own age, two millennia and more after the history in question had come to a close at long last. Yet the results need not be unduly speculative, for the themes involved pervade large areas of Mesopotamian civilization and are thus capable of repeated control. The question is whether we can reassemble the component motifs into a self-consistent pattern.

Most of the pertinent material has been treated in separate investigations by eminently competent authorities.[8] Larger portions of the total design have also been subjected to penetrating analysis.[9] All such results loom large in the presentation that follows. Yet no study to date has focused directly on the whole topic before us; although some of the territory has been well explored, large stretches of it remain untouched. To that extent therefore our argument must carry with it some of the risks and hazards of an initial effort. This is not, to be sure, a case of a writer rushing in but an instance of his

[7] *Ibid.*, p. 3.

[8] See Olmstead, *Assyrian Historiography,* University of Missouri Studies in Social Science, Ser. III, Vol. I (1916) which although antiquated and rather tangential to the present topic, being primarily a textual comparison of late annals, is still useful; Güterbock, *ZA, 42,* Pt. I, 1–91, a penetrating and pioneering discussion; Jacobsen, *The Sumerian King List,* AS 11 (1939) which is no less important, although limited to the earliest phase of the problem. Note also Mowwinckel, *Gunkel Festschrift,* pp. 278–322, and W. A. Irwin, "The Orientalist as Historian," *JNES, 8* (1949), 298–309.

[9] Cf. e.g., these major studies on the connection between religion and the state in Mesopotamia, a subject that has a pronounced bearing on the question before us: Labat, *Le caractère religieux de la royauté assyro-babylonienne;* Gadd, *Ideas of Divine Rule in the Ancient Near East;* Frankfort, *Kingship and the Gods.* See also Jacobsen, *The Intellectual Adventure of Ancient Man* (ed. H and H. A. Frankfort) pp. 125–222, and Albright, *From the Stone Age to Christianity.* Other references will be given in the course of the discussion.

having been persuaded to take the plunge. Nevertheless, the wisdom of a venture must be open to doubt when the field is one where angels have not been known to tarry.

II. THE GENERAL CULTURAL SETTING

Our task, then, is first, to seek out the principal elements which enter in one way or another into the concept of history in ancient Mesopotamia; and second, to inquire whether these sundry elements yield anything resembling a harmonious design. Before we survey the separate motifs we must touch briefly on three broader themes which furnish the essential background. These themes are civilization, religion, and government. It goes without saying that only the roughest kind of outline is possible at this time; no more than is necessary to suggest how each of these factors might affect the superimposed idea of history.

1. CIVILIZATION

Mesopotamian civilization reaches back to remote prehistoric times—an indeterminate number of centuries prior to 3,000 B.C.—and it survives as an active force until Hellenistic times. The prehistoric age, although brilliantly illuminated in some respects, must forever remain dim and inarticulate in others, notably in the social and intellectual fields.[10] This is precisely why it is prehistoric. The long historic span, however, is richly documented thanks to the presence of writing. The picture that

[10] Cf., in general, Frankfort, *The Birth of Civilization,* pp. 32 ff.; Speiser, *JAOS, 59,* suppl. 4, 17–31.

emerges is clear enough in its main contours, although innumerable details remain obscure.

Perhaps clearest of all is the fact that the underlying civilization enjoyed substantial uniformity throughout its long career. This is not to imply that it was a static civilization; its dynamic character is constantly in evidence. But the statement can be made and upheld that certain basic values present from the start retain their vitality to the very end. Dominant beliefs and practices which we notice under the Sargonids of Akkad, in the third millennium, are still in vogue in the first millennium, under the Sargonids of Nineveh. The changes that the passing centuries bring with them do not affect the main framework. For purposes of our over-all appraisal, therefore, the cultural constants outweigh the chronological variables.[11]

It is particularly noteworthy that this essential uniformity of Mesopotamian civilization throughout its historic course was maintained in spite of a great diversity of participants. For Mesopotamia, unlike Egypt or Palestine, was not the home of a single dominant ethnic group in the period under discussion. On the contrary, several significant groups pass in review, usually more than one at a time. The Sumerians, the Babylonians, and the Assyrians are the best known, but there are others. The Sumerians, moreover, inject into the scene the potentially disruptive feature of a language apart. The common

[11] It should be stressed in passing that over its long course Mesopotamian civilization confronts us with abundant evidence for discontinuity as well as continuity and that opinions differ in regard to the interpretation of these contrasting phenomena; cf. Speiser, *Hebrew Union College Annual, 23,* Pt. I, 339–56; [see above, pp. 213 ff.] Yet such differences of opinion center primarily about sundry details. The over-all structure remains uniform and self-consistent.

civilization, then, was uniquely cosmopolitan. It transcended ethnic, linguistic, and political boundaries, achieving cultural unity where disparity would be the normal outcome.

This unusual attainment of unity through disparity must be credited to the Sumerians. It is wholly immaterial in this connection what position one takes in regard to the question of ultimate Sumerian priority.[12] The long prehistoric stage lacked the means to leave to posterity definite ethnolinguistic criteria. All it could do was strew the area with material remains of several distinctive cultures.[13] Eventually, however, the survivors are drawn within a single orbit. They come to reflect the same kind of cultural content and direction in religion and literature, law and government, arts and sciences.[14] By that time the normative features are unmistakably Sumerian. These features appear early in the historic age. And whether the Sumerians had been on the scene from the very beginning or had arrived recently—which the present writer regards as an inescapable conclusion—it is they who made history beyond all dispute.

The fact, however, that the Sumerians were not alone in building up the civilization of Mesopotamia had this important consequence. For all cultural purposes, the land was bilingual: for the last two thousand years of its

[12] *Ibid.*

[13] Cf. Perkins, *The Comparative Archeology of Early Mesopotamia.*

[14] Political differences, notably between Babylonia and Assyria, could not offset the underlying cultural unity. Thus, Shamshi-Adad I of Assyria, whose concluding years dovetailed with the beginning of Hammurabi's reign, caused his own inscriptions to be couched in the style and spirit of Babylonia. His lead was followed by all Assyrian rulers after 1350 B.C.; cf. Landsberger and Balkan, *Belleten 14* (1950), 220. Analogous instances could be adduced for various other phases of the intellectual life of Assyria.

history the literate elements had to make use not alone of the Semitic Akkadian but also of the unrelated Sumerian.[15] Recourse to two languages was a broadening experience in many ways. It implied a victory over parochialism, some capacity for toleration, and a certain universality of outlook. And the eventual bearer of this heritage, in the strict cultural sense, was not properly a Sumerian, a Babylonian, or an Assyrian. He was essentially a Mesopotamian.

2. *RELIGION*

The tendency toward universalism just mentioned is most clearly evident in religion. And since the religion of Mesopotamia was in all essentials a contribution of the Sumerians, we may speak this time specifically of the Sumerian religion. Perhaps its two outstanding features are the human attributes of its gods and their identification with the powers of nature and the cosmos. It is on this last count that we have here a universalistic, and certainly a supranational, conception of religion.

Furthermore, the Sumerian saw in the society of the gods the prototype of human society. The two interpenetrated. Man took his cue from the gods at the same time that the gods were being drawn closer to mankind.[16] No one god was the sole source of power and authority. All the leading figures of the pantheon had themselves been created. None was fully secure in his status, none

[15] Hence when the combined Sumero-Akkadian vehicle proved its usefulness farther afield, as it did with the Hittites, the ultimate tool became trilingual to some extent, as any student of Hittite will feelingly confirm.

[16] Cf. the literature cited in n. 9; also Landsberger, *Fakültesi Dergisi*, 3, 151.

really omnipotent. Authority resided in the community of the gods. As a community, the gods required organization. This organization took the form of a state. The state, in turn, was a self-governing body and, as such, a safeguard against absolutism.

But the lack of absolute authority on the part of any one god led to uncertainty about the actions of the divine powers combined. Nothing was settled for all time, nothing could be taken for granted; hence the anxiety and the insecurity of the mortals, who must forever be intent on propitiating the gods in order to obtain a favorable decision. The view that nothing was permanent and that the gods were unpredictable brought with it a fitful and dramatic conception of the universe, one that called for constant watchfulness and elaborate ritual.[17] By the same token, however, there was always room for hope rather than apathy and resignation.

3. *GOVERNMENT*

Since the cosmos was conceived as a state, and since government on earth was a replica of divine government, the Mesopotamian state must correspond to the cosmic state. This principle remains valid throughout the entire history of Mesopotamia. It follows that the authority of the mortal ruler was severely circumscribed by two factors. First, his mandate stemmed from the gods to whom he was responsible for his every move. Second, the head of the pantheon lacked absolute power, in that the cosmic

[17] See Frankfort, *Intellectual Adventure,* ch. 1, and *Kingship and the Gods,* Bk. II. The fundamental fact is the limited authority of any one god, no matter how high his position in the pantheon.

state subscribed to the principle of government by assembly.[18] Hence so it must be also with government on earth.

The normative place of the assembly in the sociopolitical structure of Mesopotamia has only recently come in for proper appreciation.[19] It is a feature that combines with the overriding importance of the law to impose effective checks on unilateral authority. No major societal undertaking can be sanctioned without the prior approval of the appropriate assembly. This applied to the choice of the head of the pantheon[20] or to the grant of immortality to a mortal,[21] just as it does to political moves by human rulers,[22] whether these be legendary or historical. In this all-pervasive safeguard against autocracy lies perhaps the key to the appeal and the magnetism which Mesopotamian civilization exercised upon many neighboring cultures.

So much for the general cultural setting against which we must now endeavor to trace the idea of history in Mesopotamia. To some extent the background has already determined the scale and disclosed the outlines of the design that we seek to recover. But the whole cannot

[18] Cf. Jacobsen, *Intellectual Adventure*, pp. 125 ff., and *JNES, 2,* 159 ff. For similar results arrived at from a different starting point cf. Speiser, *Studies in the History of Science* (Philadelphia, 1941), pp. 1–13, and *Waldo Leland Volume,* pp. 51–62.

[19] In addition to the references in n. 18, cf. also, Oppenheim, *5,* 224 ff.

[20] "The Creation Epic," Tab. 3, ll. 130 ff. (*ANET,* p. 64 f.).

[21] "Epic of Gilgamesh," Tab. XI, ll. 197–8.

[22] An Old Assyrian text expresses this in a succinct formula: "Ashur is the king; Irishum is [but] the toparch [*iššakku*] for Ashur"; cf. Landsberger and Balkan, *Belleten 14,* 231. Similarly, in the Cappadocian tablets *Šarrum-kên* (*Sargon*) I of Ashur is only a *rubā'um,* or "prince," whereas the ruler of Hattum boasts the title of *šarrum,* or "king"; cf. *ibid.,* p. 231 and *Orientalia,* 20 (1951), 483. Thus, far from being despotic, as has often been alleged, the Assyrian rulers were careful to emphasize their subsidiary role in affairs of state, for even there the leading parts were reserved for the gods.

be placed in focus without due attention to the component parts.

III. NATURE OF THE SOURCE MATERIAL

Before there can be any systematic thought about history there must be sufficient interest in the past. For such preoccupation in Mesopotamia there is manifold and extensive evidence. Much of it consists of direct historical references: regnal lists, chronicles, annals. In addition to these there are literary compositions in which bare historical facts have been woven into a richer fabric of myth and legend; historical tales, in short, as opposed to straight history. That literature should go to the past for its most popular motifs is in itself significant. But echoes of remote days are not confined to literature. They are clearly audible also in a field that has no room for fancy, the deadly serious field of omens. Another form of awareness of the past is attested in certain architectural practices. And lastly, a number of Mesopotamian rulers have left us concrete evidence of their antiquarian pursuits, with an occasional hint as to motivation. These, then, are the main types of sources where we must look for the fugitive idea of history in Mesopotamia. The clue these sources furnish will be followed up later in the so-called wisdom literature. First, however, let us isolate that clue. We shall begin with the rulers whose antiquarian leanings are noted in the records.

Royal inquiries into the past are connected as a rule with religious matters. They may revolve, for instance, about the building history of major temples. Thus we are told by Shalmaneser I, an Assyrian ruler of the 13th century, that a temple at Ashur originally built by Ushpia had been rebuilt by Irishum I (i.e., Erishu), restored 159 years later by Shamshi-Adad, and reconstructed by Shalmaneser himself after a lapse of 580 years.[23] The same temple required urgent attention under Esarhaddon, who counts another 580 years between Shalmaneser's reconstruction and his own.[24] The fact that the various computations reveal some discrepancies need not concern us here. It is the detailed record of the successive restorations that is alone important in the present instance.

Of similar import is the statement by Ashurbanipal that, on capturing Susa, he was able to recover the image of the goddess Nana which the Elamite Kudur-Naḫundi had carried off from Uruk 1,635 years before.[25] Likewise related is the observation by Nabonidus, a frustrated archeologist turned king, that 3,200 years had elapsed between the burial of Naram-Sin's foundation inscription of the Shamash temple at Sippar and his own recovery of that inscription.[26] Once again the chronology does not stand up to modern audits, but the research behind such data cannot be ignored.[27]

How is this form of interest in the past to be explained? The answer is hinted at by the Old Assyrian king Irishum I, the same ruler who is cited first by Shalmaneser I, and later, by Esarhaddon. In writing about the Ashur Temple, Irishum says: "Should the building grow weak with age, and a king like me wishes to rebuild the structure, he

[23] *KAH, 1,* 13, col. 3, ll. 32 ff.

[24] A. Poebel, *JNES, 1* (1942), 290 ff.; E. Weidner, *AFO, 15* (1945–51), 89.

[25] Cf. L. W. King, *Chronicles Concerning Early Babylonian Kings* (1907), I, 12, n. 1.

[26] *Ibid.,* p. 11, n. 2.

[27] For other ancient retrospects of this kind cf. Meissner, *Babylonien und Assyrien, 2,* 363.

shall not displace the nail that I have driven in, but shall restore it to its place." [28] The nail or peg (*sikkatum*), as has recently been demonstrated, is here—and in many instances elsewhere—a symbol of the completion and dedication of a solemn project for which the protection of the appropriate deity is being invoked. It is in a sense the outward sign of a pact between the devout builder and his deity. The usage can be traced back, independently, well into the 3d millennium.[29]

We may assume, then, that temples were viewed in Mesopotamia, from early days on, as the embodiment of a covenant between a god and his community. It was vitally important for succeeding generations that the covenant, and the good will which it betokened, be maintained. Hence the original foundations must not be disregarded in later repairs and alterations. Nor must the symbol of relationship with the deity, the peg that literally nailed down the agreement, be moved from its original spot.

It thus follows that here was one practical and vital reason for the constant and exacting study for the past. That reason was the urgent need for not upsetting the friendly relations with the cosmic powers that had been established in the past. A distant echo of this policy is reflected in II Kings 17:24 ff. The people whom the Assyrians had transplanted to Israel after the fall of Samaria are instructed by the conqueror to make their peace with the god of the vanquished in order to obviate his wrath.

The principle that the past must be studied so that the present may learn how to get along is evidenced also

[28] Landsberger and Balkan, *Belleten 14,* 224 ff., ll. 19–23.
[29] *Ibid.,* pp. 252 ff.

in the process of assembling great libraries of ancient records, notably the library of Ashurbanipal.[30] There was a utilitarian purpose to that king's intellectual pretensions. He spells it out for us himself. In an itemized order for texts to be procured—looted might be a better term—in the city of Borsippa, there is included a blanket request for "rituals, prayers, inscriptions on stone, and whatever may be good for kingship," as well as "any tablet or ritual . . . that is good for my palace." [31] The phrases "good for kingship" and "good for my palace" go a long way toward defining the meaning of the past as viewed by Mesopotamian royalty. It was a case of self-interest, even enlightened self-interest, in a sense. The past was significant because it could inform the present in regard to the future. But what was the information thus gathered and the lesson obtained from it?

Before we take up this question, there still are some general points to be made in passing. The preceding remarks have stressed the fact that the Mesopotamian view of history, once it had been formulated, remained substantially unchanged through the ages. To be sure, events of the passing centuries must have left their mark on historical thinking. Yet the underlying civilization, as we have seen, continued intact in terms of basic values. In a history as long as Mesopotamia's this outstanding fact cannot be stressed too strongly. It is not surprising, therefore, that Ashurbanipal's astrologers should consult the same manuals that had been used by Hammurabi's diviners

[30] In the process of accumulating this library inferior copies were withdrawn to be replaced by better and earlier texts. For a specific reference to a Hammurabi original thus utilized cf. Olmstead, *History of Assyria*, pp. 490–1.

[31] See *CT*, 22, 1, and R. H. Pfeiffer, *State Letters of Assyria* (1935), No. 256.

more than a thousand years earlier or that historical tradition in the 1st millennium should dwell on themes that had won popularity as early as the turn of the 3d millennium. The living past was an abiding reality.

The presence of such a stock of common themes makes it easier for us to choose a particular segment of the past for closer scrutiny. History can be apprehended only in retrospect from a fixed point in time. The whole history of Mesopotamia would be too vast a span for a brief yet fruitful survey. If it is true, however, that the normative concepts of the civilization of Mesopotamia had crystallized already by the end of the 3d millennium, a convenient vantage point early in the 2d millennium should afford us all the necessary perspective. Although later periods will not be left out of account, we shall concentrate on the earlier as the basis for ideas about history.

The modern student breaks up the old sources of historical tradition into such categories as folklore, history or quasi history, theology, magic, and the like. This is a logical procedure from our standpoint. Yet we should not lose sight of the fact that to the originating civilization such categories differed from one another in emphasis and purpose but scarcely in validity. All made use of the same data of past experience. A given episode or motif is often utilized simultaneously by each. It is as if the main themes of historical tradition, before they were released to the separate disciplines of the day, had been screened and distilled by a central school of thought. The thinking of that school, and not our thoughts about the same data, must be our ideal objective. The point has been well made by R. G. Collingwood that "the historian who studies a civilization other than his own can apprehend the mental life of that civilization only by reenacting that experience for himself." [32] We should try, then, to put ourselves in the position of a native student of history of long ago—it is a synthetic and ideal abstraction, of course—and look back on the past as he saw it. In so doing, we have to take over the student's personal failures of knowledge and sympathy. Yet no stage of historiosophy, including our own, can be said to have shaken off completely the shackles of its particular environment.

IV. THE PAST AS SEEN BY THE MESOPOTAMIANS

Let us suppose, then, that a promising young scholar, say in the year 1750 B.C., desiring recognition at Ur, Nippur, or Babylon as Doctor of the Past, has been asked by his examiners to name five epochal junctures in the history of his culture. If he was thoughtful and learned beyond his years; these are the stages that he might have singled out: 1) The beginning of civilization; 2) the Deluge; 3) the crisis under Etana, the shepherd; 4) the rivalry between Kish and Uruk, culminating in the clash of Agga and Gilgamesh; and 5) the period of Sargon and Naram-Sim. Local traditions could cause some changes in such a list; [33] the accession of the given reigning dynasty would not be overlooked. But the culture as a whole would probably have agreed on these five epochs. What was the consensus about them?

1) Civilization was a gift from the gods who vouchsafed

[32] *The Idea of History,* p. 163; cf. also, pp. 282 ff.

[33] Thus the Chronicle Weidner (see the next section, cf. n. 42) assigns prominence to Marduk and Babylon at a time when neither had as yet risen above the level of mediocrity; see rev. ll. 11 ff.

it to mankind as a full-grown product. It was abroad from the day that "kingship had been lowered from heaven." [34] The primeval kings learned the necessary details through the Seven Sages.[35] But it was the presence of kingship as such that marked the difference between order on the one hand and anarchy and barbarism on the other.

2) After a hazy period of enormous length the gods saw fit to regret their gift to mankind. They sent down the Deluge, which all but swept away the last vestige of life on earth. For a number of anxious days the future of life and civilization hinged on the fate of the precarious craft that bore the hero of the cataclysm; his ark contained, providentially, "the seed of all living creatures," including "all the craftsmen." [36] Thus was culture saved from the elements.

3) The fresh start marked the beginning of an unbroken chain in which the present was but the latest link. (It meant much the same thing to the ancients that the dawn of history means to us.) Shadowy outlines of postdiluvian rulers appear on the distant horizon. The first realm to become manifest is the city-state of Kish. And the first of the new rulers to be featured by historic tradition is the shepherd Etana.

Etana's place in the traditional lore of Mesopotamia is attested in several ways. He is recognized in art,[37] figures in an omen, is prominent in a bilingual text dealing with the Seven Sages, and receives more than passing notice from the Sumerian king list.[38] Above all, however, Etana

[34] This is the introductory phrase in the Sumerian king list; cf. Jacobsen, *The Sumerian King List,* pp. 58 f.; 64, n. 119; 70.

[35] Landsberger, *Fakültesi Dergisi,* 2, 431; O. R. Gurney, *JRAS* ,1936), 459–66.

[36] "Gilgamesh Epic," Tab. XI, ll. 83, 85.

[37] Frankfort, *Cylinder Seals,* pp. 138, 139.

[38] For the epigraphic material on Etana cf. Güterbock, *ZA,* 42, 22; Jacobsen, *The Sumerian King List,* p. 80, n. 67.

is known as the hero of a celebrated epic which was to live on in at least three recensions: the Old Babylonian, the Middle Assyrian, and the Neo-Assyrian.[39] There can thus be no doubt about Etana's enduring place in the culture of his land.

What does that lasting impression signify? The popular answer is given in this repeated phrase: "Etana, a shepherd who ascended to heaven."[40] But what had caused that extraordinary journey? The epic traces the reason to a crisis in the hero's family, but it is doubtful whether learned circles were satisfied with that account. Our imaginary candidate, for instance, might be expected to refer to the proemium of the tale, which gives a different setting. Mankind, as the Old Babylonian poet informs us, had as yet to have a king. All the characteristic norms of kingship lay inactive before Anu in heaven, "there being no consultation (*mitluku*) for the people."[41] In other words, government by assembly had not yet come into being.

[39] Speiser in *ANET,* pp. 114 ff.

[40] Cf. Jacobsen, *The Sumerian King List,* p. 80, n. 67.

[41] Speiser, *ANET,* pp. 114, A–1, ll. 11–14. The norms (i.e., m e symbols) in question are virtually the same that are cited in the Sumerian m e myth discussed by Kramer, *Sumerian Mythology,* pp. 64 ff.; the pertinent lines are given in transliteration, *ibid.,* p. 116.

The myth just referred to has a further and broader significance for our present purposes. In the divine hierarchy which this myth reflects first place is held by e n, with the as yet obscure s i coming next; both are accompanied by the abstract element n a m mentioned earlier. The list continues with "godship, the tiara exalted and enduring, the throne of kingship . . . the exalted scepter, staffs[?], the exalted shrine, shepherdship, kingship" (cf. Kramer, *op. cit.,* p. 66). In other words, "god" is third in the list, whereas "king" is considerably farther down and is preceded by "shepherd." It follows that here and in related instances e n cannot simply be rendered "high priest," as is often done, nor can the derived Akkadian abstract *enūtu* (e.g., "Creation Epic," Tab. 6, l. 97) be analogously translated. The term obviously stands for "master of the universe" and is thus an exact equivalent of the West Semitic *Ba'al.* For a slightly different view see now, Jacobsen, *JNES, 12* (1953), 180 ff.

In human government the above hierarchy is reduced at the top to three positions: e n/*bêlu* "sovereign," l u g a l/*šarru* "king," and e n s i (-ak) /*iššakku* "local chief" or "toparch," the last being the representative of some

If this explanation is valid—and all signs would seem to show that it is—then the crisis under Etana was social and cultural rather than personal. It is to that juncture that historical tradition would appear to date the introduction of representative government in Mesopotamia as a basic factor in civilization. The shepherd in Etana would thus be a symbol of the king's limited authority and the source of a cultural stereotype featured in all subsequent history.

4) For further literary support of this early dating of representative government we need not go further than the end of the dynasty to which Etana himself has been assigned. According to the king list, the last ruler of the 1st Dynasty of Kish was one Agga.[42] What saves this king from being just another name in a tedious list is the fact that we know him independently from a Sumerian epic which describes his contest with Gilgamesh, lord of Uruk. Perhaps the most important thing about this particular poem is the insight which it affords into the role of the assembly in vital matters of state. Before he can embark on his perilous venture against the dominant power of Kish, Gilgamesh seeks the sanction of two separate bodies: first, the assembly of the elders, and next, the assembly of the warriors.[43] It is there that ultimate authority was evidently vested, as early as the period when history can be apprehended only through the spyglass of legend. And

---

higher authority, either divine or human. The mortal king was no more than a steward under orders from his god, a shepherd tending his master's flock.

[42] This is the Sumerian form. The Semitic pronunciation was evidently *Ak(k)a.* Cf. Chronicle Weidner, *ZA, 42,* 48, ll. 31, see Jacobsen, *The Sumerian King List,* p. 84, n. 99. Note that the name is Sumerian although the dominant local element would seem to be Semitic; cf. below n. 62.

[43] Cf. Jacobsen, *JNES, 2,* 165–6; S. N. Kramer, *ANET,* pp. 44–5.

lest one think that the assembly was little more than a hollow form, we have now the unimpeachable testimony of an Old Babylonian omen, which shows that approval in such cases was by no means automatic. The verdict of the assembly was sometimes *puḫrum ul imtagar* "the assembly will fail to reach an agreement." [44]

The poem about Agga and Gilgamesh—to dwell on it for another moment—lends color to the assumption that the hero of the cycle of Gilgamesh legends was originally an historical figure. It follows that Lugalbanda and Enmerkar,[45] two predecessors of Gilgamesh who are likewise no strangers to legend, can no longer be dismissed outright as fictional. The possibility has to be reckoned with —direct proof, of course, is not to be expected—that these three rulers of Uruk had played memorable parts in the penumbral stage of the history of Sumer. The victory of Gilgamesh over Agga, which appears to have terminated the supremacy of Kish, may well have heralded the emergence of the Sumerians as the political masters of Sumer and Akkad.[46] To the Sumerians the event was history. To us it comes through only as a weak and indistinct echo. We are not in a position, therefore, to

[44] *YOS*, Vol. 10, No. 31, col. 10, ll. 43–4; cf. also, *Orientalia*, 5 (1935), 225 f.

[45] For a recently published epic about this hero see Kramer, *Enmerkar and the Lord of Aratta*, University of Pennsylvania Museum Monograph, 1952.

[46] It may therefore be significant in this connection that the king list gives Mes-kiag-gasher, the legendary founder of this royal house—the 1st Dynasty of Uruk—the title e n as well as that of l u g a l (col. 3, "L" 1–3); the translation of the first as "high priest" is not appropriate (see above, n. 41). What this titulary would seem to imply is transition from city-state to empire. The dynasty is continued by Enmerkar, Lugalbanda, and Gilgamesh—in the order cited—each a celebrated figure in the legendary lore of Sumer, with Gilgamesh obviously regarded as the greatest of them. This is indeed an Heroic Age, as Kramer has emphasized (cf. *Proceedings of the American Philosophical Society*, 90, 120–30), not only of Sumer but also, and more particularly, of the Sumerians as such.

decide how much of the outcome may have been due to the ethnic factor—if Kish had been substantially non-Sumerian—and how much to political and cultural influences alone. We can appreciate, however, the unparalleled impact of Gilgamesh on later ages. If his historical prototype was really the founder of Sumerian supremacy, the unique vigor of the Gilgamesh motif would receive a convincing explanation.

5) The last major juncture in the early history of Mesopotamia, as listed by our imaginary informant, is the age of Akkad. To us, at a remove of over four millennia, the period of Sargon and Naram-Sin easily outweighs in importance any of the preceding eras. This is so mainly because the Akkad age is at last under the full light of history. The contemporary rulers left us original accounts of their achievements as well as various monuments which enable us to check these accounts. Claims of conquests ranging from Elam to Anatolia are substantiated by statues, stelae, and temples from the places conquered: Susa, Ashur, Nineveh, Diyarbekir, and others.[47] We can thus start out for the first time with a hard factual core.

The ancients were just as impressed with the Sargonids as we are, although not for quite the same reasons. We welcome that age because of the material it provides for concrete research. The ancients seized on it because it stirred their imagination, even though the underlying history may still have been vivid in memory and tradition had not yet strayed far from reality. The times of Sargon and Naram-Sin soon become the favorite themes of epics and folk tales, poetry and prose, admonitions and omens.

[47] Cf. Speiser, *JAOS*, 72, 97–101.

And the leading figures of the age are not merely local celebrities. Their fame spreads to other lands and cultures; it is reflected, for instance, in the literature of the Hurrians and the Hittites.[48] The civilization that had long been nurtured in southern Mesopotamia becomes an international factor, transcending ethnic, geographic, and political boundaries.

Much of this, however, is primarily source material for history. In order to appreciate the impact of the events on the idea of history we must concentrate on the secondary sources, the editorials and the columns and the sermons, so to speak, rather than the direct news accounts. Because the Sargonid era had been so rich in events, it gave rise also to a corresponding amount of reflection; hence its central place in the pattern which we are seeking to recapture. Other historical milestones should not, of course, be ignored. But it will simplify matters if, in common with the ancients, we allow the Akkad age to dominate the design of historical thought, while reserving other stages in the long career of Mesopotamia for purposes of control and elaboration.

V. TRADITIONAL VIEWS ON THE MEANING OF THE PAST

To the succeeding ages, then, the century of Sargon and Naram-Sin stood out as a period of unprecedented achievement. But it was no less memorable a fact that the power of Akkad collapsed eventually. The history of that dynasty was thus a vivid example of ebb and flow in

[48] See Güterbock, *Kumarbi*, and *JCS*, 5, 135–61; 6, 8–42.

the fortunes of an empire. It brought into sharper relief the rise and decline of other dynasties. There was an almost rhythmic regularity to this unvarying alternation. Regularity was suggestive of cosmic laws. In short, here was a ready basis on which to found a system for the interpretation of history.[49]

In its main outlines the scheme in question may have been as old as the emergence of the characteristic civilization of Mesopotamia; but the details must have been long in taking shape. Things on earth were directed from heaven, therefore history was necessarily theocratic history.[50] The victorious king was the recipient of divine favors, whereas disaster was brought upon the land by ill-fated rulers. Sargon, as the founder of Akkad's might, was obviously destiny's favorite. By the same token, Naram-Sin must have been marked for ill fortune, since the waning years of his reign were disastrous for Akkad. Similarly, the end of any dynasty was the direct result of the god's displeasure.[51]

Given the theocratic premise and the long succession

[49] See Güterbock, *ZA, 42,* 13 ff.

[50] It should be stressed, however, that Collingwood's strictures against theocratic history—in that is is not history proper—(*op. cit.,* pp. 14 ff.) apply in this instance only in part. The fundamental thing is that the supreme god of Mesopotamia is not an omnipotent being. His authority can be affected not only by the divine assembly but also by such extraneous circumstances as the theft of the Tablets of Destinies. Under the resulting system, therefore, the object of historical thinking cannot be "single and infinite," to cite Collingwood's description of theocratic thought (*ibid.,* p. 5). To some extent, at least, past events must have appeared to the traditional Mesopotamian as "final and plural," thus fulfilling some of Collingwood's criteria of historicity (*ibid.*). It would surely not be going too far to assert that in Mesopotamia history ruled the gods more than the gods ruled history. Theocratic government, in short, was to the Mesopotamian merely human government one stage removed. The local theocracy, in other words, did not of itself constitute an insuperable barrier to research and inquiry. And research and inquiry amount to a convenient paraphrase for "history."

[51] Güterbock, *ZA, 42,* 75 f.; Speiser, *JAOS, 72,* 97 ff.

of dynasties that had come and gone by the end of the 3d millennium, the social philosopher of the Old Babylonian period had every reason to see the past in terms of recurring cycles. But did he apply such findings to the future? Was Marduk certain to do to Babylon as Nidaba had done to Lagash or Enlil to the Guti? Would the timeless cure-all which spells "It cannot happen to me" have stood in the way of a tidal school of historiosophy? The question is of considerable interest, but the available data do not add up to a conclusive answer.

The past, at any rate, was high-lighted by alternating periods of bliss and disaster. As a rule, each succeeding dynasty was the instrument whereby the gods displaced the given incumbent. Occasionally, however, the gods might send a strange new people as a scourge, as happened in the case of the Ummān Manda who broke the power of the Sargonids. In other words, sequence was construed as consequence.

There had to be, of course, a reason for the dynastic changes consistent with the theocratic principle of state. The gods would forsake a mortal ruler and turn against him because he had offended them in some way (the technical Akkadian term is *qullulu*). The offender is said to have transgressed his solemn oath of office (*mamīta etēqu*) or overstepped the bounds set for him by his god (*itê ili etēqu*).[52]

The classic illustration is the well-known case of Lugalzaggesi of Umma and Urukagina of Lagash. Rivalry between these two remarkable rulers—in a prodigal generation which was to see both eclipsed by the matchless Sargon—brought about the destruction of Lagash. To the Lagash chronicler of the event the destruction of his city

[52] See *Belleten, 14,* 263.

was "an offense against Ningirsu, its god." No blame attaches to Urukagina, on whose part "there is no offense." Both Lugalzaggesi and his goddess Nidaba shall bear the consequences. Thus a political clash resolves itself into a contest between the respective patron deities, much as a dispute between shepherds might have to be settled by their masters. In practice, might was right. In theory, right was invoked to account for might.

This motif of theological offense as grounds for historic change confronts us throughout Mesopotamian history. I shall cite only two further instances, which may be less familiar than most. In a unique document from Mari, which will interest us again later on, Yasmaḫ-Addu, a contemporary of Hammurabi, solemnly affirms that no member of his family had ever "committed an offense against his god" (*ša ana ilim uqallilu ul ibašši*).[53] None had violated his oath to the deity or broken international agreements which the gods had witnessed. On the other hand, the very opposite was true of the rival rulers.[54] For their part, no doubt, the accused hastened to reverse the charges.

The same attitude animates a poetic work of the Middle Assyrian period, wherein Tukulti-Ninurta I contrasts the perfidy of Babylon with the unfailing righteousness of Ashur.[55] The Kassite king of Babylon is branded as "transgressor of the oath" (*ētiq mamīti*),[56] who admits at length that "most grievous have been the offenses of my land, numerous its sins" (*qellēt mātiya šupšuqā imīdū*

[53] *ARM,* Vol. 1, No. 3, l. 6. The king of Eshnunna is alleged to be planning a similar offense, cf. *ibid.,* No. 26, ll. 32 ff.

[54] Their guilt is termed *qullultum* (l. 18).

[55] The text has been presented in transliteration and translation by Ebeling, *MAOG,* Vol. 12, fasc. 2.

[56] *Ibid.,* col. 4, l. 20.

arnū).[57] Echoes of similar sentiments are common in the inscriptions of the 1st millennium.[58]

With so much stress on formal features, the idea of history developed against this kind of background could not readily free itself from stereotypes. To be sure, with Urukagina or Yasmaḫ-Addu or Tukulti-Ninurta I the theocratic concept of state was modified by practical needs, except that expediency sought retroactive moral sanction. With theologians, however, unsobered by every-day burdens of state, history could reduce itself under particular circumstances to a mechanism of utmost simplicity. It was all a matter of either honoring or ignoring elementary orders from on high. Everything else was incidental.

This monolithic approach is especially pronounced

[57] *Ibid.*, l. 27. Ebeling's translation of this passage cannot be right. In the first place the feminine (pl.) *šupšuqa* is not co-ordinate with the masculine *imidū;* it modifies the preceding *qellēt,* construct plural to *qillatu.* Accordingly, the initial *inanna abrā* cannot be rendered with Ebeling's translation in a transitive sense: "Jetzt (aber) habe ich die Schlechtigkeit meines Landes gesehen" (p. 17); the phrase means "Now I looked about." Cf. *ZA, 43,* 64, l. 243; *ina adnāti abrema šitnā idātu,* which Landsberger translates "As I looked about among the habitations, the signs were contradictory." Secondly, Ebeling himself renders the parallel passage in col. 6, 1. 33 in the way just advocated: "[Seine Vergehen] sind drückend, viel sind (seine) Sünden." Even in the latter passage, however, the supplemented form should be [*šu*]-*up-šu-q*[*at*], as required by the original (*Archaelogia,* Vol. 69, pl. 52), and not [*šu*]-*up-šu-q*[*u*]; the missing noun was evidently [*qillassu*] "his offense."

[58] It is not impossible that we may have the approximate wording of the king's oath on assuming his obligations under a treaty. The Etana epic, as has already been pointed out, reflects a considerable measure of interest in social philosophy. It is very suggestive, therefore, that its three extant versions—the Old Babylonian, the Middle Assyrian, and the Late Assyrian—give us the same basic oath: "He who oversteps the bounds of Shamash [note the motif of *itê ili etēqu*], may Shamash surrender him for evil to the executioner! He who oversteps the bounds of Shamash, may the mountain withhold from him its passage! May the darting weapon of Shamash, overthrow him and catch him!" Cf. *ANET,* p. 114, A–2, ll. 1–3; p. 115, B, ll. 4–7; p. 116, C–2, ll. 11–16. It is clear from the context that this solemn oath was meant to evoke a picture well known to the audience. [The view just expressed has been confirmed in the meantime by an Old Babylonian text, D. J. Wiseman, *The Alalakh Tablets* (1953), No. *1,* l. 18.]

in the so-called Chronicle Weidner.[59] The text has an Old Babylonian setting and an incurable Babylonian bias. What makes it significant, for all its stilted features, is that the chronicle is, in fact, the first Mesopotamian textbook on the idea of history; partisan, doctrinaire, and obviously below the level of the best thought of the time, but a historiosophy of a sort nonetheless.

The beginning is lost save for a few disconnected phrases,[60] just enough to indicate that the writer had started out with an exposition of general principles: "which you have commanded I have noted, and for the life of distant days . . ." (21′); "he who offends against the gods (*šá a-na i-li*^{pl} . . . *ú-qal-la-lu*)[61] of this city, his star shall not be stable in heaven . . ." (27′); "the conduct of a [?] former king that I have heard much about . . ." (30′). In other words, the purpose of the work was didactic. The past had a lesson which should be heeded for the sake of the future.

The chronicle then proceeds to a schematized survey of important stages in human history, including the time of Akka[62] of Kish and Enme(r)kar of Uruk, representatives of the first two dynasties after the Flood.[63] But the bulk of the account concerns itself with the Dynasty of Sargon and the events before and after that period.

[59] For the publication of this text and invaluable spade work on it see Güterbock, *ZA*, 42, 47 ff.

[60] *Ibid.*, p. 50.

[61] Note the telltale technical term.

[62] The corresponding form in Sumerian contexts is the aforementioned A(g)ga which need not, however, indicate any real difference in pronunciation, since the Sumerian stops do not appear to have been distinctive as to voice. Incidentally, the name itself appears to be Sumerian, whereas the earlier kings of that dynasty bear Semitic names. Does this circumstance reflect a gradual Sumerianization of Akkad?

[63] See above, Pt. IV, sec. 4 of this article. It is clear from this and other occurrences that these early Sumerian heroes maintained their hold on tradition even after the decline of Sumerian political authority.

Sargon was punctilious about the cult and so he prospered. But Naram-Sin was hostile to the people of Babylon,[64] thereby inviting divine retribution through the medium of the Gutian barbarians. Nothing could be simpler than this temple view of history; cult and ritual were the most significant factors in the affairs of state. We know, however, from the instances already cited, and from many others that can be adduced, that this was by no means the prevailing view. The gods could be arbitrary, but scarcely to such a degree. When Nabonidus, about a millennium later, refers to the destruction of Babylon by Sennacherib, he stresses Marduk's wrath against that god's favorite city, with the implication that the city got what it deserved.[65] The Chronicle Weidner is a long way behind the spirit of even that stock interpretation, not to mention the Deuteronomic formulation in such passages as Judg. 2:6 ff.

VI. OMENS AND LETTERS TO THE GODS

As we have seen, Mesopotamia developed a twofold check on the authority of her rulers. One was societal: it was inherent in the role of the assembly. The other was religious: divine bounds must not be transgressed. By extension, any major undertaking on the part of the ruler required divine sanction, in addition to approval by the assembly. How was such sanction ascertained?

The attitude of the gods was signified in the form of directions or oracles (*tērētu*) obtained through the me-

[64] The mention of Babylon in this context is an obvious anachronism which serves to circumscribe the time and place of the composition.

[65] Nabonidus Stele, col. 16, l. 36. For an instructive Hittite parallel, in a "Pestgebet" of Mursilis, cf. Götze, *Kleinasien,* Vol. 91.

dium of omens. These could be contrived with the aid of sacrifices (*tērēt nīqī*), the organs of slaughtered animals, for instance, furnishing the signs that the seer (*bārū*) went on to interpret; or they were based on observations of natural phenomena which the diviner (*mašmašu*) was trained to decipher.[66] Since the need to know what lay in store was imperative and constant, particularly in regard to the state, divination become a vital factor in the civilization of Mesopotamia and one of its outstanding characteristics. No step of any consequence could be risked without proper word from the *bārū* or the *mašmašu*.

These priests did not arrive at their decisions arbitrarily. They were guided by detailed and elaborate manuals in which virtually every possible contingency had been systematically recorded. The basis of the discipline was circumstantial association. Let us suppose that some memorable event (E) had been observed originally under a particular set of extraneous circumstances (C). Since coincidence is not admitted, any time in the future that C comes up again, E is anticipated. C is of course capable of infinite variety. These innumerable variations must be filed away for reference, not unlike our fingerprints. Now when a client calls upon his seer, that analyst identifies the problem from the omen, checks the omen readings against the file, and comes up with the answer.

The omen material is worthless as science but invaluable as raw source material. It utilizes a mass of plain facts as the basis for peculiar constructions. Stripped of these constructions, the facts stand out in stark simplicity. And since some of the events thus treated are taken from

[66] Cf. Ungnad, *AFO, 14* (1941–44), 251 ff.; Oppenheim, *Orientalia, 5* (1936), 199 ff.

history—recent history in the first instance—the omens give us an independent version of the given historical happenings and personalities.[67] They are especially useful as a check on results obtained elsewhere.

We know now that the recording of omens for future reference was an established practice by the end of the 3d millennium. The Sargonid age and the individual members of that dynasty were fully exploited. The volume of Old Babylonian omens in the Yale collection published by A. Goetze a few years ago shows how intensively the field was cultivated in that relatively early period.[68] The use to which such compendia were put may be illustrated by an example from Mari. Among the Mari letters there is one which contains a rather detailed reading of an omen on behalf of the vieroy Yasmaḫ-Addu.[69] If the *bārū* who performed the service (ca. 1700 B.C.) had been unable to consult his own reference library, he might have got almost the same results by borrowing one of Dr. Goetze's copies.[70]

There are two points about the omens that need to be stressed in the present connection. One is the fundamental fact of the ruler's abject dependence in all matters on the will of the gods. This fact, which the omens point up to an overwhelming extent, would be sufficient in itself to refute the assumption that Mesopotamia, in common with

[67] See especially, Goetze, *JCS, 1* (1947), 253 ff.

[68] *YOS*, Vol. 10.

[69] *ARM, 4,* 54; cf. also, *ibid., 5,* 65, and the comment of W. von Soden, *Orientalia, 22* (1933), 209.

[70] Some parallels to *ARM, 5,* 65, have been cited by von Soden, *loc. cit.* In commenting on *ARM, 4,* 54, von Soden (*op. cit.*, p. 204) would change the editor's translation of *tarik* from "est [de couleur] sombre" to "ist geschlagen." This is not quite adequate. The term means primarily "pinched," or "jammed," hence "bruised," or "blood-shot," and hence in a specific sense "dark" as opposed to "clear" (*nawer*).

Egypt, viewed her kings as divine. A god incarnate does not take his cue from the liver of a sheep. The other point to be emphasized is this: it is a fact that some of the kings of the Dynasty of Akkad, the 3d Dynasty of Ur, and certain other places and periods have their names written with the determinative for god and appear to enjoy other prerogatives of divinity. Yet the omens single out precisely these same rulers as human to a fault.[71]—in the way they died or in the manner in which they brought disaster upon their land. Their claim to divinity is thus found to rest on superficial attributes. We cannot be sure what the attributes may have signified in those scattered instances, but we know that the practice was not widespread and that it could not have been far-reaching in scope.[72] Above all, the mere concept of a deified ruler is incompatible with the basic features of Mesopotamia's civilization and out of keeping with its over-all character.

The problem of the ruler's divinity has an obvious bearing on the local idea of history. For history will be viewed one way if the ruler is a mere mortal, and another way if he is accepted as a god. Where government is in human hands throughout, but the state is ultimately theocratic, much will depend on the power attributed to the immortal sovereign. Because no individual god in the Mesopotamian pantheon was really omnipotent, the

[71] This applies to rulers of the Dynasty of Akkad and of Ur III—kings who are elsewhere represented as deified. As for Naram-Sin, who is likewise included in the deified group, there is ample independent information to the effect that he, above all others, was the very archetype of the ill-fated ruler, the "Unheilsherrscher" of Güterbock's penetrating analysis (cf. *ZA, 42,* 75). For a recent refutation of the deification theory, see Fish, *Bulletin of the John Rylands Library 34* (1951), 37 ff. On the question in general, cf. the references given in n. 9, above.

[72] There is, for instance, not the slightest hint of such a practice in Assyria, where we would normally be inclined to look for it first.

purposes of the cosmic society were difficult to fathom. The mortal ruler was forever intent on pleasing the cosmic powers. Often he found himself obliged to appease them. There were times when the need was urgent to establish direct contact with the distant gods. In a literate society distances can be neutralized through writing. It is logical, therefore, in these circumstances that the kings of historic Mesopotamia should write to their gods, even as they were themselves petitioned by their own subjects. Such letters to the gods add a significant touch to the underlying idea of history.[73]

Let us first cite, once again, some instances from the recently published Mari archives. In one of these, Ishme-Dagan of Ashur relates that his campaigns in hostile lands had caused concern to his personal god, or *lamassu*. Accordingly, he had written his lamassu to tell him not to worry.[74] It is noteworthy that it is the god who is being reassured, although it may be merely a case of a writer whistling in the dark. The converse is naturally more common and orthodox, as witness our second instance, which is a letter from Ishme-Dagan's brother, Yasmaḫ-Addu, a young prince whom we have met before.[75] Obviously in trouble, Yasmaḫ-Addu reviews for his god the last three generations in the history of Mari. In all that

[73] Cf. Gadd, *Ideas of Divine Rule in the Ancient Near East* (1947), pp. 61 f.

[74] *ARM* Vol. 4, No. 68, ll. 17 ff. It should be pointed out, however, that in the opinion of von Soden (*Orientalia, 22,* 205), the *La-ma-sí* of this passage can only be a proper name. Von Soden does not give his reasons for this conclusion, but it must be admitted that the form presents certain technical difficulties no matter which way it is interpreted. But the eventual solution would not affect our argument in that the Mari evidence for letters to the gods is sufficient even if this particular text is left out of account altogether.

[75] *ARM, 2,* 3. The document was recognized as a letter to a god by B. Landsberger; cf. *JNES, 11* (1952), 130.

time, his family has proved righteous and god-fearing, whereas the competing dynasty violated the rules of god and man. Parenthetically, the opponents whom Yasmaḫ-Addu accuses had a prior right to the throne of Mari and were eventually restored to power despite our writer's appeal to heaven. Presently, however—and this is our third instance—the successor, in turn, has to address a message to his own protector, the river god.[76] We happen to know that this last appeal, like the one before it, proved of no avail, inasmuch as Hammurabi took over Mari in due time. Under the circumstances, it would have been impossible to disabuse Hammurabi of the conviction that his particular brand of piety was the most efficacious of all.

The first two of the three instances just cited may throw a new light on Assyrian historiography. The writers in question were sons of Shamshi-Adad, one of the most influential kings in the early career of Ashur. The question now arises whether the practice of Shamshi-Adad's family to address the gods sporadically, in times of special need,[77] did not lead eventually to routine reports addressed to the gods at regular intervals.

The annals left us by later Assyrian rulers, from the 14th century on, were periodic accounts by definition. It has always been assumed that they were intended for posterity in general. Perhaps their most striking feature is the boastful, even bombastic, tone which the kings, writing in the first person, invariably employ. These royal writers are egocentric in the extreme.[78] Yet there

[76] See G. Dossin, *Syria, 19* (1938), 126.

[77] In turn, that practice has older Sumerian antecedents; cf. A. Falkenstein, *ZA, 49* (1939), 1 ff.

[78] Cf. e.g., Mowinckel, *Gunkel Festschrift,* p. 287; D. D. Luckenbill, *The Annals of Sennacherib* (1924), pp. 1 ff.

is something about the whole pattern that does not ring true. The normal attitude of the Mesopotamian ruler when facing his gods was one of modesty and humility. The annals were certainly not meant to be concealed from the gods. Why do they display, then, so much seeming arrogance?

I believe that by establishing a link between the annals and the letters to the gods—there is, of course, the further and long-known connection with building inscriptions[79] —we may be in a position to revise the common estimate of the Assyrian royal accounts. In point of fact, there is a concrete link between the annals and the letters to the gods. The parade example is the detailed report by Sargon II about his eighth campaign.[80] Although ad-

[79] See Olmstead, *Assyrian Historiography,* pp. 2, 64. Yet the building inscription is not of itself a logical forerunner of the annalistic account. Since the annals are first found among the Hittites, and since the Assyrian annals follow shortly thereafter, Güterbock has made out a good case in favor of deriving the Assyrian practice from the Hittites; cf. *ZA, 44,* 98 f. Goetze, *Hethiter, Churriter und Assyrer,* pp. 181 f., has contributed the further observation that the Assyrian annals incorporate mythical-epic motifs which are foreign to Hittite historical writings, but might ultimately be traced to the Hurrians. Furthermore, Goetze (*ibid.*) and others, especially Laqueur, *Neue Jahrbücher für Wissenschaft und Jugendbildung,* 7 (1931) pp. 489–506, have realized that the Assyrian and the Hittite annals show an awareness of the need for giving the deity an account of the ruler's conduct. Specific connection with the letters to the gods, however, has not been suggested so far. If the present suggestion proves valid, then the characteristic tone of the accounts might have been borrowed. But even this last supposition would now seem doubtful. We cannot, accordingly, discount the possibility that all the basic features were Mesopotamian after all, although their full potential could not be realized without Hurrian or Hittite assistance.

[80] F. Thureau-Dangin, *Une relation de la huitième campagne de Sargon,* 1912. After this paper had been presented at Yale, in the form in which it is here given, I came upon the statement by A. Moortgat (Moortgat and Scharff *Äegypten und Vorderasien im Altertum* (1950), pp. 429 f.), which voices independently conclusions very similar to mine. Moortgat, too, would see in the Assyrian annals not so much the boasts by vainglorious rulers as the glorification of the might of the god Ashur. And although the letters to the gods are mentioned in passing, the conclusions which Moortgat offers are based primarily on the testimony of art.

dressed to the gods, this is not the petition of a man in trouble but a proud account of successes achieved. Later on this report is entered, in condensed form and without the epistolary trimmings, in the composite edition of Sargon's annals.

Is there any reason to assume that this expedition alone required exceptional treatment? The facts related in this case do not depart from the pattern of other Assyrian expeditions. Furthermore, Shamshi-Adad V, a century earlier, had addressed a report about one of his campaigns to an unnamed deity, receiving this time an itemized acknowledgment from his divine addressee.[81] In other words, this kind of reporting was by no means unusual. Is it possible that the kings of Assyria, when annual reports had become customary, first composed these reports in the form of letters to their acknowledged sovereign, to be abridged in due course for purposes of a year-by-year edition?

On further examination it will be found, I think, that there is nothing inconsistent with such an assumption, whereas additional arguments can be adduced in its favor. This much, however, is worth noting: if the annals link up ultimately with letters to the gods, their egocentrism can no longer be ascribed to mere conceit. The missions

---

Our two modes of approach thus complement each other. The letters to the gods, however, suggest the ultimate form of the annals in addition to accounting for their characteristic tone.

[81] E. F. Weidner, *AFO*, 9 (1933–34), 102 f. For these and other examples cf. Gadd, *Ideas of Divine Rule*, pp. 61 f., and Labat, *Le Caractère religieux de la rayauté assyro-babylonienne* (1939), pp. 273 f. One of the most striking instances of this genre has come down to us from Ashurbanipal; see *CT*, Vol. 35, Nos. 44–5 and T. Bauer, *Das Inschriftenwerk Assurbanipals* (1933), Pt. II, pp. 83 f. (Der Gottesbrief). The colophon is highly instructive, for it reads (rev. ll. 23–6): "Message of Ashur[banipal . . .] to Ashur who dwells in E[hursaggalkurkurra], that he may accept [his] prayer, strike down his foe, slay [. . . .]."

recorded were the god's missions. They could not be undertaken except with divine sanction as signified by the omens. The words which the king used to report them were the words of the god's original mandate. The tone was exaggerated because, in phrasing the utterances of a god, man is tempted to resort to superlatives. It was boastful because the authority and valor of a god were involved in the last analysis, and not the achievements of his worshipful servant.

Thus, if the foregoing hypothesis is valid, Assyrian historiography suffered not so much from the conceit of the ruler as from his excessive piety. The material is voluminous, the language picturesque, the detail abundant—yet the coefficient of reliability is low. By the same token, Babylonia, which never had formal annals, let alone annals stylized into letters to the gods, was in a position to render a more objective performance. This is true certainly of the so-called Babylonian Chronicle. It is jejune history, to be sure, but history nevertheless in "its sobriety of presentation and its coldly impartial statement of fact." [82] That even this superior work does not approach the high level of biblical historiography is a fact too obvious to need special emphasis.

VII. THE IDEA OF HISTORY IN THE WISDOM LITERATURE

Before this rapid survey is completed there is still one last witness to be heard from. The idea of history is not likely to have been ignored by the branch of literature that deals largely with ideas. Ancient Near Eastern sources

[82] Olmstead, *Historiography,* p. 62.

devoted to speculative or didactic matters are commonly classified as wisdom literature. Extant wisdom material from Mesopotamia includes some independent works and a number of incidental passages which bear in one way or another on the problem before us. What does this testimony add up to, and how does it compare with the circumstantial evidence that has been abstracted so far?

We have seen that the ancient Mesopotamian was forever uneasy about the relation of his society to nature.[83] Because he endowed the powers of nature with most of the failings of mankind, he lacked full confidence in his gods.[84] They were unpredictable, hence mankind was doomed to be restless and insecure. The one thing that the past revealed above all others was the impermanence of all things. This note is struck with singular clarity in the Epic of Gilgamesh:

> Since the days of yore there has been no [permanence];
> The resting and the dead, how alike they are!
> Do they not compose a picture of death,
> The commoner and the noble,
> Once they have drawn near to [their fate]?
> The Anunnaki, the great gods, foregather;
> Mammetum, authoress of destiny, with them the fates decrees:
> Death and life they determine;
> Yet of death the days are not revealed.[85]

All is thus ephemeral and uncertain. Everything is in the hands of the gods, but man is kept in ignorance of their plans.

[83] This point is properly stressed by Frankfort, *Kingship and the Gods* and introduction to *Intellectual Adventure;* also by Jacobsen, *ibid.*

[84] The Babylonian Theodicy expresses this thought by the phrase *nesī milik* [*ilim*] "impenetrable is the resolve [of the god]," *ZA, 43,* 50, 58.

[85] Tab. X, col. 6, pp. 32 ff.; cf. *ANET,* p. 93.

The king, as a faithful shepherd, must strive to maintain the existing equilibrium at all costs. Any misadventure may be proof that the gods have been offended. Normally, the balance can be restored through elaborate efforts at purification and expiation. At times, it may even be expedient to set up a substitute king in order to divert the divine wrath from the established ruler.[86] There are occasions, however, when none of the known remedies will produce the desired effect. Although the king appears blameless, his land remains afflicted. The wisdom sources deal with this subject under the theme of the Righteous Sufferer.

We now know this motif from three major recensions. One of these, "I shall praise the lord of wisdom," is extant only in copies of the 1st millennium B.C.[87] Another, the so-called Acrostic Dialogue or Babylonian Theodicy[88] may perhaps go back to the end of the 2d millennium. The third, which has just been published, takes us back to Old Babylonian times.[89] The three together serve to demonstrate that the problem of unjust suffering was forever alive in Mesopotamia.

For all their differences in form, approach, and phraseology, all three compositions have this conclusion in common: although the blameless may be exposed to suffering, deliverance is sure to come to him in the end. The ways of the gods are indeed inscrutable, but the truly meritorious need never despair of ultimate salvation. The emphasis, in short, is not so much on the trials of the

[86] Cf. Frankfort, *Kingship and the Gods,* pp. 263 f.

[87] The Akkadian title is *Ludlul bêl nêmeqi;* for this work, see especially S. Langdon in *Babyloniaca,* 7 (1923), 163 ff. See also, O. R. Gurney, *AFO, 11* (1936–37), 367; R. J. Williams, *JCS,* 6 (1952), 4–7.

[88] We owe to Landsberger, *ZA, 43,* 32–76, the fundamental treatment of this composition.

[89] See Nougayrol, *RB,* 59 (1952) pp. 239–50.

sufferer as on the miracle of final deliverance.[90] Our three versions of the Mesopotamian counterpart of Job, spread though they are over a total span of more than a millenium, are in full agreement on this significant affirmation.

Is there a connection between the theme of Job and the idea of history? The established popularity of this subject in the literature of Mesopotamia, not to speak for the moment of outside echoes, suggests that the protagonist may have had an historical prototype.[91] At all events, the story of a Job is one of the strongest arguments why history should be studied. There have been kings in the past whom the gods deserted. Some never recovered, but others were eventually restored to grace. The Dynasty of Akkad was highly instructive in this respect. Old Sargon,[92] as the omens epitomize him, was "one who encountered darkness, but the light emerged for him." [93] On the other hand, the remaining rulers of that dynasty were either assassinated or lived to see their power extinguished.[94] A study of the past may help one to emulate

[90] *Ibid.*, p. 250.

[91] *Ibid.*

[92] The fact that Sargon was a usurper (originally cupbearer of Ur-Zababa, cf. Jacobsen, *Sumerian King List*, p. 107, n. 217) detracts in no way from his traditional stature. He was not, however, a legitimate king in the accepted sense of the term, which is no doubt the reason for his assuming the name *Šarru(m)-kên*, "the king is legitimate." What his real name may have been we do not know any more than we know the name of the northern neighbor of Sumer before Sargon had made "Akkad" famous. Incidentally, another known usurper is familiar to us by the name of Sargon II of Assyria. The question arises, therefore, whether Sargon I of Assyria bore that name from the start in honor of the most celebrated of Mesopotamian rulers (note that his grandson's name was Naram-Sin), or whether he assumed it later on in his life for some specific purpose; say, to break away from the more humble title of *rubā'um* (see above, n. 22) and to have himself honored as *šarrum* "king," as many of his lesser contemporaries were doing.

[93] See Goetze, *JCS*, *1*, 255 f.

[94] *Ibid.*, p. 256 ff.

the successful and avoid the mistakes of the ill-fated. The main purpose, then, of such a study is to master the formula of deliverance, for one never knows when such knowledge may prove vital.

The symbol of Job was not the only one that was held up as a source of solace. The hero of the Flood was another comforting example, for no one in the entire history of mankind had ever emerged triumphant from greater peril. In this case, however, the Mesopotamian wisdom literature goes gack a step to the father of Utnapishtim, the local Noah. For it was apparently parental wisdom that had stood Utnapishtim in such good stead. And so it is Shuruppak, the eponymous hero of the Flood city, substituting for Utnapishtim's father, who figures as the fountainhead of proverbial wisdom in Sumerian and Akkadian literature alike.[95]

The links between the heroes of the Flood and proverbial literature on the one hand, and between the Job image and the theme of deliverance on the other, combine to give a new meaning to the famous verse in Ezek. 14:14. According to that statement, Noah, Dan(i)el, and Job were the only men to emerge unscathed, because of their righteousness, from universal upheavals. Noah and Job, in Mesopotamian garb, are now known to us as celebrated wisdom personalities. Daniel's counterpart in Sumerian or Akkadian sources has yet to be identified. But the prominence of this particular theme is independently attested in Ugaritic.[96] Moreover, the biblical

[95] For this specific figure in the Sumerian wisdom material cf. Kramer, *JCS*, 1, 33, n. 208; the same name appears in an introduction to Akkadian proverbs in *KAR*, No. 27 obv. (marked rev. (?) in the copy), 1.

[96] See Spiegel *Ginzberg Jubilee Volume* (1945), pp. 305–55. On the location of *Hrnm*, the traditional home of the Ugaritic Danel, see new Albright, *BASOR*, 130 (1953), 28 f. The prominence of the biblical Daniel in the

Book of Daniel has a Babylonian setting, quite aside from the fact that Ezekiel, who cites all three names in the same breath, knew his Babylonian culture at first hand. In other words, the Mesopotamian origin of the three heroes of Ezekiel is assured beyond all doubt. The prophet's statement merely testifies to the great popularity of the underlying tradition.

How each of these heroes had proved worthy of his extraordinary distinction is not made clear. The popular explanation may perhaps be indicated in an old omen which says: "If he has abhorred sin, his god will walk with him." [97] In any case, the use of these themes in the wisdom literature suggests that they had come to symbolize the lesson of the past at the intellectual level. That lesson may be summed up as follows: the history of the heroes of old who survived great trials and disasters could, at best, help to safeguard against recurrences. At worst, it might bring a measure of comfort in the disclosure that, even in a capricious cosmos, someone is likely to be singled out to save civilization.[98]

Yet, circumscribed as such views may be, they were obviously looked upon as much too broad for official purposes. The average king, at least in late Assyrian

---

apocalyptic literature, notably the Book of Enoch, is brought out by Spiegel, *op. cit.*, pp. 336 ff. All in all, it appears certain that the Mesopotamian original of Daniel must be disguised under some other name. I would suggest with due reserve that the person in question was Adapa, who appears as an *apkallu* ("sage") in the Chronicle Weidner and has otherwise some claim to being the patron of history.

[97] *ZA*, 43, 98, l. 31: *šumma ḫaṭītam izīr ilšu ittišu ittanallak.* Note the close parallel between this saying and the biblical statement about Enoch (Gen. 5:23), where a virtually identical verbal form is used.

[98] This thought lends added force to the Ezekiel passage just cited. It should be stressed again in this connection that the three sages cited by Ezekiel were ancient Babylonian heroes of the magnitude of Noah himself, each of whom was qualified, by reason of his own extraordinary experience, to bring mankind a measure of comfort in times of cosmic distress.

times, was too chauvinistic for philosophic appraisals.[99] This is well illustrated by the concluding paragraph of the so-called Synchronistic History: "The scholar who apprehends all that is written, may he ponder it and sing the praises of the land of Ashur for all time. But as for the land of Sumer and Akkad, may he expose its wickedness to all the quarters." It is not a case of "my country right or wrong." It is rather an instance of "my country is always right and the other country always wrong." [100]

In summary, Mesopotamian civilization was faced with the same two major problems that each civilization must solve for itself. One was the relation of the individual to society, and the other was the relation of society to nature.[101] The Mesopotamian solution of the first problem proved most successful and productive. The solution of the other problem, however, was a less constructive achievement. Since the gods were unsure of themselves, no values were really enduring. The need to avoid harm gave a negative meaning to the pursuit of happiness. Ritual rather than ethics, form far more than content, promised the best protection against the schemes of heaven. Because the king and the priest alike were slaves to the mistrust and fear of nature, they were jointly the captives of the forms calculated to protect mankind from nature. In the end, this emphasis on form became a barrier to further progress. The collapse of Nineveh and of Babylon was due not so much to the heavy blows on the

[99] That such appraisals, however, were not lacking in intellectual circles is attested by a composition universally misnamed the "Babylonian Dialogue of Pessimism"; cf. Langdon, *Babyloniaca, 7,* 195 ff. I expect to show elsewhere that this work is instead a splendid parody exposing weak leaders who seeks to explain their inefficiency by recourse to threadbare clichés. See *JCS,* Vol. 8, No. 3 (1954).

[100] The Assyrian Chronicle, *CT, 34,* 41, col. 4, ll. 23 ff.

[101] See above, n. 83.

part of the Scythians, the Medes, and the Persians as to the crushing weight of the internal structure.

The Mesopotamian idea of history cannot but mirror the uneven advance of the major components of the parent civilization. It suffers from the limitations of its constituent elements. Other cultures, enriched and forwarned by the Mesopotamian experience, were to carry the study of history many strides forward. Along that course, however, the contribution of Mesopotamia marks a significant early milestone; a milestone in the progress of the idea of history as well as of the history of ideas.

[For further significant studies see now S. N. Kramer, "Sumerian Historiography," *Israel Exploration Journal,* V (1953), pp. 217–32, and J. J. Finkelstein, "Mesopotamian Historiography," *Proceedings of the American Philosophical Society,* 107 (1963), pp. 461–72.]

Authority and Law in Mesopotamia

I

THE OUTSTANDING FEATURE OF KINGSHIP IN ANCIENT MESOpotamia is the ruler's subservience to the gods throughout the long recorded history of that composite civilization. Thus in the Sumerian myth of cultural norms the attributes of kingship are listed in fourth place, after three separate divine groupings.[1] Old Assyrian inscriptions state explicitly that the real king was the god Ashur, whereas the mortal ruler was merely the god's agent (*iššakku*).[2] Other times and places likewise provide abundant evidence of similar recognition of the gods' overriding authority.[3]

Such a climate is clearly unfavorable to persistent deification of the temporal ruler. In point of fact, this practice, although often alleged, has never been established beyond dispute. It is true that some of the kings of Akkad, in common with those of the Third Dynasty

[1] S. N. Kramer, *Sumerian Mythology* (1944), 64 ff., 116.

[2] B. Landsberger and K. Balkan, *Belleten* 14 (1950), 231; cf. *Orientalia*, 20 (1951), 483.

[3] I have dealt with this general subject in a paper entitled "The Idea of History in Ancient Mesopotamia," which is scheduled for publication in the near future; [see now above, pp. 270 ff.]

of Ur and of sundry other places and periods, appear to boast certain aspects of divinity. The actual import of these instances is not altogether clear. They are, in any event, scattered and sporadic.[4] The practice was limited and atypical at best. While it does embrace a Naram-Sin or an Ibbi-Sin, it is precisely these kings on whom tradition, so far from extolling them as gods, fastened the stigma of ill-fated rulers.[5] Moreover, the Mesopotamian king remains at all times subject to the tyranny of the omens. A god incarnate would not be normally expected to take his cue from the liver of a sheep.

There are other significant details of the Mesopotamian pattern which point uniformly to the conclusion that the very concept of a deified ruler would be incompatible with the whole spirit of the underlying civilization. In the area of government, e.g., ultimate authority resided not in the given individual incumbent, but in the corporate assembly.[6] The proemium to the Etana Epic recalls a barbarous stage when mankind had not as yet had the benefit of consultative government (*mitluku*).[7] It was presumably in order to put an end to such chaos that kingship, as a constructive civilizing factor,[8] came down

[4] On this question see the comprehensive studies by R. Labat, *Le caractère religieux de la royauté assyro-babylonienne* (1939); C. J. Gadd, *Ideas of Divine Rule in the Ancient Near East* (1947); and H. Frankfort, *Kingship and the Gods* (1949). For a recent refutation of the deification theory cf. T. Fish, "Some Aspects of Kingship in the Sumerian City and Kingdom of Ur," *Bulletin of the John Rylands Library* 34 (1951), 37 ff.

[5] H. G. Güterbock, *ZA* 42 (1934), 31 f., 61, 75.

[6] L. Oppenheim, *Orientalia,* 5 (1936), 224 ff., and especially Th. Jacobsen, *JNES* 2 (1943), 159 ff.

[7] *Babyloniaca* 12 (1931), 11. 13.

[8] According to the *Sumerian King List* (Th. Jacobsen, *AS* 11 [1939], 71 ff.) 'kingship was lowered from heaven' at the very beginning of the first antediluvian dynasty. But it remained for Etana, the 'shepherd, the one who to heaven ascended, the one who consolidated all lands' (*ibid.,* 80–81. 16–18), to introduce the habits of civilization.

from heaven.[9] Etana himself, incidentally, as the traditional shepherd, personifies the abiding cultural stereotype whereby the Mesopotamian king is the "shepherd of the great people," [10] and hence responsible to his own master for the welfare of the flock.[11] Kingship, in other words, was limited here from the start by the twin checks of state and religion.

The assembly (Sum. u k k i n, Akk. *puḫrum*) is shown to operate as a safeguard against autocracy already in the penumbral stage that separates prehistory from history. Before he can embark on a fateful campaign against his rival Agga, Gilgamesh must obtain, according to a Sumerian poem, the approval of the elders as well as the townsmen of Uruk.[12] The Akkadian Epic of Gilgamesh retrojects the same condition to the days preceding the Flood; for Utnapishtim cannot start the construction of his ark until he has broached the subject to the elders and the people of Shuruppak.[13] What is more, the assembly is not just a fanciful motif appropriate to myth

[9] The fragmentary condition of the extant portions of the Etana Epic leaves wholly in the air the connection, if any, between the introduction, which refers to mankind's chaotic state, and the rest which features Etana's ascent to heaven. The suggestion may be hazarded, however, that the ascent had something to do with the bringing down from heaven of the *mitluku,* the boon of consultative government. The fabulous airlift, then, may have been part of a divine scheme to provide the necessary transportation. Needless to add, all this is but a guess. The alternative, however, of ignoring any connection between the beginning of the epic and the central tale, involves a complete *non sequitur.*

[10] Cf. B. Landsberger, *Der kultische Kalender* (1915), 119 ff.; Gadd, *Ideas of Divine Rule,* 39 ff.

[11] I doubt whether the motive of "keeping sheep as an industry gainful to the god" (Gadd, *ibid.*), had had anything to do with the matter

[12] Jacobsen, *JNES* 2, 165 f.; Kramer, *ANET,* 45

[13] Tablet XI, 35; cf. Speiser, *Leland Volume* (*Studies in the History of Culture,* Menasha, Wisconsin, 1942), p. 60. This study was first presented on September 16, 1940 at the Bicentennial Conference of the University of Pennsylvania and was published in substance on November 30, 1940 in the British magazine *Nature,* pp. 705–708.

and legend. Its reality is vouched for by the practical and sober discipline of omens. An Old Babylonian specimen informs us that in certain circumstances "the assembly has failed to reach an agreement." [14] Other instances tell repeatedly of elders gathering to advise the ruler on matters of moment.[15] Evidently, this was a right and a privilege cherished not only by the nobles but by the people at large.

It is, however, the evidence of religion that speaks most eloquently of the vital place of government by assembly in the total pattern of Mesopotamian civilization. In the Sumerian world view, which became normative for the land as a whole, divine and human societies interfused. Things on earth were but an echo of cosmic conditions and, conversely, divine doings reflected mortal pursuits. The fact, then, that the assembly was also the ultimate source of authority among the gods lends added emphasis to the enormous significance of that institution in human affairs.[16]

All the gods, even the highest ones in the hierarchy, were subject to the decisions of the cosmic body. That group alone was competent to name the head of the pantheon, to determine destinies, to regulate the length of reigns. Even the grant of immortality to a human, an Utnapishtim for example, required formal approval by the divine council.[17]

This concept of collective authority as the supreme authority is basic to our present theme. None of the gods of Mesopotamia enjoyed absolute power individually. By the same token, no mortal had a warrant for unchecked power on earth. On the one hand, the king had to satisfy

[14] A. Goetze, *Old Babylonian Omen Texts* (YOT X), 31 x 43–44.
[15] Cf. Oppenheim, *Orientalia* 5, 225 ff.
[16] Jacobsen, *loc. cit.*, 167 ff.
[17] Cf. Gilgamesh Epic, XI, 197–98.

the proper councils of his realm; and on the other hand, he must answer to the gods for the management of the affairs which they had entrusted to him.

To interpret the pleasure of the gods and to act at all times in accordance with their wishes was an ever more complex task. Only experts were competent to pass upon it. To that extent, therefore, the king was subject to the discretion of the priests. The priests imposed upon him various expiatory rituals, often to his intense discomfort and even distaste.[18] All sorts of phenomena were to the priests the means for a prognosis of the ruler's every move. Small wonder, then, that in the solemn commemoration of the New Year there was an elaborate ceremony in which the high priest administered tangible and painful proof of the king's essential unworthiness.[19] This would seem to be the utmost in constitutional safeguards.

State and religion, then, through the elders and the priests, were the instruments whereby the power of the Mesopotamian ruler was curbed. In all their essentials these two institutions are as old as the historic Mesopotamian civilization itself. They were inevitably among the most distinctive features of that civilization. Together with a third such feature they comprise the foundation of the Mesopotamian way of life. That third basic component is law.

II

Legal systems both implement and reflect the underlying concepts of state. The two are closely interrelated. All advanced societies, of course, whatever their system of government may be, have their laws. But the status

[18] Cf., e.g., ABL, 78.

[19] F. Thureau-Dangin, *Rituels Accadiens* (1921), 144. 415 ff.

of the law in each instance depends on the nature of the parent society.[20]

Mesopotamia has furnished a prodigious body of material pertaining to legal practice, but very little that bears on the theory. Such directly relevant terms as *dīnu* and *ṣimdatu* are confined to the practice in that they refer to 'decision' and to 'the process' and the results of due judicial procedure.' [21] The theory has to be reconstructed on the basis of the two general terms *kittum* and *mēšarum,* which may roughly be rendered 'truth' and 'justice.' Yet any unqualified translation of such intimate cultural rubrics is likely to fall flat, for these rubrics embody the stratification of the culture as a whole.

In essence, *mēšarum* is the process whereby law is made to function equitably.[22] This is one of the ruler's principal duties. It involves supervision, adjustment, amendments. An able administrator may find it necessary to make up-to-date compilations of normative provisions. Hammurapi did that, and so before him did Lipit-Ishtar and Bilalama, Ur-nammu and apparently also Urukagina.[23] The ruler who has fulfilled these obligations, or claims to have done so, is described as *šar mēšarim* 'the just king.' [24]

[20] Cf. Speiser, "Early Law and Civilization," *The Canadian Bar Review,* October 1953, 863–77; [see below, pp. 534 ff.]

[21] For a fundamental discussion of these and related terms see B. Landsberger, "Die babylonischen Termini für Gesetz und Recht," *Studia et Documenta,* II (1939), 219–34. A special value of *dīnāti* appears in *JEN* III, 333.31, where the word stands for 'court proceedings.'

[22] Landsberger, *loc. cit.,* 220 ff.; G. R. Driver and J. C. Miles, *The Babylonian Laws,* I (1952), 21 ff.

[23] For the pre-Hammurapian compilation cf. the literature cited in Speiser, *loc. cit.,* 867–68 and add J. Klima, *ArOr,* 19/1–2 (1951), 37–59. [Since 'Bilalama' is no longer read in the preamble to the Laws of Eshnunna, their author is at present unknown. See Goetze, *AASOR* 31 (1956) pp. 20–22.]

[24] This and not *šarru(m)-kên,* as has been often alleged, is the correct equivalent of the biblical Melchizedek; hence the divine pair Misor and Sydyk in Phylo of Byblos (for a recent reference see H. G. Güterbock,

The Mesopotamian king, however, for all his extensive judicial activity, was not the source of the law but only its agent. He was merely the faithful shepherd who tended the flock on behalf of his master. The cosmos was founded on certain eternal truths which the laws strove to safeguard. These truths applied to the ruler no less than to his subjects. The king, more than anyone else, must be ever watchful to maintain them.

The sum of such cosmic and immutable truths was called *kittum*. A king might seek to 'establish' (*šakānum*) the *kittum* just as he was bound to institute *mēšarum*.[25] Yet the final source of *kittum* was divine, not human. Shamash, the sun-god, was the prime heavenly authority in the matter the *bēl kitti(m) u mēšari(m)*. The mortal ruler could at best claim that he merited the title of *šarru(m)-kên* 'the king is legitimate,' if his office was in conformance with divine norms.[26] The fundamental distinction between *kittum* and *mēšarum*—a distinction that has not received adequate notice—is observed neatly by Hammurapi who speaks of himself as 'the just king (*šar mīšarim*) to whom Shamash committed the truths

---

Kumarbi [1946], 114 f.) would seem to stand for *mēsaru(m)* and its Canaanite gloss rather than **mēšarum u kittum*. For such "hyphenated" names note in general the Ugaritic *Kṯr-w-ḫss* and *Qdš-w-'mrr;* and for the alternate separate use of *qdš* and *'mrr cf.* the analogous use of *'l* and *šdy* in Job 8.3. Note also *'l-w-'lyn* in the Aramaic inscription from Sujin, A 11 (*AfO* 8, 2).

[25] The employment of *šakānum* with either of these nouns, or both, refers to the promulgation of laws by the given king. This is now confirmed for Lipit-Ishtar (e.g., *Sumer,* V, 58. 30–35, and the date-formula, *RLA* II, 148 [87]), and has long been known in the case of Hammurapi (CH, v, 20–22), two rulers whose compilations are extant; cf. Driver-Miles, *op. cit.,* 21.

[26] He was particularly likely to do so after usurping the throne. The parade example, of course, is Sargon of Akkad. Sargon I of Assyria appears to have modeled himself after his illustrious namesake in which practice he was followed by his grandson Narām-Sin. And although Sargon II of Assyria now appears to have been one of the sons of Tiglathpileser III (see *AfO* 9, 79), the legitimacy of his succession remains in doubt.

(*kīnātim*).[27] The king, in short, was a trustee, not an autocrat. Total law (*kittum u mēšarum*) was impersonal and above the crown. The ruler was no more exempt from the legal provisions than any average citizen.[28]

Since the law was not subject to a ruler's whims, its proper application had to be guided by collected statutes reflecting both the established tradition and the necessary topical amendments. Enough such compilations are now extant—they are not codes in the fullest technical sense of the term [29]—to indicate that the underlying legislative process reaches back to the late third millennium, and to suggest that even older instances may be assumed with confidence.[30] The arrangement into a prologue, a legal corpus, and an epilogue was itself apparently a matter of tradition. Expedience dictated that the text be available for consultation in the administrative centers of the realm; hence the number of copies in which Hammurapi's revision has come down to us.

The fact should be stressed that, although state and church interpenetrated throughout the ancient Near East, Mesopotamian law, as we know it from many sources that span score of centuries, was strictly secular.[31] It concerns itself with private and public property, trade and commerce, agriculture and land tenure, professions and wages, and the general administration of justice. It

[27] CH, rev. 25, 96–98. This view of the specific meaning of *kittum,* which was presented at the Symposium on April 14, 1954, was independently confirmed on the following afternoon by A. Goetze; the text on extispicy which he cited at that time bore out fully the above interpretation. ["The Symposium on Authority and Law in the Ancient Orient," held at the 164th meeting of the American Oriental Society in New York.]

[28] For a recent example cf. D. J. Wiseman, *The Alalakh Tablets,* No. 17.

[29] Driver-Miles, *op. cit.,* 41, 45.

[30] The legislation of Urukagina is known so far only from his historical inscriptions; but the phraseology suggests a special compilation.

[31] Driver-Miles, *op. cit.,* 39.

is not a religious pronouncement. However closely the law may blend with the total cultural fabric, it enjoys nevertheless the dignity of an independent discipline. This is perhaps one of the main reasons for its great influence and appeal. Basically, of course, the law is always *kittum* and hence an aspect of the cosmic order and an object of zealous care on the part of the meritorious king. The enforcement was the task of the governors, judges, and various other officials. As the chief steward, however—the trusted shepherd—the king bore the final responsibility and acted as the human court of the last instance. Royal correspondence abounds in examples of this particular activity.

III

Government and law comprise the means whereby civilization attempts to solve the problem of the individual's relation to society. The kind of solution employed brings out, in turn, the essential character of the civilization which evolved it.

The Mesopotamian answer, which has just been sketched in barest outline, featured a ruler who must account for his acts, first, to an assembly of his fellow-mortals and, second, to the gods, who were often unpredictable and even capricious. The supporting law concentrated on earthly security and steered clear of the doubts and anxieties which beset religion. Judging by the results, this particular solution of the societal problem enjoyed extraordinary success.

Such success is signaled in several ways. For one, we are obliged to speak of a Mesopotamian civilization rather than of separate Sumerian, Babylonian, or Assyrian cultures, precisely because the existing unifying factors outweighed the normally divisive differences of language, geography, and political boundaries; and foremost among these unifying factors were the law and the concept of state. For another, the influence of Mesopotamian society spreads far beyond the limits marked out by the Euphrates and the Tigris. The Elamites and the Hurrians, the Hittites and the Syrians—these and others show close affinities with Mesopotamia proper in regard to law and government. In law, especially, generic relationship is assured by the prevailing use of the Akkadian language, the cuneiform script, and the legal document, three outstanding features common to what has come to be called "cuneiform law." [32] For yet another, the dynamism of Mesopotamian civilization, largely through the medium of the same two factors, eventually influences also neighboring areas in matters of religion and literature, arts and sciences, and in various other aspects of society. International correspondence is conducted in Akkadian. Mesopotamia's myths and the products of its wisdom literature travel far afield. In spite of unceasing political unrest and disruption, much of Western Asia comes to reflect a community of basic cultural interests. Finally, the overwhelming importance of law as the key to a cherished way of life does not diminish with the end of the historic states of ancient Mesopotamia. The old tradition survives in part in the very name of the Babylonian Talmud and in the Islamic legal schools which flourished on Mesopotamian soil.

There is, in these circumstances, the danger of overstating the whole achievement. It is in order, therefore, to add that Mesopotamian ideas of the cosmos were not

[32] Cf. P. Koschaker, "Keilschriftrecht," *ZDMG* 89 (1936), 32.

conducive to notable ethical progress; that related cultures made independent contributions which in many respects went far beyond any comparable Mesopotamian results; and that contemporary civilizations which lived by opposing faiths were highly productive in their own way.

This inquiry, however, serves to underscore one thing in particular: material remains in themselves are not the decisive criteria of ancient civilizations that they are usually believed to be. However great may be the difference between the pyramids and the siqqurrats, and however spectacular, the principal features of the parent cultures reach deeper and loom larger. It is the societal features, and especially the respective concepts of state and of law, that afford a truly distinctive picture of a given civilization all the way back to the beginning of recorded history. Indeed, in the final analysis, it is these features that proved to make history.

The Name Phoinikes

THE PURPOSE OF THE PRESENT PAPER IS NOT TO ADVANCE yet another etymology for Greek Φοῖνιξ "Phoenician," but rather to reduce the number of acceptable suggestions with the aid of new evidence from an independent quarter. Although the material to be considered is predominantly linguistic, archaelogical sources will also be brought into discussion.

The current explanations of the ethnicon Φοῖνιξ and its immediate relatives fall into three groups,[1] as follows:

1. The term is Greek in origin, going back to φοινός "blood-red."

2. It is based on Egyptian *Fnḫ-w* "Phoenicians."

3. Both Φοῖνιξ and *Fnḫ-w* go back to a common source.

Let us first re-state briefly the arguments used by each of the above factions.

1. Φοῖνιξ is a genuine Greek word with numerous and diversified usages. It signifies the fabulous bird "Phoenix," "red purple," "palm tree" and its fruit the "date," and "a musical instrument." All these terms may have had a common origin, on the assumption of some ultimate connection with Phoenicia, or the Phoenicians. But the same can scarcely be true of the numerous in-

[1] A complete statement of the various views would require a lengthy article. With one or two exceptions, only the latest discussions of the problems at issue will be cited below.

stances in which Φοῖνιξ appears as a proper name outside Phoenicia. Thus it is found to designate a river near Thermopylae, a mountain in Boeotia and in Caria, a god and a place in Crete, not to mention the derivative formations of this term.[2] Etymologically we have here the adjective φοινός "blood-red," with the suffix *īk*, a perfectly normal construction according to W. Schulze.[3] There remains the problem of justifying the connection between "Phoenician" and "red." On this point the arguments become colorful indeed. The Phoenicians earned this distinction by being red-skinned; [4] they owe the name to the circumstance that their land, in common with Caria, was noted for red skies in the morning;[5] they were so named because of their far-famed ability to extract from murex shells a red-purple dye.[6]

2. *Fnḫ-w* is one of several names by which Phoenicians were known to the Egyptians. This became Φοίνικ-ες in Greek, and the sing. form was subsequently applied to such Phoenician articles as the palm, the musical instrument in question, and the purple dye.[7]

3. An exhaustive examination of all the passages in which *Fnḫ-w* occurs was made by the distinguished German Egyptologist Kurt Sethe.[8] He found that the bearers of that name were localized generally in Palestine and Syria; specific references to Phoenicia proper are clear in the Ptolemaic period. The name may perhaps be traced to the word *fnḫ* which occurs as early as the Old Kingdom and means something like "skilful," or as an appellative

[2] Cf. Eduard Meyer, *Geschichte des Altertums* I^2 1.97; 2.66.
[3] Berlin SB 1910, 803 f.
[4] First suggested by Pietschmann, *Geschichte der Phönizier* 107.
[5] Beloch, *Griechische Geschichte* I^2 70.
[6] Meyer, *op. cit.*
[7] First proposed by Brugsch, *Geschichte Ägyptens unter den Pharaonen* 242.
[8] *Der Name der Phönizier bei Griechen und Ägyptern* (Mitteil. d. Vorderas. Ges. 21.305 ff).

"carpenter, shipwright." [9] The specialization for "Phoenician" would not be surprising in view of the known proficiency of the Phoenicians in the art of building ships. Since the Greeks appear to have associated the Phoenicians with another local industry, viz. the production of red purple, there is a likelihood of ultimate relationship between the Greek and the Egyptian designations. But a direct connection is precluded by phonetic considerations, the respective initial consonants (*φ* and *f*) not being normally interchangeable.[10] The difficulty would disappear if we assumed an original Phoenician term from which both Φοίνικ-ες and *Fnḫ-w* were derived. Popular etymology later modified this assumed prototype into "maker(s) of red purple" and "shipwright(s)" respectively. To be sure, no such native name has been discovered as yet; but available Phoenician sources are rather scanty.

It will be evident even from this summary presentation that each of the above positions is open to serious criticism. To begin with the last one, Sethe crystallized for us the meaning of the term *Fnḫ-w* in all its ramifications. But in assuming an ultimate dependence upon a native Phoenician name he was building on an argument from silence. He was not blind, however, to this inherent weakness of his theory, which can not be said for his many excerptors.[11] In 1916, the year in which Sethe's study ap-

[9] It is interesting to note that virtually the same accomplishments are attributed to the divine artificer of the Semitic inhabitants of Ugarit; cf. Ginsberg, JRAS 1935. 49 f.

[10] As a matter of fact, the only sound that the words have definitely in common is [*n*]; the vowels of Greek ethnicon would be strange in a Semito-Hamitic word, but we are spared the necessity of further comparisons thanks to the normal Egyptian practice of vowelless writing.

[11] Cf., e.g., Peiser, OLZ 1919. 5 ff., who would see in *Kinaḫḫi* "Canaan" the prototype required by Sethe, and Eisler, ZDMG 1919. 154 ff. I am obliged to my colleague Dr. Z. S. Harris for calling my attention to several discussions on the subject.

peared, it was not unreasonable to expect the discovery of some Asiatic prototype of *Fnḫ-w*. Since then we have had, however, an enormous increase in Phoenician and other West-Semitic epigraphic materials. They have failed to affect the onomastic situation. The only known native name for the entire district remains as before "Canaan" (Phoenician and Hebrew *Kn'n,* cuneiform *Kinaḫḫi, Kinaḫna*),[12] while the people called themselves after this or that leading city (Sidon, Gubla/Byblos, Ugarit, and the like). The second view, viz. the importation of the Greek term from Egypt, betrays no worry over phonetic considerations. For this very reason Sethe himself found it untenable;[13] nor has anyone succeeded in solving the puzzle of why the Greeks should have combed Egypt in search of a suitable designation for the Phoenicians. Moreover, *Fnḫ-w* was neither the commonest nor the least ambiguous Egyptian appellation for these Asiatics or their country. Any thought of a connection between Φοίνικ-ες and *Fnḫ-w,* must therefore be given up.

We are thus back to the first interpretation of the Greek term as a strictly European development. That is to say, φοινός "red." Now we can not be concerned at present with all the usages of this term. Some of them may have had the same underlying basis,[14] and others may have arisen independently, entirely plausible alternatives once the color red has been allowed as a starting point. But how did the Phoenicians come to be regarded as "Reds"? Disregarding all fanciful attempts at explana-

[12] See Index to Knudtzon's *Amarna* 1577. The origin and etymology of *Kn'n* and its cognates are not strictly relevant to the present problem.

[13] See his explicit statement, *op. cit.* 329: 'Von einer direketen Abhängigkeit . . . kann selbstverständlich keine Rede sein.'

[14] E.g. the name of the fabulous bird "Phoenix" may have been linked with the adjective and the ethnicon under the influence of *byn-w,* the Egyptian designation for the legendary bird; cf. Sethe 307.

tion, we are left with a purely industrial set-up. φοῖνιξ came to mean "Phoenician" because the word signified "red purple" and the dyer producing this color, the Phoenicians being proficient in this form of work. This theory found a very vigorous champion in the late Eduard Meyer. It has considerable support in Greek tradition as far back as the Homeric sources, and it is in accordance with the testimony of later classical writers.[15] The principal difficulty arising from such a view is that it presupposes the naming of a people after one of its products instead of the other way about. Recent archaeological discoveries may help to obviate this particular objection. But before material sources are drawn upon, I wish to adduce another type of evidence, capable of establishing the intimate association of Phoenicia with the purple dye industry beyond any possibility of dispute.

In the cuneiform records from Nuzi, in the East-Tigris area, which date from the middle of the second millennium B.C., there occurs the adjective *kinaḫḫu* in passages dealing with wool. One published text simply uses the word as descriptive of wool.[16] Another one permits us to arrive at a closer definition of the term involved; it reads as follows: *bi-ir-me-šu-nu ša ku-zi-ti ša ki-na-aḫ-ḫu ša ta-wa-ar-wa* "the dyes of the cover (are) of *kinaḫḫu* (and) of *tawarru*." [17] The latter word (usually found in the form *tabarru*; the final *wa* in the present instance is the Hurrian genitive ending) is known to designate "deep yellow" and "red." [18] In *kinaḫḫu* we have then an adjective of some dye, presumably of a kind similar to the *tab/warru*-dye. Unpublished texts in the possession of the

[15] On purple, especially the Tyrian kind, see Pliny 9.60–63.
[16] For the text see Chiera, *Joint Expedition at Nuzi* 125.5.
[17] *Ibid.* 314.4 f.
[18] Cf. Meissner, *Beiträge zum Assyrischen Wörterbuch* I. 47 f.

Semitic Museum at Harvard help further to define *kinaḫḫu* as a sub-variety of *tabarru,* hence "a kind of red." Other passages link *kinaḫḫu* with *uqnu* "lapis, purple." [19] The combined result of these disclosures is that *kinaḫḫu* signifies "(red-) purple dye."

We have seen that the proper name *Kinaḫḫu* represents our "Canaan." The present adjective, unknown outside the Nuzi texts, is based obviously on this geographic term. To place this equation beyond a shadow of doubt, we have still another Harvard document which shows that the *kinaḫḫu*-dye was actually imported from the West.[20] It follows that the land-name "Canaan," the only one to be applied by the Phoenicians to their own country, had become in Mesopotamia an adjective meaning "purple dye" as early as 1500 B.C. The face of the Syrian coast as the home of such dyes antedates thus by centuries the oldest Greek references that point in the same direction.

Thus far we have had comparatively clear sailing. The use of geographic terms to describe local products is quite normal. In the case of Φοῖνιξ, however, the reverse process has to be assumed. Does it mean that the Greek word for "red purple" must be derived from the ethnicon Φοῖνιξ after all. In that case the latter would be left without any etymology, the equation with Egyptian *Fnḫ-w* being definitely out. Now the cuneiform evidence strongly favors a connection between the names for the people and their product. Such a connection can be maintained for Greek it we start out with "red purple"

[19] I am grateful to Prof. R. H. Pfeiffer and to Dr. E. R. Lacheman for enabling me to examine these texts in transliteration kindly furnished by them.

[20] This important document which I first read on the spot soon after it had been dug up by the late Dr. Chiera was kindly collated for me by Dr. Pfeiffer, the Curator of the Harvard Semitic Museum.

(based on φοινός "blood-red") and proceed to the Φοίνικ-ες, but not vice versa. Or have the two Greek terms really nothing in common, being merely homonyms? In view of the cuneiform parallel this would be putting an entirely unwarranted strain on the long arm of coincidence. The only available solution is to derive the Greek ethnicon from the word for "red purple."

Archaeological evidence may step into this breach with some indirect confirmation. In a suburb of the North Syrian city of Ugarit [21] (modern Râs esh-Shamrah the excavators have uncovered traces of workshops for making purple dye, to judge from the pounded murex shells left on the spot.[22] Now it is interesting that these workshops were in the Mycenaean, not the native quarter. In view of this it may be permissible to conjecture that the word φοῖνιξ was brought to Syria by the Mycenaeans who found the place an excellent source of supply of the shells required.[23] In that case the land may have been the first to be designated after the product,, Φοινίκη becoming "land of the purple dye," while the inhabitants became Φοίνικ-ες secondarily. But the main argument in favor of tracing the ethnicon to the name for the dye need not rest on such purely hypothetical grounds.

In conclusion, I may be permitted to venture an explanation of the curious Greek tradition which would derive the Phoenicians from the Persian Gulf.[24] Historically there is absolutely nothing to justify such a view. Do we have here an example of popular learning? The

[21] The importance of the purple industry of Ugarit is attested, incidentally, by a lengthy cuneiform text recently published by Thureau-Dangin; cf. his article in Syria 15. 137 ff.

[22] *Illustrated London News* 1935. 712.

[23] For the purple industry in the Aegean area see G. Casson, "Phoenicians and Purple Industry," *Antiquary* 1913. 328 ff.

[24] Herodotus 7. 89.

reasoning may have been something like this "Φοίνιξ means "Phoenician" as well as "red." Why? Because the Phoenicians came from the Red Sea (Ἐρυθρὰ θάλασσα, i.e. the Persian Gulf)." Herodotus himself need not have been the guilty schoolmaster. By his time this play on words may have attained to the dignity of tradition.

The Muškênum

THERE IS A FAMILIAR SAYING THAT "EVERYBODY TALKS about the weather but nobody really does anything about it." The same thing might be said about the Mesopotamian *muškênum*. No Assyriologist can ignore him. Many have written about him. Yet he remains essentially the poor *muškênum*, much discussed and analyzed but actually undefined. This paper, then, is an attempt to focus afresh on the problem in the hope that sufficient clarity can be attained to handle this important term with greater precision than has been the case hitherto.

There are several aspects to the issue before us. One is the etymology of the term. Another is its morphology. Still another is the exceptional popularity of the word; for it was borrowed not only by such sister languages of Akkadian as Aramaic, Hebrew, Arabic, and Ethiopic, but also by the distant Italian and French. Most important by far, however—and basic to this whole discussion—is the question of usage within Akkadian itself. It is on this last point in particular that scholars have been least able to arrive at a clear consensus.

Such differences of opinion, to be sure, affect only the specific value of *muškênum*. Its general sense has been evident ever since the publication of the Code of Hammurabi. But to say merely that this term designated a social class intermediate between the full citizen (*awīlum*) and the slave (*wardum*) is a long way from describing the actual function of the *muškênum* in Old Babylonian society. On the other hand, to call him a "plebian" or a "commoner" or the like,[1] as is often done, is demonstrably harmful, since these are transplanted concepts which are utterly foreign to the civilization of Mesopotamia. Poebel's "liegeman," as reported by Heidel,[2] would do partial justice to the actual evidence; but the reasons for this translation have not been advanced. The joint study of the Babylonian Laws by Driver and Miles[3] employs the rendering "villein,"[4] on the strength of an extensive discussion of the material. In common with "liegeman," however, "villein" would seem to imply by definition that the *muškênum* owed allegiance to given individuals who in turn were subject to higher authority; yet such is never the case in the pertinent legal sources.

Many scholars translate *muškênum* by "poor." At best, this would be a derivative value, reflecting a meaning established in the various languages which borrowed this term. But even there the question arises why a loanword was needed to express so common and ubiquitous an experience as poverty. At any rate, the Laws of Eshnunna and the Code of Hammurabi imply by *muškênum* a specific social class and not an economic status. Most doubtful of all is the view that *muškênum* could have more than one meaning in the same given source. Meek, e.g., normally renders "commoner" in his translation of

[1] Such renderings may have been acceptable in the earlier stages of the study, but they can hardly be condoned at this late date.

[2] See A. Heidel, *The System of the Quadriliteral Verb in Akkadian* (abbr. SQVA) 39 n. 7.

[3] G. R. Driver and Sir John C. Miles, *The Babylonian Laws,* 2 vols. (here abbr. D-M).

[4] D-M I 90–95.

CH, yet insists in several passages on "private citizen." [5] It will be shown presently that, whatever he may have been, the *muškênum* was never a private citizen in the strict sense of this phrase.

The problem, in short, is to determine whether there is not some common denominator which underlies the official usage of *muškênum* while accounting at the same time for its derivative values. Lack of agreement among scholars on this particular question should make it abundantly clear that the problem is real enough. Only when such a common and self-consistent pattern has been established, will it be possible to say that the sympathy which the *muškênum* could evoke in the past is no longer in order as regards present-day Assyriologists who have been struggling with this designation.

The following brief survey of the evidence will start out, as it must, with the relatively well defined legal contexts. This points directly to the Code of Hammurabi, with the Laws of Eshnunna now happily available for purposes of checking and amplifying the initial results.

Driver-Miles have already drawn the cautious inference that the *muškênum* was "in some sense a dependant of the palace." [6] Thus one who steals certain kinds of property from a *muškênum* is dealt with in common with the thief who steals from the temple or palace.[7] Identical penalties, moreover, are provided for those who assist fugitive slaves belonging either to the palace or to a

[5] T. J. Meek, ANET 166 n. 44.

[6] D-M I 92. The same general results are independently presented by I. Diakonoff, *Eos* 48 (1956) 37 ff.

[7] Between them, the temple and the palace constituted the two major branches of the state. Hence it is that the temple shares the responsibility for ransoming a captive soldier (CH 32). By the same token, fines for infringement of certain contracts were paid in Alalakh (early period) to the temple and the palace in equal amounts; cf. AT 52. 18 ff., 54.19 ff.

muškênum;[8] but the penalty is less severe if the slave belongs to an *awīlum*.[9] Again, the slave of the palace or of a *muškênum* who married a free woman enjoyed certain privileges that other slaves lacked.[10] All in all, the *muškênum* is singled out for protection by the state. Hence, when certain laws concerning him are subjoined to similar laws which involve the state, the purpose is not to make a distinction between the state and the "private citizen," but on the contrary to implement the principle that the palace has an interest in the *muškênum* above and beyond its normal interest in the *awīlum*. This is not to imply, of course, that the position of the *muškênum* was in general superior to that of an *awīlum*; it is only to suggest that the state had special obligations to the *muškênum* by virtue of the latter's services to the state.

What then were the conditions and nature of these services? The logical assumption would be that the *muškênum* was some sort of fief-holder who was bound to specified tasks in return for being a free tenant of the crown. Yet the Code, in addressing itself directly to such tenants, fails to mention the *muškênum*. The pertinent sections[11] concentrate instead on the *redûm* and the *bā'irum*. But is this omission conclusive? As matters stand, it would seem to be more apparent than real.

It happens that the passages which deal with the *redûm* and the *bā'irum* are all grouped in a section which is given over in the main to military matters.[12] If the cate-

[8] CH 15–16.
[9] CH 17–20.
[10] CH 175–76; cf. D-M I 91 for a review of these instances.
[11] CH 26–41.
[12] It is still uncertain how the *bā'irum* figures in these contexts. That this term normally designates a "fisher" is amply established, as is also the fact that fishers played an important part in the economic life of the state. Nevertheless, the bracketing together of the *redûm* and the *bā'irum* in these

gory of the *muškênum* included by chance the other two classes, there would have been no need in this instance for mentioning the *muškênum* by name. The question may be approached also from another direction. The rest of the Code is silent about armed forces. Yet what happened to a *redûm* or a *bā'irum* in case, say, of his marriage to a free woman, or when his fugitive slave was involved? If he outranked the *muškênum*, as some have asserted,[13] he could not very well be discriminated against at the same time where his wife or slave was concerned.

All such difficulties disappear once it is assumed that the communal laws about the *muškênum* applied to the *redûm* and *bā irum* as well. All three classes are linked to the lands of the crown. We know, moreover, from the Code itself, that the last two were not alone in matters of special real estate legislation. This is made clear by the sequence *redūm bā'irum u nāši biltim*,[14] which must surely be rendered "soldier, 'fisherman,' and [any such] task-bearer."[15] Now the same type of sequence recurs in a letter from Samsuiluna, where we find, however, *ša redī bāri*(!) *u muškēni*.[16] Taken together, these two passages yield the equation *nāši biltim* = *muškênum*. It would thus seem to follow that the term *muškênum* could comprise military as well as civilian fief-holders. The classes exempted from the provisions of CH 37–38, in so far as named state employees are concerned, are the *nadītum*,

---

laws would seem to preclude a strictly civilian occupation in such instances. Note especially ARM I 31 (an approximately contemporary document) where the *bā'irū* are dispatched on the state's missions fully equipped with axes and other gear (note esp. 37 f.).

[13] D-M I 94.

[14] CH 38 f.

[15] For the interpretation of the connective *u* in the sense of "any other" cf. the analogous sequence discussed in D-M I 124.

[16] TCL 17 76:13 f.; cf. ZA 42 219 f.; MAOG 15 56; JCS 6 91 n. 61.

the merchant, and the *ilkum aḫûm*.[17] The first two are mentioned in this context because they comprised the fiscal agents of the temple and the crown respectively;[18] the last, or *ilkum aḫûm*, must refer therefore to related economic personnel. All three were obviously occupations of a higher order, not to be confused with the military and agricultural rank and file.

The above results are in no way contradicted, but are in some ways confirmed, by the occurrences of *muškênum* in the Laws of Eshnunna. The field and house of the *muškênum* are protected from thieves under the pain of death.[19] If his wife or son dies as a result of unlawful seizure by a distrainer (*nepûm*), the guilty party is to be put to death.[20] And recovered slaves or animals that belong either to the palace or to a *muškênum* must be returned promptly to the capital by the appropriate officials.[21] Thus here, too, the *muškênum* is a protected person closely associated with the state. No such special provisions are made on behalf of the *awīlum*; neither is there in these laws any direct mention of the *redûm* or the *bā'irum*, at least not in the sections that are extant.

Most of the other occurrences of the term *muškênum* have been previously evaluated, without yielding conclusive results.[22] It may suffice, therefore, to draw attention only to some significant passages in recently published texts. Of greatest interest, by far, are the Mari instances, both because they are dated to the generation of

[17] CH 40.
[18] For this role of the *nadītum* cf. W. F. Leemans, *The Babylonian Merchant* 118. The laws concerning this priestess in her religious capacity are given in another section of the Code.
[19] LE (see A. Goetze, *The Laws of Eshnunna*, AASOR 26) 12–13.
[20] LE 34.
[21] LE 50; cf. D-M I 93 n. 9.
[22] D-M I 92 ff.

Hammurabi, and because they all fall into the same distinctive pattern. In one text the *muškênum*[23] complain that their lands have been assigned to the palace whereas other villages and fields have been left free.[24] Another text mentions the lands of the *muškênum* and the palace in consecutive lines, hence apparently as of equal status.[25] Still another refers to measures which are calculated to keep skilled workers (*naklum*) and the *muškênum* from starving.[26] Elsewhere reference is made to the *muškênum* of the villages[27] One laconic letter speaks of the sheep of the Ḫanaeans[28] and of the *muškênum*.[29] And lastly, a badly damaged letter voices the fear that the *muškênum* and the palace alike may be short of their normal requirements unless the neighboring woods are placed under proper protection.[30]

Once again, then, we have here a repeatedly stressed connection between the *muškênum* and the palace. The interest expressed is not on behalf of the indigent as opposed to the prosperous, but rather on behalf of the state's retainers for whom the crown feels directly responsible. These persons are grouped together with men of special skills. And although they are usually bound to the land, a distinction is made between them and the native peasants. In other words, the *muškênum* of Mari may safely be described as fief-holders charged with the

[23] The Mari texts employ this term in a collective sense.

[24] ARM II 55 29 ff.

[25] Ibid. 61 25 f., and cf. 80 9 f.

[26] ARM III 79 rev. 8 f. For this interpretation see W. v. Soden, *Orientalia* 21 86.

[27] ARM V 25 7 f.

[28] In Alalakh this name developed into a specific peasant class; cf. AT 129, 131, 148 f.; and note JAOS 74 2.

[29] ARM V 81 5.

[30] Ibid. 86 rev.

care of the lands of the crown, and by extension perhaps with other state undertakings.

Elsewhere, the Alalakh texts mention houses, of the MAŠ.EN.KAK[31] and the e r i m. m e š MAŠ.KI.EN.[32] In an Akkadian document from Ugarit we find the l ú. m e š *muškênūtum*[33] who are under the supervision of controllers (l ú. m e š UN–t ú).[34] All these texts, however, date from after the middle of the second millennium, by which time the meaning of *muškênum* appears to have undergone a change, particularly in peripheral areas. Interestingly enough, the Nuzi texts do not appear to recognize the *muškênum*. This may indicate that in a basically feudal society, of which Nuzi was a part, there was no listed class of fief-holders of the *muškênum*-type since technically all members of the state were in the same position of feudal dependence.

How do these results based on actual usage compare with the pertinent lexical and linguistic evidence? The Sumerian equivalent of the participial form *muškênum* —i.e., m a š d á, written MAŠ.KAK.EN in LE[35] and MAŠ.EN.KAK in CH and elsewhere—tells us as yet nothing about the meaning of the word. On the other hand, the corresponding verbal stem *šukênum* goes with Sum. k i. z a z a "to bow, to kow-tow."[36] The logographic writing KA + KU,[37] which *šukênu*(*m*) shares with *bulṭa*

[31] AT 188 (available in summary only).

[32] AT 180 31; 182 29 (published in JCS 8 12 f.).

[33] PRU III: 16.257 iv 17.

[34] Cf. J. Klima, *Eos* 18 73.

[35] For a tentative evaluation of this writing cf. A. Falkenstein, ZA 51 262 and I. J. Gelb, MAD 3 266; and for a résumé of the whole question see Goetze, LE 51. This writing could be phonetic.

[36] Cf. B. Landsberger, MAOG 4 306, and JAOS 69 214. E. I. Gordon kindly informs me that in one of his Sumerian wisdom texts which are soon to be published this form is applied to a groveling dog.

[37] Cf. Th. Jacobsen, JNES 2 17 n. 68.

nadānu "to offer one's life," [38] may refer to the act of placing one's hand on the mouth in a gesture of submission.[39] If this logogram is to be interpreted as s u b, we would have here a bridge to the concept of "to kiss (ceremonially)." [40] This in turn should link up with the phrase *iššiq qaqqaru maḫar/šapalšun* by which *uškên–ma* is glossed in Enūma–eliš III 69.[41] Similar glosses are found with *ikmis(i)* in the myth of Nergal and Ereshkigal; [42] and this recalls the fact that *šukênu* and *kitmusu* are elsewhere listed as synonyms.[43] Altogether, the combined lexical evidence hints strongly at a ceremonial gesture of submission.

Morphologically, as I had occasion to show recently,[44] *šukênum* is not at all an ŠD–form—a verbal form, by the way, which should be deleted altogether from the grammars and dictionaries. The force of the initial *š*– is in this case that of an "elative" morpheme, and hence eminently suitable to signify a ceremonial gesture.[45] In regard to etymology, I ventured to suggest long ago that the underlying base stem was a cognate of Heb. *ni–kna'* "he submitted." [46] Whether this suggestion is borne out or not, the original final radical had to be one of the so-called hard laryngeals.[47] At all events, the lexical evidence alone would be sufficient to establish the *muškênum* as someone who has pledged his services to a superior; hence,

[38] CT 18 30.b 26; cf. Landsberger, MAOG 4 302.

[39] For an apparent representation of this gesture cf. Goetze, LE 51 n. 2.

[40] See H. Ehelolf, *Studia Orientalia* 1 10 f. n. 2.

[41] Cf. Speiser, *Orientalia* 25 319 n. 2; The same gloss would seem to be intended in the text which underlay ST I 38 73; cf. my note in JCS 11 43 f.

[42] ST I 28 i 28; iii 49.

[43] ZA 4 30.19.

[44] JCS 6 91.

[45] Ibid. 88 ff.

[46] *Language* 11 20 ff.

[47] This is conceded by Heidel, SQVA 110 n. 16.

specifically, as the state's dependant, one who was compensated for his services by being made a fief-holder, and who was partciularly prominent in Old Babylonian society.

It remains only to recapitulate the semanitc history of the term under review. The oldest occurrence [48] would seem to date back to the period of the Fara texts.[49] The usage increases in Sargonid times,[50] but the peak is not reached until the Old Babylonian age. This accords well with the societal developments in Mesopotamia in the wake of expanding political and administrative horizons. For one should constantly bear in mind the fact that the legal status of the *muškênum* is but a reflex of social conditions in a particular age and place. A change in these might produce a shift in the meaning of the term from the technical to the general. And this is just what happened in the case of the *muškênum*.

By pledging his services to the state in return for certain economic grants, the *muškênum* was obliged to function under restrictions which pointed up his relationship of subject to ruler. So when the omens say *bēl māti . . . muškênūtam illak,*[51] they do not indicate that the king shall become a pauper—which would not constitute a genuine contrast in any case—but that "the master of the land . . . shall become a subject." Similarly, *šarru muškênu* [52] signifies "the king is nothing but a subject." Just so, too, Suppiluliuma warns Mattiwaza that, should the latter and his people violate the treaty before them,

[48] OECT 7 12 4.
[49] ZA 51 202.
[50] Gelb, MAD 3 266 f.
[51] Cf. A. L. Oppenheim, *Orientalia* 5 (1936) 207 n. 8.
[52] ABL 78 15. For a slightly different rendering of this and the following examples see Heidel, SQVA 39.

ilāni[mes] *annūtum . . . muškinnūta u errēšuta liddinkunūši* "may these gods . . . reduce you to the status of subjected peasants." [53] A state of subjection implies oppression and evokes pity. Hence *ša muškêna iḫabbilu* [54] amounts to "he who takes advantage of an inferior," and *kabtu: muškênu* [55] juxtaposes the "privileged" and the "underprivileged." From this usage it is but a short step to the nuance in *māre*[mes] *Bābili*[ki] *muškênūte ša memeni lā išū* the miserable Babylonians who have nothing at all." [56]

Finally, *muškênum* as a loanword could hardly have attained such great vogue merely on the strength of "poor." None of the borrowing languages lacked native means to signify either "poor, needy," or "humble." The loan had to fill a need with which the indigenous resources could not cope satisfactorily. The appeal of *muškênum* must have derived from its primary social sense, its secondary meaning of dejection, or both. For the former we may still have a Hebrew survival in the *ʿarēy misknōt* of Exod 1.11, where "store cities" is scarcely suitable, whereas "cities [built] by forced labor" is precisely what the context requires.[57] The secondary sense of the term

[53] KBo I 1 rev. 63 f.

[54] KAR 119 12; cf. CAD 6 4.

[55] ZA 44 163.29.

[56] ABL 340 rev. 9 f.

[57] The same might apply also to the remaining occurrences of this phrase (I Kings 9.19; II Chron 8.4, 6; 17.12). Note especially the connection between the instance in I Kings 9.19 and the phrase "forced labor" in verse 21. The usual combination of this form with Akk. *šakānu* is precarious for the simple reason that this root is present in Hebrew and did not have to be imported from Akkadian. On the other hand, the same nominal form in II Chron 16.14 is best interpreted as a loan from Akk. *maškānum* "threshing-place," which is in turn a borrowing from the Sumerian; cf. Goetze, AJSL 52 143 ff. In other words, the common Semitic root *škn* should yield Heb. *maškān,* as indeed it does. But specifically Akk. *šukênum* and the Sumerian loanword *maškānum* should find their sibilant changed to *s* in Hebrew. One of them does so certainly in *miskēn* and *miskēnut.* The other appears to have done so in the *misknēt* of II Chron 16.14.

is clearly apparent in *miskēnut* "misery," Deut 8.9, and in the adjective *miskēn* "underprivileged," Eccl 4.13, 9.15 f., as has long been recognized. It is this latter nuance that is most prominent in the other languages as well.

To sum up, the functional force of *muškênum* is that of the "state's dependant" who assumed certain onerous obligations and restrictions in return for fief-holdings. It is this meaning alone that prevails in the Laws of Eshnunna, the Code of Hammurabi, and the Mari documents. The usage goes back to a specific gesture of submission, and is in consonance with the morphology of the term. The position of "subject" in relation to "master" gave the word its derived sense of "underprivileged, pitiable." This latter development is most commonly reflected in the numerous borrowings of the term. Thus, while the person designated as a *muškênum* may have deserved sympathy, the designation itself enjoyed an unusually rich and sustained career.

[For subsequent discussions cf. F. R. Kraus, *Ein Edikt des Königs Ammi-ṣaduqa von Babylon* (1958), pp. 144–59; J. J. Finkelstein, JCS, XV (1961), pp, 96–99; D. O. Edzard, *Genava,* VIII (1960), pp. 246–47.]

The Case of the Obliging Servant

THE AKKADIAN COMPOSITION THAT HAS COME TO BE KNOWN as the "Dialogue of Pessimism" contains, nevertheless, a number of features which militate against the common modern evaluation of this literary piece. A reconsideration of the whole problem is therefore in order. It is the purpose of this paper to attempt the task.

The evidence will be presented in three sections. The basis for the argument must be, of course, the text itself. Since transliterations of it are available in two separate studies,[1] they will not be reproduced here. A new (1) *Translation*, however, is clearly justified. Because this translation differs from its predecessors on a number of points, some of which are basic to the whole argument, the reasons for such departures, as well as incidental philological notes, will be given under (2) *Annotations*. After these preliminaries we shall be ready for (3) *Interpretation.*

[1] The special abbreviations used in this paper are as follows: Eb.: Ebeling, MVAG XXIII/2 (1919) 50–70; cf. also AOT² 284–87; Jac.: Th. Jacobsen in *The Intellectual Adventure of Ancient Man* (IAAM), 1946, 216–18; Lan.: S. Langdon, *Babyloniaca* 7 (1923) 195–209; M.:B. Meissner, *Babylonien und Assyrien* II (1925) 433–34; Pf.: R. Pfeiffer in ANET (1950) 437–38; Un.: A. Ungnad, *AfO* 15 (1945–51) 74–75.
For citations of the sources see below.

The published cuneiform sources are as follows:

A = VAT 9933, KAR 96 (Plates 170–73),

B = VAT 657, Reissner, *Sumerisch-babylonische Hymnen* VI (p. 143), republished by Ebeling, MVAG XXIII /2 (1919) Plates I–II,

C = K 10523, *ibid.* Plate III,

D = K 13830, R. J. Williams, JCS VI (1952) 1. A has been dated by the editor to the late eighth century (cf. Eb. p. 50). B is evidently Seleucid. Both C and D (the two K-texts) are small fragments, yet C is valuable for the beginnings of lines in paragraphs II and III which are not preserved elsewhere, as well as for the start and apparent sequence of our paragraph IV.

TRANSLATION

I

"[Slave, oblige me!]" "Yes, y[es], my lord!"
"[Forthwith the chariot fetch and] ready for me! To the palace I will ri[de]!"
"[Ride, my lord, ride! Thine *every w*]*ish* will come to pass for thee.
[The mighty king] will defer to thee."
"[No, slave, to] the palace, in truth, I will not ride!"
"[Ride not,] my [lord,] ride not!
[*On a campaign thou didst not st*]*art* he will send thee;
[A road] thou knowest [not] he will cause thee to take.
[*In the depth*] of night he will expose thee to hardships."

II

"[Slave, obli]ge me!" "Yes, yes, my lord!"
"[Forthwith fetch] and give me water for my hands! I will feast!"
"Fe[as]t, my lord, feast! A round of banquets is the heart's relief.
[To a feast] partaken of in a joyous mood and with hands washed comes Shamash."
"No, [slave,] I will not feast, in truth!"
"Feast not, my lord, feast not!
To fast and to feast, to thirst and to gulp, goes against man!"

III

"Slave, oblige me!" "Yes, yes, my lord!"
"Forthwith the chariot fetch and ready for me! To the country I will ride!"
"Ride, my lord, ride The stalking-man's stomach stays full;
The hunting-dog has a bone to crack;
The stalking hawk feathers [his] nest;
The prowling *owl* becomes [. . . . -*li*]*ke*."
"[No,] slave, to the country, in truth, I will not r[ide!]"
"Ride not, my lord, ri[de no]t!
The stalking-man goes out of his mind;
The hunting-dog's teeth will break;
The stalking hawk's home is [a hole] in the wall;
[And] the desert is the [*h*]*ome* of the prowling *owl*."

IV

"Slave, ob[lige me!" "Yes, yes, my lord!]"
"I will build [me a house and obtain . . . !]"
"Obtain, m[y lord, obtain! . . .]"

(lacuna)

"How can I build a house!" "Build not a house!
He who acts rashly destroys his patrimony."

V

"[Slave, oblige me!" "Yes, yes, my lord!]"
"At the w[ords of my accuser I will remain silent!]"
"Be silent, my lord, be si[lent! *Silence is pleasing to Shamash.*]"
"No slave, I [will not, in truth, be silent!]"
"Be not silent, my lord, [be not silent!]
If thou openest not thy mouth, [. . .],
Thy accusers will *be shackled* on [thine] account."

VI

"Slave, oblige me!" "Yes, yes, my lord!"
"I say, 'I will commit a crime!' " "So do, my lord, [do]!
If thou committest not a crime, empty will be your (*sic*) beer jug;
Who will give thee wherewith to fill your belly?"
"No slave, I will not commit a crime!"

"[Do not, my lord, do not!]
The man who commits a crime is either killed, or comes to grief,
Or is maimed, or seized, or
Cast into prison."

VII

"Slave, oblige me!" "Yes, yes, my lord!"
"I will love a woman!" "So love, my lord, love!
The man who loves a woman forgets want and misery."
"No, slave, a woman, in truth, I will not love!"
"Love not, my lord, love not!
Woman is a snare, a trap, a pitfall.
Woman is a sharpened iron dagger
That will cut a man's neck."

VIII

"Slave, oblige me!" "Yes, yes, my lord!"
"Forthwith fetch and hand me water for my hands!
I will offer a sacrifice to my god!"
"Offer, my lord, offer! The man who offers a sacrifice to his god, his heart is glad;
He makes investment upon investment."
"No, slave, I will not, in truth, offer a sacrifice to my god!"
"Do not, my lord, do not!
Thou mightst accustom the god to follow thee like a dog,
Asking of thee either 'My due!' or 'Didst thou not ask?' or anything else."

IX

"Slave, oblige me!" "Yes, yes, my lord!"
"I will provide sustenance for our land!" "So provide, my lord, provide!
The man who provides sustenance for his land, his grain
Remains his own grain, (yet) the interest thereon is abundant!"
"No, slave, I will not, in truth, give sustenance to the land!"
"Give not, my lord, give not! Debt will eat up thy grain; thy grain
They will understate to thee and will forever abuse thee on top of all."

X

"Slave, oblige me!" "Yes, yes, my lord!"
"I say, 'I will do righteousness unto my land!' " "So do, my lord, do!
The man who does righteousness unto his land,
His righteous deeds are placed in the ring of Marduk."
"No, slave, I will not, in truth, do righteousness unto my land."
"Do not, my lord, do not!
Climb and wander about atop the ancient mounds!
Behold the skulls of the hindmost and the foremost:
Which one is an evildoer and which one is righteous?"

XI

"Slave, oblige me!" "Yes, yes, my lord!"
"Now then, what is worth while?
To break my neck and thy neck,
To plunge into the river—that is worth while!"
"Who is so tall as to come up to heaven,
Who is so broad as to encompass the earth?"
"No, slave, I will slay thee and leave thee precede me!"
"Then could my lord survive me by as much as three days?"

[Colophon: Written and collated according to its original.]

ANNOTATIONS

I: A obv. 1–9; Eb. I; Lan. A

1. The logogram for 'slave' should be read here *arad* (in the vocative, for which cf. von Soden, GAG 62l) rather than *ardu,* unless the possessive suffix (*ardi*) is to be supplied. A freer translation into English would be 'my man!'

For *mitanguranni* (and its later counterpart *muntangeranni*) various renderings have been proposed: (a) 'obey me' (Eb., M., Pf.); (b) 'gehorche mir immer wieder' (von Soden, GAG 96j); (c) 'agree with me' (Jac.); (d) 'listen to me attentively' (Un.). None is altogether satisfactory for one reason or another. 'Oblige me,' with its implicit durative connotation echoing the *tan*-form, would seem to meet all the requirements of morphology and of context.

Whether *annū* is a doublet to *anni* 'yes' (Eb.), or a demonstrative in the sense of 'this is he' (not unlike Heb. *hinnēnī* 'here I am)' with Un., its present force is 'yes' in any case.

2. The phrase *dikūmma ṣamādum* has the broader sense of 'to fetch and put to work' already in OB times; cf. VAB VI 269.2 (said of silver). In this passage, however, there may be a conscious play on words (*ṣ* meaning specifically 'to hitch'), for paronomasia is a favorite pastime with our author.

3. The text would appear to point to [*ṣa*]*m-mar-ka*.[2]

4. Since the subject in lines 7 ff., which is carried over from this line, is in the sg., *ubbala* cannot be dual (with Eb.) but must be ventive.

5. The scheme of the A-version is to announce each switch by the master by means of *-ma* (except in line 45, where B this time reads *sar-tam-ma*). The required nuance is something like 'after all, on second thought, in truth.'

7. Lan. read [*ana ašri la te-*]*bu-ú* and translated, provisionally, *'unto a place whence one cometh not up.'* The construction is impossible although the verb itself is probably right. The form *ušaṣbatka* in the next line suggests *gerra* or *urḫa* as its complement; this in turn points to *ḫarrānu* in the present instance, hence evidently to the common *ana ḫarrāni tebū* 'to undertake, start on a journey' (cf. e.g. CT 40 48. 4 ff.); perhaps, elliptically, [*a-na ḫarrāni ša la te-et-*]*bu-ú*?

8. Cf. Gilg. Th. Pl. XII 13–14.

9. Eb. proposed, with reservations, [*eklêti*[3] *mâti ašar*

[2] So apparently Eb.
[3] Eb.'s *eqlêti* is an obvious slip.

ina] *mu-ši mar-ṣa-ta ú-kal-lam-ka,* but the adduced passage in ABL 460 rev. 7 f. is not relevant and the translation '[*Die Finsternisse des Landes*(?) *wo*] es dir in der Nacht schlecht ergeht, wird er dich sehen lassen' is plainly troublesome. Lan. (followed by Pf.) read [*ur-ra u*] *mu-ši;* but the form *mūši* in this phrase is ungrammatical (although *muši u urra*—in that order—occurs). I have assumed, therefore, *ina šāt mūši.*[4]

II: A obv. 10–16; C 1–8; Eb. II; Lan. B

12. The hendiadys in *saḫēru patānu* [5] indicates 'to go in a circle, to do continuously.'

13. I supply [*ana naptani*].

16. *eli/muḫḫi amēli alāku* surely has the sense of 'to go against human nature' (so Eb.). The context, moreover, calls for a distasteful chore.

III: A obv. 17–28; C 9–20; Eb. III; Lan. C

Except for M., all translators have rendered *muttaprašsidu* in this passage as 'fugitive,' placing the *tan*-form on a par with *naparšudu*: cf. Eb. (*ad loc.* and p. 65), Lan., Pf.; A. Heidel, AS 13 69. M. renders 'hunter,' evidently from the context, without giving an explanation. But the *tan*-form presupposes an iterative-durative connotation. English 'stalk' does the same thing. The passage in V R 10. 13–16, which is cited by Heidel, *loc. cit.,* applies

[4] For *šāt mūši* cf. Meissner, AS 4 69 f.

[5] The whole subject of hendiadys in Akkadian has been badly neglected although the usage is very common. Of the various types of this construction I shall cite, for the present, only *laqū u dabābu,* Assyrian Laws B iii 13–14 'claim to possession'; *bēl adē u mamēt* 'subject to pacts under oath'; and the significant juxtaposition *ina sanāq atmē* : *sanāqa u atmē* 'by careful utterance,' PSBA 1916 136 34 and n. 95. Cf. also *dikumma ṣamādum,* above.

this particular form both to the *surdū*-bird ('falcon') and to a conquered ruler just as our text uses it to describe the hunter and the *ḫaḫḫurru*-bird (cf. below). 'Slink away' will do very well as an approximate synonym applicable to a defeated enemy.

21. The syllabaries equate *ḫaḫḫur*(*ru*) with *āribu* 'raven,' cf. Meissner, MAOG XI/1–2 11. In view, however, of *ḫ. sāmu* 'red/brown *ḫ.*' we have to posit some kind of 'hawk.'

22. The attested meaning of *akkannu* is 'wild ass,' cf. Meissner, *loc cit.* This sense is certainly possible in the present context (cf. Job 39. 5–6). Yet there is another possibility that should not be discarded. Meissner himself (*loc. cit.*) called attention to the fact that *akkannu* stands also for a bird associated with *suddinnu, āribu,* and *ḫaḫḫurru*; he found it difficult to make a choice between these two meanings in the present context, after having previously rendered 'Jagdfalke(?), (M. 433).

My slight preference for an ornithological designation in this instance is due to the following arguments: Our passage cites *akkannu* alongside *ḫaḫḫurru,* precisely as does the vocabulary just mentioned. The latter lists also the *suddinnu,* perhaps 'bat' (cf. Landsberger, *Fauna* 97 n. 3, 141; Thompson, *Devils and Evil Spirits* I 130 35, 37), and the raven. Furthermore, the terms *murtappidu* (lines 22 and 28) and *namū* (28) are both familiar in connection with *eṭimmu* 'ghost, specter,' and this seems to be the image that our writer wished to evoke in line 28. We know that evil spirits could be banished by means, and in the form, of just such birds as those mentioned above (Thompson, *ibid.,* 134 65 f.). Finally, *akkannu* as a bird is apparently connected with *akkū,* a synonym of *qadū* 'screech-owl' (cf. CT 14 6.11). All in all, the owl would seem to have a fair chance of ousting the wild ass from the present context.

In the second half of the line, only the first two signs, *i*-ME-, have been preserved out of probably six; the third sign could have been *-e* (so Eb.), in which the verb was *i-me-e*. Since a present form is required, we may have here a defective writing for *immē* similar to *e-wi* (pres.) in the Irishum inscription, *Belleten* 14 228.46 and *i-me-i* Lit. Keilschrifttexte aus Assur 62 rev. 6. In any case, this reading is supported indirectly by the occurrence of *na-mu-ú* in the counterpoint passage (28), since our writer resorts to punning skilfully and often. Now the favorite complement of *ew/mū* 'to come into the state of, to become' is that with the ending *-iš*, cf. Schott, *Vergleiche* (MVAG XXX/2) 10 ff. and von Soden, ZA 41 106 f.n. 4. It may not be mere coincidence, therefore, that what is left of the last sign could well belong to [*s/ši*]*š*; but there are too many possibilities for supplementing *x-x-s/šiš*. The general idea would be 'settled, sedate, wise, reposeful.'

27. Here M., Lan., and Pf. supply [*ḫur-ri*] with good reason. The incidental pun on *ḫaḫ*(*ḫ*)*ur*(*r*)*u* could well be deliberate.

28. The traces in the copy do not favor [*šu*]-*ba-su*, yet the context would seem to demand such a reading. Note, e.g., *šubatka bītu nadū ḫarbu* 'thy home is an abandoned, ruined house' (said of an evil spirit), Thompson, *op. cit.* 138 99.

IV: A obv. 37–38; C 21–23; Eb. V; Lan. D

The text of A is here obviously in disorder since the two concluding lines of the strophe have nothing to do with what precedes. The pertinent beginning is preserved in C, where it follows our § III, hence the present arrangement.

Eb. recognized the conflate nature of A's fourth strophe but ascribed it to the telescoping of two independent sections, his IV and V (p. 52 n. d). As a result, Eb. IV lacks a conclusion ("Fehlt wohl der Schluss des Absatzes," p. 57). Lan. tried to interpret C 21–23 + A obv. 29–38 as a unit. He was thus obliged to assume that the scheme of the resulting paragraph (his D) differed from that of the other sections, and he had to admit that "The connection between constructing a house and securing advantage over adversaries is not obvious . . ." (Lan. 201).

The arrangement here proposed proceeds from the assumption of a simple displacement in A alone: the superfluous lines came from another strophe (see under V, below). This does away, among other things, with the duplication reflected in Eb. IV and VI.

31. Since the servant always picks up his response from the last word in the master's statement (except for the last strophe where the change is in accordance with the over-all scheme; cf. under *Interpretation*), the *ri-ši* of C 23 must correspond to an antecedent *lurši*. This point has been overlooked hitherto.

32. For this force of *kē kē* (or *kī kī*) cf. Gilg. XI 179. For the use of this interjection (single) in an exclamation cf. *kī ḫabil*, *Babyloniaca* VII 177 51, where the meaning is obviously 'what a shame! too bad!' (and not 'how he is disgraced?' *ibid.*). This compares with MHeb. *ḥ^{a}bal*, Aram. *ḥ^{a}bel* (with the same sense).

33. The rebus form *i-^{d}ŠEŠ^{ki}* = *inanna* (which troubled Eb.) has been commented upon more than once; cf. Weidner, *AfO* 11 73 n. 32. The sense of *alik inanna*

would seem to be 'he who acts on the spur of the moment, hotheaded.' In *bīt abišu iḫtepi* there is a clear play on the introductory *lubni bīta*—one more argument in favor of the proposed strophe arrangement.

V: B obv. 1–7; Eb. VI; Lan. F (cf. Eb. IV)

With this strophe begins the text of B, a version which diverges from A in the order of paragraphs (cf. e.g., under VI and VII) and occasionally also in content (e.g., IX). I have assumed that A obv. 29–36 and B obv. 1–7 were originally related in their themes but differed in details much as the respective versions of IX. The adduced section of A lacks a beginning (mutilated) and an end (scribal omission). What is left deals with accusers *bēl dabābi* whom the master would 'resolutely vanquish and enchain(?)' *lu-uk-mu-ma lu-ku-uš-ma lu-ṣìl(?)-ma*. B obv. 7 refers to *bēlu dīni* 'litigants' and uses in this connection the form *uṣ-ṣa-lu*.[6] Since neither version deals elsewhere with a legal theme, it seems most likely that we have here variant statements on the same topic. The apparent contrapuntal position of *luṣilma:uṣṣalū* (assuming that both forms have been read correctly) would be a further case in point. At all events, the present translation adheres to B, where the prevailing scheme is maintained.

36. The suggested supplementation (*ṭābi eli* ᵈ*Šamaš*) is based on PSBA 1916 133 11, 13.

40. Lan. reads *uz-za-zu*; but the last sign is at best *su* if not *lu*; moreover, there is no such present form to *i/uzuzzum*. The mention of 'accusers' makes it tempting to think of *ṣēlu* 'quarrel,' for which cf. R. Kraus, AfO 11

[6] If this is the correct reading. The last sign could well be SU but the resulting form does not make sense; see note to line 40.

228 f., and this is what Ebeling appears to have done in AOT 285. Nevertheless, this cure would seem worse than the ailment, on morphological grounds in any case. I have posited in both instances an underlying *eṣēlu* and have assumed an impersonal pl. in the present passage. It must be stressed, however, that reading and interpretation remain uncertain.

VI: A obv. 39–43; B rev. 1–8; Eb. VII; Lan. E

42. On the asseverative *kī(-mi)* cf. Eb. 62.

43. That *te-ep-šu* of A is a mistake for *te-ep*<*-pu*>*-šu* and sg. subj. is proved by the *te-ep-pu-uš* of B. The pertinent possessive suffixes, however, are in the plural; the reason for this discrepancy will be pointed out below.

The last word of this line has caused much trouble. Eb. operates with *ṭītu*/*ṭittu* 'clay,' in the sense of 'dirt > corpse' (pp. 58, 62; but this does not harmonize with the *ri-iq-qa* which precedes the noun in B rev. 3. M. renders 'Topf,' apparently in the sense of 'clay (pot).' Lan. reads *ḫi-id ku-*[*ma*] (*sic*) and translates 'what *happiness* is thine?' (p. 202), which fails to take into account, among other things, the DI- of B. Pf. has 'what becomes of your clay?'; this ignores *riqqā*. R. J. Williams suggests that we read *mi-nu-u ḫi--it-l*[*u-pu-ka*] (JCS 6 1), thus obtaining a contrast between clothing and food; yet the DI- in the other version cannot be disregarded.

The only value which ḪI and DI have in common is, of course, *ṭi*; but the *ṭītu* to which such a reading would normally lead has failed to yield satisfactory results. The trouble lies not in the reading but in the rendering, for 'clay' will not provide firm ground in this instance. A better prospect is furnished by the entry DUK KAŠ.

ÚS.SA = ḪI-*it-tum*, RA 6 130, AO 2162 obv. 1.12. Since the sumerogram in question can hardly be separated from KAŠ.Ú. SA = d i d a (Hrozný, *Getreide* 146) 'a beer beverage' (cf. Oppenheim, *Eames Catalogue* 70), we cannot but link d i d a with the ḪI-*it-tum* just cited (so already Hrozný, *loc cit.* 147 n. 2), thus arriving at *ṭi-it-tum*. Whether or not there is here an ultimate connection with the common term for 'clay,' the meaning is explicit: 'a vessel for some kind of beer.' This meaning fits the present context admirably: 'empty is your beer jug' (var. 'what is [in] your beer jug?').

46. This line is missing in B (A is not available for this passage). It has been restored on the analogy of VII, where B likewise omits the first part of the reply while A has it.

VII: A rev. 1–3; B obv. 8–13; Eb. VIII; Lan. G

For this and the following strophes cf. the translation by Jacobsen (IAAM 216 ff.). Pertinent comparisons are given by Eb. 66 f. and Pf. 438 n. 2.

54. The line is missing in B.

55. The translation of Jac., which has been followed here, is supported by Prov. 7.10 f. and Eccl. 7.26.

VIII: A rev. 4–11; B. obv. 14–21; Eb. IX; Lan. H

The general sense of this strophe has been clear all along. Jac. (217) has further clarified the construction of the last line. My departures from his translation are slight: I take *lā tašāl* as a question, alluding to such requests as might be found, e.g., in letters to the gods. The overall sense is, "Be careful not to get your personal god into bad habits," or in other words, "One can teach an old god new tricks." The reference in line 64 is no more blasphemous than the familiar passage in Gilg. XI 161: 'The gods crowded like flies about the sacrificer.' The Mesopotamian's idea of reverence was plainly not the same as ours.

61. A vivid illustration of profitable investments by a person in authority is provided by the recently published *The Alalakh Tablets*, Nos. 26 ff., where Ammitakum, the local ruler, makes various loans and buys up previous debts—all against ample security and with obvious prospects of plentiful profits.

IX: A rev. 12–19; B rev. 9–14; Eb. X; Lan. I

The last three lines in A are obscured by breaks, hence the better preserved text of B has here been followed. It is evident, however, that the two versions differed considerably as to details in this particular strophe.

68 f. In B this passage contains an obvious omission which has been restored from A: *uṭṭat-su*[7] (69) *uṭtat-*[*su-ma ḫubullu-šu*] *at-ri*. A's division into verses was also plainly superior.

71. Hence *ḫubullu* denotes 'debt' in contrast (which was, we may feel sure, intentional) to the preceding line where the word carries its alternate meaning 'interest.'

X: A rev. 20–28; B rev. 15–21; Eb. XI; Lan. J

74. The force of *usātu* in this strophe approximates that of Heb. *ṣədāqā*, especially in its later sense of 'charity.' Note in particular the juxtaposition of *bēl limutti:*

[7] Perhaps *se' at/s-su.*

bēl usāti (line 81) which is matched by Heb. *rāšā':ṣaddīq*.

76. The term *kippat* (A) refers apparently to the "ring" of the god which so often forms part of the rod-and-ring motif on Mesopotamian monuments; cf. the recent treatment by E. D. Van Buren, *ArOr* 17/2 (1949) 434–50. The sense of the passage would then be that the god weighs the subject's merits and returns to him his just deserts. The reading *káp-pat* in B may either be another play on words ('palms') or a later simplification of the original idea. The mention of Marduk should have some bearing on the question of the original place of the composition.

XI: A rev. 29–37; Eb. XII; Lan. K; Un. AfO 15 74–75

Note that in this strophe the servant fails to model his reply after his master's statement. The point will be discussed presently.

86 f. This couplet reproduces an ancient Sumerian proverb; see below, p. 363.

89. Syntactically, the sentence is elliptical, the *kī* with the subjunctive having the function of a conjunction: '(I swear) that my master would (not) survive me by three days! Cf. Un. *ad loc.* and von Soden, GAG 185k. This adjurative force of *kī* (exactly like that of *šumma* in oaths) is the third distinctive use of this particle in the composition before us, alongside the asseverative (line 42, etc.), and the exclamatory (*kē kē*, line 32).

INTERPRETATION

The composition before us was no doubt familiar to the Mesopotamians under the name *Arad mitangurranni*, after its initial words, in accordance with the normal usage of the time. In assessing this unique work, modern scholarship has shown a degree of unanimity that is no less exceptional. Ebeling found it to be "tinged with extreme pessimism." [8] Langdon was the first to call it "The Babylonian Dialogue of Pessimism," [9] with Jacobsen,[10] Pfeiffer,[11] and Williams [12] concurring. Meissner saw in this piece an expression of the futility of all human endeavor,[13] for all that it might seem to be rather burlesque to our tastes. Similarly, Ungnad regarded the work as basically pessimistic, if not an example of philosophic resignation.[14]

The question may first be posed whether any outright "denial of all values" [15] would have been sanctioned by the meticulously pious Mesopotamians. The extant witnesses of the text represent, as we have seen, four separate sources. The oldest of these—and the longest (A)—contains, moreover, a colophon which refers to a still older original. The composition, in short, was not only popular

[8] Eb. 50: "höchst pessimistisch gefärbt."

[9] Lan. 195.

[10] Jac. 216.

[11] Pf. 437.

[12] JCS VI 1.

[13] M. 433.—[There has just been called to my attention the article by F. M. Th. de 1. Böhl on "Die Religion der Babylonier und Assyrer," in *Christus und die Religionen der Erde* II (ed. F. König, Vienna 1951), 441–498, which includes a brief statement on the composition before us (493 f.) It is Böhl's opinion that the objective of the work was caricature. To that extent, therefore, our respective results coincide; the coincidence is made even closer by the fact that my first formal discussion of the piece, outlining the present conclusions, was likewise presented in 1951 (Spring) before a local faculty seminar on the Wisdom Literature of the Orient. In his particular context Böhl did not have the opportunity to give the full evidence on which his assessment is based so that a detailed comparison is not possible at this time. In any case, however, Böhl's general statement is welcome in this connection in that it constitutes independent support of the conclusions offered herewith. E.A.S.]

[14] Un. 75.

[15] *Loc. cit.*

but enjoyed also something like canonical status. It could not, in these circumstances, have sponsored views that threatened to subvert the tenets of contemporary orthodoxy.[16] Nowhere else in Akkadian literature can one find unrelieved heresy of the kind that this piece is alleged to reflect. The *Theodicy* ends on a note of hope.[17] Even that catalogue of human misery which bears the name *Ludlel bēl nēmeqi* leads up, as the name suggests, to a paean of praise for Marduk.[18]

Could it be, then, that the prevailing imputation of abject pessimism is not justified in the present instance? Because I believe that such is indeed the case, and because I owe it to my fellow-Assyriologists with whose opinions on this subject I herewith beg to differ, I offer the following arguments in favor of a revised assessment.

The common ascription of a pessimistic philosophy to the work before us is at best only a half-truth. On each of the projects which the master announces the servant has two opposite opinions. The one is just as positive as the other is negative; each is given in the same axiomatic manner. If the man is a pessimist in the second instance, he must be by the same token an optimist in the first instance. And lest it be asserted that what is really pessimistic is the net result, it should be recalled that each of these diametrically opposed views is pronounced with like finality. This is not close reasoning but outright ambivalence.

There is, furthermore, nothing spontaneous about the servant's responses. Each strophe is introduced with the unvarying command, 'Slave, oblige me!' The servant does

[16] Even *Ecclesiastes,* centuries later, had considerable difficulty in being admitted to the OT Canon.

[17] Cf. Landsberger, ZA 43 (1936) 72; cf. also the comment, *ibid.* 42.

[18] KAR 10 rev! 14 ff.

merely as he is bidden. He has little choice in the matter. His personal views are not for publication. The man is truly the "Obliging Servant" in every sense of the phrase.

On further probing we learn also that the replies are far from original. 'Climb and wander about atop the ancient mounds' [19] is an all too obvious borrowing from the Gilgamesh Epic.[20] The public for which the dialogue was intended surely had no difficulty in spotting the allusion; it must have heard this lesson from archaeology many times. In lines 86–87 we have another ancient saying of which the Sumerian original is happily available. This was pointed out by Kramer [21] and it has since been stressed by Jacobsen.[22] Other passages, too, are linked with the wisdom literature not only to Mesopotamia but of other parts of the ancient Near East as well.[23]

The servant, then, does little more than cite familiar sayings. It is this trait above all others that characterizes his replies; indeed, it is the key to the nature of the composition as a whole. Perhaps the strongest proof of the mechanical manner of the replies is contained in the couplet found in lines 43–44. The possessive suffixes in that passage are in the plural—'*your* beer jug,' '*your* belly,' not 'thy . . .'—although only one person is addressed and the singular is employed everywhere else. The proverb involved was evidently construed in the plural; it was too well known, apparently, to be tampered with

[19] Above, line 79.

[20] Gilg. I i 16; XI 303.

[21] BASOR 96 (1944) 24 and JCS I (1947) 35 n. 215. Mr. Edmund I. Gordon was good enough to collect for me additional material on this point, but the present references would seem sufficient.

[22] Jac. 218.

[23] Cf. Eb. 66–70. Note also such links with Akkadian proverbs as the sequence *epru* and *usātu* in K 33851 obv. ii 13, 16 (PSBA 1916 133).

for grammatical purposes. Nothing could better illustrate rigid adherence to familiar quotations.

If our literate servant deals thus in clichés and copybook maxims, what could be the object of the effort before us? Was it to demonstrate for the first time on record that "The devil can cite Scripture for his purpose"? Perhaps so, but hardly with the implications that Shakespeare had in mind. Strophe V is a good case in point. The master had just declared his resolve to remain silent at the words of his accuser. To this the servant, faithful to his custom to cling to his master's last word, replies, 'Be silent, my lord, be silent!' This may seem innocent and dutiful at first glance. Let us bear in mind, however, that *sukut* also means 'hush,' just as its cognates do elsewhere in Semitic. A situation in which a servant could say this to his master and do so in all propriety must have been a source of much merriment in an oriental setting. It is scarcely credible that the double meaning in this instance was purely accidental. The trap appears to have been set with care if not with malice aforethought. If so, the aim of the work, or at least one of its main aims, was humor. We would seem to be here in the realm of broad satire, and not of ponderous philosophizing.

This brings us to the last strophe, which is basic to the evaluation of the piece as a whole. That particular section differs from all the others in tenor and in scheme. The master starts out with a question instead of announcing a plan. The servant, in sharp contrast with his previous behavior, fails to pick up the cue. He comes back instead with a time-honored proverb that must have worn threadbare from the use and abuse by countless generations: 'Who is so tall as to come up to heaven, who is so broad as to encompass the earth?' What has this to do with the breaking of necks? Clearly, nothing. It is a plain *non sequitur.*

I submit that this reply by the servant was deliberately off the mark and that it was intended to underscore the farcical bearing of all that had preceded. Indeed, it is altogether probable that the audience was treated at this point to a visible sign of a change in mood, inasmuch as the piece may well have been designed for oral presentation by two performers. For the "master's" retort comes very close to sounding like, "I will kill you, you reprobate, and have you precede me to the Nether World!" Whereupon the "slave," steps out of character with this irreverent parting shot: "And do you really think, my precious lord, that you could last three days without me?"

Just who or what may have been the butt of this satire is another matter. Perhaps it was the weakling in a position of authority, or the cliché expert, or the incompetent in any walk of life. But whatever the target, the strictures of this unusual ancient work must have given great pleasure to the community at large, to judge from the number of extant sources. It is a pleasure that should not be lost on the modern reader.

In any event, *The Obliging Servant* surely has no close affinity with an Aethelred the Unready or a Hamlet, a Schopenhauer or a Spengler. One could make out a case for listing Jonathan Swift as a spiritual descendant of our ancient author.[24] All in all, the characters in our piece are

[24] Cf. his *Complete Collection of Genteel and Ingenious Conversation:* "I can faithfully assure the reader that there is not one single witty phrase in the whole Collection which has not received the Stamp and Approbation of at least One Hundred Years, and how much longer it is hard to determine; he may therefore be secure to find them all genuine, sterling and authentic." Aldous Huxley, who quotes this passage (*On the Margin,* New York, 1923, p. 88) calls the work "a diabolic picture of the social amenities" and "a never-ceasing stream of imbecility."

related in some ways to that pair of worthies who have been working overtime for P. G. Wodehouse, namely, the Hon. Bertie Wooster and his matchless man-servant, the imperturbable Jeeves.

The defense rests!

[The older view is defended, at least in part, by W. G. Lambert, *Babylonian Wisdom Literature* (1960), pp. 139–49.]

LINGUISTIC STUDIES

Secondary Developments in Semitic Phonology: An Application of the Principle of Sonority

THERE ARE TWO TYPES OF SECONDARY DEVELOPMENTS WITH which I propose to deal in the present study, viz., the occurrence of new vowels, and the development of the so-called secondary gemination. The former phenomenon is observable in one form or another in all the Semitic languages; the latter is restricted in the main to Hebrew and to the Aramaic dialects. I further hope to prove in the course of the present investigation that the two phonetic changes go back to one and the same principle which will figure in the following pages as the principle of sonority.

Both the problem of secondary vowels and the development of new geminate consonants have been to the Semitic philologist a cause of much trouble and confusion. To the problem of secondary vowels Brockelmann has devoted a separate chapter in his *Comparative Grammar of the Semitic Languages.*[1] But, for all the examples

[1] C. Brockelmann, *Grundriss der vergleichenden Grammatik der Semitischen Sprachen* (Berlin, 1908), I, 209 ff. To be quoted hereafter as *GVG.* Works which are referred to frequently in the present study are quoted in full in the first reference, and an abbreviated form is also given in the brackets to be used in further citations.

which are recorded in that work, the author does not seem to notice any closer connection between the causes of all those phenomena. As for Hebrew, where various types of secondary vowels have resulted in a considerable number of secondarily extended forms, the problem has received, to be sure, a good deal of attention. Nevertheless, little light has been hitherto shed upon the origin of those sounds, and upon the conditions under which they are prompt to arise, with the possible exception of the so-called Ḥatephs. So much so that the author of one of the latest and most complete studies of Hebrew phonology finds enough reason to complain that many of the instances with such vowels (Ḥatephs with non-laryngeals) betray "neither consistency in their treatment nor even a trace of a recognizable principle."[2] The same writer states in connection with his discussion of secondary gemination in Hebrew that no definite laws have been established for that language to determine the precise relationship between long vowels and geminate (lengthened) consonants.[3]

There is, however, one important branch of philology which has not been sufficiently explored for the explanation of the phonetic changes just mentioned. I am referring to the science of phonetics as it is understood and applied in the study of Indo-European languages. The nature and properties of a number of sounds as well as their behavior and influence in syllables and groups of syllables should be subjected to a close study before an answer to the questions outlined above can be attempted with any measure of success. Those developments are obviously phonetic and not morphological. It is, consequently, in the study of sounds where alone an explana-

[2] G. Bergsträsser, *Hebraische Grammatik* (Leipzig, 1918), § 21 w. (Brg.).
[3] *Ibid.*, 24*b*.

tion of such phenomena should be looked for and expected.

It is also essential to deal with the above changes as a whole rather than separately. Furthermore, it is of importance to compare the same new phonetic development in more than one related dialect, wherever it is observable as a clearly defined type and not as some isolated phenomenon. Only when proved related to a large family of similar sound-changes can any given type of them be explained with a satisfactory show of reason as to its nature. Similarly, with an appreciable number of examples from different stages of the change, the successive steps may be marked through which the development was most likely to go. In fine, it is from a phonetic angle and with a comparative method that the problems should be investigated.

Before I take up the question in detail one more introductory remark remains to be made. The phonetic changes alluded to above are, of all the Semitic languages, best observable in Hebrew. This is especially true, of course, of the secondary lengthening of consonants, in which Hebrew is particularly concerned. As regards the development of new vowels there is added another important consideration in favor of Hebrew as the starting-point for the discussion. As is well known, all the Semitic systems of writing are, with the exception of Assyrian, originally consonantal. The marking of the vowels is invariably a later development. Now in the case of Hebrew we have a methodical and thoroughgoing, even if occasionally too schematic, system of vocalization in the so-called Tiberian texts. Apart from that—and this second point is of still greater importance—we have in the case of Hebrew considerable sources for checking up the Masoretic tradition. In the first place, there are the differently vocalized Babylonian texts with many interesting and important variations from the Tiberian system.[4] Secondly, there is the comparatively scanty, but very valuable, transcriptional material, especially the recently discovered remnants of the second column of the Hexapla. In the Greek and Latin transcriptions of Hebrew the vowels are, naturally, indicated. Since the most recent of the Greek sources (the transcriptions of Origen) antedate the Hebrew systems of vocalization by at least four centuries their importance for the knowledge of Hebrew vowels cannot be overstated.[5] It will be, therefore, most advisable to base the discussion of secondary Semitic vowels primarily on Hebrew examples while analoga from other Semitic languages will be adduced as often as may be desirable and possible.

For the understanding of the changes to be discussed below one must bear in mind the effect of the *principle of relative sonority* upon the order of sounds within a given syllable. A comprehensive account of the subject is given in O. Jespersen's *Lehrbuch der Phonetik.*[6] In the present connection it will suffice to state, that if highly sonorous sounds such as liquids and nasals come to stand between consonants with a relatively smaller amount of sonority, the former become automatically syllable-forming.[7] I shall quote only one prominent instance. Latin *agellus* "a small field" goes back to the

[4] Cf. especially P. Kahle, *Der Masoretische Text des Alten Testamentes nach der Überlieferung der Babylonischen Juden* (*MT*) (Leipzig, 1902), and *idem, Masoreten des Ostens* (*MO*) (Leipzig, 1913).

[5] For the Hexaplaric material (Hex.) cf. especially Field, *Origenis Hexaplarum* (Oxford, 1875), and H. A. Redpath, *Supplements to the Concordance of the Septuagint* (Oxford, 1900–1906), pp. 199 ff.

[6] Cf. O. Jespersen, *Lehrbuch der Phonetik* (*J Ph*), (Leipzig, 1904), 191 ff.

[7] In the present discussion the terms "consonant," "vowel," "emphatic sounds," etc., are employed for simplicity's sake in their traditional signification. Spellings of words like *Qames, Hateph* are also conventionalized.

diminutive form **agro-los*. The intermediate changes may be set down as follows. First the *o* of the stem was lost through syncope as the result of a strong stress-accent which rested in primitive Italic on the first syllable. In the form **agrlos* which thus resulted the *r* was between two consonants with a smaller amount of sonority. That sound had, therefore, to assume vocalic function (the process is called by the Sanskrit name *samprasāraṇa*). Next developed an anaptyctic vowel *e* yielding the form **agerlos*. From there it was only a question of time to reach the form *agellos* > *agellus* through assimilation (*rl* > *ll*) and vowel-weakening (*o* > *u*).

The development of secondary vowels may be traced almost invariably to the presence of highly sonorous sounds in their immediate neighborhood.[8] It may be attributed from the phonetic standpoint to two main causes, viz., (*a*) the occurrence of relatively more sonorous sounds between two other consonants, (*b*) the increase in sonority in the neighborhood of sounds with a high quantity of resonance.

A. SECONDARY VOWELS IN THE SEMITIC LANGUAGES

It will be best to begin the discussion of the problem of secondary vowels in the Semitic languages with an attempt at classifying the main types of such vowels as they

[8] Another point must be also borne in mind. The frequent variations in the tradition of various languages as regards the presence or absence of secondary vowels confirm the theory that anaptyxis is largely dependent upon the tempo of speech. This in turn varies, of course, according to the subject, so that where an *allegro* pronunciation might not be productive of a secondary vowel, a *lento* pronunciation will often result in a *Svarabhakti*. As compared with the vowels that are etymologically required the appearance of secondary vowels is, so to speak, accidental.

are found in that group of dialects. I propose to deal with the subject under the following heads:

1. Prothetic vowels, i.e., anaptyctic sounds which have been developed before consonants at the beginning of a word, e.g., gen. Sem. *ʾarbaᶜ* from the stem *rbʿ* "four," Heb. *ʾezrōaʿ:zᵉrōaʿ* "arm," Syr. *ʾarqīʿā* for *rᵉqīʿā;* "firmament."

2. Anaptyctic vowels in medial syllables which in turn may be subdivided in to two groups.

a) before a single consonant, e.g., Heb. *tōḵalennā* from *ʾkl* "to eat."

b) before two consonants, e.g., Heb. *qāroḇᵉḵem* Deut. 20:2 < *qorbᵉḵem* "your approaching," Syr. *madenḥā*: *madnᵉḥā* "sunrise."

3. The so-called segolates, i.e., anaptyctic vowels with two final consonants, e.g., Heb. *boqer* = Hex. βοκρ Ps. 46:6, Arab. *mahal* < *mahl* "rest," Eth. *falag* < *falg* "stream," Akk. *ṣalmu* cstr. st.: *ṣalam* "statue."

4. Anaptyctic vowels formed under the influence of the laryngeals, e.g., Heb. *yeḥᵉzaq:yeḥzaq, mōšīaʿ*, Hex. μωσι, Ps. 18:42, Eth. *samāʿeku* > *samāʿku* "I have heard."

1. *Prothetic Vowels*

While such secondary vowels may at times develop in Semitic (*a*) before single initial consonants, they are found as a rule (*b*) before two consonants at the beginning of a word.

a) As is the case with the Indo-European languages (see above) prothesis before single consonants is especially favored with liquids. Cf. Syr. *ʾarezlē* "feet," J. Aram. *ʾarē* < *rē* < *rəʾe* "behold," Mand. *ʾarāmaṯa* "hills," Eth. *ĕrāḥ* as compared with Arab. *rāḥat* "palm of the hand." [9]

[9] *GVG*, pp. 213, 217.

Instances of prothetic vowels before less sonorous consonants are rare and isolated, and therefore may have to be attributed to causes other than phonetic.

b) Prothesis before two consonants is well known in Semitic. We have seen that within the syllable there obtain certain definite rules concerning the order of the consonants, and that a word beginning with two consonants prefers the more sonorous one next to the usual syllabic apex, viz., the vowel. The initial sounds of such words are in consequence possessed of comparatively little resonance. Now in Semitic, syllables began originally with one consonant.[10]But linguistic change would often cause two consonants to appear together initially, as when, e.g., the Arab. Perf. *inqatala* developed secondarily from the form **nqatala* which in turn was due to analogy with the Impr. *ianqatilu*.[11] In cases like **nqatala* an additional syllable was immediately necessary, as the sonorous *n* could not remain in the same syllable with the following sound unless the latter were of equal or higher sonority, hence in a comparatively small number of cases. But the prothetic vowel, being required in the great majority of the *inqatala* forms, was naturally extended, on the analogy of the latter, to the few groups of forms where it was dispensable phonetically.

A new syllable may develop with two initial consonants, with the aid of an anaptyctic vowel after the first consonant, as well as through a prothetic vowel. As is well known, some Semitic dialects chose to follow the former course. The treatment of the Imp. Qal forms may serve as an example. Over against Arab *uqtul* we have Heb. and Aram, *qətol,* Akk. *kušud.*

It is not my present intention to advance the theory

[10] *Ibid.*, p. 61.
[11] *Ibid.*, p. 209.

that all anaptyctic vowels with two initial consonants, recognized in the respective morphologies of the various Semitic languages, are due solely to purely phonetic and mechanical causes. That with the aid of analogy such a state of affairs would not be impossible has been shown in the case of *inqatala*. The customary explanation for these phenomena has been hitherto found in an alleged aversion on the part of the Semitic languages to syllables beginning with two consonants. From the point of view of phonetics such arguments are of necessity metaphysical. The fact, however, remains that not every linguistic change is explainable on phonetic grounds alone. If one cares to introduce into our discussion the argument of a disinclination in the linguistic consciousness of the speakers of the Semitic dialects to the unoriginal biconsonantal groups of initial sounds, we have no means of disproving such a contention. It is, however, a fact that, apart from all the other possible considerations, the necessity of anaptyctic vowels in a vast number of such groups is from a *phonetic standpoint* demonstrably certain. If the principle of sonority was here not the only cause of the change, it was without any doubt the most important contributing factor.

Instances of prothetic vowels developed in nouns before two consonants are comparatively rare for the following reason. In cases like *uqtul* or *inqatala* the first of the two consonants was vowelless before prothesis set in. But in words like *z*^{e}*rō*$^{a‘}$ there had been, to begin with, a vowel after the first consonant (*ḏirā‘*). That vowel was later reduced under the influence of the stress-accent. It is only under special conditions that a complete loss (syncope) of the reduced sound may have been phonetically desirable, as, e.g., in the construct state where the word-accent is made secondary, thus removing the main stress at least two syllables further (*ḏrōa). The urge for prothetic vowels would be, therefore, primarily felt in words with a highly sonorous initial consonant followed by Shwa and used frequently in the construct state.

Let us now examine the more prominent examples of such nouns with prothetic vowels to see whether these theoretical prerequisites are actually borne out by facts. We find that Hebrew, and especially Syriac, develop prothetic vowels before such nouns when they begin with a liquid. E.g., Heb. *'argaz* "coffer," *'almānā "widow,"* [12] *'armōn* "palace," [13] Syr. *'arḥīmā* "beloved," *'ardīdā* "upper garment," *'ar'ē* "contented," [14] J. Aram. *'arkubbā* "knee," *'arzīlā* "gazelle," [15] and many others. We know that *š* is in this respect closely akin to the liquids and there are indeed instances of prothetic vowels before that sound, cf. Syr. *'aštīn,* and *štīn* "sixty," *'eštī* "drank," [16] Hex. αρσαειμ *r^ešā'īm* Ps. 1. 1. So far, therfore, the examples are perfectly in accordance with the phonetic principles outlined above. The vocal Shwa which followed the first consonant before the development of the anaptyxis is naturally sacrificed for the full prothetic vowel.

Now one might conceivably ask the question as to what grammarians have had so far to say on the subject

[12] Barth, *Nominalbildung,* 151*a.*

[13] The author, *JQR* (NS), XIV, 329.

[14] Nöldeke, *Kurzgefasste Syrische Grammatik* (Nöld.), Leipzig, 1898, 51.

[15] G. Dalman, *Grammatik des Jüdisch-Palästinischen Aramäisch* (Dalm.),

[16] Nöld., *loc. cit.,* J. Aram. *'eštāqad* "last year" which Dalm., *loc. cit.,* lists among his examples of words with a prothetic vowel does not belong here at all. The same applies to Heb. *'etmōl* "yesterday" which Berg. (23*e*) cites in a similar connection. The initial sound of both words is *etymologically* justified as it is a development of the Akk. preposition *ina*> *en* "in" found in the corresponding (and cognate) expressions *ina šattaqad* "last year," *ina timāli i-timāli* "yesterday." Cf. Jensen, *ZA,* XI, 352, Pick, *OLZ,* XII (1909), col. 165, Perles, *ibid., XII* (1918), col. 67. To this may be added Heb. *'emeš "yesternight."* Cf. Akk. *ina muši.*

of prothetic vowels in the Semitic languages. On closer investigation it will be found that the subject is taken cognizance of in very few works, and is particularly neglected in those that deal with Hebrew grammar. For the Aramaic dialects men like Nöldeke and Dalman have contented themselves with a brief and accurate presentation of facts, without going deeper into the phonetic side of the problem.[17] In the case of Hebrew, Brockelmann (who is followed by Bauer-Leander) has attempted to set up a law which cannot but appear misleading and inaccurate upon closer investigation.[18] According to the author of the *Comparative Grammar of the Semitic Languages* a secondary syllable develops in Hebrew before a sibilant followed by a vocal Shwa. The examples he quotes are *'ezrōᵃ'* "arm" and *'eṣ'āḏā* "bracelet." This statement would naturally give the impression that secondary vowels develop regularly before a sibilant + Shwa and that prothetic vowels should not be expected with Hebrew nouns before a non-sibilant. Yet neither of the cases is strictly true. In the first place, we have seen prothetic vowels before *r* as in *'argaz, 'armōn*. Secondly, the sibilant in both *'ezrōᵃ'* and in *'eṣ'āḏā* has very little to do with the prothetic vowel. The reason for the latter is rather to be sought elsewhere. It has been pointed out in the introductory pages of the present article that certain sounds are under special conditions especially conducive to the development of anaptyctic vowels. We have seen that this statement applies particularly to sounds with a relatively high amount of resonance, as, e.g., liquids and nasals. It has been also indicated above, and it will be

[17] Nöld., p. 37; Dalm., p. 94.

[18] *GVG*, p. 215. Bauer und Leander, *Historisch Grammatik der Hebräischen Sprache des Alten Testamentes*, Halle, 1922 (*B-L*), p. 210. See, however, the valuable contribution of Frank R. Blake, *JAOS*, XXXVI, 217–22.

further substantiated in the course of the present study, that the Semitic laryngeals are often responsible for new vocalic developments. In *z^e^rō^a^ʻ* and in *ṣ^eʻ^ʻāḏā,* which are variants of the above forms with the prothetic vowel, it was the liquid (*r*) and the laryngeal (ʻ) that were responsible for the tendency to develop a stronger anaptyctic vowel than the vocal Shwa that preceded them. As a full vowel in place of the Shwa could not have been tolerated in Hebrew in that position for accentual reasons, the anaptyctic vowel could have developed only before the first consonant of either word. It is purely accidental that in either case that first consonant happens to be a sibilant. But that any other consonant could have done as well is proved by examples like Heb. *'abneṭ* "girdle," Syr. *'eglīdā* for *g^e^līdā* "ice," J. Aram. *'aḏmā* (Heb. *dām*) "blood" and especially *'eḏrāʻēh* "his arm," *'eḏrāʻāḵ* "thine arms,"[19] both being forms of the cognate to the Hebrew *z^e^rō^a^ʻ*, yet without the sibilant of the Hebrew, in accordance with the consonantal correspondences of Hebrew and Aramaic. The above examples illustrate the fact that the consonants in question may be at times instrumental in the development of anaptyctic vowels not only in a contiguous position but also when separated by another sound.

Lastly should be mentioned such prothetic vowels as have developed in the Semitic languages in loan words with two initial consonants, e.g., Arab. *'Aflātun:* πλάτων, J. Aram. *'isṭrāṭā:* Lat. *strata,* Mishnic *'aḵsanyā:* Gr. ξενία "inn." The cause of such prothesis, however, is in these cases psychological rather than phonetic, as is shown by the fact that the languages from which those words had been borrowed had no need of such a sound. It may be explained by a certain degree of effort with which people

[19] Dalm., pp. 94–95.

will attempt to reproduce the sounds of a foreign language. As an interesting parallel may be cited the fact that the English and French, who do not usually begin an initial vowel with a glottal catch (') as do the Germans, will produce such a sound when they learn a foreign tongue.[20]

2. *Anaptyctic Vowels in Medial Syllables*

This group too is best treated under two separate heads, (*a*) anaptyctic vowels with single consonants, and (*b*) with two consonants.

a) It has been stated above that the phonetic basis for a secondary vowel with a single consonant is an increase of resonance in the neighborhood of that sound, provided that the latter itself is distinguished by a high amount of sonority. It should also be indicated that such conditions might arise, among others, during especially solemn recitations or else on occasions in which the emotions of the speaker have been particularly stirred. At any rate such developments presuppose a greater stress on the given syllable than the latter is ordinarily entitled to, and this in turn is, barring colloquialisms, not to be expected in the free speech of the usual daily intercourse. In the case of Hebrew, conditions favoring the development of such vowels obtained notably in the pronunciation of the synagogue, especially that of the poetical portions of the Scriptures. Those vowels are consequently of a comparatively recent date. They have never attained to the dignity of full vowels and are therefore marked with the Ḥateph-signs which are otherwise reserved for secondary vowels with laryngeals.

[20] *JPh*, 76, end.

For the Ḥatephs with non-laryngeals the Masorete Ben Asher[21] lays down the following rules. Ḥateph-Pathaḫ is placed (1) after Metheg in a word with a conjunctive accent, e.g., *'im*^{a}*rōṯ* Ps. 12:7 (No. 27). (2) Between like consonants after Metheg, e.g., *b*^{e}*riḇ*^{a}*ḇōṯ* Mic. 6:7 (No. 33). (3) With the *m* of the participles preceded by a Metheg, e.g., *ham*^{a}*lē'īm* Isa. 21:20 (No. 34). (4) In all forms of *hlk* before the so-called *Dagesh conjunctivum*, e.g., *'el*^{a}*ḵā-nā* Exod. 4:18 (No. 50). And lastly (5) in a number of isolated instances, e.g., *'uš*^{a}*laḥ* II Kings 9:17 (No. 14).

As regards the Ḥateph-Qames after non-laryngeals it will suffice to indicate in the present connection that the vowel is found (*a*) primarily before laryngeals and the partially related emphatic sounds (*q, ṣ, ṭ*) when followed by an *o*-vowel, or (*b*) as a remnant of a reduced *u/o*. E.g., (*a*) *wa'ešm*^{o}*'ā* Dan. 8:13, *'ešš*^{o}*qā-nā* I Kings 19:20, (*b*) *'amm*^{o}*niyyōṯ* I Kings 11:1 (from *'ammōniyyōṯ*), *ṣipp*^{o}*rīm* Lev. 14:4 e.a. (from *ṣippōr*).

A detailed discussion of all the groups indicated above would carry us disproportionately far afield. Among others it should not be forgotten that there are considerable variations between the lists of Ben Asher and the Masoretic texts, as regards the placing of the Ḥateph-Pataḫ with non-laryngeals (cf. especially König, *Lehrgebäude*, pp. 71 ff., Bergsträsser, *op. cit.*, No. 21 u, bb). Such variations existed no doubt among the Masoretes themselves, as is but natural in the case of this particular type of secondary vowels. I may be, therefore, permitted to sum up the matter as briefly as possible, in so far as it bears on our present problem. Cases like Ḥateph-

[21] See Ahron ben Mosheh ben Asher, *Diqduqqē-hatt*^{e}*'āmim,* ed. by S. Bauer and H. L. Strack (Dikd.), Leipzig, 1879.

Pathaḥ (2) and Ḥateph-Qames (*a*) are self-explanatory. Between like consonants a secondary vowel was required to prevent such consonants from coalescing into one long consonant (*ribᵃbōt* into **ribbōt*). The Ḥateph-Qames before the laryngeals and the emphatic sounds, especially the back-sound *q*, requires no further explanation. Now with these groups out of the way, the remaining ones disclose a very interesting fact. We find that all the other *secondary Ḥatephs with non-laryngeals are found all but exclusively with the sonorous sounds.* This is, of course, particularly true of the forms of *hlk* before the *Dagesh conjunctivum* (Ḥ.-P. 4) and of the examples with the *m* of the participles (Ḥ.-P. 3). But also as regards the other groups there are very few exceptions to the above rule. Thus among the examples of Ḥateph-Pathaḥ with non-laryngeals which is the rule—according to Ben Asher—after a Metheg if the word contains a conjunctive accent, there are listed in the Diqduqqē Haṭṭᵉāmîm (No. 27) seven cases with liquids and nasals against only two with other consonants, i.e., *wᵉlišᵃkēnay* Ps. 31:12, *ebᵃḥar* Job 29:25. Of these latter, the first has a Ḥateph with a *š*, hence is also in conformity with the principle of sonority. It should be noted that the Metheg is indispensable for the above examples, a fact which accounts immediately for the increase in the amount of sonority in the neighborhood of the sounds in question. In No. 14 of the abovementioned work are listed isolated instances with a similar Ḥateph which cannot be classified as a special type (excepting words containing a Ḥateph between like consonants which have been discussed above). Now of the 14 examples which are given there, 11 may be attributed to an adjoining liquid, nasal, or *š*. In the carefully compiled list of words with a non-laryngeal Ḥateph-Qames in place of a reduced *u/o* vowel, which is given in Bergsträsser (*op. cit.,* No. 21 bb), there are 11 examples with the same sonorous sounds against 4 with other consonants. These data (particularly as regards the lists of Ben Asher) are of course incomplete, but they will suffice for an approximate comparison of the ratio of sounds with a relatively high amount of sonority against that of the less sonorous sounds, where secondary vowels of the above type are concerned. There can be, therefore, very little doubt that relative sonority was here too the principal factor in the development of secondary vowels, in medial syllables before single consonants.[22]

[22] Another important trace of the influence of the sonorous sounds should be noticed in the present connection. It has been observed that the majority of cases with the so-called *Dagesh forte dirimens* show the secondary vowel indicated thereby, after a *liquid or a nasal.* cf., e.g., *hall^{e}qē-* "smooth," Isa. 57:6, *'inn^{e}ḇē-* "grapes," Lev. 25:5 (see *GVG,* p. 215, *B-L,* pp. 214–15). This type of Dagesh has, of course, nothing to do with gemination, being employed to indicate a Shwa-vowel, as the sign for the latter (ְ) had become ambiguous (*quiescens* and *mobile*). The phonetics of the process should now be perfectly clear. At the same time another knotty problem of Hebrew grammar receives a good deal of light. I am referring to the so-called "Shwa medium." As is well known, Sievers (MS, pp. 22–23, 294) has concluded on metrical grounds that there could not have been any Shwa medium, as a syllable is either closed or open but not half-closed and half-open. The theory of Sievers has since found all but general acceptance (for literature cf. Brg. 21q). Some opposition, however, has been started by E. *König, ThLBl,* 1909, 581–82 (followed by Brg.), who seems to object to Sievers' argument on the ground that, whatever be the phonetic objections to the Shwa medium theory, such a Shwa exists nevertheless. We are now in a position to see that there is some measure of truth in both views. Etymologically (and hence originally) syllables are of course either closed or open. So far Sievers is right. But we have seen that vowels may develop secondarily as a purely phonetic product, and this is undoubtedly the case with the sounds indicated by so-called *Dagesh forte dirimens.* This, in turn, is clearly established by the afore-cited fact that the vowel in question is most frequent after sounds with a high degree of sonority. In such cases, then, the so-called Shwa medium actually represents a vowel-sound. However, there is no need to operate with the precarious concept of a "loosely closed syllable." What has actually taken place here is the secondary development of a vocal Shwa out of a *Shwa quiescens.* We thus arrive at a simple explanation which is both phonetically incontestable and at the same time in accordance with the actual facts of the case. It will now be readily

The fluctuations in manuscripts and in editions of the Bible as regards the placement of Ḥatephs with non-laryngeals unquestionably justify the assumption that the process leading to such developments was still operative at the time of the Masoretes. However, the beginnings of that tendency may be traced as far back as the time of Origen. Of the Hexaplaric examples that may have a bearing on the present subject the least doubtful are *αφαδανω*/*appad̲nō* Dan. 11:45 *θ*, *ιοχαλευ*/*yuk̲lū* 18:39, *εμαραθ*/Heb. *'imrat̲* Ps. 18:31 and *λσαχηναυ*/Heb. *lišk̲ēnāw* Ps. 18:42. Now it is most noteworthy that the last two words are also found with a secondary vowel (Ḥateph) in the traditional texts, but this time not in the same passages in which the anaptyxis was heard by Origen *ʿim*^{a}*rōt̲* Ps. 12:7, *w*^{e}*liš*^{a}*k̲ēnay* Ps. 31:12). One important point is made thereby perfectly clear. If the same word may be found with a secondary syllable in this passage according to one recension and in that passage in another recension, that word must be generally liable to such secondary developments. On the other hand, such fluctuations prove also that the need for secondary vowels was not imperative in those cases, the presence of the latter being rather dependent upon outward conditions, as, e.g., the purely relative urge to raise the pitch or to increase the stress in the word in question.

---

understood why the vocalization presupposes a vowelless consonant in a number of cases before Shwa medium (cf. Brg. 21s). It is equally clear why the *bgdkpt* should in some cases be spirantized after the Shwa in question while in other cases the stops are left unchanged (cf., e.g., *bin*^{e}*p̄ōl* Job 4:13, but *kizkōr* Jer. 17:2). For we have seen that secondary vowels, dependent as they are on so many external, largely phonetic, factors, will appear in some instances, while their absence may be noted in other cases, which are apparently similar. In fine, the whole problem becomes incomparably simpler as soon as we realize that the so-called Shwa medium indicates a sound which is secondary and not etymological.

b)Anaptyxis in medial syllables with two consonants. In contrast with the former group, secondary vowels with two consonants are with medial syllables often internally required. From a phonetic point of view *such developments are to be expected if the first of two consonants placed at the beginning of a syllable is more sonorous than the second one.* The Semitic languages are not exceptions to this phonetic rule. Let us first take one typical example. From the root *dnḥ* Syr. forms the noun *madenḥā* "sunrise." In the second syllable of that word the first of the two consonants (*n*) is the more sonorous one, hence a new syllable is required. For a while *n* itself assumes a vocalic function (*samprasāraṇa*), the word becoming actually tri-syllabic (*maḏṇḥā*). But at length an additional vowel develops and the new syllable is thereby permanently fixed (*maḏenḥā* = *maḏenḥā* < *maḏṇḥā*). The same process is responsible for the form of the word in question in J. Aramaic (*MDYNḤ'*). The development of secondary vowels has been recognized in Syriac grammars (however, without an adequate phonetic explanation), and there is consequently no need here to multiply examples. Significant is the remark of Nöldeke[23] that the phenomenon is most frequent when one of the letters is a liquid or ', ', *h*, *y*, *w*. As for the *M*ᵉ*hagg*ᵉ*yānā* (the stroke which indicates in this case an anaptyctic syllable) with the semi-vowels *w* and *y*, the phonetic explanation of the phenomenon is not far to seek. *W* and *y* are even more capable of *samprasāraṇa* than are the liquids and nasals and there are parallels for anaptyxis with those sounds in the Indo-European languages.[24] The other sounds responsible for the development of secondary vowels are laryn-

[23] Nöld., 51 B.

[24] Brugmann, *Kurze vergleichende Grammatik*, p. 270.

geals and, although the results are the same as in the case of the semi-vowels and the sonorous sounds, the causes of the change are in this case quite different from a phonetic point of view. In a study of the secondary developments in the Semitic languages this distinction should be constantly borne in mind. For more details see below under laryngeals. One may also note the very interesting fact that the "insertions" under discussion are never found in Syriac between sibilants and dentals.[25] As has been shown in the course of the present discussion there is no phonetic reason whatever to expect anaptyxis between such sounds. The principle of sonority both postulates the above type of anaptyxis where it is actually found here and accounts for the absence of similar vowels with other specified consonants. The above examples illustrate once more the general truth that what is often considered in language as an irregularity from the point of view of the empirical philologist, will often turn out to be perfectly regular when the problem is investigated from a historical and a comparative angle.

Since the secondary developments described above have been shown as attributable to general phonetic causes it would be indeed surprising if the former were confined to a single dialect in a given group of languages.[26] This

[25] Nöld., *loc. cit.* Anaptyxis is very common in Mandaic. Nöldeke's *Mandaic Grammar* is full of such examples.

[26] That the phenomenon is not confined to any single family of languages has been pointed out above. It may be often observed in our present-day speech. Take, for instance, the case of English "pretty." The word is heard not infrequently as "prty" (with *samprasāna*). While colloquially the phonetic change has advanced even further, so that the pronunciation "pərty" may be heard frequently, hence with anaptyxis). Cf. the spelling "purty" often resorted to wherever an attempt is made to reproduce the colloquial pronunciation, showing at the same time that instinctive feeling for phonetics which is responsible for the representation of the new vowel as the labial *u* after the labial stop *p*. The same example illustrates another fact which is

is, however, not the case. J. Aram. shows many similar developments. As examples may be here given nouns like *mazzirqayyā* "basins," *mašeryān* "camps," and such verbal forms as *yāp̱ilḥūn* "they will work," *tap̱iršūn* "you shall separate."[27] In Spanish Arab. we find the same phenomenon with the identical sounds, e.g., *maçuruq* "stolen."[28] In Akkadian it is again the liquids and nasals that are instrumental in the development of secondary vowels in medial syllables. Cf. among others *epru* alongside of *epiru* "dust," *uznu* and *uzunu* "ear."[29] And lastly, there is abundant evidence to show that the same type of anaptyctic vowels was not unknown to Hebrew.

First there are some isolated examples in the traditional texts with the Tiberian vocalization. Cf., e.g., *qārob^{e}ḵem* Deut. 20:2 < *qorb^{e}ḵem, qāḇol'ām* II Kings 15:10 < *qāb^{e}l'ām*. However, it is the evidence of the texts with Babylonian vocalization that is most instructive in this connection. Medial anaptyxis with two consonants is here illustrated by a wealth of instances. Cf., e.g., with *r* *b^{e}'oḇorḵem* (for Tib. *b^{e}oḇr^{e}ḵem*) Deut. 27:12, *hay^{a}ḥoḇerḵā* (for Tib. *hay^{e}ḥoḇr^{e}ḵā*) Ps. 94:20. *map̱iršē* (for Tib. *map̱r^{e}śē*) Job. 36:29. With *l, w^{e}n^{o}šolḥā* (for Tib. *w^{e}nišl^{e}ḥā*) I Sam. 11:13, *mamilḵōṯ* (for Tib. *maml^{e}ḵōṯ*) I Chron. 29:30. With nasals. *t^{o}šom'ū* (for Tib. *tišm$^{e'}$ū*) Deut. 11:13,

not unimportant in the historical study of language. Much of what is considered today as "slang," whether pertaining to the phonology or the morphology of a given language, may be nothing else than an advance notice of certain tendencies in language which are on their way to be raised to the dignity of "regular" manifestations of speech. Lat. * *agerlos* and Heb. *mamilkoṯ* may have been also considered at one time as "slangy." The Babylonian pronunciation may have been felt in many instances as colloquial by the Tiberian Masoretes. On the subject of slang see Jespersen, *Language* (New York, 1924), pp. 299 ff.

[27] See Dalm., pp. 94, 272 ff.

[28] *GVG*, p. 211.

[29] *Ibid.*, p. 219.

weyešim'ū (for Tib. *wayyišmᵉ'ū*) I Sam. 4:6.[30] In each of the above examples the Babylonian texts point to an anaptyctic vowel before a sonorous sound where the Tiberian vocalization has no vowel at all. In the case of the Tiberian Masoretes it may have been the reluctance to introduce a construct state like *mamilkōt* by the side of the absolute state *mamlākōt* that was mainly responsible for the smaller vogue of anaptyxis in the system of the former. In actual pronunciation the tendency to such developments was doubtless much more in evidence. Hexaplaric examples of the type of anaptyxis discussed above are furnished by the transcription of *yiqrᵉṣū* Ps. 35:19 as *ικερσου*, *yiśmᵉḥū* 35:24 as *ιεσεμου*.[31]

The examples which have been adduced in the present discussion show conclusively how inaccurate it is to explain the secondary vowels which are found in medial syllables before two consonants, as an attempt at separating three otherwise contiguous consonants. The imposing number of *yiqṭᵉlū*-forms and the like, is a convincing proof of the fact that such vowels could be dispensed with in the great majority of cases that answer to the above conditions. Instead of accusing groups composed of any three contiguous consonants of disagreeable behavior culminating in the expulsion of the first one of the trio by means of an imported vowel, the phenomenon may be described with greater accuracy as follows: An anaptyctic vowel often develops in medial syllables before two consonants if the first of the two consonants is more sonorous than the second one. The few cases of anaptyxis where this is not the case may be due to analogy.

[30] Kahle, *MT,* p. 26, *MO,* pp. 165, 185.
[31] Cf. Margolis, *AJSL,* XXI, 68.

3. *The Segolates*

In any study of the so-called segolates in the Semitic languages one is bound to run up against serious difficulties as soon as a discussion of the formation and treatment of the former is attempted. The origin of the secondary vowel before the final consonant of some originally monosyllabic nouns (Arab. *mahl* > *mahal* "quiet," Heb. **sifr* > *sefer* "book"; the formation of the plural of the segolate nouns in Hebrew (*məlāḵīm* from **malk* as contrasted with the Syriac form *malḵē*); the spirantization of the *bgdkpt* in the plural construct state of the Hebrew segolate nouns (*malḵe* but Syr. *malkai*); the date of the segolatization of the individual types of segolates (monosyllabic forms are found in Hebrew as late as the time of Origen, cf. κοδς = *qods*/Heb *qodeš* Ps. 29:2);[32] these are but a few of the many problems that must be still considered as debatable in spite of the manifold attempts to solve each individual point. As may be gathered from the few examples listed above, Hebrew has been more affected in this respect than the other Semitic languages. In the present study it will be, of course, relevant to discuss only those points that have a direct bearing upon the question of the secondary developments in the Semitic languages.

The most obvious case of a secondary vowel is in this connection furnished by the anaptyctic vowel which has been developed between two final consonants. The latter had come in turn to stand at the end of a word after the loss of original case endings (cf., e.g., Heb. **malku* > **malk*). Anaptyxis has set in here primarily

[32] Sievers, *Metrische Studien*, pp. 261 ff.

in nouns of the type *qatl, qitl, qutl* (cf. Heb. **malk* > *melek* "king," **sifr* > *sefer* "book," **qudš* > *qodeš* "holiness," Arab. *mahl* > *mahal* "quiet," Akkadian construct state *puḫur* from *puḫru* "totality," etc.) Further in feminine forms like Heb. *yōšébeṯ* from *yōšabt,* and lastly, in the apocopated forms of the verbs *tertiae wy,* as, e.g., Heb. *yíben* < **yibn* as compared with *yibne* from *bny* "to build." As the *Segol*-sign is the traditional form of the vowel in question as regards the Hebrew "extensions," it has become customary to apply the term "segolates" to all the similarly treated formations.

Semitic philologists have been hitherto satisfied, as far as Hebrew is concerned, with a make-shift explanation of the phenomenon which cannot but prove unsatisfactory upon the first casual glance at the facts. If we accept the current theory that secondary vowels developed in Hebrew with any two final consonants, we are immediately forced to declare as exceptions the numerous cases in which anaptyxis has not set in under similar circumstances. Cf., e.g., nouns like *qošṭ* "truth," *nerd* "nard," the short imperfect forms of the verbs tertiae *wy* like *yift, yešt,* and especially the 2nd person fem. of the perfect forms (the entire group *qāṭalt*). In order to explain away the "exceptions" Brockelmann [33] (again followed by Bauer-Leander) [34] sets up a mythical phonetic law according to which [(*way*)*yišb*] "and he captured," *qāṭalt* "thou hast slain" are made out to consist "in reality of two and three syllables respectively." According to such a law English "felt" or "theft" would also have to be presented with another syllable, a procedure which the most charitable of phoneticians could not risk very well.

[33] *GVG,* p. 216.
[34] *B-L,* p. 213.

If such erroneous views were not so widespread as they are, it would be entirely gratuitous to marshal here some of the available facts. As it is, however, I may be permitted to do so as briefly as possible.

1. We have seen that in Hebrew the segolate vowel is (*a*) developed generally with nouns of the type *qatl, qitl, qutl* (excepting a few cases before a final stop, as, e.g., *qošṭ*) ; (*b*) is regularly omitted in forms of the type *qāṭalt;* and (*c*) in the short imperfect forms of the verbs *tertiae wy* anaptyxis sets in generally before liquids and nasals (e.g., *yigel, wattemer, yiḇen, yip̄en;* it is omitted however, before a final stop (e.g., *yešt, wattéḇk.*

2. In Akkadian the nouns which are liable to segolatization are treated as they are in Hebrew, e.g., *zikir* for *zikr* "name," *kalab* for *kalb* "dog."

3. In classical Arabic and in Ethiopic the segolate vowel develops usually before, but sometimes also after, a liquid or nasal; cf., e.g., Arab.*mahl* > *mahal* "quiet," *'udn* > *'uḏun* "ear," infinitive forms like *ṭalb* > *ṭalab* "to seek"; Eth. *baql* > *baqal* "mule," *ᶜarab* Heb. *ᶜereb* "evening." [35]

4. In the neo-Arab. dialects anaptyxis is usually absent if the first of two final consonants is a liquid or a nasal, e.g., Tunis. *qalb* "dog," *milḥ* "salt"; but if the sonorous sound is the final one, the secondary vowel usually develops, e.g., Syr.-Arab. *tibin* "straw." [36]

There is hardly any need to adduce more examples from the Semitic languages. The above facts become self-explanatory as soon as we recall the phonetic rule (see above) that of two final consonants, the first is the more sonorous one if both sounds belong to the same syllable.

[35] *GVG,* 210, 213.
[36] *Ibid.,* 212.

If the reverse is the case a new syllable will develop (cf. Eng. *whims,* one syllable, but the end *-ism* [*izem*], two syllables. Before summing up, however, the conclusions regarding the segolates in Semitic I wish to cite a few interesting parallels from the Indo-European languages. They will further bear out the statement made in the introductory section of the present study that certain general phonetic principles are traceable in every language, and that for the proper understanding of certain phenomena in a single language it is of the greatest importance to compare the corresponding occurrences, first in the remaining dialects of a given linguistic family, and then, if possible, in other known languages.

There are cases in Germanic which parallel, one might say, sound for sound some of the examples of segolatization in Semitic. A secondary vowel may develop in the languages of the former group before the final consonant provided that the latter is a liquid or a nasal following a stop or a sibilant. Cf., e.g., Goth. nom *akrs* acc. *akr,* (Gr. αγρο-ς, αγρο-ν) which become *acchar* in OHG. *æccer* in Ags. "field," Goth. nom. *fugl* acc. *fugls* acc. *fugl* over against OHG. *fogal,* Ags. *fuǧol* (German Vogel) "bird," Goth. nom. *ibns,* acc. *ibn* as compared with OHG. *eban,* Ags. *efen* "even." [37] The parallels are sufficiently close to require no further explanation.

The conclusions concerning the origin and development of the segolates in Semitic may now be assumed as follows: When two consonants were left in the Semitic languages at the end of a word, there arose the need to develop a secondary vowel in the final syllable if the last consonant was more sonorous than the preceding one. For practical purposes it may be said that this was the case between a

[37] Cf. Brugmann, *GIE,* 385, 446–47.

stop or sibilant and a following liquid or nasal. Thus arose forms like Arab. *mahal,* Heb. **'aben* > *'eben,* Akk. *ṣalam.* That there was no phonetic need for the development of a segolate vowel if that order of consonants was reversed is proved by the fact that in modern Arabic there is no anaptyxis under such conditions, hence we get here forms like *qalb, milḥ.* The same is true of the short imperfect of the Hebrew verbs of the type *tertiae wy,* hence *yiben* occurs in that language alongside of *yard* and *yešt.* Later anaptyxis was extended to forms in which either of the final consonants was a sonorous one, so in Arab. *ṭalab* by the side of *'udun,* Eth. *baqal* as well as *ᶜarab.* And finally, in some languages the vowel was extended to all nouns capable of segolatization, notably in Hebrew where *'ebed* is now found by the side of *'ozen, geber.* In the *qātalt* forms there never was an urge to develop the segolate vowel before that final *t.* For in this case no consonant that could possibly have preceded the *t* of *qātalt* would be possessed of still less sonority, since it could be a spirant or higher. Consequently, the absence of segolatization in the Hebrew *qātalt*-forms is regular according to the very same phonetic law which makes anaptyxis necessary in *régel* or in *yíp̄en.*

The small number of exceptions to the above rules which may be found in the individual Semitic languages does not call for additional explanations. The Hebrew forms of the type *qotélet* probably owe their anaptyctic vowel to the analogy of the type *qām* : *qāmā* in which the feminine participle has one more syllable than the corresponding masculine form.

Before leaving the interesting province of the segolates mention may be made of a seldom considered suggestion of Ungnad's [38] concerning the origin of the plural form

[38] *ZA,* XVII, 333–43.

m^e^lāḵīm with an unoriginal vowel in the penult. He would explain the latter as a case of *Svarabhakti* before the word-accent with subsequent reduction of the first syllable, hence **katlim* > *kat^a^līm* > **katalīm k^e^tālim*. The process may have originated—he thinks—with combinations of sounds which were particularly difficult to pronounce. I believe that Ungnad was on the right track, which he did not, however, follow up sufficiently. A suggestion will not merit deeper consideration if the only basis for discussion be some hypothetical groups of sounds and a footnote containing the statement—wholly irrelevant as it stands—that the *Svarabhakti* is also known to the Indo-European philologists. What is necessary to prove in order to make such a suggestion plausible is, in the first place, the fact that the *Svarabhakti* was here indispensable in a great number of cases. Parallels from other languages must be shown, on the other hand, to apply exactly to the case under discussion if they are to carry enough weight. It is very likely that upon a further and more methodical study of the question anaptyxis may be shown to have played a very important, if not a deciding, part in the formation of the plural of the segolate nouns in Hebrew.

4. Secondary Vowels With Laryngeals

This type of new vowels has been studied rather thoroughly. To be sure, there still remain here some problems which will bear further investigation. In the present connection, however, it may suffice to indicate the main difference between the secondary vowels attributable to the influence of the laryngeals, and those which have been hitherto considered. Two examples will serve to illustrate my point satisfactorily. Let us first consider a case like

Heb. *mōšiaʿ* "delivering." In the last syllable a final laryngeal (ʿ) is preceded by a long, heterorganic vowel (*ī*). From the place of articulation of that front vowel the organs must get in position to produce the laryngeal ʿ back in the larynx. It is quite natural that the on-glide to that sound should assume the form of the glide-sound *a* which is homorganic with the laryngeals. This is borne out by another fact. The Hexaplaric transcription of the cited Hebrew word is μωσι without the glide. Other considerations also point to an older period in which the glide in question was either absent or, at least, very indistinct. The secondary vowel became necessary, it appears only after the laryngeal had become sufficiently weak to require its aid. It is, therefore, primarily the weakening of the laryngeal coupled with the peculiar nature of the latter that accounts for the development of a secondary vowel in the afore-mentioned instance.

Now let us compare the medial anaptyxis in ικερσου, *yiqerṣū* with the one found in *yàʿaz̲b̲ū* "they left." The circumstances leading up to the development of the former have been discussed above at some length. The same conditions do not obtain in the case of *yàʿazb̲ū*. However, the first of three medial consonants is here the laryngeal ʿ. The whole group is, undoubtedly, comparatively hard to pronounce. As long as the laryngeal retained a good deal of its original strength there was no cause for anaptyxis. At the time of the Hexapla there seems to have been no serious difficulty in pronouncing the word as *yàʿazbū*, since Origen transcribes the verb in Ps. 89:31 as ιεζεβου. The weakening of the ʿ had not yet become, then, sufficiently marked. It is apparently post-Origenic.

The main difference, therefore, between the secondary developments with the laryngeals as against those with the sonorous sounds may be expressed as follows. In the case of sounds with a relatively high amount of resonance it is the sonorous *strength* of those consonants that is mainly responsible for the developments of anaptyctic vowels in their neighborhood. As regards the laryngeals, however, secondary developments are here primarily due to the *weakness* of the latter sounds. The general results are similar in both cases, but the actual causes are appreciably different.[39]

B. SECONDARY GEMINATION

The problems which have been discussed in the preceding pages required a comparatively detailed exposition of phonetic principles with a bearing on the subject under discussion. As there is a general phonetic connection between secondary vowels and the phenomenon which is to be discussed presently, it will not be difficult to sum up very briefly the problems that are connected with the subject of secondary gemination in the Semitic languages.

First, a few words will be in place as regards the term "gemination." This is one of those misnomers which denote in most instances a phonetic process different from what its term might lead one to imply. For double consonants are, in the strict sense of the word, groups of two like sounds which are marked off by a decrease in sonority in the first sound with a following increase in the second member of the group. To speak, e.g., of double stops is

[39] For a fuller treatment of the subject the reader may be referred to the present author's monograph on *The Pronunciation of Hebrew according to the Transliterations in the Hexapla* (now in press) which is to appear shortly among the publications of Dropsie College. [See JQR XVI (1926), pp. 343–82; XXIII (1933), pp. 233–65; XXIV (1933), pp. 9–46.]

phonetically correct only when the explosion incidental to the pronunciation of those sounds actually takes place within the group, after which the same sound is pronounced again. This, however, never happens, say, in English and in German.[40] What is usually mistaken for gemination is simply an increase in the quantity of the sound and the proper term is here really lengthening of sounds instead of gemination. Similarly, it is only the lengthening of consonants in Semitic whose secondary appearance will be discussed below. The word gemination has been hitherto used in the present study to avoid further misunderstandings.

By secondary lengthening of consonants is implied that increase in the quantity of the latter which is not the result of assimilation, coalescence of two like consonants, or lastly, and this applies particularly to the Semitic languages, a morphological indication of certain special forms, as, e.g., the intensive formations of the verb.[41] As examples of unoriginal lengthening in Semitic might be cited Hebr. $g^e mall\bar{\imath}m$ as compared with $d^e\underline{b}ar\bar{\imath}m$, $t^el\bar{u}nn\bar{o}\underline{t}$ from $l\bar{u}n$ etc.; Syr. $t^el\bar{a}l\bar{a}$ "shadow," J. Aram. $q\bar{a}r\bar{\imath}\underline{b}\bar{a}$ "relative," '$umm\bar{a}n$ "artist."

Now it is a well-known fact that a long vowel + a short consonant may be substituted at times for a short vowel + a long consonant, and vice versa, in which process the quantity of the syllable remains, of course, unchanged. Hence a form like Lat. *Juppiter* for an earlier *Jū-piter* (< the vocative **dieu pəter* alongside the nom. *Diēspiter*) [42] offers no difficulties from a phonetic point of view. The metathesis is, naturally, easiest when the length-

[40] *JPh.* 204.
[41] *Brg.*, 24*a*.
[42] Walde, *Lateinisches Etymologisches Wörterbuch*, p. 399.

ening of the syllable itself is of secondary origin. (Cf., e.g., Hebr. *g^e^mallīm* : *k^e^tālīm* > *katalīm* > *kátalīm*.) What is not obvious in these cases of metathesis in Semitic, is not the quantitative exchange itself between the given vowels and consonants, but the laws that govern the distribution of length, in some cases upon the vowels, and in others upon the consonants in question. The problem is indeed a very complicated one, and all we can hope for is to gain a certain degree of insight into these matters rather than to trace exact laws which governed those phonetic phenomena. In the final analysis, language itself is often undecided as to which of the sounds is to be favored in the given syllable.

It has been often observed that, whereas the voiceless sounds are, in specified positions, usually long after short vowels, the length is, in the case of voiced consonants, frequently distributed evenly between the vowel and the consonant.[43] It is self-evident that such even exchanges would be particularly favored in the case of consonants with a high amount of sonority. In English *man,* for instance, it is sometimes the vowel, and at times the consonant, that partakes of the greater length in the syllable; often, however, neither is in this respect singled out particularly.[44] This element of instability as regards the precise quantity of contiguous groups of vowel + consonant is one of great importance in the study of secondary lengthening.

Before drawing final conclusions for the phenomena of secondary lengthening in Hebrew and the Aramaic dialects, I may be permitted to make one more general remark. The conditions described above obtain primarily

[43] *JPh.,* 187.
[44] *Ibid.*

within the same syllable. Quantitative metathesis would not be normal between a vowel of one syllable and a consonant belonging to the following syllabic group. This fact requires no further comment. It is for that very reason that quantitative metathesis is best studied in the case of final syllables. Here, however, another important point should be made. There is no phonetic norm by which we could determine whether in instances like in German *harte, feste,* the respective syllables are *har-te, fes-te* or rather *ha-rte, fe-ste.* The difficulty is even greater in cases with one long consonant instead of two dissimilar short ones, as, e.g., in *komme hatte.*[45] All we can claim for such combinations of two syllables is the fact that they possess two distinct apexes with one intervening low-point. But it is entirely futile to worry as to whether that low-point belongs entirely to the first syllable or to the second, or perhaps is partly appropriated by the first and partly by the second syllable. It follows, therefore, that the interrelationship discussed above is quite possible in groups of sounds distributed among more than one syllable.

We may now take up the discussion of the main types of examples in which secondary lengthening of consonants is observable. It will be seen that in the majority of cases where we have a long consonant instead of a preceding long vowel, *the lengthened sound is a liquid or a nasal.* This is true of syllables with an originally long vowel, as well as of those syllabic groups where the lengthening is of secondary origin.[46] The lengthening of the consonant is, of course, secondary in both cases. Cf. Heb. *tᵉlunnōṯ* from *lun; 'ammūḏ, ṣinnōr, limmūḏ; lᵉhummām* Zeph. 1:17 (var.) and *niḥummīm* Zech. 1:13 (var.) over

[45] *Ibid.,* 205.
[46] *Brg.,* 24*a.*

against *l^e ḥūmō* Job 20:23 and *niḥūmay* Hos. 11:8 (the variant spellings are significant in the light of the preceding discussion); forms like *g^e'ullā, ʿ^a gullōṯ, ʿērūmmīm, qardummīm, qarsullay; '^a gammīm, g^e mallīm, 'ōpannim, q^e ṭannā; raʿ^a nannīm, šaʾ^a nannīm, '^a ḏamdammōṯ, ʿ^a qalqallōṯ*. After the article *hā* the lengthening was extended to all cases by analogy with the forms before a liquid or nasal. The same may, perhaps, be said of the few cases of the passive of Qal, which were likely to have been influenced by forms like *yullaḏ*.[47]

However, secondary lengthening of a consonant need not necessarily be due to a quantitative metathesis with a preceding vowel. It may also be caused by accentual conditions, as, e.g., in cases which resisted reduction in syllables distant from the main word-accent. Lengthening acts then as a preservative measure by rendering the given syllable secure from any further accentual pressure. Now it is again the liquids and nasals which first helped those syllables to resist reduction and weakening. This fact may be best observed in Hebrew in connection with the weakening of short Hebr. *a* to *i* in unstressed syllables, as, e.g., when *maḏbar* becomes *miḏbar* "desert." It is very interesting that most of the exceptions in which the *a* has remained are due to a following liquid and nasal (cf. Heb. *malbūš, mal'āḵ, malmaḏ, mamlāḵā, malqōš*). The preservative doubling came subsequently (especially in Syriac and in Aramaic. Cf., e.g., Sr. *tennāyā* "smoke," *ṣennartā* "hook," *ṭellālā* "shadow";[48] J. Aram. *summāq* "red,"

[47] On the subject of alleged intensive noun-formations in Semitic, a highly interesting paper was read by Professor J. A. Montgomery at the meeting of the American Oriental Society in New Haven, April, 1925. The author of that communication pointed out the influence of the liquids and nasals upon the secondary lengthening of the forms in question.

[48] Nöld., 116.

qallīl "light," *ṣannīn* and **qarrīr* > *qārīr* "cold," *ḥillūp̱īn* "changes,"[49] and the like.

It is not necessary to multiply examples. Nor is it my intention to advance the claim that all cases of secondary lengthening in Hebrew are directly attributable to the principle of sonority. To be sure, analogy came undoubtedly into its own in this case as in so many others. The possible influence of sounds characterized by a high amount of relative duration (not to be confused with sonority) has not been considered in the present study. The prominent part which the sound ṣ plays in connection with secondary gemination would, no doubt, receive some light from that quarter. The influence of laryngeals remains to be further investigated. The entire field of Semitic phonology has been sorely neglected and many problems concerning the habits and nature of the sounds of the Semitic languages will yet bear a thorough investigation. If this brief study helps to arouse the interest of philologists in this not ungrateful task the present writer will consider himself amply rewarded for the many tedious hours which it took in making.

[*Addendum.* Aside from a few minor proofreader's corrections, no substantial change has been made in this paper as published nearly forty years ago. Semitic terms, however, have been transliterated to save trouble and expense.

Today, my statement on the *Shwa medium* would be expressed more crisply and shaded differently, but the fundamental evaluation would remain much the same. No modification would seem to be called for in regard to the origin of the "segolate" forms. Nothing has come

[49] Dalman, pp. 163 ff.

up in the intervening years to cause me to alter my view that forms like **'a/ebn* were of necessity disyllabic from the start alongside monosyllabic form of the type **ma/elk*. The former came to be formalized as *'eḇen,* and the like, which brought on *meleḵ* by analogy, there being no phonologic reason for such a change. The few monosyllabic survivals of the type *qošṭ* are precisely the kind of exceptions that help to prove the rule.]

Studies in Semitic Formatives

THE FORMATIVES, OR NON-INFLEXIONAL PREFIXES AND AFfixes, constitute perhaps the most neglected field in the study of comparative Semitic grammar. The treatment of these elements is confined as a rule to mere tabulations. We find lists of prefixes, affixes, and occasionally of infixes, capable of modifying the meaning of nominal and verbal bases in one form or another, but little has been done towards ascertaining the original values and functions of such determinants. Of late there have been isolated indications that the subject may soon come into its own. Concrete results cannot be expected, however, for some time to come. It will require the concerted efforts of many scholars and much constructive discussion and criticism before real progress has been made in this particular department of Semitic linguistics.

At two successive annual meetings of the American Oriental Society I discussed certain aspects of this problem and submitted general conclusions. My principal purpose was to direct attention to a virtually untapped field. The subjects discussed were "The So-called Causative Conjugation" and "The So-called Feminine Ending (*a*)*t*." The inadequacy of our knowledge of these topics is reflected fairly well by these qualified titles. To test the validity of my tentative conclusions these papers are now summed up in printed form. The statements are far from complete. A thorough treatment of each subject would call for a monograph of respectable proportions. The next best thing is to confine illustrative material and references [1] to the barest minimum and to concentrate instead on a brief presentation of the actual problems. Requirements of space dictate the latter course.[2]

I. THE "CAUSATIVE" CONJUGATION

As is well known, Semitic contrives to enrich its basic vocabulary by means of derivative conjugations which modify, shade, or emphasize in one respect or another the primary meaning of a given verbal base. Grammarians have come to designate these secondary stems as intensive, reflexive, causative, and the like. These terms are convenient for purposes of general classification; but they convey no more than a very superficial idea of the wealth of nuances that a secondary conjugation in Semitic is capable of expressing. Particularly inadequate from this standpoint is the label "causative," attached by grammarians to a derivative stem which is represented promimently in all Semitic languages.

[1] The following abbreviations are used below: Bauer-Leander, *GBA* = *Grammatik des Biblisch-aramäischen; HGH* = *Historische Grammatik der Hebräischen Sprache.* Bergsträsser, *Einfuhrung* = *Einführung in die semitischen Sprachen; Verbum* = *Hebräische Grammatik* II: *Verbum.* Brockelmann, *GVG* = *Grundriss der vergleichenden Grammatik der semitischen Sprachen.* Gardiner, *Eg. Gr.* = *Egyptian Grammar.* Gray, *ICSL* = *Introduction to Comparative Semitic Linguistics.* Meinhof, *Hamiten* = *Die Sprachen der Hamiten. MO* = *Le Monde Oriental.*

[2] Wherever a single example from any given language of the group is a sufficiently clear illustration of the entire category under discussion, no other illustrations have been cited.

This stem is developed from the primary base with the aid of one of several prefixes, in the choice of which the various members of the family display a certain degree of individuality. Thus Akkadian (Akk.) employs the prefix *š*-, Minaean (Min.) has *s*-, Hebrew (Heb.), Sabaean (Sab.), and Mehri use *h*-, and Arabic (Arab.) and Ethiopic (Eth.) have the glottal stop ʾ; all four elements are found among the Aramaic (Aram.) dialects, while Phoenician (Phoen.) acquires in course of time a *y*-prefix. The causative connotation is present throughout, to be sure: the addition of the proper prefix to, say, *qbr* 'bury' imparts to the stem the meaning 'cause to bury.' But this particular significance of the new stem is only one of many. The same conjugation may yield on occasions a factitive, declarative, or perfective sense; it may express momentary action as opposed to the durative connotation of the primary stem; it may have even the value of a passive, as when it is employed to indicate the result of action in the case of certain verbs.[3] In short, the term "causative" is wholly inadequate. If we retain it in the present discussion it is so mainly for the sake of convenience; the designation has been in use too long to be readily displaced.[4] It will be demonstrated, I trust, that the numerous and apparently unrelated uses of the stem under discussion

[3] Cf. H. S. Nyberg, "Wortbildung mit Suffixen in den semitischen Sprachem," *MO* XIV (1920). 250 ff. Nyberg's monograph (*ibid.* 177–290) is an extensive historical treatment of the Semitic prefixes which is sound methodologically and thoroughly consistent with the requirements of modern linguistic science. Although I am unable to accept the author's final conclusions with regard to the origin of the causative stem, and while I must take exception to a number of his etymologies, particularly in the Akk. group, I herewith make grateful acknowledgement of the stimulating effect of this admirable study.

[4] Nyberg, *op. cit.*, employs the phrase "the fourth form," which is suitable for Arab., but awkward and misleading in the case of the other Semitic languages.

derive directly from the peculiar origin of this conjugation.

It should be made clear at the outset that the causative stem is proto-Semitic and that it has an exact counterpart in Hamitic. The same wide range of meanings confronts us throughout, and the morphological relationship of the respective bases is equally apparent in all instances. The only divergence, then, is in the choice of the characteristic prefix. We have seen that several of them are in use. It may be added that their semantic functions are identical. For whether *pqd* 'heed' is equipped with an initial *š*- in Akk., *h*- in Heb., or '- in Aram., the meaning will be in each case 'put in charge,' or the like. The disparity is solely on the phonetic side. It is not as wide, however, as might seem at first. To begin with, *š* and *s* represent one original sound: Semitic *š* maintains itself in Akk., but changes to *s* in the South Semitic group (represented here by Min.) in accordance with a perfectly normal sound-shift. Within the Akk. group Assyrian exhibits a dialectal shift to *s*, and the sporadic *s* of Aram. may be ascribed to dialectal influences.[5] Since Phoen. *y* does not represent an original prefix,[6] we are left ultimately with three causative prefixes: one sibilant (*š*/*s*-) and the laryngeal ones (*h*-, '-).

The question now arises whether a further reduction could not be justified by the laws of Semitic phonology. In the case of *h*- and '- the problem is comparatively

[5] Cf. Brockelmann, *GVG* I. 526 and Bauer-Leander, *GBA* 92 k. The Aram. causatives with the prefix *š*- may safely be ascribed to Akk. influence, cf. *ibid.* 116 y. The original Aram. causative prefixes are thus reduced to the laryngeal group, on which see below. For the causative elements in the dialect of Ras Shamra see note 17.

[6] For this causative element the reader may be referred to the forthcoming *Grammar of Phoenician*, by Zellig S. Harris (American Oriental Series, vol. 8).

simple. In Aram. *h-* is found in the older dialects, while *'-* comes to prevail at a later stage. In the South Semitic group we have *h-* in Sab. and Mehri, but *'-* normally in Arab. and Eth.[7] Do we have instances of a direct shift from *h* to *'*? Such a change cannot be demonstrated as yet as a regular procedure, certainly not in Arab., although the correspondence is observable there in certain isolated words. But an *'-* prefix might develop from *h-* by the process of back-formation: since the "impf." **yu-haqtilu* may lead, as it actually does in Heb., to a form simplified through elision (**yu/aqtilu*), the "perf." modeled after it would be **'aqtala*. Arab. and some of the Aram. dialects would thus have specialized this secondary prefix, while *h-* was restored in Heb. and Bibl. Aram. on the analogy of the "perf." [8] In other words, the two laryngeal causative prefixes go back in all probability to a single one (*h-*). This would leave us with two formatives, *š-* and *h-*.

Attempts have been made to effect further simplification by postulating an original connection between these two sounds: the *h*-prefix is regarded as a phonetic de-

[7] We are concerned at present with the principal prefix in each language, presumably representing, or developed from, its original causative element. For traces of rival elements see Nyberg, *op. cit.* Such sporadic occurrences may be due to a variety of causes: material inherited from the proëthnic period, later interdialectal borrowing, etc.; but they are confined to the noun class, except for Aram. and Ras Shamra, where Akk. influence, easily accounted for on geographic and cultural grounds, is to be assumed. The point to be made at present is that '- is the sole living causative prefix in Arab. and Eth. just as *h-* alone is operative in Heb. and *š-* in Akk. The history of the Aram. dialects shows '- to be later than *h-*, and this chronological sequence is of value for the purposes of the discussion below.

[8] This position is taken by Bauer-Leander in *HGH* 228 é, cf. *GBA* 62 r, though the authors later express some misgivings, *ibid.* 113. Nevertheless, it is the only theory that accounts at once for the developments in both Arab. and Aram. It is true that in later Aram. dialects, such as Mandaic, *h* is reduced to a glottal stop; but this reduction would not apply to earlier times. The assumption of an analogic back-formation provides therefore the most satisfactory explanation.

For the "perfect" and "imperfect" see below, p. 418.

velopment from an earlier sibilant element, which maintained itself, however, in certain dialects. But for all the ingenuity displayed by the advocates of such a phonetic change,[9] the two sounds have not been successfully united.[10] It is quite true that the sibilant occurs in Akk., the oldest documented member of the Semitic family, and that it is characteristic of the Hamitic group,[10a] which has retained many archaic features of the larger Hamito-Semitic stock. The difficulty is that there is no evidence for a common Semitic shift of *š* (or *s*) to *h* in any position. Thus e.g., 'nine' is *tīšu* in Akk., *tis'u*^{n} in Arab., and *téša'* in Heb.; no trace here of any dialectal shift to *h*. The same holds true of practically all the available comparative lexical material.[11] Since, then, the languages that employ a laryngeal causative prefix do not show any tendency to a normal shift of *š*/*s* to *h* in any position whatever, a phonetic relationship between the causative prefixes in question must definitely be ruled out. This is indeed the prevailing opinion among the latest writers on the subject. Some of them would go even further: a common origin of the causative elements having proved impossible, they see no immediate reason for reducing the number of prefixes to two; they would concede independence to '- as well.[12] In the final analysis, two causa-

[9] Cf. P. Joüon, *Mélanges de la Faculté orientale de l'Univ. St.-Joseph à Beyrouth* 1913. 125–28; Barton, *Semitic and Hamitic Origins* 22 and 365 f.; I inclined to a similar view in *JQR* NS. XXIII. 248, note 90.

[10] Brockelmann, *GVG* I. 521; Barth, *Pronominalbildung* 13; Bergsträsser, *Verbum* 107.

[10a] Cf. Gardiner, *Eg. Gr.* 212, and Meinhof, *Hamiten* 18. Cf. also Barton, *op. cit.*, and the very useful comparative tables at the end of that work.

[11] For the initial consonants in the personal pronouns see below. In Mehri *ś* changes in certain roots to h, cf. Bergsträsser, *Einführung* 126. But the limited number of these changes and the comparative lateness of the dialect make it impossible to regard these phenomena as survivals from the earliest period of Semitic; we have here instead late and isolated developments.

[12] Nyberg, *MO* XIV. 250; Bauer-Leander, *GBA* 62 r.

tive prefixes in Semitic represent the irreducible minimum, and quite probably also the original maximum.[13]

It is clear that the semantic functions of these elements must have been identical. This circumstance is evidently responsible for the usual statement that each causative prefix had the value of 'cause, make.' [14] Does this mean that we have violently reduced forms of so many verbs, each with the same original connotation, but none apparently preserved in full in historic times? [15] Such a theory is not only transparently simple but also manifestly untenable. For the causative significance is, as we have seen, but one of many functions of the conjugation in question. If we operate exclusively with 'make,' we shall not get very far in our effort to account for the remaining connotations of our stem.

A solution of the problem is indicated, rather unexpectedly, from a different quarter. The Semitic personal pronouns for the third person exhibit virtually the same variations of initial sounds that we have found in the causative prefixes. One group of dialects employs *š*/*s*-, while the remaining languages use *h*-. Thus Akk. has *šū* 'he,' *šī* 'she,' and Min. uses *s*-forms; elsewhere we find *h*-pronouns, with the exception of Mehri which presents both types in *he* 'he' and *se* 'she.' [16] Apart from this single departure we find that the sibilant pronoun occurs precisely in those languages in which there is also a sibilant causative prefix, while the *h*-pronoun is accompanied in

[13] An ultimate connection of *h* and ʾ is indicated by Bergsträsser, *Einführung* 12.

[14] Cf. e.g., Haupt, *JAOS* 28. 114, and the criticism of Brockelmann, *GVG* I. 521.

[15] Is the statement of Bauer-Leander, *HGH* 283 to be understood in this sense?

[16] Cf. Brockelmann, *GVG* I. 302 f.; Barth, *Pronominalbildung* 14 ff.

the other dialects by a corresponding causative element.[17] This noteworthy harmony pervades also the Hamitic group; e.g., by the side of the Egyptian causative prefix *s*- we find the pronouns *św* 'he' and *śy* 'she.' [18] Such striking regularity over a wide field seems to preclude any possibility of mere coincidence. Apparently, there is a deeper connection between these seemingly heterogenous elements.

At first one might again be tempted to operate with the theory of phonetic relationship. Could not the laryngeal go back, after all, to a sibilant in both instances? It has been indicated, however, that Semitic does not show a regular shift of *š*/*s* to *h*. Against this correspondence of the two sounds in two grammatical categories we have the uniformly negative testimony of the entire lexical material. Moreover, Mehri employs both forms of the pronoun; if the masc. had been subjected to the shift, there is no sound reason why the fem. should have been spared. To sum up, a phonetic explanation must be ruled out in both cases; and to ascribe such manifold correspondence to mere coincidence would require more faith than linguistic study can afford to utilize.

[17] It is significant in this connection that the languages employing a causative prefix with '- have *h*-pronouns (in Eth. the initial *h* was subsequently lost). This may be regarded as an indirect confirmation of the view that within the causative elements the '- developed from an earlier *h*-. Moreover, where several prefixes occur at the same time, as in Aram., the pronoun is likely to point to the original causative element. The dialect of Ras Shamra is a case in point. There we encounter a number of *š*-causatives, but these are confined for the most part to verbs of cultic use and are thus evidently Akk. loanwords; cf. Montgomery and Harris, *The Ras Shamra Mythological Texts* 22. On the other hand, causatives with a laryngeal prefix are definitely established in such tertiae-' verbal forms as *ymṣi'* (with an *i*-containing '), while other occurrences are certain from the context (loc. cit.). It is noteworthy, therefore, that the pronoun 'he' was probably *hwt* (*ibid.* 19).

[18] Gardiner, *Eg. Gr.* 45.

In this contingency only one solution remains open to us: there must be an ultimate semantic connection between the Semitic causative prefixes and the personal pronouns of the third person. In other words, if it could be shown that these pronouns entered into the make-up of the causative stems, our principal difficulty would disappear. Let us concentrate for the moment on the pronouns. If Heb. *hū'* did not develop from the prototype of Akk. *šū*, it follows that primitive Semitic had both forms available for the purpose of indicating the third person. Just how this duplication originated is beyond our present means to ascertain; we may have here specialization of two out of several originally demonstrative pronouns. At all events, the conviction is gaining ground that *h* occurred originally with mascs., *š* with fems., the earlier forms being **hū'a* 'he' and **šī'a* 'she.' [19] Since the difference in vowels was sufficient to indicate the gender,[20] the consonantal distinction was given up, one group of dialects ultimately retaining the sibilant while the other chose the laryngeal. Both types can be traced back, at any rate, to primitive Semitic. Now if these pronouns were used in the causative stem, the prefixes would reflect necessarily the consonantal dichotomy. After the equipment had been simplified through the operation of linguistic economy, those dialects that had retained the sibilant pronouns

[19] The situation in Mehri (see above; but cf. note 11) is responsible for the now practically universal view that the original division was *h-* for the masc. and *š-* for the fem.; cf. Brockelmann (who cites Jensen and Ungnad), *GVG* I. 302 f., Barth, *Pronominalbildung* 13, Bauer-Leander, *HGH* 249, Bergsträsser, *Einführung* 8. In view of this well-established position I cannot understand the statement of Gray, *ISCL* 63, note 1, that he is indebted for the same hypothesis to one of his pupils, even though the latter's reasoning is somewhat different (and, incidentally, not uniformly clear).

[20] I take it that Gray, *loc. cit.*, implies the same thing.

would naturally show also a sibilant causative, with analogous results in the laryngeal group.[21] So far the reasoning has been comparatively simple. The main problem, however, is to show what business the pronouns had with the causatives.

The problem is not properly one of phonology or morphology, but essentially one of syntax. Derivative stems are often shortened or elliptical forms of what were formerly fuller sentences. In causatives we have really the remains of compound sentences. Thus Akk. *ušabni* 'he caused to build' implies that A had ordered or induced B to build (a house, shrine, or whatever the case might be). We have here two distinct subjects. A is the superimposed subject, the principal actor, while B is the secondary agent,[22] impersonal unless otherwise specified (by means of special suffixes). B stands thus for 'someone, anyone else'; this agent is expressed by the stem prefix.

The above analysis applies, of course, exclusively to transitive verbs, and consequently to causative stems proper. The matter becomes more complicated when we consider other functions of the Semitic stem in question. Let us first examine the type having a declarative value. Heb. *hiršīʿa* may be translated by 'he declared (or denounced) as guilty.' Our translation is plainly incapable of conveying the force of the original, of which it is merely a paraphrase. It is the direct result of the elliptical nature of the underlying sentence, infinitely flexible because any number of predicates of the superimposed subject could

[21] The one exception to this rule (discounting sporadic rival forms like the Aram. š-causatives) would be the Arab *istaqtala* conjugation. Here, however, the addition of the *t*-infix was apparently responsible for the selection of the *s*-element, *st* being simpler to pronounce than *ht*. I hesitate to make chronological deductions concerning the time of final specialization of the one or the other causative prefix on this basis alone.

[22] Cf. Nyberg, *MO* XIV. 250.

be implied: A has declared, demonstrated, or the like, that B is guilty. Again our nondescript B is represented by the so-called causative prefix.

Other types of our stem may be analyzed in the same manner. They will be found to represent original clauses following verbs expressing causation, command, belief, putation, and the like. The numerous nuances of the stem are obviously due in large measure to the possible multiplicity of the implied governing verbs.

The stem is not limited, however, to the function of verbal sentences. Such a form as Heb. *he'ĕdīm* 'has turned red' is clearly the equivalent of a nominal sentence that has nothing to do with the type of clauses discussed above. Is it not strange, then, that the same stem should be employed for two such heterogeneous types of sentence? The answer is bound up intimately with the peculiarities of Semitic syntax; and it promises to furnish a satisfactory solution of the whole problem.

It has been abundantly demonstrated that nominal sentences predominate in the early stages of Semitic. There is no specific copula. For purposes of particular emphasis, however, the pronoun of the third person might serve as copula. To call attention to the fact that 'the wool is actually, unexpectedly, outstandingly, or permanently white' the ancient Semite would use the equivalent of 'the wool, *it* white.' Here we see rather plainly the original demonstrative value of the later personal pronoun. This pronoun can be interposed even when a different person expresses the subject; cf. e.g., Aram. *ănaḥnā himmō 'abdōhī* 'we, they His servants,' i.e., 'we are truly His servants.' [23]

We have now an adequate explanation for the use of

[23] Cf. Bergsträsser, *Einführung* 15.

this "pronoun of separation" or "pronoun of support," as it is called by Arab grammarians,[24] in the type of verbal sentences mentioned in the foregoing discussion. It must be borne in mind that in place of hypotaxis the ancient Semite resorted to paratactic or asyndetic construction. The phrase 'A orders (wishes, etc.) that B build a house' was actually construed as 'A orders, B builds the house,' In such asyndetic *that*-clauses particular emphasis was needed to make clear that a given action was to be performed by someone, or that a given quality was attributed to someone or something. The pronoun of the third person, a demonstrative in origin, was evidently the only available means of conveying this idea. It was unavoidable, therefore, that this pronoun should become associated with the *that*-clause in the linguistic consciousness of the speaker. This intimate association made it possible to dispense in course of time with the governing verb. The specialization of the pronoun, always in a rigidly observed syntactic sequence, as the corollary of the clauses in question, and the frequency and variety of such sentences, led at length to the emergence of the characteristic pronominal element [25] as a prefixed stem determinant. In

[24] *Al-faṣlu,* or *al-ʿimādu,* cf. Wright, *Arabic Grammar* II. 258 ff.

[25] I use the term advisedly because I do not wish to imply the joining of the entire pronoun to the verbal base. In that case we should have to explain the origin of the vowel *a* which invariably follows the consonantal element of the prefix. While the presence of this vowel could be connected with the final *a* of the pronouns themselves (**hūʾa, *šīʾa* becoming **ha* and **ša* as proclitics), such a view would presuppose deeper insight into proto-Semitic phonology than we can possibly claim at present. Nyberg (*MO* XIV. 263) regards the causative prefixes as original demonstratives (**ha, *ša,* and **ʾa*), which were joined to a base like **qitil* to yield one of two possible meanings: 'he of slaying,' or 'he who slays.' Such ambiguity was possible, he holds, because verb and noun had not become separated as yet. I doubt that much can be accomplished when one has to go back to the mythological stages of language; were causatives required at so lawless a period? Finally, as Bauer-Leander remark (*GBA* 92 f.), such an assumption would not account for the basic causative connotation of the stem. On the other hand, the syntactic conditions referred to above are

the meantime a similar coalescence was taking place in certain nominal sentences of a declarative character. The ultimate result was the formation of quasi-quadriradical verbal stems, since the new prefix constituted in effect a fourth radical in what had been for the most part a triradical base.[26] It is certainly not without significance tha the new stem was inflected like other quadriradicals, and this fact accounts for the nature of the vowels in the "causative stem." [26a]

Two final points may be made by way of illustration. The first concerns the connection of the causative prefix with independently ascertained elements of emphasis. Such a relationship has been seen by few between the causative element of the Arab. verb and the proclitic *'a-* of the elative form of the Arab. adjective.[27] A similar adjectival formation, though not as regular as in Arab., occurs in Akk. where we have, e.g., *pašqu* 'steep,' by the side of *šupšuqu* 'too steep'; here *š-* is used for both the causative and the elative.[28] An emphasizing function underlies the prefix in both instances.

The other illustration is found in Sumerian. Here the

---

demonstrable facts. The coalescence of pronominal and verbal elements which we have assumed would be guided by the analogy of available verbal forms, leading to the standardization of the stem as a whole.

[26] This would presuppose, of course, that such forms with doubling or repetition of the second or third radical, quadriradicals in effect, were earlier than the causatives, an altogether plausible assumption, since the introduction of foreign elements (causative prefix) is likely to be later than operation with available radicals. Causative stems would thus be compartively late developments of proto-Semitic.

For the treatment of sibilant causatives as "quadriliterals" in Aram. cf. Dalman, *Aramäische Grammatik* 250, and in Egyptian, Gardiner, *Eg. Gr.* 212.

[26a] I.e., *yušaqtilu* on the analogy of *yuqattilu* and *yuqatlilu.*

[27] Cf. Nyberg, *op. cit.,* 269.

[28] Christian has published an article entitled "Die kausative Bedeutung des semitischen Steigerunsstammes" in *Analecta Orientalia* 12. Unfortunately, this work is not available to me and I do not know whether our conclusions are similar in this respect.

causative elements are *-n-* and *-b-*, precisely the same as the two, and only two, subject elements of the third person sing. of the preterite tense. Indeed, Poebel regards the causative elements of Sumerian as accusative infixes of the third person.[29] So complete a parallel between two totally different linguistic stocks brings into bolder relief the mode of reasoning that may lead to the formation of causative and related stems.

To sum up, we have noted the correspondence between Semitic causative prefixes and the pronouns of the third person. There being no phonetic justification for these parallel occurrences, and chance correspondence being out of the question, an underlying functional relationship was sought. A common ground has been found in the employment of the pronouns in question as elements of emphasis. Peculiarities of Semitic syntax led to the development of these pronominal elements into so-called causative prefixes.[30] The various connotations of the causative stem become intelligible when we take into consideration the variety of possible verbs implied in the governing verbal sentence, and the character of the Semitic nominal sentence.

II. THE SO-CALLED FEMININE ENDING

The facts concerning the means of expressing gender in Semitic are well known and they are listed in the

[29] Cf. his *Sumerische Grammatik* 210 and 173. The syntactic function of the Sumerian causative prefixes would thus be slightly different, but their pronominal origin is virtually certain. Incidentally, I had overlooked this exceedingly gratifying parallel when this paper was read in April 1934.

[30] It should be pointed out that I do not seek the basis of the stem in full sentences such as 'the king commanded that the house be built.' The final standardized form would represent the ultimate abstraction based on innumerable related statements, in all of which the emphasizing pronoun played a leading part.

standard grammars.[31] Their chronological relationship is less clear. In re-stating briefly the relevant details we shall seek to arrange them in a historical sequence, so far as this is possible. This is an essential prerequisite for our present investigation. For only by establishing the relative date of the ending *-(a)t* can we hope to obtain some insight into its origin.

To judge from the interrogative, the earliest classification in Semitic recognized animates and inanimates. At least, the pronoun for person is not further differentiated with regard to masculine and feminine;[32] this may be due, however, to the fact that such distinctions were of no use to the speaker. A similar situation confronts us in the case of the personal pronoun of the first person. Here again gender is not indicated, being at all times obvious to the audience. But when a person was being addressed, the gender was specified: by the side of the masc. **'antā* 'thou' we have the fem. **'antī,* where *ī* obviously serves as gender determinant. This distinction is extended subsequently to the nominal phrase, e.g., **qaribtī* 'thou art near' (fem.), and to the verbal phrase, as in **tápqidī*[33] 'thou heedest.' In all of these categories *ī* serves to indicate the feminine.

The third person, in the pronoun as well as in the verb, displays a marked degree of individuality. It is not bound

[31] Brockelmann's *GVG* I. 404 ff. contains the most complete statement; for a recent analysis cf. Gray, *ISCL* 48 ff.

[32] This applies only to the common *m-pronoun;* cf. Barth, *Pronominalbildung* 137 ff.

[33] That forms like * *tápqidi* go back to an earlier * *ta-pa/iqid-i* is obvious. But the composite verbal form suffered syncope of the second vowel at some remote stage. At any rate, we need not refer to the possible prototypes of * *tápqidi,* which are immaterial for our discussion; the processes with which we are concerned in the present investigation are comparatively late developments of primitive Semitic. The accent on the preformative syllable has been indicated in order to call attention to the loss of a vowel in the following syllable.

by the same laws that govern the other two persons.[34] The clearest evidence for this split is furnished by the verb. Here we must distinguish clearly between an originally nominal aspect, the so-called perfect (e.g., 'be near') on the one hand, and a primarily verbal aspect, the so-called imperfect (e.g., 'heed') on the other. The two constitute ultimately the Semitic system of "tenses." [35] Inasmuch as the significance of these "tenses" is not historically uniform, it will be best to designate them in the present discussion in accordance with their external characteristics, which render them mutually exclusive. The "perfect" will be termed therefore the suffix conjugation, while the "imperfect" will figure as the prefix conjugation. Now the suffix conjugation forms its first and second persons with the aid of pronominal elements (e.g., **qarib-tā*: **'an-tā*); the prefix conjugation yields such forms as **tá-pqid-u*). There can be no doubt that the pronominal elements so used were ultimately the same in both groups.

As regards the third person, however, there was no such harmony in treatment. Here the suffix conjugation shows **qarib-a* 'he is near,' while the prefix conjugation has **yá-pqid-u* 'he heeds.' There is no etymological connection between the above formatives, nor are they related morphologically, as we shall see. Moreover, neither bears

[34] Cf. Bergsträsser, *Einführung* 8.

[35] The historical difference between the "perfect" and "imperfect" is now generally recognized as is also the inadequacy of the above designations. Bauer-Leander substitute therefore "nominal" and "aorist" respectively, see *HGH* 269, while Gray (*ISCL* 91) has suggested "telic" and "atelic" under the influence of M. Cohen's "accompli" and "inaccompli." Now while "nominal" is entirely acceptable, and suggestive of earlier conditions when the form was primarily a "qualitative" (cf. the formal parallel between this "tense" and the noun in the common employment of suffixes), the term "aorist" restricts unduly the freedom of the "imperfect." Since no single set of terms will do justice to the functional character of the two main aspects of the Semitic verb, it seems best to base our designations on purely external, and definitely contrasted, characteristics.

any relation to the established Semitic personal pronoun of the third person (masc. **hū'a* or **šū'a*; fem. **šī'a* or **hī'a*); at best, the feminine forms of this pronoun may contain the same characteristic feminine element *ī* that has been noted also in the personal pronoun of the second person. In short, the third persons of the two "tenses" of Semitic were formed independently of each other and without the assistance of the known personal pronouns. In the first and second persons, however, there is a definite connection between personal pronoun and verb.

This sharp disparity is manifestly the result of differing linguistic stratification: the third person belongs to a later stratum.[36] The personal pronoun of the third person had not been definitely established at the time when the verbal system was on its way to schematization, and another original demonstrative (**ya*) was used to indicate the third person in the prefix conjugation. But the suffix conjugation never did succumb to this particular system, because it had its own peculiar way to designate the third person.

The *-a* of forms like **qarib-a* 'he is near' cannot be associated directly with the personal pronoun.[37] There is, however, another explanation for this element, which has hitherto been overlooked. Its occurrence in the suffix conjugation is due to the requirements of Semitic syntax. It so happens that the accusative is the normal case of the predicate in a nominal sentence,[38] i.e., after a copula, whether the latter is expressed or implied; cf. Arab. *kāna*

[36] For this chronological difference in the suffix conjugation cf. Bergsträsser, *Einführung* 14.

[37] One might think in this connection of the final vowel in the pronouns ** hū'a* and ** šī'a;* but no special significance appears to attach to it and it may be itself secondary.

[38] Cf. Bergsträsser, *op. cit.* 15.

qarība^{n} 'he was a companion, near.' Now **qarib-a* is in effect such a sentence; and the accusative ending is *-a*. The presence of this ending does away with the need for a special pronominal determinant of person. [This point, however, turns out to be much more complicated. It requires special treatment.]

It follows that the above form is later than the case endings of Semitic. This result is not surprising, for we have had other indications that the third person of the Semitic verb is a comparatively late development. In the suffix conjugation a case-ending came to designate the person in question owing to the nature of that conjugation and the special laws of Semitic syntax. But since syntax is not restricted by gender, a verbal ending thus obtained would apply automatically to masculine and feminine alike. If, then, the third person feminine was to be differentiated from the corresponding masculine form, a special distinguishing characteristic had to be introduced. Quite appropriately, this new element is also borrowed from the noun. For the *-at* in **qarib-at* 'she is near,' or at least the characteristic *-t*, cannot be dissociated from the feminine ending *-(a)t* of the noun group.

What is the origin of this feminine element? Shared by the noun and the verb, and equally prominent in the Semitic and in the Hamitic languages, this ending would seem capable of a satisfactory explanation. Nevertheless, all attempts at deriving the formative from some plausible source have failed thus far. As the transcription *-(a)t* shows, we are not even clear as to its original form. For by the side of *-at* we find also *-t* (as in **bín-t-u* 'daughter'). The variation between the two forms is explained usually by postulating originally different accentual conditions.[39]

[39] Brockelmann, *GVG* I. 405.

But other explanations have not been lacking, and a recent student regards it as probable that *-at* represents a combination of two distinct elements (*-a-* and *-t*), both intended to indicate the feminine.[40] The problem is clearly far from settled.

At this stage of our inquiry it will be well to eliminate from further consideration certain sources that are ordinarily likely to produce a specific feminine ending. We have seen that the personal pronoun cannot be held responsible in the present instance; its feminine element was *ī*. Nor does *-(a)t* owe its origin to some prominent designation of beings naturally female. In the earliest stages of Semitic such beings were signified not by the addition of special endings, but by individual stems.[41] The employment of *-(a)t* to mark beings as female belongs to a later period, and the ending is thus obviously not original with the natural feminine. Later still must be its connection with the grammatical feminine.

The question of grammatical gender in Semitic, to restrict the problem to this specific case,[42] has led to much speculation. The grammatical feminine is said to be due to the association of female animate beings with things which the primitive mind may consider female, and things inactive and inanimate. Together with abstracts, collectives, diminutives, and pejoratives, the entire group was viewed as inferior when contrasted with the active, male animates, and was consequently classed as feminine.[43] The ending *-(a)t* would thus have spread to inanimates after it had become a mark of inferiority through associa-

[40] Gray, *ISCL* 51 f.; cf. my review of this book in *Language* XI. 258.

[41] Cf. Brockelmann, *op. cit.* 416.

[42] For the same problem in Hamitic cf. the views of Meinhof, *Hamiten* 22 ff.; for the situation in Indo-European see Hirt, *Indogermanische Grammatik* III. 320 ff.

[43] So most recently Gray, *op. cit.* 48.

tion with passive, female animates.[44] Since designations for beings specifically female are not burdened with feminine endings in the earlier stages of Semitic, it has also been suggested that this implied higher rating may reflect a matriarchal organization of society.[45] With such sociological and, to a certain extent, metaphysical speculations we cannot be concerned at present. Generalizations about the workings of the primitive mind are out of place here, primarily because the linguistic data by which they have been inspired do not characterize a particularly early stage of primitive Semitic. We have seen that the ending -(*a*)*t* is the product of a comparatively late, though still prehistoric period. Its introduction and subsequent wide distribution are relatively datable. To operate with concepts such as matriarchy is likely to involve us in anachronisms. And while the ending in question may have been specialized in course of time for names of weak or timid beings, diminutives, pejoratives, and the like, this function is but one of many; inferior classification will not account for the other usages. In short, too much mystery seems to be made of our feminine ending.[46]

To return to our matter-of-fact inquiry, it will be best to review the larger groups that are typified by the ending -(*a*)*t*. Since these classes are well known and copiously illustrated in grammars, a minimum of examples will suffice. The categories to which they belong are the main thing.

[44] *Ibid.* 51.

[45] Cf. Brockelmann, *GVG* I. 417.

[46] It should be stressed again that our present problem is not to analyze the Semitic feminine endings in general, but only the spread of the element -(*a*)*t*. It is altogether likely that early Semitic possessed originally a larger number of nominal categories than are found in the historical period. The wealth of such classes in Hamitic is justly suggestive, though in our ignorance of historical Hamitic grammar we cannot be sure what has been acquired from other African families.

1. The ending is used to form abstracts from adjectives, numerals, and verbs.

1a. **kull*- 'all': Akk. *kull-at*- 'totality'; Akk. *kēn*- 'just': **kēn-t*- 'justice'; Heb. *ra'* 'bad': **ra'-at*- 'evil'; Arab. *ḥasan*- 'good': *hasanat*- 'goodness.'

1b. **ḫamiś*- 'five': **ḫamiś-at*- 'quintet.'

1c. **wṯb* 'dwell': **ṯib-t*- 'dwelling'; Akk. *nb'* 'call': *nibī-t*- 'nomination, call': Heb. *qny* 'acquire': inf. **qanay-at*.

2. Participles yield collectives. Names of occupations, often specifically masculine, use collective forms for plurals, with secondary lengthening of the vowel of *-at*; this form is the same as the fem. pl. ending, a secondary specialization, as proved by its sing. case endings.[47]

2a. **'āriḫ*- > Heb. *'ōrēaḥ* 'wanderer, guest': **'āriḫ-at*- 'caravan'; **bahīm* 'dumb (?)': **bahīm-at*- 'cattle, beasts'; Arab. *kāfir*- 'unbeliever': coll *kafar-at*- (with secondary shortening of the first vowel).

2b. Akk. *ḫazān*- 'governor': *pl. ḫazān-āt*-; *ikkar*- 'cultivator': pl. *ikkar-āt*-; Eth. *kāhen* 'priest': pl. *kāhen-āt*.

3. Conversely, collectives become nomina unitatis.

Heb. *śē'ār* 'hair': **śa'r-at*- 'single hair'; Arab. *baqar*- 'cattle': *baqar-at*- 'single head of cattle'; with pl. endings, Heb. *lĕḇēn-īm*[48] 'brick': **lĕben-at*- 'single brick'; Aram.[49] *se'ār-īn* 'barley': *se'ār-ṯ-ā* 'single grain.'

[47] Cf. Brockelmann, *op. cit.* 441, and Gray, *ISCL* 52.

[48] The plural ending in such collectives is pleonastic and clearly secondary. Arabic did not feel the necessity for so marking its "broken plurals." In the dialect of Ras Shamra, however, the plural ending is present, but the fem. sing. is employed for the predicate; cf. e.g., *nḫl-m t-lk nbtm* 'the rivers flow (sing.!) with honey,' Poem A iii. 13. Here too, then, we have proof that the collective "plural" was in function a fem. sing. Significant is also the fact that the pleonastic plural ending is masc. and not fem., plainly the heritage of a period in which special endings for the fem. pl. had not yet come into existence.

[49] Here and elsewhere in this discussion "Aram." is used for Syriac as well.

4. The ending is found in diminutives and related classes; cf. Heb. **yāniq-* 'sapling': **yāniq-at-* 'twig.'

Even from this schematic presentation it is apparent that the ending under discussion lent itself to a variety of uses. It should be emphasized, however, that the formation of abstracts is demonstrably its most prominent function, so much so that we may regard the class of abstract nouns as the one from which it was extended to other categories. Further analysis reveals two interesting facts. In the first place, the ending has at this stage of its progress no connection whatever with the feminine gender. It is used to form numerical substantives (**ḫamiś-at-*), which are employed subsequently with masculine nouns only ('a quintet of men'); when the dichotomy into two genders had at length won through, the original numeral (**ḫamiś-*) is assigned to the feminines.[50] The same independence of any definitely feminine connotation is seen in those names of occupations (cf. group 2b) that from their "plurals" with *-ā(i)*. And finally, this condition is echoed in such phrases as Akk. *nibīt Enlil anāku* 'I am the appointee of Enlil' (Hammurabi Code I. 52), which a thoroughly masculine ruler of Babylon applies to himself.

The other important fact about our ending is its remarkable versatility: it forms, among others, not only collectives but also their precise opposite, i.e., *nomina unitatis* (group 3). It is this seeming inconsistency that furnishes the necessary clue for the appreciation of the principal function of *-(a)t*. This was not to mark inferior classification, or to form abstracts, collectives, diminutives,

[50] This seems to me the simplest explanation of the curious behavior of the Semitic numerals for 'three' to 'ten.' Barth, *Pronominalbildung* 87, fails to see the connection between the *t*-endings of the numeral and noun because he regards the Eth. *tū*-suffix as original; it was borrowed, however, from the pronouns, cf. Bergsträsser, *Einführung* 98.

or the like, but plainly to construct derivative stems with some special modification of the original meaning. To be sure, abstracts could thus be formed most readily, because of the underlying value of the formative, as will be shown later on; they were based on adjectives or verbs. But once the formative had gained prominence, it was the derivative signification that facilitated its expansion. The starting point was the decisive thing. Participles, agent nouns, and names of occupations formed collectives with the aid of *-(a)t*; but when the original form represented a collective (sometimes equipped with the plural ending), the derivative formation would signify a *nomen unitatis*. In other cases the ending could be used conveniently for diminutives and pejoratives. In other words, our formative became the simplest means of producing derivative nouns whose specialized meanings depended mainly on the primary values of the simple bases. In these circumstances the influence of analogy must have been an important factor in the gradual development of distinct and schematized categories.

All this must have taken place before *-(a)t* had acquired the function of a feminine ending, that is before it had come to designate female beings, thus leading to the emergence of the grammatical feminine. These advanced stages in the career of our formative are no longer difficult to follow. Its specializing connotation was before long found to be of value in modifying relationship terms. By the side of **'abu-* 'father,' **'aḫu-* 'brother' and **bin-* 'child, son' there were formed **'abu + at-*, **'aḫu + at-*, and **bin + at-*. The meaning of the new words would depend on the needs of the language. A word like **'abāt-* might come to signify 'fatherhood,' as an abstract, or 'parents' as a collective. In Heb. it is preserved in the sense of 'fathers.'

Similarly, **'aḫāt-* and **bin(a)t-* could yield abstracts or collectives. Now as collectives these words would refer simultaneously to males and females. If the corresponding simple plurals had been in vogue too long to be easily displaced, the new derivatives could be specialized for the females alone, yielding respectively 'sister' [51] and 'daughter.' [52]

It is impossible, of course, to determine the precise channel through which *-(a)t* gained admittance to the group of names of animates. The above remarks are intended simply as a likely illustration. But what with the restrictive value of the element *-(a)t* on the one hand, and the inconvenience of separate stems to designate beings respectively male and female on the other, the ultimate specialization of our ending as the feminine elements was merely a matter of time. From here it is only a step to the grammatical feminine. Since the addition of *-(a)t* to any given name of an animate being may introduce the female of the species, other words with the same ending will soon also be regarded as feminine. Analogy is here the main factor. This does not mean that in his progress towards grammatical gender the Semite was guided by no other principle. There are numerous words without spe-

[51] Cf. e.g., the juxtaposition of German *Schwester* and *Ge-schwister.*

[52] The *t*-form of **'abu-* could not displace the indispensable **'umm-* 'mother.' It is worthy of notice that while the latter word has the same meaning in all Semitic language, * *bint-* is not the usual word for 'daughter' in Akk., and was specialized in another sense in the South Arabic group. Lastly, the explanation of the ending of Heb. *'aḇōṯ* (< **'abāt*) as due to polarity with *nāšīm* 'women' can now be given up without compunction; the contrast of 'fathers' and 'women' is hardly one of direct opposites. In *'aḇōṯ* we have simply an old collective in which the long vowel is due to the contraction of the vocalic termination of the base and the *-a* of the ending. It is no more a real plural than *'aḥōṯ* 'sister,' where the quantity of the second vowel has precisely the same origin. As for the ending of *nāšīm,* we have observed it in the capacity of a pleonastic element in collectives as early as Ras Shamra.

cial endings whose gender in historic times requires explanation. Our present task, however, has been to explain the origin of the grammatical feminines in -(*a*)*t*, and in this we need not look further than formal analogy.

Bearing in mind the fundamental function of the element -(*a*)*t*, viz., that of opposing secondary meanings to primary ones, we may postulate the following chronological stages in the progress of this ending.

1. Formation of abstracts from adjectives, numerals, and verbs.
2. Formation of collectives from participles and nouns.
3. Formation of derivatives in general, restricting in some way the value of the primary word (*nomina unitatis*, **'aḫāt-*, **'abāt-*).
4. Designation of the natural feminine (**bin-(a)t-* 'daughter').
5. Inclusion of all words ending in -(*a*)*t* under the grammatical feminine; spread of the ending to the verb (masc. **qarib-a*: fem. **qarib-at*).
6. As a final link in this chain we may add the development of the feminine plural. On the analogy of the masculine (sing. *-u*: pl. *-ū*), the feminine formed a plural *-āt-* by the side of the singular *-at-*.[53]

It has been indicated that our ending owed its later prominence to its association with abstract nouns. The reason for this association is still to be investigated. We know that **kull-* 'all' becomes *kull-at-* 'totality,' and we may deduce from this the approximate force of the formative. But how did -(*a*)*t* acquire that force? In other words, what is the origin of this element?

Our search is necessarily limited to sources other than

[53] For references see note 47.

the noun and the verb. Moreover, there is no independent Semitic particle to which the ending under investigation could be related. There are, however, possible analogues among certain component elements.

Barth has established for Semitic the existence of an adverbial element occurring as *-ta* and *-t*: It is used with such words as Arab. *rubbata/t* 'occasionally,' Heb. *rabbaṯ* 'greatly,' and Aram. *kĕmaṯ* 'namely,' and probably also Aram. *'eryaṯ* 'in a state of nakedness.' [54]. Perhaps Akk. *eli'at* 'over and above' is to be included with this group. This suffix is generally identified with the feminine ending, but the derivation from the latter is justly rejected by Barth. If there is a connection between the two, borrowing from the adverbs would have to be assumed. Semantically, an adverbial element would not be out of place as a formative in abstract nouns.[55] But since this *-ta/t* is rare, obviously secondary, and obscure as to origin, we cannot attach to it much weight.

A much more tangible element is the *-t-* which appears as an accusative exponent in Akkadian to form independent pronominal forms indicating the direct object.[56] Thus *yā-t-i* means 'me,' and *kā-t-i* 'te.' The original full form of this element is not quite certain. It appears to require an initial *a-*,[57] and it is followed by *-i* or*-u*, both of which may be due, however, to the influence of the nominal declension. The composite form has to be given as - (*a*) *t* (*i*/*u*), where *-t-* is at any rate invariable; its ac-

[54] *Pronominalbildung* 87 ff.

[55] Cf. the use of Heb. *ḥinnām* 'gratis' (containing the common adverbial-accusative element **-am*) with a preceding noun in the construct state; e.g., *'ēḏ ḥinnām* 'witness of falsehood, false witness.' Conversely, abstract nouns may yield the sense of an adverb, as in Akk. *balṭussūnu* 'their state of being alive,' i.e., 'they alive.'

[56] For this exceedingly important element, first noted by Bertin in 1885 (*JRAS* XVII. 65 ff.), see Barth, *Pronominalbildung* 25 ff.

[57] Note *šu-a-ti* 'him.'

cusative function is equally constant. Akkadian is unique in its use of such independent pronominal forms, the other Semitic languages employing possessive afformatives instead, without case exponents. But that these pronominal case endings (in addition to the accusative *-t-*, there is a dative *-š-*) are not Akkadian innovations, but rather survivals from the oldest period of Semitic, is proved by their occurrence in Hamitic. In the Agau group of the Cushitic branch we find the same element *-t* (in certain instances *-tī*) with precisely the same significance; cf. *yi-t* or *ye-t* 'me,' *ku-t* 'te.'[58] This complete correspondence between two widely separated linguistic divisions of Semitic and Hamitic respectively is one of the strongest arguments in favor of an underlying Hamito-Semitic stock.

This reference to Hamitic brings up an important point. Since an ultimate relationship between Hamitic and Semitic is now generally regarded as certain,[59] it follows that a morphological element prevalent in both families must go back to primitive Hamito-Semitic. The ending *-(a) t* is such an element; its origin must therefore be traceable to the proëthnic period. A given theory as to that origin will gain in plausibility if the assumed source is still represented in each of the two main subdivisions. In the light of these remarks the pronominal accusative element *-t-* acquires added interest.

That case elements are capable of assuming wider formative functions is a fact too well known to need special emphasis. This is particularly true of the accusa-

[58] Cf. Barth, *ibid.;* Reinisch, *Das persönliche Fürwort und die Verbalflexion in den chamito-semitischen Sprachen* 266 ff.

[59] For the latest discussion of this question see M. Cohen, "Les résultats acquis de la grammaire comparée chamito-sémitique," *Conférences de l'Institut de Linguistique de Paris,* 1933 (1934), 17 ff. For the question in general see Barton, *Semitic and Hamitic Origins.* Werner Vycichl, "Was sind Hamitensprachen?" *Africa* VIII. 76 ff., goes entirely too far for the present state of our knowledge.

tive because of the manifold uses of this case. A reference to Arabic syntax, e.g., will remind us of the existence of accusatives of comparison, of limitation or determination, of motive or cause, of state or condition, of time, place, salutation, adverbial accusatives, and so forth. The nominal accusative ending was frequently employed in Semitic to form independent adverbs.[60] As the direct object or "passive" case the accusative may lead to the formation of neuters, as seems to have occurred in Indo-European.[61]

There is, consequently, no semantic difficulty in deriving the Semito-Hamitic formative -*(a)t* from a Semito-Hamitic accusative element -*t*-. This ending may have been employed at first for adverbs, of which sporadic survivals[62] have been mentioned above. No less probable is a direct borrowing by the noun for the purpose of forming abstracts, a use to which the case lends itself admirably; in fact, any one of several functions of this "adverbial" case might easily influence the transfer of its ending to the class of derivative nouns.[63]

The contribution of Hamitic to our study is not exhausted by the aforementioned parallels. Other interesting possibilities are suggested by the behavior of the

[60] For the general question cf. Torczyner, *Die Entstehung des semitischen Sprachtypus.*

[61] This view is rejected provisionally by Hirt, *Indogermanische Grammatik* III. 95. The specific illustration for Semitic as chosen by Gray, *ISCL* 51 f., is incorrect; cf. *Language* XI. 258.

[62] It is an interesting coincidence that von Soden, *ZA* 41. 119 f., seeks the origin of the Akk. adverbial ending -*š* in the dative element -*š* of the same pronominal class, which is related in turn to the -*s* of the Agau languages. The formative possibilities of pronominal case elements are evidently beginning to be appreciated. If our theory is correct, the accompanying -*t* of the accusative enjoyed an infinitely more varied career than the -*š*/*s* of the dative, owing of course to the greater semantic flexibility of the accusative case.

[63] Torczyner, who has perhaps overemphasized the significance of the accusative, derives the feminine ending from an entirely precarious -*tam;* cf. *Enst. d. sem. Sprachtypus* 250 ff.

"feminine" ending under discussion. The Agau languages employ this element not only as an affix, but occasionally also as a prefix.[64] This reminds us that the *-t-*, which acts as a pronominal accusative exponent in Akkadian, finds a wider application as an element in several prefixed *notae accusativi* of West Semitic; cf. Heb. *'eṯ, 'ōṯ,* Aram. *yāṯ,* and perhaps Phoen. *yt.*[65] The same juxtaposition in Hamitic of affix and prefix suggests also a closer parallel in the Semitic noun. There the origin of the prefix *-t-* is yet to be explained. Its principal function is the formation of abstract nouns from verbs. When it is realized that this is also one of the most important uses of the ending *-(a)t,* the ability of Hamitic to use this formative at the beginning or at the end of certain bases assumes an unexpected significance. It should be borne in mind that Semitic can form verbal nouns with *-(a)t* (**ṯib-(a)t-*, *qatal-at-*), as well as with *t-* (*ta-qtīl*); there is scarcely any difference in meaning between Heb. **neḥam-at* and *ta-nḥūm* 'comforting.' We do not know enough about primitive Semitic to determine the laws which governed the distribution of prefixes and affixes respectively. We are entirely in the dark as to why the accusative *-t-* was affixed in Akkadian while the *notae accusativi* were prefixed in Semitic nor why the definite articles occur proclitically in Hebrew or Arabic and enclitically in Aramaic. But the underlying correspondence in meaning, and the Hamitic analogues, make it difficult to dissociate

[64] Cf. Reinisch, *op. cit.* (note 58) 278. This procedure is known also from the Berber languages.

[65] Cf. Barth, *Pronominalbildung* 95, where the connection with the accusative *-t* is, however, not recognized. Gray's (*ISCL* 56) proposed etmyology for Heb. *'ōṯ* is far-fetched; moreover, Akk. *yāti* (*ibid.*) has nothing to do with accusative particles, being an independent oblique case of the pronoun of the first person. The Heb. *notae accusativi* are compared with the Hamitic *t-* elements by Meinhof, *Hamiten* 24, note 1, and 227, note 2. Though he confuses the two particles of Hebrew, he was clearly on the right track.

-(*a*)*t* from *t*-. It goes without saying that the further development of the formative in these two positions did not proceed along strictly parallel lines; in course of time the prefix and affix can even be used pleonastically.[66]

Having reached this concluding stage of our investigation, we are in a better position to inquire about the original form of the ending; was it -*t* or -*at*? The evidence of Hamitic, which in our present state of knowledge of Hamitic phonology need not be regarded as conclusive, would favor -*t*. In Semitic a preceding *a*- is found in most positions, but the vowel may be heterogeneous. A clear-cut decision in the matter is therefore impossible for the present.

Finally, the question may be raised anew as to the origin of the *t*-stem in the verb. So long as *t*-nouns were considered an isolated class, the connection of their characteristic element with that of the reciprocal conjugation was viewed as impossible: the disparity in meaning was much too wide.[67] The matter is placed in a different light now that the formatives *t*- and - (*a*) *t* may both be derived from an old accusative ending. For a semantic relationship between accusative and reciprocal elements is not beyond the realm of probability. But this is as far as we can afford to go. There are other possibilities worthy of consideration, if one cares to indulge in speculations of this kind. Short of some such striking indication as was provided by the correspondence of sibilants and laryngeals in the causative conjugation and in the personal pronoun of the third person, there can be no assurance that we are on the right track.

[66] That is, nouns with the preformative *t*- may have also the feminine ending -(*a*)*t*.

[67] Cf. Brockelmann, *GVG* I. 383.

The Pitfalls of Polarity

THE TERM "POLARITY" WAS ADOPTED FOR LINGUISTIC PURposes by Carl Meinhof, who introduced it in his comparative account of the Hamitic languages,[1] published in 1912. Slow at first in gaining currency, this designation has steadily been increasing in popularity; today it stands for a widely recognized principle said to be operative alike in the Hamitic and Semitic languages.

This is what Meinhof himself has to say on the subject:

> If under certain conditions A becomes B, B will become A under the same conditions. I call this process polarity for the following reason. The magnet has a positive pole (A) and a negative pole (B). If the positive pole becomes negative under the influence of a stronger magnet, i.e., if A becomes B, the negative pole will turn positive, B becoming A.[2]

[1] Die Sprachen der Hamiten (Abh. des Hamburgischen Kolonialinstituts) 9. Strictly speaking, Meinhof does not seem to have been the first to use polarity in a linguistic sense. It is clear, however, from his elaborate statement that he was unaware of any other secondary application of this term. Moreover, Meinhof suspects the operation of polarity in phonetic and morphological developments, whereas others would use the term in connection with (Greek) syntax and stylistics. Since the advocates of polarity in the Hamito-Semitic field, with which the present discussion is concerned, are all avowed followers of Meinhof, the term will be used here in the sense in which it was independently adopted by him.

[2] Ibid. 19.

The author goes on to suggest an explanation for the process. The speakers of the languages involved divide things into two principal categories, such as male and female. A change in classification entails transfer from one category to the other. In Meinhof's own words: "To put it pointedly,[3] what is not a man is necessarily a woman, and what is not a woman must be a man; tertium non datur."

This formulation is based on phenomena observed in three out of the seven groups of Hamitic languages with which the book deals. But even in those three Meinhof notes important exceptions to the general rule.[4] The author seeks to strengthen his case by adducing illustrations from the social practices of certain African groups,[5] but such instances can have no direct bearing on linguistic problems.

What Meinhof started out to do was to describe certain contrasted situations observed among several Hamitic languages. The term "polarity" suggested itself as a convenient designation for such cases. The name implies, however, also a degree of interpretation. Meinhof was thus compelled to find a reason for his linguistic facts, and to do that he had to enlist the aid of psychology. It should be emphasized that the author was fully aware of the subjective nature of his argument. The same cannot be said of many of Meinhof's followers, some of whom have gone so far as to regard polarity as a linguistic law. We can have no serious quarrel with the term if it is understood to be purely descriptive, a convenient label and nothing more. But when one reads and hears with

[3] 'drastisch ausgedrückt.'

[4] For numerous unexplained exceptions in Ful see ibid. 41; in Šilh feminines take 'not infrequently' masculine plurals (ibid. 95); in Somali only collectives to masculine singulars are feminine (ibid. 171).

[5] Ibid. 19–20.

increasing frequency that polarity explains this or that set of facts in Hamitic and Semitic, and realizes at the same time that the facts in question happen to include some of the problems which so far have been eluding all attempts at interpretation, one is prompted to inquire more closely into this linguistic panacea.

Let us disregard for the moment Meinhof's interpretation of polarity, since it is admittedly subjective, and concentrate instead on his definition of the process. This definition requires two sets of linguistic features to have exchanged places, the interchange being interdependent and simultaneous. In other words, A must have started out as B, and B must once have been A; the respective shifts of A to B and of B to A were mutually conditioned; they were also related chronologically. Unless all of the above conditions obtained, the process described as polarity cannot be said to have taken place.

Since a chronological factor is implicit in the definition of polarity, the term can properly be applied only to languages which have been studied historically. Where our knowledge of a given language, or group of languages, is largely empirical, the time element cannot be checked. For this reason it is not advisable to operate with the concept of polarity in the Hamitic languages. The comparative study of Hamitic would have to be much further advanced than it is today before we could speak with confidence of detailed historical processes within this group. At all events, it is significant that Meinhof has been able to utilize his theory only for a part of the Hamitic family, although he circumvents more than once the requirements of his own definition. The historical criterion is at no time mentioned, let alone applied.

It is no less significant that in Egyptian, a Hamito-

Semitic language for which we have ample historical material,[6] polarity has yet to be demonstrated. A recent attempt to identify the process in Egyptian[7] is likely to embarrass rather than please the advocates of the theory. Confronted with more than two sets of features which he would explain by polarity, the author is forced to set up a "polar cross,"[8] which is a curious contrivance at best. He adds that in its operation polarity seems to resemble the process of analogy. But if analogic change furnishes an explanation which students of language will understand, why does one need to have recourse to a principle which is linguistically obscure? For as an explanation of linguistic processes polarity narrows down to a principle of contrariness; something like "you have taken my sheep, so I am going to take your sheep."

It is however, primarily[9] in the Semitic languages that polarity has been assigned of late a place of honor, not only as a term descriptive of certain contrasted conditions but as the principle behind them. To concentrate only on instances which have become stock examples in works by competent scholars,[10] we find that the operation of polarity is seen in: 1. The "broken plurals" of Arabic; 2. The plural endings in the Hebrew words for "fathers" and "women"; 3. The system of tenses in West Semitic;

[6] For a convenient summary of the affinities of Egyptian see A. H. Gardiner, Egyptian Grammar 2–3 (1927).

[7] H. Brunner, Das Gesetz der Polarität in der ägyptischen Sprache, Zeitschrift für ägypt. Spr. 72. 139–41 (1936).

[8] Ibid. 140.

[9] Prof. R. G. Kent has called my attention to the fact that the term (in Meinhof's sense) has been making headway also in Indo-European linguistics.

[10] The principal advocates of the theory have been, in addition to Meinhof, W. H. Worrell and G. Bergsträsser. The three sets of examples adduced by Bergsträsser will be discussed below under sections 2–4. Worrell's principal argument is detailed under section 1; his remaining illustrations are covered, for the sake of completeness, in footnote 30. I first expressed my misgivings about Worrell's position in JAOS 49. 181 (1929).

4. The syntax of the Semitic numerals from "three" to "ten." If polarity is really responsible for the present conditions in the above four classes, the operation of that principle should be comparatively easy to follow, because Semitic furnishes ample material for historical investigations. On the other hand, uniformly negative results will not be wholly satisfactory until adequate explanations are substituted in each case for those which are now current.

1. The most vigorous advocate of polarity as a factor in the development and gender of the so-called broken plurals of Arabic has been W. H. Worrell.[11] As is well known, these forms are original singular abstracts which gradually came to be used in a concrete and collective sense, and hence pass for plurals.[12] Grammatically, the gender of these forms is feminine. According to Worrell "the broken plurals are feminine, not only because they are abstracts and collectives, but because they must be polaric opposites to their masculine singulars."[13] In other words, *kilāb "dogs"* (plur., fem.) is said to be the polaric opposite to *kalb* "dog" (sing., masc.) in number as well as in gender. The contrast in number ceases to impress, however, when it is realized that *kilāb* is morphologically a singular[14] just as plainly as *kalb*. Nor is the opposition of the genders other than accidental. The normal ending of abstracts and collectives in Semitic is *(a)t*, which came to be the general designation of the feminine gender in

[11] The Formation of Arabic Broken Plurals, Am. Jour. Se. Lang. 41. 179–82 (1925); A Study of Races in the Ancient Near East 61–4 (1927).

[12] W. Wright, Comparative Grammar of the Semitic Languages 148 (1890); Grammar of the Arabic Language[3] I. 199–234 (1896). A thoroughly satisfactory treatment of the nature of these forms was given by J. Barth, Nominalbildung 417–83 (1889).

[13] Races 64.

[14] It is based on infinitives of the type *qital*, cf. Wright, Arabic Grammar I, 111 no. 26; 202–5.

all branches of this linguistic family.[15] The analogy of the abstracts and collectives in -(*a*)*t* is entirely sufficient to account for the gender of those collectives which have no formative suffix: Arabic *kilāb* "dogs" is feminine by signification because it belongs to a class which is commonly in Semitic, and not infrequently in Arabic itself (e.g., *ǧamā'at-* "totality"), feminine by form.

The "broken plurals" are thus in no way abnormal with regard to number or gender. It remains only to examine the differences in form which distinguish these collectives from their respective nomina unitatis. The situation will be clarified if we first cite an illustration involving Semitic languages other than Arabic. Hebrew *śē'ār* "hair" is a collective to which the nomen unitatis is *śa'ărā* "single hair"; the latter yields the constr. plural *śa'ărôt* "hairs." *śa'ărā* is "feminine" on account of its ending (< -*at*), which had become specialized as the designation of the feminine gender, *śē'ār* is "masculine" because it lacks the one common Semitic suffix of the grammatical gender; it is an "internal" collective, in that no formative is required to convey the meaning. But in Akkadian the corresponding form is *šārt*(*u*), with the abstract-collective ending -*t*; by reason of that ending it is also "feminine." In other words, Hebrew could and did make use of the ending (*a*) *t* to designate a single specimen of the class "hair," because that ending had not been employed by the collective in question; in Akkadian the same formative was needed to express the collective. Consequently, Semitic **śa'arat* comes to represent opposed grammatical subdivisions in Hebrew and Akkadian respectively.

Now in Arabic (and South Semitic in general) the

[15] See Speiser, Studies in Semitic Formatives, JAOS 56. 33–46 (1936) [cf. above, pp. 403 ff.]

internal collectives are specialized to a degree not approached elsewhere in Semitic. Whereas in Hebrew these forms are rudimentary[16] and supported for the most part by pleonastic plural endings,[17] the process of forming "broken plurals" is a living one in Arabic, so much so that modern loanwords are readily assigned to one of the numerous stem-forms of this type.[18] These stem-forms comprise no less than twenty-nine comparatively common classes.[19] It is easy to see, therefore, how plurals (with the idea of individuality wholly suppressed, however[20]) might be expressed in Arabic by forms that had originally been reserved for abstracts, although the normal Semitic plural formed with the suffix *-ū-* is by no means rare.

The number of stem-forms encountered with the "broken plurals" is exceeded by the number of forms used to express verbal nouns. There are forty-four[21] recognized types of verbal noun which may be formed from the ordinary triradical verb. Since such abstract nouns on the one hand, and collectives on the other, are often related semantically, frequent correspondences in

[16] Although by no means as rare as is generally supposed; for a recent list of collectives in Hebrew see L. H. Gray, Introduction to Semitic Comparative Linguistics 53 (1934). These forms are represented frequently by 'segholates' of the type *qitl* and *qutl*. A good, but unnoticed, example is *kofĕr* 'villages' (type *qutl*), I Samuel 6.18. An older instance is *sefĕr* 'writing, book' (type *qitl*), which Hebrew borrowed from Akkadian.

[17] Here belong most of the singulars in **-at* which form their plurals with *-îm;* for examples of such forms see H. Bauer and P. Leander, Historische Grammatik der hebräischen Sprache 1.515–6. The segholate plural *qᵉtāl-îm* is most likely of the same origin.

[18] Thus a modern Arabic term for 'Egyptologists' is *barāgiš,* which is based on the name of the German Egyptologist *Brugsch;* see Meinhof, Die Entstehung flektierender Sprachen 55 (1936). I have heard many formations of the type *panākik* < Engl. *pancake.*

[19] This is the number of the more common forms cited by Wright, Arabic Grammar 1. 199.

[20] Ibid. 233.

[21] Ibid. 110–2, the list being only 'nearly complete'.

form are perfectly natural. These correspondences merely bear out the theoretical premise that infinitives may be expected to represent abstracts. Thus *qitāl,* a very common type of "broken plural," [22] occurs also as an infinitive.[23] In Hebrew, an original *ấ* (> *ô*) in the second syllable is evidenced in such pleonastic collectives as *d^eḇôr-îm* "bees" and *ś^eʿôr-îm* "barley".[24]

We now come to the form of the singulars which occur with the "broken plurals". From among the wealth of classes of these secondary plurals Worrell has selected eight which he juxtaposes with their respective singulars in order to illustrate the underlying principle of contrast.[25] Since Worrell's groups 5–8 depend on the use of formatives, and thus weaken the argument by introducing an outside element into the discussion, I shall consider for the present only the first four groups. Taking the first example in each group, we get the following picture:

	singular	"broken plural"
a.	*kalb* "dog"	*kilāb*
b.	*kitāb* "writing"	*kutub*
c.	*šarīf* "noble"	*širāf*
d.	*ṣāḥib* "friend"	*ṣiḥāb*

The difference in number within each group is said to rest "upon the principle of contrast maintained between two members of a two-class system," [26] the contrast being attained by varying the quantity, character, or position of the vowels in question. But even in this schematic presentation there is apparent a complete disregard of uniformity which violates the "tertium-non-datur" clause

[22] Ibid. 202–5.
[23] Ibid. 111 no. 26.
[24] See note 17.
[25] Races 62–3.
[26] Ibid. 63.

of Meinhof's definition. For if we start out with the "plural" forms, we find the base *qitāl* in three out of four groups cited; but the corresponding singulars represent three different bases (*qatl, qatīl, qātil*). Moreover, in group (b) the singular also shows the form *qitāl;* the plural, however, exhibits yet another base (*qutul*). In other words, in each of the above four classes *qitāl* furnishes one of the two forms listed, while the corresponding opposites are all different. There is not a trace left of the purely mechanical principle of contrast.

The plain fact is that tabulations of this kind are misleading because they are superficial and incomplete. One of the examples given by Worrell under group (a) is *'abd* "servant," with *'abīd* as its plural. A non-Semitist is likely to conclude from this statement that no other plural form is used in this particular instance. It so happens, however, that *'abīd* is one out of no less than fifteen "broken plurals" found with *'abd.*[27] Finally, one singular may have several irregular plurals and a normal plural (in *-ūna*) besides, each form being often specialized for one particular shade of meaning.[28]

It follows that no classification that is based solely on external criteria of form will account for the complex picture which the "broken plurals" present. We have seen that these forms started out as singulars used in a collective sense. A language will have as many forms of such virtual plurals as it has stems capable of carrying a collective connotation. Arabic happens to have forty-four varieties of verbal nouns which may occur with the primary form of the verb; fully in keeping with this luxurious development is the existence of twenty-nine

[27] Wright, Arabic Grammar I. 225.
[28] Ibid. 225–6.

stems (many of which are identical with the verbal nouns) employed for collectives.

In a final analysis of the situation accidents of semantic change must be taken into account. If we follow Worrell's classification we shall regard the word *kitāb* (group b) as a normal singular. But the word is in reality an infinitive of the verb "to write" and hence identical morphologically with the *qitāl* "plurals" found in the other three groups. But whereas abstract forms of the nouns for "dog," "noble," and "friend" came to denote the respective collectives and then plurals proper, *kitāb* was to become specialized in the sense of "book;" another plural had to be added. From a historical point of view, some nouns started out as collectives and developed their nomina unitatis later on; others substituted collective stems for plurals formed with the aid of a special ending; still others were original abstracts which had acquired a concrete meaning, with the result that a new "plural" had to be formed from some other abstract stem. In each case the choice of a given secondary stem may have been influenced by a number of factors, such as primary form, meaning, and analogy. With a wealth of forms to choose from, the contrast in meaning could easily be preserved.[29] The contrast in form was at best a secondary consideration.[30]

[29] Barth's statement on the subject, published nearly fifty years ago (Nominalbildung 417–31), is still substantially correct.

[30] Worrell cites two other positive instances of polarity. One is the use of 'the inferiority sign *t*' to distinguish 'the relatively unimportant second person and feminine from the first person and masculine respectively' (AJSL 41.182; Races 64). The fact is that the *t* which is used as a pronominal element in the second person of the verb represents the personal pronoun *'an-tā/tī* 'thou', while the *t* in the feminine forms *qatal-at, ta-qtul,* and the like, is based on the feminine ending *-at*. The respective formatives for person and gender are absolutely heterogeneous. The other instance concerns the use of *banāt* 'daughters' in plurals of compounds with *ibn*

2. Another instance of alleged polarity in the use of genders has been seen in the formal contrast between Hebrew *'āḇôṯ* "fathers" (with fem. pl. ending) and *nāšîm* "women" (with masc. pl. ending).[31] But "fathers" and "women" are not proper opposites, and it can be shown that the two words in question had nothing to do with one another's plural ending. The respective suffixes were acquired independently. *nāšîm* contains an old collective of the word for "human being" (cf. Arabic *nās*), which had been specialized for "women," and the plural ending *-îm* which was added pleonastically to strengthen the collective connotation. Similar combinations are found in the Hebrew words for "bricks," "bees," "fig-cakes," "barley," and a number of others, not one of which bears the slightest semantic relation to "fathers."[32] The norm in all these cases is: collective form + masculine plural ending. Why the corresponding feminine ending was not used for this purpose is open to speculation. It is a fact, at any rate, that the latter suffix (*-āt*) is secondary development from the singular ending (*-at*).[33]

The view that *'āḇôṯ* contains the feminine plural suffix

'son' when these compounds are used for names of animals and other objects (Races 63–4), but not of persons (Wright, Arabic Grammar 1.196). Thus *ibnu dā'irin* 'son of the lewd,' 'young stallion camel' appears in the plural as *banātu dā'irin,* without any regard for the actual sex of the object. But in this case *banāt-* is not properly a feminine plural; it is an original singular collective form of * *bin* 'son,' viz., * *binat-* whose present form is due to the analogy of *banat-* 'daughters'. Such a use of the collective 'sons' would have its exact parallel in Arabic *'iḫwat* (sing.) 'brothers' and Hebrew *'aḇôṯ* 'fathers,' for which see below.

[31] G. Bergsträsser, Einführung in die semitischen Sprachen 15 (1928); Hebräische Grammatik, Verbum 5 (1929); Meinhof, Enstehung flekt. Sprachen 75; Bauer and Leander, Hebr. Gramm. 1. 515, explain the ending of *'āḇôṯ* as due to the analogy of **'immôṯ* 'mothers'.

[32] See note 17, and Bauer and Leander, Hebr. Gramm. 1.515–6.

[33] Speiser, JAOS 56. 41 [see now above, p. 427] and the references there given.

is due, however, to wrong analysis. **abū*[34] belongs to the small class of proto-Semitic kinship-terms whose stems ended in a vowel; another such term is **'aḫū* "brother." Now **'aḫū* + the abstract ending *-at* (which was to become the common feminine suffix) develops in Hebrew the form *'āḥôṯ* (< **āḫātu*) and the value "sister:" The long *ô*-vowel is the result of contraction (of the final stem-vowel and the *a*-vowel of the ending). The absolute form "sisters" does not occur in Biblical Hebrew; but construct forms of this word presuppose **'ăḥāyôṯ*,[35] from an original **'aḥū+at*. Hence the plural for "fathers" should be **'ăbāyôt*. Our *'āḇôṯ* is just as plainly singular in form as *'āḥôṯ* "sister," not "sisters." The failure to regard these two words as morphologically identical must, of course, be ascribed to the ultimate differentiation in number: whereas *'āḥôṯ* means "sister" (sing.), *'āḇôṯ* stand for "fathers" (pl.).

I have elsewhere attempted to show how the word for "father," equipped with an abstract formative, came to have in Hebrew a collective sense.[36] The underlying meaning was probably "parentage." [37] A semantic extension of the same basic word in another direction may be seen in Akkadian *abūtu* "fatherhood, parentage," which

[34] The exact character of the final vowel is unknown since we find it only in contractions with case-endings. These contractions in the masculine forms result in Hebrew in *î* (from the genitive), in Aramaic in *â* (from the accusative). Arabic lost the final vowel of these stems (*'ab, 'aḫ*). However, various derivative forms with *-w-* favor an original stem-ending *-ū*.

[35] Josh. 2.13; Ezek. 16.52; Job 42.11; I Chron. 2.16.

[36] JAOS 56.40 [above, p. 425 f.].

[37] Arabic does precisely the same thing with *'aḫ* 'brother,' whose abstract form is specialized for the plural: *'iḫwat* 'brothers'; cf. C. Brockelmann, Grundriss der vergleichenden Grammatik der semitischen Sprachen 1.427 (1908). In this case, however, the plural ending could not be suspected, as it has been in the parallel Hebrew form *'āḇôṯ*, because the stem-ending of the Arabic word assumed consonantal function, thus preventing contraction.

develops in the Nuzi dialect the value "co-parentage," and thence "(adoptive) mother." [38]

It takes thus a singularly unilateral view to make polaric opposites out of Hebrew *'āḇôṯ* : *nāšîm*. By the same token English forms of the type *foot* : *feet* should also reflect the principle of polarity. Historical data, however, show the English forms to be due to conditioned vowel alternation and subsequent analogic leveling.[39] By considering historical processes the correct perspective is restored. The introduction of polarity as a factor in Hamito-Semitic linguistics is traceable all too frequently to a lack of historical perspective.

3. The verbal system of West Semitic presents numerous problems to the student of comparative Semitic linguistics.[40] After eliminating secondary developments of a phonetic, morphological, and semantic nature we are left with the basic question of the rise of an active afformative conjugation (theme *qatal-tā*). A corollary of this development, in which Akkadian proper did not share, is the difference in the vocalism of the active themes on the one hand and the neuter themes on the other, a difference which gives the impression of premeditated contrast:

[38] See Speiser, Annual of the American Schools of Oriental Research 10.11. The semantic changes exhibited by the respective abstract forms of the two kinship-terms under discussion are illustrated in the following schematic grouping:

Basic Form	Abstract Form
*'*abŭ̌* 'father'	Hebr.: fatherhood'; 'fathers' Akk.: parentage'; 'mother(hood)'
*'*aḫŭ̌* 'brother'	Hebr.: 'Geschwister-; 'sister' Arab.: 'brotherhood'; 'brothers'.

See also JAOS 56.40 [above, p. 425 f.].

[39] Cf. Sapir, Language 197–203 (1921).

[40] For the latest literature see Bergsträsser, Verbum 9–10, and Driver, Problems of the Hebr. Verb. Syst. 155–7.

	Afformative Conjugation ("Perfect")	Preformative Conjugation ("Imperfect")
Active:	*qatal-tā*	*ta-qti/ul*
Neuter:	*qati/ul-tā*	*ti-qtal*

It is evident that within a given stem there is disagreement between the thematic vowels of the two tenses: *qatal-tā* : *ta-qti/ul* (*a* : *i/u*); but there is complete correspondence between the respective thematic vowels of the active perfect and neuter imperfect: *qatal-tā* : *ti-qtal* (*a* : *a*), and vice versa: *qati/ul-tā* : *ta-qti/ul* (*i/u* : *i/u*). No satisfactory explanation of this contrast in vocalism has yet been offered. Compelled thus to rely in the main on purely mechanical factors, Bergsträsser joined the school of Meinhof and injected wholesale doses of polarity into his reconstruction of the West Semitic verb.[41] Since the original definition of the process was not elastic enough for his needs, Bergsträsser had to lift some of its restrictions; his plea of "guilty" scarcely minimizes the offense.[42] But even if we grant all of Bergsträsser's premises, the solution will not be a permanent one. It will be at best a stop-gap, because polarity, as used by him, is in the last analysis descriptive and not explanatory.

A more recent attempt to solve the problem under discussion is that of G. R. Driver. He reproduces much of Bergsträsser's argument,[43] but concludes that polarity may not have been the sole arbiter in the matter of vocalism.[44] Other causes are found in phonetic influences and in the suitability of a given vowel to express the required

[41] Verbum 10–4, 89, 92.
[42] Ibid. 6.
[43] Cf. e.g., Driver, Problems 17–20 and Bergsträsser, Verbum 10–4.
[44] Problems 72–3.

meaning. Driver's presentation is not made lucid by his adherence to the theory of vowel symbolism.[45]

The following schematic sketch is organized on a strictly historical basis, making use of recognized chronological stages which Bergsträsser himself did much to clarify. It is my contention that the same basic factor, viz., the underlying sentence-type, determined the systematization of the vocalism throughout the history of the Semitic languages. In other words, the development of the active form *qatal-,* which we witness in the second millennium B.C., is the logical and consistent application of a principle that was at work in pro-ethnic times.

a. There are two traceable types of primitive Semitic sentence: [46] the verbal, which employed the actor-action form **ta-q(a) ti/ul-* "thou -st" (pronominal element + verbal theme), and the nominal, expressed by the equational scheme [47] **qati/ul-tā* "x (art) thou" (noun + implied verbal copula + pronominal element).[48] Although

[45] I can see no linguistic advantage in statements to the effect that a given form was vocalized 'with the soft or light *i* to express stativity or passivity and the hard or heavy *a* to express activity'; see ibid. 72.

[46] It is not necessary to contribute here to the rather academic speculation as to which particular verbal form (imperative, preterite, infinitive, each of which has its supporters) was the earliest in the language. Nor does it matter whether verbal and nominal forms existed side by side from the beginning, or not. For our present purposes it will suffice to go back to that late, although still prehistoric, period when the two basic sentence-types were fully established.

[47] For the terminology see L. Bloomfield, Language chap. 11 (1933).

[48] Logical considerations compel the use of the second-person forms as paradigmatic in historical discussions, instead of the third-person forms, as is commonly done. In both types of Semitic conjugation (preformative and afformative) third-person forms are demonstrably later than the other two. The same pronominal elements underly in both conjugations the forms for the first and second persons respectively, whereas the third person employs in the preformative conjugation a dissimilar pronominal element, and in the afformative conjugation no pronoun at all. Moreover, in the latter conjugation there are accentual differences between the first and second persons on the one hand, and the third person on the other (cf. Arab. *qatál-tu, qatál-ta,* but *qátala*), which are the indirect result of the disparate origin of the

either type of predication may have exhibited externally several vowel-sequences, one such sequence prevailed demonstrably in both sentence forms:

a-i/u,

since it becomes basic in the two resulting "conjugations," the preformative, or active (**tá-q(a)ti/ul* > **tá-qti/ul*), and the afformative, or neuter (**qatí/úl-tā*). So far from any contrast in this respect, we have absolute identity instead.[49] The only decisive element was the position of the pronoun, which clearly was conditioned by the sense stress (actor-action as against nominal equation).

b. In crystallizing these forms into a verbal system East Semitic (Akkadian) and West Semitic (Aramaic, Canaanite, Arabic) pursued divergent paths. The Akkadian system is objective and impersonal, the verb thus assuming stative character.[50] The neuter afformative conjugation becomes the "permansive," and the active preformative verb is established as the "preterite," which is joined presently by a cognate durative "present" (*taqáta/i/ul*).[51] The closer association of the two original categories results in the addition of neuter forms to preformative themes, with a necessarily neuter or passive sense (*nadin* "given" to *ináddin* "is, was giving"), and in supplementing afformative themes with verbal forms

---

forms in question. Finally, the second person influenced in West Semitic the consonantal afformative of the first (*t* instead of *k*). To start with * *qátala* rather than * *qatál-tā* would, therefore, be anachronistic and generally disadvantageous.

[49] Again it would be futile to speculate how and why the vowel-sequence *a-i/u* came to prevail. The fact is that it did.

[50] To use 'stative' as a term descriptive of 'Aktionsarten'; for the contrast between objective and subjective verbal systems see Bergsträsser, Einführung 11 (based on Landsberger, Die Eigenbegrifflichkeit der babylonischen Welt, Islamica 2.355–72[1927]).

[51] For the position of the dialect of Ras Shamra see A. Goetze, The Tenses of Ugaritic. JAOS 58.266–309.

(*imruṣ* "suffered" alongside *maruṣ* "painful"). These extensions were achieved by purely external means. **qati/ul-tā* > *qatlā-ta* added a verbal class on the analogy of *ta-qti/ul,* while the latter acquired a nominalized class after the model of *qati/ul-*. The vocalism of the new forms was borrowed from their respective prototypes. Subsequent individual adjustments are due to phonetic and semantic considerations.

The West Semitic system, on the other hand, bears a personal and subjective character which imparts to the verb a temporal orientation. The neuter conjugation becomes the "perfect," the active conjugation the "imperfect." In such a system neuter forms will soon require means for aspective and temporal differentiation; the afformative class adds thus preformative by-forms. West Semitic accomplishes this extension of the paradigm in a manner quite different from Akkadian. Corresponding to the psychological contrast between the underlying sentence-types and the consequent syntactical reversal of the position of the pronominal elements, there is here also the internal reversal of the stem-vowels: *qatíl-tā* > *tíqtal-*; *qatúl-tā* > *túqtal-*.[52] The stress-accent, which rests in early West Semitic on the non-final long syllable nearest the end, may have been a contributory factor in this transposition. For with the accent thus determined by position, the accented thematic vowel of the afformative class is transferred to the accented position in the preformative class, while the unaccented vowels exchange positions automatically.

The next step is easy to follow. West Semitic tended

[52] The possibility of such a reversal shook Bergsträsser's confidence in polarity; cf. Verbum 13. See also F. R. Blake, The Internal Passive in Semitic, JAOS 22. 45–54 (1901), and A. Ungnad, Zeitschr. d. deutsch. morg. Ges. 59.766–8 (1905). The part which sentence-types may have played in these changes has not been considered thus far.

to specialize its two neuter forms in that *qátil-* signified a temporary state or condition, while *qátul-* indicated a permanent state of a naturally inherent quality; this is still the situation in Arabic.[53] Accordingly, the new form *túqtal-* developed a passive function and came to be used for passives with transitive themes; on the other hand, *tíqtal-* became the common imperfect to *qátul-* as well as *qátil-*.

At the end of this stage the basic verbal system of West Semitic appears as follows:

	Afformative Conjugation (Perfect)	Preformative Conjugation (Imperfect)
Active:	*x*	*táqti/ul*
Neuter:	*qatíl-tā*	*tíqtal* (> with *qátil-* and *qátul-*)
	qatúl-tā	*túqtal* (> passive with transitives)

c. The final stage in the completion of this pattern was the addition of an active perfect to *táqti/ul*. By the process of analogic back-formation the accented vowel of the imperfect became the thematic vowel of the perfect: *qxtál/tā*. In the choice of the first vowel the analogy of the long-established forms *qatíl-tā*[54] and *qatúl-tā,* where the *a*-vowel is constant, was decisive; *qatál-tā* was the inevitable result.

4. Perhaps the strongest argument which advocates of polarity have used in support of their theory is the disagreement between the gender of the numerals "three"

[53] Cf. Wright, Arabic Grammar 1.30; Driver, Problems 12; see also F. R. Blake, The so-called Intransitive Verbal Stems in Hebrew, JAOS 24.145–204 (1903).

[54] It is perhaps pertinent to stress once again the fact that according to the above account the origin of the second *a* of *qatál-tā,* the chief difficulty in previous discussions, was determined automatically. The same principle which led to *tí-qtal-* and *tú-qtal-* in the neuter forms was responsible for *qatál-tā* in the active class.

to "ten" and that of the things numbered. For "five sons" the Semite would say **ḫámišat- banī,* i.e., with the numeral in the feminine, while "five daughters" is **ḫámiš-banāt-,* the numeral lacking the feminine suffix. This syntactical disagreement furnishes the only instance where the conditions are precisely as demanded by Meinhof's theory. Furthermore, it is also the only time that a process linked with polarity [55] is common to Semitic in general instead of affecting but a part of this linguistic group. It follows that if this curious behavior of the numerals was indeed due to polarity, the process was in evidence in primitive Semitic.

Upon closer examination,[56] however, polarity proves to be once again a misleading label. The ending *-at* found with these numerals was originally an abstract formative which had nothing to do with gender; its feminine connotation was demonstrably a later development. **ḫámišat-* meant "pentad" "quintet," **árbaʿat-* "quartet," and so on,[57] the digits "three" to "ten" having started out as abstract nouns, without any relation to gender. This is made clear by the fact that these forms precede the thing numbered, while "one," which is expressed adjectivally, follows its noun.[58] Furthermore, Akkadian may express "the four regions of the world" by *kebrāt erbettim* "the regions of the quartet," thus emphasizing the character of the numeral as an abstract noun. Originaly, **ḫámišat-*

[55] Cf. Bergsträsser, Einführung 15; Driver, Problems 72.

[56] See JAOS 56.39 [above, p. 423.]

[57] The priority of the ('feminine') forms in *-at* was not disputed by the older grammarians; see the summary in Sven Herner, Syntax der Zahlwörter im Alten Testament 4–12 (1893). A different view is taken by Reckendorf and approved by Brockelmann, Grundriss 2.274–5.

[58] 'Two' is also an adjective, but it frequently follows the analogy of 'three' to 'ten' in behaving like a noun that governs a genitive; cf. Brockelmann 273.

must have been capable of numbering both male and female beings.[59]

The present syntactical peculiarity has to be connected with the development of grammatical gender in Semitic. The old abstract and collective ending _-at_ had been specialized as the designation of the feminine, and the thoroughgoing dichotomy of genders which followed embraced not only adjectives and such nouns as now employed _-at_ for purposes of grammatical differentiation, but also those nouns which had long used this ending formative.[60] Thus, "one daughter" became _*bín-(a)tu áḥad-(a)tu,_ alongside _*binu 'áḥadu_ "one son." At the same time, however, the abstract noun _*ḫámišat_ "pentad," and the analogous forms for the other digits from "three" on although they were now feminines grammatically, could still be used with both _*banī_ "sons" and the new form _*banāt-_ "daughters," because they appeared in a possessive phrase and not as appositions; the position was the same as in _*kull-at- banī_ "the totality of sons, all the sons," and _*kull-at- ban-āt-_ "all the daughters."

In course of time, however, the circumstance that the inherited class formative of the digits in question was the same as the new feminine designation brought about the correlation of such groups as:

*binu 'áḥadu (masc.)
*bín-(a)tu 'áḥad-(a)tu (fem.) and _*ḫámiš-at-_ { _banī_ / _ban-āt-_.

The analogy of the adjectives, and especially of the numeral "one," introduced dichotomy into the other digits. "Two" appeared as _*ṯínay_ and _*ṯín(a)tay,_ the latter with feminines. It is this regular use of _-(a)t_ in the feminine forms for "one" and "two" that rules out immediately

[59] This is still often the case; cf. Herner, op. cit.
[60] See Speiser, JAOS 56.37–41 [above, pp. 420–427]

any possibility of polaric contrast in the numerals. For if the irregular syntax of the digits "three" to "ten" is ascribed to polarity, the regular behavior of the two remaining digits would, paradoxically, now have to be explained.

In reality, "two" was to escape confusion of genders because the formative *-(a)t* was overshadowed in this instance by the final dual ending *-ay*. But with the numerals "three" to "ten" dichotomy led to analogic creation based on the pattern

**banī* : **ḫ̮ámiš-at-*
= **ban-āt-* : *x*,

whence the introduction of the form **ḫ̮ámiš-*, i.e., without the ending *-at*. There remains only the question why the genders were not brought into agreement after the splitting up of the digits. In other words, why did not *ḫ̮ámiš-* go with **banī* and **ḫ̮amiš-at-* with **ban-āt-*? The answer is bound up with the history of the respective forms. We know that both **ḫ̮ámiš-at-* and **banī* were old forms, while **ban-āt* is considerably later than the feminine signification of *-at,* from which the plural *āt* subsequently developed. The neologism **ḫ̮ámiš-* was assigned, therefore, to the other neologism **ban-āt-* and not to the ancient masculine form; the two secondary formations were brought together.

To sum up, polarity as a linguistic principle cannot be established for the Semitic languages. It has been linked by some writers with the tendency of Semitic towards dichotomy in number and in gender, but whereas that dichotomy is consistent and thoroughgoing, polarity could be suspected only in a few isolated instances. Moreover, the favorite examples of polarity turn out to be illustrations of well-established linguistic processes;

other examples prove to present no contrast whatever, when viewed historically. But even if a given problem, which polarity has been called in to solve, should happen to elude explanation, that problem will not be a case of polarity merely because it is difficult. This would be a lazy man's way out. At best, polarity may be regarded as a label for certain contrasted linguistic phenomena empirically viewed. Even in this limited sense, however, the designation is dangerous in that it may hamper ultimate solution by conveying a false sense of security. It should be abandoned altogether.

A Note on the Derivation of *šumma*

The derivation of words used as sentence markers involves more than mere etymology. Beyond the origin of the given word there arises in such instances the question of a whole sentence type. A word of this kind is Akkadian *šumma,* which introduces the normal equivalent of the conditional sentence; it is always followed by the verb in the indicative.

For nearly half a century *šumma* has been traced back to the root *šym* "establish." It will be shown that this etymology is unsatisfactory on a number of counts. I believe that another derivation, which will be proposed later, suffers from none of the objections that can be raised against the current etymology. On the contrary, the negative arguments in the one case become supporting reasons in the other. The point should be stressed however, at the outset that the evidence on either side is as yet only cumulative and circumstantial, not direct. The problem cannot be conclusively settled, but it should be raised just the same. For this purpose a brief note should suffice.

In ZA 17 (1903) 362-63 A. Ungnad explained *šumma* tentatively as a permansive formation from *šym,* in the D-stem, third feminine plural. Six years later (Hammurabi's Gesetz II 171) he felt justified to take a more positive stand at the expense of a slight modification in his earlier theory: he now viewed *šumma* as a verbal adjective from the D-stem of *šym* followed by the "emphatic *-mà*," the sense remaining "gesetzt." This interpretation has enjoyed almost universal acceptance ever since. F. Thureau-Dangin, for instance, gave it his unqualified approval (Syria 15 [1934] 143-44 fn. 3). T. J. Meek agrees with Ungnad's explanation, but formulates it more precisely by taking *šumma* as "the third masculine singular, the impersonal permansive plus the particle *-ma*" (JBL 44 6; JNES 5 64).

I

The main misgivings concerning this derivation of *šumma* may be listed as follows:

1. On formal grounds, there is the serious problem whether the D-permansive of *šym* would appear with *-u-* not only in Babylonian but also in Assyrian. Furthermore, an impersonal permansive in the required context would function as an adverb. Yet the one adverbial term of possible relevance—in that it may go back to *šym*—appears to show the direct personal form; the term in question is *tušām(a)* "verily" or the like, which has been explained as the second masculine present from the D-stem of *šym*.[1] The semantic development may have been something like this: "you establish" > "one establishes" > "in fact" > "verily."

2. The instance of *tušām(a)* merits closer attention also for another reason. For it carries, potentially, stronger support of the prevailing derivation of *šumma* than has

[1] C. Bezold, Glossar 261b.

yet been offered by any of its advocates. Both words have been alleged to derive from *šym*. What is more, *tušāma* has been explained as an oath particle; now precisely this usage is well attested for *šumma,* which introduces positive oaths when followed by *lā,* but negative oaths when *lā* is absent.[2] Thus Paul Kraus translates *tu-ša-ma am-tu-ut ba-al-ṭa-ku* "ich bin *wahrlich nicht* gestorben, ich lebe!" (italics his).[3] If this view is right, then the striking correspondence between *šumma* and *tušāma* in highly intricate usage would securely establish the further etymological connection, particularly since we should be dealing in both instances with the identical stem (D). On the other hand, if *tušāma,* granting its derivation from *šym,* is functionally not what it seems to be, then the derivation of *šumma* from *šym* might similarly be due to misleading appearances.

The function of *tušāma* is clarified to a degree by the use of its Akkadian analogues *mindē, appūna, pīqa*(*t*), and *ra-i-ma,* all of which have been lumped by the Akkadian grammarians as equivalents of Sumerian n a n / m g a "verily."[4] We find here one base that is plainly nominal (*appūna,* cf. its doublet *apputtum*[5]), one transparent verbal base (*mindē* and its numerous variants[6]), and two forms which appear to be verbal in origin

[2] E.g., Ungnad, VAB 6 (1914) 205h; J. J. Stamm, Die akkadische Namengebung (MVAeG 44 [1939]) 135–6; especially at Nuzi, cf. Chiera-Speiser, JAOS 47 (1927) 55; Gordon, Orientalia 7 (1938) 47–8.

[3] MVAeG 3 6 (1931) 209.

[4] Cf. Jacobsen, JNES 5 (1946) 137 fn. 17.

[5] B. Landsberger, ZA 43 (1936) 73 fn. to line 16.

[6] Thureau-Dangin, RA 31 (1934) 30. The underlying root is obviously *idūm* 'to know' in agreement with the Hebrew and Aramaic analogues of this particle. Beyond this the morphology of the Akkadian forms remains to be clarified. According to P. Jensen, KB 6 (1900) 5 68–9, the stem in question is **madū*. The West-Semitic analogues, however, point strongly to a fusion of the verb with the interrogative pronoun; cf. Heb. *madduaʿ* <*mā*(*h*) *yādūaʿ* "wherefore?" A like development in Akkadian cannot be

(*pīqa*[*t*] and *ra-i-ma*[7]). Of these terms, perhaps the most significant in the present connection is *pīqa*(*t*), which Ungnad is content to view as a synonym of *šumma*.[8] Thureau-Dangin, however, following H. Zimmern and mindful of the Sumerian equivalent, takes the word as an adverb of emphasis and translates "vraiment." [9] The key passage occurs in the bilingual text K 4347, iv 42–45. The pertinent Akkadian part—a frequently discussed saying—is given below in transliteration and translation.[10]

pi-qa a-ma-at-man	Truly I may die;
lu-ku-ul	Then let me spend!
pi-qa a-bal-lu-uṭ[*-man*][11]	Truly I may live;
lu-uš-kun	Then let me put by!

The sentiment expressed here is not far from Isaiah's "Let us eat and drink for tomorrow we shall die," or our "You can't take it with you." And in choice of phrase at least it recalls the passage from the Old Babylonian letter quoted above, viz.,: *tu-ša-ma am-tu-ut ba-al-ṭa-ku*, which may now be translated, "I might indeed have died, (yet) I am still alive."

It follows that both *tušām*(*a*) and *pīqa*(*t*)—and their analogues as well—are adverbs of a strictly attributive character which cannot have any relational bearing on the context. They do not alter the sense of their clauses. And they could be omitted without appreciable loss to meaning.

discounted. The components in that case would be either the animate form of the pronoun and the preterite, in the sense of "who knows?," "perhaps" (preterite for present in this verb for "know" much as in Indo-European); or the inanimate form of the pronoun and the permansive in the sense of "what is known?"

[7] For *ra-i-ma cf.* Jacobsen, JNES 5 137 fn. 17.

[8] Babylonisch-assyrische Grammatik ^{2} 72; ZA 38 (1929) 71.

[9] Analecta Orientalia 12 (1935) 308.

[10] See ibid. 307–10 for literature and comments.

[11] Ibid. 308.

The sharp contrast between such adverbs and *šumma* must by now be fully apparent. Although this particle has not the grammatical force of a conjunction, and hence is not followed by the subjunctive, it is obviously the distinctive element in its clause. This divergence in function alone should be sufficiently striking to cause us to look for the background of *šumma* in entirely different surroundings.

3. Two other objections to connecting *šumma* with *šym* will be mentioned in passing. One concerns the semantics involved. Akkadian *šâmu* means "to establish, decree," and is not independently attested in the sense of "to assume, suppose, posit." The close parallel of, say, German "setzen: gesetzt" is suggestive but by no means conclusive. Further, since *tušām(a)* (granting once again its derivation from *šâmu*) indicates emphatic affrmation, there is doubt whether the same stem would also yield readily a term introducing a hypothesis. It is yet to be proved that this particular semantic development is as natural to Semitic as it is to Indo-European.

The other objection arises from the syntax of the *šumma*-clause. Could the sense "supposing (that)" be expressed in Akkadian without the aid of the subjunctive? It is noteworthy, at any rate, that "you assert that" or the like is *tuššâm(m)a ki*,[12] that is, with a subordinating particle.

4. None of the arguments cited thus far need be conclusive individually, but their cumulative force can hardly be ignored. One final argument is still to be adduced, however, the bearing of which should be sufficient to carry the point unaided. I refer to the normal method by which the conditional sentence is expressed throughout Semitic.

[12] Cf: Meissner, SAI 2650; Deimel, Šumerisches Lexikon 142 330.

Actually, there are two such methods, although the same linguistic process underlies both. This process consists in giving the protasis as a direct statement. The methods employed are:

(a) Asyndesis [13] or, as a variation on this, the use of the ordinary copula; cf., e.g., Heb. *wᵉrāītī mā(h) wᵉhiggadtī lāk* (I Samuel 19 3) "If I see anything I shall tell thee."

(b) The use of special particles to mark the protasis. Wherever their origin is immediately apparent, these particles can be promptly identified as ordinary demonstrative elements. Thus Mehri *hän,* Bib. Aram. *hen,* and Syr. *'en* are all cognates of Heb. *hinnē* "behold," [14] itself no stranger to conditional sentences.[15] Similarly, Ugaritic *hm* is employed both as an interjection and as the initial element in protases.[16] And while the origin of Arab. *'in* and Heb. *'im* remains to be clarified, the probability is near at hand that we have here a usage in close accord with the above instances. In short, so far as our evidence goes, the Semitic conditional sentence—disregarding Akkadian for the moment—was introduced either asyndetically or by means of some demonstrative element.

Returning now to Akkadian, the asyndetic condition is no less at home here than elsewhere within the Semitic family.[17] An added example may be cited from the same bilingual text which was drawn upon earlier in a similar connection:

lu-uš-kun Should I put by,

[13] Cf. C. Brockelmann, Grundriss 2 (1913) 482–4. See also P. Friedrich, Die hebräischen Konditionalsätze (1884).

[14] Brockelmann, op. cit. 635.

[15] Cf. e.g., I Samuel 9 7: *wəhinnē nēlek̲* "if we go (what shall we bring the men?)." For *hinnē* in the apodosis cf. S. R. Driver, Hebrew Tenses [2] 205.

[16] Cf. C. H. Gordon, Ugaritic Grammar (1940) 76, 78.

[17] Brockelmann, op. cit. 484.

ik-ki-mu	They will take it away.
lu-ut-ter-ma	And should I squander,
ma-an-nu i-nam-din	Who will make it up? [18]

One would expect, then, that with so much general agreement between Akkadian and the rest of Semitic, in regard to the conditional sentence, the harmony should extend also to the type of particle employed. Yet if *šumma* is an adverb based on *šym,* the common chain is broken and the Akkadian usage becomes atypical. Nor would it help in this particular case to invoke the aid of Sumerian. For Sumerian t u k u n - b i, the all but exclusive equivalent of *šumma,* has a definite pronominal aspect, the final - b i being employed either in the possessive sense "its" or demonstratively as "this, that"; if the latter is the case, the Akkadian correspondent is *šū, šuati.*[19] The word as a whole means according to Poebel something like "its case (is as follows)," [20] or perhaps "this is the case."

There is thus no comfort in Sumerian for those who would advocate a verbal derivation of *šumma.* Quite the contrary, it would not be unreasonable to suppose that, if one should be disposed to question the inner-Sumerian development of t u k u n - b i , the model for this term might well be sought in Semitic. At all events, neither Semitic nor Sumerian lends color to the current etymology of *šumma.* And we have seen that there are weighty objections to this derivation within Akkadian itself.

II

In preparing my "Studies in Semitic Formatives" (JAOS 56 22–46 [—above, pp. 403ff.]), published in 1936,

[18] Analecta Orientalia 12 310–11.
[19] A. Poebel, Sumerische Grammatik 83.
[20] Ibid. 157.

I arrived at the opinion that *šumma* consists of the demonstrative *šū* plus the particle *-ma*. Since then I have discussed the matter on various occasions with several colleagues. The response has been cautious interest in some cases and a measure of scepticism in others, which is all that might be expected from a hasty oral presentation on my part. To go to print, however, required some positive evidence in favor of the new derivation in addition to the circumstantial case that could be made out for it coupled with the formidable negative evidence against the old view. As stated at the outset, strictly conclusive evidence is still lacking. Nevertheless, some new material has turned up which appears to have sufficient positive bearing on this problem to tip the scales and justify publication at this stage.

The explanation of *šumma* as a compound of the demonstrative *šū* and the particle is free, of course, from the various objections that are inherent in the derivation of the term from *šym*. Further, the assumed pronominal origin would account automatically for the syntax of the *šumma*-clause; such an element would necessarily form part of the main clause. And finally, agreement with the rest of Semitic—not to mention parallelism with Sumerian—would be complete: The conditional sentence is (a) asyndetic; or (b) one which has a particle meaning "this is (so)," "behold" in the protasis, while the apodosis carries with it an implied "then," "in that case."

For all these advantages, however, this derivation of *šumma* could not qualify as an acceptable candidate until one significant phonologic detail had been cleared up. As is well known, Akkadian *š* may represent either an original Semitic sibilant (*š* or *ś*) or the spirant *ṯ*. What is less commonly recognized is the further fact that some

Akkadian syllabaries managed to reflect, in one way or another, that original distinction [21]. Thus the dem. *šū*, e.g., is verified as containing an inherited sibilant, while the relative *šū ša* is shown to trace back to an earlier form with an initial spirant. Hence, should the *š* of *šumma* be derived from a spirant, any connection with the demonstrative pronoun would be disproved once and for all. And one should then be obliged to reconsider the possibility of equating *šumma* with Arab. *tamma* "therefore."

Today this particular contingency is no longer possible. For Goetze has pointed out recently that two of the Mari liver models, whose orthography distinguishes between the respective antecedents of Akk. *š*, show that *šumma* (written *šu-ma* in these particular instances) and the demonstrative *šū* share the same initial sound, an original sibilant in both cases.[22] The strongest potential argument against relating these two terms has thus been eliminated.

The exceptional spelling *šu-ma* brings up the question of the double *m*, which is the regular Akkadian writing in this word and which occurs also on other Mari livers. Is the double *m* of *šumma* original or secondary? The two Mari examples of single writing are not necessarily suggestive because the very texts in question fail to employ double writing even where it is etymologically justified.[23] The double sound, therefore, has to be considered on an independent basis.

At first I proposed to interpret this doubling as sec-

[21] A. Ungnad, Materialien zur altakkadischen Sprache (1916) 21; Thureau-Dangin, RA 23 (1926) 28, and RA 30 (1933) 93; Speiser, JAOS 58 (1938) 187; Goetze, Lang. 14 (1938) 137, and JCS 1 (1947) 79.

[22] Goetze, loc. cit. The Mari livers (RA 35 [1938] 36 ff.) are numbered 14 and 19 respectively.

[23] Note, e.g., *a-ni-um in* No. 19. Isolated single writings of the *m* in *šumma* are found outside Mari.

ondary. For one, the fusion of *šū* and *-ma* into an inseparable form, with a long vowel followed by an enclitic, might furnish in itself valid grounds for doubling. For another, I thought, a deictic *šumma* would be subject to the analogic influence of the common deictic particle *umma.* Goetze has pointed out, however, in a private communication, that *šumma* is already attested at a time when *umma* still occurs as *enma.* He suggests as a possibility an original **šū'* plus *-ma.* It would seem that one need not look any further, especially in view of the posited PSemitic forms **hū'a* "he" and **šī'a* "she," [24] both with the alif-sound to which Hebrew still bears positive testimony.

This is as far as one can go at present. In conclusion, a caution appears to be in order in regard to the translation of *šumma.* The rendering "supposing" leans, either implicitly or explicitly, on the explanation of the term as proposed by Ungnad. This translation can hardly be adequate, even if one chooses to reject the present explanation. For it stresses—unduly, in my opinion—the purely conditional character of what follows. Yet *šumma* is used also with oaths (see above, note 2), the strongest possible form of asseveration. A conjunction like Heb. *'im* "if" has the range to serve as a full-fledged hypothetical element, but it is doubtful whether "supposing" could be credited with like flexibility. Whatever the origin of *šumma* may be, and whatever the syntax of the *šumma*-clause, it is a fact that the term came to possess the force of "if." There is no need for circumlocutions, especially when these imply a derivation which bids fair to be wholly erroneous.

[24] G. Bergsträsser, Einführung in die semitischen Sprachen (1928) 8.

The "Elative" in West-Semitic and Akkadian

1. The present paper links up with one that I read before the American Oriental Society in 1934[1] and published in JAOS two years later.[2] The subject of that study was the origin of the so-called causative in Semitic. The conclusions pertinent to this discussion were briefly as follows:

(a) Semitic formed its causative stems by means of morphemes which ultimately may be reduced to two, one with a sibilant initial, as in the Akkadian šafʿel, and the other with a laryngeal initial, as in the Hebrew hifʿil.[3]

(b) Within the Semitic languages there is a striking correspondence between this verbal morpheme and the initial sound of the third-person pronoun. The prevailing regularity of this correspondence[4] precludes any possi-

[1] JAOS 54 (1934) 334.

[2] Ibid. 56 (1936) 22–33 [above, pp. 404–416].

[3] Subsequent development of *h*- > ʾ- is demonstrated for the causative unambiguously within Aramaic and less directly in Arabic. G. Bergsträsser, Einführung 12, takes it for granted; cf. also JAOS 56.25. I cannot accept the conclusion of C. H. Gordon, Ugaritic Handbook (1947) 72, that "Proto-Northwest-Semitic apparently contained all three types" (i.e., *ś*-, *h*-, and ʾ-); cf. next note.

[4] This statement finds striking support in Minaean where *ś*- characterizes both the third person pronoun and the causative, as distinct from Sabaean where the same functions are performed by *h*-. In Aramaic the limited num-

bility of coincidence.

(c) An interrelationship is thus established which is morphologic but not phonologic.[5] It follows that the pronoun *šū* entered into the formation of the šafʻel just as *hū(')* underlay the formation of the hifʻil.

(d) This specialized application of the pronoun is explained by the fact that the morphemes in question, originally demonstratives, functioned also as pronouns of emphasis.

(e) This explanation, in turn, helps to account consistently for other phenomena usually regarded as unrelated: the use of the Hebrew hifʻil for such non-transitive concepts as colors, physical states, and the like; the formation of Arabic adjectives of color or enduring qualities by means of a morpheme that is identical, at least in form, with the preformative of stem IV (*'aqtala*); and lastly, it accounts also for the Arabic elative proper, with the same preformative, which marks off adjectives from their positive grade.

---

ber of *š*-causatives can be, and generally has been, traced to šafʻels borrowed from Akkadian. The only notable exception to the rule would seem to be Ugaritic, because here the šafʻel is clearly established (alongside the *h*-pronoun), whereas the *h*-causative is rudimentary (see especially Z. S. Harris, JAOS 58 [1938] 103–11). Yet the presence of some causative *h*-forms should suffice to mark the correct historical sequence in Ugaritic, suggesting a specific local development in which the *š*-form (whether imported with prominent culture words from Akkadian—as is the case in Aramaic—or otherwise domiciled) "came to be favored over the common *h(')* stem" (Harris, loc. cit. 111).

[5] And hence also not etymological, a point which cannot be stressed too strongly. If the conditional particle *hm* of Ugaritic is cognate with *šûm*-in Akkadian *šûmma,* as recently maintained by A. Haldar (JCS 4 [1950] 64), then the same *h*:*š* correspondence would have to apply to the respective *h*- and *š*-phonemes in general, at least initially; yet note West-Semitic *šm,* South-Semitic * *šm,* Akk. *šumu* "name" and the countless other instances of the same kind. We cannot, of course, estimate conditions in remote Hamito-Semitic stages. In historic times, at any rate, the pronouns and causative morphemes with sibilant and laryngeal respectively are morphologically parallel but phonologically distinct.

(f) It follows that the Semitic causative is a relatively late form which owes its origin to but one of several prominent applications of specialized morphemes of emphasis.

The discussion below will deal primarily with another type of these emphatic forms, one which the earlier article could take up only in passing. Whereas the first paper dealt largely with the verb, the present analysis will concern itself in the main with adjectives and stative forms related to adjectives. For the sake of convenience I shall apply the term "elative" in a broad sense to the several types to be discussed. On formal grounds this designation commends itself immediately in that the several classes to be discussed relate in one way or another to the recognized elative. An attempt will be made, moreover, to demonstrate that the relationship extends also to meaning as well. The material utilized will be limited to Arabic, Hebrew, and Akkadian. For one, it is in these three languages that the forms involved would seem to have attained their most characteristic development. And for another, Akkadian, Hebrew, and Arabic between them offer ample assurance that a phenomenon common to all three belongs to the field of Comparative Semitic.[6]

[6] With regard to the problem here under discussion, this fact is amply stressed in H. S. Nyberg's study on Wortbildung mit Präfixen in den semitischen Sprachen, Le Monde oriental 14 (1920) 177 ff., where an impressive amount of relevant material has been gathered and analyzed. My conclusions coincide with Nyberg's, and those of K. Vollers, ZA 17 (1903) 321–32, before him, in finding a close connection between the elative and the causative. We diverge sharply in respect to many details, but most notably in this: Nyberg views all causative prefixes of Semitic as having equal validity in each subdivision of the family, whereas I am able to ascribe this function to but one favorite morpheme in each instance. This is not said to depreciate Nyberg's stimulating and often pioneering efforts; nor can the circumstance be held against him that in dealing with Akkadian he could barely scratch the surface and had to rely on many illustrations that are not relevant.

2. The thesis, then, here to be defended is

(a) that Semitic in general had once an elative or emphatic form indicated by a special prefix, and

(b) that the prefix in question was homogeneous with that of the so-called causative.

Such a view is by no means self-evident. Not only is the presence of an elative in Akkadian unrecognized in Akkadian grammars, but even the antiquity of the form within Arabic itself has been subjected to conflicting estimates.

Some modern students of Arabic hold that the *'aqtal* form of the adjective is a specifically Arabic, and hence recent, development.[7] Others would associate *'aqtal*(*u*) with the verbal stem *'aqtala* (IV),[8] thus assuming an older background for the elative. A common West-Semitic source was advocated as early as 1889 by Paul de Lagarde,[9] who adduced for comparison Hebrew denominatives of the hif'il class which are notable for their intransitive, non-causative connotations. Cognate forms outside Arabic would establish, of course, automatically the pre-Arabic origin of the formation as a whole.

Before we glance at the Arabic-Hebrew correspondences that are involved, it will be useful to break down the *'aqtalu* class into three types: (A) colors, e.g., *'abyaḍ* "white' ; (B) bodily defects and other lasting qualities or conditions, e.g., *'aḫras* "dumb"; (C) elatives proper, e.g., *'aḥsan* "fairer" : *hasan* "fair." On this basis Arabic and Hebrew compare as follows:

[7] Cf. C. Brockelmann, Grundriss 372; F. Rosenthal, Festschrift für Leo Baeck (1938) 175–81, where the problem is clearly stated and the necessary literature cited.

[8] As suggested already by the Kufic grammarians, cf. ZA 17.312.

[9] Übersicht über die im Aramäischen, Arabischen und Hebräischen übliche Bildung der Nomina 120 f.

	Arabic		Hebrew	
Type A	*'abyad*	"white"	*hilbīn*	"became white"
Type B	*'aḫras*	"dumb"	*heḥrīš*	"became still"
Type C	*'aḥsan*	"fairer"	[o]	

Each example stands for its entire type. The formatives employed for the purpose by both languages are precisely the same that are used in their respective causatives. Arabic, however, has reserved the formation for adjectives (all three types, whereas Hebrew has confined it to denominatives corresponding to Types A and B.[10] Each language fills out the pattern in its own particular way. Arabic denominatives to *'aqtalu* take the form *iqtalla* (IX) or *iqtālla* (XI). On the other hand, Hebrew adjectives of Type A appear in the basic stem-form *(lābān* "white"); Type B occurs usually in the form *qittil* (*ḥērēš* "dumb"); [11] Type C has no morphologic representation in Hebrew, being expressed instead either syntactically or by means of prepositions.

It is obvious that the above correspondences are incomplete, however suggestive they may appear to be. They are not sufficient in themselves to demonstrate an underlying generic connection. The possibility of similar though independent developments must be entertained until all chance of coincidence has been eliminated. It so happens that Akkadian has a distinctive contribution to make on this very problem. Special circumstances render

[10] See especially G. Bergsträsser, Hebräische Grammatik II (Verbum) pp. 102–04.

[11] Occasionally *qattul,* as in *šakkulā* "childless," with corresponding verbs in the qal as well as hif'il. In Akkadian the favorite nominal class with this function is *quttulu.* Note also the doubling of the third radical in the Arabic stems IX and XI, which configurate with *'aqtal;* further Heb. nominal forms of the types *ša'nan* "peaceful" and *'umlāl* "languishing," as well as the *htqtll* verbs, including * *hštḥww* "bowed down."

the Akkadian evidence decisive and far-reaching in more ways than one.

One point above all others is basic to the following discussion. Alongside the established correlation between the causative prefix and the third-person pronoun in Semitic we have seen so far indications of a similar ultimate correlation between the causative and the elative prefixes in Arabic and Hebrew. If Akkadian is to bear out these indications, it too must possess an elative; moreover, that elative has to be homogeneous with the morpheme of the Akkadian causative. It should, furthermore, be remembered that each Semitic language had at any given time no more than one productive causative morpheme. In other words, while Semitic as a family yields jointly the causative morphemes *h*, *'*, *š*, and *s* (descriptively stated), only one of these is at home in a given individual language. Accordingly, it is unsound and futile to posit all four for any one language, as has been done,[12] or even to combine any two of these locally.[13] Conversely, if only the specific causative morpheme of the given language proves to correlate with the third-person pronoun on the

[12] E.g., by Nyberg, with serious harm to his central thesis. His view that **'arba'-* "four" is a Common Semitic instance of the elative-causative morpheme (p. 224) is, of course, untenable because (1) only one numeral is affected, and (2) a phonologic explanation accounts for the form very well. A similar role for the initial in * *šamay* "heaven" (p. 210) seeks the support of an unsupportable etymology.

[13] The customary props for an elative '- in Hebrew, namely, *'ak̠zāb̠* "deceitful," *'ak̠zār* "cruel," and *'ayt̠an* "enduring" (cf. J. Barth, Nominalbildung [1899] 224) collapse for lack of native etymologies (with the possible exception of the first example which may well be mere coincidence), and more especially because of the more numerous instances where such an '- can be nothing else than prothetic and hence phonologic; cf. Bauer-Leander 487. Even Barth is obliged to concede (loc. cit.) that the reason for an elative in these isolated instances is not apparent. The elative element in Hebrew has to be *h*-, and is indeed found in this form in the numerous examples of the intransitive hif'il.

one hand[14] and the elative morpheme on the other, the underlying significance of such a correlation should be immediately apparent.[15]

3. Since the Akkadian causative morpheme is *š* plus a a vowel, the posited Akkadian elative should have the same initial consonant if the correlation advocated above is valid. As a matter of fact, Akkadian possesses a large number of nominal forms with an initial non-radical *š*. The first attempt at a comprehensive explanation of these forms was made, more than thirty years ago, by H. S. Nyberg.[16] Although much of Nyberg's detail is now out of date and out of focus, which makes his specific conclusions untenable, his general approach was sound in that he sought to relate pertinent phenomena in the pronominal, nominal, and verbal categories. Nyberg viewed the nominal forms with *š*-initial as the product of relative *ša* plus genitive. The relative particle he connected ultimately with the demonstrative *šū*.[17]. The question, however, of a possible Akkadian elative was not pursued.

It is clear today that Akkadian nominal forms with *š*- go back to more than one source. It remains to be established whether among these forms there exists a sufficient number with clearly elative connotation. I ventured an express reference to the elative in Akkadian in the afore-mentioned paper of 1934,[18] and W. Eilers made the same suggestion independently in a paper read in

[14] For the apparent exception of North Arabic (South Arabic remains regular) see above, note 4. The disparity within Ugaritic has been dealt with in note 4.

[15] The three main types of Arab. *'aqtal* could not, then, be regarded with Brockelmann, Grundriss 372 as "ganz junge, speziell arabische Bildungen."

[16] Op. cit. (note 6) 191 ff.

[17] The two, moreover, cannot be related for phonemic reasons; cf. JCS 1 326 [above, pp. 462 f.].

[18] P. 32.

1936.[19] In their translations of given š-forms some contemporary Assyriologists consistently indicate an elative force; others, however, have not observed this usage. The problem calls, therefore, for a systematic inquiry.

At this point the reminder may not be amiss that the term "elative" is being used here in the broader sense of some specially emphasized connotation. It has to be applied in Arabic to a group of adjectives which we had reason to subdivide into three types (cf. A, B, and C, above). The pertinent Hebrew examples are stative verbal forms. The Akkadian instances to be adduced will be found to include nominal forms (substantives, adjectives, and verbal nouns), stative verbs, as well as transitive forms. They will prove to correspond in part to typical Arabic forms, particularly Type C, and in part to characteristic Hebrew forms; in some instances moreover, Akkadian turns out to possess elative types not known elsewhere in Semitic.

Because of inner-Akkadian conditions the distinction between adjectival and stative verbal bases in Akkadian is even less sharp than in Hebrew or Arabic. Adjective and "permansive" are often interchangeable in that the "permansive" functions as an adjective predicatively employed, while the converse use of apparent "permansives" in an attributive sense (equipped with the nominative ending) is also well attested. For our present purposes the ultimate difference between the two is immaterial. What matters only is the question whether a given š-form attributively used might not be regarded as a "permansive" of the causative stem. In most such instances the context will normally suggest the correct division: an š-form in apposition to clear adjectives will

[19] ZDMG 89 (for 1935) 18 *. But it is the šaf'el as such that constitutes the starting point in Eilers' opinion.

usually have to be classified as an adjective.[20] Moreover, a form like *ušalbar* (see below) which can mean only "becomes old," and not "is made old," establishes conclusively and independently the existence of non-causative *š*-forms even with the verb. The evidence, in short, is cumulative in the main.

The examples listed below are by no means exhaustive. They have been singled out primarily for the relative clarity of their meaning and context. Marginal or ambiguous cases have been left out altogether. The intent throughout has been to emphasize the typical rather than the exceptional. In order to hold the presentation down to manageable proportions, citations for each example have been limited to the necessary minimum.

4. The first group to be considered consists of bases whose adjectival connotation is usually apparent. The basic sense may be described in general as normative, in that the qualities or states in question are (a) meliorative, or (b) deteriorative. The *š*-form signifies in each instance some intensification of the basic meaning.

a. The šurbū Class

rabū "great" : *šurbū* "supreme"

As an epithet of gods and goddesses *(šurbūtum)* passim.[21] Not "magnified"[22] which would scarcely be the most suitable divine epithet as applied by mortals. Cf.

[20] As it must be also in such phrases as *ašru šupšuqu* for reasons of grammar (scarcely a predicative construction) as well as of meaning. The significant passage (Sennacherib, Or. Inst. Prism i 69, 71) reads: *eqel namraṣi ina sisī arkabma . . . ašru šupšuqu ina šēpēya remaniš attagiš* "where the terrain was difficult I rode on horseback . . . ; where it was too steep I made my way on foot like the wild-ox." There can be here no question of the terrain having been made difficult (permansive).

[21] For examples cf. M. Weir, L(exicon of) A(ccadian) P(rayers) 353 f.; see also ibid., s.v., for other illustrations of the terms listed below.

[22] So translated by Weir and others.

E(nūma)-e(liš). VII 94: *ša ina ilī*^pl *aḫḫī*^pl*-šu šur-bu-u e-tel nap-ḫar-šú-un* "who is supreme among the gods his brothers, the lord of them all." [23] Alongside the common adjectival forms (used either attributively or as predicates), we have also the abstract, e.g., *šur-bu-ut-ka Igigi* "thy preeminence are the Igigi" KAR 25 obv. ii 15.

(w)atru "exceeding" : *šūturu* "surpassing"

Attributive: *Marduk [bēlu] kab-tu šu-tu-ru* "Marduk [the lord], puissant, surpassing" BA V/3 349.21; similarly, *šu-tu-ru ta-a-šu* "the surpassing spell against him" E-e I 62.[24] Predicative: *šu-tur la-a-an-šu* "surpassing was his stature" ibid. I 99; *e-nu-su lu-u šu-tu-rat* ibid. VI 107 "his sovereignty [25] is indeed surpassing." [26] Note also the constructs or similar compounds which further enhance the elative meaning, e.g., *šu-tur uz-ni/a* ibid. I 59 and *šu-tu-ru ḫa-si-su* King, SCT I 205.6 "surpassing in wisdom, understanding." These epithets are applied to an Ea or a Marduk. Lower creatures (men or animals) may be given the epithet *atram/atar-ḫasīs* (without *š*-).

šaqū "lofty" : *šušqū* "exalted"

šu-uš-qu [27] *ma-'-diš e-li-šu-nu a-tar mim-mu-[ma]* "greatly

[23] W. von Soden, ZA 47 14. For greater simplicity, the line count in E-e is given after R. Labat, Le Poème babylonien de la Création.

[24] Note also the Old Babylonian passage . . . *šu-tu-ru-um ša er-pí-e-tim* "the excessive . . . of the clouds" ZA 43 310.21.

[25] This rather than "high priesthood" would seem to be the correct meaning of *enūtu;* note especially that en outranks both dingir and lugal in such passages as Kramer, Sumerian Mythology 116.3. The elevation of Marduk (and of Enlil before him) in the E-e passage cited above clearly harks back to such celestial rankings.

[26] This force of *šūturu* should help to explain the Hebrew cognate in the disputed form *tôṯar* Gen 49.4 in which a textual error has often been suspected. It makes admirable sense as it stands ("thou shalt [not] excel"). The pertinent verses (3–4) may therefore be rendered: "Reuben, thou art my first-born, my might and the first fruits of my strength, exceeding (*yeṯer*) in rise and exceeding in power. Unstable as water, thou shalt not excel, etc."

[27] Variant gives the permansive *šu-uš-qī.*

exalted was he [Marduk] above them, exceeding throughout" E-e I 92. Cf. also *lu-u šu-uš-qú-ma ma-ru* . . . "verily exalted is the son . . . [Marduk]" ibid. VI 106. The base stem alone was felt to be sufficiently "elative" in force to serve as a favorite divine epithet; cf. Tallqvist, Akkadische Götterepitheta 229 f. Marduk, however, requires superlatives as is shown by *šušqū* and the added emphasis of *mādiš* and *elišūnu*.

(w)aqru "precious" : *šūquru* "most precious"
[*š*]*u-ut-tum šu-qu-rat* "the dream is most precious" Gilg. Th. Pl. 18.39; *šap-tan šu-qu-ra-a-tuš* "whose lips are most precious" Thureau-Dangin, TU 51.42; [N]A$_4$[^{pl}] *ni-siq-tú* NA$_4$ *šu-qu-ra-tú* "choice stones, most precious stones" Nabonidus, Eski-Harran iii 25 f.[28]

As the above examples indicate, most occurrences in this group are references to gods. Each constitutes a suitable analogue of Arabic *'akbar*, i.e., an elative of Type C.

b. The šupšuqu Class

pašqu "difficult" : *šupšuqu* "most difficult"
pa-aš-qat né-bir-tum šup-šu-qat ú-ru-uḫ-ša "difficult is the crossing, most difficult the way thereto" Gilg. Th. Pl. 39. 24. This is an instance of what may be called climactic parallelism wherein the second member of a sequence introduces a heightened aspect of the first. Cf. also *áš-ru šup-šu-qu* "terrain unusually difficult, too steep" D. D. Luckenbill, Sennacherib 166.71 (see above, note 20); *le-é-as-su šup-šu-qat-ma* "his wisdom is most difficult" ZA 43 66.257. Note particularly *šapšaqu*, a plainly independent nominal formation, e.g., *ilī*^{pl} *ab-bé-e-šu i-ṭe-ru ina šap-ša-*

[28] B. Landsberger, Halil Edhem Volume (1947) 128.

qí "the gods his fathers he rescued in distress E-e VI 127, and cf. the parallel *i-na pu-uš-qí dan-ni* ibid. VII 23.

marṣu "ill, suffering" : *šumruṣu* "sorely afflicted, painful"

mar-ṣu šum-ru-ṣu arad-ka "ill, sorely afflicted is thy servant" King, Magic 22.11, once again with the gradation base stem : elative. For the fem. of this common term cf., e.g., *al-kat-su-nu lu-u šum-ru-ṣa-at-ma* "be their conduct ever so painful" E-e I 46.

anḫu "weary" : *šūnuḫu* "exhausted"

ana-ku al-si-ki an-ḫu šu-nu-ḫu šum-ru-ṣu arad-ki "I called to thee, thy weary, exhausted, sorely afflicted servant" KB VI/2 128.42 [29] Here we have a succession of three adjectives, the first in base stem, the second an elative of the first, and the third an elative of a synonymous term. Note, further, [*u*]*l i-ba-aš-ši ina gi-mir* ^{d}*I-gi-gi ša šu-nu-ḫu ba-li-ka* followed by [*ina*] *ilī*^{pl} *napḫar ki-iš-ša-ti ša šu-tu-ru ki-ma ka-a-ta* "there is none among all the Igigi more exhausted than thou, (none) among the gods of all the world as surpassing as thou" ibid. 98.45 f. Cf. also *u*$_4$*-mu šu-ta-nu-ḫu mu-šu gir-ra-a-né-e* "the day is extreme weariness, the night weeping" K 3291 (Babyloniaca 7, Pl. XI) 20.

adru "dark, disturbed" : *šu'duru* "in mourning, in consternation"

pal-ḫa-ku-ma ad-ra-ku u šu-ta-du-ra-ku "I am afraid and disturbed and in consternation" V. Scheil, Sippar 6.9 and the various references in Weir, LAP 5; *ilū*^{pl} *lu-u šu-'-du-ru e-liš u šap-liš* "the gods above and below shall be in consternation" E-e VI 143 (ZA 47 7).

In each of the above instances the *š*-form emphasizes some outstanding quality or condition. The elative force

[29] For other occurrences cf. Weir, LAP 22.

involved is brought out with particular clarity by the graded pairs *pašqu-šupšuqu, marṣu-šumruṣu, anḫu-šūnuḫu, adru-šūduru.* The Arabic form *'aqtal* constitutes once again a good analogue.[30] It should be stressed, however, that the Arabic type remains productive throughout whereas the Akkadian examples form a limited and closed group. On the other hand, the obvious popularity of the *š*-form in such compositions as Enūma-eliš points up this usage as one of the characteristics of the so-called hymnal-epic dialect, which goes back to Old Babylonian times.[31]

Closely allied are *š*-forms from what are predominantly stative verbal stems, which yield a durative connotation:

pašiḫ "is at rest, at peace" : *šupšuḫu* "peaceful"

ur-ri-iš la šu-up-šu-ḫa-ku mu-ši-iš la ṣa-al-la-ka "I have no repose by day (or) rest by night" E-e I 38; note the parallel *ṣallāku* (without *š*-) which confirms the non-causative force of *šupšuḫāku.* Cf. also *(ul-tu) šu-up-šu-ḫi-iš i-nu-uḫ-ḫu* "(after) he had rested peacefully" E-e I 75; *nu-uḫ ti-šab šup-ši-iḫ* "rest, sit down, be at peace" KAR 58 19.

dalip "is restless" : *šudlupu* "agitated"

an-ḫu šu-nu-ḫu šu-ud-lu-pu arad-ka "thy weary, exhausted, agitated servant" RA 25 112.5; cf. also JCS 5 65.

etiq "has passed" : *šūtuqu* "surpassing"

šu-tu-qá-at i-la-tim "surpassing among the goddesses" VS X 214 ii 4; *šu-tu-qa-at be-le-e-ti* "surpassing among the mistresses" LSS II/4 p. vi 1.

na'du anxious, reverent" : *šanūdu* "illustrious"

ša-nu-da-at i-la-ti "most illustrious of the goddesses" KAR

[30] In the verb, stem XI in particular provides close semantic parallels. The corresponding Akkadian form appears as *šutaqtulu,* cf. von Soden, ZA 49 178.

[31] Cf. von Soden, ZA 40 170 ff.

158 ii 31. This last example (cf. ZA 41 167) is particularly instructive in that it constitutes a strictly adjectival formation (with *ša-/šu-*), unless the hymn in question is assigned to an Assyrian source.

5. The examples in this section feature once more the non-causative use of *š-*. The connotation, however, is declarative rather than adjectival, with the intransitive hif'il of Hebrew providing here a closer parallel than can be found in Arabic *'aqtal.* Some of the pertinent forms are transparent denominatives; others are based on stative verbs and show either an elative or a durative connotation.

labīru "old" : *e-nu-ma aš-ru šu-ú ú-šal-ba-ru-ma e-na-ḫu* "when this place should become old and weak" (i.e., "weak with age" [31a]) AOB I 70.10 f., and similarly 72.33 f., etc. No causative meaning could readily be forced on this type of occurrence, especially with stative *ēnaḫ(u)* in apposition. This usage should suffice by itself to explode the view that the *š*-form must signify "to cause someone to do something." [32] The analogous Heb. *hizqīn* (in common with many other intransitive hif'ils) carries precisely the same stative connotation achieved by identical morphologic means.

šēru "dawn, morning"; *šumšū,* alongside *mūšu* "night": On account of *i-še-e-er ú-ša-am-ša* "he will be about at dawn, at night" MSL I 53.33 f., cf. ibid. 169, we must translate *ú-šam-šam-ma ù ú-šeš-še-ram-ma* (cf. Meissner, BAW II 46) "(when the moon becomes visible) late or early." [33] Meissner cites the Arabic parallels *'aṣbaḥa, 'am-*

[31a] A usage alanogous apparently to the type *uštašannama utar* CH xr 58, 73 "shall double and return, shall return double," wherein the first of two coordinate verbs serves as an adverbial complement to the other.

[32] E.g., Or. Inst. AS 13 94, 107, 108; cf. JNES 4 248.

[33] Not (with Meissner, loc. cit.) "is dark (like the night), or light (like the morning)."

sā, but fails to adduce the equally significant Hebrew phrase (the syntactic difference is immaterial) *haškēm weha'rēḇ* 1 Sam. 17.16 "morning and evening." In view of the context and the context and the extra-Akkadian evidence, the Akkadian forms cannot, of course, be interpreted with Meissner as causatives (ultimately "to make a night, etc.") with consequent mistranslation of the passage in question. The non-causative meaning, moreover, is independently confirmed within Akkadian by the semantic identity of *išēr-ušešēr;* note also the Arabic cognate *'asḥara* which is used in the same sense.[34] The complete correspondence of Arabic, Hebrew, and Akkadian usage in instance such as these merits particular attention.

There are other declarative forms which may be pertinent in this connection. Cf., e.g., *šumma šu-tam-ṭa-šu balāṭa ur-rak akla i-še[b-bi] šumma šu-uk-lu-la-šu šumma mūtu šum-ma lu-úp-n[u]* ZA 43. 102.26 f. (in an omen composition edited by F. R. Kraus) "if he is brief (in his speech) he will have long life and satisfying food; if he is elaborate, (that means) either death or poverty.[34a] Perhaps likewise worthy of note is *šumma le-mun šu-šur* "if he (in his speech) is wicked (yet) effective" (or the like) ibid. 33. For the first passage cf. the significant Hebrew passage *welō he'dīf hammarbē wehammam'īṭ lō heḥsīr* Ex. 16.18 "he that gathered much had nothing left over, and he that gathered little had no lack." [35] The first of these four hif'il forms corresponds approximately to *šuklulašū* (with an elative nuance in both instances), the fourth to *šutamṭāšū.* Both pairs are clearly intransitive, a fact which would seem to be independently confirmed for the

[34] Cf. H. S. Nyberg, Le Monde oriental 14 260 f.

[34a] This interpretation, with its specific reference to speech (the subject of the composition) rather than to general events ("suffers want: fares well"), I owe to a suggestion by Goetze.

[35] See G. Bergsträsser, Verbum 103.

Akkadian instances by the dative *-šū*. For *šūšur* we may have a close Hebrew analogue in *hiṣlī(a)ḥ*, which often has the stative value of "is, was successful."

6. Like the preceding groups, the present one consists of quadriconsonantal forms, the first consonant being *š*. Unlike the others, however, the fourth consonant is identical with the third: *šlbb, šrbb, šḫrr, šqmm*. In the first two of these instances there exist within Akkadian corresponding nominal forms without *š*-; accordingly, the initial must be a formative and not a radical. In the last two instances Akkadian appears to lack pertinent *š*-less bases.[36] This fact, among others, has led A. Heidel to list them as "quadriliterals,"[37] with *š*- as their first radical. All four terms, however, in spite of two different structural types which are here involved, are interrelated in that each designates a particular emotional-physical state. Moreover, *šḫrr* and *šqmm* have significant morphologic parallels elsewhere in Semitic. In these circumstances, therefore, the *š*- in each instance has to be regarded consistently as formative so that there can be no question of actual quadriliteral stems in any one of these. This is confirmed by further examination.

šalbubu, šalbabu "overwrought" : *labbu* "angry"

ᵈEn-líl ša-al-bu-bu-ú-um (OB) "Enlil, the overwrought" AfO 13 pl. II 10 (and p. 47); *ᵈMarduk šal-ba-bu* "Marduk the overwrought" KAR 59.3

šarbabu "abject" : *rabbu* "humble"[38]

a-mi-ir-šú-nu šar-ba-ba (var. *šar-ba-bi-iš*) *li-iš-ḫar-mi-mu*

[36] For suggested Semitic cognates see Goetze, JNES 4 248.

[37] The System of the Quadriliteral Verb in Akkadian, AS 13. Heidel's argument (p. 94) that the "quadriliteral" *šuḫarruru* cannot go back to a "triliteral" base because Akk. *ḫarāru* means "to dig" is irrelevant since it would presuppose a total absence of homonymous bases.

[38] Cf. B. Landsberger, apud von Soden, ZA 41 153 n. 1.

/im "he who beholds them shall perish abjectly" E-e I 138, etc.; *šar-ba-bi-iš uš-ḫa-ra-am-ma-mu-šu* "they shall make him perish abjectly" ZA 43 70.286. The corresponding factitive (i.e., II-stem from the non-thematic *š*-form) is *lišrabbib* "may he humble" E-e I 161, etc.

šaḫurru "still, numb with fear"; abstract:
šaḫurratu; stative: *šuḫarruru*
šaqummu "still, silent"; abstract:
šaqummatu; stative: *šuqammumu*

The pertinent occurrences have conveniently been listed by Heidel.[39] Heidel's analysis, however, is borne out only in part. It is a fact, of course, that the types *šaḫurru* and *šuḫarruru* exist side by side. According to Heidel both are patterned after "the pure Šafʿel of the triconsonantal verb." [40] This view does not begin to account for all the irregularities involved. Least of all do we find here a convincing explanation for the use of *ša-* in contexts that are mainly Babylonian (some actually Old Babylonian), in place of the expected *šu-*. The difficulties disappear once we have posited as the starting point the adjective *šaḫur(r)u* or the corresponding abstract *šaḫur(r)atu*.[41] The pertinent verbal forms would then be denominatives with quadriconsonantal bases. They are not quadriradicals, however, inasmuch as the first consonant

[39] Op. cit. 26 ff. From the Old Babylonian (Susa) version of the Zū Epic add *šu-ḫa-ru-ur* *dEn-lil* RA 35, 20.2; note the single writing of *-r-* in a text which normally expresses doubling.

[40] AS 13 104.

[41] See the review by Goetze, JNES 4 246–48 and the later account by von Soden, ZA 49 330 ff. Both reviewers view the adjectival forms as the starting point. But whereas Goetze regards the *š-* as ultimately related to the prefix of the šafʿel (p. 248), von Soden is inclined to see here a "numinose Steigerungsform" with the third radical doubled, thus partly supporting Heidel's interpretation. Since we have, however, so many other forms in which the *š-* is neither radical nor causative, it is hazardous to make exceptions of these particular cases, especially in view of the morphologic and semantic parallels in Hebrew and Arabic (for which see below).

is no more radical here than it is in *šarbabu* (or *šaḫluqtu,* for which see below). The sound in question is a special augment, identical in origin with the *š*- of the šafʻel, yet by no means the causative morpheme functionally. Further, it is related in function to the ʼ- in Arabic *ʼaqtal* and the *h*- in Hebrew *hilbīn* which are homogeneous in turn with the respective causative prefixes. Yet the causative function in each instance is only a specialized application within the verbal system.

Hebrew in particular has a significant bearing on the present discussion. In *heḥšā* and *heḥrīš* "became still" [42] we have not only morphologic but also precise semantic parallels to *šḫrr* and *šqmm;* note also Heb. *hiskīṯ,* Arab. *ʼaskata* "became, was quiet." The same means, then, were resorted to in each of these languages in order to convey the idea of "motionless, still," namely, the morpheme of emphasis which recurs as the fixed stem-marker with the causative. All in all, it is scarcely sound to deny to *šḫrr* and *šqmm* underlying bases without *š*- just because these are either lacking in Akkadian or have not been found in the expected meanings.[43]

The fact should be stressed again that the forms under discussion go back to the older periods of the language, being attested in Old Babylonian and common in the hymnal and epic material. This circumstance, apart from testifying to the antiquity of the formation, has a bearing also on the single or double writing of the third consonant involved; for it is precisely in the older periods that doubling is not always expressed with regularity in the texts. Now Heidel states categorically that "the

[42] In the sense of "silent" as well as of "motionless," cf. G. F. Moore, Judges 350.
[43] See above, note 37.

doubling of the third radical" (counting *š*- as the first) is a feature of these forms.[44] Yet a review of his own examples shows that such a rule is by no means self-evident in the present and preterit forms: [45] out of ten forms cited under *šḫrr*,[46] eight are undoubled and only two show *-rr-*; under *šqmm* the count is 2:1.[47] Yet the very same texts will normally write *lišrabbib* (note also the examples cited in the next section). The reason for this disparity in treatment is not clear, to be sure, but the fact should be pointed out nevertheless.

It goes without saying that the present form of the type *ušḫarrar* requires doubling of the first *-r-* regardless of how that form is actually expressed in writing; the question that concerns us here is whether such doubling would be on a par morphologically with the doubled radical in *lišrabbib* and the like. It is a fact, at any rate, that between *šuḫarruru* and *šurabbubu* there is a noteworthy difference in meaning. The first is stative [48] ("became still"), the other factitive ("shall humble"); the one is stem I of a base augmented by *š*- (and hence treated as a quadri-radical), the other is stem II with the same *š*-complement. In other words, the doubling in each case would be of different origin, hence the unequal treatment in writing. But in both instances *š*- is neither radical nor stem-forming,[49] but merely an added lexical element or

[44] P. 93.

[45] The permansive and the infinitive are functionally close to the adjective (*šaḫurru*) and the abstract (*šaḫurratu*) and hence influenced by them in the use of *-rr-* (or *-mm-*).

[46] For Heidel's Type A (pp. 26 ff.). Add also the undoubled occurrences listed in note 39, above. In type B conditions for doubling do not obtain in the present and preterit.

[47] Pp. 34 f.

[48] For the terminology see Goetze, JAOS 64 5.

[49] That is, the meaning which it imparts here is not a regular feature of the established verbal system.

base-complement. As such this *š-* modifies in a specified way a limited number of essentially adjectival types. The augmented base is then taken over by the corresponding denominatives. Since the modifier *š-* is not on a par morphologically with the causative (III-stem) *š-* (in that it does not form a separate verbal stem), *ušḫarir* cannot be described unqualifiedly as a III-stem; neither can *ušrabbib* be similarly described as a III/II-stem. The question may now be posed whether Akkadian ever recognized such a synthetic category as "šafʿel-piʿel" or "causative/factitive."

7. So-called III/II-forms may roughly be divided into three classes: (a) with middle *u/ī* verbs, e.g.,*ušdīk;* (b) with certain strong verbs, e.g.,*ušrabbī;* (c) with *šk'n* and *šp'l*. Type (a) is nothing more than a III-stem whose vocalization coincides with that of the II-stem on purely phonologic grounds: *ušdīk* < **ušadīk*.[50] Group (c) will be discussed in the next section. For the present we are concerned with Type (b).

One of the many distinctive contributions of von Soden's work on the "Hymnal-Epic Dialect of Akkadian" is the convincing demonstration that *š*-forms of the type *ušrabbī* (with no vowel after *š-*, and with the middle radical of the base doubled) are a special feature of that dialect and are all but confined to it; further, that such forms predominate with adjectival bases.[51] It should be stressed here that the doubling of the middle radical is expressed in this instance in an overwhelming majority of the occurrences, in sharp contrast to the single writing in the verbal forms based on *šḫrr, šqmm*. The examples

[50] Goetze, JNES 4 249 n. 15. The same conclusion is reached by A. Poebel, Studies in Akkadian Grammar (AS 9) 71, but by a different process.
[51] ZA 41 151 ff.

cited by von Soden are listed below, without duplicating his references. The respective underlying bases have been in parentheses.

From adjectival bases: *uš-mal-li* (*malū* "full"), *uš-rab-bi* (*rabū* "great"), *liš-rab-bi-ib* (*rabbu* "humble"), *muš-na-me-er* (*namru* "bright"), *mu-uš-pa-az-zi-ir* (*pazru* "secret").[51a]

With stative verbs: *uš-rad-di* "he added" *(redī), lu-uš-ḫal-liq* (*ḫalqu* "missing").

From later texts: *tuš-na-as-si* (*nesū* "distant"), *uš-pa-áš-šaḫ* (*pašḫu* "at rest"), *uš-rap-piš* (*rapšu* "wide").

It is immediately apparent that all of the above examples fall within the same semantic categories that have been encountered in the preceding sections. The corresponding forms outside of the dialect in question appear normally in the II-stem, and they are by no means rare within the dialect alongside the *š*-forms. It remains to be determined whether any appreciable difference exists between the plain II-forms and the *š*/II-forms. Von Soden could find no such distinction. If we bear in mind, however, the results of our analysis so far, a definite difference will not be hard to find.

The following example should prove highly significant: *u-ša-aš-qi* ᵈ*Kin-gu i-na be-ri-šu-nu ša-a-šu uš-rab-bi-iš* E-e I 147, II 34, etc. "She exalted Kingu, made him the greatest among them." The superlative is required here by the context as well as by the syntax. The purpose of the passage is to show that Tiamat made Kingu chief and not just great, which is an attribute that could well have been applied to most of her entourage. Furthermore,

[51a] Von Soden's list included also a form which he read *mu-uš-ta-aq-qi-in* CH iv 11 and connected with *taqnu* "proper, equipped" (ZA 41 143). Subsequently, however, the interpretation was changed to a I*tn* form of *šakānu* (Arch Or 17/2 360 f.).

the normal force of an adjective plus preposition in Semitic is that of a superlative (cf. the use of Heb. *mi(n)* and *b-* in such cases and note the example with *ina* under *šurbū*, above). In consequence, Tiamat can say to Kingu: *lu-u šur-ba-ta-ma ḫa-'-i-ri e-du-ú at-ta* ibid. 154, etc. "thou art indeed chief, my only spouse art thou." The pair *ušrabbiš* : *šurbāta* provides a precise proportion of action: result. In other words, *ušrabbī* is the factitive (II-stem) of *šurbū*, from which alone it must be directly derived, and not the III/II-stem from *rabū*, with which it has only an indirect connection.

The other examples in this group can be interpreted consistently in the same fashion. We have seen already that *ušrabbib* is a factitive based directly on *šarbabu*. To match *ušpaššaḫ* we have *šupšuḫu*, above. For *ušḫalliq* the abstract *šaḫluqtu* "utter destruction" may now be adduced. The forms *mušnam(m)er* [52] and *ušrappiš* conform readily to the adjectival group *šurbū*, and *ušgallit* is semantically related to the pair *šḫrr-šqmm*. The meaning of the *š*/II-stem (avoiding the misleading designation III/II) may, then, be indicated (in slight modification of von Soden's definition) as follows: "to make the object into something that is expressed by the underlying adjectival or stative forms with *š*-." With adjectival bases the sense will be for the most part elative; [53] with stative bases the

[52] While the underlying nominal base may be lacking in Akkadian [note, however, *lū šuwwurā* Gilg. YOT 250, and cf. 256], it would seem to be attested indirectly in Hebrew. Biblical *sanwērīm* "blindness" is surely an abstract based on a borrowed * *šanmurtu* > * *sanmurtu* "intensive, blinding light." The source could only be Akkadian, more specifically Assyrian—on account of the initial *s*.

[53] This sense is already approximated in Goetze's suggestion, JNES 4 248 n. 13 that "the ŠD *ušrabbī*, means 'cause (someone/something) to be made great(er), larg(er), enlarged.'" But no causative stem is involved and no ellipsis (someone/something) is necessary. All we have here is a factitive

emphasis would be on the durative feature of the state or condition involved. Or to put it differently, the former are factitives to what would be in Arabic the *'aḥsan* type; the latter have Hebrew *heḥrîš* as their intransitive analogue. In either instance the *š*- is non-causative, functioning only as a specialized morpheme of emphasis.

One concluding observation has to be made in this connection. The *š*/II-forms just surveyed are favored by a special group of texts: Enūma-eliš, hymns, and royal inscriptions influenced by these religious compositions. Whether or not one concedes the existence of a hymnal-epic dialect, the fact remains that together with the other *š* forms here discussed this material goes back to Old Babylonian times, from which direct examples are not lacking. The class as a whole, then, is traceable to the older stages of the language, becoming rudimentary or altogether inactive in later times. The evidence clearly precludes a late development. This fact lends added importance to the pertinent Semitic analogues, illuminating as they may be in themselves. For the relative antiquity of the Akkadian material in question is further proof that the underlying usage has a common Semitic origin.

8. A brief discussion is now in order concerning *šukēnu* and *šupēlu*. The necessary examples for the various forms of each of these terms have conveniently been listed by Heidel [54] and need not be duplicated. Once again, however, Heidel's interpretation cannot be accepted. He

(stem D or II) to *šurbû* "greater, greatest." Poebel's view (AS 9 69) that the type *ušrabbî* resulted from the identity of meaning of stems III and II is erroneous, as is also his theory (71 ff.) that this formation was of vernacular origin. Its antiquity and its use in the poetic and archaizing compositions are, on the contrary, the marks of an old literary style which is the opposite of popular usage.

[54] Pp. 37 ff.

declines to view the initial *š* as a formative on the ground that *š*-forms could only mean "to cause someone to do something," [55] which is not here the case. Consequently he regards *š*- as radical and concludes that "the forms of *šukēnu* and *šupēlu,* like those of the group *šuḫarruru,* were first adapted to the old šaf'el but that the forms which have come down to us are already on the way toward being modified after the šaf'el-pi'el." [56] This complex explanation reflects to some extent the formal irregularities which these forms actually exhibit, but it fails to account for them. We have seen that the mechanical approach to the *š*-form as an unvarying causative breaks down in scores of instances; the common *šulburu,* to cite but one, is undeniably a "šaf'el," yet it does not mean to "cause to become old," but only "being old." The answer, in short, has to be sought along the same lines as with the groups previousy discussed: *š*- can be non-radical without expressing the causative.

Both *šukēnu* and *šupēlu* have one extraneous feature in common that needs stressing at the outset. They are prominent "culture terms," the one adapted to the social and the other to the economic life of the land. As such, both had a pronounced legal bearing, which in turn may have had much to do with the specializing meaning developed by each. Suitable morphologic emphasis would likewise seem indicated in these circumstances.[57]

Now one of Heidel's objections to taking the *š*- of *šukēnu* and *šupēlu* as a formative is the fact that the posited *š*-less forms have not been found. That this is

[55] Pp. 107, 108.
[56] P. 111.
[57] Note, e.g., the group of juristic terms which take the form *qutullā',* von Soden, Koschaker Volume, 199–207.

not a valid argument has been shown in connection with *šḫrr*. Furthermore, we do have a plausible cognate for at least one of the assumed basic forms. As I had occasion to point out twenty-five years ago,[58] Heb. *peʿullā* "compensation" may give us both a semantic and an etymological parallel to Akk. *šupeultu*. The Hebrew abstract, incidentally, has nothing to do in form with the puʿal. The doubling could well be purely phonologic (as is frequently the case after short *-u-*), a suggestion that is borne out by the synonymous term *poʿal* and the absence of piʿel forms of this particular base. The basic form, then, may be set down as **puʿl* and **puʿlat* respectively (with **puʿullat* as a possible second choice). One of the meanings of *pʿl,* therefore, was "earn a return for services rendered." It goes without saying that such a meaning is admirably suited to Akk. *šupeultu, šupēltu* "exchange." The positing of an underlying Akk. **pʿl* would thus seem to be well justified.

If we assume, then, (all attempts to account for *šupēlu-šukēnu* have to start out with some basic assumption) that oldest Akkadian possessed an abstract **puʿultum* or **puʿullatum,* with some such general meaning as "return for services," the formation **šapʿultum* in the sense of "legally valid, permanent exchange" would be entirely normal. The factitive to this would have to be **ušpaʿʿil* "made an exchange, exchanged," yielding the abstract **šapaʿʿul(la)tum;* note the MA form *šu-pa-ul-ti* KAJ 175.6. With the change 'ʿ>' the historic results could not but be *ušpēl, šupeultu, šupēltu.* The frequency of the transactions involved, moreover, and their established legal standing would soon have eliminated the unaug-

[58] JAOS 47 (1927) 46 (with E. Chiera).

mented **pu'ultu* leaving only the appertaining *š*-forms. The verb in question would be inevitably a II-stem (not a III/II-stem) from an augmented *š-p'l*.

The case of *šukēnu* is more complicated, but so also is its societal background. To start with the established meanings, the term connotes supplication whereby an inferior acknowledges by a special gesture[59] his abject dependence on a superior. In view of the enormous political changes brought about by the conquests under the Dynasty of Agade, it is not surprising that this term should first confront us in the Old Akkadian period.[60] Consequent changes in the social structure created a need for a special term describing a member of the class of feudal dependents (of the crown or temple), as distinct from slaves; *muškēnu* filled this need admirably and the meaning "dependent" is the only one that consistently fits the several uses of this form.[61]

Turning now to the debatable etymology, I suggested some time ago that the underlying form might be **kēnu* < **kan'u* (cf. *zēru* < **zar'u*), a possible cognate of Heb. *ni-ḵna'* "he submitted."[62] Whether or not this combination is an apt one is not important. The fact remains that

[59] The ceremonial background of *šukēnu* is duly stressed by H. Eheholf, Studia Orientalia I 10 f., n. 2. It is immaterial whether the accompanying gesture was performed by the hand (ibid.), or consisted in some form of proskynesis, as the Sumerian group k i-(a-) za-(z a) would seem to indicate, cf. Landsberger, MAOG IV 306; for the ideograms with KA cf. Jacobsen, JNES 2 171 n. 68.

[60] Cf. Landsberger, loc. cit.; note the synonym *bulṭa nadānu* CT 18 30.b26 ("to offer one's life"?).

[61] Note especially the parallel passages *rēdûm ba'irum ù naši biltim* CH 12.22 f. and *ša rēdi ba'iri* (!) *ù mu-uš-ki-ni* TCL 17 76.13 f. which yields the equation "feudal servant = *muškēnu*." From this start there is a clear path to "member of the intermediate class," "subject (of the crown or the temple)," and finally, outside the immediate orbit of Babylonian law, "indigent, etc." [*Addendum.* A. Falkenstein, *Genava,* VIII (1960), p. 310, would derive *šupēlum* from Sum. š u -b a l. But the Akk. stem, especially in the form *šupeultu* points to a medial laryngeal. Moreover, the Akk. product of Sum. š u-b a l would have to be **šuballû,* on the analogy of *šubarrû* < š u-b a r.]

[62] Language 11 (1935) 20–22.

šukēnu has to be traced back to some **ka'nu* > **kēnu,* a term which could not have been distinguished from the heterogeneous but very common *kēnu* "firm, true." The resulting ambiguity might alone have sufficed to differentiate the first **kēnu* by means of *š*-. The socio-legal bearing of the word would be another valid reason. In any case, there would seem to be adequate grounds for assuming some such form as **šak'untum* "act or gesture of submission" with the corresponding factitive **uška''in,* which yielded in turn *uškēn, muškēnu.* Since the performance of the act and the resulting status, rather than the gesture as such, were the really significant factors, the factitive forms become established in the language while the underlying abstract disappeared.[63] Interestingly enough, because of the meaning involved *šukēnu* never takes an object, in marked contrast to *šupēlu.* The *š*- is no more causative here than it is in the type *ušrabbī.*

In passing, a comment is called for in regard to the term *šḫ̮ḫ̮n.* Its semantic identity with *šukēnu* is self-evident as has been stressed recently by H. Lewy[64] and von Soden.[65] Heidel would see in *šḫ̮ḫ̮n* yet another "quadriliteral" with *š*-.[66] Goetze remarks in rebuttal that the word can hardly be genuinely Akkadian and that its forms are hence "inconsistent with themselves and do not fit any pattern of Akkadian morphology."[67] It is precisely such inconsistencies that once led me (in AASOR 16 [1936] 72) to view *šḫ̮ḫ̮n* as a composite West-Semitic form under Hurrian influence. This may well have been

[63] The fact that no such nominal form has been preserved does not necessarily militate against this theory. Actual occurrences of *šukēnu* prior to Old Babylonian and Old Assyrian times are rare as it is. With the specialized development of *šukēnu* the need for the assumed * *šak'untum* would have disappeared, unlike *šupēltum,* where the act or transaction as such, and not the resulting state or condition, remains a primary factor.

[64] Orientalia 11 (1942) 330 n. 2.

[65] ZA 49 332.

[66] AS 13 111 f.

[67] JNES 4 249.

a hazardous guess, not nearly so hazardous, however, as the positive statements by H. Lewy and von Soden[68] according to whom direct Hurrian transformation of *šukēnu*-forms are here involved. Hurrian is not quite so much of a blank as to allow us to posit such wholesale phonetic upheavals in Akkadian dialects. The equation finds no support in Hurrian phonology on the one hand or in Nuzian usage on the other. The farthest one is entitled to go in this instance is to see in *šukēnu* a model which influenced a base of unknown origin and composition. In these circumstances nothing can be asserted one way or another concerning the *š*- of *šḫḫn*.

9. It may prove useful to summarize, in conclusion, the main results of this paper:

(a) Akkadian *š*-, when not a radical, is not limited to causative stems. It occurs also in restricted use with a variety of other forms.

(b) With some adjectives and statives *š*- brings out the sense of "more, most, especially," e.g., *šurbū, šūtuqu, šupšuqu, šumruṣu*. This class corresponds most closely to the Arabic elative of Type C, which is not reflected in Hebrew.

(c) It forms denominative verbs from nouns and adjectives which indicate periods or duration of time, e.g., *ušalbar, ušešer, ušamšā*. This application is paralleled in West-Semitic semantically, sometimes even etymologically; cf. Heb. *hizqīn, haškēm weha'rēḇ*, Arab. *'asḥara, 'amsā*.

(d) It may be used with forms denoting stillness (lack of sound or motion, sometimes resulting from fear), e.g., *šḫrr, šqmm*, cf. Heb. *heḥša, heḥrīš, hiskīṯ*, Arab. *'askata*.

[68] In the publications just cited.

(e) A distinctive Akkadian usage is the formation of factitives from elatives, e.g., *ušrabbī, lišrabbib*. Similar factitives from *š*-forms are *šukēnu* and *šupēlu*. The complementary employment of *š*- in these forms disproves the existence of a III/II-stem as a dual category, we have here only II-forms from augmented bases.

Further comparison with West-Semitic shows

(f) that Akkadian does not use the relative *š*- for colors, whereas Arabic regularly employs in such cases its elative *'a*- (with adjectives) and Hebrew its *h*- (with stative verbal forms).

(g) The correspondence of the elative and causative morphemes is strictly maintained throughout:[69] Arabic *'a-*, Hebrew *h*- (but not '- or *š*-), Akkadian *š*- (but not '-).

(h) This far-reaching correspondence between the elative elements (in the broad sense of the term) and the particular causative morpheme in each instance establishes the ultimate identity of the respective prefixes.

(i) Two important conclusions follow: first, that the Arabic elative, in common with its Hebrew and Akkadian analogues, goes back to Primitive Semitic; and second, that the causative as a common Semitic category is necessarily a specialized, and hence later, application of the morpheme used for the elative, a morpheme which can be identified independently as a pronoun of emphasis.

[*Addendum*. A particularly clear sequence of factitive-elative derived from the Heb. adjectives *qāšê* "hard, difficult" (synonym of Akk. *pašqu*) occurs in Gen. 35.15 f.: *watt^eqaš b^elid̲tāh wayy^ehī b^ehaqšō̲tāh b^elid̲tāh* "She had hard labor. And when her labor was at its hardest (elative) . . ."]

[69] Not counting loanwords, or possible Arabic elatives with *h*-, the source of the causative and elative '-.

The Terminative-Adverbial in Canaanite-Ugaritic and Akkadian*

NEW MATERIAL CAN PROVE UPSETTING TO LONG-CHERISHED theories, in linguistics no less than in other fields of study. A case in point is the so-called *"hê-locale"* of Hebrew. This form used to be connected almost universally[1] with the Semitic accusative ending *-a*. The evidence of Ugaritic, however, has conclusively disproved this derivation.[2] By combining the relevant data of Ugaritic with the results of his independent investigation of prevailing Biblical usage, T. J. Meek has been able to show that the Hebrew ending in question is essentially terminative and should

* This paper is published in Hebrew in *Eretz-Israel,* 3, 1953 (Cassuto Memorial Volume), pp. 63–66.

[1] Cf. W. Gesenius-E. Kautzsch: *Hebräische Grammatik.* 28th ed. Leipzig, 1909, p. 259; K. Brockelmann: *Grundriss der vergl. Grammatik der sem. Sprachen,* I. Berlin, 1909, p. 464; H. Bauer & P. Leander: *Historische Grammatik der hebr. Sprache.* Halle a. S., 1922, p. 529; G. Bergsträsser: *Einführung in die sem. Sprachen.* München, 1928, p. 44; L. H. Gray: *Introduction to Semitic Comparative Linguistics.* New York, 1934, p. 57.

[2] H. L. Ginsberg: *Kithvey Ugarith.* Jerusalem, 1936, p. 80. (Hebrew); *Orientalia,* 7, 1938, p. 9; F. Rosenthal, *ibid.,* p. 167, n. 1; C. H. Gordon: *Ugaritic Handbook* (Analecta Orientalia, 25). Roma, 1947, p. 88. For originally consonantal *-h* in this form see already B. Stade: *Lehrbuch d. hebr. Grammatik Leipzig,* 1879, p. 35. For its non-accusative origin (and derivation from the type *šámāh,* cf. C. Sarauv, *Zeitschr. f. Assyriol.,* 20, 1907, pp. 183–89.

hence be renamed "terminative *hê*." [3] The standard grammars plainly need correcting on this point.

The main purpose, then, of this brief note is not so much to restate an observation that has already been made, as to review the situation in the light of Comparative Semitic and perhaps to advance the discussion a step further. First, however, it will be necessary to present the basic facts in briefest schematic outline.

The ending which eventually came to be expressed as *āh* in Hebrew [4] represents:

(a) Normally, "the place towards," as in *'arṣāh* "earthwards" (Gen. xi, 31; xii, 5; etc.); *haššāmáymāh* "heavenwards" (Gen. xv, 5; etc.).

(b) Less often, "the place where," perhaps under the influence of *šāmāh* which can mean either "thither' or "there," [5] e.g., *hammizbēḥāh* "on the altar" (Ex. xxix, 13, 25; etc.).

(c) Occasionally, "the time until," as in *(miyyāmīm) yāmímāh,* "from year to year" (Ex. xiii, 10; Judges xi, 40; etc).

(d) The variant *lyl,* alongside the usual *láylāh* "night," shows clearly that the ending in this instance has nothing to do with the feminine suffix. This conclusion is confirmed by the stress on the penult and the masculine gender of the word. T. Nöldeke's attempt to derive the form in *-h* from a reduplicated *lyly* [6] fails to account for the abnormal position of the accent. Moreover, the occurrence of *bllh* in Mesha 15 could not readily be analyzed in this fashion, especially in view of the prevailing *defec-*

[3] *Journ. Amer. Orient. Soc.,* 60, 1940, pp. 228–29.

[4] The silent *-h* of this ending is now definitely established as secondary.

[5] Cf. W. von Soden, *Zeitschr. f. Assyriol.,* 42, 1934, p. 121, n. 1.

[6] Th. Nöldeke: *Mandäische Grammatik.* Halle, 1875, p. 127; cf. Brockelmann, *op. cit.* (supra, n. 1), 260.

tiva scriptio in that inscription. What we have here, therefore, is in effect a specialized form of type (c) above. Just as the goal of motion can be equated morphologically with the place itself, so too can the goal of time be identified with the period in question "at night > night."

(e) Lastly, the original terminative connotation may be lost altogether; cf., e.g., the pleonastic use of the prepositions for "to" and "in," and particularly the occurrences with "from," as in *miṣṣāfōnāh* "from the north" (Jos. xv, 10).

Two features of the form before us call for special emphasis. First, the basic meaning, to judge from the majority of the instances, was the goal of motion; closely allied to it was the goal of time. In other words, the original connotation was indeed terminative, as Meek has shown. In stressing this underlying usage, however, Meek would seem to go too far in asserting that it was exclusive.[7] It is inherently probable that "whither" may on occasions shade off into "wherein," so that a locative develops from a terminative. Such was demonstrably the case in Akkadian, as will be pointed out presently. Type (b) above appears to reflect just such a development, even though some of the individual examples (including the comparable instance of *lylh*) might be explained otherwise. At any rate, the traditional *"hê-locale"* is a misnomer in that it stresses secondary usage at the expense of the original function.

The other significant feature of the form is its treatment as an enclitic with the result that it remains unaccented. This is a detail that has not received proper attention so far. Yet it provides us with a valuable cri-

[7] *Op. cit.* (supra, n. 3), p. 229.

terion for separating heterogeneous forms, notably the present suffix from the feminine ending *-āḥ*. To follow this lead a step further, we find that those formatives of Hebrew which may be said to fuse with the root are all subject to the same accentual treatment: not only the feminine ending but also the markers of number and gender and the normal pronominal suffixes invariably came to bear the word stress. Indeed, the assumed survivals in Hebrew of the Semitic accusative of the type *ḥinnā́m* "gratuitously,"[8] and the possible Hebrew reflexes of the locative proper (e.g., *hᵃlṓm* "hither"[9]) have their stress on the suffix. By contrast, the unstressed terminative suffix is thus revealed as a juxtaposed rather than a fusing element, corresponding to the prepositional particles; it is enclitic for the same reason that the prepositions are proclitic. The contrast between *hᵃlōm* "hither," with final stress, and the terminative *hālᵉʼāh* "thither, further," where the suffix is unstressed, becomes thus highly instructive.

That the consonantal value and the terminative function of the *-h* in the forms under discussion are today established beyond any doubt is due first and foremost to the evidence of Ugaritic. There we find such forms as *arṣh* "earthwards" and *šmmh* "heavenwards," precisely as in Hebrew; and in a temporal sense we have *ʻlmh* "forever."[10] Since Ugaritic does not use any vowel letters, the *-h* must be radical. The same has to be posited,

[8] Brockelmann, *op. cit.* (supra, n. 1), p. 474; Bauer & Leander, *op. cit.* (supra, n. 1), p. 529, would see here the possessive suffix of the third person plural, surely a far-fetched derivation.

[9] Brockelmann, *op. cit.* (supra, n. 1), p. 245; cf. von Soden, *op. cit.* (supra, n. 5), p. 118, n. 1. See also E. J. Young, *Westminster Theol. Journ.*, 1951, p. 152; his paper was in most respects anticipated by von Soden.

[10] Gordon, *op. cit.* (supra, n. 2), p. 88.

accordingly, for the *-h* of the original Hebrew terminative. The eventual loss of its consonantal value was plainly a secondary development. One aspect of the problem has thus been settled: instead of representing a specialized application of the inherited Semitic accusative, the terminative was an independent formation which employed a morpheme of its own. But the background of this morpheme is as yet obscure. It poses a new and distinct problem.

Outside Canaanite proper and Ugaritic, the terminative as an independent form is found within the Semitic family most prominently in Akkadian. There the pertinent suffix appears as *-iš*. Until recently, Assyrologists interpreted this form basically as an expression of comparison, in the sense of "like," since this is its dominant function with adjectives.[11] Thanks, however, to the researches of J. Lewy, A. Schott, B. Landsberger, and especially W. von Soden,[12] we know now that with substantives the primary use of the suffix was to indicate the goal of motion or of time; e.g., *il-iš* "to the god," *dār-iš* "forever." Closely related to this use is the employment of *-iš* with infinitives, as in *amāriš* "for beholding," *nadāniš* "for giving." In other words, the suffix fulfills here the function of the prepositions *ana* "unto" and *ina* "in." The more strictly locative connotation may have originated with such forms as *ašar-iš* "to the place > there," *el-iš* "to on high > up," or the like. The comparative meaning with adjectival bases might well have come about by way of "to the degree, to the point of," until *mād-iš* came to mean simply "greatly,"[13] *kên-iš* "truly,"

[11] W. von Soden: *Grundriss der akkadischen Grammatik* (Analecta Orientalia, 33). Roma, 1952, p. 89 (e).

[12] *Zeitschr. f. Assyriol.*, 42, 1934, pp. 103–130.

[13] von Soden, *ibid.*, p. 109, and n. 3, analyses this form as based on infinitives rather than adjectives.

and so forth. With substantives, the comparative connotation of *-iš* is demonstrably secondary and late. In view of the chronological factor and the known flexibility of adverbial forms, it is logical to conclude with von Soden that *-iš* got its start as an outright terminative.

In seeking to explain the origin of this form, von Soden rightly rejects any connection with Sumerian *-šè*, even though it is superficially analogous with Akkadian *-iš*.[14] He does so on the ground that the respective functions of the two morphemes do not fully coincide, that the two languages are poles apart structurally, and that actual borrowing by Akkadian of Sumerian grammatical elements has not been proved independently.[15] A more promising lead suggests itself to von Soden in the dative suffix *-ši* of the Akkadian pronouns (as in *yā-ši* "to me," etc.), the close relationship of dative and terminative requiring no further comment.[16] Since the pronominal dative, moreover, in Akkadian has long been known to be related to the pronominal dative of the Kushitic branch of Hamitic, and since Kushitic has also a corresponding dative with substantives, the further connection between the Akkadian terminative and the dative of the Kushitic noun, von Soden argues, has much to recommend it.[17]

Leaving this particular question aside for the moment, how does the Akkadian terminative compare with the analogous Canaanite/Ugaritic form? The functional correspondence of the two could scarcely be overstressed. It is so close and intimate, in fact, as to raise the question

[14] Proposed tentatively by A. Schott, *Mitt. Vorder-Asiat. Ges.*, 30, 1925, p. 36.

[15] *Zeitschr. f. Assyriol.*, 42, 1934, p. 121, n. 2.

[16] von Soden, *op. cit.* (supra, n. 11), p. 88 (67a) regards the original identity of the two forms as established.

[17] *Zeitschr. f. Assyriol.*, 42, 1934, p. 119 f., n. 1.

of a possible etymological relationship. Such a connection, however, must be ruled out promptly by the facts of Semitic phonology: Akkadian *š* does not correspond to West Semitic *h* phonologically. If it did, we should expect all or most of the occurrences of *š* which do not go back to the Semitic interdental spirant to configurate with an *h* in the Western branch of the family, which is not, of course, the case. Unless, therefore, another link is found, the striking parallelism between the Akkadian terminative is *-iš* and the Canaanite terminative in *h* will have to be charged to coincidence, implausible as this might seem. In short, the proposed Kushitic analogue has little bearing on the problem so long as the more immediate issue of inner-Semitic correspondence continues unclarified. Moreover, if the Akkadian and Canaanite/Ugaritic terminatives should prove to have a generic connection, any further cognate would have to be related not only to *-iš* but also to *h*.

Now there happens to be one area of contact between Akkadian *š* and West Semitic *h*. The relationship in question is not phonologic but morphemic, and the morphemes involved are restricted to certain demonstrative pronouns. In other words, Akkadian (and in part also South Arabic) employed a pronominal type with *š*- (or *s*) where West Semitic used corresponding pronouns with *h*-.[18] Since the pronouns in question enjoyed wide currency in each group—as bound forms as well as independent forms—they might give rise to the superficial impression that there was some sort of phonologic connection between *š* and *h*. As has been indicated,

[18] Minaean has *s;* Modern South Arabic (Mehri, Šḫauri, Soqotri) has *se* for 'she', while the masculine is represented by laryngeal forms. For these apparent exceptions to the West Semitic norm see infra, n. 20.

however, such a conclusion is absolutely untenable.[19] Wherever there is a real interdialectal link between these two sounds, the reason for it is not to be sought in etymology. Thus far, morphology has been able to supply a satisfactory answer; more specifically, the same set of morphemes has proved to figure in each of the instances involved.

The clearest instance is afforded by the respective pronouns of the third person, which are properly demonstratives. Starting with separate and etymologically unrelated forms of this pronoun, **hū'a* for the masculine and **šī'a* for the feminine, the Semitic languages proceeded to equalize the initial sounds by adopting either *š-* or *h-* for both genders.[20] The resulting dichotomy of Semitic has left us with a useful dialectal criterion; so much so that we are justified, on the familiar analogy of Indo-European, in dividing the family into a *hū*-group and a *šī*-group respectively. What this means is that an actual interdialectal correspondence of *h* and *š* presupposes mediation by the pronouns in question.

This assumption has so far proved valid on several occasions. Nearly twenty years ago I argued—I believe successfully—that the causative morphemes *š/s-* and *h-* were pronominal in origin because their distribution in Semitic corresponds strikingly to the incidence of third person pronouns with *š/s-* and *h-* respectively.[21] In a recent article I obtained similar results in regard to the

[19] That a sibilant may become *h* in Modern South Arabic [Bergsträsser, *op. cit.* (supra, n. 1), p. 126; W. Leslau: *Lexique Soqotri.* Paris, 1938, p. 32 f.] is irrelevant, because that development is irregular and secondary.

[20] Bergsträsser, *ibid.*, pp. 7–8. Modern South Arabic still maintains the original Semitic distribution. In Old South Arabic, Minaean has the sibilant and Sabaean the laryngeal, showing how the equalizing process operated in Semitic in general.

[21] *Journ. Amer. Orient. Soc.*, 56, 1936, pp. 23–33 [above, pp. 404 ff.].

"elative,"which promise to have a substantial bearing on a number of points in Semitic linguistics.[22] There is, furthermore, the probability—more than that I did not venture to claim—that the Akkadian particle *šumma* "if" was basically pronominal.[23] One might perhaps be inclined to ask at this point why Semitic should have imposed such heavy service on a single set of pronouns. I would answer that the set in question happened to be specialized for deictic purposes, and that deixis would seem to have played a particularly important part in Semitic morphology. In any event, there appears to be no other way of accounting consistently for the actual facts: the observed interdialectal correspondences under discussion are not phonologic but morphemic; the morphemes involved perform precisely the same functions in two respective groups; their distribution follows the distribution of the third person pronouns; they must be related accordingly to those pronouns.

Let us see now whether the above premises are borne out in regard to the terminative, which is *-iš* in the "*šî*-group" and *-h* in the "*hû*-group" of Semitic. Once again, within each group there is the necessary phonetic agreement, in that the one utilizes the sibilant *š*[24] and the other the laryngeal *h*. In order, however, to establish the likelihood of a morphologic relationship between the two terminatives, it is necessary to show also that terminative and deictic functions are or can be interrelated. It is my opinion that this can be asserted with a considerable show of reason. But the nature of the evidence and the character of the problem are such as to render the proposed solution no more than highly probable. A speculative

[22] *Journ. of Cuneif. Studies*, 6, 1952 pp. 81–92 [above, pp. 465 ff.].
[23] *Ibid.*, 1, 1947 pp. 321–28 [above, pp. 455 ff.].
[24] For the *š*- causatives in Aramic and Ugaritic cf. *ibid.*, 6, 1952, p. 81, n. 4 [above, p. 465 n.4].

element is always present whenever we are obliged to go back to the pro-ethnic stage of a given linguistic family.

The formative we are tracing would seem to have started out with some such meaning as "away towards a specific point." The pronoun with which I would link it —*š*/*s*- in the one group and *h*- in the other—is known to be demonstrative or deictic in origin. It is assumed that for "earth-towards," or the like, Semitic employed "earth-that." This assumption, not implausible in itself, gains a measure of support from two circumstances: (1) Landsberger has observed that *-iš* does not occur at all with suffixes of the first person, and is found but rarely with those of the second person. This might well be the natural consequence of the presumed deictic origin of this element.[25] The underlying significance would be "not here, with me (or thee), but there, with him, her, it." (2) In Ethiopic, a South Semitic language of the "*hu*-group," there is a deictic suffix *-hā* which is not to be confused with the normal accusative in *-ā*. Dillmann-Bezold[26] describe this element as follows: 'This is an impersonal demonstrative particle with the force of "here" or "there," and in origin it is certainly identical with the Hebrew *āh* of direction.' A favorite use of this morpheme is with proper names, where it has an explicative force not unlike that of Akkadian *-ma* in similar context. Ethiopic helps thus not only to attest the presence in South Semitic of what had once been a terminative, but also to connect that element with deictic forms.

We have, then, complete agreement between Canaanite

[25] Apud von Soden, *Zeitschr. f. Assyriol.*, 42, 1934, p. 120, n. 1.

[26] A. Dillmann & C. Bezold: *Ethiopic Grammar.* 2nd. ed. (Transl. by J. A. Crichton.) London, 1907. The connection has not been overlooked by Rosenthal, *op. cit.* (supra, n. 2). On the other hand, the dative prefix *he-*, which Modern South Arabic uses with pronouns, is probably of different origin; cf. Leslau, *op. cit.* (supra, n. 19), p. 137.

proper and Ugaritic as regards a terminative in *(a)h*, coupled with indications that Ethiopic had at one time observed the same usage and employed the same morpheme for the purpose. On the other hand, there is in Akkadian a terminative in *-iš*, which is by and large identical in usage with its West Semitic counterpart, but differs from it etymologically. That difference reflects the same dichotomy into *š:h* groups which is particularly notable in the third person pronoun, and extends also to the causative and, to a more limited degree, to the elative. The ultimate source of this phonologic split as against the funtional identity of the morphemes involved has to be traced to respective choices of the underlying pronominal elements: *h-* in the one case and *š-* in the other.

How do these findings affect von Soden's suggestion that the Akkadian terminative is to be connected with the dative suffix *-ši* of the independent pronouns of Akkadian and with the similar suffix in Kushitic? On the face of it, the suggestion remains plausible in that here, too, we would be dealing with pronominal morphemes. Nevertheless, support for such a view cannot be adduced as yet. The problem concerns, as we have seen, not only Akkadian but also West Semitic. Since the '*hū*-group' does not present us with dative suffixes analogous to Akkadian *-ši*, there is no means of checking von Soden's hypothesis within that group. In any event, the issue has broader ramifications than von Soden appears to have realized.

In conclusion, there remains to be noted one difference in detail. The Canaanite/Ugaritic terminative in *-āh* (paralleled by the *-hā* of Ethiopic) and the Akkadian analogue in *-iš* do not employ the same vowels. I have no explanation for this divergence. It goes without saying that it is the consonants and not the vowels that are distinctive in this instance. The *-i-* of Akkadian could well be a secondary local development. It may therefore be significant in this connection that Akkadian possesses also the adverbs *aḫrataš* and *ṣitaš,* where *-aš* occurs in place of the usual *-iš*.[27] To be sure, these are isolated forms, perhaps late; they are certainly incapable, on present evidence, of offsetting the abundant record in favor of *-iš* There is no warrant, however, for discarding altogether the possibility that the exceptions rather than the norms reflect in this instance the original situation. At any rate, the relationship of the Akkadian terminative with its analogues elsewhere in Semitic has been established securely on independent grounds. It could hardly be said to be in the balance by reason of its specific vocalic content.

[27] *Zeitschr. f. Assyriol.,* 42, 1934, p. 128.

The Durative Hithpa'el: A *tan* Form[1]

One of the features of the Semitic verbal system is its extensive use of the morpheme *-t-*, prefixed or infixed. The commonest function of the *t*-stems would seem to be reflexive or middle. Akkadian, however, stands apart by and large. In common with its sister languages, it subjects some of its *t*-forms to reciprocal use, e.g., *mitḫurum* "to face one another," *mitgurum* "to come to agreement with"; but generally the Akk. *t*-stems are separative or reversing, e.g., *atlukum* "to go away," *itabulum* "to take away." [2]

Everywhere except in Hebrew the number of *t*-forms is in the plural. Arabic has four (V, VI, VIII, X); South Arabic (including the Ethiopic group has three such non-

[1] The main conclusions of this paper were arrived at years ago and they have been cited in seminars on a number of occasions. The impetus for the present formal presentation—in compact form, necessarily—was provided by the essay "On First Reading Genesis," which Mr. Edmund Wilson published in *The New Yorker,* issue of May 15, 1954, pp. 117 ff., and specifically by two paragraphs, *ibid.,* 118–19. Mr. Wilson was puzzled by the for of ***mištā'ê*** 'gazed at,' Gen. 24.21 and of *h/yitḫallek̠* 'walked (with),' *ibid.,* 5. 22, 24; 6. 9. There was no apparent reason for the use in these cases of intensive or reflexive forms. He was perfectly right on this score and acute in spotting the difficulty after only a brief acquaintance with Hebrew. Since the grammars fail to explain the problem, a statement on the subject would seem overdue.

[2] Cf. A. Goetze, *JAOS,* LVI, 322 ff.; W. von Soden, *Grundriss der akkadischen Grammatik* (*GAG*) 120 f.

causative formations and more than one causative *t*-class;[3] there are three *t*-forms in Aramaic; in Canaanite dialects other than Hebrew there are at least two *t*-forms. Hebrew alone is credited formally with but a single *t*-class, the Hithpa'el or Dt, i.e., the *t*-stem of the doubling form.

On a comparative-historical basis, therefore, there can be little doubt that Hebrew had subjected its inherited *t*-stems to drastic reduction. The traditional vocalization still reflects vestigial traces of Bt (*t*-stem of the Qal) in *hiṯpāqᵉḏū* (Judg. 20. 17), and place-names like *'eštā'ōl* are to be similarly interpreted. Elsewhere, the original character of the given Hithpa'el can be determined only by adducing the corresponding form without *-t-*: thus *hiṯnaddev* "to volunteer" goes with the Qal *nādav, hiṯḥazzeq* "to make oneself strong" with the Pi'el *ḥizzeq,* and *hiṯ'allem* "to hide oneself with the Hif'il *he'līm.* The Hithpa'el, in short, combines several independent *t*-stems, their merger being due on the one hand to the successful competition on the part of the Nif'al and the Hof'al, and on the other hand to specific phonologic and morphologic circumstances.[4]

The problem so far has been one of simple analysis and description. The situation becomes involved, however, when we come to consider a residue of Hebrew *t*-forms in which the function of the infix can hardly be reflexive, middle, or reciprocal. Most of these are immediately betrayed as atypical by the fact that the corresponding stems without a *t*-morpheme—in the Qal or the Pi'el, as the case may be—appear to perform the same duty as the *t*-forms.

[3] Cf. Dillmann-Bezold, *Ethiopic Grammar,* 151 ff.; M. Bittner, *Mehri-Studien* II (SAW Wien, 168, 1911) 43 ff.

[4] Relation of *ă* plus single consonant to *ă* plus doubled or long consonant; metathesis of the *-t-;* borrowing of the prefix *h-* from the Hif'il—all these being leveling influences.

This is true, among other instances,[5] of the respective Qals and Hithpa'els of *'bl* "to mourn,"[6] *'np* "to grow/ be angry,"[7] *g'š* "to shake,"[8] *nḥl* "to inherit,"[9] *'ṭp*[10] "to grow/be weak, faint," **š'y/š'y* "to gaze";[11] and of the respective Pi'els and Hithpa'els of **'wy* "to desire,"[12] *hlk* "to wander,"[13] *'ll* "to act (often adversely)."[14]

On closer examination, all these atypical Hithpa'els turn out to connote repeated or continuous action. This special nuance is some times underscored by an added phrase in the context: Jacob "mourned his son *for many days*" (Gen. 37.34); David "mourned his son *all the days*" (II Sam. 13;37); "*how long* will you mourn for Saul?" (I Sam. 16.1); there is he "who covets greedily *all the day long*" (Prov. 21.26). In each of these instances the verb is in the Hithpa'el. For the most part, however, the *t*-stem alone is sufficient to express the habitative function; e.g., *hiṯnaḥḥel* "to come into and remain in possession."

[5] All of the following roots except **š'y* are cited (although without references) in G. Bergsträsser, *Hebräische Grammatik, Verbum,* 98. The references given below have been limited, as a rule, to a pair in each instance.

[6] E.g., Amos 9.5: I Sam. 15.35, etc. In II Sam. 14. 2, however, we may have an instance of a genuine Hithpa'el.

[7] E.g., I Kings 8.46: Deut. 1.37.

[8] Ps. 18.8: II Sam. 22.8. Note Jer. 5.22 "and although its waves batter continuously, they cannot prevail."

[9] E.g., Ex. 23.30: Nu 33.54 (both with [the same] object, whereas such a construction is unusual with normal *t*-forms).

[10] Isa. 57. 16: Ps. 142.4.

[11] Accepting the prevailing view that ** š'y* and ** š'y* are identical, Isa. 31. 1: Gen. 24.21. Akk. *ištene'i* (CH rev. 5) has the nuance of 'he shall keep on searching' as compared with the Heb. 'gazing steadfastly.'

[12] E.g., Prov. 21. 10: Deut. 5. 18 (with obj. suffix).

[13] See below.

[14] Lam. 1.22: Ex. 10.2 (with object). It should be stressed that most of the Qals and Pi'els under review could be viewed as reflecting a durative meaning, which is precisely why they appear to differ little from the corresponding Hithpa'els. What is really significant is the fact that practically all the Hithpa'els of this group are durative and are clearly intended to convey that aspect. The original distinction, however, must have become obliterated in course of time.

The group of Hithpa'els just cited, once their special force has become apparent, points immediately to the *tan*-class of Akkadian, which expresses repeated or continuous action.[15] Since medial *-n-* assimilates to a following consonant in Akkadian as well as in Hebrew, it could be preserved only where a vowel intervened, notably in the Akk. present *iptanárras*. Elsewhere in Akkadian, and everywhere in Hebrew, *-tan-* was or would be bound to surrender its *-n-*, with the consequent doubling of the following radical. Hence it was that all such disguised *tan*-forms remained unrecognized by modern scholars in Akkadian itself, in spite of the telltale *tan*-present, until 1939, and even then it required all of Poebel's insight and ingenuity to drive home the point.[16] That the corresponding discovery in Hebrew, which lacks a morphologic present, should have lagged behind is in these circumstances easy to understand.

The main argument, then, for separating the normal Hebrew Hithapa'el from its heterogeneous homonyms under review may be summed up as follows: (1) The atypical occurrences show no trace of the ordinary uses of the *t*-stems. (2) They differ from the concurrent Qals and Pi'els in that they emphasize iterative and habitative aspects. (3) Morphologically, they coincide with the *tan*-stems of Akkadian. (4) Phonologically, they cannot be told apart from original Hithpa'els. What is yet to be shown is a prevailing agreement in usage between such secondary Hithpa'els and the Akk. *tan*-forms. For this purpose there is no better illustration than the shared root **hlk* "to go," since the pertinent forms are prominent both in Akkadian and in Hebrew.

[15] See v. Soden, *GAG* 119 f.
[16] *A(ssyriological) S(tudies)* 9, 1–64.

(a) "to walk about"

Akk.: [Lord,] "wanderer in the night" (*muttallik mušī*); [17]

Heb.: [God] "walking in the garden (*mit̲hallek̲*) toward the cool of the day," Gen. 3.9.

(b) "to wander (aimlessly)"

Akk.: [chariots with their riderless horses] "wandered to and fro' (*ittanallakā mitḫāriš utirrā*), Sen. *OIP* VI, 22; [17a]

Heb.: "from roaming over the earth and wandering on it to and fro (*ūmehit̲hallek̲ bāh*), Job 1.8; 2.2;

(c) "to proceed"

Akk.: "the mighty hero who proceeded by the authority of Ashur . . ." (*ša . . . ittallaku*);[18]

Heb.: "and I have walked (*weʾhit̲hallak̲tī*) in Thy truth," Ps. 26.3.

(d) "to follow"

Akk.: "he will follow you like a dog" (*arkika ittanal[l]ak, KAR* 96 rev. 10; [19]

Heb.: "those who walk (*hammit̲hallek̲īm*) after my lord," I Sam. 25.27.

(e) "to walk before, in the presence of"

Akk.: "to walk in the presence of Enlil and Ninlil" (*ina maḫar . . . atalluka*); [20]

Heb.: "Yahweh, in whose presence I walked (*hit̲hallak̲tī*), Gen. 24.40.

(f) "to walk with, commune"

[17] *Ibid.*, 36.

[17a] For the use of the present in late Assyrian historical inscriptions cf. Poebel, *ibid.*, 49 ff.

[18] *Ibid.*, 19.

[19] Cf. *JAOS*, LXII, 8 n. 75.

[20] *AS* 9, 8.

Akk.: "[If he rejected sin,] his god will walk with him (*ilšu ittišu ittanallak), ZA* 43, 98.41; [21]

Heb.: "And Enoch walked with God" (*wayyiṯhallek̠ Ḥanōk̠ 'eṯ-hā'ᵉlōhīm*), Gen. 5.22,24; cf. Gen. 6.9.

This last pair of examples is especially instructive. Not only is the idea of intimate association between a deity and a mortal expressed in each language by the same form, but the entire phrase is made up both times of exactly the same etymological elements. You might say that in this instance Hebrew walked with Akkadian.

I have elsewhere had occasion to refer to the detailed interrelationship that has just been discussed.[22] The same point had previously been broached by Goetze in another connection.[23] We agree independently on the form and function of the end product, but we differ in our respective estimates of the starting point.[24] Goetze would ascribe the underlying continuative force to an *n*-infix alone (Akk. **yu-ra-n-qid,* Heb. **ya-ha-n-lik*). The result, according to him, was a secondary D-stem or Piʻel.[25] Where a *-t-* was further added, it would have its usual function. Goetze's view, attractive as it is, raises several difficulties:

[21] Cf. R. C. Dentan, ed., *The Idea of History in the Ancient Near East* (AOS 38), 71 n. 97.

[22] *Ibid.*

[23] *JAOS,* LXII, 7 f.

[24] The one pair of instances that Goetze actually cites is *KAR* 96 rev. 10 (cf. above under [d]) for Akkadian and Kilamuwa 9/10 for West-Semitic. If the latter is pertinent, we would have proof of the use of *tan*-forms in Phoenician, in addition to Hebrew. The reading of the verb, however, is disputed. Lidzbarski, *Ephemeris* 3.233 prefers *ytlkn;* but Harris, *Grammar of Phoenician,* 42, and Friedrich, *Phönizisch-Punische Grammatik* 58 (135) read *ytlwn.* Happily, the issue does not hinge on this canine reference; the phrases which refer to the deity (cf. above under [f]) should be convincing enough.

[25] In other words, the starting point, as Goetze sees it, was a * Bn-form which led to a secondary D-stem; Btn was a *t*-extension of * Bn.

(1) The iterative-durative force of an infixed *-n-* by itself is nowhere unambiguously demonstrated.[26] (2) The Akk. present might be expected to show some traces of such an *-n-* in the secondary D-stems just as it does in the *tan*-form of the B-stem.[27] (3) The added *-t-* of the *tan*-stem would still require on this assumption a special explanation.[28]

It would thus seem best to start out with an unatomized *tan*-element in its amply attested normal sense. The resulting stem would coincide with the Heb. Hithpa'el in every instance, as well as in all Akk. forms other than the present. The small group of stems of the type of Heb. *hillek̠* and Akk. *ruppudum* [29] need not cause any serious

[26] The small group of verbs of the type *naparrurum* 'to disperse,' which v. Soden cites, *GAG* 135 f. (101 g), as examples of the ingressive-durative class, is composed of Ntn-stems. Simple "ingressive" *n*-stems could be durative only in an incidental way.

[27] Even if we grant the hypothetical * *yu-ra-n-qid* (> uraqqid), would not the corresponding present have been something like * *yu-ra-n-aqqud* > * *ya-r-n-áqqud,* so that the *-n-* would be preserved just as it was in Btn? Outside of Akkadian, incidentally, the theoretical possibility of maintaining the *tan*-morpheme intact existed only in the South Arabic group, where the indicative of the prefixing tense is a morphologic analogue of the Akkadian present. But the respective forms of Ethiopic III 2 and of Mehri *k-t-ôteb* are too ambiguous phonologically for any safe conclusions.

[28] One would have to show, among other things, how a reflexive or reciprocal *t*-morpheme (the separative is restricted within Semitic to Akkadian) came to be linked with a continuative infix without retaining any of its original function. The "nomina professionis," which Goetze adduces (*ibid.,* 7 n. 67), are at best of dubious relevance in this connection. Although their use becomes widespread eventually, their origin would seem to be far more circumscribed. Arabic, e.g., appears to have taken over this class from Aramaic (cf. Nöldeke, *Mand. Gr.* 120; Barth, *Nominalbildung* 49). Moreover, this formation features many strictly nominal roots and may well be nominal in origin. Indeed, there is even the possibility that the initial impetus may have been provided by prominent nouns which had been borrowed in the first instance from another language. Such household terms, e.g., as *naggar* 'carpenter' or *e/ikkar* 'farmer' might conceivably have given rise to the entire class; yet in both the doubling is secondary (< *nangar, engar*). At all events, the nominal form *qattal* cannot illuminate phenomena of the verbal D-stem.

[29] To the list of such stems in Akkadian (cf. *JAOS,* LXII, 6 f.) may be added the durative D-stems which v. Soden has cited, *GAG* 116 (h).

difficulty. Heb. *hillek̲* may be derived from *yit̲-hallek̲* through analogic back-formation,[30] i.e.,

Heb. *yit̲ḥazzeq* : *ḥizzeq* — *yit̲hallek̲*
(<**yahtanlik*) : *hillek̲*

As for Akk. *ruppudum,* and the like, the numerous forms of the *quttulum*-class could well have been a powerful analogic factor.[31] The Akk. personal names, or rather nicknames, of the type *Ḫuzzumum* "Deaf" and *Ḫummurum* "Blind" are immediately to be assigned to the formation which specialized in bodily defects, namely, Akk. *quttul-,* parallel by Heb. **qittil* (e.g. *'iwwēr* "blind") A natural sequel to these names of a common adjectival type would be onomastic formations from cursive verbal roots such as *Lussumum* "Speedy," *Lupputum* "Loiterer,"[32] *Dullupum* "Fidgeter,"[33] and the like. These names in turn could scarcely fail to be identified with the homophonous *purrusum,* the infinitive of the D-class, yielding thus D-stem verbs "to gallop," "to loiter," "to fidget," and so forth; and by extension also *ruqqudum* "to dance," *ruppudum* "to rove," if indeed these par-

[30] The question whether the *tan*-form has left survivors in West Semitic languages other than Canaanite (cf. above, n. 24) is beyond the scope of this brief note. In conclusion, however, it is worth calling attention to the various non-reflexive stems of the *taqattala* form of Arabic which corresponds to the Hithpa'el of Hebrew; cf. Wright, *Arab. Gr.* (3rd ed.), I 37 (b). These verbs, which are noteworthy syntactically in that they can take the accusative, are nearly always pronounced duratives. The only means by which a stem like *tafawwaqa* 'to milk, suck at intervals' could be expressed in Akkadian would be a *tan*-form. To be sure, assimilation of *-n-* is not the rule in Arabic; it does occur, however, with sonorous sounds (cf. *mimmā, 'illā,* etc.). The influence of such duratives as *taṭallaba* 'to seek' and the pull of genuine VI-stems could have sufficed to place original *tan*-forms, if such actually occurred in Arabic, in the *taqattala*-class. The problem merits a thorough investigation.

[31] See H. Holma, *Die assyrisch-babylonischen Personennamen der Form* quttulu.

[32] Goetze, *JAOS,* LXII, 6 f.

[33] Cf. Speiser, *JCS,* V, 65 ff.

ticular forms did not start out as nicknames in the first place.

In the light of the foregoing remarks there may be more than mere coincidence in the fact that cursive D-stems in Akkadian are relatively rare [34] whereas *tan*-forms of the base stem are common. Just so, the number of durative Hithpa'els is greater than the number of the corresponding Pi'els; moreover, as a group, the durative Hithpa'els configurate more frequently with ordinary Qals.

In any case, an original *tan*-form resulting in a secondary Hithpa'el would be an idiomatic way of saying that "Enoch walked steadfastly with God," or that Elieᶻer "gazed fixedly" (and in silence) at Rebekah.

[*Addendum*. A particularly persuasive example of the durative use of the form is *hiṯnappel* in Deut. 9.18, 25. The condition involved is stated explicitly to have lasted forty days. This automatically eliminates the reflexive, since one cannot keep on throwing oneself to the ground for forty days and nights; and the reflexive would be even more out of place. The sense is unavoidably "to lie prostrate," that is, something inherently durative.

The original statement appears, on rereading, too compact for clarity. It may, therefore, be spelled out schematically, as follows:

In the ordinary *Hithpa'el* the commonly admitted development was **taqattala* > **itqattil* (with the last vowel taken over from the Pi'el) > *hitqattel* (*h*- from Nif'al; cf. Berg., *Verbum* 18k).

In the present instance, the indicated reconstruction is this: **qa-tan-tala* > **qatattala* > *'*iqtattala* > *hitqattel* (the last step under the influence of the Hithpa'el proper).]

[34] Goetze, *JAOS*, LXII, 6 f.

PERSPECTIVES

Some Sources of Intellectual and Social Progress in the Ancient Near East[1]

LATEST ADVANCES IN THE STUDY OF THE PAST HAVE LENT fresh emphasis to the traditional view that the oldest known historic civilizations evolved in Egypt and Mesopotamia. It is equally clear that intellectual and social progress in these two centers kept pace with material developments. The question of relative priority is injected all too often into discussion on this subject. For the time being, at least, such a question is not capable of a satisfactory solution. It is doubtful indeed whether an answer can be expected at all, in view of the dynamic character of both civilizations and the consequent diffusion of vital innovations and inventions from the one center to the other. There are, however, certain characteristic aspects of progress in the two respective areas which stand out by contrast, and it is to one particular set of such contrasted characteristics that I wish to address myself at present. I refer to the background of progress in science.

[1] The substance of this paper was presented in 1940 before the University of Pennsylvania Bicentennial Conference and published in a volume on *Studies in the History of Science* (University of Pennsylvania Press, Philadelphia, 1941) under the title of "Ancient Mesopotamia and the Beginnings of Science." The present is a revised and somewhat expanded version of that paper.

The following remarks will embody four main propositions: (1) Available evidence points to Mesopotamia as the oldest center of scientific observation permanently recorded. (2) Whatever its immediate objectives, this activity comes to include such widely separated fields as education and language study, jurisprudence, and the mathematical and natural sciences. (3) The divers elements in this broad advance are basically interrelated. The common underlying factor is a concept of society whereby the powers of the state are restricted and the rights of the individual receive a corresponding degree of emphasis. (4) It is significant that under the opposed order of authoritarian Egypt early scientific development differed in scope as well as in degree; although notable in selected fields, such as medicine and engineering, it lacked the breadth and balance manifested in contemporary Mesopotamia.

It should be made plain at the outset that the scientific detail cited in this statement is negligible in amount and derivative in character. My principal objective will be rather to demonstrate that there were forces in the social structure of early Mesopotamia which tended to promote intellectual progress. The results happen to constitute the first recorded evidence of scientific performance known to us today. To this extent we are justified in touching here upon the beginnings of science, including the natural sciences. But this account is concerned not so much with the results as with the background: a combination of forces conducive to concerted intellectual activity rather than the disciplines affected by that activity. The background provides us in this instance with the all-important starting point. It is thus more significant than the eventual achievement.

Our interest, then, will center on a given cultural stage at which there were at work forces that led to extensive scientific developments and provided the predisposition to these developments. Accordingly, we shall ignore the sporadic achievements of a still more remote age, for instance, the invention of the wheel, the introduction of the brick-mold, and perhaps the use of instruments in effecting accurate geometric designs on very early forms of painted pottery. We may have here Mesopotamian inventions which were to play substantial parts in the subsequent progress of engineering, architecture, and possibly geometry. But these inventions represent isolated contributions of discontinuous civilizations which scarcely had any immediate bearing on intellectual progress. This statement will confine itself, therefore, to subjects which had a common origin in a well-defined period and area; which involve from the start habits of observation, classification, and analysis; and which enter then and there upon a continuous course of development.

The locale of our inquiry is Lower Mesopotamia, the land of Ancient Sumer. More specifically, it is the area which extends southeast from the environs of Babylon, past Uruk—the biblical Erech—and on along the Euphrates to the metropolis of Ur. The time is the middle of the fourth millennium B.C. The period can be established with relative accuracy because it coincides with a clearly stratified cultural stage that is marked off sharply by distinctive material remains. Soon thereafter we begin to get inscribed records which tie up before long with regnal years and thus afford data for an absolute chronology.

Our first inscribed documents come from a building level dated to about 3500 B.C. and constituting one of a long series of strata which represent the remains of ancient Uruk. It is among these documents, written on clay, that we find a small collection of scientific records, the earliest known to man to date. That similar records of still greater antiquity will ever turn up outside Mesopotamia is improbable. All available evidence favors the conclusion that the scientific notations with which we are concerned were compiled as a direct consequence of the introduction of writing itself. To be sure, this evidence applies only to the script of Mesopotamia. But writing from all the other ancient centers of civilization is demonstrably later. In Egypt it follows by some centuries the appearance of script in Mesopotamia, and the earliest evidence of writing in India is well within the third millennium B.C. As for China, there is nothing to indicate that its script antedates the second millennium. It follows, therefore, that the scientific notations on our earliest Mesopotamian tablets constitute not only the first evidence of intellectual activity in Sumer but at the same time also the oldest recorded effort of this kind from anywhere in the world. With this significant fact in mind let us turn now briefly to the records themselves.

What is it that would justify the use of the term "scientific" as applied to a few of the primitive inscribed documents from Mesopotamia? The answer is bound up with the nature and purpose of these special texts. Each contains lists of related entries. But these lists have nothing in common with the customary inventories of a strictly economic type. They serve an intellectual rather than material purpose. They are to enjoy, however, the sort of continuity and diffusion that will set them off sharply from the usual run of business documents which can claim only ephemeral and local importance. The lists in question are destined to be copied and recopied for many centuries and in more than one city or country. Actual samples of such copies, often modified and expanded but still in a clear line of descent from the very first prototypes, have been dug up in Mesopotamian sites of much later age, and in the foreign Elamite center of Susa. We have here the beginning of a family of scholarly documents notable at once for their continuity, distribution, and purposeful adherence to an established tradition.[2]

In this recording of accumulating experience and the manifest applicability of such records to centers separated by time and space we have the essential ingredients of scientific performance. What branches of science did that activity include? We shall see presently that the primary purpose of the lists under discussion was to aid in the preservation of the knowledge of writing. Before long, philological studies become an added objective, owing largely to the complex ethnic and linguistic background of early historic Mesopotamia. But natural sciences, too, soon come in for their share of attention.

For regardless of their original purpose, our lists happen to include, quite early in their history, groupings of birds, fish, domestic animals, plants and the like. It is worth stressing that these compilations presuppose careful observation and imply organization and analysis of the accumulated data.[3] As part of the cumulative tradition of the land these compilations are subject to expansion and revision. Moreover, such texts lead in course of time to the independent study of the subject matter in-

[2] These facts are brought out in full by A. Falkenstein whose *Archaische Texte aus Uruk* (Berlin, 1936) is the basic work on the earliest documents from Mesopotamia, cf. especially pp. 43 ff.

[3] Careful observation is evidenced also by the accurate drawings of the early pictographs, particularly where exotic animals or specific plants are concerned.

volved. The fields thus affected are zoology and botany, and later geology and chemistry. The first recognition of all these subjects as so many separate disciplines may be traced back, therefore, to the oldest inscribed documents of Mesopotamia. That recognition was due ultimately to the fact that man had just discovered in writing a way to arrest time and was bending all his effort and ingenuity to the task of keeping this method alive.

The subsequent progress of the individual sciences just mentioned has to be traced by specialists. We are concerned at present with the initial impetus alone and the time and circumstances in which that impetus arose. A few details, however, may be brought out in passing for purposes of illustration. In the light of the foregoing remarks botanists should not be surprised to learn that many of the terms which they use today go back to Mesopotamian sources. These terms include "cassia" (cuneiform *kasû*), "chicory" (*kukru*), "cumin" (*kamûnu*), "crocus" (*kurkânu*), "hyssop" (*zûpu*), "myrrh" (*murru*), "nard" (*lardu*), and probably many others. The zoological compilations which are available in cuneiform contain hundreds of names systematically arranged and presented in two columns, the first giving the Sumerian term and the other its Akkadian counterpart.[4] The scholastic tradition in chemistry[5] results in such texts as the one which has come down to us from the early part of the second millennium B.C., wherein a formula for glazing pottery is preserved in the guise of a cryptogram so as to remain hidden from the uninitiated.[6] The importance of the

[4] See B. Landsberger (with I. Krumbiegel), *Die Fauna des alten Mesopotamien* (Leipzig, 1934).

[5] On this subject cf. R. Campbell Thompson, *A Dictionary of Assyrian Chemistry and Geology* (Oxford, 1936).

[6] R. C. Thompson and C. J. Gadd, in *Iraq* III (1936), pp. 87 ff.

natural sciences for the study of medicine is self-evident; it was not lost on Babylonian and Assyrian medicine.

So much for the indirect benefits derived from the lists under review. But the primary objective of these compendia was not neglected in the meantime. On the contrary, the direct results are reflected in an immensely fruitful advance in another field of intellectual progress.

It was indicated above that our lists were conceived as a means of maintaining the knowledge of script. By the very nature of its origin in concrete pictographs, early writing was an elaborate medium which comprised thousands of items. To each new prospective user it represented a code which could not be deciphered without the right key. The lists were calculated to furnish that key. They were analytical catalogues of signs arranged according to outward form. Since each sign was at first a reflection of something specific in the material world, these catalogues came to constitute systematic arrangements of related objects; hence their incidental value for the natural sciences, as we have just seen. The immediate purpose, however, of the sign-lists was pedagogical; they are our oldest manuals of a basic branch of education.

With the study of the script there was linked perforce the study of language. It is evident from the material at hand that the pictographs were not meant merely to be seen but to be sounded. They were associated with concrete words or groups of words on an auditory rather than visual basis. This is made clear by the ability of the early writers to use given graphs for purely phonetic values. For instance, the first lists contain a graph which appears to represent a carpenter's drill and thus comes to be sounded as *ti*. Now Sumerian had a word for "life" which also was pronounced *ti* in certain positions. But the concept "life" is not as readily depicted by a pictograph as a concrete artisan's tool. The protohistoric Sumerian did not hesitate to use the tool-sign when he wanted to express the word "life." [7] It is this freedom in the use of specific pictorial symbols for abstract phonetic values that accounts for the rapid progress of Sumerian writing as a medium for recording any required type of utterance. After the Semitic-speaking Akkadians had joined the Sumerians in building up the civilization of Mesopotamia the resulting bilingual background caused linguistic studies to rise to exceptional heights.

The deep-rooted respect for scholarly tradition, implicit in a conscious dependence on the contributions of the past, had much to do with the unprecedented achievements of ancient Mesopotamia in the field of linguistics. For it meant that Akkadians, Babylonians, and Assyrians alike must fall back upon records in the wholly unrelated tongue of Sumer. The knowledge of that language had to be preserved for cultural reasons long after its speakers had lost all political power and eventually disappeared from the scene altogether. For the first time in history translators are busily at work to commit their renderings to writing. This activity called for the creations of various auxiliary manuals: syllabaries giving the phonetic value, form, and name of each given sign; vocabularies containing the Sumerian pronunciation, word-sign, and Akkadian equivalent of each word or group of words; lists of synonyms, commentaries on selected word-signs, interlinear translations, and the like. Nor was this all. The scientific analysis of Sumerian took the form of grammatical works arranged in paradigms according to parts of speech and explicit down to such minutiae as

[7] Cf. note 2, p. 38.

the place of the accent. Differences in the dialects of Sumerian were carefully recorded. And most of this formidable apparatus was available and in use more than four thousand years ago! It is to this apparatus that we of today owe our knowledge not only of the various dialects of Sumerian and Akkadian but also of such languages as Hittite, Hurrian, Urartian, and Elamite. As linguistic material these languages may be of interest only to a small group of specialists. But as the media for expressing the thought of a large portion of the ancient world over a period of three millennia—a period one and a half times as long as the whole of the present era—they have a deep significance for the whole of the civilized world.

The foregoing outline has had as its main theme the demonstration that many forms of scientific progress in Mesopotamia were influenced and linked together by a scholarly tradition which was in turn a byproduct of the invention of writing. Our survey has not included thus far mathematics and astronomy, two fields for which Mesopotamia has long been celebrated and is today honored more than ever before owing to the discoveries of modern investigators.[8] It goes without saying that these two subjects were affected no less than the other disciplines by the same forces which made for a broad cultural advance in general. But the primary cause of the extraordinary development of mathematical and related studies in Mesopotamia is to be sought, I believe, in conditions which antedate the introduction of writing. In fact, I would add, the origin of writing as well as the interest in mathematics are to be traced back in this instance to a

[8] Especially Otto E. Neugebauer, whose paper on "Some Fundamental Concepts in Ancient Astronomy" is included in the *Studies in the History of Science* (cf. note 1).

common source. This source will be found inherent in the society and economy of proto-historic Sumerians.

We know today that the Sumerians came upon the idea of writing through their use of the cylinder seal. Such seals were engraved with a variety of designs and were employed as individual personal symbols for religious and economic purposes, say, with temple offerings. In this representational function the decorative motifs on the seals come to be applied also to cities, temples, gods, all for purposes of identification; the designs are thus converted into graphs. Their employment is gradually extended to represent animals, plants, and objects in general. The graphs are soon associated wtih specific words and the gap between picture and word is bridged. The next step is to divorce the given sign from the specific underlying picture and to use signs not only for complete words but also for component syllables, the advance leading thus from the concrete to the abstract, as was illustrated above. Complete flexibility of the new medium is attained very early in the third millennium when administrative and historical documents are produced with equal ease. It is scarcely a coincidence that this advanced stage of writing should mark for us the beginning of the historical age.

When we look back now on the successive stages in this complex process, a process which could be sketched here only in its barest outlines, an interesting fact comes to the fore. The early Sumerians had not set out at all to invent anything like writing. They were driven to this result by a combination of peculiar circumstances. The outcome had hardly been planned or foreseen. The achievement of the discoverers lay chiefly in their ability to recognize and seize their opportunity. This they did with no little ingenuity and perseverance. But they had this opportunity to begin with because of the way in which their society functioned. The underlying system can now be reconstructed from a wealth of diversified evidence. Only a rough summary can be attempted at present.

We have seen that the immediate ancestor of Mesopotamian writing was the cylinder seal which was first and foremost the Sumerian's mark of ownership. Impressed on clay or cloth it served to safeguard in the eyes of gods and men one's title to possessions or merchandise. We have here a clear indication of a strongly developed sense of private property and thereby of individual rights and individual initiative.[9] The curious shape of the cylinder seal, original with the Sumerians, is explained by its employment as a mark of individual ownership. For such objects are well suited to cover uneven surfaces with their distinctive designs.[10]

Wholly consistent with this economic origin of writing is the fact that the earliest written documents are given over to temple economy. Later texts branch out into the field of private business. Both these uses testify independently to the importance of property rights. Records of a non-economic character are the last to appear in the developmental stages of script, except for the lists discussed above which served as direct aids to writing. The first inscribed documents were used, accordingly, for economic ends, precisely as the cylinder seals themselves. It is easy to understand why the oldest pictographs were so often identical with the designs on the seals.

[9] Cf. E. A. Speiser, "The Beginnings of Civilization in Mesopotamia," Supplement 4, *Journal of the American Oriental Society,* Vol. 59 (1939) pp. 17 ff. (esp. 25–28).

[10] See H. Frankfort, *Cylinder Seals* (London, 1939) p. 2.

It follows that Mesopotamian writing, the oldest script known to man, was the unlooked for outgrowth of a social order founded on the recognition of personal rights. This basic feature of Sumerian society is attested overwhelmingly in cuneiform law, perhaps the most characteristic and abundant expression of ancient Mesopotamian civilization. In the last analysis this law rests on individual rights. Under this system proof of ownership becomes a vital necessity. Incidentally, the rigid requirement of such proof is the principal reason for the hundreds of thousands of legal documents recovered from the buried sites of Mesopotamia; the forces responsible for the introduction of writing emerge as the main factor in the subsequent popularity of this means of communication and attestation.

The law applies to ruler and subjects alike. The king is at first no more than a "great man," as is shown by the Sumerian etymology of the term and the form of the corresponding pictograph. He may become the administrator of a vast empire, but even then he is still the servant, not the source of the law and is responsible to the gods for its enactment. There is here no encouragement of absolute power. The law is the constitution which guides the ruler and safeguards the subjects. The king cannot increase his holdings by the simple process of requisition or expropriation. Even members of the powerful Sargonid Dynasty, which flourished about the middle of the third millennium and strove to raise kingship to a superhuman status, had to pay for the lands which they would have. An impressive business record of Manishtusu, a member of that dynasty, testifies to the absence of special privileges in transactions of this kind.

This brings up the question of the divine rights of

kings which some works of a general character still read into Mesopotamian history. Careful study of the entire material [11] shows conclusively that this view cannot be upheld. It is true that under the Sargonids attempts were made to arrogate for the king the prerogatives of the gods. The success of the founder of the dynasty, Sargon of Akkad, in establishing a mighty empire may have served as an incentive to such aspirations. At any rate, the deification of the king was never a complete success. The effort is repeated towards the end of the third millennium, and sporadic attempts in the same direction are made a few centuries later. None of these ventures left a permanent impression on Mesopotamian civilization. Each in turn was to fail to strike root; it was a thing alien and unassimilable. One need point only to the fact that the Assyrian kings, whose conquests bespeak unprecedented military power, are foremost in their subservience to the gods whose aid they ceaselessly invoke.

Mesopotamian literature provides ample independent evidence of the limited powers of the ruler. This is true not only of the human kings but also of the leaders in the divine hierarchy, which is no more than an idealization of conditions on earth. In heaven and in the netherworld alike the ranking gods draw their authority from the "assembly" in which ultimate power is vested. Just so, the great hero Gilgamesh, legendary king of Uruk, has to consult the elders of his city. And Uta-Napishtim, the hero of the Mesopotamian account of the Flood, tells us plainly that he must have the consent of the city which he rules before embarking on a journey: "What am I to say to the city, the people and the elders?" [12] The rule

[11] Cf. R. Labat, *Le Caractère Religieux de la Royauté Assyro-Babylonienne* (Paris, 1939).

[12] Gilgamesh Epic, Tablet xi, line 119.

of the city is vested in "the people and the elders," the identical source of power which we are to recognize, thousands of years later, in "the senate and the people." The system of government, then, is a rule by the assembly or delegates of the citizens. We may call it politocracy.[13]

We have seen that this system was capable of promoting intellectual progress on an extensive scale. Its inherent vitality is attested by the ease with which this order maintains itself for tens of centuries in spite of a succession of political changes under the Sumerians, Akkadians, Gutians, Babylonians, Kassites, and Assyrians. Nor is its further expansion hindered by ethnic or linguistic barriers. Distant and unrelated peoples are attracted time and again to the orbit of the civilization of Mesopotamia. Among the newcomers we find the Elamites, the Hurrians, and the Hittites, the last-named a people of European ancestry and Indo-European speech. Incidentally, it is to the influence of Mesopotamia upon the Hittites that we owe today our oldest records of any Indo-European language. The newcomers proceed to copy the law, use the script, and enjoy the other benefits of the adopted civilization.

To sum up, there existed an intimate relation between intellectual progress in Mesopotamia and the mainspring of historic Mesopotamian civilization. Underlying all was a social order resting on the rights of the individual, embodied in a competitive economy, and protected by the supreme authority of the law. This system brought about the evolution of writing, henceforward a decisive factor

[13] Similar conclusions, based on cuneiform literary sources, but proceeding from different illustrations, were presented by Dr. Thorkild Jacobsen at the meeting of the American Oriental Society held in Chicago in April, 1941. The independent nature of our respective results tends to enhance their validity.

we are fortunate to possess in the original rather than in some copy of much later date, was already utilized and revered about 1700 B.C. or approximately as many years before the age of Moses as separate the time of Columbus from our own day.

The term "code," it may have been noticed, has not been used at all in the preceding remarks. The omission is not accidental. The handful of jurists who have so far given their attention to this material seem agreed that what we have before us is not properly a code or digest, but "a series of amendments to the common law of Babylon."[10] It is advisable, therefore, to speak here only of the "Laws of Hammurabi." The responsible authorities, then, were drafters rather than codifiers. Nor is the end product a pioneering effort, as many would still seem to believe. As far back as 1917, the distinguished German legal historian, Paul Koschaker, was able to show on internal evidence that the Laws of Hammurabi contain various interpolations and duplications—convincing proof that the document had a considerable history behind it.[11] This deduction was supported by known fragments of laws which were the work of the Sumerians, who flourished in that area before the Babylonians and spoke a language that had no generic relationship with Semitic. On independent cultural grounds, moreover, some of us have long held that enactment comparable to the Old Babylonian laws must have been current back in the third millennium. For the legal structure was an integral phase of the historic civilization of Mesopotamia, and that civilization reaches in all its essentials well back into the third mil-

[10] *Ibid*, p. 41.
[11] See his Rechtsvergleichende Studien zur Gesetzgesbung Hammurapis.

lennium.[12] Accordingly, in a popular article written in 1949 and published in January 1951 I ventured to lay a representative legal scene in the 21st century B.C.[13] We now have direct proof that such expectations were in no wise too sanguine.

As of this date we know of at least three collections of Mesopotamian laws which are anterior to Hammurabi's.[14] In 1947, F. R. Steele discovered in the University Museum of Philadelphia new fragments of Sumerian laws which in conjunction with previously published specimens add up to the "Laws of Lipit-Ishtar," featuring a preamble, a central legal portion and an epilogue, precisely as in the case of Hammurabi.[15] Lipit-Ishtar was a king of the South Mesopotamian city of Isin who ruled nearly two centuries before Hammurabi. Thus the famous Babylonian ruler had a solid precedent for his own legal project; not only is his arrangement the same as Lipit Ishtar's, but there is an intimate relationship in contents wherever the individual enactments can be compared. In 1948 there was brought to light a still older body of laws, thanks to the efforts of A. Goetze of Yale in association with the Iraq Department of Antiquities.[16] The place of origin was this time the city of Eshnunna, east of Baghdad. The language

[12] Cf. my paper entitled, Some Sources of Intellectual and Social Progress in the Ancient Near East (1942), in Studies in the History of Culture (Menasha, Wisconsin) pp. 51–62; [see above, pp. 517 ff.].

[13] In the National Geographic Magazine issue of that date, pp. 78–79.

[14] For fragments of still another collection, the Old Assyrian, see G. R. Driver and J. C. Miles: The Assyrian Laws (Oxford, 1935) pp. 1–3.

[15] See his The Code of Lipit-Ishtar (University Museum, Philadelphia, 1948).

[16] Published in Sumer (Baghdad), Vol. 4, pp. 63–102. For recent translations of most of the collections here mentioned see Ancient Near Eastern Texts Relating to the Old Testament (ed. J. B. Pritchard, Princeton, 1950) pp. 159–198. The respective translators are S. N. Kramer, A. Goetze and Th. J. Meek.

of the Laws of Eshnunna, however, is once more Akkadian rather than Sumerian, in spite of the antiquity of the text. Finally, S. N. Kramer of the University of Pennsylvania and its museum was able to announce in 1952 the discovery of a yet older body of laws, bearing the name of Ur-Nammu, the founder of the Third Dynasty of Ur.[17] This gives us a second Sumerian legal work, alongside the two in Semitic. And the date of this particular collection is the 21st century B.C., or exactly as some of us had anticipated.

Aside from these early juridical works, which date from the end of the third and the early second millennium, there are collections of cuneiform laws from later periods. Extensive portions of the Middle Assyrian laws have come down to us on several clay tablets dating from the last quarter of the second millennium,[18] and the following millennium is represented by a single clay tablet containing some of the Neo-Babylonian laws.[19] As their names indicate, both these collections were phrased in respective dialects of Akkadian, which is the collective name for the principal Semitic speech of Mesopotamia. But cuneiform "codes" were not restricted to Mesopotamia proper. The Hittites, who employed the same form of writing in recording their own language, which has unmistakable Indo-European affiliations, had an analogous collection of laws of which two extensive tablets are now extant.[20]

Legislative compilations, however, make up only a negligible part of the total cuneiform legal material that

[17] Cf. provisionally The Scientific American 188 (1953) pp. 26 ff. [See now *Orientalia* 23 (1954), pp. 40–51.]

[18] Driver and Miles: The Assyrian Laws.

[19] Cf. Pritchard, *op. cit.*, pp. 197–198 (translation by Meek).

[20] *Ibid.*, pp. 188–197 (translation by Goetze).

has been brought [illegible] the appropriate [illegible] and [illegible]

[illegible]

has been brought to light. Incomparably more numerous are the documents pertaining to the actual practice of law. Their total mounts up to countless thousands. They date all the way from the third millennium down through the first, and they cover a formidable array of legal types. Nor do they stem from Mesopotamia alone. Vast numbers of legal documents have come down to us from neighbouring areas representing all sorts of ethnic groups and languages. Yet even here the cuneiform script became standard equipment and Akkadian the normal legal language. Thus the Hurrians, who were linguistically and ethnically distinct from Sumerians, Semites and Hittites alike, resorted for official purposes to Akkadian, both in the region of modern Kirkuk and in their more widespread settlements in Syria. The Elamites—yet another distinct group—did likewise in their Iranian homeland. Thousands of cuneiform legal documents, written in Akkadian, have turned up in Cappadocia. Even Palestine has yielded material of the same kind.[21]

What we have thus before us is a picture of unprecedented cultural expansion, which is especially vivid in its legal details. Invariably prominent in this picture are the following three features: a common script, a common language, and the obligatory employment of the legal document. The external criterion of writing permits us to apply to this community of cultural interests the designation "cuneiform culture," however incongruous this phrase might be on other grounds.[22] The prevailing use of Akkadian, notably in the second millennium B.C., has more recent analogues in the use of Latin for legal purposes or of French in international diplomacy.

[21] Cf. the brief survey in Koschaker, Keilschriftrecht, pp. 1–20.
[22] *Ibid.*, pp. 26–29.

Shurkitilla, the son of Tehiptilla, went to court before the judges with Taya, the son of Rimusharri. Thus Shurkitilla: 'Kawinni, the son of Kunadu, and Ithapu, the son of Puhishenni, had adopted my father Tehiptilla for (the transfer of) two acres of land in the district of Shulmiya.[24] Now Taya has sued me by swearing out against me a royal warrant, and has had me evicted from that land.'

Thus Taya: 'I have no connection (with the land) either by inheritance or by lot or in any other manner. (But) Hanate, the wife of Shanhari delegated me with these instructions: "Go and sue Shurkitilla by swearing out against him a royal warrant, and evict him from that land." So in accordance with Hanate's instructions I swore out against him a royal warrant and had him evicted from that land.'

Then the judges questioned Hanate, saying: 'Did you delegate Taya to swear out against Shurkitilla a royal warrant?' Thus Hanate: 'I sent Taya to Shurkitilla with these instructions: "Sue Shurkitilla by swearing out against him a royal warrant, and have him evicted from that land." '

Thereupon the judges dismissed Taya from the court proceedings. To Hanate the judges declared: 'Argue the case with Shurkitilla!'

Thus Hanate: 'When my husband Shanhari provided for me in his will, he deeded that land to me.' Then the judges examined Hanate's records of the will whereby Shanhari had deeded his land to his wife. But neither the name of Kawinni nor the name of Ithapu, who had adopted Tehiptilla, was inscribed in the records of Hanate.

Thereupon Hanate declared as follows: 'Kawinni died earlier; and later on Shanhari, in providing for me in his will, deeded that land to me.' [25]

Then the registrars[whose five names are officially recorded] deposed before the judges: 'That land used to belong to Kunadu. Now Kawinni was Kunadu's eldest son and Kani was a younger son.' Then Hanate made this statement: 'That land did belong to Kunadu. Kawinni was Kunadu's eldest son, and Kani, the father of my husband Shanhari, was indeed a younger son.' [26]

[24] Since land holdings were inalienable under the local law, the only means of selling real estate was through the legal fiction of adoption, for a suitable consideration. The seller became the adoptive father, and the purchaser was recorded as the adoptee.

[25] Note the emphasis on alleged prior rights.

[26] The share of the firstborn was double and preferential.

It would have been helpful to illustrate the main types of the extant cuneiform legal records, for no description can match the flavour and the impact of actual examples. But anything like a representative number of citations, together with the necessary minimum of explanatory notes, would carry us too far afield. Before we go on, however, to broader considerations, I may perhaps be allowed to adduce a single illustration in order to convey, to a very limited degree, something of the legal problems and procedures that these records reflect. The specimen which I have selected for translation (from the local dialect of Akkadian) has been taken from among the archives found in the area of Kirkuk, because these happen to reflect the spread of Mesopotamian concepts to adjoining regions and peoples. The document records a lawsuit. If it seems involved at first, it is mainly because many of the details were fully familiar to the parties concerned and required no elaboration. It will be noticed that the court was most careful in identifying the principals and in tracing the case, step by step, to its inception two generations earlier. The decisive bearing of the written records is brought out very pointedly. Incidentally, the tablet dates from the fourteenth century B.C., over a hundred years before the time of Moses. Yet it was not very long ago that critics doubted the possibility of complex legislation in the Mosaic age on the ground that those times were too primiitve and that the knowledge of writing was at yet unequal to the task. Indeed, our perspective has changed radically within the past few decades.

Here is the translation of the first sixty-eight lines of the tablet: [23]

[23] The cuneiform text is given in E. Chiera: Proceedings in Court (Publ. of the Baghdad School, Texts, Vol. IV, Philadelphia, 1934), No. 333.

Whereas, therefore, Shanhari had deeded to his wife land that was not his, in that the names of Kawinni and Ithapu were not inscribed in his records, the judges ordered Hanate to surrender that land and assigned the land to Shurkitilla. And whereas she had a royal warrant sworn out against Shurkitilla, (evicting him) from his own land, the judges committed Hanate to Shurkitilla for the payment of one bullock as fine.

[The judges take certain additional steps to clear the title to the land under dispute. There follow the seals of the officials and the signature of the scribe.]

To get back to our main argument, how can one account for the unprecedented cultural influence of Mesopotamia, emanating as it did from a relatively small center in the South? It should be stressed that this expansion was by no means co-extensive with political authority. Even in Mesopotamia proper, the South and the North were traditional enemies. The Elamites and the Hurrians on the fringe pursued their own political ways. The Hittites represented an independent power; nor were the various states of Syria and Palestine ordered about by a Mesopotamian power until the emergence of Assyrian might, in the first millenium. Yet all these diverse elements, in spite of their underlying differences, were drawn into the orbit of a single civilization, notably in such essentials as the concept and practice of law. Is there a plausible explanation for this phenomenon?

III. LAW AS THE TOUCHSTONE OF A CIVILIZATION

Legal systems not only help to implement but also serve to reflect the underlying concepts of government. In the ancient Near East state and religion were inseparable. The two interfused. Between them they embodied the individual society's way of life. Hence the pertinent legal systems have to be viewed in conjunction with the over-all social philosophies which the respective societies had evolved.

The great impact of the legal thinking and practice of Mesopotamia on other parts of the Near East must be bound up, accordingly, with the kind of society that was characteristic of Mesopotamia. And, conversely, the failure of the other legal systems of the area to achieve similar prominence should be rooted in their respective sociocultural backgrounds.

The pre-classical Near East has left evidence of only one major juridical structure that may be said to have competed with that of Mesopotamia, namely, the Egyptian. To be sure, the effect of Biblical law can hardly be overestimated; nor does Hittite law appear to have played a negligible rôle. These two systems, however, were not in competition with Mesopotamian law. On the contrary, they were related to it in several ways: the Biblical in its framework, spirit, as well as in many individual provisions; and the Hittite still more closely by reason of the use of the cuneiform script and the stress on the written document. There is thus no genuine cleavage until we come to Egypt. The civilization of Egypt is found to be in sharp contrast with the cultural complex of that portion of Western Asia which has conveniently been designated as the Fertile Crescent. The contrast stems not so much from material ways as from differences in the way of life. And these differences are brought into sharp relief by the respective legal systems.

Readers of John Henry Wigmore's *A Panorama of the World's Legal Systems* may be still under the impression that the Egyptian system is the oldest known to man and that it can be documented as far back as 4000 B.C.[27] The jurist repeated in this case an understandable error of earlier orientalists. Scholars have since been obliged to lower the date for the beginnings of recorded Egyptian history by about a thousand years. In the present context, however, the absolute antiquity of Egyptian law is not nearly as important as are its nature and place in the over-all scheme of things. It is on these counts that the differences from the Mesopotamian system are most clearly apparent.

One highly significant point of contrast is noticeable at first glance. Egypt has not left to posterity a formal body of laws comparable to the Laws of Lipit-Ishtar or Eshnunna or Hammurabi, the Old Assyrian or the Middle Assyrian or the Neo-Babylonian systems, or the Hittite and Hebrew analogues. What is more, alongside the countless thousands of records relating to the practice of law in Mesopotamia and affiliated areas, there is barely a trickle from Egypt before the Persian and Greek periods. This is no mere argument from silence. The soil and climate of Egypt were kind to materials far more perishable than those that were employed for writing. The negative evidence of many centuries has in these circumstances a substantial cumulative bearing. Then there is compelling internal evidence. The local society was so constituted that it set far less store by the written legal document than could possibly have been the case in Mesopotamia. Nor is the reason for this Egyptian attitude far to seek.

In a paper read in 1940, and subsequently published and reprinted several times, I sought to sum up the situa-

[27] (Chicago, 1928) pp. 5–12.

tion as it presented itself to an assyriologist.[28] We are on firmer ground today in that we can refer to a statement by one of our most distinguished egyptologists. In the lucid words of John A. Wilson's *The Burden of Egypt*,[29] the pharaoh was the essential nucleus of the state:

> He, as a god, *was* the state. . . . To be sure, it was necessary for a new state to have rules and regulations for administrative procedures and precedent, but our negative evidence suggests that there was no codification of law, impersonally conceived and referable by magistrates without consideration of the crown. Rather, the customary law of the land was conceived to be the word of the pharaoh. . . . In later times there was visible no impersonal and continuing body of law, like one of the Mesopotamian codes, until we come down into Persian and Greek days; the centralization of the state in the person of the king apparently forbade such impersonal law. The authority of codified law would have competed with the personal authority of the pharaoh.

In other words, since the pharaoh was regarded as a god, there could be no authority, personal or impersonal, superior to his own.

In sharp contrast to the authoritarian position of the pharaoh, the Mesopotamian ruler was viewed as an ordinary mortal who was accountable to the gods for his every move. His powers were further circumscribed, since the beginning of history, by the requirement that each major public undertaking must have the prior consent of the appropriate assembly, either of the elders or of the warriors. All this is intimately related to the Mesopotamian concept of the cosmos, that is to say, religion.[30]

[28] Cf. *supra*, footnote 12, for the latest publication.

[29] (Chicago, 1951) pp. 49–50.

[30] Cf. Thorkild Jacobsen in Frankfort *et al.:* The Intellectual Adventure of Ancient Man (Chicago, 1946) pp. 125–222; H. Frankfort: Kingship and the Gods (Chicago, 1948) pp. 215–267.

State and religion were the two normative aspects of the way of life, just as in Egypt and elsewhere in the ancient Near East. What made the real difference in each case was the kind of religion and government involved. In Egypt the result was authoritarianism. In Mesopotamia the trend was towards democracy. And the mechanism whereby that democratic orientation was controlled and safeguarded made up the Mesopotamian legal system.

How such fundamentally opposed ways of life had arisen in two contemporaneous and otherwise related civilizations is a question that is altogether beyond the scope of this paper. Some of the answers, incidentally, are as yet concealed from us by deep layers of pre-history. At any rate, the fact is that these far-reaching differences existed and that they profoundly affected the historic careers of the two great civilizations.[31] Although sundry details of these careers are still obscure, the principal features of the Mesopotamian experience fall into a clear pattern.

Since the kings of Mesopotamia lacked absolute authority—indeed even the Mesopotamian gods could not boast unlimited power—the position of the subjects was correspondingly enhanced. This shows itself with telling force in the ubiquitous recognition of private property and the prevailing respect for it. Nowhere is this last-named feature more sharply reflected than in § 7 of the Laws of Hammurabi:

> If a man has purchased or received for safekeeping either silver or gold or a male slave or a female slave or an ox or a

[31] In this connection attention may be called to my paper on The Ancient Near East and Modern Philosophies of History (1951), 95 Proc. Amer. Philos. Soc. 583–588.

sheep or an ass or anything whatsoever from the hand of a citizen or the slave of a citizen, without witnesses or a written contract, that man shall be put to death for he is a thief.

Time and practical considerations may eventually have modified this drastic provision. It is all too plain, however, that on more than one occasion possession of proper legal records was literally a matter of life or death. Small wonder, therefore, that the mounds which pockmark the landscape of Mesopotamia became repositories of hundreds of thousands of documents executed in strict conformity with the law of the land. The law rather than accidents of discovery and the use of a durable writing material accounts for the presence of all these tablets.

There is, furthermore, a strong probability that writing itself came to be invented in the first place in conjunction with age-old practices pertaining to temple and private economy. The cultivation of writing in turn —a highly intricate process before the introduction of the alphabet—has considerable bearing on the advance of other sciences. Progress was thus being registered on a broad front. But it was the law that remained the zealous guardian of the distinctive Mesopotamian way of life throughout the many centuries.

In passing, a few words may be in order concerning the Akkadian phrase which is used to express both the nature and the function of law. The reference in question is *kittum u mēsharum*. The first word means "that which is firm, established, true"; the third word (following the particle for "and") means "equity, justice." In other words, the whole phrase stands for something like "impersonal and immutable order tempered with equity and fairness." This is how Hammurabi describes his own legal effort. We could scarcely improve on it in seeking to characterize the whole legal philosophy of Mesopotamia.

IV. THE DYNAMICS OF MESOPOTAMIA LAW

In the discussion so far I have spoken repeatedly of Mesopotamia, although this term stands for no ethnic, linguistic or political unit. Quite the contrary; for on all these counts the Biblical tale of the Tower of Babel comes closer to the mark, in that it hints at a confusing variety of tongues and peoples. In the several millenniums of its pre-classical history various mutually antagonistic peoples pass in review and several unrelated linguistic stocks are encountered. There is, however, an underlying cultural unity which transcends the conventional boundaries and gradually embraces the entire valley, to spread thence to adjoining areas. The composite product cannot properly be ascribed to any one people or center. It was, in effect, Mesopotamian.

The question was broached earlier whether this spectacular cultural dynamism can be explained. We have seen that characteristic legal features were the normal witnesses of the advancing Mesopotamian civilization: collections of laws and documents pertaining to legal practice. Those features had come in their native vessels, so to speak: the cuneiform script and the Sumerian language, which soon gave way to Akkȧdian. It may be added in passing that an itinerant language is not the same thing as an international scientific formula. The language may be said to carry with it an accumulation of cultural genes. Thus the Hittites of Antolia, in acquainting themselves with Akkadian and rudiments of Sumerian, exposed themselves not only to the appertaining laws but to religion, literature and the sciences as well. And so they proceeded to translate Akkadian myths and epics. Indeed, some Babylonian tales which had reached the Hittites through Hurrian mediation turn up eventually in Greek mythology.

To get back, however, to the possible causes of this cultural expansion, it should be made clear that the problem is not capable as yet of a conclusive solution. In the nature of things, perhaps, some uncertainty will always attend any answer that may be attempted. The following remarks, which bring this paper to its conclusion, should be viewed therefore, as has already been indicated, as a working hypothesis. The test of such hypotheses has to be pragmatic. Let us see how this one works.

The outward signs of foreign dependence on Mesopotamian law are the script, the language and the document. Yet such formal indebtedness fails to reveal the secret of Mesopotamia's appeal. Magnetism on so large a scale would seem to suggest that content as well as form played here a substantial part. Nevertheless, the Hittites certainly did not simply adopt the laws of Hammurabi or the Old Assyrian laws. And the Hebrews remain even further apart; for they either never acknowledged the influence of the cuneiform script or they soon emancipated themselves from it in committing their own laws to writing. In content, then, there is nothing like a one-to-one correlation between the laws of Mesopotamia and Hittite or Hebrew law.

Yet too much store can be set, I believe, by this circumstance. Complete interdependence in details is not the only valid criterion of close substantive relationship. No less significant, I submit, would be affinity in ideas and spirit if that could be demonstrated and shown to be sufficiently far-reaching. Now law, as was pointed out earlier, serves to reflect the fundamental spirit of the given civilization. Mesopotamian civilization, by restricting the authority of the ruler, did much to emphasize and to protect the rights of the individual in relation to society and the cosmos. In this significant respect the social philosophies of the Hebrews and the Hittites had much in common with the Mesopotamian outlook on life. Their civilizations were related not only materially and intellectually but also, to a pronounced degree, spiritually. It is on this last count that the contrast between the Fertile Crescent and Egypt shows up in sharpest relief. And in each case the law is the key to the civilization.

It would appear, therefore, that the dynamism of Mesopotamian civilization was due in the last analysis to
Mesopotamian civilization was due in the last analysis to
its distinctive way of life. We cannot tell at this time whether other civilizations found the Mesopotamian way appealing because it was similar to theirs, or whether they had first to be converted to that way under Mesopotamian influence. Be that as it may, we have now a better insight into what converted Mesopotamia itself into an integral cultural unit. We are no longer surprised by the fact that the stela of Hammurabi should have turned up at Susa. What is more, we have a clearer perspective on the characteristic Biblical term *torah*. That term does mean "law," as it is commonly rendered. But it means also a great deal more than such a rendering would generally suggest. *Torah* corresponds also to the Babylonian *kittum u mésharum,* and beyond that, and more particularly, it stands also for a specific way of life. In addition, we are entitled to ask whether the remem-

brance of the bondage in Egypt, which runs through the Old Testament as a recurrent refrain, reflects no more than the experience of a small number of Hebrews during a relatively short period of their pre-history. In view of all that has been said so far, there is the inherent probability that the bondage in this instance was so exceptionally severe because it involved basic spiritual values and had resulted from a clash between fundamentally incompatible ways of life.

To be sure, we do not know, nor do I wish to assert, that the Biblical estimate of the law as the key to a vital civilization was due to direct influence from Mesopotamia. It is significant, however, that tht peak in the study of Biblical law was reached, in later times, not in Palestine but in Babylonia, and was embodied in a major work which still bears the name of the Babylonian Talmud. Analogously, the most fruitful period in the development of Islamic law was witnessed when Baghdad was the capital of the Ismalic world. The vitality of legal tradition in Mesopotamia survived thus by a number of centuries the end of the historic Mesopotamian civilization.

In conclusion, a word may be in order concerning the possibility that classical law may have owed some inspiration to oriental prototypes. With the unexpected expansion of juridical horizons as a result of recent discoveries, it was but natural that some writers should turn against the traditional views and seek to derive the classical law from Mesopotamia. But the leading workers in the field have refused to be driven to such extremes.[32] Direct Roman borrowing from Mesopotamian legal sources is precluded, of course, by the fact that the civilization of Mesopotamia had come to the end of its independent

[32] See Koschaker, Keilschriftrecht, pp. 29–32.

course before Rome became an oriental power. That specific cultural elements may have filtered through, by one route or another, from the Fertile Crescent to the classical world is quite another matter. And that legal items were not left out in the process is suggested by certain Babylonian loanwords in the West. The really important thing is that Mesopotamia had experienced more than two millenniums of notable legal progress before classical civilization began. That experience could not have been without some effect on Europe. Finally, the kind of law which Mesopotamia evolved proved its capacity to serve as an aid to the democratic process. To the extent, therefore, that the Fertile Crescent as a whole contributed to the evolution of democracy, it placed under indebtedness not only ancient Greece but our modern western civilization as well.

Religion and Government in the Ancient Near East

WE LIVE IN AN AGE OF TECHNOLOGICAL MIRACLES AND OF intellectual and moral confusion. Viewed from some distant star, where our smallest unit to be picked out might be a state or a society, we could well appear as a group of strange creatures, half penguin and half ostrich. This, one would be perfectly right to observe, is a weird idea even for science fiction. It is all of that, no doubt. The one thing about it, however, that has more in common with science than with fiction, and is not at all weird, is the fact that man's behavior can best be sized up in perspective. And our only source of adequate perspective is history

Human history is in reality nowhere near as long as it may appear to be at first glance, provided that by history we mean the only kind that is fully articulate, namely, recorded history. Man's career as a food-gatherer began, it would seem, about half a million years ago. His first traceable steps toward concerted social activity reach back some fifty thousand years. But recorded history spans only five thousand years. It takes up at most a mere one per cent of an immemorial total, a partly remembered and partly forgotten yesterday with a direct and immediate bearing on today. Such a small segment is scarcely enough for a true perspective. Yet it is all that we have when it comes to the larger questions of life and destiny and it is our obvious task to use this modest store as fully and as wisely as we can.

All societies advanced enough to leave their stamp on history have had to face two issues above all others. One is the relation of the individual to society. The other is the relation of society to the universe. The former is the foundation of government. The latter is the heart of religion. The standing of a given civilization depends primarily on the way in which it has solved these two issues. The most pressing political and economic problems of the day become secondary and ephemeral by comparison.

This is, of course, an old and familiar conclusion. The point has been made many times, most often in terms of "God, man, and the state." The only thing about it that may seem novel to some is the fact that the twin problems of government and religion—in the broadest sense of each term—should have been as acute at many critical junctures of the past as they are in our own time. Students of history, however, have long been familiar with this very fact, particularly if they have been careful, as Lord Acton so aptly put it, to "study problems, not periods." For the fundamental problems of mankind cannot be limited to any one age. They are timeless and universal.

Strangely enough, however, some of the most celebrated historians of our day have not taken this precept sufficiently to heart. Monumental erudition and a lucid style are not in themselves infallible tools where facts are distorted by preconceived theories so that problems cannot be seen for the periods. In the words of R. G. Collingwood, whose penetrating philosophy of history was first presented nearly twenty years ago, "This is the origin of all the schemes and patterns into which history has time and again, with surprising docility, allowed itself to be forced by [various men] . . . down to Flinders Petrie, Oswald Spengler, and Arnold Toynbee in our own time . . ." This kind of history is, in Collingwood's judgment, pigeon-holed and scissors-and-paste history. Overriding issues such as those of government and religion can be neither pigeon-holed nor cut up and reassembled. They observe no chronological boundaries, and they are the masters, not the slaves, of any given era.

There is thus much to be gained from viewing the ever-present issues of religion and government, in the perspective that the past affords, as constant aspects of otherwise variable civilizations. It may be in order to emphasize in this connection that such continuity is not at all an instance of history repeating itself, for the observation still holds good that history does not repeat itself, but that it is only the historians who repeat one another. Rather is this an instance of history that has never paused and of pressing questions that have confronted mankind as long as civilization can remember. These questions have never been solved for all time because, although the problems remain the same, civilizations do not. We can see such issues, however, in a clearer light if we allow the present to be informed by the living past at the same time that the past is illuminated for us by the deep-rooted present.

Now the one region above all others where the past has never stopped or, alternatively, where the present got its start a long time ago, is the Near East. It is there that history began and there it continues to be made every day. And it is there, too, that many of the most vital questions of today were first raised, among them, inevitably the basic questions about the universe and man and the state. Nowhere else is the record so rich or the work sheets so full, for the whole has taken five thousand years to compile—all the years in fact that man has had control of that greatest and most far-reaching of all means of communication, the knowledge of writing.

What has come down to us from yesterday is thus in large measure our heritage from the Near East. This heritage comprises an enormous accumulation of sundry items. Yet if we were asked to single out the Near East's greatest gifts to today's civilization, we should have to name, significantly enough, two contributions which stand out from all the rest. One pertains to intra-societal relations, or government, and it bears the imprint of Mesopotamia. The other is the religious achievement which crowned the long and dedicated efforts of ancient Israel. These two legacies, which jointly supply an answer to one of civilization's basic needs have been drawn upon and fought over ever since they were first made available. Their abiding vitality has remained unaffected.

Mesopotamia came up with its distinctive approach to society at the very dawn of recorded history. It proved to be a singularly successful solution in that it was highly constructive at home and widely adopted abroad. It came to be modified and refined by many successive societies, but it has never been superseded in its essentials. This Mesopotamian answer to the problem of government deserves a much fuller account than can here be given. It marks a significant milestone in the progress of world civilization; yet primary credit for this advance has been misdirected to Greece. The evidence is so abundant, manifold, and unambiguous as to be beyond reasonable dispute. Nevertheless, we sometimes shrink from new findings when these involve a revision of worn-out textbooks. And mental habits of long standing often take a long time to readjust.

In any case, according to the Mesopotamian world-view, human society was an exact replica of the society of the gods. Now none of the gods of Mesopotamia was really omnipotent, not even the head of the pantheon. Ultimate authority was vested in the gods as a body, and no given chief could command absolute power. The example of the gods thus precluded autocracy on earth. The mortal ruler was subject, first, to the will of the gods and, second, to the decisions of the assembly of his own elders. A third check against autocracy on earth was the supreme authority of the law which was impersonal and absolute. The king was but the humble servant of the law, and its just enactment was one of his principal responsibilities. The wide use to which writing was put served as an added guarantee against abuses and distortions on the part of the ruler, for the law could now be given expression in permanent form. Written compilations of laws have been witnessed in a series of codes which reach back to the third millennium and in some instances antedate by several centuries the celebrated Code of Hammurabi. Such prologues to these collections as have come down to us invariably stress the king's solemn duty to effect justice in the land under divine protection and supervision.

What is implicit in this Mesopotamian concept of state is a form of democracy. For government by assembly, restricted royal power, and the overriding authority of the law can scarcely add up to anything else. This recognition of the essentially democratic nature of the historic civilization of Mesopotamia is of relatively recent date. But it was arrived at independently by several students, each approaching the subject from a different angle, the starting points being law, literature, and art. Yet the conclusions converge in a most convincing manner. The newness of this discovery should not cause too much surprise. We have all been brought up on the traditional notion that the Orient has always been synonymous with despotism. No less firmly entrenched has been the view that Greece was the cradle of democracy. Small wonder, therefore, that the mere suggestion of a democratic trend in Mesopotamia runs up against instinctive disbelief, even among some cuneiformists. The signs are multiplying, nevertheless, that this particular stereotype will soon be adjudged an intellectual liability. The Mesopotamian concept of state was the very antithesis of autocracy. It was instead a pioneering experience in democracy.

The Mesopotamian way just described, with its emphasis on the rights of the individual and on the dependent position of the ruler, is furthermore the key to the steady expansion of that civilization. Locally this system helped to mold a Babel of tongues and races into an integrated and dynamic whole. And abroad it was copied widely by more and more of Mesopotamia's neighbors, as far as the borders of Europe, and down to the period of the Hellenistic civilization.

Nevertheless, a productive philosophy of government is but half the answer to a society's major dilemma. It is, so to speak, a half-truth. The inner strength of a civilization depends ultimately on the harmony of its societal and religious components. In the case of Mesopotamia, religion failed to keep pace with secular advances, in that the religious concepts did not promote spiritual security. Since no Mesopotamian god was truly omnipotent, the gods as a body were likewise unsure of themselves. They were arbitrary and capricious, not just. Hence in his relations with nature the Mesopotamian lacked the solace of genuine ethical standards. Religion and government were not in balance.

In sharpest contrast with the Mesopotamian system was the Egyptian way. In Egypt, the head of the cosmos was a sublime autocrat whose absolute rule was reflected on earth in a king in whom the creator was perpetually incarnate. Because the land was thus ruled by a king who was himself a god, and because there was no check on his authority, the ruler on earth was not answerable to any higher power. The law was his tool not his master. The pyramids are an awesome monumental reminder of the pharaoh's limitless totalitarianism. Once again, then, government and religion were not in equilibrium, with the important difference, however, that in Egypt religion overshadowed government and blocked social progress. Small wonder, therefore, that the Egyptian way was sterile at home and abhorred abroad. Totalitarian efficiency is in the long run no match for unregimented inspiration.

The ancient Hebrew way evolved against the contrasted backgrounds of Egypt and Mesopotamia. The Mesopotamian order had proved highly constructive in matters of law and government, but it was unproductive in matters of religion. In this light, Abraham's departure from Mesopotamia assumes a new significance. The Patriarchs were in large measure the nurselings of the cosmopolitan civilization of Mesopotamia. They had absorbed many of the cultural norms of their original homeland, notably in regard to law and government, and they showed no hesitancy in retaining these particular features and in subscribing to their underlying philosophy. The religious vacuum, however, of the Mesopotamian way of life drove the Patriarchs to move to other climes in search of more enduring truths. This is after all the meaning of God's covenant with Abraham, a pact that is one of the two persistent motives of the Hebrew Bible. The other such motive is bondage in Egypt, and it comes up time and again as a recurring refrain. For if the Mesopotamian system was regarded as inadequate, in spite of its democratic features, then the Egyptian way with its unrelieved autocracy and its deified kings could be nothing short of abomination. And so the quest for valid spiritual truths went on.

That such truths were arrived at in time is a matter of pragmatic test quite apart from being an article of more than one faith. They were to prove their strength by anchoring the Hebrew way of life and by nurturing two subsequent world religions; and they were to sustain a scattered people through continuous trials without parallel in all history. These truths are just as valid today as they were half of history ago when they had first been proclaimed. No age, certainly, aside from our own, could have had greater need of their comfort and guidance. They ring out with utmost clarity. In a cosmos which everywhere mirrors the omnipotence of God, they affirm, the only viable norm is universal justice, the one supreme grace, peace. Peace and justice on a universal scale are possible through a perfect alignment between society and nature, which must therefore be man's highest ideal and his fondest hope. This is the substance of the message though not its exact phraseology. It is a message that has often been disparaged and strayed from. Yet mankind invariably comes back to it and reaches out for it. For you cannot surpass something that you have not even begun to attain.

There cannot be, of course, a ready formula for discoveries of this kind. They cannot be produced in a laboratory, for their essence stems from the alchemy of history, not its chemistry. The basic ingredients, however, are not hard to identify. Israel had inherited from Mesopotamia a philosophy of government which made for notable social progress. What was wanting in that heritage was commensurate spiritual content: a concept of religion which society could not outstrip, as it did in Mesopotamia, yet one which would not at the same time expose society to strangulation, as in Egypt. Israel had somehow found the inspiration, the perseverance, and the capacity for self-sacrifice to fill that need. The vital balance between temporal and spiritual factors was attained in the age of David and it is reflected in more ways than one. Politically, Israel progressed from abject defeat to an all-time peak of prosperity. Culturally, the age was graced by those nameless men of genius who left us the narrative accounts of the Pentateuch and the matchless history of the Davidic era itself with its stirring events and its unforgettable personalities. And spiritually, that same period was destined to be looked back upon as the Messianic ideal of not one but two religions, whose sway was not to be restricted to the little land of their origin.

It is one thing, however, to attain the all-important balance between religion and government, and quite another thing to hold it. The delicate equilibrium is in constant danger of being upset as these two factors interpenetrate. Indeed, the succeeding centuries were never to be free from that threat. Yet no lasting damage was suffered; on the contrary, the gains were refined, consolidated, and rendered enduring and universally valid. This was the unique achievement of the Prophets. There is no proved method, happily or unhappily, for dissecting flaming genius. Significantly enough, however, all the great Prophets had this in common: they were committed neither to the government position nor to the claims of the official representatives of contemporary religion. Independent of the throne and the altar alike, the Prophets held each of these in check until norms could be discovered which were valid for any society. And so it came about that when the parent states had lost their political independence, the way of life which had evolved in Israel and Judah was no longer in danger from the temporal forces which had prevailed. What went thus down with the Temple at Jerusalem, under the impact of Babylon's ephemeral might, was in a broader sense not a shrine but a barrier. The destruction was at the same time also, and much more so, a release. The insights that had matured in the meantime were no longer tenuous and parochial. They were now imperishable and universal. They belonged not to any one nation but to the world at large.

The journey's end for ancient Israel and Judah is but the mid-way mark in the continuous interaction of government and religion through the overall history of the Near East. The first half had been in the nature of a heroic experiment which led to positive results at long last. But it is the second half that concerns us more intimately for the simple reason that it is our own half. It witnesses, moreover, the appearance of Christianity and of Islam on the always active Near Eastern stage. And finally, the latest episode features also the return of Israel to the same old stage, a stage as old in fact as recorded history itself.

In thus turning the spotlight for a brief moment on a region that has been both the beneficiary and the victim of history and geography combined, and which has known the blessings and the curses of both, we should not lose sight of the fact that what we are trying to trace is not the picture as a whole, in all its mass of detail, but only the two prominent features of government and religion. Nor is this intended as an evaluation of each of these two institutions individually. Such an attempt would be far too ambitious in the case of government; and in the case of living religions any analysis is at best a fumbling tool. The sole quesiton before us is how these two parallel factors have interacted, one with the other, during history's latter half, and more particularly since the rise of Christianity.

As a spiritual force Christianity became and has remained a paramount world influence. As a social institution, however, Christianity was bound to be affected by the political careers of the component societies. In the Near East this interpenetration of the spiritual and the temporal became a serious drawback as soon as government took it upon itself to take sides in doctrinal disputes. "Unhappily," writes James Parkes, "[the Church] succumbed entirely to the idea that theological questions can be settled by the short cut of imperial legislation and civil punishment—aided by violence which the side supported by the imperial court could be sure would be overlooked. It was only a step . . . to the decision of Theodosius the Great . . . that it was an imperial prerogative to proclaim by law what should be the orthodoxy of its subjects, and to treat those who disagreed as enemies of society to be proscribed, banished, robbed of their property and, if the situation seemed to warrant it, killed. Within a couple of centuries the Emperor Zeno could write . . . on the same issue that "thousands have perished in the massacres and not only the earth but the air is red with blood." ' The theological controversy resulted in successive split-offs of the Eastern Churches, a rift that has not been healed to this day. And the unceasing anarchy and bloodshed into which the Byzantine Empire had been plunged left the Near East a physical and moral wreck. It was this weakness, far more than the strength of the opposing forces, that accounts for the singular sweep of the new order of Islam and the relative ease with which the Muslim armies achieved their conquests. We have here yet another instance of what can happen in a power vacuum. This time, however, the vacuum was not brought on primarily by material factors. Its source was largely theological.

Islam, for its part, was from its very inception not only a religion but also a political and social system, it being Muhammad's conviction that his mission included the task of founding a community which should be a State as well as a Church. Accordingly, the blending of the two is more intimate and firm in Islam than in any other major community. By now, Islam as a spiritual experience has stood the test of some thirteen centuries. It numbers today well over 300 million adherents. But the secular content of the traditional Islamic system has not held up nearly as well. Social solutions designed in the seventh century for a small body of followers in the recesses of the Arabian Peninsula could not be expected to satisfy the needs of a world communtiy in the fifteenth, let alone the twentieth century. The long-term results have been detrimental in precisely those fields in which religion has encroached on the independent functions of government. Behind the mass poverty that points up the sick state of the Islamic societies today lies the ominous factor of social and cultural stagnation. Education in theocratic countries is of necessity slanted, limited, and reactionary. Political progress, international relations, and even economic development are hampered by numerous injunctions that were anachronisms a thousand years ago. The organic weakness of the Islamic community today stems, in short, from the temporal features of the underlying religious system.

Since the Near East is the traditional world center of gravity—a role it has had to play since history began—by reason of its location, its natural and human resources, and the chain reaction of its history, a stable and healthy Near East is vital to the peace and security of the whole world. Our diplomats and our political scientists know this well enough. What they fail to recognize all too often is the root cause of the ills which stand in the way of a healthy and stable Near East. Because so much is at stake, they are all impatient for a quick cure, after but a surface diagnosis. At times they would ascribe the major ailment to oil; at other times they would trace it to the Suez Canal. Most prominent of all in recent years has been the diagnosis based on the so-called Palestine controversy. This is not to minimize the importance of all such issues, for each has been a serious and dangerous irritant, and one of them still is. Yet none of these issues should be charged with a major share of the blame, not even the colonialism of recent and still vivid memory. Each should be seen as a symptom, and not as the cause, of the internal ills. For if all these irritants combined should be wiped out miraculously with a single stroke, the area would still be a threat to world stability so long as the basic ailment continues unresolved.

Progressive elements throughout the Muslim world have long recognized that what is urgently needed, instead of scapegoats and divisionary tactics, is religious reform as the first step towards social reform. The example of Turkey has borne this out. Once the proverbial sick man of Europe, Turkey did not start on its way back to health until Church and State had been separated so that each could function without undue interference from the other. No lasting improvement can be looked for in the other Islamic states until each has acted with like honesty and resoluteness. It required, therefore, no exceptional insight, nor a gift of prophecy, to say—as I did in writing several years ago—that the Arab states in which traditional Islam has remained a dominant force are faced with a new form of the three R's, one of which will have to be adopted sooner or later: Reform, Revolution, or Russia. Each of these three choices has already been sampled by one state or another, but only to a very limited degree so far. It should be apparent, however, that nothing less than the wholehearted application of religious reform is in the best interests of the local population.

In these circumstances one cannot but regard as curious a statement by Arnold Toynbee which he made a few years ago in a chapter on "Islam and the West." After deploring the disruptive influence of Western nationalism, Toynbee went on to express the hope that "the spread of this Western political malady may be arrested by the strength of a traditional Islamic feeling for unity." That nationalism can become a virulent obsession is all too evident in this day and age, and Toynbee's wish that this disease be checked can only be echoed with fervor. What makes his statement curious is the substitute which he suggests. The ideal of Islamic unity could not easily be divorced from pan-Islamism, which in turn is nationalism under the aegis of a militant religion. If political nationalism is a villain, then religious nationalism is even more offensive in that it seeks to give spiritual sanction to political excesses. Pan-Islamism has proved harmful to its followers in the past and would hardly be likely to improve their lot in the future. It has been a serious liability precisely because under it the tie between government and religion has failed to bring about a balance between the political and the spiritual factors. It is a union which the Islamic world must strive to loosen rather than cement.

We come, lastly, to modern Israel. It goes without saying that the problem of religion and government in our age is not confined to the Islamic world in general and the Arab world in particular. It is an ever-present issue in many other communities, quiescent when these two factors are in balance but eruptive when the equilibrium between them has been upset.

In modern Israel, a new state with old traditions but very young institutions, the question has a very special pertinence. In no other state could religion hold a comparable appeal, because no other nation is indebted for its very existence, and in such overwhelming measure to the spiritual treasures of the past. This means that religious tradition, under whatever guise it may manifest itself, is in Israel a historical and sentimental influence even where it is not an apparent spiritual factor. The reasons for this sort of attachment are not far to seek. The survival of the Jews in the Diaspora—under widely different and constantly changing conditions, through many ages, and in circumstances of prevailing adversity on a scale unparalleled in the annals of mankind—would be unthinkable without the sustaining and enduring values of Israel's spiritual heritage. Among those of the survivors who went on to establish modern Israel, the hard-headed rationalists may look upon the long intervening centuries as a historical anomaly; the devout among them may see here the gradual fulfillment of a confidently expected miracle. In either case, each camp pays thus, in its special way, its own kind of tribute to religion.

Now one of the inevitable consequences of the Diaspora has been the dissolution of the traditional tie between religion and government. In each instance, the sovereign society would naturally impose its own political norms and its own form of government. Judaism became a stateless community, cherishing its spiritual and cultural heritage, and sustained in turn by that heritage, while its secular life was now wholly in the service of the various adoptive states. And this is what Judaism has remained to this day: a living demonstration, as it were, that religion and the state are ultimately independent entities. To be sure, neither occurs, or is known to have occurred, without some form of accommodation to the other. But as that bold experiment on the part of history which we know as Judaism has shown, religion and government can coexist in more than one possible combination. The two need not have grown up together. This is the principal reason why Judaism and Israel cannot be synonymous, although they will always remain related. They can never undo, even if they wished to, their common spiritual background. But the political and social content must differ inevitably from country to country. And modern Israel has yet to strike its own balance between religion and government.

When Israel addresses itself to the old question of God, man, and the state, the evidence of the past—Israel's own past as well as that of the Near East as a whole—is surely uniform and unambiguous. It is etched sharp, in fact, on all of history's pages to date. What this evidence adds up to is this: Many forms of government have been tried, many different systems of religion. The solution that went into the Biblical way of life has retained its fundamental validity to this day and is still subscribed to in substance by a large portion of mankind. It is a solution based on a delicate balance between the component spiritual and sociopolitical factors. But interdependence of government and religion, as a matter of a common philosophy, must not be mistaken for the domination of the one by the other. Whenever that was permitted to take place, the delinquent society has faced bankruptcy, and one of the immediate consequences has been political receivership.

Yes, this lesson of the past is unmistakable. And no community is in a position to decipher its import better than Israel.

Oriental Studies and Society

THE SECOND WORLD WAR MAY BE SAID TO HAVE BROUGHT about the rediscovery of the Orient by the western world. To be sure, this has not been a planned development. Circumstances had much to do with it. Of the two war theatres, one engulfed in the main the Far and Middle East while the other extended to the Near East for the major part of the conflict. East and West met thus all along the line. Now the post-war world is finding out that the twain cannot be separated.

This unscheduled prominence of the Orient drew the orientalist under the spotlight during the war, a role to which he was wholly unaccustomed and for which his training had failed to prepare him. The chasm between the orientalist's normal studies and his emergency duties was perhaps nowhere more pronounced than in this country. For American concern with the Orient had been traditionally—and, one may add, proverbially—academic, more so certainly than was true of Britain, or France, or the Netherlands, not to mention Italy and Germany. The American orientalist, moreover, was primarily a student of the ancient East. The relatively few who had chosen to specialize in the modern Orient did so usually as humanists. The war could not but expose this unbalanced coverage of the field. In consequence, an Egyptologist had to take charge of research on the Arab world, a cuneiformist was sidetracked to Afghanistan, a Sanskritist was obliged to turn to Burma and Malaya, and a student of Chinese philosophy was plunged into the very thick of the strictly mundane affairs of Sinkiang. What is more, nearly all of these dislocated specialists found it necessary to branch out, as part of their new work, into such unfamiliar fields as psychology, economics, communications, and public health. If in so doing they added little to the sum of knowledge, it should be said in their defence that these tasks went to them by default and were accepted with marked reluctance.

All this makeshift is now a thing of the past. The whole discipline of Oriental studies is back on its pre-war course. In some isolated instances there may have been an increase in numbers. The underlying conditions, however, are no longer the same as they once were. For the events which have taken place in the meantime impose a drastic change in the relation of Oriental studies to society. The orientalist still has his responsibility to himself and his subject; but he has been left also with another major obligation, namely, that as citizen.

A moment's reflection should convince those who may not have given much thought to the matter so far that we as a group, if not necessarily as individuals, are faced with an urgent need for reorientation. Until recently ours had been a field which carried little general appeal and which called for special tastes and interests. Society ignored us with virtually complete impunity. Yet, as often as not, we were satisfied with this situation; at least, we were reconciled to it. This state of mutual aloofness broke down during the war. Now it cannot be restored even though the status quo might be tempting to both sides.

Oriental studies must not be allowed to lapse back to the spotty coverage which characterized them in pre-war days. The Orient has become too vital for that. Not only does it hold more than half of the present population of the world, but it is also well on its way towards closing up the political and economic gaps which once gave the West such an enormous advantage over the regions of the East. Moreover, the strategic and political centers of gravity have shifted from Europe to the Orient. The Near East has resumed its former role as the key to world power, the possession of which was sought and fought over in this area by Alexander and Pompey, Timur i Leng and Napoleon, not to mention more recent would-be conquerors. Today the attraction of the Near East seems stronger than ever. The evidence is spread on the front pages of your daily newspaper. Some of the reasons are new, some old, but none is far to seek. For in addition to its overland routes and its waterways, the Near East now commands all-important air communications and boasts fabulous underground treasures—quite apart from those which beckon to the archaeologist. India ranks second among the countries of the world as regards population, and—what is not generally realized—high in respect to industry. China's right to consideration as a major power cannot be and is not being disputed. Thus each of the three principal regions of the Orient has outstanding present-day significance. None is as yet close to realizing its full potential strength. Yet each already figures more prominently in the new global set-up than it did before the war. It is not difficult to foresee what their collective weight may amount to in the near future. In short, one can hardly overstate the importance of the

Orient to the nations of today and, more particularly, to the world of tomorrow.

This country has had very little experience with the Orient, less than any other major power. Obviously, this situation cannot continue. It is not simply a matter of intellectual or cultural curiosity but rather one of world peace and security. The latest war was rehearsed in Manchuria, Ethiopia, and Spain. That peace is indivisible is now a stark truth, not just an apt phrase. And peace may be at stake at this very moment in Iran or Turkey, Manchuria or Korea. We cannot therefore know too much about these states and provinces, or about any others where common interests meet and clash. Contrasted with these needs is the plain fact that most of the basic knowledge about the Orient which this country possesses, or can obtain independently, resides in the relative handful of members who make up this Society. Much other information of likely significance is not available at all, here or elsewhere. It is for these reasons that a heavy burden of responsibility now rests on Oriental studies.

II

That basic research about the Orient must be conducted and correlated by the various branches of Oriental studies is a point that needs no stressing. There may be some question, however, as to whether this task sums up the orientalist's obligation in the manner. Personally I am convinced that it marks the full extent of our responsibility. We deal with the subject as scholars. It is our business to ferret out, integrate, keep up-to-date, and make available all the pertinent data about our subject. What is done with our material once it has fallen into other hands is entirely beyond our control. We neither can nor would we wish to be held accountable for the operational or diplomatic uses to which some of our results may be put. Attempts on our part to reach over into other spheres of activity would cause our legitimate contribution to be viewed with suspicion and possible resentment. Yet if we fail to supply the facts, the way will have been left open for obsolete and injurious substitutes. Or foreign policy might be improvised with dogma taking the place of data. If such procedure is unenlightened, you don't find out about it until it is too late to repair the damage. In other words, it should be our aim, as scholars and citizens, to make our study of the Orient as comprehensive as possible, without encroaching on alien, not to say hostile, fields.

What it comes down to, then, is the application of the principle of area studies to the entire Orient. Because the several major regions which the Orient comprises have been chronically understudied, we have farther to go, to begin with, than do other disciplines. Moreover, the ground to be covered is vast in extent geographically as well as historically. Since the Orient is the home of the oldest historic cultures, the study of its component regions is necessarily more complex than that of other areas. Above all, the matter is one of mounting urgency owing to the strategic position in world affairs which the Orient occupies today and the very real prospect that its importance is due to be enhanced in the near future.

In the light of these general needs our existing assets, considerable though they may be in individual instances, do not loom large in an over-all survey. The stated goal is adequate coverage of the whole field—in space and in time. In our empirical progress to date we have tended to concentrate on a relatively small number of salients while neglecting much intervening territory. The resulting lacunae are many and varied. They confront us as we move from region to region, from period to period, and from discipline to discipline. All will have to be filled in somehow before we can regard Oriental studies as a truly integrated field.

Geographically, we find many spaces which, from the standpoint of scholarship, have been either poorly explored or left practically blank. Ethiopia and its environs is one such space, and the fringes of the Arabian Peninsula are another. We know far too little about Anatolia, the Caucasus, and large stretches of Iran. For such regions as Afghanistan, Central Asia, Southeast Asia, and Korea we have had to rely on very scanty and fragmentary information, mostly at second hand. It is true that our own experience with regard to these hitherto out-of-the-way countries is not altogether typical. Italy had been applying herself to Ethiopia, Britain to Arabia and Southeast Asia, Russia to territories on either side of her Asiatic borders. But in none of these instances was such application comprehensive or wholly scientific. Furthermore, while the free interchange of knowledge is an ideal devoutly to be desired, the goal is as yet by no means in sight. Even if all the known details were accessible here, we should still want experts to assimilate the material and to transmit it to wider circles. Since we are obliged to live with the Orient, and want to understand it, information on the subject cannot remain much longer the exclusive property of the graduate schools. It will have to reach down to more popular levels through the medium of properly qualified specialists. Lastly, much more work remains to be done than has yet been attempted anywhere, and there is every reason for a proportionate contribution on our part.

Within the established cultural areas the historical gaps may be less pronounced than the inter-regional blank spots in our information. The transition from period to period is nevertheless far from smooth. Your student of the ancient Near East, for instance, is seldom more than correct in his attitude towards his neighbor at work on Hellenistic or Early Christian history, and his manners become strained to the limit by the time he meets the Islamist. The feeling is cordially reciprocated all around. The result is a sort of occupational isolationism.

Now no serious student whose special field lies within a great cultural tradition can be expected to be at home in all the multitudinous phases of that tradition. The maintenance of proper contact along the line is for the whole group to provide. It is a question of adequate liaison between the various sections. Without it the general perspective is bound to suffer, the distortion increasing with each successive stage. The modern Near East has its roots deep in antiquity. Arabic and Hebrew still share, among countless other elements, the terms for 'chair' and 'carpenter,' not as part of the common Semitic stock but as a legacy, through diverse channels, from the distant and unrelated Sumerian. When Premier Nahhas Pasha of Egypt and Prime Minister Nuri Pasha of Iraq vied with each other a few years ago for the leadership of the Arab Unity movement, their rivalry was made all the more acute by the recollection of the conflict between the Egyptian Necho and the Babylonian Nebuchadrezer twenty-five centuries earlier. In addressing the President of the United States the ruler of Saudi Arabia reached back all the way to the ancient Canaanites in support of his particular argument. That this digression into ethnic origins cannot be viewed as an unqualified scientific success does not affect the basic premise, which is, that the modern Near East senses the importance of its links with the past. In this case it is the student who failed the statesman by providing him with rash conclusions. And in last analysis, this failure, in common with others like it, is essentially the result of faulty liaison between the modern and the ancient fields.

The lack of balance which characterizes Oriental studies in their regional and chronological coverage is paralleled by a top-heavy concentration on a few of the many relevant functional aspects. As a result the specialist in language, history, or religion is forced to try his hand at jurisprudence, sociology, economics, and the natural sciences. The species known as sloppy polyglot is happily nearing extinction, but its place may be taken by latter-day encyclopaedists because the requisite division of labor has been wanting. It is clear, of course, that without fuller cooperation between the humanities and the social and natural sciences our understanding of the Orient, modern as well as ancient, will remain segmental. As individual students we can only try to get along as best we can. But as a group we must endeavor to attract and develop the personnel capable of dealing at first hand with all the aspects that enter into the life of a culture or a nation.

It will be granted then, I think, without further argument—if indeed any argument was called for at all—that Oriental studies today stand in need of greater integration and of very considerable expansion. The expansion would concern primarily the study of the modern Orient, in which field the need is most apparent. The question may be raised whether the indicated additional emphasis on the modern East would not affect adversely the older fields of Oriental studies. It is difficult to see how this could happen. Sumerian civilization, or Buddhism, or Confucianism—to mention only a few instances—belong to the major experiences of mankind along wtih Judaism, Christianity, and Islam. The forces underlying these historic movements are still descernible in the countries of their origin, however disguised or transposed they may now appear. The modern Orient is a product of its past probably in a more intimate sense than any other part of the world. We cannot hope to understand it if we arbitrarily splinter off the present from its antecedents. The Egyptologist and the cuneiformist, the Sanskritist and the student of ancient China, cannot be expected to close up shop, cut across a few thousand years of progress, and make a fresh start in the field of the contemporary East. This would be a good way to impede rather than promote progress in the field as a whole. It would seem that a more active market for oriental ware in general is bound to stimulate the demand for the older product. The problem to date has not been one of over-specialization. It is more a question of too few specialists to go around and of insufficient concert among them.

III

So far we have been considering the gap between what has been realized and what is desirable in Oriental studies. The distance between the fact and the ideal is indeed prodigious. Yet because of the stakes involved we cannot eye the goal with the usual academic detachment. This appears to be an age when the scholar and the scientist have to be practical because those charged with the conduct of worldly affairs have not justified their pretensions to a monopoly on realism. Orientalists can see what lies ahead in that half of the world to which their labors relate. The task before them is complex. It calls for long-range planning and development. It will involve also substantial financing: This brings up the question of ways and means.

The required expansion of Oriental studies concerns in the first place the orientalist himself, the scope of his work, and the opportunities for making this work more meaningful. But it is also of definite interest to society. The government was made aware of this fact when it found out during the war that it needed more specialists in various phases of Oriental studies than were available or could be produced on short notice. The demands of the post-war era have not curtailed this need. To the contrary, the problem threatens to grow more acute as the Orient moves towards its rightful place in the world. It would seem to follow that the furtherance of Oriental studies in this country, especially along lines of particular interest to the work of the government, should have active federal support. Logical though it may appear, however, this solution is not in prospect, at least for the time being. Moreover, even if government assistance to Oriental studies were forthcoming at this time, it is doubtful whether, under existing circumstances, such a development could be wholeheartedly approved by the orientalist.

This statement is intended as an explanation, not as a criticism. As a country we have not had enough time to discover that basic research about the rest of the world is one of the preliminaries to an effective foreign policy. The idea is still entertained in some quarters that you can gauge the mood and temper of another country—its needs and aspirations, and its potential contribution to international well-being—from the ephemeral conclusions of itinerant diplomats. There has certainly been no time to learn from experience that such an approach is particularly futile when it comes to the manifold intricacies of the East. The concept that the behavior of another and to us relatively strange people is conditioned by an infinite variety of unfamiliar factors, each of which is significant and none of which remains static—this concept may be allowed in theory but is not honored in official practice. Admittedly, the whole thing may look too remote to invest money in, the more so since the returns from such an investment would have to be classified as intangible.

At any rate, were federal funds to be made available for area studies, and especially for Oriental studies, it is probable that such work would be restricted and slanted in a manner uncongenial to the best type of student. The experience of fellow-specialists in another, and currently far more fateful field of inquiry, has shown that science and government have divergent views about what scientists should do and how they should do it. The most complacent humanist, if tried beyond endurance, may be driven to rebellion against the assembly-line methods and the scissors-and-paste technique to which all too often he is expected to submit. Under such conditions government supervision cannot but become a stultifying and corrosive influence. The conditions may change as the harm which they cause becomes apparent to all concerned. One can only hope that this discovery will not prove to be a long process.

In the meantime, with government aid as yet unlikely, and not wholly desirable, the problem is thrown back upon private enterprise. This does not mean individual effort. It is plainly a task which requires group initiative. For even on a greatly reduced scale the program will involve planning and priorities, in order to insure economy of effort and expenditure and to guard against wasteful duplication. The American Oriental Society is the obvious choice to undertake the preliminary labor. But the Society can not progress very far unaided. Since the matter involves the close cooperation of several disciplines it will require the concerted support of such organizations as the American Council of Learned Societies and the Social Science Research Council. Grants and Fellowships made available in sufficient volume and strategically allocated would be a constructive start in the right direction. The next step would be the establishment of a National School of Modern Oriental Studies.

The fact that we still lack such a school is proof that in our thinking about the Orient we are far behind a number of European countries. To be sure, the European schools in question were organized in connection with specific colonial interests. For this reason they have had the benefit of continued support by their respective governments. If neither of these sources of stimulation has been an unmixed blessing, the cause of knowledge has not suffered in the process. By the same token, the absence of a similar school in this country must be regarded as a loss to the cause of international understanding.

World events are forcing the orientalist to give up

his comfortable place in the ivory tower. There is no appeal against the eviction. Nor would a demurrer be likely in any case. As a scholar the orientalist will be engaged in making his work reflect the essential unity of his subject, which is part of the greater unity of human learning. And as a citizen he now has the obligation as well as opportunity to perform a very vital service in behalf of world unity.

Bibliography of the Writings of Ephraim Avigdor Speiser

BOOKS

Mesopotamian Origins, University of Pennsylvania Press, 1930.

Excavations at Tepe Gawra, Volume I, University of Pennsylvania Press, 1936.

One Hundred Selected Nuzi Texts, Annual of the Americal Schools of Oriental Research, Volume XVI (with R. H. Pfeiffer), 1936.

Introduction to Hurrian, Annual of the American Schools of Oriental Research, XX, 1941.

The United States and the Near East, Harvard University Press, 1947, 1950.

At the Dawn of Civilization (ed.), The World History of the Jewish People Vol. I, Rutgers University Press, 1964.

Genesis, translated with an Introduction and Notes, The Anchor Bible, Doubleday & Co., 1964.

ARTICLES

1924

1. "The Etymology of *'Armōn*," *JQR* XIV, p. 329.
2. "The Hebrew Origin of the First Part of the Book of Wisdom," *ibid.*, pp. 455–482.

1925

3. "Hosea 2:7," *JBL* XLIV, pp. 189–191.
4. "Vocalic *N* in Assyrian," *Language* I, pp. 107–108.

1926

5. "The Pronunciation of Hebrew Based Chiefly on the Transliterations in the Hexapla, I," *JQR* XVI, pp. 343–382.
6. "Secondary Developments in Semitic Phonology: An Application of the Principle of Sonority," *AJSL* XLII, pp. 145–169.
7. "A New Factor in the History of the Ancient East" (with E. Chiera), *AASOR* VI, pp. 75–92.

1927

8. "Prehistoric Mounds in Northern Iraq," *BASOR* 27, pp. 11–12.
9. "Slected 'Kirkuk' Documents" (with E. Chiera), *JAOS* 47, pp. 36–60.

1928

10. "Soundings at Tepe Gawra," *BASOR* 29, pp. 12–15.
11. "Southern Kurdistan in the Annals of Ashurnasirpal and Today," AASOR VIII, pp. 1–42.
12. "Report from Iraq," *BASOR* 31, pp. 12–14.

1929

13. "Preliminary Excavations at Tepe Gawra," *AASOR* IX, pp. 17–94.

14. "Some Prehistoric Antiquities from Mesopotamia," *JQR* XIX, pp. 345–354.
15. "A Letter of Saushshatar and the Date of the Kirkuk Tablets," *JAOS* 49, pp. 269–275.
16. Traces of the Oldest Cultures of Babylonia and Assyria," *AfO* V, pp. 162–164.
17. "An Archaeologist in Kurdistan," *Art and Archaeology* XXVIII, pp. 151–160.

1930

18. "The Name 'Bildad,'" *AfO* VI, p. 23.
19. "New Kirkuk Documents Relating to Family Law," *AASOR* X, pp. 1–74.

1931

20. "The Excavation of Tell Billa," *BASOR* 44, 2–5.
21. "The Excavation of Tepe Gawra," *ibid.*, pp. 5–8.

1932

22. "Tell Billa," *ibid.* 45, pp. 32–34.
23. "Excavations at Tell Billa and Tepe Gawra," *ibid.* 46, pp. 1–9.
24. "The Joint Excavations at Tepe Gawra," *ibid.* 47, pp. 17–23.
25. "The 'Chalice' Ware of Northern Mesopotamia and Its Historical Significance," *ibid.* 48, pp. 5–10.
26. "On Some Important Synchronisms in Prehistoric Mesopotamia," *AJA* XXXVI, pp. 465–471.
27. "New Kirkuk Documents Relating to Security Transactions," *JAOS* 52, pp. 350–367; 53, pp. 24–26.

1933

28. "The Pronunciation of Hebrew Based on the Hexapla [con't]," *JQR* XXIII, pp. 233–265; XXIV, pp. 9–46.

29. "Ethnic Movements in the Near East in the Second Millennium B.C.," *AASOR* XIII, pp. 13–54 (Off-print Series no. 1).

30. "The Pottery of Tell Billa," *Museum Journal* XXIII, pp. 249–308.

31. "New Assyrian Eponyms," *BASOR* 49, pp. 14–15.

32. "An Inscribed Lance-Butt From Tell Billa V," *ibid.* 50, pp. 11–13.

33. "The Ethnic Background of the Early Civilizations of the Near East," *AJA* XXXVIII, pp. 459–466.

34. "First Steps in Mesopotamian Archaeology," *BASOR* 52, pp. 15–18.

35. "The Historical Significance of Tepe Gawra," *The Smithsonian Report for 1933*, pp. 415–427. Reprinted in Smithsonian Treasury of Science III, (1960), pp. 945–968.

1934

36. "An Assyrian Document of the Ninth Century B.C. from Tell Billa," *BASOR* 54 pp. 20–21.

37. "Impression of a Cylinder Seal from Gawra VI," *Ibid.* 55, pp. 2–3.

38. "A Rare Brick of Sennacherib," *ibid.*, pp. 22–23.

39. "A Figurative Equivalent for Totality in Akkadian and West-Semitic," *JAOS* 54, pp. 200–203.

40. "Ur Excavations," *Antiquity* VIII, pp. 448–452.

41. The Continuance of Painted Pottery in Northern *Mesopotamia*," *AfO* IX, pp. 48–50.

1935

42. "The Archaeological Promise of the Zagros Region," *Bulletin of the American Institute for Persian Art and Archaeology* 6, pp. 3–4.

43. "The Season's Work at Tepe Gawra," *BASOR* 58, pp. 4–6.

44. "Notes to Recently Published Nuzi Texts," *JAOS* 55, pp. 432–443.
45. "The Etymology of 'Meschino' and its Cognates," *Language* XI, pp. 20–22.
46. "When the Past Broke Its Silence," *The Scientific Monthly,* XL, pp. 366–369.

1936

47. "The Name *Phoinikes,*" *Language* XII, pp. 121–126.
48. "Studies in Semitic Formatives," *JAOS* 56, pp. 22–46.
49. "Report on the Assyrian Campaign," *BASOR* 64, pp. 4–9.

1937

50. "Progress of the Joint Assyrian Expedition," *ibid.* 65, pp. 2–8.
51. "Three Reports On the Joint Assyrian Expedition," *ibid.,* pp. 2–19.
52. "Excavations in Northeastern Babylonia," *ibid.* 67, pp. 2–6.
53. "Mesopotamian Miscellanies," *ibid.* 68, pp. 7–13.
54. "Excavations at Tepe Gawra During the Season of 1936–7," *Bulletin of the American Institute for Iranian Art and Archaeology* V, pp. 1–6.
55. "The Archaeologist," *Asia* 1937, pp. 837–840.

1938

56. "The Oldest City in the World," *Science Digest* 3, pp. 45–47.
57. "Notes on Hurrian Phonology," *JAOS* 58, pp. 173–201.
58. "The Pitfalls of Polarity," *Language* XIV, pp. 187–202.
59. "Progress of the Joint Expedition to Mesopotamia," *BASOR* 70, pp. 3–10.

60. "The Cuneiform Tablets from Tell Billa," *ibid.*, pp. 23–24.

61. "I Samuel 1:24," *ibid.* 72, pp. 15–17.

62. "Closing the Gap at Tepe Gawra," *Asia* 1938, pp. 536–543. Reprinted, *The Smithsonian Report for 1939*, pp. 437–445.

63. A Scholar's Progress," *The University of Pennsylvania Library Chronicle* VI, pp. 18–23.

1939

64. "Gleanings from Billa Texts," *Koschaker Volume*, pp. 141–150.

65. "Studies in Hurrian Grammar," *JAOS* 59, pp. 289–324 (Offprint Series no. 10).

66. "The Beginnings of Civilization in Mesopotamia," *JAOS Supplement* no. 4, pp. 17–31.

67. "Progress in the Study of the Hurrian Language," *BASOR* 74, pp. 4–7.

1940

68. "Of shoes and Shekels," *BASOR* 77, pp. 15–20.

69. "Phonetic Method in Hurrian Orthography," *Language* XVI, pp. 319–340.

70. "A New Hurrian Pronominal Form," *JAOS* 60, pp. 265–267.

71. "Ancient Mesopotamia and the Beginnings of Science," *Nature* (London) CXLVI, pp. 705–709. Reprinted in *Studies in the History of Science*, University of Pennsylvania Bicentennial Conference (1941), pp. 1–11; *The Scientific Monthly*, LV (1942), pp. 159–165.

1942

72. "Some Sources of Intellectual and Social Progress in the Ancient Near East," *Studies in the History of Culture, Dedicated to Waldo Gifford Leland*, pp. 51–62.

73. "An Intrusive Hurro-Hittite Myth," *JAOS* 62, pp. 98–102.
74. "The Shibboleth Incident (Judges 12:6)," *BASOR* 85, pp. 10–13.

1946

75. "Oriental Studies and Society," *JAOS* 66, pp. 193–197.

1947

76. "Challenge in the Near East," *The General Magazine and Historical Chronicle,* 1947, pp. 234–240.
77. "Near Eastern Studies in America 1939–1945," *Archiv Orientální* XVI, pp. 1–15.
78. "A Note on the Derivation of *šumma,*" *JCS* I, pp. 321–328.
79. "A Note on Amos 5:25," *BASOR* 108, pp. 5–6.

1948

80. "Hurrians and Subarians," *JAOS* 68, pp. 1–13.
81. "The United States and the Near East—Study Guide," Harvard University Press.

1949

82. "A Note on Certain Akkadian Terms for Door-Equipment," *JCS* 2, pp. 225–227.
83. "Ground Swell in Arab Lands," *Foreign Policy Bulletin 18* no. 14, pp. 2–4.
84. "James Alan Montgomery (1866–1949)," *BASOR* 115, pp. 4–8.

1950

85. "On Some Articles of Armor and Their Names," *JAOS* 70, pp. 47–49.
86. "Bibliography of James Alan Montgomery," *BASOR* 117, pp. 8–13.
87. "Akkadian Myths and Epics," *Ancient Near Eastern Texts* . . . ed. Pritchard, pp. 60–119. Reprinted in part in I. Mendelsohn, ed., *Religions of the Ancient Near East* (1955), pp. 19–125.

88. "An Analogue to II Sam 1:21: *'AQHT* I 44–45," *JBL* LXIX, pp. 377–378.

1951

89. "Ancient Mesopotamia: A Light That Did Not Fail," *National Geographic,* Jan., pp. 41–105.
90. "A Note on Alphabetic Origins," *BASOR* 121, pp. 17–21.
91. "The United States and the Arab World: A Problem in Depth," *The General Magazine and Historical Chronicle* LIII, pp. 155–162.
92. "The Semantic Range of *dalāpu,*" *JCS* V, pp. 64–75.
93. "Damascus as *ša imērišu,*" *JAOS* 71, pp. 257–258.
94. "The Ancient Near East and Modern Philosophies of History," *Proceedings of the American Philosophical Society* 95–6, pp. 583–588.

1952

95. "The Contribution of Max Leopold Margolis to Semitic Linguistics," *Max Leopold Margolis Volume,* pp. 27–33.
96. "The Sumerian Problem Reviewed," *HUCA* XXIII, pp. 339–355.
97. "The 'elative' in West-Semitic and Akkadian," *JCS* 6, pp. 81–92.
98. "Some Factors in the Collapse of Akkad," *JAOS* 72, pp. 97–101.

1953

99. "Cultural Factors in Social Dynamics in the Near East," *Middle East Journal* 7, pp. 133–152. Reprinted in S. N. Fisher ed., *Social Forces in the Middle East* (1955), pp. 1–22.
100. "A Vivid Sidelight on the Machpelah Episode," *Israel Life and Letters* I, pp. 56–59.
101. "Comments on Recent Studies in Akkadian Grammar," *JAOS* 73, pp. 129–138.

102. "The Middle East: A Problem in Re-education," *University of Pennsylvania Bulletin* 54/5, pp. 26–34.
103. "Early Law and Civilization," *Canadian Bar Review* XXXI, pp. 863–877.
104. "The Terminative-Adverbial in Canaanite, Ugaritic and Akkadian," (in Hebrew), *Eretz-Israel* III, pp. 63–66. English version in *IEJ* 4 (1954), pp. 108–115.
105. "The Hurrian Participation in the Civilizations of Mesopotamia, Syria and Palestine," *Journal of World History* I, pp. 311–327.

1954

106. "On the Alleged *namru*, 'fair-skinned,'" *Orientalia* 23, pp. 235–236.
107. "The Alalakh Tablets," *JAOS* 74, pp. 18–25.
108. "The Case of the Obliging Servant," *JCS* 8, pp. 98–105.
109. "Authority and Law in Mesopotamia," *JAOS Supplement* 17, pp. 8–15.

1955

110. Corrected and expanded "Akkadian Myths and Epics," *ANET*, pp. 60–119, 514–516.
111. "The Idea of History in Ancient Mesopotamia," in *The Idea of History in the Ancient Near East, AOS* 38, pp. 37–76, 361–362.
112. "Nuzi or Nuzu?," *JAOS* 75, pp. 52–55.
113. "The Durative Hithpa'el: A *tan*-Form," *JAOS* 75, pp. 118–121.
114. "Akkadian Documents from Ras Shamra," *JAOS* 75, pp. 154–165.
115. "I Know Not the Day Of My Death," *JBL* LXXIV, pp. 252–256.
116. "'*Ed* in the Story of Creation," *BASOR* 140, pp. 9–11.

1956

117. "Nuzi Marginalia," *Orientalia* 25, pp. 1–23.
118. "Ancient Near East: Cradle of History," in R. N. Anshen ed., *Mid-East: World Center,* pp. 29–42.
119. "Government and Religion in the Near East," *Hebrew Union College Booklet.*
120. *"YDWN,* Gen. 6:3," *JBL* LXXV, pp. 126–129.
121. "Word Plays on the Creation Epic's Version of the Founding of Babylon," *Orientalia* 25, pp. 317–323.
122. " 'Coming' and 'Going' at the City Gate," *BASOR* 144, pp. 20–23.
123. "A(dvisory) E(ditorial) C(ommittee) Report," *Jewish Publication Society Bookmark,* Dec. 1956, pp. 2–4.

1957

124. "New Light on the Eternal Book," Jewish Publication Society pamphlet.
125. "Sultantepe Tablets 38:73 and Enuma Eliš 3:69," *JCS* 11, pp. 43–44.
126. *"ṬWṬPT," JQR* XLVIII, pp. 208–217.
127. "The Biblical Idea of History in its Common Near Eastern Setting," *IEJ* 7, pp. 201–216.

1958

128. "The *muškênum,*" *Orientalia* 27, pp. 19–28.
129. "Census and Ritual Expiation in Mari and Israel," *BASOR* 149, pp. 17–25.
130. "Gilgamesh 6:40," *JCS* 12, pp. 41–42.
131. "In Search of Nimrod," *Eretz-Israel* V, pp. 32*–36*.
132. "Hurrians" (in Hebrew), *Encyclopedia Biblica* (Jerusalem) III, pp. 58–62.
133. "New Horizons in Bible Study," Baltimore Hebrew College Booklet.

1959

134. "The Most Fateful Commencement in History," Baltimore Hebrew Teacher's College pamphlet.

135. "The Rivers of Paradise," *Festschrift Johannes Friedrich,* pp. 473–485.

1960

136. "Three Thousand Years of Biblical Study," *Centennial Review* IV, pp. 206–222.
137. " 'People' and 'Nation' of Israel," *JBL* LXXIX, pp. 157–163.
138. "Leviticus and the Critics," *Yehezkel Kaufmann Jubilee Volume,* pp. 29–45.
139. "An Angelic 'Curse': Exodus 14:20," *JAOS* 80, pp. 198–200.

1961

140. "The Verb *SḤR in* Genesis and Early Hebrew Movements," *BASOR* 164, pp. 23–28.

1962

141. "Horites," "Man, Ethnic Divisions of," "Nineveh," "Nuzi," in *The Interpreter's Dictionary of the Bible.*
142. "Mesopotamian Motifs in the Early Chapters of Genesis," *Expedition* V, pp. 18–19, 43.

1963

143. "Background and Function of the Biblical *Nāśī,*" *Catholic Biblical Quarterly* 25, pp. 111–117.
144. "The Wife-Sister Motif in the Patriarchal Narratives," in A. Altmann ed., *Studies and Texts: Volume I, Biblical and Other Studies,* Philip W. Lown Institute of Advanced Judaic Studies, Brandeis University, pp. 15–28.
145. "The Stem *PLL* in Hebrew," *JBL* LXXXII, pp. 301–306.
146. "A Significant New Will from Nuzi," *JCS* 17, pp. 65–71.
147. "Unrecognized Dedication," *IEJ* 13, pp. 69–73.
148. "Cuneiform Law and the History of Civilization,"

Proceedings of the American Philosophical Society 107, pp. 536–541.

1964

149. "Prologue"; "The Regional Environment"; "Akkadian"; "Semites"; "Hurrians and Hittites"; "Amorites and Canaanites"; "Mesopotamia—Evolution of an Integrated Civilization; "Epilogue"; in *At the Dawn of Civilization,* pp. 3–4, 93–96, 112–120, 135–141, 153–161, 162–169, 173–266, 345–349.
150. "Geschichtswissenschaft" in *RLA* III, pp. 216–220.
151. "The Syllabic Transcription of Ugaritic [ḫ] and [ḥ]," *BASOR* 175, pp. 42–47.

1965

152. "*Pālil* and Congeners: A Sampling of Apotropaic Symbols," in *Studies in Honor of Benno Landsberger on his seventy-fifth birthday* (*AS* no. 16). pp. 389–393.

REVIEWS

1927 S. Langdon (ed.), *Oxford Edition of Cuneiform Inscriptions,* in *JQR* XVII, 481–482.

1929 T. Bauer, *Die Ostkanaanäer,* in *JAOS,* 49, 325–326.

G. Contenau, *Manuel d'archéologie orientale, I,* in *JAOS,* 49, 323–325.

Martin David, *Die Adoption im altbabylonischen Recht,* in *JAOS,* 49, 182.

C. J. Gadd and L. Legrain, *Ur Excavations, Texts I: Royal Inscriptions,* in *JAOS,* 49, 322–323.

W. H. Worell, *A Study of Races in the Ancient Near East,* in *JAOS,* 49, 181.

1930 G. Bergsträsser, *Einführung in die semitischen Sprachen,* in *JAOS,* 50, 269–271.

V. Gordon Childe, *The Most Ancient East,* in *JAOS,* 50, 79–81.

Adolf Dirr, *Einführung in das Studium der kaukasischen Sprachen,* in *JAOS,* 50, 268–269.

J. Obermeyer, *Die Landschaft Babyloniens im Zeitalter des Talmuds und des Gaonats,* in *JAOS,* 50, 267–268.

1931 G. Furlani, *Religione dei Yezidi,* in *JAOS,* 51, 334–335.

R. Campbell Thompson and R. W. Hutchinson, *A Century of Exploration at Nineveh,* in *JQR* XXI, 188.

R. P. Dougherty, *Nabonidus and Belshazzar,* in *JQR* XXI, 188.

P. Jensen, *Das Gilgamesch-Epos in der Weltliteratur,* in *JQR* XXI, 189–190.

Alfred Jeremias, *Handbuch der Altorientalischen Geisteskultur,* in *JQR* XXI, 188.

M. v. Tseretheli, *Die Neuen haldischen Inschriften König Sardurs von Urartu,* in *JQR* XXI, 188.

C. Leonard Woolley, *The Sumerians,* in *JQR* XXI , 187–189.

1932 P. Koschaker, *Über einige griechische Rechtsurkunden aus den östlichen Randgebieten des Hellenismus,* in *JAOS,* 52, 255–257.

R. H. Pfeiffer, *The Archives of Shilwateshup, son of the King,* in *JAOS,* 52, 257–260.

1933 H. Frankfort, *Archeology and the Sumerian Problem,* in *JAOS,* 53, 359–360.

R. P. Dougherty, *The Sealand of Arabia,* in *AJA,* 37, 173–174.

M. Pezard, *Quadesh: Mission Archéologique à Tell Nebi Mend, 1921–22,* in *AJA,* 37, 343–344.

1934 Edgar H. Sturtevant, *A Comparative Grammar of the Hittite Language,* in *JAOS,* 54, 206–208.

M. v. Oppenheim, *Tell Halaf,* in *AJA,* 38, 609–610..

James Henry Breasted, *The Oriental Institute,* in *JHE,* 173–174.

C. Leonard Woolley, *Ur Excavations Vol. II,* in *Antiquity.*

1935 H. de Genouillac, *Fouilles de Telloh: Tome I,* in *AJA,* 39, 413–414.

Sir Flinders Petrie, *Palestine and Israel: Historical Notes,* in *AJA,* 39, 413.

L. Gray, *Introduction to Comparative Semitic Linguistics,* in *Language,* 11, 252–260.

1936 Driver and Miles, *The Assyrian Laws,* in *JAOS,* 56, 107–108.

Mallowan and Rose, *Excavations at Tall Arpachiyah,* in *JAOS,* 56, 109–110.

W. Andrae, *Die Jungeren Ischtar-Tempel in Assur,* in *AJA,* 40, 170–171.

G. Contenau, *La Civilisation des Hittites et des Mitanniens,* in *AJA,* 40, 170.

T. Jacobsen and S. Lloyd, *Sennacherib's Aqueduct at Jerwan,* in *AJA,* 40, 394.

R. S. Lamon, *The Megiddo Water System,* in *AJA,* 40, 394.

S. Langdon, *Babylonian Menologies and the Semitic Calendars,* in *AJA,* 40, 173.

H. G. May and R. M. Engberg, *Material Remains of the Megiddo Cult,* in *AJA,* 40, 393–394.

John Strong Newberry, *The Prehistory of the Alphabet,* in *AJA,* 40, 172–173.

1938 E. Grant (ed.), *The Haverford Symposium on Archaeology and the Bible,* in *JAOS,* 58, 670.

G. E. Wright, *The Pottery of Palestine from the Earliest Times to the End of the Early Bronze Age,* in *JAOS,* 58, 671–673.

1939 P. W. Ireland, *Iraq: A Study in Political Development,* in *JAOS,* 59, 117–118.

E. Schmidt, *Excavations at Tepe Hissar, Damghan,* in *JAOS,* 59, 115–117.

1949 George E. Kirk, *A Short History of the Middle East,* in *The Nation,* 113.

R. Mikesell and Hollis B. Chenery, *Arabian Oil: America's Stake in the Middle East,* in *The Nation,* 617–618.

J. Parkes, *A History of Palestine from 135 A. D. to Modern Times,* in *AJHS,* 39, 194–196.

Kermit Roosevelt, *Arabs Oil and History,* in *Jewish Social Studies,* 312– 313.

1950 Kenneth W. Bilby, *New Star in the Near East,* New York Herald Tribune (August 27).

R. T. O'Callaghan, *Aram Naharaim,* in *JAOS,* 70, 307–309.

1951 R. N. Frye (ed.), *The Near East and the Great Powers,* New York Herald Tribune (October 28).

Philip K. Hitti, *History of Syria,* in *Middle Eastern Affairs,* 2, 370–371.

Theophile J. Meek, *Hebrew Origins* (revised edition), in *Jewish Social Studies,* 13, 350–351.

Sidney Smith, *The Statue of Idrimi,* in *JAOS,* 71, 151–152.

1952 H. V. Cooke, *Challenge and Response in the Middle East,* New York Herald Tribune (August 10).

Majid Khadduri, *Independent Iraq,* in *Middle East Journal,* 6, 351–352.

E. R. Lacheman, *Excavations at Nuzi V,* in *JAOS,* 72, 94–95.

George Lenczowski, *The Middle East in World Affairs,* New York Herald Tribune (July 13).

T. Cuyler Young (ed.), *Near Eastern Culture and Society,* in *Crozier Quarterly,* 29, 217–218.

1953 J. C. Hurewitz, *Middle East Dilemmas,* New York Herald Tribune (April), 5.

Hurewitz, Kirk, and R. N. Frye, *Iran,* in *the Yale Review* (Autumn), 158–160.

George Kirk, *The Middle East in the War, 1939–1946,* in New York Herald Tribune (February 1).

Emil Lengyel, *World Without End,* in New York Herald Tribune (April 12), 5.

H. St. J. Philby, *Arabian Highlands,* in *The Yale Review,* 620–622.

1954 I. J. Gelb, *A Study of Writing, JBL,* 73, 257–259.

Linda Braidwood, *Digging beyond the Tigris,* in *Middle Eastern Affairs,* 5, 65–66.

F. W. Fernau, *Moslems on the March: People and Politics in the World of Islam,* in *The Yale Review* (Autumn), 143–145.

Richard H. Sanger, *The Arabian Peninsula,* in *The Yale Review* (Autumn), 143–145.

1955 E. Ebeling, *Literarische Keilschrifttexte aus Assur,* in *Orientalia,* 24, 178–182.

H. Paper, *The Phonology and Morphology of Royal Achaemenid Inscriptions,* in *Language,* 32, 540–541.

1957 *The Assyrian Dictionary* of the Oriental Institute of the University of Chicago, in *Language*, 33, 475–479.

1958 A. Finet, *L'Accadien des Lettres de Mari,* in *Journal of Semitic Studies,* 4, 65–68.

ADDENDA TO REVIEWS

1930 W. Andrae, *Farbige Keramik aus Assur und ihre Vorstufen in altassyrischen Wandmalereien,* in *JQR* XX, 197.

S. Langdon, *Excavations at Kish,* in *JQR* XX, 198.

G. Contenau, *La Glyptique Syro-Hittite,* in *JQR* XX, 200.

G. Contenau, *Manuel d'Archeologie Orientale,* in *JQR* XX, 202.

E. Chiera, *Sumerian Religious Texts,* in *JQR* XX, 203.

P. M. Witzel, *Hethitische Keilschrift-Urkunden in Transkription und Uebersetzung mit Kommentar,* in *JQR* XX, 206.

E. A. Speiser: An Appreciation*

The task before me this evening is probably the most overwhelming one with which I have ever been faced. This is not only due to the emotion inherent in the occasion, or to my own association with E. A. Speiser as pupil, colleague, and friend. It is due most of all to the eagerness—which all of us here feel—to render homage to a most extraordinary man and scholar, realizing at the same time the sheer impossibility of presenting in the span of a few minutes a portrait that would evoke and capture the man in his uniqueness and distinctiveness in a manner that would satisfy all of us who have known him closely, and impart a suggestion of an authentic image of the man and his work to those who have not had the fortune of knowing him personally or of studying under him.

That E. A. Speiser was one of the most distinguished humanistic scholars of this generation, one of the great Semitists of our time, I need not document here in any detail. This is universally recognized by his peers, the world-wide academic community, and the public and private institutions whose major function it is to foster, recognize, and reward extraordinary scholarly distinction. It is gratifying to be able to state that such recognition

* Read at the Memorial Meeting for Professor Speiser at the University of Pennsylvania, November 10, 1965.

and honor came to him from the very beginning of his career to his last living moments. If I may be permitted to recall but two of them here, it is because he was visibly affected by these honors, which came to him as a complete surprise, and which he accepted in humility. These were the award of the American Council of Learned Societies Special Prize in 1959, and his being named University Professor by his own institution here just two years ago.

His scholarly career illustrated a kind of grand dialectic. Beginning in the field of Semitic philology, and concentrating on Biblical text criticism, he very soon branched out into Ancient Near Eastern History, Assyriology, Archeology, even Hittitology—in short, everything that came within the purview of the ancient civilizations of Western Asia—but never losing sight of his point of departure. In his last years the the focus of his efforts returned to Biblical studies, this time informed by an unexcelled command and deep understanding of the intellectual and cultural milieu of the entire ancient Near East, without which, he believed, the Bible, as the major source of Western spiritual values, could not be properly understood. It cannot be doubted that this was his overriding passion; in a letter to me just a few years ago he put it quite simply and characteristically in a single sentence: "Sooner or later, the intellectual fortunes that we amass in peripheral fields get to be wisely invested in the Bible." Now, as most of us know, Speiser was not a religious man in any conventional sense. But with respect to the Bible he was a man with a mission. He was convinced of the uniqueness of its value system, indeed as the bonding agent of the moral fabric of Western Civilization. Above all, however, he felt that the Bible must be understood as a human document created and accumulated over many centuries by a real society in a tangible and broad geographical, cultural, and historical environment, and as the final distillation of the response of this society to its experience. In order to appreciate and to bring into better focus those elements in the Biblical tradition that constituted its own unique contribution, it was imperative to know a good deal about the experience of the major civilizations of the Ancient Near East—not for the sake of invidious comparisons that had all too often characterized extra-Biblical Near Eastern studies in the past, but for understanding's own sake; to perceive and ungrudgingly acknowledge the cultural, spiritual, and intellectual legacy upon which Biblical tradition continually drew; to observe how a younger society adopted, assimilated, transformed, and built upon the larger cultural heritage of which it was the heir, and which indeed continued to flourish all around it. To know as much as possible about both is to understand and appreciate the difference all the more. This approach to Biblical studies had barely begun when Speiser began his work; it is due in no small measure to his example and to his achievement that no aspiring Biblical scholar today would consider ignoring this approach to the major object of their study. The closing years of his life—despite our awareness that many years of creative scholarship would still have awaited him—nevertheless witnessed a true synthesis of his work as he himself envisioned it. His part in the widely hailed new translation of the Pentateuch of the Jewish Publication Society may be discerned on every page, in almost every verse. At almost every point in the primeval history, and the patriarchal narratives, the various legal codes, etc., where a new departure in interpretation can be detected, the controlling factor will usually be found to be Speiser's bringing to bear on it some insight out of the store of Mesopotamian legal or cultic literature, some parallel and amplifying social institution or custom, or some comparative linguistic or lexical datum. Of his widely admired and distinctive literary gift, which is equally evident on every page of this translation, we shall speak later. The harvest of his method in Biblical study came in only with the publication last year of his translation of and commentary on the book of Genesis, the first published volume of the Anchor Bible series. It may fairly be said that this volume incorporates Speiser's credo and philosophy in the realm of Biblical study. It is explicit in demonstrating the profound influence of the ancient Near Eastern—especially the Mesopotamian—cultural milieu upon the earliest and most formative of the traditions of ancient Israel. Speiser would have been the last to claim that his commentary is the only valid one. It was not meant to replace the scholarly and even the semi-popular commentaries that proceed along the more accepted methodological lines; it was meant to complement them in a twofold way. The emphasis on the historical and cultural background of the civilizations of the Near East was deliberate; it might seem to some excessive, but only because of the paucity of such considerations in the more traditionally oriented commentaries. Secondly, it is precisely through such a socio-historical approach that Speiser believed he could reclaim for the Bible the attention of the intelligent and basically secular modern public, to both its intellectual and aesthetic profit. And this, it might be noted, is the stated aim of the editors of the Anchor Bible series as a whole.

In a real sense, the Genesis translation and commentary is Speiser's final orchestration of materials previously realized with individual instruments. In almost forty years of unbroken effort Speiser became the acknowledged authority on Hurrian civilization, language, and influence throughout Upper Mesopotamia, Syria, and even in Asia Minor through much of the second millennium B.C. Indeed, from the purely technical point of view, his grammar of the Hurrian language, published almost twenty-five years ago, is the high point of his achievement as a grammarian and linguist; it immediately became the standard work on the subject, and will probably remain so for many years to come. In the interpretation of the legal and administrative texts of the Hurrians, written in a peculiar and difficult dialect of Akkadian, Speiser has probably accomplished more than have all other scholars put together who have ever worked on the subject. And a great part of his store of knowledge in this area bore fruit in the form of published doctoral dissertations prepared under his guidance. Yet he felt that his greatest triumph with the Hurrian material was his demonstration of its deep penetration into the social patterns of the time of the Biblical patriarchs.

His profound understanding of Mesopotamian cosmology and the epical and religious literature of Babylonia reached its high point in his translation of the most important Babylonian literature, such as the Gilgamesh and Creation epics as well as shorter pieces, in *Ancient Near Eastern Texts,* a volume which in its fifteen years has achieved the status of a classic; Speiser's translations in that volume are conceded to be at once a most faithful rendering of the sense of the original, and a tour de force of English style. Yet his greatest satisfaction again came in his utilization of these same documents in the illumination of the first ten chapters in Genesis—the primeval history from the creation to Abraham.

It is generally acknowledged that Speiser was among

the most acute of Semitic grammarians in this generation, and it is a source of deep regret that he did not live to offer a comprehensive treatment of any major phase of the subject. His separate studies, however, especially those on aspects of the verbal systems of Hebrew and of Akkadian, are among the finest contributions of their kind to the historical grammar of the Semitic languages. But his mastery of the field is demonstrated to its most impressive effect once again in the Genesis commentary, for in it not only was his unexcelled understanding of Hebrew verb morphology put to practical use, but it afforded the best possible vehicle to display his equally unrivalled understanding of Hebrew syntax and prosody, and in general a sensitivity to all the subtleties of the idiom of Biblical Hebrew.

Above all, what Speiser strove for in his work in extra-Biblical fields as well as in his Biblical studies was the identification of the human values that were reflected and preserved in the literary remains of these ancient civilizations. Grammatical study, archaeology, even philology on a larger scale, were to him ultimately no more than the necessary means to get at the human, ethical, moral, and spiritual values that animated all their activity, and thereby to bring them face-to-face with modern man for all that he could derive from such confrontation. The Bible was to him only the most eloquent of such documents, having much more cogency and immediacy for contemporary civilization. It needed only a presentation as a document written by pulsating humans about flesh-and-blood persons and not as source-texts or proof-texts for edifying sermons. I should like to quote one example from Speiser's translation of Genesis that illustrates what I mean, and those who knew Speiser and the way he worked will, I am sure, immediately recognize in it both the man and his style. I quote first the Authorized Version as the most familiar, then the new JPS translation, and then Speiser's own rendering. The scene is the death of Rachel as she gave birth to Benjamin, in Ch. 35, Vs. 18 in the familiar AV renders: "And it came to pass, as her soul was departing (for she died), that she called his name Ben-Oni." The new JPS: "As she was breathing her last—for she was dying—she named him Ben-Oni." Speiser: "With her last gasp—for she was dying—she named him Ben-Oni." Now it is clear that the JPS rendering is as faithful to the original Hebrew as Speiser's (both, of course, abandon the image of the departing soul, for the modern connotative accretions to the word "soul" have no place in the Hebrew text, where the word *nefesh* meant no more than breath, the breath of life). Yet in the JPS the scene is as passive as it is in AV; it conveys a mood of resignation, a kind of calm—which might be just the right tone when the scene is viewed from the somewhat distant liturgical perspective. But Speiser sensed directly what kind of scene it was, and was intent upon rendering it in all its human impact. Here was a woman in the most excruciating moments of childbirth, which the Biblical text is at pains to make explicit: it happened "when her labor was at its hardest." In the flash realization that she was dying she uttered with her last breath the child's name as a rueful exclamation upon her fate: "Son of my woe." When Speiser translated "with her last gasp" it was not out of the desire to sound dramatic; the drama was in the occasion, an all too human and all too common occasion. Rachel was gasping, as women have ever done in the throes of difficult childbirth. Her terror and panic were increased by the awareness of approaching death, and her final exclamation constituted something of a protest. All this came across in Speiser's four plain words: "With her last gasp," as it does in no other rendering; the *human* scene is evoked, and its impact upon the reader is immediate. At the same time the style, directness, the stark simplicity, the animation, is as evocative of Speiser himself as it is a perfect rendering of the Biblical scene.

One of the most enviable gifts, especially in scholarship —and Biblical scholarship particularly—is the ability to see old familiar things in a fresh, new light. For the most part it is difficult to discard the baggage of accumulated tradition that affects our view often without our being aware of it. But this is a gift that Speiser had in great abundance. It enabled him, despite his awareness of the impact of AV upon the English language, and the fact that one cannot even think of a rendering of Biblical Hebrew verse without that language automatically interposing itself, to translate the Book of Genesis into English almost as if it were being done for the first time. To have attained such an effect, apart from its faithfulness to the Hebrew, is perhaps as great an achievement as anything else that Speiser did.

For Speiser the man and the teacher, the illustration of his translation of the passage just cited might serve equally well as a bridge. For it illustrates his directness in expression, his antipathy for superfluous verbiage in any context or situation. In the first paper I ever wrote for publication, the manuscript of which he reviewed first, he struck out practically every adverb and a good proportion of the adjectives; it was a lesson in verbal economy that still has its impact. In presenting papers before meetings of learned societies he took particular pains to stay within the fixed time limit, even allowing himself a margin; he was never known to exceed that limit. He felt that any point that could be made in twenty minutes could be made in fifteen or less, if the speaker would devote the effort to it. When in the chair at such a session he was therefore not excessively tolerant of transgressors of the rule. On such occasions his fabulous wit would be brought into play; the arrow, however, was rarely intended to explode the balloon; it was designed only to expedite its return to earth—with a safe landing.

Speiser was not a sentimental, or "soft," person. That too would have been out of character for one who insisted on directness and avoidance of ambiguity wherever possible. But I doubt if I shall ever again encounter anyone with a truer understanding of humans and the nobility of spirit that must accompany it if such understanding is to be put to constructive rather than destructive ends. Towards such an end sentiment can only act as an obstruction, and sympathy, which itself is but true understanding, was to be rationed to the patient in judicious quantities only, like medicine. As a teacher and as a friend Speiser was the best doctor. With students he was quick to sense weakness and strengths, and it was the strengths that he would play to from that time onward. Only pretense, if intractable and sustained, could turn him against a student or anyone else. Being as careful and lucid in his lectures and his explanations to the class as he was in his writings, he fostered the same qualities in his students. Persistent longwindedness could drive him to distraction, but in the classroom he was more forgiving of it than with his peers. Above all, he was an optimist in the most serious sense of the term. He believed in progress, though with a lower case, not a capital, P. He was aware, like the rest of us, that in a field as unyielding as the study of the ancient Near East, very rarely do we attain the satisfaction of sensing that we have for once really penetrated the veil and achieved definitive comprehension even in small matters; the turn of a single spade of earth can make a mockery of our most carefully reasoned deductions and apparently brilliant insights. The frustrations of our field have, at times, prompted the most pessimistic appraisals of its achievements and its prospects. Yet to Speiser such a response was the most alien of all. Aware of the pitfalls, he remained intent on bridging them, for such to him was the essential condition of humanity at large. The obstacles served only to sharpen the challenge; the engagement was itself the only true evidence of vitality, in scholarship as in life in general. It was the quest that mattered, not the awareness that the desired goal would never be attained. And each honest attempt, based on competence, devotion, and thorough immersion in the subject, is itself an advance in that it discloses another facet of the object sought after, even if the "ultimate truth"—whatever that might mean—remains as distant as ever. And this attitude Speiser carried over with him into his private and social life. He never saw any situation as utterly black. He exemplified his view, as he liked to put it, in a very simple way: There are two responses to the sight of a glass containing some desirable substance. One may see it as "half empty" or one may see it as "half full." Objectively both views are accurate. Yet one is negation, the other affirmation. To Speiser no situation, either in the contemporary world or in the field of scholarship of the Ancient Near East, or the potentialities of any student, was cause for despair.

In the field of Ancient Near Eastern Studies, in this

country, this approach had its effect. In more recent years, especially as Speiser's own work attained its fullest maturity, the department here began to attract the liveliest young minds, since under Speiser the study of the ancient Near East, including Biblical studies, took on challenging intellectual dimensions as well as scholarly ones. Classes in Assyriology and Sumerology were growing to unprecedented proportions, doctoral dissertations of impressive quality were flowing out in increasing numbers, and, perhaps most significant of all, graduates of the department were being placed in significant academic positions at a rate that equalled or exceeded that of any comparable department in the country. It is perhaps too much to say that Speiser had developed a distinctive "school" of Assyriology and Biblical studies, in the German style, for example. Had he lived to complete his full tenure at the University, this too might have developed in a more pronounced form. As it is, Speiser's legacy as a teacher is reflected in certain features that are common to those who had their graduate training under his guidance and went on to publish independently. These features may be summed up in the simple and widely used metaphor: the conviction that it is important from the very first to plunge deeply into the woods, analyzing the vegetation closely, even microscopically, but that it is equally important that one early and often climb up to the highest branch to survey the shape and dimensions of the forest. In other words, Speiser insisted on the simultaneous concentration upon analysis and synthesis; the first without the second he deemed sterile, the second without the first an empty playing with words. Nor did he believe that synthesis, or the attempt at it, should come only after a lifetime of concern with details, for by that time intellectual atrophy would probably have set in. The ultimate questions about one's work, one's entire field, must be posed early, even though the answers and the formulation of the questions themselves will be constantly modified with ever-increasing control of details. Speiser's insistence on such concerns, so eloquently exemplified in his own work, was, I believe, the most distinctive and certainly the most enduring part of his legacy as a teacher. There is hardly a former student of his now a scholar in his own right—whether in Biblical or in other ancient Near Eastern fields of study—who is not always conscious of his dual responsibility in this manner, whatever degree of success he might have in the attempt to live up to it. If ever our field—and here I must speak of Assyriology alone, as my particular area—is to have anything of value to contribute to the history of social institutions in general, to jurisprudence, sociology, the history of religion—in short, when Assyriologists will have a great deal of serious consequence to contribute to scholars and persons other than their fellow Assyriologists, the credit will be due to a philosophy of scholarship of which, as regards the study of the ancient Near East, Speiser was the greatest champion.

Ephraim Avigdor Speiser, as a witty, warm, and almost ineffably wise human being, lives on as an especially satisfying glow in the memory of those who were close to him personally. As teacher and scholar, he will live on more tangibly so long as Biblical and Ancient Near Eastern studies themselves live on as significant humanistic enterprises of the intellectual and scholarly world of Western civilization.

J. J. Finkelstein

DATE DUE

FEB 2 '73			
MAY 28 '75			
DEC 14 '83			
MAR 4 '87			
OCT 28 '87 RESERVE			
SPRING			
RESERVE			
SPRING 88 Reserve 89 Sp			